Contemporary Perspectives on Rhetoric

Third Edition

Sonja K. Foss
Karen A. Foss
Robert Trapp

WAVELAND

PRESS, INC.

Prospect Heights, Illinois

For information about this book, contact:
Waveland Press, Inc.
P.O. Box 400
Prospect Heights, Illinois 60070
(847) 634-0081
www.waveland.com

Photograph of Jean Baudrillard © Peter Hamilton

CONTENTS

ACKNOWLEDGMENTS

Just as the development of rhetorical thought is an ongoing conversation, so was the process of writing this book. We are indebted, first of all, to the scholars included in this book. Special thanks to Ernesto Grassi, Stephen Toulmin, Fela Perelman, Noemi Perelman Mattis, Thomas McCarthy, and Mike Gane, who helped in varying ways by supplying biographical material; unpublished sources; and, in Grassi's case, by granting an interview and reading drafts of the chapter about him. Others contributed by commenting on various chapters: Lewis Bright, Wayne Brockriede, Brant Burleson, George Cheney, Martha Cooper, Robert Martin, Karen Massetti-Miller, and Stephen W. Littlejohn.

We would also like to thank those who helped in various ways with the preparation of this book. The following individuals helped us locate sources: Eric Berson, Wayne Brockriede, Trudy Burtis, Ming-chu Chen, Leslie Fagre, Meryl Anne Fingrutd, Walter Fisher, Laura K. Hahn, Christine M. Hanson, Peg Ingolia, Richard Johannesen, Marla Kanengieter, Niki Lilienthal, Britta Limary, Noemi Perelman Mattis, Yoshi Miike, Kelly O'Connor, Catherine J. Ondek, Richard Rieke, John Paul Russo, Craig Schultz, Tsai-Shan Shen, Giorgio Tagliacozzo, Donald Philip Verene, David Werling, and Daniel Wildeson. Belle Edson, Brad Golphenee, Dorothy Mettee, Kathaleen Reid, and Nancy Reist helped check the accuracy of the sources included in the bibliography. Polly Weaver, Noemi Perelman Mattis, Fela Perelman, John Paul Russo, Julie Yingling, Peter Hamilton, Mike Gane, Beacon Press, the Intercollegiate Studies Institute, Random House, South End Press, and the University of California Press were helpful in securing photographs of the theorists. Stephen W. Littlejohn, Bonnie Mesinger, Marianne Pennekamp, Roswitha Kima Smale, and Luisella Corbellari helped translate correspondence from and about Grassi, and Susan Stakel translated correspondence to Foucault.

Special thanks to our publishers, Carol Rowe and Neil Rowe, for their support, confidence, and patience. Above all, we are grateful for the love, encouragement, and support of our families, Anthony J. Radich, Stephen W. Littlejohn, Hazel M. Foss, Erin Trapp, Judy Bowker, Hilary Jones, and Parker Jones.

1

AN INTRODUCTION
TO RHETORIC

When the word *rhetoric* is used today, the meaning frequently is pejorative. More often than not, it refers to empty, bombastic words with no substance or trivial talk. A typical use of the term occurred in an article in *The Toronto Star*, in which the Canadian prime minister was criticized for suggesting the use of "tough love" on Western Canadians to stem their growing alienation from the rest of Canada. In response, Stockwell Day, a leader of the Canadian Alliance, suggested that Western Canadians want to "'feel the love' Prime Minister Jean Chrétien speaks of through actions, not rhetoric."[1]

Rhetoric, however, should not engender only negative connotations. In the Western tradition,[2] the study of rhetoric dates back to the fifth century B.C. and has a distinguished history of largely positive meanings. For those of us who have chosen to study rhetoric, it is an art and a discipline that facilitates our understanding of the nature and function of symbols in our lives. How we perceive, what we know, what we experience, and how we act are the results of our own symbol use and that of those around us; *rhetoric* is the term that captures all of these processes. For us, rhetoric is the human use of symbols to communicate. We believe this definition is broad enough to cover most contemporary uses of the term, including the perspectives offered by the theorists who are the subjects of the chapters that follow. To clarify this definition, we will discuss each of the key components of this definition—*human, symbols*, and *communicate*.

Our definition of rhetoric features the use of symbols by humans. As far as we know, humans are the only animals who create a substantial part of their reality through the use of symbols. Some people debate whether or not symbol use is a characteristic that distinguishes humans from all other species of animals, pointing to research with chimpanzees and gorillas in which these animals have been taught to communicate using signs or systems of signs such as American Sign Language. Although many of the theorists whose ideas we will discuss in this book argue that symbols are uniquely human, we believe that the debate over whether animals use symbols is unresolved and perhaps unresolvable. Most would agree, however, that the difference between humans and other animals with regard to symbol use involves such a difference in degree that whether or not it is also a difference in kind is largely irrelevant to the position that the human is the symbol-using animal. Even if certain primates can be taught signs that operate in some fundamentally symbolic ways, these species do not create any substantial part of their realities through their use of symbols.

We take seriously the notion that humans create their realities through symbols. Put another way, humans construct the world in which they live through their symbolic choices. This does not mean that there is no objective reality—that this book, for example, is simply a figment of our imagination. Rather, we mean that the symbols through which our realities are filtered affect and perhaps determine our view of the book and how we are motivated to act toward it. The frameworks and labels we choose to apply to what we encounter influence our perceptions of what we experience and thus the kinds of worlds in which we live. Is someone an alcoholic or morally depraved? Is a child misbehaved or unable to concentrate because of attention deficit disorder? A move to a new state can be a struggle or an adventure, a coworker's behavior can be seen as irritating or not worthy of attention, and a child's interruption can be greeted with frustration or seen as a chance for a break. The choices that an individual, a community, and a culture make in terms of how to approach alcoholism, children's fidgetiness, a relocation, or interruptions—to continue with these examples—are critical in determining the nature and outcome of interactions. Every word choice we make—every perspective we choose to apply—results in seeing the world one way rather than another. In each case, the experience will be different because of the symbols used to frame it. Because we create our worlds through symbols, changing our symbols changes our worlds. Gloria Anzaldúa describes the process of changing the world as one of shifting metaphors—choosing new terms to label and thus create experience. The outcome is control over the situations in which we find ourselves and the ways in which we respond to them: "People in possession of the vehicles of communication are, indeed, in partial possession of their lives."[3]

The second concept in our definition of rhetoric is symbol, by which we mean something that stands for or represents something else by virtue of relationship, association, or convention. Symbols are distinguished from signs by the degree of direct connection to the object represented. Smoke is a sign that fire is present; there is a direct relationship between the fire and the smoke. Similarly, the changing color of the leaves in autumn is a sign that winter is coming; falling leaves are a direct indicator of a drop in temperature. A symbol, by contrast, is a human construction connected only indirectly to its referent. The word *kitchen*, for example, has no natural relationship to the place where meals are prepared. It is a symbol invented by someone who needed to refer to a place where food is cooked. Words are symbols that stand for objects to which there usually is no literal connection. A *kitchen* could have been labeled a *fish*, for example. That the word *kitchen* was selected to refer to a particular room in a house is totally arbitrary.

The case of a heart attack further clarifies the distinction between a symbol and a sign. A woman is awakened in the middle of the night by a severe pain in her arm and chest and calls an ambulance to take her to the hospital. The doctor who examines her concludes that, on the basis of her heart rate and rhythm, she has suffered a heart attack. In this case, heart rate and rhythm are signs. If someone goes to a doctor because she is suffering from pain in her chest and arm, explains the nature and location of the pain, and the doctor diagnoses her condition as a heart attack, the patient is using symbols to communicate. In the first example, the symptoms (heart rate and rhythm) were signs directly connected to the woman's illness; they were not conscious choices. The second example involved the conscious use of symbols to communicate a particular condition. Of course, in reality, this distinction is never this clear. In all likelihood, the woman taken to the hospital by ambulance would use words to communicate—assuming she is conscious—in addition to the signs of a heart attack evident in her body.

That signs and symbols often intertwine is typical of human communication. For instance, a tree standing in a forest is not a symbol; it does not stand for something else. It simply is a tree, although the word chosen to represent the thing standing in the forest is a symbol. The tree could be a sign of regeneration after a forest fire of the previous summer when it sprouts new leaves in the spring. The tree also becomes a symbol—an instance of rhetoric—when it is cut, for example, for use as a Christmas tree. The act of bringing a tree into the house and decorating it symbolizes certain aspects of the Christmas holiday, but Christmas trees can be used symbolically to express other meanings as well. Some people choose real rather than artificial Christmas trees to symbolize their disdain for anything fake or artificial. Some people keep a live Christmas tree in a pot that can be reused year after year to symbolize their respect for nature and the need to preserve the world's natural resources. Humans use all sorts of nonrhetorical objects in rhetorical ways, turning them into symbols in the process.

Rhetoric often involves the deliberate and conscious choice of symbols to communicate with others, but actions to which rhetors do not consciously attend also can be interpreted symbolically. Humans often choose to interpret something symbolically or rhetorically that the sender of the message did not intend to be symbolic. In this case, someone chooses to give an action or an object symbolic value, even though the sender does not see it in symbolic terms. Often, in such cases, the meanings received are quite different from what the rhetor intends. When the United States deploys an aircraft carrier off the coast of a Central American nation to warn its government not to install a weapons system that could endanger North America, the United

States has performed a rhetorical action that is designed to be read symbolically by both sides, and there is no doubt about the meaning of the message. If a United States reconnaissance plane accidentally strays over North Korea without the purpose of communicating anything to North Korea, however, the pilot is not engaged in rhetorical action. In this case, however, the North Koreans could choose to interpret the event symbolically and take retaliatory action against the United States. Any actions, whether intended to communicate or not, can be taken as symbolic by those who experience or encounter those actions. This is one reason why many claim that we "cannot not communicate." Any human action can be received and interpreted rhetorically. We are constantly using symbols to communicate with those around us, and we are assessing and evaluating the symbol use of others.

The third primary term in our definition of rhetoric is *communicate*. For us, rhetoric is another term for communication. Some scholars make rigid distinctions between rhetoric and communication, suggesting that rhetoric refers to intentional, purposive interactions, while communication covers all kinds of meanings, whether intended or not. For us, however, they are essentially synonymous terms, and the choice of whether to use the term *rhetoric* or the term *communication* is largely a personal one, often stemming from the tradition of inquiry in which a scholar is grounded. Individuals trained in social scientific perspectives on communication, for example, often prefer the term *communication*, while those who study symbol use from more humanistic perspectives tend to select the term *rhetoric*.[4]

Classical Theories of Rhetoric

Although this book deals with contemporary treatments of rhetoric in the West, the focus of this chapter is primarily a history of Western rhetoric. This history is intended to provide context and background for the study of the contemporary theories of rhetoric that follow. In some instances, the contemporary theories relate directly to the classical rhetorical tradition, developing or extending some of the same constructs in similar ways, as is the case with Ernesto Grassi's focus on *ingenium*. Other theorists expand constructs and theories beyond their conceptualizations in the rhetorical tradition, as Kenneth Burke and Jean Baudrillard do in defining symbolicity in broad terms that extend far beyond traditional conceptualizations. In other instances, contemporary rhetorical theorists ignore and even challenge rhetorical history as they develop constructs that were not even part of the discussion about rhetoric in traditional theories. Michel Foucault's discursive formation offers one example of a concept that did not exist in classical times.

We begin with the fifth century B.C., where the art of rhetoric in the West is said to have originated with Corax of Syracuse. A revolution in about 465 B.C. in Syracuse, a Greek colony on the island of Sicily, was the catalyst for the formal study of rhetoric. When the dictators on the island were overthrown and a democracy was established, the courts were deluged with conflicting property claims about rightful ownership and had to sort out whether a piece of land belonged to its original owner or to the one who had been given the land during the dictators' reign. The Greek legal system required that citizens represent themselves in court—they could not hire attorneys to speak on their behalf as is the practice today. The burden, then, was on the claimants in these land disputes to make the best possible case and to present it persuasively to a jury.

Corax realized the need for systematic instruction in the art of speaking in the law courts and wrote a treatise called the "Art of Rhetoric." Although no copies of this work survive, later writers suggest that the notion of probability was central to his rhetorical system. He believed that a speaker must argue from general probabilities or establish probable conclusions when matters of fact cannot be established with absolute certainty. He also showed that probability can be used regardless of the side argued. For instance, to argue that someone convicted of driving under the influence of alcohol probably is guilty if arrested for a second time on the same charge is an argument from probability. So is the opposing argument—that the person convicted once will be especially cautious and probably will not get into that same situation again. In addition to the principle of probability, Corax contributed the first formal treatment of the organization of speeches. He argued that speeches consist of three major parts—an introduction, an argument or proof, and a conclusion—an arrangement that was elaborated on by later writers about rhetoric.[5]

Corax's pupil, Tisias, is credited with introducing Corax's rhetorical system to mainland Greece. With the coming of rhetorical instruction to Athens and the emerging belief that eloquence was an art that could be taught, the rise of a class of teachers of rhetoric was only natural. These teachers were called *sophists*, a term derived from *sophos*, which means knowledge or wisdom. A sophist, then, was a teacher of wisdom. Sophistry, not unlike rhetoric, acquired a tarnished reputation that had its origins in the sophists' reception in Athens. This reputation persists today in the association of sophistry with fallacious or devious reasoning.

The Greeks' distrust of the sophists was due to several factors. Because the sophists were itinerant professors and often foreigners to Athens, some distrust existed simply because of their foreign status. They also professed to teach wisdom or excellence, a virtue that the Greeks traditionally believed could not be taught. In addition, the sophists charged for their services, a practice not only at odds with tradition but one that made sophistic education a luxury that could not be afforded by all. Some resentment may have arisen among those who could not afford to study with the sophists. In large part, however, the continuing condemnation accorded the sophists can be attributed to an accident of history—the survival of Plato's dialogues. Plato was a strong critic of the sophists, and several of his dialogues make the sophists look silly.[6] Although Plato's views now are considered unjustified in large part, his dialogues (discussed below) perpetuated an antisophistic sentiment that has continued to the present.[7]

For the sophists, absolute truth was unknowable and perhaps nonexistent and had to be established in each case according to the perspective of the individual involved.[8] This perspective privileged language because the incomplete, ambiguous, and uncertain world could be interpreted and understood only by means of language. According to the sophists, truth and reality do not exist prior to language but are creations of it: "Speech is a powerful lord [that] can stop fear and banish grief and create joy and nurture pity."[9] The sophists valued figurative and poetic language in particular because of its capacity to appeal directly to the senses through images, thus providing alternative possibilities for understanding and experiencing the world.

Protagoras of Abdera (c. 480–411 B.C.) is considered to be one of the earliest sophists. He is remembered for the statement, "Man is the measure of all things," which indicates the interest the sophists collectively placed on the study of humanity as the perspective from which to approach the world. Gorgias, another important sophist, was the subject of one of Plato's disparaging dialogues on the sophists. Originally from Sicily, Gorgias established a school of rhetoric in Athens and became known for his emphasis on the poetic dimensions of language. He also is called the father of impromptu speaking because this was a favored technique at his school.[10]

Another sophist whose work is significant in the history of rhetorical thought is Isocrates (436–338 B.C.). He began his career as a speechwriter for those involved in state affairs because he lacked the voice and nerve to speak in public. In 392 B.C., he established a school of rhetoric in Athens and advocated as an ideal the orator active in public life. He believed that politics and rhetoric could not be separated; rather, both disciplines were needed for full participation in the life of the state. Unlike many other teachers of his day, Isocrates encouraged his students to learn from other teachers—to take instruction with those best qualified to teach them.[11]

While the sophists offered the beginnings of a philosophical position on rhetoric, the codification of rhetoric was left to those who followed. The work of the Greek philosopher Plato (427–347 B.C.) provided the foundation for such developments, despite his opposition to the sophists and their relativistic perspectives on rhetoric. Plato was a wealthy Athenian who rejected the ideal of political involvement in favor of philosophy after the death of his teacher and mentor Socrates. At his school, the Academy, Plato espoused a belief in philosophical thought and knowledge, or dialectic, and rejected as unreal any form of relative knowledge or opinions. The two dialogues in which Plato's views on rhetoric emerge most clearly are the *Gorgias* and the *Phaedrus*. In the *Gorgias*, Plato set Gorgias and others against Socrates to distinguish false from true rhetoric. Plato faulted rhetoric for ignoring true knowledge; for failing to work toward the good, which Plato believed was the end toward which all human pursuits should be directed; and because it was a technique or knack rather than an art.

In Plato's later dialogue, the *Phaedrus*, he used three speeches on love as analogies for his ideas about rhetoric. The first two speeches illustrate the faults of rhetoric as practiced in contemporary Athens. Either a speech fails to move listeners at all, or it appeals to evil or base motives. With the third speech, however, which Plato had Socrates deliver, he articulated an ideal rhetoric. Such a rhetoric is based on knowing the truth and the nature of the human soul: "any man who does not know the truth, but has only gone about chasing after opinions, will produce an art of speech which will seem not only ridiculous, but no art at all."[12] In addition to his concern for content, Plato also commented on organization, style, and delivery in the *Phaedrus*, thus paving the way for a comprehensive treatment of the rhetorical process.

Plato's student Aristotle (384–322 B.C.) was responsible for first systematizing rhetoric into a unified body of thought. In fact, his *Rhetoric* often is considered the foundation of the discipline of communication. Although Aristotle could not avoid the influence of Plato's ideas, he diverged significantly from his teacher in his treatise on rhetoric. Some of these differences are due to Aristotle's scientific training. Rather than attempting a moral treatise on the subject, as did Plato, Aristotle sought to categorize objectively the various facets of rhetoric, which he defined as "the faculty of discovering in the particular case what are the available means of persuasion."[13] The result was a philosophic and pragmatic treatise that drew upon Plato's ideas and those of the sophistic tradition.

Aristotle devoted a large portion of the *Rhetoric* to invention, or the finding of materials and modes of proof to use in presenting those materials to an audience. He dealt as well with style, organization, and delivery—the pragmatic processes of presentation. Thus, he incorporated four of what later would be identified as the five major canons of rhetoric. The canons consist of invention, the discovery of ideas and arguments; organization, the arrangement of the ideas discovered by means of invention; elocution or style, which involves the linguistic choices a speaker makes; and delivery, the presentation of the speech. Memory, memorizing the speech for presentation, is the fifth canon, which Aristotle did not mention in his rhetorical theory.

No major rhetorical treatises survived in the 200 years after Aristotle's *Rhetoric*. This was a time of increasing Roman power in the Mediterranean, and, not surprisingly, the next extant work on rhetoric was a Latin text, the *Ad Herennium*, written about 100 B.C. The Romans were borrowers and, as they did with many aspects of Greek culture, they adopted the basic principles of rhetoric developed by the Greeks. The *Ad Herennium* appears to be a representative Roman text in that it is essentially Greek in content and Roman in form. A discussion of the five canons constitutes the essence of this schoolboys' manual, but the practical aspects, not their theoretical underpinnings, are featured. The systematization and categorization that characterized the *Ad Herennium*'s approach to rhetoric were typical of the Roman treatises that followed. The Romans added little that was new to the study of rhetoric; rather, they organized and refined it as a practical art.[14]

Cicero (106–43 B.C.) represents the epitome of Roman rhetoric because, in addition to writing on the art of rhetoric, he was himself a great orator. His earliest treatise on the subject was *De Inventione* (87 B.C.), which he wrote when he was only 20 years old. Although he considered it an immature piece in comparison to his later thinking on the subject, it offers another model of the highly prescriptive nature of most Roman rhetorical treatises. Cicero's major work on rhetoric was *De Oratore* (55 B.C.), in which he attempted to restore the union of rhetoric and philosophy by advocating that rhetoric be taught as the single art most useful for dealing with all practical affairs. He drew heavily on Isocrates' ideas in advocating an integration of natural ability, comprehensive knowledge of all the liberal arts, and extensive practice in writing. As a practicing orator, Cicero developed the notion of style more fully than did his predecessors and devoted virtually an entire treatise, *Orator* (46 B.C), to distinguishing three types of style—the plain, the moderate, and the grand.[15]

Another Roman rhetorician who contributed theoretically and practically to rhetoric was the Roman lawyer and educator M. Fabius Quintilian (35–95 A.D.). In his *Institutes of Oratory* (93 A.D.), Quintilian described the ideal training of the citizen-orator from birth through retirement. He defined the orator as "the good man speaking well," and his approach was not rule bound as was the case with many Roman rhetorics.[16] Quintilian was as eclectic and flexible, drawing from Plato, Aristotle, Isocrates, and Cicero and also integrating his own teaching experiences into traditional theory. His work was so systematic that it not only served as an excellent synthesis of Greek and Roman rhetorical thought, but it was an important source of ideas on education throughout the Middle Ages.

With the decline of democracy in Rome, rhetoric entered an era when it essentially was divorced from civic affairs. A series of emperors ruled, and anyone who spoke publicly in opposition to them was likely to be punished. Rhetoric, then, was relegated to a back seat and became an art concerned with style and delivery rather than with content. This period, from about 150 to 400 A.D., often is referred to as the *second sophistic* because of the excesses of delivery and style similar to those for which the early sophists were criticized.

The Middle Ages (400–1400 A.D.) followed the second sophistic and, during this period, rhetoric became aligned with preaching, letter writing, and education. The concern with preaching as an oratorical form began with St. Augustine (354–430 A.D.), who often is viewed as a bridge between the classical and medieval periods. During the Middle Ages, as Christianity became increasingly powerful, rhetoric was condemned as a pagan art. Many Christians believed that the rhetorical ideas formulated by the pagans of classical Greece and Rome should not be studied and that possession of Christian truth was accompanied by an automatic ability to communicate that truth effectively. Augustine, however, had been a teacher of rhetoric before converting to Christianity in 386. Thus, in his *On Christian Doctrine* (426), he argued that preachers need to be able to teach, to delight, and to move—Cicero's notion of the duties of the orator—and that for Christianity to accomplish its ends of conversion effectively, rules of effective expression should not be ignored.[17] Because Augustine believed such rules were to be used only in the expression of truth, he revitalized the philosophic basis of rhetoric that largely had been ignored since Quintilian's time.

Letter writing was another form in which rhetoric found expression during the Middle Ages. Many political decisions were made privately through letters and decrees, and letter writing also became a method of record keeping for both secular and religious organizations as they increased in size and complexity. Letter writing, too, was necessary to bridge the distances of the medieval world, which, in contrast to the classical period, no longer consisted of a single center of culture and power.[18] Thus, principles of letter writing, including the conscious adaptation of salutation, language, and format to a particular addressee, were studied as rhetoric.

Finally, rhetoric played a role in education in the Middle Ages as one of the three great liberal arts. Along with logic and grammar, rhetoric was considered part of the *Trivium* of learning, much as the three Rs of reading, writing, and arithmetic function today.[19] Rhetoric was paired with the *Quadrivium* (arithmetic, geometry, astronomy, and music) to form the seven liberal arts, equivalent to a baccalaureate degree. As part of the *Trivium*, the teaching of rhetoric generally emphasized classical figures of speech and other facets of style. Rhetoric, then, was a practical art that provided the foundation of a basic liberal education.

The Renaissance, from 1400 to 1600, signaled the end of the Middle Ages and gave rise to humanism, a movement that encompassed a diverse group of thinkers and writers. Although the term *humanism* today has a broad meaning—concern for and interest in humans and their activities—during the Renaissance, it referred to a scholarly interest in the learning and languages of classical antiquity, especially in the fields of history, moral philosophy, poetry, and rhetoric. The movement began and reached its height in Italy, where the humanists were the professional successors of the medieval monks who had served as letter writers and secretaries, copying rediscovered texts from antiquity and recording the deeds of the present. Unlike the monks who lived and worked in seclusion, however, the humanists were active participants in civic life; they were lawyers, historians, grammarians, and teachers as well as intellectuals and scholars. Thus, although required to perform technical writing as part of their professions, humanists pursued philosophical and literary interests in their leisure time and developed a theory of rhetoric not unlike that of the sophists.[20]

Interested in the human world as constructed through language, rather than in the natural world, the humanists gave the human as knower a central position. They highlighted the world of human culture and language, believing and delighting in the power of the word not only because it gives those with a command of it special advantage in practical affairs but because of its inherent capacity to disclose the world to humans.[21] The Italian humanists believed rhetoric, not philosophy, to be the primary discipline because humans gain access to the world through language. Poetry, not the rational proofs of logic, was considered the original source of intelligibility and inspiration, capable of transforming the world.

Francesco Petrarcha (1304–1374), the Italian poet and essayist whose name is often translated into English as Petrarch, is perhaps the best known of the Italian humanists. Particularly interested in ancient Roman literature, he revived the style of great Roman writers in his own works. Coluccio Salutati (1331–1374) was a prominent disciple of Petrarcha; among his works was *De laboribus Herculis*, in which he argued that only through poetry does human history emerge. Lorenzo Valla (1407–1457)—scholar, polemicist, and pamphleteer—is another representative of Italian humanism. In his *De ver falsoque bono*, he argued for privileging everyday language over formal, arcane usage, suggesting values of rhetorical accessibility, flexibility, and responsiveness. The work of Giambattista Vico (1668–1774) often is seen as the culmination of Italian humanist thought, although he was separated from the mainstream of humanism by almost a century.

A second trend in rhetoric—rationalism—also began during the Renaissance and dominated the rhetorical theories that followed. Rationalists sought objective, scientific truths that would exist for all time and, not surprisingly, had little patience for rhetoric. Poetry and oratory might be aesthetically pleasing, but they were seen as having no connection to science and truth. Two major contributors to rationalism were Peter Ramus (1515–1572) and René Descartes (1596–1650). Ramus was a French scholar who made rhetoric subordinate to logic by placing invention and organization under the rubric of logic and leaving rhetoric to focus only on style and delivery.[22] This dichotomizing and departmentalizing of knowledge made for easy teaching, and Ramus's taxonomy was perpetuated for generations through the educational system. Descartes believed that to reach certain knowledge, the foundations of thought provided by others had to be abandoned.[23] He was willing to accept only that which would withstand all doubt. Thus, he rejected truths established in discourse, relegating language to the role of communicating the truth once it was discovered.

Dominated by the rationalism instituted by Descartes and Ramus, rhetoric in the modern era, generally equated with the Enlightenment period of the sixteenth through eighteenth centuries,[24] was considered to be subordinate to science and philosophy. A prominent rhetorician of this period, Francis Bacon (1561–1626), sought to promote a revival of secular knowledge through an empirical examination of the world. He introduced ideas about the nature of sensory perception, arguing that sensory interpretations are highly inaccurate and should be subjected to reasoned, empirical investigation. Likewise, he rejected narratives, myths, and fables as simply tales of the past that had no bearing on a rational world. His definition of rhetoric suggests his effort to bring the power of language under rational control: "the duty of rhetoric is to apply Reason to Imagination for the better moving of the will."[25]

Three trends in rhetoric characterized the modern period—the epistemological, belletristic, and elocutionist. Epistemology is the study of the origin, nature, methods, and limits of human knowledge, and epistemological thinkers sought to recast classical approaches to rhetoric in terms of modern developments in psychology. George Campbell (1719–1796) and Richard Whately

(1758–1859) exemplify the best of the epistemological tradition. Campbell was a Scottish minister, teacher, and author of *The Philosophy of Rhetoric* (1776). He drew on Aristotle, Cicero, and Quintilian as well as on the faculty psychology and empiricism of his time. Faculty psychology was characterized by an effort to explain human behavior in terms of five powers or faculties of the mind—understanding, memory, imagination, passion, and will—and Campbell's definition of rhetoric was directed to these faculties: "to enlighten the understanding, to please the imagination, to move the passions, or to influence the will."[26] Campbell's approach to evidence also suggests his ties to the rational, empirical approach to knowledge. He identified three types of evidence—mathematical axioms, derived through reasoning; consciousness, or the result of sensory stimulation; and common sense, an intuitive sense shared by virtually all humans.

Richard Whately, like Campbell, was a preacher, and his *Elements of Rhetoric*, published in 1828, often is considered the logical culmination of Campbell's thought.[27] His view of rhetoric was similar to Campbell's in its dependence on faculty psychology, but he deviated from Campbell by making argumentation the focus of the art of rhetoric: "The *finding* of suitable arguments to prove a given point, and the skilful [*sic*] *arrangement* of them, may be considered as the immediate and proper province of Rhetoric, and of that alone."[28] He also is remembered for his analysis of presumption and burden of proof, which paved the way for modern argumentation and debate practices. The epistemologists, then, combined their knowledge of classical rhetoric and contemporary psychology to create rhetorical theories based on an understanding of human nature. They offered audience-centered approaches to rhetoric and paved the way for contemporary concerns with audience analysis.

The second direction rhetoric took in the modern period is known as the *belles lettres* movement. A French term, *belles lettres* literally means fine or beautiful letters. It referred to literature valued for its aesthetic qualities rather than for its informative value. Belletristic rhetorics included within their purview spoken discourse, written discourse, and the criticism of discourse. Scholars of this school believed that all the fine arts, including rhetoric, poetry, drama, music, and even gardening and architecture, could be subjected to the same critical standards. Thus, rhetoric gained a critical component not seen in earlier approaches.

Hugh Blair (1718–1800) stands as a representative figure of the belletristic period. In his *Lectures on Rhetoric and Belles Lettres*, based on a series of lectures he delivered at the University of Edinburgh, Blair presented an overview of the relationship among rhetoric, literature, and criticism. One of his most innovative contributions was his discussion of taste, which he defined as the faculty that is capable of deriving pleasure from contact with the beautiful. Taste, according to Blair, is perfected when a sensory pleasure is coupled with reason—when reason is used to explain the source of that pleasure.[29] Blair's ideas on rhetoric proved extremely popular and laid the foundations for contemporary literary and rhetorical criticism.

The elocutionary movement, the third rhetorical trend of the modern period, reached its height in the mid-eighteenth century and represented an effort to restore to prominence the canon of delivery, neglected since classical times. It developed in response to the poor delivery styles of contemporary preachers, lawyers, and other public figures. Like the epistemologists, the elocutionists were concerned about contributing to a more scientific understanding of the human being and believed that their observations on voice and gesture—characteristics unique to humans—constituted one such contribution. The elocutionists also sought to determine the effects of delivery on the various faculties of the mind, thus continuing the link with modern psychology. Despite a stated concern for invention, however, many elocutionary treatises were prescriptive, using highly mechanical techniques for the management of voice and gestures.

Gilbert Austin's guidelines are representative of the highly stylized approach to delivery of the elocutionists. For instance, he offered this advice to the speaker about eye contact and volume: "He should not stare about, but cast down his eyes, and compose his countenance: nor should he at once discharge the whole volume of his voice, but begin almost at the lowest pitch, and issue the smallest quantity; if he desire to silence every murmur, and to arrest all attention."[30] Another example is provided by James Burgh, who categorized 71 emotions, believing that each emotion could be linked to a specific, external expression. Thomas Sheridan (1719–1788), who wrote *A Course of Lectures on Elocution* in 1762, was perhaps the most famous elocutionist. Sheridan was in the forefront in terms of criticizing the speakers of his day, and he sought to establish a universal standard of pronunciation for the English language, in addition to offering the usual techniques for delivery.[31] The elocutionists have been criticized for their excesses in terms of style and delivery and for the inflexibility of their techniques. Their efforts to derive an empirical science of delivery based on observation, however, foreshadowed the use of the scientific method to study all aspects of human communication.

Each of the trends in the development of rhetoric in Europe and Great Britain had its counterpart in the approaches taken toward rhetoric in the United States. The earliest rhetorical instruction in the United States, offered at Harvard in the seventeenth century, was based on the work of Ramus. *A System of Oratory*, published by John Ward in 1759, did much to generate a renewed interest in the rhetorics of antiquity in the United States. Widely used as a text until the late eighteenth century, this book dealt with all of the classical canons—invention, organization, style, delivery, and memory—and thus restored invention to a place of primacy in rhetorical education.[32] The rediscovery of the classics prompted an increased attention to rhetoric in U.S. colleges that lasted into the early years of the nineteenth century. Seen as a broad art of communication, the discipline of rhetoric integrated ideas from a variety of areas and provided the basis for a liberal education. Chairs of rhetoric were common and were held by some of the most respected American scholars. Among them was future president John Quincy Adams, who served as the first Boylston Professor of Rhetoric at Harvard in 1806 and published *Lectures on Rhetoric and Oratory* in 1810.

With the rise of the *belles lettres* and elocutionary movements, however, rhetoric again began to decline as a subject of study as these movements emphasized style and aesthetic appreciation over issues of substance. Simultaneously, the college curriculum became more specialized. Separate departments formed, including departments of English, and there no longer was a place for rhetoric as a multidisciplinary art. Colleges also shifted from testing students orally to giving written examinations, thus making written skills more important than competence in public speaking.[33] All of these developments furthered the image of rhetoric as associated primarily with composition, style, and standards of usage. Any instruction in speech at the turn of the twentieth century was available in departments of English, where it was considered secondary to the teaching of written composition.

A major shift again occurred in the approach to rhetoric in 1910, when a small group of public speaking teachers, housed in English departments, broke away from the National Council of Teachers of English. Interested in restoring the richness and breadth of the study of rhetoric to their classrooms, these teachers established in 1914 a new association, the National Association of Academic Teachers of Public Speaking.[34] This organization remains the national association for professors and students of communication, although its name has undergone several changes since its inception. Today, it is called the National Communication Association.

The development of the field of speech adopted the humanistic/scientific dichotomy that first appeared in the Renaissance. Members of the Cornell school of rhetoric, which began with a graduate seminar on classical texts offered by Everett Hunt at Cornell University in 1920, believed the discipline should focus on public speaking or oratory, with an emphasis on classical principles and models from a humanistic perspective. The Midwestern school of speech, associated with James O'Neill at the University of Wisconsin and Charles Woolbert at the University of Illinois, was influenced by the research methods of behavioral psychologists. Members of this school advocated specialized and scientific studies of the process or act of speaking, thus following in the footsteps of the rationalists in the Renaissance who sought to understand the world through scientific principles.[35] Both schools were concerned with recapturing the substance of communication for the discipline but disagreed on what that substance should be. The Midwestern and Cornell schools initiated a split between rhetoric and communication that continues today in various aspects of the discipline.

World War II prompted yet another set of issues for the emerging discipline. An international concern with persuasion and propaganda arose during the war, with scholars from journalism, political science, sociology, and information science directing their attention to all aspects of rhetorical processes as part of the war effort. This multidisciplinary effort eventually resulted in the emergence of the field of mass communications.[36] As a new source of material about the communication process, the field of mass communications was bolstered by European critical theory, the result of the emigration of the Frankfurt School to New York during the war.

The rapprochement of rhetorical, philosophical, literary, psychological, and mass communications studies that characterizes contemporary approaches to rhetoric is evidence of yet another revival of interest in the study of rhetorical processes. Whether or not the scholars in these disciplines use the term *rhetoric* to define their interests, they share a concern for how symbols function—personally, socially, and epistemologically—in the human world. They formulate theories of rhetoric that investigate the possible relationships between thought and discourse as well as pragmatic theories that explore what humans do with discourse. Whatever aspect of the rhetorical process receives attention, there is a recognition that rhetoric is both the use of symbols and a "mode of approaching the phenomena of discourse."[37] The individuals whose work is discussed in the following chapters represent the diversity that exists among those who study human symbols.

Contemporary Theories of Rhetoric

In the following chapters, we present the theories of I. A. Richards, Ernesto Grassi, Chaïm Perelman and Lucie Olbrechts-Tyteca, Richard Weaver, Stephen Toulmin, Kenneth Burke, Jürgen Habermas, bell hooks, Jean Baudrillard, and Michel Foucault. We do not see these theorists as comprising a necessary or best list of contemporary rhetorical scholars. Rather, the theorists were chosen for inclusion because they met at least two of three criteria. Our first criterion for selection of these theorists was that they not only have some important things to say about rhetoric but have developed a somewhat coherent body of knowledge relevant to the study of symbolicity. All of the theorists included meet this criterion. The individuals included here also meet one or both of two additional standards: they intended to develop a perspective on or theory of rhetoric, and scholars in the discipline of rhetoric see their work as contributing in important ways to the subject of rhetoric. The works of Richards, Weaver, Burke, Perelman and Olbrechts-Tyteca, and Grassi are directed intentionally toward the development of perspectives on rhetoric; thus, they meet the former standard. Toulmin, Foucault, Baudrillard, Habermas, and hooks did not deliberately develop rhetorical perspectives, but people in the discipline of communication have interpreted their works as relevant to the study of communication. Thus, these writers meet our third criterion.

The theorists are arranged by the breadth of their theories about rhetoric. This schema is designed to provide readers with a sense of the development and evolution of the various perspectives that constitute the study of contemporary rhetoric. The theorists who are the subjects of the early chapters, such as Richards, Grassi, and Perelman and Olbrechts-Tyteca, tend to single out a particular concept or dimension for attention, while later chapters deal with theorists such as hooks, Baudrillard, and Foucault who have developed theories of rhetoric that are more comprehensive or explore a number of rhetorical processes.

We begin with I. A. Richards. In 1923, he co-authored *The Meaning of Meaning* with C. K. Ogden, which focused on the process of meaning creation in symbols. Ernesto Grassi, the subject of the third chapter, focuses on a revitalization of humanism as rhetorical philosophy. Chaïm Perelman and Lucie Olbrechts-Tyteca are discussed next; their focus is on a rediscovery of the classical rhetorical approach to argumentation. The next chapter deals with the ideas of Stephen Toulmin, whose theory includes the nature of everyday argumentation, argumentation in ethics, an evolutionary view of science, and the humanization of modernity. Richard Weaver offers a values-based perspective in the chapter that follows and also explores the intersection of rhetoric with culture. A chapter on Kenneth Burke follows; he is a theorist who presents a comprehensive treatment of rhetoric as a foundation for humanness and as a primary motive for human action. We have placed Jürgen Habermas next because of his interest in a rationality inherent in speech acts that can serve as the basis for consensual decision making. Next, bell hooks introduces notions of gender, race, and class as they inform rhetorical production and reception, as well as suggesting the importance of standpoint in the development of rhetorical theory. Jean Baudrillard, the focus of chapter 10, extends rhetorical theory into a concern for consumerism, objects, and the mass media as they interact in a postmodern age. The final chapter in the book is about the theory of Michel Foucault, who makes rhetoric key in the creation and maintenance of systems of knowledge and power.

Our intent in this book is not to limit the conversation about rhetoric by stating definitive conclusions about the nature of contemporary rhetorical thought or by suggesting that contemporary thinking about rhetoric is confined to the theories presented here. We hope the ideas of the theorists included here provide you with an entry point for contemporary conversations about rhetoric. We hope the summaries offered here intrigue, puzzle, and challenge you so that you, too, will contribute to this conversation and to the continual expansion of rhetorical theory.

Endnotes

1 Anne Dawson, "Day Rips PM for Western Dejection/Says Stop 'Tough Love,'" *The Toronto Star*, January 3, 2001, p. 18.

2 We acknowledge that there are many rhetorical traditions outside the Western one, which has its origins in ancient Greece. We only will be dealing with the Western tradition here, however. For an example of ethnocentrism on the part of Western rhetorical scholars, see John L. Morrison, "The Absence of a Rhetorical Tradition in Japanese Culture," *Western Speech*, 36 (Spring 1972), 89–102. Morrison argues that "Japanese culture before World War II evidenced no rhetorical tradition." His claim is based, among other things, on the "predominantly intuitive and emotional tendencies in the Japanese language" that "mitigate against a rhetorical development" (p. 101). Similarly, James J. Murphy suggests that rhetoric is "an

entirely Western phenomenon." According to Murphy, "no evidence of interest in rhetoric exists in the ancient civilizations of Babylon or Egypt, for instance. Neither Africa nor Asia has to this day produced a rhetoric." See James J. Murphy, ed., *A Synoptic History of Classical Rhetoric* (Davis, CA: Hermagoras, 1983), p. 3. For examples of treatments of non-Western rhetorics, see George A. Kennedy, *Comparative Rhetoric: An Historical and Cross-Cultural Introduction* (New York: Oxford University Press, 1998); and William J. Starosta, "Roots for an Older Rhetoric: On Rhetorical Effectiveness in the Third World," *Western Journal of Speech Communication*, 43 (Fall 1979), 278–87. The Japanese tradition is described in: Satoshi Ishii, "Buddhist Preaching: The Persistent Main Undercurrent of Japanese Traditional Rhetorical Communication," *Communication Quarterly*, 40 (Fall 1992), 391–97; Satoshi Ishii, "Thought Patterns as Modes of Rhetoric: The United States and Japan," *Communication*, 11 (December 1982), 81–86, 97–102; and Roichi Okabe, "Cultural Assumptions of East and West: Japan and the United States," in *The Rhetoric of Western Thought*, 7th ed., ed. James L. Golden, Goodwin F. Berquist, and William E. Coleman (Dubuque, IA: Kendall/Hunt, 2000), pp. 390–404. For examples of treatments of Chinese rhetorics, see: Xing Lu, *Rhetoric in Ancient China, Fifth to Third Century B.C.E.: A Comparison with Classical Greek Rhetoric* (Columbia: University of South Carolina Press, 1998); Xing Lu and David A. Frank, "On the Study of Ancient Chinese Rhetoric/Bias," *Western Journal of Communication*, 57 (Fall 1993), 445–63; and D. Ray Heisey, ed., *Chinese Perspectives in Rhetoric and Communication* (Stamford, CT: Ablex, 2000). In a special section in *Communication Quarterly* about communication practices in the Pacific basin, several articles discuss communication practices in Australia, Hong Kong, Korea, and the Philippines. See *Communication Quarterly*, 40 (Fall 1992), 368–421. The text *Rhetoric in Intercultural Contexts*, edited by Alberto González and Dolores V. Tanno (Thousand Oaks, CA: Sage, 2000), describes the intersection of rhetoric and intercultural communication, situating rhetoric within the cultures that produce and nurture it.

[3] Gloria Anzaldúa, "Metaphors in the Tradition of the Shaman," in *Conversant Essays: Contemporary Poets on Poetry*, ed. James McCorkle (Detroit, MI: Wayne State University Press, 1990), p. 100.

[4] For additional information on the meanings of the terms *rhetoric* and *communication*, see: Gerald R. Miller, *Speech Communication: A Behavioral Approach* (Indianapolis, IN: Bobbs-Merrill, 1966); Wayne E. Brockriede, "Dimensions of the Concept of Rhetoric," *Quarterly Journal of Speech*, 54 (February 1968), 1–18; Walter R. Fisher, "Narration as a Human Communication Paradigm: The Case of Public Moral Argument," *Communication Monographs*, 51 (March 1984), 1–22; and Nancy L. Harper, *Human Communication Theory: The History of a Paradigm* (Rochelle Park, NJ: Hayden, 1979), p. 71.

[5] George Kennedy, *The Art of Persuasion in Greece* (Princeton, NJ: Princeton University Press, 1963), pp. 58–61; and Bromley Smith, "Corax and Probability," *Quarterly Journal of Speech*, 7 (February 1921), 13–42.

[6] Kennedy, *The Art of Persuasion in Greece*, pp. 13–15; and Lester Thonssen and A. Craig Baird, *Speech Criticism: The Development of Standards for Rhetorical Appraisal* (New York: Ronald, 1948), pp. 36–37.

[7] That Plato's negative view of the sophists was unjustified has been asserted by numerous scholars. His views in the *Gorgias*, in particular, have come under frequent re-examination. See, for example: Bruce E. Gronbeck, "Gorgias on Rhetoric and Poetic: A Rehabilitation," *Southern Speech Communication Journal*, 38 (Fall 1972), 27–38; Richard Leo Enos, "The Epistemology of Gorgias' Rhetoric: A Re-examination," *Southern Speech Communication Journal*, 42 (Fall 1976), 35–51; Susan C. Jarratt, *Rereading the Sophists: Classical Rhetoric Refigured* (Carbondale: Southern Illinois University Press, 1991); and Mark Backman, *Sophistication: Rhetoric and the Rise of Self-Consciousness* (Woodbridge, CT: Ox Bow, 1991).

[8] Kennedy, *The Art of Persuasion in Greece*, p. 13; and Philip Wheelwright, ed., *The Presocratics* (Indianapolis, IN: Odyssey/Bobbs-Merrill, 1966), pp. 238–40.

[9] Gorgias, *Encomium on Helen*, trans. George Kennedy, in *The Older Sophists*, ed. R. K. Sprague (Columbia: University of South Carolina Press, 1972), p. 52.

[10] Thonssen and Baird, p. 38.

[11] Russell H. Wagner, "The Rhetorical Theory of Isocrates," *Quarterly Journal of Speech*, 8 (November 1922), 323–37; and William L. Benoit, "Isocrates on Rhetorical Education," *Communication Education*, 33 (April 1984), 109–20.

[12] Plato *Phaedrus* 262.

[13] Aristotle *Rhetoric* 1.2. 1355b.

[14] George Kennedy, *The Art of Rhetoric in the Roman World* (Princeton, NJ: Princeton University Press, 1972), pp. 106–08.

[15] For a summary of Cicero's style, see Thomas R. King, "The Perfect Orator in *Brutus*," *Southern Speech Journal*, 33 (Winter 1967), 124–28.

[16] Thonssen and Baird, p. 92.

[17] James J. Murphy, "Saint Augustine and the Debate About a Christian Rhetoric," *Quarterly Journal of Speech*, 56 (December 1960), 400–10; and Saint Augustine *On Christian Doctrine* xvii, 34.

[18] Harper; and James J. Murphy, *Rhetoric in the Middle Ages: A History of Rhetorical Theory from Saint Augustine to the Renaissance* (Berkeley: University of California Press, 1974).

[19] Donald Lemen Clark, *Rhetoric in Greco-Roman Education* (Westport, CT: Greenwood, 1957), p. 12.

[20] John F. Tinkler, "Renaissance Humanism and the *genera eloquentiae*," *Rhetorica*, 5 (Summer 1987), 279–309.

[21] Samuel Ijsseling, *Rhetoric and Philosophy in Conflict: An Historical Survey* (The Hague, Neth.: Martinus Nijhoff, 1976), p. 55.

[22] Wilbur Samuel Howell, *Logic and Rhetoric in England, 1500–1700* (New York: Russell and Russell, 1956), p. 148.

[23] Ijsseling, p. 64.

[24] The period of the modern often is equated with the Enlightenment and a focus on rationality at the turn of the eighteenth century. Berman, however, identifies three distinctive historical eras in the emergence of modernity: (1) from the beginning of the sixteenth to the end of the eighteenth centuries, when elements of what are considered modern life begin to emerge; (2) the French Revolution and the social and political upheavals that followed it; and (3) the development of a global process of modernization that extends into contemporary life. See M. Berman, *All That is Solid Melts into Air* (London, UK: Verso, 1983).

[25] Hugh C. Dick, ed., *Selected Writings of Francis Bacon* (New York: Modern Library, 1955), p. x; and Harper, pp. 100, 109.

[26] George Campbell, *The Philosophy of Rhetoric*, ed. Lloyd F. Bitzer (Carbondale: Southern Illinois University Press, 1963), p. 1.

[27] Douglas Ehninger, "Introduction," in *Elements of Rhetoric*, by Richard Whately, ed. Douglas Ehninger (Carbondale: Southern Illinois University Press, 1963), p. xv.

[28] Richard Whately, *Elements of Rhetoric*, ed. Douglas Ehninger (Carbondale: Southern Illinois University Press, 1963), p. 39.

[29] Hugh Blair, *Lectures on Rhetoric and Belles Lettres* (London, UK: William Baynes, 1825), p. 24.

[30] Gilbert Austin, *Chironomia or a Treatise on Rhetorical Delivery*, ed. Mary Margaret Robb and Lester Thonssen (Carbondale: Southern Illinois University Press, 1966), p. 94.

[31] Thomas Sheridan, *A Course of Lectures on Elocution* (London, UK: W. Strahan, 1762).

[32] Robert J. Connors, Lisa S. Ede, and Andrea A. Lunsford, "The Revival of Rhetoric in America," in *Essays on Classical Rhetoric and Modern Discourse*, ed. Robert J. Connors, Lisa S. Ede, and Andrea A. Lunsford (Carbondale: Southern Illinois University Press, 1984), p. 1.

[33] Connors, Ede, and Lunsford, pp. 3–4.

[34] George Gerbner and Wilbur Schramm, "Communications, Study of," *International Encyclopedia of Communications*, vol. 1, ed. Erik Barnouw (New York: Oxford University Press, 1989), p. 360.

[35] For descriptions of the Cornell and Midwestern schools, see W. Barnett Pearce, "Scientific Research Methods in Communication Studies and Their Implications for Theory and Research," in *Speech Communication in the Twentieth Century*, ed. Thomas W. Benson (Carbondale: Southern Illinois University Press, 1985), pp. 260–64.

[36] The emergence of the field of mass communications is described in James Carey, "Graduate Education in Mass Communication," *Communication Education*, 28 (September 1979), 282–93.

[37] Donald C. Bryant, "Literature and Politics," in *Rhetoric, Philosophy, and Literature: An Exploration*, ed. Don M. Burks (West Lafayette, IN: Purdue University Press, 1978), p. 107.

2

I. A. RICHARDS

"What I feel is that if there is a way of doing things which is obviously much better than what anyone else has to offer then, in a bad enough emergency, everyone will jump at it. I've been only concerned to produce something really better than anyone else has."[1] This statement by I. A. Richards suggests the motive for much of his work in the areas of rhetoric, linguistics, and literature. He seeks to help solve the problems confronting society, many of which he sees as directly related to a lack of effective communication.

Ivor Armstrong Richards was born in Sandbach, Cheshire, in England, on February 26, 1893, the son of William Armstrong Richards and Mary Anne Haigh Richards. An early interest in language developed when he

became ill with tuberculosis in his early teens and read poetry for amusement during his period of recuperation. He pursued a college education at
Magdalene College at Cambridge, intending to specialize in history. He
turned from history, however, at the end of his first year, when he went to
his advisor "one morning in a grim mood" and said he "didn't think History ought to have happened" and "didn't see why we should study it."[2]
His advisor introduced him to C. K. Ogden, a senior, and as a result of
their discussion, Richards decided to specialize instead in moral sciences
or philosophy.

At Cambridge, Richards was supervised in his studies by the idealist philosopher J. M. E. McTaggart and the logician W. E. Johnson. The most powerful influence on him, however, was G. E. Moore, whose lectures on the
philosophy of mind were not understood, for the most part, by the students
in the class, including Richards. Moore reawakened Richards's interest in
language because Richards felt "something must be done to stop the leakage
of information" or the lack of understanding in his classroom.[3] Moore was
convinced that "few indeed could possibly *mean what they said*." Richards
silently disagreed with him, believing that people "could not possibly *say*
what they *meant*."[4]

Richards obtained a First Class in the Moral Science Tripos (the equivalent of a bachelor's degree) in 1915, left Cambridge, and experienced a recurrence of tuberculosis. While recovering in northern Wales, he became
interested in mountaineering and found that he was "fairly good at floating
up difficult rocks."[5] When he regained his health, he returned to Cambridge
and studied biology, chemistry, psychology, and physiology with the intention of pursuing a medical career as a psychoanalyst.

In 1918, Richards renewed his acquaintance with C. K. Ogden, and they
began to discuss language and meaning, outlining one of the books they were
to coauthor, *The Meaning of Meaning*. Ogden had been publishing a penny
weekly digest of world news as an aid to the war, but he turned it into a quarterly journal, which he used as a means of publishing *The Meaning of Meaning*. Because each issue of the quarterly contained a portion of the work,
Richards and Ogden wrote the book "in bits and pieces quarter by quarter."[6]

Tired of living in poverty and suffering from what Ogden called "Hand
to Mouth Disease,"[7] Richards dropped his medical studies in 1919 and
asked Mansfield Forbes, a professor at Clare College, to write letters of rec-
ommendation for him for a position as a professional mountaineering guide
on Skye, an island of Scotland. After the letters were written, Forbes and Richards began to discuss literature. Two hours later, Forbes tore up the letters and invited Richards to lecture on the contemporary novel and the
theory of criticism in the English School of Clare College, enabling him to
"collect fifteen shillings a head from anyone who came six times to the
course."[8] He was appointed Lecturer in English and Moral Science in 1922
by Magdalene College at Cambridge and became a Fellow of the College
four years later.

Richards became interested in aesthetics as a result of an experience in the summer of 1920. He usually spent his summers in the Alps, but he suffered a fall on an early expedition and returned to Cambridge to recuperate. There he met Ogden's friend, painter James Wood, and the three of them decided to form a triumvirate, sorting "out this art talk."[9] The result was the coauthorship of *The Foundations of Aesthetics*, published in 1922.

Richards and Ogden's next project together was Basic English, a language composed of 850 English words that they believed covered the needs of everyday life. While writing the chapter on definition in *The Meaning of Meaning*, they discovered that "with under a thousand words you can say everything" simply by substituting descriptive phrases for specific words: "If a word can be defined in a descriptive phrase of not more than ten words, you can substitute the descriptive ten words for the word and get rid of it."[10] Ogden spent a great deal of time talking to people who were experts in a variety of fields, finding out which words were essential and which could be dropped from the vocabulary. The result was his *General Basic English Dictionary*, in which more than 20,000 words are defined using the 850 words of Basic English.

Richards became interested in promoting Basic English as an international auxiliary language and as a method for teaching English as a second language. He spent several years in China trying to establish Basic English as the method for teaching English there, serving as a visiting professor at Tsing Hua University in Peking (now Beijing) from 1929 to 1930 and as director of the Orthological Institute of China from 1937 to 1938.

In 1939, Richards received an invitation from Harvard University to direct the Commission of English Language Studies (later Language Research) and to produce Basic English textbooks and train teachers in the method of Basic English. While working on these projects under a three-year endowment, he decided that television might be an important part of the teaching method because it allows the eye and ear to cooperate in the learning process. He received a grant from the Rockefeller Foundation to study cartooning and animation at Walt Disney's studios, where he worked on developing a universal simplified script in which various situations can be expressed. With his collaborator, Christine M. Gibson, Richards produced a number of textbooks over the years for teaching Basic English in a variety of languages. Despite its promising beginnings, however, Basic English never was accepted as the standard method of teaching English in any country. The efforts to disseminate the language were stymied by the start of World War II; the support of Winston Churchill and Franklin D. Roosevelt, which seemed to hinder rather than help the movement; and a series of misrepresentations that developed about the language.

At the age of 60, Richards added another dimension to his career when he began to write poetry. He was writing a play, *A Leak in the Universe*, and "it seemed definitely to require a lyrical component."[11] He went on to write several volumes of poetry, including *Goodbye Earth and Other Poems* (1958) and *The Screens and Other Poems* (1960).

Richards's voice often has been noted as one of his most distinguishing characteristics: "It was the sound of him, above all, that mattered. In form he was unremarkable, but you could not forget the voice, which was high-pitched and musical, utterly unaffected and effortlessly flexible. It would make little sense to say he flowered on a platform, since he never quite seemed to be off one."[12] Watson elaborates:

> He was incandescent. His voice rose and fell like the plashing waters of a fountain, and his face, especially on a public platform, glowed as if from an inner light. It hardly mattered what he said, since he said it so well; and when he read a poem the effect was brilliant, with a brilliance of a highly inimitable kind. He would atomize it, uttering the chief words between marked pauses and at independent pitch, often with an emphatic movement of an arm or of the whole figure that could make a word seem, for a fleeting moment, a matter of supreme significance. I would not recommend this mode of public utterance to anybody, and would confidently predict that anyone who tried it would sound and look ridiculous. With Richards it was spellbinding.[13]

Richards made his home in Cambridge, England, until his death on September 7, 1979. He maintained a passionate interest in mountaineering throughout his life, and with his wife, Dorothea Pilley Richards, he climbed the Matterhorn; Mont Blanc; Adam's Peak in Ceylon; Mount Hermon in Lebanon; Mt. Hood in Oregon; the Japanese Alps; the Canadian Rockies; the Andes; and mountains in China, Greece, and Alaska.[14] Richards's climbing has been called a metaphor for his intellectual life: " 'Poking about corners for something new' was said of him on Welsh rocks, but seems as true of the corners of his mind. . . . As he delighted in crossing a ridge to come down into a new valley, so we can see him in his critical works raiding across the ridges that divide one academic discipline from another, adventuring into new country."[15] "He was never interested in well-trodden paths. He was a pathfinder,"[16] a characteristic applicable in his contributions to rhetorical theory.

Objections to Traditional Rhetoric

Richards objects to the traditional view of rhetoric in the classical rhetorical tradition: "So low has Rhetoric sunk that we would do better just to dismiss it to Limbo than to trouble ourselves with it."[17] Richards rejects the works of such traditional rhetorical theorists as Aristotle and Richard Whately, which provide the basis for much of the contemporary study of rhetoric, because he believes they are largely irrelevant for the study of how rhetoric functions today. The study of rhetoric associated with such theorists revolves around learning a collection of rules about how to speak and write effectively, such as, "be clear, yet don't be dry; be vivacious, use metaphors when they will be understood not otherwise; respect usage; don't be long-winded, on the other hand don't be gaspy; avoid ambiguity; prefer the energetic to the elegant; preserve unity and coherence." The study of such rules, however, is not what the study of rhetoric should be: a "philosophic inquiry into how words work in discourse."[18] _'why' as opposed to 'how'_

A second objection Richards has to the traditional study of rhetoric is that its central theme is persuasion; it often has been "the theory of the battle of words and has always been itself dominated by the combative impulse."[19] Richards sees persuasion as only one of the many aims of rhetoric, among them exposition. He believes that narrowing the study of rhetoric to only one function does not encourage scholars of rhetoric to study the larger problem of how language works.

how words should be used

Proposal for a New Rhetoric

The traditional study of rhetoric, Richards believes, should be replaced by a view of rhetoric as "a philosophic discipline aiming at a mastery of the fundamental laws of the use of language."[20] Echoing the nineteenth-century rhetorical theorist George Campbell, Richards defines rhetoric as "the art by which discourse is adapted to its end"; its task is "to distinguish the different sorts of ends, or aims, for which we use language, to teach how to pursue them separately and how to reconcile their diverse claims."[21] In short, rhetoric "should be a study of misunderstanding and its remedies."[22] Such a rhetoric would offer explanations for questions such as how losses in communication can be measured, how good communication differs from bad communication, and how much of communication is distorted by outdated assumptions about and habitual attitudes toward words.[23]

Richards suggests that three major requirements must be met if a new rhetoric is to offer such explanations. One requirement is that the assumptions of rhetoric must be questioned and evaluated. Many of the assumptions of rhetoric were inherited from other disciplines, and without a questioning of their validity, rhetoric relies on terminology, data, and presuppositions that may prevent a much-needed innovative and comprehensive examination of how discourse operates.

Richards also advocates that the study of rhetoric begin with an analysis of words, the smallest units for conveying meaning.[24] This focus on words makes Richards's perspective different from that of traditional scholars of rhetoric, whose focus is largely on arguments, speeches, and how groups of words function. Richards believes, however, that if individuals first understand how words function, they will be able to put together larger messages for whatever end they desire—whether to persuade, to explain, to create a particular relationship with an audience, or to write poetry.

A third requirement for a new rhetoric is that it must be viewed and studied as holding a central place in the order of knowledge. It should not be seen as a discipline that is peripheral or irrelevant to other studies. Rhetoric can provide the core of a sound educational curriculum at a time when nothing is central and primary in the educational curriculum. Nothing holds it together or provides a center around which all subjects studied can be grouped. The study of rhetoric—the "systematic study of *the inherent and necessary opportunities for misunderstanding* which language offers"[25]—can serve as this center, Richards believes. Such a study would involve a knowledge of how central intellectual terms such as *being, have, cause,* and *same* can shift their meanings and thus give rise to varied misunderstandings and how misinterpretations in one field illuminate misinterpretations in others. The same problems in interpretation exist in all fields, and a discovery of patterns of meaning and misunderstanding in different areas of study would provide a unifying theme for education.[26]

Meaning

Much of Richards's perspective on rhetoric is concerned with how words come to mean what they do. Richards sees meanings of words as central to a theory of rhetoric not only because they are the essential components in the function of language but also because of the ways in which meanings serve the users of words. Meanings mediate or serve as a screen for individuals in their thinking, feeling, and willing—between all cognitive, affective, and volitional activities and the actuality with which these activities are concerned. Meanings are what individuals think of and think with when they contemplate happiness, what they feel when they dread an exam, and what they want when they envy a wealthy individual.

In addition to mediating for individuals in their thinking, feeling, and wanting, meanings mediate among individuals. They constitute the common world for people because they serve as common representatives of reality. Although no two individuals have exactly the same meanings for words, there are words—such as *president, post office,* and *stove*—whose meanings are used to create and maintain a somewhat common world.[27]

Richards begins his exploration of meaning with a discussion of other theories about how words come to have meaning. These theories usually involve some type of association whereby ideas or images become associated with words. For example, individuals learn what the word *cat* means by seeing an actual cat at the same time that they hear the word, and thus a link is formed between the sight of the cat and the particular sound of the word *cat.* The next time they hear the word, an image of a cat comes to mind. Because contact with different kinds of cats is likely, however, this type of theory next suggests that actual images eventually are relegated to the background, and something imprecise, such as the idea of a cat, becomes associated with the word.[28]

Richards objects to associational theories of meaning because to say that images and ideas cluster around a word in the mind does not really answer the question of how a word comes to have meaning. Such a theory only leads to the question of how an image or an idea comes to mean what it does.[29] Richards sets out to answer these questions and to develop a more satisfactory theory of meaning as a result.

Richards's explanation of meaning begins with the process of perception. Human beings are responsive to incoming sensory data from the perceived environment, and every stimulus that is received through the senses leaves an imprint, a trace, or what Richards calls an *engram* on the mind that is capable of being revived later.[30] To explain how sensory perceptions are developed into meanings, Richards introduces the notion of context. Context is a "cluster of events that recur together"[31] or "*a set of entities (things or events) related in a certain way.*"[32] In every perception, a context is formed that is composed of the sensations being experienced.

Whenever any part of a context appears, the possibility exists that the entire context will be called up and remembered because the various perceptions of the context have left residual traces in the mind. When part of the context appears, that part serves the function of a sign, affecting the individual as though the whole context were present. A sign, for Richards, is a thing that is understood to refer to something else. For example, dark skies, thunder, lightning, and rain once may have constituted a context for an individual. Following the experience of that context, when that person hears thunder, the sensation that comes to her through sound becomes a sign of rain, and she carries an umbrella or makes plans to stay indoors. Signs come to have meaning, then, because they previously have been components of a context that once affected the individual as a whole.

Words function in the same way that signs do. Because words are used as instruments of thought and for purposes of communication by humans, Richards calls them *symbols* rather than *signs*.[33] Like signs, words derive meaning through belonging to a context and serve as substitutes for the part of the context that currently is not present. For example, upon hearing the word *scissors*, an individual focuses on and sorts back through his category of scissors and draws up past contexts in which he has had experiences with scissors. The word fills in the missing parts of those contexts—all that is not currently present—from past experiences with scissors.[34]

Semantic Triangle

Richards illustrates his theory of meaning in a diagram called the *semantic triangle*. At each of the three corners of a triangle are the three major components in the process of meaning—symbol, reference or thought, and referent or the object of thought. At the top of the triangle, *reference* indicates the realm of memory where recollections of past experiences and contexts occur. *Referents* are the objects that are perceived and that create the impressions stored in the thought area, and *symbol* is the word that calls up the referent through the mental processes of the reference.[35]

Different kinds of relationships exist among the three components of the triangle. Between the reference and the symbol, a causal relationship exists. When individuals speak, the symbols they choose to use are caused partly by the references they are making and partly by social and psychological factors in the present, such as the purpose of the reference, the proposed effect of the symbol on the audience, and individuals' attitudes. Similarly, when they hear something that is said, the symbol causes them to perform an act of reference and to assume an attitude that will be more or less similar to the act and attitude of the speaker.

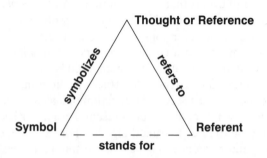

The relation between the reference and the referent can be either direct or indirect. It is direct when individuals think about something they are perceiving—for example, the color of a house. It is indirect when they think about something not immediately present—such as the shootings at Columbine High School in Colorado—and that may require a long chain of interpretations of signs or symbols that lead to other signs or symbols, such as bullying, alienation, violence, gun control, and safety.

Between the symbol and the referent, however, only an indirect relation is possible because these two entities are not connected directly. Thus, the relation is indicated by the dotted line at the base of the triangle. The exceptional case is when the symbol essentially is equivalent to the referent for which it is used—for example, an onomatopoeic word such as *buzz* or an explicit gesture or drawing. In these instances, the triangle is complete because its base is solid.[36] In the typical situation, however, no such direct relation holds between the symbol and the referent.

Not only does the semantic triangle summarize the process of meaning, but it serves as a reminder that no direct connection exists between a word and the object it symbolizes. For example, there is no particular relation between the word *plate* and the object from which food is eaten at the dinner table; it could just as easily be symbolized by the word *fort*. The belief that a connection exists is encouraged when this particular symbol occurs in a context with the flat, round object that holds food.

The semantic triangle also serves as a warning not to assume that the person to whom an individual is talking has identical thought processes around a symbol and referent as the speaker does. For example, assume a man was bitten by a dog as a child. He avoids dogs, rarely pets them, and is uncomfortable in their presence. For him, the meaning of the word *dog* may be represented in the semantic triangle in this way:

**Dangerous animal;
avoid any contact (Thought/Reference)**

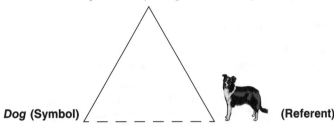

Dog **(Symbol)**   **(Referent)**

Another person, however, has a very different reference for dog. She grew up among dogs, her family owned several dogs while she was a child—all of them friendly—and she generally enjoys dogs. For her, the meaning of the word dog may be expressed in the semantic triangle in this way:

**Friendly, affectionate,
soft creature (Thought/Reference)**

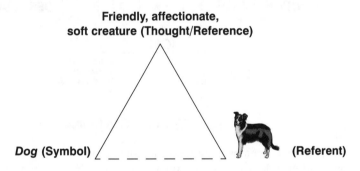

Dog **(Symbol)**   **(Referent)**

When these two people are discussing dogs, they are using the identical symbol, and they are reacting to a similar referent—an animal that barks and has four legs and a tail. But their thoughts or references about that animal, based on their individual experiences with dogs, are very different. If each assumes that the other person has the same meaning, there will be many opportunities for misunderstanding in their conversation about dogs.

Richards gives the label *Proper Meaning Superstition* to the belief that a word has a meaning all its own about which everyone should agree.[37] This belief is not uncommon. Generally, "whenever we hear anything said we spring spontaneously to an immediate conclusion, namely, that the speaker is referring to what we should be referring to were we speaking the words ourselves."[38] The semantic triangle is a practical tool for refuting the Proper Meaning Superstition because it makes clear that meanings exist in people rather than in the symbols themselves. Only "when a thinker makes use" of a word does it "stand for anything, or . . . have 'meaning.' "[39] Contexts determine and shape the meanings of words, and because every human being is a unique entity who has had different experiences, each person attaches somewhat different meanings to the same words.

Model of Communication

Richards presents another diagram to illustrate how meaning operates when people are attempting to communicate with one another:

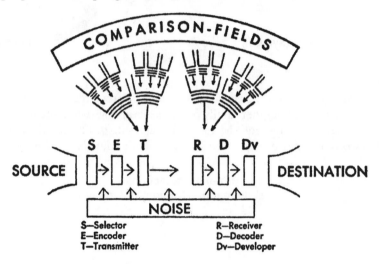

UTTERANCES-in-SITUATIONS

This model includes a source—the communicator—who selects mental images and encodes or translates them into words that can be transmitted to people who receive them. These receivers then decode or translate the words into mental images in accordance with their past experiences. In short, the process can be viewed in this way: Source Experience → Source Mind →Environment →Destination Mind →Destination Experience. Noise, in the model, refers to foreign elements that may interfere with the intended meaning—for example, a cough, illegible handwriting, or static in the electronic signal.[40]

All of the elements of Richards's model are common in communication models; what makes Richards's model different from many is the addition of the notion of comparison-fields. Comparison-fields are the various experiences of the people involved in the communicative effort—the contexts from which the symbols derive their meaning. The units of the comparison-fields consist of utterances-within-situations, represented by the open boxes and lines in the model. The "comprehending of any utterance is guided by any number of partially similar situations in which partially similar utterances have occurred."[41] His model shows how similar utterances in similar situations are brought together (represented in the synthesis of boxes and lines) to represent a more or less similar experience and thus to assist in the interpretation of the message. This process, of course, may not be a conscious one: "The past utterances-within-situations need not have been consciously remarked or wittingly analysed; still less need they be explicitly remembered when the comprehending occurs."[42]

The source's experience may be similar to or very different from the destination's experience, but the closer the comparison-fields or experiences of a source and a receiver, the more similar their interpretations of meaning are likely to be and thus the greater probability of successful communication. Communication, if defined as strict transference of or participation in identical experiences, does not occur. Communication is "a use of symbols in such a way that acts of reference occur in a hearer which are similar in all relevant aspects to those which are symbolized by them in the speaker."[43] In other words, an experience occurs in the hearer's mind that is like the experience in the speaker's mind. Communication results in misunderstanding, then, when there is a lack of common experience. If people are to communicate effectively, "long and varied acquaintanceship, close familiarity, lives whose circumstances have often corresponded, in short an exceptional fund of common experience" are needed.[44]

Feedforward

Although not explicitly included in his model of communication, Richards's concept of feedforward is an integral part of his theory of meaning and perspective on communication. Feedforward is the process by which receivers affect themselves, in contrast to feedback, which is the effect of receivers on a source. Feedforward is "some sort of preparation for, some design arrangement for one sort of outcome rather than another."[45] It is a readiness to act in one way or another. Feedforward is present when a person walks downstairs, for example, and expects and readies her advanced leg to meet the stair under her toe. Usually, this feedforward is fulfilled, and there is confirmatory feedback at the end of each step taken—her foot finds the expected step of the stair. Sometimes, however, the expected feedback does not come, as when she believes there is one more stair at the bottom of a dark staircase when there is not. Her foot then hits the floor with a thud, suggesting that her feedforward was not accurate.

Meaning in a communicative exchange functions, in part, on the principle of feedforward. As individuals hear the words spoken by the source of a message, their past experiences and contexts lead them to choose certain meanings as more salient and relevant than others. Their ability to select meanings similar to those envisioned by the source depends on their previous choices of meanings. Feedforward prepares them to attribute particular meanings to words rather than other possible meanings. When the word's meaning for an individual seems roughly equivalent to that expected by the speaker or writer, confirmatory feedback is received, and the person is more likely to symbolize that meaning with that word again in the future.[46] "The entirety of activity . . . seems to consist of *choices*," Richards asserts. "Initial choices would be free; but, when choice has been made, the subsequent choices are bound thereby while the choice is held."[47] Feedforward is the pattern of meanings accumulated from past experiences applied to subsequent encounters with the same word symbol.

Functions of Discourse

The process of comprehending meaning becomes more complex as Richards introduces various functions that discourse serves for the source and the receiver. To explain how words work from both perspectives, Richards suggests that language performs a variety of tasks so that whether "we know and intend it or not, we are all jugglers when we converse, keeping the billiard-balls in the air while we balance the cue on our nose. . . . Language . . . has not one but several tasks to perform simultaneously."[48] The four functions of language from the point of view of the speaker are:

1. Sense: Words function to direct listeners' attention to some state of affairs and to cause them to think about selected events or items.

2. Feeling: Words express feelings or attitudes toward the referent. Only in exceptional cases—as in the language of mathematics—is no feeling conveyed through an utterance. Feeling also involves the degree of certainty or confidence the speaker has in the soundness of the statement being made.

3. Tone: Words convey the attitude of the speaker toward the audience.

4. Intention: Words express the aim or outcome desired by the speaker or writer—whether this is conscious or unconscious.[49]

Just as words function in various ways for the speaker, they also have various functions for the audience. Richards suggests that if comprehension is to occur, an audience must distinguish among seven[50] functions or activities of language:

1. Indicating: A message points to or selects which items are to be the focus of attention.

2. Characterizing: The utterance says something about the items on which attention is being focused, sorting among various characteristics and qualities.

3. Realizing: Realizing concerns the degree and vividness to which the utterance makes an audience sense the particular item: "what is in question is the nearness and fulness [*sic*] with which something is to be present to us."[51] This activity deals with the nature of the presentation, whether the subject is presented "vividly or plainly, excitingly or quieteningly, close up or remotely."[52]

4. Valuing: Valuing is the raising of the question, "SHOULD this be so?"[53] Valuing functions to assign a positive or negative value to the item under discussion.

5. Influencing: At issue in this function is whether the audience would like to maintain or change the status quo. Encouraging an audience to change a situation and persuading it to become adjusted to a set of circumstances are major activities of this function.

6. Controlling: Controlling is the management and administration of the other activities or functions so that they do not interfere too much with one another.

7. Purposing: In this function, the end, aim, or intention that is being pursued in the discourse is revealed to the audience.

Any full utterance, Richards asserts, does all seven of these activities at once and invites all of them in the listener. In some types of discourse, however, some aspects are emphasized more than others. In mathematics, for example, the activities of indicating, controlling, and purposing are predominant functions. In the act of swearing, the functions of valuing, influencing, and purposing are the focus.

The seven constituent parts of the process of comprehending help to explain why communication often goes awry. Misunderstanding may occur, for example, if the communicators do not agree about the subject of their interaction (indicating), do not realize the implications of what is being said (realizing), do not accept the proposals that are offered (influencing), do not understand or will not agree about the way in which a proposal should be carried forward (controlling), or do not agree about the purpose of their interaction (purposing).[54]

A complete model of how Richards sees the process of communication, then, might look like this:[55]

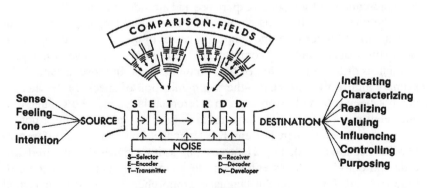

UTTERANCES-in-SITUATIONS

Emotive versus Referential Language

The type of discourse involved affects the process by which communicators come to comprehend. Richards distinguishes between two uses of language—the referential and the emotive—that correspond roughly to the discourses of science and poetry.[56] Each of these involves the seven comprehending activities to varying degrees. Although the referential and emotive uses may occur together in an utterance, they function in very different ways.

The referential function of language involves words used primarily for the references they evoke. In contrast, the emotive function of language involves the expression or excitation of feelings and attitudes.[57] "The house has seven rooms" is an example of referential use, while "you go, girl!" is emotive. Most language, of course, is mixed or rhetorical as opposed to purely referential or emotive. "The majestic mountains sparkled against the blue sky" exemplifies the rhetorical use of language, which is the type used in most discourse.

The distinctions among the three types of language can be seen in these sentences:

1. The Mississippi River is 3,960 feet wide at Baton Rouge where the ferry crosses.

2. The lovely Mississippi glides smoothly into the Gulf.

3. Old Man River, that old man river, he just keeps rolling along.[58]

Referential language can be tested by reference to objective reality. The depth and width of the Mississippi River, for example, can be measured to determine the truth of the first statement, which is referential. The second statement is rhetorical; it contains some words with specific referents—*gulf*, for instance—and some without. *Lovely*, for example, does not have a referent in the environment that can be assessed objectively. A rhetorical statement, then, contains some referential and some emotive words. The third sentence, in contrast, "has no objective truth whatsoever. It is not intended to have any. It is merely a faithful representative of someone's experience and attitude or feeling."[59]

The differences between emotive and referential language are particularly important in terms of the mental processes of meaning and comprehension. Individuals fail to comprehend referential language when the references differ in the minds of the communicators. In those instances, the primary aim of the discourse—the communication of specific references—has not been attained. Moreover, in referential language, the connections and relations of references to one another must be logical and must not interfere with one another. For emotive language, however, wide differences in reference are of little importance as long as it produces the required attitude and emotion. The essential consideration is the character of the attitude aroused. For referential language, comprehension consists of factual accuracy; agreement or comprehension in emotive language is accomplished by what Richards calls *engagement of the will*.[60]

There are greater opportunities for misunderstanding in emotive language use because of the likelihood that the symbols may not lead the communicators to precisely the same emotional responses. Each type of language use emphasizes different aspects of comprehension. In referential language, the functions of indicating and characterizing are predominant, while emotive language emphasizes the functions of realizing, valuing, and influencing.[61]

Elimination of Misunderstanding

Richards's recognition of the many ways in which communication may be ineffective leads him to suggest some means by which communicators may work to prevent misunderstandings. Among these are metaphor, definitions, literary context, and specialized quotation marks.

Metaphor

For Richards, metaphor is more than a figure of speech used for stylistic effect in discourse. It holds a central place in his theory of meaning and is a major technique for facilitating comprehension. He objects to traditional conceptions of metaphor; in particular, he disagrees with Aristotle's view of metaphor in the *Poetics*. In this work, Aristotle says that the use of metaphor is a gift that some people have and some do not, and it cannot be imparted or taught. In addition, Aristotle calls the metaphor something special and exceptional in the use of language, a deviation from its normal mode of working.[62]

Richards refutes these notions in his definition of metaphor, which he sees as using a grouping of things related to one another in a particular way to discover a similar relationship in another group. The thought process, then, is metaphoric. When individuals attribute meaning, they notice in a new context an aspect similar to that encountered in an earlier context. Two thoughts of different things are "supported by a single word, or phrase, whose meaning is a resultant of their interaction."[63] In this process, the principles of sorting, categorization, comparison, and abstraction are employed.

When individuals encounter a moving vehicle with four wheels and an engine, for example, they sort back through their contexts to discover when they have encountered similar objects and come up with the word *car* to stand for their various thoughts about the vehicle in question. The meaning for car is derived from "the attraction of likes" or from a recognition of the similar characteristics that both things have in common.[64] The symbol pulls together thoughts about various cars, and the meaning of the word *car* is the result of the interaction among the thoughts. This is the basic process of metaphor.

Not only is metaphor the means by which meaning is developed, but it is a method by which a communicator may provide listeners with the experience needed to elicit similar references for a particular symbol. In cases where "the speaker must himself supply and control a large part of the causes of the listener's experience,"[65] metaphor is used to supply the experience: "But what is needed for the wholeness of an experience is not always naturally present, and metaphor supplies an excuse by which what is needed may be smuggled in."[66] For example, suppose a professor is attempting to communicate with graduate students about the process of writing a doctoral dissertation. The professor might use a metaphor to supply some of the needed experience and to help develop a meaning for *dissertation* in their minds similar to the meaning she holds: "Writing a dissertation is writing a series of term papers."

Richards proposes two terms to enable metaphor to be analyzed and discussed easily. *Tenor* is the term he uses to refer to the underlying idea or principal subject of the metaphor—what is meant. *Vehicle* is the means of conveying the underlying idea, the borrowed idea, or what the tenor resembles. *Metaphor* refers to the double unit as a whole.[67] In the metaphor "the sun is a red balloon," the tenor is the sun and the vehicle is the balloon, which attributes the characteristics of redness and roundness to the sun.

In the analysis of metaphor, Richards cautions that metaphor does not depend for its operation only on resemblances or correspondence between the tenor and the vehicle. A metaphor works "through disparity as well as through likeness."[68] Although the action of the vehicle certainly invites a recognition of the similarities with the tenor, it also invites a consideration of differences. In the metaphor of the sun and the balloon, the balloon invites readers to note similarities between a balloon and the sun, but it also implicitly warns them not to take the resemblances too strictly—not to ignore the differences. They do not see, for example, the sun as something that holds air and can be popped with a pin, something that can be attached to a string, or something that is a toy. They must play "an incessant game with the discrepancies" in metaphor.[69]

In addition to resemblance and discrepancy, the relationship suggested by metaphor may be based on a common attitude held toward the tenor and vehicle. Richards gives as an example calling someone a *duck* in an endearing manner. The intent is not "to imply that she has a bill and paddles or is good to eat"[70] but that the speaker views ducks and the person in a similar way—as, perhaps, with a "tender and amused regard."[71]

Definition of Words

For Richards, defining words is another means for eliminating misunderstanding. Clear definitions of references can make discussion more profitable by bringing individuals into open agreement or disagreement with one another. Some words such as *beauty* or *truth*, for example, actually are not single words at all; rather, they are sets of discrepant symbols. Yet, if people use them as if only one meaning is possible, misunderstanding is likely to result. Similarly, Richards suggests, to examine and analyze a concept seriously, individuals should begin with as complete a list as possible of the different uses of the word. Without "a map of the separable fields covered" by the term, it "is liable to be confused with another, to their common detriment, or to yield an apparent contradiction of purely verbal origin."[72]

Definition involves finding the referent for a symbol through the substitution of a symbol or symbols that are better understood than the one being defined. It involves the selection of referents with which the listener is familiar and the drawing of connections to the word being defined. Richards suggests several methods of definition or possible routes to reach an understanding about an unclear or unknown referent.

Symbolization is the simplest, most fundamental means of definition. Using this route to define *apple*, for example, someone could take an actual apple, point to it, and say, "*Apple* is a symbol that stands for this."

In definition by similarity, a relation of likeness is used to connect the concept to be defined to the familiar referent. *Purple* could be defined, for example, by pointing to something that is purple and saying, "Anything that is like this in color is purple."

Spatial relations also may be used to define terms. Words such as *in, on, above, between, beside, to the right of, near, bigger than*, or *part of* are used in such definitions to connect a symbol by spatial relations to another referent. A definition of *library* using spatial relations could be: "The library is the building to the east of the student union."

Temporal relations can be used to connect unknown referents to known ones. Using this method of definition, *yesterday* can be defined as "the day before to-day," and *Sunday* can be defined as "the first day of the week."[73]

Causation is another route of definition. Definitions of physical causation indicate a physical cause-and-effect relationship between referents. For example, *thunder* can be defined as "what is caused . . . by certain electrical disturbances,"[74] and *sunburn* can be defined as "a burn on the skin caused by overexposure to the sun." Definitions of psychological causation indicate a psychological cause-and-effect relationship between referents. The term *pleasure* might be defined as "the conscious accompaniment of successful psychic activity."[75] Psycho-physical definitions involve both psychological and physical causation; using this method of definition, *a perception of orange* can be defined as "the effect in consciousness [psychological effect] of certain vibrations falling on the retina [physical cause]."[76]

Another type of definition Richards suggests is that in which the object of a mental state is described. Examples of this type of relation are referring, desiring, willing, and feeling. Using such a definition, *piteous things* are those things "towards which we feel pity" or sympathy, and *good things* are defined as "those which we approve of approving."[77]

Legal relations provide the basis for definitions that frequently are employed in courts of law. They are subject to the test of satisfying the judge and generally involve terms such as *belonging to, subject of, liable to*, and *evidence of*. A definition of *abandonment* in a lease agreement for the rental of an apartment, for example, uses legal relations: "The premises shall be conclusively presumed to be abandoned permanently by the tenant if the same are apparently unoccupied for a period of fifteen (15) days or more."

Aware that some concepts may not be able to be defined easily using only one of these methods, Richards suggests that definitions also can be developed from combinations of the various methods in a form he calls *common complex relations*. *Imitation*, for example, can be defined as "the act of modeling or copying," which implicitly relies on the methods of similarity (doing an act that is like another act) and psycho-physical causation (a desire to repeat an observed behavior causes the behavior in the observer).[78]

In summary, Richards suggests that unclear references be symbolized by means of various routes of definition. In the definitional process, the starting points are familiar things that occur freely in ordinary experience and then are linked to unclear or new words to facilitate the understanding of their meanings. The list is not exhaustive, however, and Richards makes clear that other relations can be used to define, including shape, function, purpose, and opposition.

Literary Context

Literary context is another way to eliminate misunderstanding in communication. Words never appear in isolation but instead occur in literary contexts, with sentences, phrases, or paragraphs dependent upon one another to provide clues to possible meanings of the words. This mutual dependency or interaction, which Richards calls the *interinanimation* of words, constitutes their literary context.

The process of paying attention to literary context is one in which human beings engage unconsciously, but Richards hopes to bring it to conscious attention as a device to aid in the comprehension of meaning. The process operates in this manner: An individual comes to a word in a sentence that has a disputable or unclear meaning for him—as nearly all words do. At this point, he notes a reservation about it, leaving unsettled for a time what the meaning is going to be. Richards calls this use of a word—the creating of a gap to be filled later—the *Mesopotamian* use. This term comes from a "story about an old woman who told her pastor that she 'found great support in that blessed word *Mesopotamia*.'"[79] Just as the reader of the story waits to see what meaning the woman gives to *Mesopotamia* (and Richards does not say), so readers wait to discover what meanings words have until they become acquainted with their literary context. A word generally keeps to a Mesopotamian use for only a brief moment as it quickly has its immense field of possible meanings narrowed down by the influence of the other words that accompany it.[80]

Richards's concept of literary context reinforces his notion that a word does not have a meaning of its own or a fixed correct usage. Because a word is always a cooperative member of a group of words, the meaning for a word comes to it only with respect to the meanings of the other words that surround it. Just as a note in a musical phrase takes its character from and makes its contribution only with the other notes about it and a color is what it is only with respect to the other colors with it in a painting, so meanings of words must be considered only in literary context. Words cannot be judged correct or appropriate in isolation but only in their literary contexts.

The principle of literary context holds not only for the meanings of words but also for other elements of communication such as a speaker's attitude and tone. As with the meanings of words, the attitude and tone conveyed in "the opening words" of a speech are "likely to be ambiguous."[81] Only when the speaker has continued to speak and more context is revealed can the audience tell if the tone of the speech is sarcastic or serious, confident or hesitant.

The mutual dependence of words, of course, varies with the type of discourse. At one end of the scale, with discourse that is technical and scientific—referential language—many of the words are independent. They tend to mean the same regardless of the words with which they are combined. If they fluctuate, they move only into a small number of stable positions. At the opposite end of the scale, in poetic discourse—emotive language—words are likely to have no fixed and settled meanings separable from those of the words with which they occur.[82]

Specialized Quotation Marks

To assist the reader further in discovering the intended meaning of a word, phrase, or sentence, Richards devised a set of special symbols to take the place of the usual quotation marks. Metasemantic markers are small letters placed, as quotation marks are, around the words, phrases, and sentences they single out. Believing that quotation marks must perform a great number of functions, Richards advocates these marks "as a technical notation by which we could better keep track of the uses we are making of our words." He used the system in much of his own writing and was "persuaded of the usefulness of this device."[83]

w...w indicates that the word itself is being talked about; these "marks are equivalent to 'the word.' For example, ^{w}table^w may mean an article of furniture or a list."[84]

r...r indicates that the author is referring to some special use of the word or phrase, as " ^{r}Nature^r for Whitehead is not Wordsworth's ^{r}Nature.^{r} "[85]

nb...nb "indicates that how the word is understood is a turning point in the discussion, and usually that it may easily be read in more than one way or with an inadequate perception of its importance."[86] It is short for *nota bene* or note well. American automobile companies, for example, have lost a share of the American market to the Japanese and Europeans because they have failed in the ^{nb}art^{nb} of automobile manufacture.

i...i indicates that other meanings "the word may have in other occurrences may intervene" in the meaning the writer is attempting to convey. "The marks are equivalent to 'Intervention likely.' "[87] For example, Kenneth Burke defines *piety* as *"the sense of what properly goes with what."*[88] When writing about Kenneth Burke's concept of piety, these marks could indicate that the reader's knowledge about the religious meanings of [i]piety[i] could intervene and conflict with Burke's meaning of the term.

hi...hi   means "Helpful intervention."[89] It signals that meanings the word is likely to have in other occurrences may intervene, and such intervention is likely to help in understanding the meaning of the word in this situation. For example, in "the organization implemented a [hi]democratic[hi] system of decisionmaking," the marks would indicate that the usual meanings of the word should be utilized in determining the meaning of *democratic*.

t...t   means "technical term"[90] and the meaning is fixed. In the sentence, "she has formulated several notions about politics but has not devised a [t]theory,[t]" for example, these marks indicate that the word is being used in a specialized, technical way.

!...!   indicates surprise or astonishment that people can write or talk in such a way. It signals "'a Good heavens! What-a-way-to-talk!' attitude. It may be read [!]shriek[!] if we have occasion to read it aloud."[91] The marks indicate astonishment at an idea, as in: "He claimed that his theory was [!]the only legitimate theory that had been developed in the communication discipline.[!] "[92]

For Richards, the goal of communication—for communicators to attribute similar meanings to symbols—is difficult to achieve. An awareness of and use of metaphor, definition, literary context, and specialized quotation marks do not guarantee that communication will be effective but serve as a starting point to aid in the elimination of the misunderstandings that inevitably occur.

Commentary

"Few thinkers in our century have left their imprint so visibly on the scenes of literary and rhetorical criticism as Ivor Armstrong Richards,"[93] asserts Stephen H. Browne. Although many of Richards's notions about rhetoric today seem commonplace such that reading him now "is an odd experience, rather like watching a home movie and missing the technical finesse of modern Hollywood,"[94] his ideas have had lasting impact on rhetorical theory. He created and put into circulation a number of terms and assumptions about rhetoric that are truisms of the communication discipline, including tenor, vehicle, emotive and referential language, and the idea that the meanings of words are in people. As Browne explains, "The point may seem obvious to us now, but at the time Richards and Ogden saw themselves battling a centuries-old habit of mistaking the word for the thing and of assuming that words contain one and only one proper meaning."[95] His microscopic perspective on rhetoric also was an innovative approach to a discipline largely concerned with patterns, characteristics, and functions of composite discourse such as debates, speeches, and rhetorical acts.[96] By providing a much-needed microscopic supplement to the study of rhetoric, Richards encourages rhetorical theorists to study rhetoric in a more holistic fashion, examining, in essence, both the pieces of the puzzle and the completed puzzle itself.

Yet another characteristic of Richards's contributions is his use of a variety of disciplines and fields to develop his perspective on rhetoric. As Stanley Edgar Hyman notes, "Perhaps more than any man since Bacon, Richards has taken all knowledge as his province, and his field is the entire mind of man."[97] He continues: "Not only is he thoroughly familiar with the dozen fields . . . that he has staked out as his own, but he has invaded almost every other area of knowledge. To make a minor point, he is apt not only to quote theoretical physics with authority, but to quote Lenin's *Materialism* and *Empirio-Criticism* against it with equal authority."[98] Browne notes that psycholinguistics and cognitive rhetoric, domains of inquiry to which Richards points, "would bear rich fruit several decades later. In practical terms, this emphasis on the relationship between the structure of language and mind, and of both to the world, allowed Richards to develop an approach to interpretation that was, if not entirely unique, distinctive and so forcefully expressed as to shape generations of literary critics."[99]

"A sense of mission always made him seem far more, and far other, than an academic,"[100] notes George Watson, recognizing Richards's contribution of conceptualizing rhetoric as an instrument for the diagnosis and remedy of social problems. He "sought to accord the subject a seriousness of mission heretofore unrealized," notes Browne, who asserts that "his insistence that rhetoric serve purposes beyond teaching the young how to score debating points remains a position ignored only at peril to rhetoric's growth and vitality."[101] Richards's primary aim is to furnish a means to improve social life or civilization in general through the improvement of communication.[102] He views the ailments of the world primarily as verbal ones with verbal remedies. Richards proposes to accomplish his goal of improving civilization through education, thus joining "the ranks of those who would save mankind from its verbal frailties by pedagogical dogma."[103] He has "faith in education, and particularly the humanities, as *the* way of improving verbal understanding, both in the metaphoric or dialectic shaping of messages and in the dialogical or balanced reception of them."[104] Richards summarizes this position as "while you're teaching beginning English, you might as well teach everything else." He elaborates: "That is to say, a world position, what's needed for living, a philosophy of religion, how to find things out, and the whole works—mental and moral seed for the planet. In this way the two-thirds of the planet that doesn't yet know how to read and write would learn in learning how to read and write English, the things that would help them in their answers to 'Where should man go?' "[105] Richards believes his goal of improving civilization can be accomplished specifically through the educational tools of world literacy programs and Basic English, the 850-word language he developed with Ogden.

Richards's goals concerning rhetoric—to solve the problem of understanding and misunderstanding and to launch a new rhetoric—also have been attacked as pretentious and as failing to yield the results he promised. "But the general effect . . . is . . . of a largeness of promise and an impressiveness of operation quite disproportionate to anything that emerges," suggests F. R. Leavis. "Moreover this effect is such as to impose the regretful conviction that had the ambition been less the profit might very well have been greater."[106] One example of this largeness of promise is Richards's assertion that no "revolution in human affairs would be greater than that" initiated by observance of the distinction between prose and poetry.[107] To attribute such results to this distinction seems an exaggeration, Max Black notes, when what Richards actually has done is simply to "recognize that scientific discourse is not the sole significant mode of human communication."[108] Hyman suggests, for example, that rather than solving the problem of the "breakdown of our civilization" through educational means, Richards actually formulates a method for teaching reading more effectively in the schools—a considerably lower achievement than the one for which he aimed.[109] Neither is Richards concerned with the pragmatics of education that would have to be addressed were education to serve the vital role he suggests—pragmatics such as variations in instructors' abilities to teach the breadth in content he requires and varying levels of students' abilities. As Donald K. Enholm explains, "None of these problems is necessarily insolvable, but they are problems not dealt with by Richards, and they should indicate that between his proposals for improving verbal understanding and our hopes for realizing them, lies considerable distance, most of it uphill."[110]

Others of Richards's ideas also have been the subject of criticism. One complaint that has been leveled against his works concerns the "looseness" of his discussions.[111] In some instances, his understanding of a particular subject seems superficial or even incorrect. His attack on traditional rhetoricians, for example, has been described as "more dogmatic than accurate" because ancient and modern rhetoricians "consider rhetoric and the use of language in terms quite as functional as Richards's."[112] In many cases, Richards provides little evidence or support for his assertions. Another complaint about Richards's writing is that many of the crucial terms in his theory "are so vague as to be virtually undefined."[113] "His theories flutter past like bright butterflies, endless evidence of a darting intelligence, but offering no lasting good," suggests Watson. "His books look as if they were written at high speed, garrulous rather than eloquent, and often needlessly long."[114]

Another problem concerning looseness that the reader of Richards is likely to note is that his works sometimes contain incongruities. As B. Aubrey Fisher explains, what he asserts in one work is different from his assertions in another.[115] Hyman describes this tendency as a "curiously dilettantish irresponsibility toward ideas" and "an inability to hold to a consistent point of view at any given time."[116] This problem is evident, for example, when Richards cites different numbers of functions of comprehending.

There are seven listed in *Practical Criticism* and only four in *Interpretation in Teaching*, a discrepancy he does not address. Incongruities also are evident in Richards's "frequent changes in vocabulary," which, according to John Paul Russo, produce "a confused effect."[117] These incongruities, however, may be less a problem of clarity of thought and writing than they are evidence of Richards's own "healthy growth."[118] Richards's views on aspects of his ideas appeared to change over time, and these discrepancies can be viewed simply as evidence of the evolution of his thought.

Richards also has been criticized for an overemphasis on science in his ideas and for his apparent desire for a science of symbolism and criticism. That he weights his ideas—particularly his early ideas—in favor of science is reflected in his psychological approach to the problem of meaning, which draws on a variety of psychological theories, including "physiological and neurological psychology, behaviorism, Pavlov's conditioned-reflex psychology, psychoanalysis, Gestalt, and snips and snatches from every other psychological theorizer or experimenter."[119] This scientific focus well may have been due to the influence on Richards of his early collaborator, Ogden, a renowned psychologist.[120]

Richards's scientific bias was lessened, to some degree, in his later works, although he never explicitly renounced his early theory of the science of symbolism and continued sporadically to adapt pieces of scientific models in his later writings. He seems to have retired his "psychological model" of meaning "from active duty—retired with honorable discharge, not court-martialed"[121]—after the middle 1930s, suggesting a shift away from a behavioristic theory with mechanical metaphors of stimulus and response to notions more influenced by humanism.

Richards's transition from a commitment to the development of a theory of criticism and meaning to a preoccupation with education—particularly Basic English—that took place gradually from 1929 to 1939 is difficult to explain. Russo suggests his motive may have been "the need to be challenged and to be creative in response to challenge," as well as a desire to investigate the lower levels of education, since his career until then had focused on the upper levels.[122] His background as a literary critic, however, seems contradictory in many ways to the very concept of Basic English. As Hyman explains: "To put it bluntly, there seems to be no way of reconciling the two, and to the extent that he continues working with Basic he renounces criticism and abdicates his position as our foremost living critic. The concept of Basic in Criticism . . . seems to be at its best superfluous and at its worst a fraud, and even in the hands of Richards . . . it has produced no critical insights particularly worth having."[123]

Richards appears to have solved the conflict between Basic English and his more theoretical work in rhetoric and criticism by giving "up the writing of literary criticism" and theorizing about rhetoric.[124] As John Needham notes, "It is hard to think of any other English critic who might be described as 'major,' whose interest in literature is so peripheral," and he cites the "corresponding absence of any deep or prolonged study of a given body of literature."[125] Watson concurs: "Strangest of all, there survives from his hand no account of any poem, play, or novel that one could regard as classic or even notable. The critical effort always lay in the future, as he saw it: it was one day to be done—and was not done. Pupils who entered the subject under the spell of his personality continued to love him and to miss him; but they knew that Basic English had not worked and that nothing else he had proposed had worked."[126] His failure to continue to develop his notions in these areas well may be a reason why Richards's ideas, which constituted original and significant starting points for a new rhetoric, in the end did not have the impact on contemporary rhetoric many had believed they would. That Richards did not continue to develop his perspective on rhetoric in his later works does not denigrate, however, his earlier achievements in this area. As Hyman asserts, "we shall still have, in his early books, work to rank with the finest of our time, as well as a whole dazzling body of work stemming out of it. Those are in no danger."[127]

Bibliography

Books

Basic English and Its Uses. New York: W. W. Norton, 1943.

Basic in Teaching: East and West. London, UK: Kegan Paul, Trench, Trubner, 1935.

Basic Rules of Reason. London, UK: Kegan Paul, Trench, Trubner, 1933.

Beyond. New York: Harcourt Brace Jovanovich, 1973.

Coleridge on Imagination. London, UK: Kegan Paul, Trench, Trubner, 1934.

Design for Escape: World Education Through Modern Media. New York: Harcourt, Brace and World, 1968.

Development of Experimental Audio-Visual Devices and Materials for Beginning Readers. Cooperative Research Project No. 5,0642. Cambridge, MA: Harvard University, 1964–65. (With Christine M. Gibson.)

English Through Pictures, Book I. New York: English Language Research, 1945. (With Christine M. Gibson.)

English Through Pictures, Book II and a Second Workbook of English. New York: Pocket, 1973. (With Christine M. Gibson.)

A First Book of English for Chinese Learners. Peking: Orthological Institute of China, 1938.

First Steps in Reading English: A First Book for Readers to Be. New York: Pocket, 1957. (With Christine M. Gibson.)

First Steps in Reading Hebrew. New York: Language Research, 1955. (With David Weinstein and Christine Gibson.)

A First Workbook of English. New York: Language Research, 1959. (With Christine M. Gibson.)

A First Workbook of French. New York: Pocket, 1957. (With M. H. Ilsley and Christine M. Gibson.)

A First Workbook of Russian. New York: Pocket, 1963. (With Evelyn Jasiulko Harden and Christine Gibson.)

A First Workbook of Spanish. New York: Pocket, 1960. (With Ruth C. Metcalf and Christine Gibson.)

The Foundations of Aesthetics. London, UK: George Allen and Unwin, 1922. (With C. K. Ogden and James Wood.)

French Self-Taught Through Pictures. New York: Pocket, 1950. (With M. H. Ilsley and Christine M. Gibson.)

French Through Pictures. New York: Pocket, 1950. (With M. H. Ilsley and Christine Gibson.)

General Education in a Free Society: Report of the Harvard Committee. Cambridge, MA: Harvard University Press, 1946. (With Committee on the Objectives of a General Education in a Free Society.)

German Through Pictures. New York: Pocket, 1953. (With I. Schmidt Mackey, W. F. Mackey, and Christine M. Gibson.)

Hebrew Reader. New York: Pocket, 1955. (With David Weinstein and Christine M. Gibson.)

Hebrew Through Pictures. New York: Pocket, 1954. (With David Weinstein and Christine M. Gibson.)

How to Read a Page: A Course in Efficient Reading with an Introduction to a Hundred Great Words. New York: W. W. Norton, 1942.

Interpretation in Teaching. New York: Harcourt, Brace, 1938.

Italian Through Pictures, Book I. New York: Pocket, 1955. (With Italo Evangelista and Christine M. Gibson.)

Learning Basic English: A Practical Handbook for English-Speaking People. New York: W. W. Norton, 1945. (With Christine M. Gibson.)

Learning the English Language, Books I–III. Boston: Houghton Mifflin, 1943. (With Christine M. Gibson.)

Learning the English Language, Book IV. Boston: Houghton Mifflin, 1953. (With Christine M. Gibson.)

The Meaning of Meaning: A Study of the Influence of Language Upon Thought and of the Science of Symbolism. London, UK: Kegan Paul, Trench, Trubner, 1923. (With C. K. Ogden.)

Mencius on the Mind: Experiments in Multiple Definition. London, UK: Kegan Paul, Trench, Trubner, 1932.

Nations and Peace. New York: Simon and Schuster, 1947.

The Philosophy of Rhetoric. New York: Oxford University Press, 1936.

Plato's Republic. Cambridge, UK: Cambridge University Press, 1966. (Trans. and ed. I. A. Richards.)

Poetries and Sciences. London, UK: Routledge and Kegan Paul, 1970.

Poetries: Their Media and Ends. Ed. Trevor Eaton. The Hague, Neth.: Mouton, 1974.

The Portable Coleridge. New York: Viking, 1950. (Ed. I. A. Richards.)

Practical Criticism: A Study of Literary Judgment. London, UK: Kegan Paul, Trench, Trubner, 1929.

Principles of Literary Criticism. London, UK: Kegan Paul, Trench, Trubner, 1924.

Republic of Plato: A Version in Simplified English. London, UK: Kegan Paul, Trench, Trubner, 1948.

Russian Through Pictures, Book I. New York: Pocket, 1961. (With Evelyn Jasiulko and Christine Gibson.)

Science and Poetry. London, UK: Kegan Paul, Trench, Trubner, 1926.

So Much Nearer: Essays Toward a World English. New York: Harcourt, Brace and World, 1960.

Spanish Self-Taught Through Pictures. New York: Pocket, 1950. (With Ruth C. Metcalf and Christine M. Gibson.)

Spanish Through Pictures, Book II and A Second Workbook of Spanish. New York: Pocket, 1972.

Speculative Instruments. Chicago: University of Chicago Press, 1955.

Techniques in Language Control. Rowley, MA: Newbury, 1974. (With Christine Gibson.)

Words on Paper: First Steps in Reading. Cambridge, MA: Language Research, 1943. (With Christine Gibson.)

The Wrath of Achilles: The Iliad of Homer, Shortened and in a New Translation. New York: W. W. Norton, 1950.

Articles

"Basic English." *Fortune*, 23 (June 1941), 89–91, 111–12, 114.

"Basic English and Its Applications." *Royal Society of Arts Journal*, 87 (June 1939), 735–55.

"Basic English Can Be Learned Easily by All." *Rotarian*, 63 (December 1943), 30, 56–57.

"Belief." *Symposium*, 1 (1930), 423–39.

"Between Truth and Truth." *Symposium*, 2 (1931), 226–41.

"Can Education Increase Intelligence?: I. But We Can Be Taught to Think." *Forum*, 76 (October 1926), 504–09.

"The Changing American Mind." *Harper's*, 154 (January 1927), 239–45.

"Chinese Personal Nomenclature: The Advantages of an Ambilateral System." *Psyche*, 12 (July 1931), 86–89.

"The Chinese Renaissance." *Scrutiny*, 1 (September 1932), 102–13.

"A Common Language." *Vital Speeches of the Day*, 10 (December 15, 1943), 158–60.

"Communications: Art and Science—I." *Athenaeum*, June 27, 1919, pp. 534–35.

"Communications: Emotion and Art." *Athenaeum*, July 18, 1919, pp. 630–31.

"Communications: The Instruments of Criticism: Expression." *Athenaeum*, October 31, 1919, p. 1131.

"'A Cooking Egg': Final Scramble." *Essays in Criticism*, 4 (January 1954), 103–05.

"Design and Control in Language Teaching." *Harvard Alumni Bulletin*, 59 (June 8, 1957), 673–74.

"Emotive Language Still." *Yale Review*, 39 (September 1949), 108–18.

"The Eye and the Ear." *English Leaflet*, 47 (May 1948), 65–72.

"First Steps in Psychology." *Psyche*, 2 (1921), 67–79. (With C. K. Ogden.)

"The Future of Reading." In *The Written Word*. Ed. Brian L. McDonough. Rowley, MA: Newbury, 1971, pp. 27–59.

"Gerard Hopkins." *Dial*, 81 (1926), 195–203.

"God of Dostoevsky." *Forum*, 78 (1927), 88–97.

"Idle Fears About Basic English." *Atlantic*, 173 (June 1944), 98–100.

"Instructional Engineering." In *The Written Word*. Ed. Brian L. McDonough. Rowley, MA: Newbury, 1971, pp. 61–86.

"Introduction." In *Opposition: A Linguistic and Psychological Analysis*. By C. K. Ogden. Bloomington: Indiana University Press, 1967, pp. 7–13.

"Introduction." In *Semantics: The Nature of Words and Their Meanings*. By Hugh R. Walpole. New York: W. W. Norton, 1941, pp. 11–19.

"Language and World Crisis." *Harvard Graduate School Association Bulletin*, 6 (1961), 8–14, 24. (With Christine M. Gibson.)

"Letter from I. A. Richards to Richard Eberhart, from Magdalene College, Cambridge, December 15, 1938." *Furioso*, 1 (Spring 1940), 43.

"The Linguistic Symbolism." *Cambridge Magazine*, 10 (Summer 1920), 31.

"Literature for the Unlettered." In *Uses of Literature*. Ed. Monroe Engel. Cambridge, MA: Harvard University Press, 1973, pp. 207–24.

"The Lure of High Mountaineering." *Atlantic*, 139 (January 1927), 51–57.

"Mechanical Aids in Language Teaching." *English Language Teaching*, 12 (October/December 1957), 3–9.

"Mr. Eliot and Notions of Culture: A Discussion." *Partisan Review*, 11 (Summer 1944), 310–12.

"Mr. I. A. Richards Replies." *American Speech*, 18 (1943), 290–96.

"The Mystical Element in Shelley's Poetry." *Aryan Path*, 30 (July 1959), 290–95.

"The Mystical Element in Shelley's Poetry." *Aryan Path*, 30 (June 1959), 250–56.

"Nineteen Hundred and Now." *Atlantic*, 140 (September 1927), 311–17.

"Notes on the Practice of Interpretation." *Criterion*, 10 (April 1931), 412–20.

"On Reading." *Michigan Quarterly*, 9 (1970), 3–7.

"On TSE: Notes for a Talk at the Institute of Contemporary Arts, London, June 29, 1965." *Sewanee Review*, 74 (Winter 1966), 21–30.

"Our Lost Leaders." *Saturday Review of Literature*, 9 (April 1, 1933), 509–10.

"Passage to Forster: Reflections on a Novelist." *Forum*, 78 (1927), 914–20.

"Percy Bysshe Shelley." In *Major British Writers*. Vol. 2. Ed. G. B. Harrison. New York: Harcourt, Brace, and World, 1954, pp. 235–50.

"A Philosophy of Education." *Wellesley Alumnae Magazine*, 53 (1969), 21, 41.

"Poetic Process and Literary Analysis." In *Style in Language*. Ed. Thomas A. Sebeok. Cambridge, MA: MIT Press, 1960, pp. 9–24.

"The Poetry of T. S. Eliot." *Living Age*, 329 (April 4, 1926), 112–15.

"Preface to a Dictionary." *Psyche*, 13 (1933), 10–24.

"Psychopolitics." *Fortune*, 26 (September 1942), 108–09, 114.

"Religion and the Intellectuals: A Symposium." *Partisan Review*, 17 (February 1950), 138–42.

"The Secret of 'Feedforward.'" *Saturday Review*, February 3, 1968, pp. 14–17.

"Some Recollections of C. K. Ogden." *Encounter*, 9 (September 1957), 10–11.

"The Spoken and Written Word." *Listener*, October 16, 1947, pp. 669–70.

"The Teaching of English." *New Statesman*, July 23, 1927, p. 478.

"Technology to the Rescue: Elementary Language Teaching by Film and Tape." *Harvard Alumni Bulletin*, 63 (April 15, 1961), 548–50. (With Christine M. Gibson.)

"The Two Rings: A Communication." *Partisan Review*, 10 (1943), 380–81.

"A Valediction: Forbidden Mourning." In *Master Poems of the English Language*. Ed. Oscar Williams. New York: Trident, 1966, pp. 111–13.

"What is Involved in the Interpretation of Meaning?" In *Reading and Pupil Development: Proceedings of the Conference on Reading Held at the University of Chicago, Vol. II*. Ed. Williams S. Gray. Chicago: University of Chicago Press, 1940, 49–55.

"William Empson." *Furioso*, 1 (Spring 1940), Supplement: "A Special Note."

Collected Works

Coleridge's Minor Poems. Lecture delivered in honor of the 40th anniversary of Professor Edmund L. Freeman at Montana State University, April 8, 1960. Folcroft, PA: Folcroft, 1970.

Complementarities: Uncollected Essays. Ed. John Paul Russo. Cambridge, MA: Harvard University Press, 1976.
Richards on Rhetoric: I. A. Richards: Selected Essays (1929–1974). Ed. Ann E. Berthoff. New York: Oxford University Press, 1991.
Selected Letters of I. A. Richards. Ed. John Constable. Oxford, UK: Oxford University Press/Clarendon, 1990.
Wyndham Lewis and I. A. Richards: A Friendship Documented: 1928–57. Ed. John Constable and S. J. M. Watson. Cambridge, UK: Skate, 1989.

Poetry and Fiction

Goodbye Earth and Other Poems. New York: Harcourt, Brace, 1957.
Internal Colloquies, Poems and Plays. New York: Harcourt Brace Jovanovich, 1971.
Lighting Fires in Snow. Poem sent as a holiday greeting by Harcourt, Brace. New York: Harcourt, Brace, 1958.
New and Selected Poems. Manchester, UK: Carcanet, 1978.
The Screens and Other Poems. London, UK: Routledge and Kegan Paul, 1961.
Tomorrow Morning, Faustus!: An Infernal Comedy. New York: Harcourt, Brace and World, 1962.
Why So, Socrates? A Dramatic Version of Plato's Dialogues: Euthyphro Apology Crito Phaedo. Cambridge, UK: Cambridge University Press, 1964.

Interviews

Brower, Reuben. "Beginnings and Transitions: I. A. Richards Interviewed by Reuben Brower." In *I. A. Richards: Essays in His Honor.* Ed. Reuben Brower, Helen Vendler, and John Hollander. New York: Oxford University Press, 1973, pp. 17–41.

Endnotes

[1] I. A. Richards, *Complementarities: Uncollected Essays*, ed. John Paul Russo (Cambridge, MA: Harvard University Press, 1976), p. 268.
[2] Reuben Brower, "Beginnings and Transitions: I. A. Richards Interviewed by Reuben Brower," in *I. A. Richards: Essays in His Honor*, ed. Reuben Brower, Helen Vendler, and John Hollander (New York: Oxford University Press, 1973), p. 19.
[3] Brower, p. 20.
[4] Brower, p. 20.
[5] Brower, p. 20.
[6] Brower, p. 34.
[7] Brower, p. 23.
[8] Brower, p. 23.
[9] Brower, p. 24.
[10] Brower, p. 34.
[11] Brower, p. 37.
[12] George Watson, "The Amiable Heretic: I. A. Richards 1893–1979," *Sewanee Review*, 54 (April–June 1996), 248.
[13] Watson, pp. 255–56.
[14] Biographical information on Richards was obtained from the following sources: Brower, pp. 17–41; and Janet Adam Smith, "Fare Forward, Voyagers!," in *I. A. Richards: Essays in His Honor*, ed. Reuben Brower, Helen Vendler, and John Hollander (New York: Oxford University Press, 1973), pp. 307–17.

[15] Smith, p. 316.

[16] Watson, p. 250.

[17] I. A. Richards, *The Philosophy of Rhetoric* (New York: Oxford University Press, 1965), p. 3.

[18] Richards, *The Philosophy of Rhetoric*, p. 8.

[19] Richards, *The Philosophy of Rhetoric*, p. 24.

[20] Richards, *The Philosophy of Rhetoric*, p. 7.

[21] I. A. Richards, *Interpretation in Teaching* (New York: Harcourt, Brace, 1938), pp. 12, 13.

[22] Richards, *The Philosophy of Rhetoric*, p. 3.

[23] Richards, *The Philosophy of Rhetoric*, pp. 3–4.

[24] Richards, *The Philosophy of Rhetoric*, pp. 9–10.

[25] I. A. Richards, *Speculative Instruments* (Chicago: University of Chicago Press, 1955), p. 74.

[26] Richards, *Speculative Instruments*, pp. 74–76. Richards also discusses requirements for the new rhetoric in *The Philosophy of Rhetoric*, p. 23.

[27] I. A. Richards, *So Much Nearer: Essays Toward a World English* (New York: Harcourt, Brace and World, 1960), p. 131.

[28] Richards, *The Philosophy of Rhetoric*, pp. 13–14.

[29] Richards, *The Philosophy of Rhetoric*, pp. 14–17.

[30] C. K. Ogden and I. A. Richards, *The Meaning of Meaning: A Study of the Influence of Language Upon Thought and of the Science of Symbolism* (New York: Harcourt, Brace, 1930), p. 53; and I. A. Richards, *Principles of Literary Criticism* (New York: Harcourt, Brace, 1930), p. 103.

[31] Richards, *The Philosophy of Rhetoric*, p. 34.

[32] Ogden and Richards, p. 58.

[33] Ogden and Richards, p. 23.

[34] The meaning of words as missing parts of context is discussed in Ogden and Richards, pp. 174–75; and Richards, *The Philosophy of Rhetoric*, p. 34.

[35] Ogden and Richards, pp. 10–12.

[36] Ogden and Richards, p. 12.

[37] Richards, *The Philosophy of Rhetoric*, p. 11.

[38] Ogden and Richards, p. 15.

[39] Ogden and Richards, p. 10.

[40] This model is described in Richards, *Speculative Instruments*, pp. 22–23; and Paul R. Corts, "I. A. Richards on Rhetoric and Criticism," *Southern Speech Journal*, 36 (Winter 1970), 119–21.

[41] Richards, *Speculative Instruments*, p. 23.

[42] Richards, *Speculative Instruments*, p. 24.

[43] Ogden and Richards, pp. 205–06.

[44] Richards, *Principles of Literary Criticism*, p. 178.

[45] Richards, *Complementarities*, p. 247.

[46] Feedforward is discussed in Richards, *Complementarities*, pp. 246–53.

[47] Richards, *Speculative Instruments*, p. 19.

[48] I. A. Richards, *Practical Criticism: A Study of Literary Judgment* (New York: Harcourt, Brace, 1939), p. 180.

[49] Richards, *Practical Criticism*, pp. 181–83. The functions of discourse for the speaker also are discussed in Ogden and Richards, pp. 226–27.

[50] Richards proposes four—rather than seven—functions of comprehending in *Interpretation in Teaching*, p. 196: to point to or name things, to express feelings about them, to represent acts, and to indicate directions.

[51] Richards, *Speculative Instruments*, p. 28.

[52] Richards, *Complementarities*, p. 101.

[53] Richards, *Speculative Instruments*, p. 28.

[54] Keith Jensen, "I. A. Richards and His Models," *Southern Speech Communication Journal*, 37 (Spring 1972), 312.

[55] Corts, p. 122.

[56] Richards discusses referential and emotive language in *Complementarities*, pp. 88–97; Ogden and Richards, pp. 234–35; and *Principles of Literary Criticism*, pp. 261–71.

[57] Richards sometimes seems to use the term *emotive language* simply to mean language that is used nonreferentially. For a discussion of Richards's various uses of *emotive*, see Jerome P. Schiller, *I. A. Richards' Theory of Literature* (New Haven, CT: Yale University Press, 1969), pp. 50–61.

[58] Marie Hochmuth Nichols, *Rhetoric and Criticism* (Baton Rouge: Louisiana State University Press, 1963), p. 101.

[59] Nichols, p. 101.

[60] For a discussion of comprehension in referential and emotive language, see Richards, *Principles of Literary Criticism*, pp. 268–69; and Richards, *Complementarities*, pp. 93–94.

[61] Richards, *Complementarities*, pp. 92–93.

[62] Aristotle *Poetics* 22; and Richards, *The Philosophy of Rhetoric*, pp. 89–90.

[63] Richards, *The Philosophy of Rhetoric*, p. 93.

[64] Richards, *Interpretation in Teaching*, p. 49.

[65] Richards, *Principles of Literary Criticism*, p. 178.

[66] Richards, *Principles of Literary Criticism*, p. 240.

[67] Richards, *The Philosophy of Rhetoric*, pp. 96–97.

[68] Richards, *Interpretation in Teaching*, p. 133.

[69] Richards, *Interpretation in Teaching*, p. 133.

[70] Richards, *The Philosophy of Rhetoric*, p. 117.

[71] Richards, *The Philosophy of Rhetoric*, pp. 117–18.

[72] Ogden and Richards, p. 132. For additional discussion of the notion of definition, see Ogden and Richards, pp. 246–47.

[73] Ogden and Richards, pp. 118–19.

[74] Ogden and Richards, p. 119.

[75] Ogden and Richards, p. 119.

[76] Ogden and Richards, p. 119.

[77] Ogden and Richards, p. 119.

[78] Various means of definition are discussed in Ogden and Richards, pp. 117–21.

[79] Richards, *Interpretation in Teaching*, p. 248.

[80] Richards also discusses literary context in *The Philosophy of Rhetoric*, pp. 47, 53–55, 69.

[81] Richards, *The Philosophy of Rhetoric*, p. 50.

[82] Richards, *The Philosophy of Rhetoric*, pp. 49–50.

[83] Richards, *Speculative Instruments*, p. 29.

[84] Richards, *So Much Nearer*, p. x.

[85] Richards, *So Much Nearer*, p. x.

[86] Richards, *So Much Nearer*, p. xi.

[87] Richards, *So Much Nearer*, p. xi.

[88] Kenneth Burke, *Permanence and Change: An Anatomy of Purpose* (Indianapolis: Bobbs-Merrill, 1965), p. 74.

[89] Richards, *So Much Nearer*, p. xi.

[90] Richards, *So Much Nearer*, p. xi.

[91] Richards, *So Much Nearer*, p. xi.

[92] Richards also explains his system of specialized quotation marks in *Speculative Instruments*, pp. 29–30; and *Complementarities*, p. 98.

[93] Stephen H. Browne, "I. A. Richards (1893–1979)," in *Twentieth-Century Rhetorics and Rhetoricians: Critical Studies and Sources*, ed. Michael G. Moran and Michelle Ballif (Westport, CT: Greenwood, 2000), p. 304.

[94] Watson, p. 261.

[95] Browne, p. 306.

[96] Marie Hochmuth, "I. A. Richards and the 'New Rhetoric,'" *Quarterly Journal of Speech*, 44 (February 1958), 16.

[97] Stanley Edgar Hyman, *The Armed Vision: A Study in the Methods of Modern Literary Criticism* (New York: Alfred A. Knopf, 1948), p. 287.

[98] Hyman, p. 324.

[99] Browne, p. 306.

[100] Watson, p. 253.

[101] Browne, p. 304.

[102] William G. Hardy, *Language, Thoughts, and Experience: A Tapestry of the Dimensions of Meaning* (Baltimore: University Park Press, 1978), p. 62.

[103] Hardy, p. 67.

[104] Donald K. Enholm, "Rhetoric as an Instrument for Understanding and Improving Human Relations," *Southern Speech Communication Journal*, 41 (Spring 1976), 232.

[105] Richards, *Complementarities*, pp. 268–69.

[106] F. R. Leavis, "Advanced Verbal Education," rev. of *The Philosophy of Rhetoric*, by I. A. Richards, *Scrutiny*, 6 (September 1937), 212.

[107] Richards, *Principles of Literary Criticism*, p. 274.

[108] Max Black, *Language and Philosophy: Studies in Method* (Ithaca, NY: Cornell University Press, 1949), p. 203.

[109] Hyman, p. 286.

[110] Enholm, p. 233.

[111] Schiller, p. 68.

[112] Hardy, p. 95.

[113] Max Black, "Some Objections to Ogden and Richards' Theory of Interpretation," *Journal of Philosophy*, 39 (May 21, 1942), 287.

[114] Watson, p. 260.

[115] B. Aubrey Fisher, "I. A. Richards' Context of Language: An Overlooked Contribution to Rhetorico-Communication Theory," *Western Speech*, 35 (Spring 1971), 111.

[116] Hyman, p. 324.

[117] John Paul Russo, "I. A. Richards in Retrospect," *Critical Inquiry*, 8 (Summer 1982), 745.

[118] Hardy, p. 96.

[119] Hyman, p. 287.

[120] Hyman, p. 314.

[121] Russo, p. 749.

[122] Russo, p. 755.

[123] Hyman, p. 322.

[124] Hyman, p. 323.

[125] John Needham, *The Completest Mode: I. A. Richards and the Continuity of English Literary Criticism* (Edinburgh, Scot: Edinburgh University Press, 1982), p. 22.

[126] Watson, pp. 260–61.

[127] Hyman, p. 326.

ERNESTO GRASSI

When we look at today's scientific panorama, philosophy hardly appears still to play a role, and rhetorical speech is recognized only outside the framework of scientific discourse as the superficial art of persuasion. . . . But let it be remembered that it is only within the limits of human communication and the tasks that arise from it that the problems of philosophy and the function of rhetoric can be discussed.[1]

This statement captures the core of Ernesto Grassi's conception of rhetoric. He continually seeks to return to and retrieve the ideas of the Italian

51

humanists, showing how the starting point for humans is not rationality or logic but language. The language through which humans grasp and express the "sense of reality" is prior to the process of defining the nature of things. Language is not "merely the tool but the very stuff" of human response to existence.[2]

Ernesto Grassi was born in Milan, Italy, on May 2, 1902, the son of Giovanni Battista Grassi and Caterina Luce Grassi. His interest in philosophy developed as a result of a serious illness as a youth, when thoughts about his own mortality led him to ponder the nature of reality and the place of humans within the world. Grassi pursued the study of philosophy, earning his doctorate from the University of Milan in 1925. He married Elena Stigler in the same year and moved to France to study with philosopher Maurice Blondel. This was the beginning of a long career in philosophy, all of it spent as an emigrant.[3]

After Grassi's studies in France, he moved to Marburg, Germany, to study with Edmund Husserl and Martin Heidegger at the University of Freiburg. He had visited Freiburg while a student at the University of Milan to meet with Husserl, a phenomenologist and "the acknowledged authority of Western philosophy."[4] At that earlier meeting, Husserl had encouraged Grassi to take seriously his Italian background in his approach to philosophy. His advice was prophetic for Grassi's eventual focus on Italian humanism: "Young man, as an Italian you are particularly predestined for philosophy. . . . Because you Italians approach the phenomenon itself; because of your sense for the concrete in philosophy; you do not start from abstract, *a priori* thinking and systematic historic schemata as do we German philosophers."[5] While at Freiburg, Grassi served first as a lecturer and then as an associate professor of Italian literature.

When Martin Heidegger succeeded Husserl in the endowed chair at Freiburg, Grassi began what would be a 10-year period of study with Heidegger. Grassi was the first Italian philosopher to write about Heidegger; much of his career was devoted to working with, disseminating, evaluating, and incorporating the works of Heidegger into his own scholarship. He also dedicated his book *Renaissance Humanism*, published in 1988, to the memory of Heidegger, and many of his ideas reflect basic aspects of Heideggerian thought.[6] Heidegger's rejection of Latin thought, however, especially in terms of his dismissal of the significance of the Italian humanists, eventually led Grassi to move away from Heidegger's beliefs and to articulate his own philosophical perspective at odds with that of Heidegger.

In 1938, Grassi was commissioned to found the Institute *Studia Humanitatis* under the patronage of the Royal Italian Academy in Berlin. He moved to that university in 1939, and the institute formally opened on December 6, 1942.[7] The essence of what would become Grassi's philosophical position first was published during this period in a 1940 essay titled *"Der Beginn des modernen Denkens."* With the rise of Hitler and National Socialism, publishing research on humanistic topics became increasingly difficult, however.

After two years of publication, the Nazi regime prohibited publication of *Geistige Überlieferung*, the yearbook Grassi edited as director of the institute. Fearing persecution from the Nazi regime, Grassi resigned his directorship of the institute and left the country.[8] He went first to Florence, Italy, and then to the University of Zurich in Switzerland, where he served as a visiting professor in philosophy from 1943 to 1946.[9] At various times in his career, Grassi served as a visiting professor at the University of Valparaiso in Chile, the University of Buenos Aires, the University of San Paolo, the University of Caracas, Columbia University, Pennsylvania State University, and Mount Allison University in Canada. In 1948, Grassi returned to Germany to become a professor at the University of Munich and director of the Center for the Study of Philosophy and Humanism. He was the first recipient of a chair, endowed in 1962, for the study of "Philosophy and Intellectual History of Humanism."[10]

During his tenure at the University of Munich, Grassi published the bulk of his writing on humanism, beginning with *Macht des Bildes: Ohnmacht der rationalen Sprache Zur Rettung des Rhetorischen* published in 1970, which laid the groundwork for his view of the primacy of rhetoric over rational speech. He also published *Rhetoric as Philosophy: The Humanist Tradition* (1980), a collection of essays on humanism, and *Heidegger and the Question of Renaissance Humanism* (1983), based on a series of lectures Grassi gave at the Medieval and Renaissance Center at Barnard College. In these essays, he explores Heidegger's antihumanistic attitude and reinterprets many basic Heideggerian concepts from the perspective of humanism. In *Folly and Insanity in Renaissance Literature*, coauthored with Maristella Lorch and published in 1986, Grassi and Lorch demonstrate the process of humanistic philosophizing in their treatment of the concept of folly.

In his 1988 book, *Renaissance Humanism: Studies in Philosophy and Poetics*, Grassi returns to a discussion of the place of humanism as a philosophical enterprise and Heidegger's reaction to it. Grassi sees this book as "a continuation and, in a certain way, the conclusion" of his efforts to come to terms with Heidegger's stance and to develop his own perspective on humanism. A fifth book, *Vico and Humanism: Essays on Vico, Heidegger, and Rhetoric* (1990), is a collection of essays previously published elsewhere. Beginning with Grassi's first essay published in English, the book spans two decades of Grassi's writing, elaborating his commitment to Vico and the humanism Vico represented. This book was followed in 1994 by *The Primordial Metaphor*, an English translation of a 1990 text, *La metafora inaudita*, in which Grassi analyzes various literary texts to clarify his notions of metaphor, the primacy of passion and imagery in the human world, and the place of language in bringing that world into reality.[11]

In addition to his books on philosophy, humanism, and rhetoric, Grassi was the organizer, with German psychologist Hugo Schmale, of a series of philosophical seminars that served as the foundation for a set of volumes called *Zürcher Gespräche*. These seminars brought together participants from diverse areas of inquiry—economics, linguistics, semiotics, anthropology, and religion—to "overcome the banal assumptions of everyday life . . . to make possible new angles of insight from which diverse subject matters can become mutually illuminating." [12] For Grassi, these seminars represented humanism in action—"creative humanistic research" designed to construct a common contemplative experience to facilitate new knowledge across disciplines. [13] In particular, they were designed to address the isolation and sterility of contemporary thought by using a remedy from the Italian humanists— "the cultivation of discourse that is imaginative and even fantastic." [14]

The dialogues, funded by a wealthy industrialist, were held at a villa in Zurich. To encourage the diverse perspectives Grassi sought, he brought Zen Buddhists together with Hebrew theologians, Indian anthropologists with business analysts and literary critics. [15] Also in keeping with Grassi's personal interests, topics were generally metaphoric, promoting "imaginative play rather than . . . the pursuit of preordained and controllable subjects." [16] As an example, one topic was "On the Dealing with Borders," which prompted one participant to talk about borderline cases in psychiatry, another about the boundaries that fixed concepts impose in metaphysics, and another about Jacques Derrida's model of deconstruction as applied to a painting of the Crucifixion. These dialogues were "Grassi's Experiment," [17] an effort to address the impoverished state of human interaction that characterizes modernity through the practical application of Italian humanism.

Upon his retirement, Grassi spent winters in Munich—where he continued to write and lecture as an emeritus professor—and summers at his home on the island of Ischia in Italy. Grassi died in Munich on December 22, 1991. [18]

Italian Humanism

Grassi did not set out deliberately to formulate a theory of rhetoric. Rather, circumstances of birth and education brought together for him two opposing philosophical traditions—German idealism and Italian humanism. The tension between the two led him to explore his intellectual roots and eventually to conceive of rhetoric not simply as persuasion or expression but as constituting the philosophical foundation of human thought.

Grassi's exploration of Italian and German thought had its beginnings in his early years as a lecturer on Italian literature at the University of Freiburg. At the time, philosophy was dominated by the thinking of German philosophers—especially Georg Hegel, Edmund Husserl, and Martin Heidegger— and was rooted in the rational tradition formulated by René Descartes. Grassi describes the prevalence of this approach to philosophy: "Neither when Descartes calls upon the 'cogito' as an original axiom for the definition of knowledge, nor when Kant deduces knowledge from original forms of experience and thought, nor when Hegel gives his *a priori* dialectical deduction of the real do we ever leave this model of rational deductive thought." [19]

The assumption of the superiority of German thought brought into focus for Grassi the contrast between his philosophical heritage as an Italian and his German educational background. He singles out two experiences that heightened this contrast. The first occurred when he read a statement by Bertrando Spaventa, an Italian philosopher of the late nineteenth century, which succinctly captured prevailing German sentiments about the differences between the German and Italian philosophical traditions: "The development of German thought is natural, free, and independent, in a word, it is critical. The development of Italian thought is unsteady, hindered, and dogmatic. This is the great difference." [20]

Grassi's decade of study with Heidegger also provided him with a constant source of contrast between Italian humanism and German idealism because Heidegger consistently rejected Italian thought as being without philosophical importance. [21] Heidegger defined humanism as "a movement that arrives at re-discovering the inherent values of mankind by way of literature, philology and rhetoric"—a definition that "precludes any original thinking from the very outset." [22] Grassi ultimately rejected this view—and the priority given to rational philosophy by German idealism generally—in favor of Italian humanism.

The Scientific Paradigm

Scientific thought, as represented by the German tradition, is based on the presumption that objective knowledge is both possible and desirable and that reason is the preferred tool for comprehending reality. Also referred to as *logical, analytic,* or *modern* thought, it is characterized by the use of the scientific method, which seeks to discover or deduce self-evident axioms that are universally valid: "statements are scientifically valid only if they can be strictly deduced from an unquestionable, ultimate axiom in a necessary and universally valid manner." [23] The ideas of René Descartes often are considered the starting point for the scientific tradition; he considered his statement, *cogito ergo sum* (I think; therefore, I am), to be one such self-evident axiom. The human power to apprehend reality by means of reason was, for him, the key to understanding the world. [24]

Grassi discusses various characteristics of the scientific paradigm, all of which he considers to be limitations of science in terms of knowing the world. The scientific method seeks to discover first principles, yet it does not examine the source of such principles. In other words, knowledge exists within the boundaries of the system under examination, but no attempt is made to understand the origins of the system itself. [25] Grassi elaborates: "science is only applicable within the range of a system based, in each field, on its own particular premises, and of course these premises cannot be proved because they form the system's own foundation." [26] For Grassi, the original or foundational proof of any system lies with language, metaphor, and the nonrational—characteristics that are critical for human nature and human evolution. To ignore these origins is to ignore a large part of what constitutes human reality, which is, for Grassi, the most serious shortcoming of the scientific tradition.

A second difficulty with scientific thought for Grassi is that it is concerned only with universals and not with individual cases or situations. Science deals with claims that are valid for all times and places and thus ignores the concrete details of the particular situation: "Traditional philosophy claims to be able to identify objectivity through rationality and, consequently, attempts to exclude from its realm all that can distract from the rational determination of individual beings, namely, every thought and every word connected to sensibility, time, place, passions." [27] Grassi describes the rational paradigm as a "desperate effort of freeing oneself from relativity, from the subjectivity of what appears through the senses." [28] It is a way of knowing that does not take into account the particular contexts, needs, and variations that are part of the experience of life. Grassi offers a simple example to illustrate his point: "The color *red* has one meaning in the traffic code, another in the political code, a third in optics, another in the set of rules regulating human relations. A lover offers a red rose to his beloved." [29] The objectivity and generalizability demanded by the rational paradigm simply are unable to deal with such distinctions.

In its privileging of the universal, objective, and rational, Grassi also suggests another limitation of the scientific paradigm: it dismisses the contributions of virtually all humanistic disciplines because any discipline that is not grounded in logical processes is denigrated:

> This approach leads to a repudiation of *history*, for the latter is not in a position to contribute to knowledge or truth, since all discussions as to how events have taken place or how they are described by historians remain merely within the framework of "possibility." Nor can *philology* be attributed any philosophical significance; it can at most serve as a useful means for the understanding of ancient or foreign texts. . . . Still more dangerous is the inclusion of *art* and *poetry*, because they represent possibility rather than truth; *rhetoric*, a discipline which acquired great significance in Humanism, fares no better, because the passions impair the clarity of thought and consequently are not to be taken into account.[30]

The privileging of science that characterizes the contemporary Western world is problematic for Grassi because it means a devaluing of anything that cannot be proved scientifically and ignores the starting point of human knowledge:

> Today we glory in science and in cybernetic instruments, entrusting our future to them, forgetting that we still have the problem of finding "data," of "inventing them," since the cybernetic process can only elaborate them and draw consequences from them. The problem of the essence of the human genius and of its creativity cannot be reduced to that of rational deduction, which modern technology is developing to improbable depths.[31]

The attitude of the primacy of science also has led to the atomic age, characterized by the discovery, technological applications, and sociopolitical consequences of instruments of domination and destruction. Grassi acknowledges that the attitude of rational calculation has assumed different forms throughout the history of Western thought, but he sees the present epoch as its ultimate manifestation.[32] The discovery of and application of the atom is an almost perfect expression of the desire for domination over nature. The individual who has atomic control has the power not only to dominate other beings but to destroy the entire world. The rational, scientific approach to the world that has dominated Western philosophy leads Grassi to conclude pessimistically: "we have lost and we are still losing the 'match' of the Western world." [33]

The attitude of superiority that accompanies the rational paradigm has consequences, according to Grassi, for interactions worldwide: "If this calculating and purely rational attitude, about which Western culture is so proud, were called into question, then a new inroad to understanding foreign cultures that do not have this basic attitude would result. Here I am thinking of Far Eastern cultures whose relationship to things is imagistic and metaphorical."[34] Rather than presuming the benefits of technology and the "inferiority" of "underdeveloped" countries, Grassi encourages a consideration of what systems based in metaphor and imagery can offer. At present, however, the dominance of the rational attitude precludes any genuine understanding of cultures that begin from different starting places.

The scientific method is only one tool for understanding the world and, for Grassi, it is a limited and partial approach compared to that offered by the philosophy of humanism. From the standpoint of science, humanism typically is considered nothing more than the confused anticipation of Descartes's approach. In other words, the humanist philosophers were believed to be searching for and moving toward the position advocated by Descartes; he was seen as clarifying their ideas.[35] Yet, science is unable to ask and answer fundamental questions regarding the nature of humanity—questions "continually raised by the Italian humanists."[36] Grassi seeks "a proper appreciation of humanism's rejection of the rational"[37] and devotes himself to showing how humanism, despite its domination by science, in fact offers perspectives not available to science.

Humanism

When Grassi speaks of humanism, he does not mean the broad and rather ambiguous meaning given the word today, in which "almost any kind of concern with human values is called 'humanistic.' "[38] Nor does he mean only the Renaissance rediscovery of the literature, art, and civilizations of ancient Greece and Rome and the corresponding renewal of interest in the study of the human being. Although a rediscovery of the classics was one of the interests of the humanists, it is not what is most important about humanism for Grassi.

Perhaps the oldest meaning of the term *humanism* derives from the phrase *studia humanitatis*, used by ancient Roman authors such as Cicero to describe a liberal or literary education.[39] By early in the fifteenth century, the *studia humanitatis* referred to a group of scholarly disciplines, including grammar, rhetoric, history, poetry, and moral philosophy, that involved the "reading and interpretation of its standard ancient writers"—mostly Latin but some Greek as well.[40] In the sixteenth century, the term *humanista* was used to denote a professor, teacher, or student of the humanities. In 1808, the German educator F. J. Niethammer coined the term *humanismus* to describe the emphasis on Greek and Latin classics in secondary education and to distinguish the study of these liberal arts from scientific training.[41] Generally speaking, the humanists of the Renaissance were professional rhetoricians—teachers at universities and secondary schools, secretaries to princes or of cities, or wealthy amateurs "who combined their business or political activities with the fashionable intellectual interests of their time."[42] They were interested in reviving classical texts not simply as an academic pursuit but because they found in them issues parallel to their own situations and interests. More significantly, however, as practitioners, they believed in civic participation and in the need to remain "rooted in practical human concerns."[43]

The humanists' concern with texts and language was part of their civic and pragmatic perspective. The text was considered "an integral, concrete experience in the past"[44] through which individuals could understand the exigencies of the human condition and the responses of a particular culture toward them. As translators and interpreters of texts, the humanists were in an excellent position to observe how language functions: "They experienced how the same word in the writings of one author has a particular specific meaning but receives a different meaning in the context of another author's works."[45] In their analysis of texts, then, the humanists sought to understand the ways in which humans respond to a set of claims or demands made on them by the world and the kind of world revealed to them as a result of linguistic choices. They labeled such language *rhetorical* because it seeks to strategically manage the "essential concerns of existence . . . matters of life and death."[46] Thus, they came to value literature as a means of knowing about the human condition: "literature is a way of forming a meaning without losing the details and emotions of an event. . . . The fable, the tale, the narration has a universal meaning, but this meaning is achieved through the relating of particular events and qualities."[47]

Just as literature was seen as a way of knowing the human condition by the humanists, so was history. History was a form of knowledge whose basic problem is meaning not truth; it is the set of responses humans have made to persistent human situations. History involves understanding experience as expressed through a particular author's account, which makes issues of language again important. The past always is experienced "as mediated" through language rather than something naively, uniformly, and accurately handed down.[48] The historian is a mediator, moving between events and their presentation in language to create an image of or knowledge about those events.

Both literature and history teach that the exigencies humans face are not limitlessly new, so historical and literary patterns can serve as the basis for future action. Coluccio Salutati, one of the many humanist scholars whom Grassi studied, captured this notion well: "Believe me we create nothing new, but like tailors we refashion garments from the oldest and richest fragments which we give out as new."[49] The humanists, then, ultimately sought "timely, not the timeless, verities"—patterns of knowledge realized in concrete particulars and not in abstract universal responses.[50]

The manner in which literary and historical truths are framed was equally important as their substance for the humanists. Thus, eloquence was seen not as superficial attention to style but as a genuine part of content itself. Content was not apart from its presentation in language, and knowledge was considered "a spark brought to visibility and efficacy by eloquence."[51] Eloquence was viewed as a creative, fluid reality of "content-in-form,"[52] a combination of the text itself, its interpretation, and its application in language to the contemporary situation. Thus, the humanists' worldview offered a positive view of rhetoric, in contrast to many conceptions, in which rhetoric was considered only the art of expression or a technical doctrine "to be appreciated primarily from outside, for *pedagogical reasons*, that is, as aids to 'alleviate' the 'severity' and 'dryness' of rational language."[53] Instead, for the humanists, rhetoric was an integrated approach to the world that took into account both substance and form.

Through their interests in classical texts, the humanists addressed the nature and importance of human history, the place of human beings in the universe, and the significance of language in creating reality. Although these are issues that have been and continue to be addressed by philosophers, there has been considerable debate about whether the humanists themselves should be called *philosophers*. This debate undoubtedly impacted the reputation of the humanists and the low esteem in which they were held by many scholars and, in fact, may have negatively impacted Grassi's reception as a scholar. This debate was raised explicitly by Renaissance scholar Paul Kristeller in a 1955 lecture series when he declared that Renaissance humanism was not "a philosophical tendency or system, but rather a cultural and educational program which emphasized and developed an important but limited area of studies. This area had for its center a group of subjects that was concerned essentially neither with the classics nor with philosophy, but might be roughly described as literature."[54] In 1964, however, Kristeller published a book about eight philosophers of the Italian Renaissance, in which he suggested that he had come to see philosophical merit in some of the works produced by the Renaissance humanists. Although unwilling to regard humanism as a singular philosophical movement, he states that the "study of Renaissance philosophy will be of continuing, and even increasing, interest both to the student of the Renaissance and to the student of philosophy and its history" because it provides ways to understand the different cultural and intellectual movements of the time.[55]

Jerrold Seigel suggests that the answer to whether the Renaissance humanists were philosophers depends on "how the term 'philosopher' is defined." He suggests that if, to be called a philosopher, "it is enough to discuss some of the traditional problems of philosophy, to enter into debate with philosophers, and to influence the subsequent course of the history of philosophy," then the humanists deserve this label. On the other hand, if the label is applied only to those who "place themselves within one of the great philosophical traditions, or who actually try to find solutions to philosophical problems through reasoned and consistent discourse," the humanists cannot lay claim to this label. Seigel suggests that despite their often contradictory approaches to philosophical problems per se, the humanists were united by "their rhetorical approach to philosophical problems."[56]

Grassi enters the debate about the philosophical importance of the humanists clearly on the side of the humanists as philosophers. Choosing to focus on Italy from the second half of the fourteenth century to the final third of the fifteenth century, Grassi is interested in writers whose concern was with "the problem of words, of metaphorical thought, and of the knowledge of the philosophical function of rhetorical thinking and speaking that was perfected as a new way of philosophizing."[57] Grassi's intention in his work with the Italian humanists was to demonstrate the philosophical interests and importance of these scholars and to advocate their ideas as critical for the contemporary world. Through close, critical textual analysis and interpretation, he offers the humanists' writings as the basis for a philosophical system that he believes has been dismissed and neglected because of the domination of scientific, rational thought. In the process, Grassi not only offers the humanists' system for consideration but expands the philosophical importance of many thinkers who traditionally are not placed within the rubric of philosophy. He turns to such diverse sources as Longinus, Sigmund Freud, and the book of Ecclesiastics in the *Bible* to demonstrate the existence of a persistent philosophical humanistic thread throughout history.[58] Grassi's interest in the philosophy of Italian humanism unavoidably led him to a study of rhetoric because the Italian humanists did not separate rhetoric and philosophy.

Giambattista Vico: A Source for Grassi's Rhetoric

Grassi's views of philosophy and rhetoric are based largely on the work of Giambattista Vico, an eighteenth-century Italian philosopher whom Grassi believes represents the thought of Italian humanism most fully. Although Grassi devoted much of his scholarly work to humanism, his particular interest in Vico emerged late. What he came to call his "Vichian career" began when he was invited to contribute to a symposium on Vico held in

January, 1976, in New York City. Grassi describes the significance of this event in a letter to the symposium organizer, Giorgio Tagliacozzo: "Since then, starting with the essay presented at that symposium, and continuing with the articles that I published for you, I have re-discovered Vico's significance and the essence of our humanistic tradition which culminated with Vico. This is why I am so grateful to you." The last 15 years of Grassi's life were characterized by "uninterrupted and intense activity" in which he "tried to make up for the time he had lost in the long years spent struggling against Heidegger and almost ignoring Vico."[59]

Vico, born in 1668, was a professor of rhetoric at the University of Naples from 1699 to 1741.[60] His major philosophical works are *De nostri tempori studiorum ratione* (1709), *De antiquissima Italorum sapienta* [(1710), and *Scienza nuova prima* (1725). Grassi describes Vico's place in and influence on philosophy this way: "At the end of the humanist period Vico—in whose theories the whole humanist tradition reached its highest philosophical consciousness—is in radical opposition to Descartes and tries to reestablish the connection between philosophy and rhetoric and, at the same time, to reinstate the humanistic branches of knowledge . . . by rendering their philosophical significance."[61]

Vico's intention was to develop a new science or critical art that responded to and moved beyond the narrowness of Cartesian philosophy. Vico did not so much oppose Descartes's emphasis on logic and rationality as much as he did Descartes's singular attention to the rational mode of thinking. According to Vico, Descartes's emphasis on the analytic outcome of an individual thinker (I think; therefore, I am) leaves out critical aspects of what today are called *standpoints*—the history or context of the thinker as part of a social community. Furthermore, analytic methods, such as those offered by Descartes, ignore language. Yet, only through language does the self have "access to its own nature as a social being—to the ways the human self confronts its own nature in the world of its own making."[62] Vico's criticism of Descartes, then, is that he fragmented knowledge and constructed an understanding of the world in a way unnatural to the human mind, errors Vico attempted to correct with his discussion of history and the arts by which humans learn about, understand, and construct their world. Vico proposed a pedagogy and a new method of studies that began with those arts that "make human community possible" and then proceeded to analytic thought.[63]

The basis of Vico's worldview is his notion of imaginative universals as a fundamental way in which humans respond to the world: "The world is not first thought with the intellect, but felt through the passions and the senses."[64] The world experienced through the senses is formed into images, which in turn are translated into words or names that give form and definition to the world. Vico gives as an example early humans' experience with lightning, which they named *Jove, God,* or some other word to signify a supreme being, creating in the naming process not only the first human thought but the first god.[65] This example demonstrates a basic metaphoric process of transfer. Feelings are translated into words, and words are organized to form perspectives on or particular approaches to the world. Metaphor is thus fundamental to the formation of the human world for Vico. [66]

Vico's starting point for how humans learn their world also introduces the notion of myth. Vico believes that the science of metaphysics, or the study of being, must begin where the idea of being is first recognized—in the myths that are the beginnings of any community: "In human experience being is first apprehended in poetic form by the human power of imagination. . . . Metaphysics requires an art whereby this original apprehension of being or Jove can be recovered and seen as a principle of the human world in its development from its beginnings." [67] Vico's notion of how humans come to know the world is in stark contrast to Descartes's view, in which an individual being comes to know god or to have a notion of being not by grasping it in engagement with life but by constructing it through a process of formal reasoning. [68]

For Vico, the rise of human history is the basic problem of philosophy. History is the realm in which individuals understand human action from its original feeling impulses through its interpretation into language, myth, and culture. Once humans become conscious of their intellectual powers and their abilities to make choices, to express themselves through a language, and therefore to direct their own destinies, they begin to make adjustments in nature. Vico terms this process the *humanization* or *historicization* of nature: "We can only attain a 'humanization' and 'historicization' of nature by giving meaning to the phenomena that our sensory tools offer to us." [69]

Vico suggests that the humanization process occurred gradually and was distinguished by three major phases. In the cultural age, humans did not see themselves as separate from the natural world or capable of action apart from the influence of that world. Rather, they attributed all events that occurred to divine beings. The second stage, which Vico calls the age of heroes, was characterized by superhuman benefactors—combinations of humans and gods—who were seen as helping humans by introducing social institutions and laws. In the age of humanity, the third stage, humans realized that they could control nature on their own without assistance from superhuman or divine powers of any kind. This stage represents the awakening or revelation of free will and choice—of confronting nature and imposing control over it. [70]

Vico's conception of the emergence of human societies relies on the basic process of *ingenium* or ingenuity. Ingenuity is the capacity to see relationships—to make connections among things—and to give shape to the dimensions of the human social world. *Ingenium* is the capacity to grasp what is common or similar among objects, ideals, or experiences. It is the "original and generating power of mind" that enabled the first humans "to transpose what they sense and feel through their bodies into the orders and relationships they express in their fables." It is a faculty whereby thought achieves "its beginning point or principles." [71]

For Vico, the development of human community by means of *ingenium* is the basic process taught in the study of rhetoric. It is "the ability to think from the individual situation to the features of the truth that lie within it, rather than thinking from the particular situation to an abstract principle of which it then becomes an instance."[72] For Vico, this process is eloquence— the joining of thought and word such that a situation can be understood as a whole without losing touch with particulars: "What is eloquence, in effect, but wisdom, ornately and copiously delivered in words appropriate to the common opinion of mankind?"[73]

Grassi's Philosophical and Rhetorical System

Grassi begins with the basic components of Vico's philosophy and translates them into contemporary terms. His starting point is the concrete situation that characterizes human existence: particular events, objects, and experiences appear to and thus make their claims on humans. These claims or appeals are essentially needs or challenges "which humans have to face in different situations";[74] they demand a response or a strategy for handling those challenges.

The senses are the vehicles through which needs become known to humans in any given situation. The world thus is experienced concretely, passionately, and intimately on a continuum from pleasure to pain: "Boredom, fear, pleasure and pain . . . are all expressions, warnings, passionate indicative signs; they are, therefore, sensible phenomena through which we swim, either with sensual enjoyment or with despair." Through these experiences, the "original horizon we inhabit opens up."[75] For Grassi, the "passionateness"—the particular emotional engagement humans have with the world through the senses—is their first exposure to the meaning of the world. The senses direct attention to particular stimuli or phenomena, to which humans then assign varying degrees of significance: "We thus find ourselves bent over the mysterious coming to presence of phenomena in order to listen to and identify the meaning of visions, words, images; floating on the waves of the senses, we reach the island of our sensible world" and "seek out the multiplicity of existential occurrence."[76]

The grounding of basic human meaning in the senses is primary to Grassi's articulation of a philosophy based on the particulars of human experience rather than in the abstractness of rational thought: "no sensory perception hovers isolated in mid-air, in abstract, rarefied space. On the contrary, it becomes crystallized in various situations."[77] Grassi summarizes by quoting Aristotle: "For it is astonishment which initially and even today leads people to philosophize."[78]

The process by which humans meet the demands or claims of the world is the process of *ingenium*, a term Grassi adopts directly from Vico.[79] Grassi elaborates on Vico's discussion of *ingenium*, citing Cicero's description of *ingenium* as an archaic, primal, nonreducible power. Grassi sees *ingenium* as the capacity that allows humans to process the sensory world of phenomena that presents itself to them. He emphasizes the importance of *ingenium* to human choice: as humans make connections among situations and choose coping responses, they are ingenious, responding with versatility and agility to the situation before them.[80] Donald Verene summarizes Grassi's view of *ingenium* as a capacity that "allows us to 'see' with the word, to make connections in experience we have not before made and which we need in order to think new thoughts."[81] *Ingenium* frees humans to create and order their own lives, to choose how to respond to life's changing demands.

There are three basic ways in which *ingenium* is manifest in the human world—in imagination, in work, and in language. By *imagination*, Grassi does not simply mean the ability to form mental images of things not present or the capacity for creativity. Rather, imagination is fundamentally and uniquely a human process that embodies *ingenium* and depends on the creation of new images and relationships. Grassi cites Vico to make his point: "Imagination collects from the senses the sensory effects of natural phenomena and combines and magnifies them to the point of exaggeration, turning them into luminous images to suddenly dazzle the mind with their lightning and stir up human passions in the thunder and roar of their wonder."[82] In turn, the images produced are translated into larger fables, stories, or myths—imaginative universals. The truth of a myth, fable, or narrative comes from its formation through feeling; imagination "makes into a 'truth' what it feels in the world."[83] The story—literature of any kind—is thus a way of forming meaning without losing the details of an event: "The problem of every philosophical system is to make its reasonings concrete, to keep the system in touch with the world."[84]

Imagination also is significant because of its role in the emergence of human history. Through imagination, humans realize they are not bound to nature in the same way that animals are: "It is shown in and through imagination that the human being, unlike the animal, does not stand under the dominion of ruling patterns which give sense perceptions an unequivocal meaning. He therefore can, and does, give sensory phenomena the most varied interpretations."[85] Imagination allows humans to explain the world around them in a multiplicity of ways.

The way imagination functions in the face of fear to allow humans to cope with an unknown situation is cited by Vico as one example of humans' use of interpretation to understand and explain their world. Vico suggests that the basic human response in the face of things not understood is fear: Humans break "out of nature through startling fear at the experience of . . . alienation from nature . . . in order to create the first place of . . . historicity, the 'new' world and its institutions, which arise from . . . ingenious and fantastic activity."[86] The human imagination causes humans to begin making adjustments in nature or constructing an order by which to understand the world: "Thus it was fear which created gods in the world"—not fear awakened in humans by others but fear awakened in them by themselves.[87] Imagination, then, allows humans to select certain interpretations of sensory experiences and to use them to define or order the world in certain ways. The ultimate result of this interpretation process is an entire system of reality or history that is uniquely human.

Work is the second manifestation of *ingenium* or means by which humans make connections among or interpret sensory phenomena. While imagination allows humans to conceptualize needs apart from those of animals, work allows for the fulfillment of these needs: "By establishing relationships (similitudes) between what man needs (e.g., to quench a thirst) and what his senses report to him in each specific concrete situation in nature (e.g., the availability of water), man works out the transfer of meanings leading him to the appropriate action (e.g., looking for water and making it available to himself)."[88] Work is another way of conveying a meaning to natural things or of making connections between the world of the senses and its meaning in the human world. When humans plant gardens or cultivate apple trees, for example, they are giving that patch of land and the apple trees more complex meanings than before they engaged in those tasks.

Vico chooses the figure of Hercules as a symbol for how work functions to allow humans to step out of or transform nature, and Grassi follows Vico's lead in calling Hercules the traditional symbol of human "ingeniousness."[89] Hercules, who performed 12 feats for King Eurystheus of Mycenae in return for immortality, is seen by Vico and Grassi as the founder of human society: "The myth of Hercules lies at the base of the making of history, because that mythical figure has always been . . . the first to carry out the humanization of nature."[90] Work, like imagination, is a form of self-assertion and control over the natural realm.

The notion of work emphasizes the necessary grounding in concrete experience that is the starting point for human knowledge and philosophy for Grassi. Work is another example of how the "transformation *(metamorphose)* of any material . . . does not happen on the basis of the contemplation . . . of abstract ideas, but of 'usus' and 'experientia,'" or use and experience. [91] Human work is a powerful demonstration of the basic human condition of encountering a new situation and responding to it in light of the particulars of that situation: "Human work is understood as a response to demands" made on humans in the situations in which they find themselves, and "at the same time, as the celebration of being in the context of the situation at hand, in which this work appears with ever new meanings." [92]

Grassi uses the metaphor of the theater to elaborate on the similarities and differences between imagination and work as vehicles through which humans know the world. Both imagination and work allow the human world to be made manifest; they allow the individual "to be at the same time a creature and something different"—a human being.[93] What Grassi calls the *theater of the imagination*, however, deals with the story invented by individuals—the way individuals process and interpret the unfolding drama of the world before them.[94] The theater of existence, in contrast, is the stage of the world, the stage where pragmatic action in conjunction with others—work—creates larger social stories. Humans don various masks or roles to participate in these stories: "in the function of the role of the moment they are given the necessary masks" that allow them to respond to the situations presented to them by the world. [95]

In addition to imagination and work, language is a third manifestation of *ingenium* for the humanists. It is another way of creating human history because it is another way of assigning meaning to the world. When humans name an object a *cat*, for example, they can talk about that object even when it is not present. Before they gave it a label or name, they were able to deal with the cat only by pointing to it or interacting with it when it was around. Naming it creates a symbolic, abstract reality that exists apart from the object. Language does more than simply create a symbolic world, however. For the humanists—and for Grassi—meaning cannot be understood without a simultaneous examination of the words used, the person using those words, and the context in which the object or situation arises: "the meaning of things arises in their concrete relationship to people and their human endeavor to come to grips with them." [96]

Grassi discusses the importance of language by offering the metaphor of language as a game. Any game has certain elements in common—instruments by which the game is played, rules, and actions. A game might use "cards, dice, a football, colors, sounds" as instruments. [97] The rules of the game prescribe the use to which the instruments are to be put. In addition, each game has its actions to be performed, and these differ depending on whether, for example, the game of dice or the game of football is being played.

The game of language also has its rules and its instruments—in this case, sounds or language. [98] Unlike other games, where the rules are determined beforehand, however, the rules of language are experienced and emerge "as the game is being played, on the basis of the first *originary indications*" or original perceptions provided by the senses. [99] As individuals experience and play the game of the world, they come "to presence" or are disclosed as individuals. [100] They essentially do not exist as human beings prior to language but "it is in and through language" that they make the game—their world—known. Unlike games in general, then, where "diversion, escapism, or relaxation" is the end, the language game "is extremely intense and requires our full concentration; it is the originary effort and the burden of our existence." The stakes, in fact, could not be higher: "in the matches of history, we play for and lose . . . the possibilities of our individuality and our world." [101] With language, the possibilities revealed are not just trivial options within the rules of the game but the whole range of possibilities available to humans: "Language makes real the announcement, which is forever new, of a world, of an order, of a cosmos, and of our corresponding historical world." [102]

Although the humanists studied imagination, work, and language and the roles of these in the development of human history, their focus clearly was on language—how *ingenium*, the basic human faculty for seeing relationships, operates linguistically. For the humanists, the operation of *ingenium* in language best is captured by the metaphor. The metaphor is the most important figure of speech because it embodies the notion of transfer and movement from internal personal space to external domain that is at the heart of *ingenium*.

The humanistic emphasis on metaphor contrasts with most approaches to metaphor, and Grassi devotes considerable time to metaphor's function to counter these other perspectives. In medieval conceptions, for example, truth was "concealed under the veil of metaphor"—metaphor was seen as obstructing rather than contributing to the search for truth. The primary usefulness of metaphor, in most philosophic traditions, is "to induce those incapable of rigorous thinking into accepting rational truth"; [103] rational cognition "surpasses the metaphor inasmuch as the metaphor remains attached to the superficiality of the image." [104] German idealists such as Heidegger and Hegel "took Humanism to task" for its focus on the senses, images, and metaphors—which they saw only as expressions of fantasy. Metaphor was considered to be a " 'distracting' element which has nothing to do with reality." [105] Grassi describes how this view of metaphor is completely overturned in the humanist tradition, in which metaphor discloses "what rational thought and discourse are unable to unveil. Again and again, metaphor, 'pointing' but not 'proving,' gives notice of or realizes human reality." [106]

The metaphor is powerful, according to Grassi, because it allows for the transfer of insights on several levels. At the most fundamental level, metaphor is the basic process of human thinking: it is a grasping of similarities between two unrelated things. When frost is called "mother nature's paintbrush" or the sky a "blue ceiling," commonalties between things of the human world and things in nature are highlighted. Thus, metaphor operationalizes *ingenium*, the primary means by which humans grapple with the world of nature because it enables them to make connections between the world of the senses and the human realm. Vico reinforces this point when he notes that humans tend to describe the inanimate aspects of the world through metaphoric references to the human body, giving their special human interpretation to nature: "It is noteworthy that in all languages the greater part of the expressions relating to inanimate things are formed by metaphor from the human body and its parts. . . . Thus, head for top or beginning; the brow and shoulders of a hill; the eyes of needles and of potatoes; mouth for any opening; the lip of a cup or pitcher; the teeth of rake, a saw, a comb; the beard of wheat; the tongue of a shoe; the gorge of a river; a neck of land; an arm of the sea." [107]

Metaphor is important at yet another level: it is the basic process embedded in the nature of language. Language is fundamentally a process of connecting a symbol to an experience. When one word rather than another is selected to refer to an event, the process of metaphor is involved: "the spoken word is a metaphor which originates from the transference . . . of meaning, of an indicative sign, to sound." [108] Metaphor, then, is the essence of human life—the entrance to the human world. It is the basic process by which humans understand their worlds. Humans make connections among experiences, both in imagination and in language, and thereby create a particular version of a world on the basis of metaphoric transferences.

For Grassi, the capacity of *ingenium* to see different possibilities—to manifest in imagination, work, and language—ultimately is realized in the concept of folly. Although folly typically is viewed as "thinking, speaking or acting without well-grounded reasons,"[109] for Grassi, it is just the opposite. Folly is the ability, through language, to choose what perspective to take on a situation and to imagine the self in different possibilities: "It is folly which allows the projection of . . . one's own desires, hopes, worries, expectations, fears . . . on the stage of life, the stage where our own interactions with the environment take place."[110] Verene elaborates:

> To see human affairs as folly is to have an ontological insight into what is possible in any situation; that is, to see all as folly is to realize that things are never what they seem. What appears to be solid reality, the real nature of things, is not so; through folly it is seen to be just as much its opposite. But this opposite interpretation of events cannot be reached by a logical deduction. It can be reached only by a situation, where things can just as well be true in a sense opposite to what they are. This opens the human world. We are human only when we can see beyond what is there to its opposite truth.[111]

Folly is not a loss of contact with reality but an engagement with life at its fullest and most fundamental—with the passion, emotion, and wonder of *ingenium*. Folly captures the means by which humans, in their most engaged sense, approach life—in awe of the many possibilities the senses make available, appreciative of the passions and emotions in directing their attention to certain aspects of the world, and ever cognizant of the many responses they can make to that world. Grassi concludes: "To live in folly is the profound reason for existence."[112]

Rhetorical versus Rational Speech

After establishing the basic process of *ingenium* as critical to human thought and speech and to his rhetorical system, Grassi proceeds to discuss the differences between rhetorical language—grounded in the ingenious function—and rational speech or language. These two types of speech exemplify the contrast between Grassi's perspective on rhetoric and rhetorics grounded in science and logic. Rhetorical speech is "immediate, not deductive or demonstrative, illuminating, purely indicative."[113] It is figurative, metaphoric, and pathetic. Rational speech, on the other hand, is deductive, demonstrative, and "without any pathetic character"[114] and achieves its effect through logical demonstration rather than through images: "The deductive process is completely closed within itself and as such cannot admit other forms of persuasion which do not derive from the logical process."[115]

A major difference between rhetorical and rational speech is that rhetorical speech is directly connected to the sensory images upon which humans come to know and create their world. Rhetorical speech "shows" by manifesting the basic original principle of *ingenium*—pointing out similarities between different things. Rhetorical speech, then, is grounded in metaphor:

"The metaphor lies at the root of our human world. Insofar as metaphor has its roots in the analogy between different things and makes this analogy immediately spring into 'sight,' it makes a fundamental contribution to the structure of our world."[116]

Grassi uses the story of Iris in Greek mythology to explain the metaphoric basis of rhetorical speech. Iris, which means to speak or announce, was personified as the rainbow, with her colors spanning the sky between the heavens and earth. Her role was that of mediator between the divine or inexplicable realm and the human one. As the one who spreads "the word," Iris showed the way between the inexplicable, original, wondrous images that humans encounter and the way in which they make sense of them in the concrete realities of human life.[117] Imagistic or rhetorical language—made concrete in metaphor—allows humans to capture those original images and interpret them using language. In contrast, rational language can explain the sequence of events by which something comes to be but not the impulse or idea—the original sensory experience—that gave rise to that experience. A sound, for example, might be explained causally—it was produced by the human voice, by hitting two sticks together, or by ringing a bell. These explanations offer no clue, however, as to the reason for producing the sound—is it an expression of fear, excitement, or joy?[118]

Another way Grassi distinguishes rational from rhetorical speech is on the basis of the openness of the systems involved. He develops this difference through an extended example of the concept of a code: "A code is a system of signs whose elements receive their meanings within this system. . . . A code is a kind of structure that is applied to phenomena in order to give them an order and a particular meaning."[119] The dots and dashes of a call for help are decoded, for instance, by means of the Morse code; the code provides the means by which to interpret the message. Similarly, any language is a code in which things come to have meaning within that framework. Grassi likens a code to rational speech in that it "establishes the governing system of relations that are already given and on the basis of which something is interpreted."[120]

No code, however, "can lead to a *new* code because its essence consists in 'fixing' certain things into place" so that they can be understood within that system. What counts as "real is 'read' on the basis of a previously given code."[121] In other words, both a code and rational speech lack an inventive function. The metaphor supplies such invention because it does not simply move within the established code to determine meaning but finds new codes and structures: "The function of a metaphor, unlike that of a code, does not consist merely in applying an interpretation but also in 'finding' the new code on the basis of which reality is rendered. It gives us a new perspective of relationships between beings. Metaphor's function is that of invention—the seeing of new relationships. It is metaphor that produces each new code."[122]

Yet another difference for Grassi between rhetorical and rational speech is the level of generality and engagement each offers. Rational speech deals with the universal and generalizable, while rhetorical speech always engages the particulars of an issue or situation. For instance, to define a Canadian dogwood, a scientist would refer to it as a *Cornus canadensis*. *Cornus* is the genus or category of all dogwoods, and the species is *canadensis*, which is a particular type of dogwood. By defining it in this way, the dogwood is considered in its universality; the definition does not ask the individual to think of a particular dogwood that blooms profusely along a favorite hiking trail. For Grassi, rhetorical speech deals with objects as they exist in a particular time and space, while scientific speech treats objects as abstract, universally definable phenomena. Rhetorical speech achieves an emotional identification with specific images that simply does not occur with rational speech. Grassi equates rational speech to monologue; a person delivering a monologue can proceed without input from or concern for others present or for situational factors.[123] Rhetorical speech, on the other hand, is likened to dialogue because it must take the world—in this case, the particular, profusely blooming dogwood—into account.

For Grassi, rhetorical speech is the primary, original, and thus superior form of speech. Based on the act of metaphor, it leads humans from the sensory images of their biological roots to a realization of their humanness. Rational speech, in contrast, always must be grounded in rhetorical speech because it is based on the acceptance of certain premises that are not knowable in rational terms. Because the power of any message derives from its starting point in images, rhetoric—and not logical deduction—is the true philosophy.

Rhetoric is the discipline that grapples with the fundamental questions of human existence—questions grounded in basic processes of *ingenium* and metaphor by which humans know, interpret, and create their worlds. All other ways of knowing depend on "metaphors, on the basis of the ingenuity which supplies the foundation of every rational, derivative process."[124] The primacy of rhetoric as Grassi conceptualizes it reverses the commonly held view of rhetoric as only an art of making logical reasons palatable to an audience. Instead, rhetoric is the foundation of logic because it is the means by which humans translate their foundational experiences and perceptions into language and from there into logical systems.

Commentary

Grassi's ideas about rhetoric have not had widespread impact on the field of communication; he is best known to scholars interested in Vico and in Renaissance humanism. The lack of attention to Grassi's work may be attributed in part to his philosophical orientation and style of presentation. His preferred mode of discussing the themes important to the Italian humanists is to elucidate them through comparative reflection on various texts rather than presenting them directly in a systematically argued treatise. Grassi's last two books, however, do provide more fully developed elaborations of his position, which will be helpful in making Grassi more accessible to rhetorical scholars.[125]

Efforts by scholars in all fields to explore alternatives to the scientific paradigm also are likely to call attention to Grassi's work because of his articulation of humanism as an alternative to rational, scientific approaches. Grassi's work has many similarities with social constructionist theories of communication and epistemic notions of rhetoric—theories that privilege the role of language in creating human social worlds—and he undoubtedly will be given more attention from scholars working within these paradigms. There are also parallels between Grassi's perspective on humanism and Eastern conceptions of rhetoric; Grassi himself believes that the humanistic tradition "could facilitate a new access to Chinese and Japanese philosophy." [126]

Perhaps Grassi's most important contribution is his "rehabilitation" [127] of the humanist tradition and the kind of philosophy it manifests. Despite the various ways Grassi has approached the topic of humanism, he "remains remarkably constant in his outlook." [128] Grassi rejects traditional conceptions of philosophy that strive for "universally valid propositions" in favor of philosophy as a "constantly renewed response to ever-changing situations." [129] For Grassi, to take into account the here and now of any situation means attending to the nonrational foundations by which humans come to know. These nonrational foundations—the creative insights available through *ingenium*—are what give form to human reality. Grassi's focus, then, is on those thinkers who "denounced with considerable foresight the serious limits" of all visions "based on rationalism, individualism, the abolition of *pathos*, the presumption of the natural sciences, the appeal to a procedure deducible from a single principle, the denial of a sense of the concrete and the empirical, the subtraction of models of awareness, to the flux of time and history." [130]

Grassi does more, however, than simply revive and reassert the humanist tradition. He "invents" it based on his own particular background and interests, showing it to be an undercurrent of thought throughout philosophical history that still is applicable today. Several of the speakers at a conference organized in memory of Grassi in Ischia, Italy, in October 1993 suggest the distinctive contribution that Grassi's scholarship makes. In particular, the juxtaposition of Italian and German perspectives creates a particularly independent and insightful view of humanism. Ebherhard Bons notes that Grassi's dual study of German philosophy from an Italian perspective and Italian philosophy from a German perspective allowed him to "observe mutual convergences and divergences" [131] and made him an independent thinker. Richard Winer similarly comments on the special edge that the balance between German and Italian brought to Grassi's thinking: "His Latin origins . . . drove him to measure himself against the German 'essence.' " The constant comparison of the two was not a limitation but a stimulus "to overcome" the limitations of both the Italian and German traditions. [132] Andrea Battistini suggests that the outcome of this German/Italian juxtaposition is a humanism that is " 'nocturnal,' 'disturbing,' 'dramatic,' 'conflictual,' and 'at times even subversive' " in opposition to the " 'sunny,' 'serene,' and 'balanced'" decoding often given to humanism.[133] Grassi's work continues to show how humanism always has been part of history but was "covered over completely by the Western rationalism of Platonism and Aristotelianism"—and yet is increasingly vital to dealing creatively with the problems that "the West can no longer discuss alone."[134]

Grassi's humanism contributes in particular to critiques of contemporary culture precisely because it is a perspective that demands attention to the concrete experience of the present situation. The focus of humanism on the role of "imaginative connections" that create truth "in a living, experiential way"[135] requires Grassi to apply humanism to the experiences of modern life. For Grassi, modernity, with its emphasis on scientific rationality, provides only a "temporarily stabilizing center" that neglects the most important questions "of human interaction."[136]

Grassi looks to the humanists for a model of how to provide the needed sense of centering,[137] and his Zurich dialogues—a "combination of the Existentialist notion of personal encounter with the Renaissance humanistic love of 'ingenium' or creativity"[138]—were one way he achieved this. Grassi not only is interested in critiquing contemporary culture but in finding ways to overcome its limitations. For Grassi, the kind of dialogue the Zurich dialogues made available—communication that depends on "the release of imaginative metaphors"—can promote new connections and divergent points of inquiry and "a human exchange of psychic energy and of unexpected angles on things."[139] To Grassi, the need to engage the problems of contemporary culture is critical, and the reintroduction of humanism offers one such means of engagement.

Yet, the contributions that many scholars see Grassi making in his discussion and application of Italian humanism are seen by others as weaknesses. Karl Popper's critique was one of the earliest and the most damaging: he charged Grassi with "incoherence and lack of clarity," essentially ignoring the philological and philosophical dimensions of Grassi's theory.[140] Domenico Pietropaolo suggests that Popper's critique was so vitriolic precisely because Popper "understood that the tradition from which it [Grassi's work] stemmed was alive and potentially dangerous for the cause of critical rationalism if it had been allowed to enter the arena of serious philosophical discussion in the Anglo-American world."[141] Popper's response, however selfishly motivated, kept Grassi's work from receiving attention from philosophers in the United States until the 1970s.

Charles Fierz, in seeking to determine whether Grassi actually offers a new philosophical foundation in his revival of Italian humanism, suggests that Grassi's background, rather than serving as the impetus for a more expansive definition of humanism, limits Grassi's philosophical contributions. Because Grassi was first a teacher of Italian literature, he naturally chose to focus on rhetoric: "It is his rhetorical background that 'favors' Grassi's perspective. It is also the factor that limits his ability to take a fully developed philosophical perspective."[142] Fierz, in particular, criticizes Grassi's notion

that rhetoric is prior to reason and instrumental in determining first premises, arguing that "rhetoric is not so original: each part of a persuasive effort,
to be appealing, must contain attractive images, metaphors. It does not,
therefore, attain its truth as ontology, but is an embellishment that may help
lead to truth."[143] Fierz suggests that Grassi's lack of elaboration of this philosophy leaves his system in the realm of common sense, lacking the rigors of
other philosophic systems.

Although Grassi may have chosen to point to rather than to elaborate
fully the ways in which Italian humanist thought is applicable in the current
world, Grassi's interest in and re-creation of Italian humanism as philosophy
offers a perspective worth considering. Not only does he attempt to recover
themes generally ignored in the dominance of scientific rationalism—" *ingenium*, imagination, memory, the ideal of folly, the role of metaphor, the primacy of human speech that forms a particular event of our social
world"[144]—but he constructs these concepts into a perspective useful for
contemporary consideration:

> Grassi's thesis asks us to choose Vico over Descartes, the humanities
> over science as our master key to understanding the power of language.
> In an age in which philosophy is dominated by conceptual analysis,
> Grassi's view calls us back to remember what has been denied in the
> modern basing of philosophy and knowledge on logic and not on the
> imagination. He brings forth from his account of antiquity, the Renais-
> sance, and Vico a whole world that has been lost.[145]

Bibliography

Books

Folly and Insanity in Renaissance Literature. Binghamton, NY: Medieval & Renais-
sance Texts & Studies, 1986. (With Maristella Lorch.)
Heidegger and the Question of Renaissance Humanism: Four Studies. Trans. Ulrich
Hemel and John Michael Krois. Binghamton, NY: Medieval & Renaissance
Texts & Studies, 1983.
The Primordial Metaphor. Trans. Laura Pietropaolo and Manuela Scarci. Bingham-
ton, NY: Medieval & Renaissance Texts & Studies, 1994.
Renaissance Humanism: Studies in Philosophy and Poetics. Trans. Walter F. Veit. Bing-
hamton, NY: Medieval & Renaissance Texts & Studies, 1988.
Rhetoric as Philosophy: The Humanist Tradition. Trans. John Michael Krois and
Azizeh Azodi. University Park: Pennsylvania State University Press, 1980.
Vico and Humanism: Essays on Vico, Heidegger, and Rhetoric. New York: Peter Lang, 1991.

Articles

"Appendix: A Philosophical Correspondence on Heidegger and Taoism." Correspondence between Michael Heim and Ernesto Grassi. *Journal of Chinese Philosophy*, 11 (December 1984), 324–35.

"Can Rhetoric Provide a New Basis for Philosophizing? The Humanist Tradition." Part I. Trans. John Michael Krois. *Philosophy and Rhetoric*, 11 (Winter 1978), 1–18.

"Can Rhetoric Provide a New Basis for Philosophizing? The Humanist Tradition." Part II. Trans. John Michael Krois. *Philosophy and Rhetoric*, 11 (Spring 1978), 75–97.

"The Claim of the Word and the Religious Significance of Poetry: A Humanist Problem." *Dionysius*, 8 (December 1984), 131–54.

"Critical Philosophy or Topical Philosophy? Meditations on the *De nostri temporis studiorum ratione*." Trans. Hayden V. White. In *Giambattista Vico: An International Symposium*. Ed. Giorgio Tagliacozzo and Hayden V. White. Baltimore: Johns Hopkins Press, 1969, pp. 39–50.

"The Denial of the Rational." Trans. A. Azodi and U. Hemel. *Man and World*, 16 (1983), 91–103.

"Humanistic Rhetorical Philosophizing: Giovanni Pontano's Theory of the Unity of Poetry, Rhetoric, and History." *Philosophy and Rhetoric*, 17 (1984), 135–55.

"Italian Humanism and Heidegger's Thesis of the End of Philosophy." Trans. John Michael Krois. *Philosophy and Rhetoric*, 13 (Spring 1980), 79–98.

"Marxism, Humanism, and the Problem of Imagination in Vico's Works." Trans. Azizeh Azodi. In *Giambattista Vico's Science of Humanity*. Ed. Giorgio Tagliacozzo and Donald Phillip Verene. Baltimore: Johns Hopkins University Press, 1976, pp. 275–94.

"The Originary Quality of the Poetic and Rhetorical Word: Heidegger, Ungaretti, and Neruda." Trans. Lavinia Lorch. *Philosophy and Rhetoric*, 20 (1987), 248–60.

"The Philosophical and Rhetorical Significance of Ovid's Metamorphoses." *Philosophy and Rhetoric*, 15 (Fall 1982), 257–61.

"The Priority of Common Sense and Imagination: Vico's Philosophical Relevance Today." Trans. Azizeh Azodi. *Social Research*, 43 (1976), 553–75.

"The Problem of Death: *Alcestis* by Euripides." *Philosophy and Rhetoric*, 30 (1997), 121–49.

"The Rehabilitation of Rhetorical Humanism: Regarding Heidegger's Anti-Humanism." Trans. R. Scott Walker. *Diogenes*, 142 (Summer 1988), 136–56.

"Remarks on German Idealism, Humanism, and the Philosophical Function of Rhetoric." Trans. John Michael Krois. *Philosophy and Rhetoric*, 19 (1986), 125–33.

"Response by the Author." Trans. Azizeh Azodi. *Social Research*, 43 (1976), 577–80.

"Rhetoric and Philosophy." Trans. Azizeh Azodi. *Philosophy and Rhetoric*, 9 (Fall 1976), 200–16.

"Vico as Epochal Thinker." Trans. Roberta Piazza. *Differentia*, 1 (Autumn 1986), 73–90.

"Vico, Marx, and Heidegger." Trans. Joseph Vincenzo. In *Vico and Marx: Affinities and Contrasts*. Ed. Giorgio Tagliacozzo. Atlantic Highlands, NJ: Humanities, 1983, pp. 233–50.

"Vico Versus Freud: Creativity and the Unconscious." Trans. John Michael Krois. In *Vico: Past and Present*. Ed. Giorgio Tagliacozzo. Atlantic Highlands, NJ: Humanities, 1981, 144–61.

"Why Rhetoric is Philosophy." Trans. Kiaran O'Malley. *Philosophy and Rhetoric*, 20 (1987), 68–78.

Endnotes

[1] Ernesto Grassi, *Rhetoric as Philosophy: The Humanist Tradition*, trans. John Michael Krois and Azizeh Azodi (University Park: Pennsylvania State University Press, 1980), p. 68.

2 Domenico Pietropaolo, "Grassi, Vico, and the Defense of the Humanist Tradition," *New Vico Studies*, 10 (1983), 5–6.

3 Eugen Baer, "Introduction," in "Noetic Philosophizing: Rhetoric's Displacement of Metaphysics *Alcestis* and *Don Quixote*," by Ernesto Grassi and Emilio Hidalgo-Serna, trans. Eugen Baer, *Philosophy and Rhetoric*, 30 (1997), 107.

4 Ernesto Grassi, *Renaissance Humanism: Studies in Philosophy and Poetics* (Binghamton, NY: Medieval & Renaissance Texts & Studies, 1988), p. xi.

5 Grassi, *Renaissance Humanism*, p. xi.

6 Baer, p. 107.

7 Baer, p. 109.

8 Heidegger adopted the ideology of National Socialism, a stance Grassi never was able to accept although he understood it within Heidegger's philosophical framework. According to Grassi, Heidegger's embrace of National Socialism was not "so much a political as a philosophical decision, one of principle." Heidegger believed that Anglo-Saxon and Marxist philosophies were responsible for the demise of Western thought, a demise he believed could be "overcome by the ideology of National Socialism." Grassi, *Renaissance Humanism*, p. xiv.

9 Grassi, *Renaissance Humanism*, p. xviii.

10 Grassi, *Renaissance Humanism*, p. xix.

11 Most of Grassi's publications have not been translated into English. For a complete bibliography of his Italian, German, and Spanish publications, see Emilio Hidalgo-Serna and Massimo Marassi, *Studi in memoria di Ernesto Grassi*, vol. 2 (Naples, It.: La Città del Sole, 1996), pp. 777–838.

12 Michael Heim, "Grassi's Experiment: The Renaissance through Phenomenology," *Research in Phenomenology*, 18 (1988), 246.

13 Heim, "Grassi's Experiment," p. 249.

14 Heim, "Grassi's Experiment," p. 241.

15 Heim, "Grassi's Experiment," p. 245.

16 Heim, "Grassi's Experiment," p. 248.

17 Heim, "Grassi's Experiment," p. 236.

18 Biographical material on Grassi was obtained from the following sources: *Who's Who in the World* (Chicago: Marquis Who's Who, 1976), p. 308; Ernesto Grassi, *Rhetoric as Philosophy*, acknowledgments, p. 2; Baer; Grassi, *Renaissance Humanism*, pp. ix–xix; Ernesto Grassi, letter to Karen A. Foss, October 17, 1983; personal interview with Grassi in Munich, West Germany, conducted by Karen A. Foss, August 21, 1983; Gianni Vattimo, "Grassi tra Vico e Heidegger," trans. for Karen A. Foss by Luisella Corbellari, *La Stampa* [Turin, It.], December 27, 1991, p. 16; and "Announcement," *Philosophy and Rhetoric*, 25 (1992), n. pag.

19 Ernesto Grassi, "Italian Humanism and Heidegger's Thesis of the End of Philosophy," trans. John Michael Krois, *Philosophy and Rhetoric*, 13 (Spring 1980), 83.

20 Bertrando Spaventa, *La fiosofia italiana nelle sue relazioni colla filosofia europa*, quoted in Grassi, *Rhetoric as Philosophy*, p. 2.

21 Grassi, *Rhetoric as Philosophy*, p. 4.

22 Grassi, *Renaissance Humanism*, p. 5.

23 Ernesto Grassi, "The Priority of Common Sense and Imagination: Vico's Philosophical Relevance Today," trans. Azizeh Azodi, in *Vico and Contemporary Thought*, ed. Giorgio Tagliacozzo, Michael Mooney, and Donald Phillip Verene (London, UK: Macmillan, 1980), p. 164.

24 René Descartes, *Meditations on First Philosophy*, trans. Laurence J. Lafleur (Indianapolis: Bobbs-Merrill, 1951), p. 26.

25 Grassi, "The Priority of Common Sense and Imagination," p. 166.

26 Grassi, *Renaissance Humanism*, p. 1.

27 Ernesto Grassi, *The Primordial Metaphor*, trans. Laura Pietropaolo and Manuela Scarci (Binghamton, NY: Medieval & Renaissance Texts & Studies, 1994), p. 95.

28 Ernesto Grassi, "The Originary Quality of the Poetic and Rhetorical Word: Heidegger, Ungaretti, and Neruda," trans. Lavinia Lorch, *Philosophy and Rhetoric*, 20 (1987), 248.

29 Grassi, "The Originary Quality of the Poetic," p. 249.

[30] Ernesto Grassi, "Marxism, Humanism, and the Problem of Imagination in Vico's Works," trans. Azizeh Azodi, in *Giambattista Vico's Science of Humanity*, ed. Giorgio Tagliacozzo and Donald Phillip Verene (Baltimore: Johns Hopkins University Press, 1976), p. 276.

[31] Ernesto Grassi, "Critical Philosophy or Topical Philosophy?: Meditations on the *De nostri temporis studiorum ratione*," trans. Hayden V. White, in *Giambattista Vico: An International Symposium*, ed. Giorgio Tagliacozzo and Hayden V. White (Baltimore: Johns Hopkins Press, 1969), p. 50.

[32] Ernesto Grassi, *Heidegger and the Question of Renaissance Humanism: Four Studies*, trans. Ulrich Hemel and John Michael Krois (Binghamton, NY: Medieval & Renaissance Texts & Studies, 1983), p. 43.

[33] Ernesto Grassi, "Why Rhetoric is Philosophy," trans. Kiaran O'Malley, *Philosophy and Rhetoric*, 20 (1987), 75.

[34] Grassi, *Heidegger and the Question of Renaissance Humanism*, p. 44.

[35] Grassi's contemporary critics also have used this argument. Perhaps the best known is Karl Popper, who, in an essay called "Humanism and Reason," attacked Grassi's work, suggesting that at the heart of "true humanism" is "the domain of reason, rehearsing its full power of criticism on the constructs of imagination in order to bring them into the proximity of truth." For Popper, humanism means "man's growth to ever greater rationality." See Karl Popper, "Humanism and Reason," *Philosophical Quarterly*, 2 (1952), 166–71. Popper's argument and its impact are discussed in Pietropaolo, pp. 2–3.

[36] Grassi, "Marxism, Humanism, and the Problem of Imagination," p. 294.

[37] Charles L. Fierz, "Philosophical Implications of Ernesto Grassi: A New Foundation of Philosophy?," *Philosophy and Rhetoric*, 27 (1994), 106.

[38] Paul Oskar Kristeller, *Renaissance Thought: The Classic, Scholastic, and Humanistic Strains* (New York: Harper, 1961), p. 8.

[39] Kristeller, *Renaissance Thought*, p. 9.

[40] Kristeller, *Renaissance Thought*, p. 10.

[41] Kristeller, *Renaissance Thought*, p. 9.

[42] Kristeller, *Renaissance Thought*, p. 122.

[43] Albert Rabil, Jr., "The Significance of 'Civic Humanism' in the Interpretation of the Italian Renaissance," in *Renaissance Humanism: Foundations, Forms, and Legacy*, vol. 1, ed. Albert Rabil, Jr., (Philadelphia: University of Pennsylvania Press, 1988), p. 142.

[44] Nancy S. Struever, *The Language of History in the Renaissance: Rhetoric and Historical Consciousness in Florentine Humanism* (Princeton, NJ: Princeton University Press, 1970), p. 74.

[45] Ernesto Grassi, "Remarks on German Idealism, Humanism, and the Philosophical Function of Rhetoric," trans. John Michael Krois, *Philosophy and Rhetoric*, 19 (1986), 128.

[46] Grassi, "Remarks on German Idealism," p. 128.

[47] Donald Phillip Verene, "Preface," in Ernesto Grassi and Maristella Lorch, *Folly and Insanity in Renaissance Literature* (Binghamton, NY: Medieval & Renaissance Texts & Studies, 1986), p. 10.

[48] Struever, p. 93.

[49] Coluccio Salutati, *Epistolario*, quoted in Struever, p. 97.

[50] Struever, p. 153.

[51] Struever, p. 61.

[52] Struever, p. 99.

[53] Grassi, *Rhetoric as Philosophy*, p. 26.

[54] Kristeller, *Renaissance Thought*, p. 10.

[55] Paul Oskar Kristeller, *Eight Philosophers of the Italian Renaissance* (Stanford, CA: Stanford University Press, 1964), p. 3.

[56] Jerrold E. Seigel, *Rhetoric and Philosophy in Renaissance Humanism: The Union of Eloquence and Wisdom, Petrarch to Valla* (Princeton, NJ: Princeton University Press, 1968), p. 256. The humanists themselves probably would have rejected the label *philosophers*. They preferred to call themselves *grammarians* because they saw philosophers as dealing with the abstract human condition and ignoring the realm of individual action. For them, the study of philology

or grammar was the new form of philosophizing because grammar requires an understanding of the whole sentence and its context—subject, verb, and background—that brought the sentence into being. Grassi, "Marxism, Humanism, and the Problem of Imagination," p. 284.

57 Grassi, "Remarks on German Idealism," p. 125.

58 Freud, Longinus, and *Ecclesiastes* are discussed in Grassi, *Primordial Metaphor*.

59 Ernesto Grassi, letter to Giorgio Tagliacozzo, October 8, 1986, trans. for Karen A. Foss by Luisella Corbellari, quoted in Giorgio Tagliacozzo, "L'istante iniziale della carriera vichiana di Grassi," in *Studi in memoria di Ernesto Grassi*, by Emilio Hidalgo-Serna and Massimo Marassi, vol. 1 (Naples, It.: La Città del Sole, 1996), pp. 379–83.

60 Henry Thomas, *Biographical Encyclopedia of Philosophy* (Garden City, NY: Doubleday, 1965), p. 248.

61 Grassi, *Rhetoric as Philosophy*, p. 37.

62 Donald Phillip Verene, *The New Art of Autobiography: An Essay on the Life of Giambattista Vico Written by Himself* (Oxford, UK: Clarendon, 1991), p. 136.

63 Verene suggests that Vico's method of studies "is not new in the sense of intending to be something novel." Rather, it was an attempt to "revive something old—the interest of the ancients in self-knowledge and the basis self-knowledge has in the teaching and practice of humane letters." Verene, *The New Art of Autobiography*, p. 136.

64 Verene, *The New Art of Autobiography*, p. 151.

65 Verene, *The New Art of Autobiography*, p. 169.

66 Verene, *The New Art of Autobiography*, p. 152.

67 Verene, *The New Art of Autobiography*, p. 154.

68 Verene, *The New Art of Autobiography*, p. 154.

69 Ernesto Grassi, "Vico *Versus* Freud: Creativity and the Unconscious," trans. John Michael Krois, in *Vico: Past and Present*, ed. Giorgio Tagliacozzo (Atlantic Highlands, NJ: Humanities, 1981), p. 147.

70 Giambattista Vico, *The New Science of Giambattista Vico*, trans. and ed. Thomas Goddard Bergin and Max Harold Fisch (Ithaca, NY: Cornell University Press, 1968), par. 374–84.

71 Verene, *The New Art of Autobiography*, p. 169.

72 Verene, *The New Art of Autobiography*, p. 148.

73 Giambattista Vico, *On the Study Methods of Our Time*, trans Elio Gianturco (Ithaca, NY: Cornell University Press, 1990), sec. XV.

74 Grassi, *Renaissance Humanism*, p. 23.

75 Grassi, *Primordial Metaphor*, p. 24.

76 Grassi, *Primordial Metaphor*, p. 26.

77 Grassi, *Primordial Metaphor*, p. 134.

78 Aristotle, *Metaphysics*, quoted in Grassi, *Renaissance Humanism*, p. 39.

79 Grassi, *Renaissance Humanism*, p. 124.

80 Grassi, *Renaissance Humanism*, p. 23.

81 Donald Phillip Verene, "Response to Grassi," *Philosophy and Rhetoric*, 19 (1986), 135.

82 Giambattista Vico, *"Orazione in morte di donn'Angela Cimmino marchesa della Petrella,"* quoted in Grassi, "The Priority of Common Sense and Imagination," p. 173.

83 Verene, *The New Art of Autobiography*, p. 152.

84 Verene, "Preface," p. 10.

85 Grassi, "Marxism, Humanism, and the Problem of Imagination," p. 290.

86 Grassi, *Heidegger and the Question of Renaissance Humanism*, p. 26.

87 Vico, *The New Science*, par. 382.

88 Grassi, "The Priority of Common Sense and Imagination," p. 175.

89 Grassi, *Renaissance Humanism*, p. 100.

90 Grassi, "The Priority of Common Sense and Imagination," p. 174. The 12 feats performed by Hercules were: (1) killing the Nemean lion; (2) destroying the Lernaean Hydra, a monster reared by Hera as a menace to Hercules; (3) capturing the Ceryneian Hind, a creature with golden horns like a stag; (4) capturing alive the boar that haunted Mt. Erymanthus; (5) cleaning King Augeia's filthy cattle yard in one day; (6) removing the man-eating Stymphalian

birds; (7) capturing the Cretan bull; (8) capturing the four savage mares of King Diomedes; (9) fetching the golden girdle worn by the Amazon queen, Hippolyte; (10) fetching the cattle of Geryon from Erytheia; (11) fetching fruit from the golden apple tree in Hera's garden; and (12) bringing the dog Cerberus up from Tarturus. Robert Graves, *Greek Myths* (London, UK: Cassell, 1955), pp. 462–520.

[91] Grassi, *Renaissance Humanism*, p. 104.
[92] Grassi, *Renaissance Humanism*, p. 105.
[93] Grassi, *Renaissance Humanism*, p. 92.
[94] Grassi, *Primordial Metaphor*, p. 53.
[95] Grassi, *Renaissance Humanism*, p. 92.
[96] Ernesto Grassi, *Die Macht des Bildes*, quoted in Walter Veit, "The Potency of Imagery—the Impotence of Rational Language: Ernesto Grassi's Contribution to Modern Epistemology," *Philosophy and Rhetoric*, 17 (1984), 235.
[97] Grassi, *Primordial Metaphor*, p. 103.
[98] Grassi, *Primordial Metaphor*, p. 107.
[99] Grassi, *Primordial Metaphor*, p. 108.
[100] Grassi, *Primordial Metaphor*, p. 109.
[101] Grassi, *Primordial Metaphor*, p. 108.
[102] Grassi, *Primordial Metaphor*, p. 108.
[103] Grassi, *Primordial Metaphor*, p. 20.
[104] Grassi, *Renaissance Humanism*, p. 27.
[105] Grassi, *Primordial Metaphor*, p. 20.
[106] Grassi, *Renaissance Humanism*, p. 114.
[107] Vico, *The New Science*, par. 405.
[108] Grassi, *Primordial Metaphor*, p. 17.
[109] Grassi and Lorch, p. 37.
[110] Grassi and Lorch, p. 89.
[111] Verene, "Preface," p. 11.
[112] Grassi and Lorch, p. 113.
[113] Theresa Enos and Stuart C. Brown, *Professing the New Rhetorics: A Sourcebook* (Englewood Cliffs, NJ: Prentice Hall/Blair, 1994), pp. 92–93.
[114] Enos and Brown, p. 93.
[115] Grassi, "Critical Philosophy or Topical Philosophy?," p. 39.
[116] Grassi, *Rhetoric as Philosophy*, p. 33.
[117] Ernesto Grassi, "Humanistic Rhetorical Philosophizing: Giovanni Pontano's Theory of the Unity of Poetry, Rhetoric, and History," *Philosophy and Rhetoric*, 17 (1984), 146.
[118] Grassi and Lorch, p. 40.
[119] Grassi, *Heidegger and the Question of Renaissance Humanism*, p. 68.
[120] Grassi, *Heidegger and the Question of Renaissance Humanism*, p. 69.
[121] Grassi, *Heidegger and the Question of Renaissance Humanism*, p. 69.
[122] Grassi, *Heidegger and the Question of Renaissance Humanism*, p. 70.
[123] Grassi, *Rhetoric as Philosophy*, p. 113.
[124] Grassi, *Rhetoric as Philosophy*, p. 34.
[125] Grassi, *Renaissance Humanism*; and Grassi, *The Primordial Metaphor*.
[126] Michael Heim, "A Philosophy of Comparison: Heidegger and Lao Tzu," *Journal of Chinese Philosophy*, 11 (1984), 328.
[127] Ernesto Grassi, "The Rehabilitation of Rhetorical Humanism: Regarding Heidegger's Anti-Humanism," trans. R. Scott Walker, *Diogenes*, 142 (Summer 1988), 136–56.
[128] Pietropaolo, p. 4.
[129] Baer, p. 106.
[130] Franco Ratto, rev. of *Studi in memoria di Ernesto Grassi*, ed. Emilio Hidalgo-Serna and Massimo Marassi, *Forum Italicum*, 31 (Spring 1997), 244.
[131] Ebherhard Bons, quoted in Ratto, p. 239.
[132] Richard Winer, quoted in Ratto, p. 242.

[133] Andrea Battistini, quoted in Ratto, p. 244.
[134] Heim, "A Philosophy of Comparison," p. 331.
[135] Heim, "Grassi's Experiment," p. 240.
[136] Heim, "Grassi's Experiment," p. 240.
[137] Heim, "Grassi's Experiment," p. 238.
[138] Fierz, p. 114.
[139] Heim, "Grassi's Experiment," p. 243.
[140] Pietropaolo, pp. 2–3.
[141] Karl Popper, p. 377, quoted in Pietropaolo, pp. 3–4.
[142] Fierz, p. 114.
[143] Fierz, p. 114.
[144] Donald Phillip Verene, "Remarks on Ernesto Grassi's Work," unpublished paper available from Karen A. Foss, 1983, p. 2.
[145] Donald Phillip Verene, rev. of *Die Macht der Phantasie* and *Rhetoric as Philosophy*, by Ernesto Grassi, *Philosophy and Rhetoric*, 13 (1980), 282.

4

CHAÏM PERELMAN AND LUCIE OLBRECHTS-TYTECA

The publication of *The New Rhetoric: A Treatise on Argumentation* was one of the most substantial twentieth-century contributions to rhetorical thinking—especially to argumentative perspectives on rhetoric. Oddly, students of argumentation and rhetoric know a great deal about one author,

Chaïm Perelman, and very little about the other, Lucie Olbrechts-Tyteca. Perhaps one of the reasons is that he was a professor with doctorates in both law and philosophy, while she held the equivalent of a B.A. degree. Another reason is that after completion of their major project, *The New Rhetoric*, Perelman traveled throughout Europe and the United States, delivering lectures and seminars about the subject, while Olbrechts-Tyteca stayed home in Brussels. Students of argument also have made a greater effort to learn about Perelman's life because of his "inclination to assume ownership of the [*New Rhetoric*] project as well as a cultural predilection to believe him."[1]

Chaïm Perelman was born in Warsaw, Poland, on May 20, 1912; his family moved to Belgium in 1925.[2] Perelman was exposed to the study of rhetoric in secondary school, including Richard Whately's *Elements of Rhetoric* (1828), and he studied such diverse topics as the syllogism and figures of style. These topics later seemed to Perelman to be conspicuously unrelated to one another: "Since then I have often wondered what link a professor of rhetoric could possibly discover between the syllogism and the figures of style with their exotic names that are so difficult to remember."[3] Perelman completed his education at the Free University of Brussels, where he earned a doctorate in law in 1934 and a doctorate in philosophy in 1938.

Perelman was a person of action as well as of ideas. During World War II, he and his wife, Fela Perelman, "played an heroic role in the underground during the Nazi occupation"[4] of Belgium. At the conclusion of the war, he was offered a number of medals for heroism, but he refused them, saying, "My heart was on fire. I simply picked up a pail of water to douse the flames. I want no medals."[5] After the war, Perelman returned to the Free University as a professor of logic, ethics, and metaphysics. At the age of 36, he was the youngest full professor in the history of the university. Later, he served as director of the Center for the Philosophy of Law and the National Center for Logical Research at the Free University. He also received honorary degrees from the University of Florence and the Hebrew University of Jerusalem.

Because of his interest in law, Perelman studied the nature of justice early in his professional career. His studies of justice led him to develop the concept of formal justice, which he defines as "*a principle of action in accordance with which beings of one and the same essential category must be treated in the same way.*"[6] Perelman soon discovered that application of this principle to particular cases led to an exploration of values and to the question, "How do we reason about values?"

Perelman found the answers provided by the philosophical literature about reason and values highly unsatisfactory. He could think of no way to resolve questions of value on rational grounds: "Indeed, as I entirely accepted the principle that one cannot draw an 'ought' from an 'is'—a judgement of value from a judgement of fact—I was led inevitably to the conclusion that if justice consists in the systematic implementation of certain value judgements, it does not rest on any rational foundation."[7] Unable to reconcile justice with formal logic, Perelman turned to other ways in which people reason about values such as justice. James Crosswhite claims that a part of Perelman's motivation to take up the study of argumentation was "a direct result of the impasse he reached in his work on the theory of justice. . . . In his Genoa lectures, translated as *Justice* (1967), Perelman describes his one-time skepticism as absolute: 'As for the value that is the foundation of the normative system, we cannot subject it to any rational criterion: It is utterly arbitrary and logically indeterminate.' "[8]

Perelman's work on justice and on argumentation was motivated both by the failure of philosophy to deal with reason and by the "actual historical situation of Europe's undergoing the physical and moral-political devastation of World War II. Nationalist and ethnic allegiances had overwhelmed the modern political project of articulating more universal, transnational principles that might protect the rights of individuals and help mediate conflicts among groups."[9] Thus, Perelman's work in law and in rhetoric was connected to his philosophical interests and to his work in the Belgian resistance. In this light, his work can be seen as "a philosophical response to a postmodern Europe shaped by systemic (and systematic) violence and unconstrained fragmentation, where the massive counterviolence of the war might prove to be only a temporary hedge against the future."[10] Motivated by the horrors of the holocaust, Perelman turned away from logic in seeking answers to his questions about justice and about how humans reason about all values.

In 1962, Perelman accepted an invitation to visit the United States as a distinguished visiting professor at Pennsylvania State University. He came at the joint invitation of Henry W. Johnstone, chair of the Department of Philosophy, and Robert T. Oliver, chair of the Department of Speech. "I was very perplexed," noted Perelman, "for I knew nothing of 'speech,' a discipline entirely unknown in European universities. . . . I chose as the title of my course, 'The Philosophical Foundations of Rhetoric,' but I could not prepare my lessons, because I did not know what the preoccupations of the members of the Department of *Speech* were."[11]

Prior to his visit to the United States, Perelman assumed that rhetoric and argumentation were neglected subjects and knew nothing of a profession in the United States devoted to the study and teaching of rhetoric. Perelman developed close ties to the communication discipline, beginning with that first visit, that he maintained until his death. His last official visit with the profession was his attendance at the annual convention of the Speech Communication Association (now the National Communication Association) in Louisville, Kentucky, in 1982. According to Johnstone, Perelman's close association with colleagues in communication partially explains "why a Belgian philosopher who made a number of trips to North America was so seldom welcomed by the philosophy departments on this continent."[12] Johnstone claims that philosophy departments in North America tend to "draw a sharp distinction between philosophy and rhetoric, denigrating the latter and pursuing the former on the assumption that rhetoric had nothing to do with it."[13] This polarity is probably less sharp today than it was in Perelman's time.

Perelman's death came "just as he was getting ready to write the great synthesis that he had been preparing for several years, which he wanted to title *From Metaphysics to Rhetoric*."[14] On December 5, 1983, King Baudouin I of Belgium awarded Chaïm Perelman and Fela Perelman the titles of Baron and Baroness in recognition of their work in the Nazi resistance movement, his work in philosophy, and the subsequent renown he had brought to Belgium.[15] Following a dinner on January 22, 1984, to celebrate the honor with some of his close friends, Perelman died of a heart attack in his home.

Lucie Tyteca was born into a wealthy Belgian family in 1899.[16] Her father was a prominent psychiatrist and founder of the Tyteca Institute for Neuropsychiatry. In 1925, she received her degree in social science and economics from the Free University of Brussels. That same year, she married a statistician, Raymond Olbrechts, and took the name *Lucie Olbrechts-Tyteca*. Although she "read widely in French and German literature and in sociology, social psychology, and statistics," Olbrechts-Tyteca did not work toward a graduate degree. After hearing Perelman discuss his ideas at various social gatherings during the 1940s, she became interested in his work. They began *The New Rhetoric* project in 1947,[17] working together on it for the next 10 years. Following this collaboration, Olbrechts-Tyteca published in French "at least four more articles and a book" as a single author, none of which has been translated into English. Although not as prolific as Perelman, Olbrechts-Tyteca was a serious student of argumentation, and her *vita* at the end of her career very likely would have "qualified her to be appointed to the senior faculty of most major research institutions."[18] Olbrechts-Tyteca died under mysterious circumstances in 1988. According to Perelman's daughter, she " 'disappeared,' having been whisked away to the countryside by her caretakers in the year before she died."[19]

Perelman and Olbrechts-Tyteca's most important work is *La Nouvelle Rhétorique: Traité de l'Argumentation*, published in French in 1958 and translated into English in 1969 as *The New Rhetoric: A Treatise on Argumentation*. As a team, Perelman and Olbrechts-Tyteca complemented one another well. Perelman was the "philosopher and theorist," and Olbrechts-Tyteca was the "empiricist and analyst."[20] Perelman, with his expertise in both logic and law, provided the overall theoretical framework and its justification, permitting him to "identify the relations between formal logic and quasi logic and to make a significant distinction between the rational and the reasonable."[21] Olbrechts-Tyteca excelled at "fine-grained description of discourse" and provided "examples, description, and 'middle-level' theory" so essential to the project.[22] Her background in French and German literature as well as in sociology helped her "to discuss the argumentative function of stylistic devices and discursive structures"[23] and provided expertise for the "close study of the uses of values in discourses, in particular, philosophical pairs, value hierarchies, and dissociation."[24] Because a sizeable majority of *The New Rhetoric* is devoted to the structures of argument, Barbara Warnick has argued that Olbrechts-Tyteca was a major contributor to *The New Rhetoric*.

Perelman and Olbrechts-Tyteca's methods closely followed those of German logician Gottlob Frege, who studied examples of reasoning that mathematicians use to cast new light on logic. They decided to investigate the ways in which authors in diverse fields use argument to reason about values. Their methods included the study of specific examples of argumentation texts concerning questions of value. They also studied specific examples of political discourse, philosophical discourse, reasons given by judges to justify their decisions, and other daily discussions involving deliberations about matters of value. "For almost ten years, Mme. L. Olbrechts-Tyteca and I conducted such an inquiry and analysis," Perelman explained. He summarized their results: "We obtained results that neither of us had ever expected. Without either knowing or wishing it, we had rediscovered a part of Aristotelian logic that had been long forgotten or, at any rate, ignored and despised. . . . We called this new, or revived, branch of study, devoted to the analysis of informal reasoning, *the new rhetoric.*"[25]

Perelman and Olbrechts-Tyteca rejected the term *the new dialectic* in favor of *the new rhetoric* for three reasons: Use of the term *dialectic* would be confused with modern uses of that term such as the use of dialectic in Marxist theories; the term *rhetoric* was available for development because *rhetoric* had fallen in such disrepute that it no longer was used in substantial philosophical literature; and the notion of audience was central both to ancient theories of rhetoric as well as to their own. According to the editors of *The Great Ideas Today*, "more than any single item, this work aroused a renewed interest in the idea [of rhetoric]."[26]

Need for a New Rhetoric

Perelman and Olbrechts-Tyteca suggest that a new approach to rhetoric is needed because traditional rhetoric emphasizes matters of style at the expense of matters of rationality.[27] The contemporary state of disrepute of rhetoric is due to this emphasis, which they trace to attitudes about rhetoric in classical Greece: "Among the ancients, rhetoric appeared as the study of a technique for use by the common man impatient to arrive rapidly at conclusions, or to form an opinion, without first of all taking the trouble of a preliminary serious investigation."[28] Thus, because rhetoric seems to be concerned more with matters of style than with matters of rationality, the subject is not one that historically has commanded respect, particularly among philosophers.

Perelman and Olbrechts-Tyteca trace the connection of rhetoric to style (and its current disrepute) largely to Aristotle's "misleading analysis . . . of the epideictic or ceremonial form of oratory."[29] Aristotle divides rhetoric into forensic, deliberative, and epideictic oratory. Forensic or judiciary oratory is speaking in a court of law; it is concerned with matters of the past, such as whether or not a certain act has occurred. Deliberative oratory, or speaking in a legislative assembly, is concerned with matters of the future, such as what courses of actions are advisable. Epideictic oratory, or ceremonial speaking, such as a Fourth of July address, concerns speaking about matters of praise and blame.

The audiences for both forensic and deliberative oratory are expected to judge a speech on the merits of its content. "Was it or was it not true that a certain person committed an act of murder?" is a question that might concern the forensic speaker. "Is it or is it not advisable for the state to enact this policy or that policy?" are questions a deliberative speaker might answer. In epideictic oratory, however, the audience is expected to judge on the basis of the orator's skill: "Such set speeches were often delivered before large assemblies, as at the Olympic Games, where competition between orators provided a welcome complement to the athletic contests. On such occasions, the only decision that the audience was called upon to make concerned the talent of the orator, by awarding the crown to the victor."[30] Although deliberative and forensic speaking are concerned with matters of policy and fact, epideictic oratory is concerned with matters of value. Consequently, no explicit standards for judging the content of the epideictic speech exist, and audiences are instructed to judge it on matters of skill. Although audiences are capable of judging matters of fact and policy on their merits, the classical treatment of rhetoric views audiences as incapable of judging matters of value in the same way.

Because the form of speaking most closely associated with values—epideictic oratory—is judged on style instead of content, Perelman and Olbrechts-Tyteca suggest that a theory of argument is needed in which values, like facts and policies, can be assessed rationally. They believe that questions of value are especially important to rhetoric: "The epideictic genre is not only important but essential from an educational point of view, since it too has an effective and distinctive part to play—that, namely, of bringing about a consensus in the minds of the audience regarding the values that are celebrated in the speech."[31] How speaker and audience argue about values is of particular interest to Perelman and Olbrechts-Tyteca, an issue they believe best is dealt with by rhetoric than by logic.

Argumentation and Logic

Perelman and Olbrechts-Tyteca's theory of rhetoric is a theory of argumentation. For them, however, argumentation is not the same as logic; Perelman and Olbrechts-Tyteca believe that argumentation is separate and distinct from demonstration or formal logic. Demonstration involves calculation made according to rules accepted by formal, deductive logic, while "argumentation is the study of the discursive techniques allowing us *to induce or increase the mind's adherence to the theses presented for its assent.*"[32] Demonstration uses mathematical language such as that contained in the mathematical formula $a/b = c/d$, while argumentation uses naturally ambiguous human language. Thus, demonstration allows the production of a conclusion by reasoning from premises, while argumentation attempts to gain audience adherence to a claim.

One of Perelman's elaborations on the distinction between argumentation and demonstration involves contrasting the terms *rational* and *reasonable*.[33] For Perelman, the term *rational* is related to abstract systems and is aligned more with formal logic than with argumentation: "The *rational* corresponds to mathematical reason, for some a reflection of divine reason, which grasps necessary relations, which knows *a priori* certain self-evident and immutable truths."[34] The reasonable, on the other hand, is more aligned with common sense and practical argumentation. According to Perelman, "the idea of the reasonable in law corresponds to an equitable solution in the absence of all precise rules of adjudication."[35] Thus, the rational corresponds more to demonstration, while the reasonable corresponds more to argumentation.

The primary difference between argumentation and demonstration is that demonstration is impersonal, while argumentation is personal. Demonstration or formal logic is conducted according to a system that largely is unrelated to people, but argumentation is a person-centered activity. The aim of demonstration is calculation—the deduction of formally valid conclusions by conforming to a particular set of rules—while the aim of argumentation is not calculation but adherence to a thesis, which presupposes a "meeting of minds."[36] The conclusion of demonstration is assumed to be certain, while the conclusion of an argument is a probable one. Demonstration begins with axioms that are assumed to be true regardless of an audience's agreement with them. Argumentation, on the other hand, is personal because it begins with premises that the audience accepts. The conclusion of demonstration, then, is a self-evident one, while the conclusion of argument is one that is more or less strong, more or less convincing. The central concept separating argumentation from logic is the audience.

Audience

Perelman and Olbrechts-Tyteca's concern with argumentation as opposed to demonstration leads them to focus on the audience.[37] All argumentation must be planned in relation to an audience: "A speech must be heard, as a book must be read."[38] Sometimes, groups such as scientists assume they do not address an audience and merely report the facts. Perelman and Olbrechts-Tyteca reject such an attitude because it "rests on the illusion, widespread in certain rationalistic and scientific circles, that facts speak for themselves."[39] Perelman and Olbrechts-Tyteca insist that facts do not "speak"; "facts" only become facts when an audience consents to view them as facts.

Perelman and Olbrechts-Tyteca believe that an audience is necessary for argumentation to occur. A contact of the minds or, in their words, a "formation of an effective community of minds"[40] must exist. This meeting of the minds is an intellectual contact that requires people engaged in argumentation to share some frame of reference. In some cases, of course, contact of minds can be inadequate. They use the example of Alice in *Alice in Wonderland* to show how failure to have this contact of minds results in ineffective or nonexistent argumentation. Alice is unable to communicate effectively with the characters in Wonderland because the rules of conversation are so different from those in Alice's natural environment. A shared frame of reference between speaker and audience does not exist.[41]

In defining the concept of audience, Perelman and Olbrechts-Tyteca first consider whether the concept should be limited to the speaker's physical audience. Perelman and Olbrechts-Tyteca do not impose this limitation on their definition, explaining that "a member of Parliament in England must address himself to the Speaker, but he may try to persuade those listening . . . throughout the country."[42] At the same time, however, situations exist where the speaker may choose to ignore certain persons to whom argumentation is actually addressed because they are beyond appeal. For example, a candidate for political office may realize the futility of attempting to persuade a group of people carrying signs for her opponent even though those people are actually present for the speech. Thus, Perelman and Olbrechts-Tyteca define the audience, "for the purposes of rhetoric, as *the ensemble of those whom the speaker wishes to influence by his argumentation*."[43] Their concept of audience refers to the speaker's mental conception of the audience rather than to the physical presence of a group of people assembled to hear a speech.

Perelman and Olbrechts-Tyteca distinguish between particular and universal audiences. The universal audience is composed of all reasonable and competent people; a particular audience is any group of people whether or not they are reasonable or competent. The particular audience may range from people who are physically present and who are addressed at a particular time to a specific group of persons whom the speaker is attempting to influence. The particular audience for a politician, for example, may include all the voters of the precinct, even though the speech is presented only to an assembly of the League of Women Voters. For a doctor, a particular audience may be the patient, even if the entire family is present. Sometimes, a particular audience is composed of so many varied elements that it should be considered a "composite audience."[44] Because members of a composite audience may hold a variety of different values or at least may arrange their values differently, the speaker should use a multiplicity of arguments to gain their adherence.

In contrast to the particular audience, the universal audience "may be all of humanity, or at least all those who are competent and reasonable . . . which may itself be made up of an infinite variety of particular audiences."[45] The universal audience is a mental concept the speaker constructs; thus, every culture and perhaps every speaker has a different universal audience. The universal audience generally is not an elite audience or even an audience of experts in a subject area. Those who wish to appeal to elite audiences may consider elite audiences to be above common people: "The elite audience embodies the universal audience only for those who acknowledge this role of vanguard and model. For the rest it will be no more than a particular audience. The status of an audience varies with the concepts one has of it."[46] An elite audience may or may not embody the universal audience, depending on the attitude of the speaker.

The universal audience does not have to be composed of many people; it can be one person or even oneself. Argumentation before a single hearer might include one philosopher attempting to convince another to accept her position on the question of ethics. Similarly, most people occasionally argue with themselves. These instances constitute argumentation before the universal audience only when the speaker chooses arguments and appeals that merit consideration beyond the particular audience. In these cases, "the interlocutor in a dialogue and the man debating with himself are regarded as an incarnation of the universal audience."[47] The distinguishing feature of the universal audience "does not depend upon the number of persons who hear the speaker but upon the speaker's intention; does he want the adherence of some or of every reasonable being?"[48] The speaker may envision those to whom the speech is delivered—even in an instance of private deliberation—as the universal audience.

The concept of the universal audience serves two purposes for the speaker. First, it serves as an aid in the choice of arguments and appeals—as a "metaphor which functions as an inventional tool."[49] The speaker begins with a concept of the universal audience and from that concept makes decisions regarding the types of appeals that seem most appropriate for that audience. In selecting appeals and arguments, the speaker actually is selecting the audience—universal or particular—toward whom the argumentation is directed.

A second purpose of the universal audience is that it serves as a norm or a standard for differentiating good arguments from bad arguments. This purpose is more relevant to philosophical argument than to everyday argument. For philosophical arguments, the universal audience provides a sense of rationality because it gives its assent to good arguments and withholds it from those it considers bad. Perelman and Olbrechts-Tyteca do not consider truth and validity in argumentation to be absolute and assert that argumentation must provide for a variety of interpretations for reality: "To reconcile philosophic claims to rationality with the plurality of philosophic systems, we must recognize that the appeal to reason must be identified not as an appeal to a single truth but instead as an appeal for adherence of an audience."[50] Various audiences and various members of the audience, of course, have different conceptions of what must be provided before assent will be given.

The concept of the universal audience implies that the quality of argument depends on the quality of the audience that accepts the thesis of the speaker. Although adherence of a particular audience may not be indicative of an especially good argument, adherence of the universal audience is the ultimate in rationality in Perelman and Olbrechts-Tyteca's theory. Thus, an argument addressed to a particular audience may be persuasive to that audience but not to the universal audience. An argument that would persuade members of the National Rifle Association, for example, to oppose gun control might not be one that would convince all reasonable and competent people that gun control is unwise.

Starting Points of Argumentation

The purpose of argumentation is to move an audience from agreement about premises to agreement about some conclusion. The process of argumentation, then, is different from that of demonstration, where the purpose is to produce "Truth." In Perelman's words, "the aim of argumentation is not, like demonstration, to prove the truth of the conclusion from premises, but to transfer to the conclusion the *adherence* accorded to the premises."[51]

Although the conclusions of argumentation may be uncertain, contingent, and unacceptable to an audience, the argumentation process begins with premises the audience accepts. Although the arguer's claim may be controversial, such as the value of a nuclear test ban treaty, the argument must begin with agreed-upon premises such as, for example, the value of peace. An audience's rejection of the premise of an argument is tantamount to refusing to let the argument begin.[52] Once the audience accepts the premises, the next step is to encourage the members of the audience to adhere to the conclusion in the same way it agrees with the premises. This is accomplished by "the establishment of a bond between the premises and the theses whose acceptance the speaker wants to achieve."[53]

Premises of various kinds serve as the starting points of argument.[54] Perelman and Olbrechts-Tyteca distinguish between starting points that deal with reality and those that concern the preferable.

Starting Points Dealing with Reality

Starting points dealing with reality reflect the universal audience's beliefs about things as they actually are rather than as they ought to be. Facts, truths, and presumptions are the starting points of argumentation that deal with reality.

Facts. These starting points are "characterized by objects that already are agreed to by the universal audience."[55] Because something's status as a fact depends on agreement by the universal audience, there is no way "to define 'fact' in such a manner that would allow us, at any time, to classify this or that concrete datum as a fact." A fact is a fact only by the agreement accorded it by the universal audience. Although its actual correspondence to the structures of reality is not the issue, universal agreement is achieved when persons perceive data to be rooted in those structures of reality. "From the standpoint of argumentation," Perelman and Olbrechts-Tyteca assert, "we are confronted with a fact only if we can postulate uncontroverted, universal agreement with respect to it."[56]

Because facts are given universal agreement, they are not subject to argumentation. Adherence to a fact requires no justification, and an audience expects no reinforcement for it. Facts have a privileged status in argumentation that easily can be lost; if a statement is questioned or justification is called for, the datum loses its status as a fact that enjoys universal agreement.

In other words, a fact loses its privileged status as a fact when it is the conclusion rather than the starting point of argument. Although argumentative conclusions are uncertain and contingent, the starting points of argumentation require agreement; thus, agreement is precisely the criterion that defines a fact. In the days prior to Christopher Columbus's voyage to North America, for example, a well-accepted fact was that the earth was flat. This idea was granted the status of fact not because of its enduring truth but because of the agreement accorded to it.

Truths. Similar to facts, truths enjoy universal agreement. Perelman and Olbrechts-Tyteca use the term *fact* to refer to a particular datum and the term *truth* to refer to a broader principle that connects facts to one another. The two terms are different in that truths involve "more complex systems relating to connections between facts. They may be scientific theories or philosophical or religious conceptions."[57] Both facts and truths serve as starting points of argument that concern the nature of reality. Depending on the audience, an argument concerning the development of the human species might be based on a premise that assumes the truth of evolution or the truth of divine creation.

Presumptions. The third starting point of argument deals with the nature of reality. Presumptions are related to "what is normal and likely. . . . Until there is proof to the contrary, it is presumed that the normal will occur, or has occurred, or rather that the normal can safely be taken as a foundation in reasoning."[58] Presumptions, like facts and truths, enjoy universal agreement, but the audience's adherence to presumptions falls short of being maximum; thus, presumptions, unlike facts and truths, can be reinforced by argumentation. Speakers engage in preliminary argumentation to establish certain presumptions or to reinforce those presumptions in the minds of the audience. According to Perelman and Olbrechts-Tyteca, audiences expect that which is normal and likely, and presumptions are based on these expectations. For example, audiences expect good people to commit good deeds, evil people to commit evil deeds, truthful people to tell the truth, liars to lie, and reasonable people to act in prudent ways. Although individuals presume that good people will commit good deeds, exceptions are often encountered. A number of U.S. leaders have served their country well while leading less than exemplary private lives. Thus, presumptions can be violated, whereas facts and truths cannot.

One of the important advantages associated with the use of presumption in argumentation is that it "imposes the burden of proof upon the person who wants to oppose its application."[59] The presumption of innocence in the U.S. legal system is an example of this advantage. Juries are supposed to accept the presumption of innocence on the part of the defendant until proven otherwise. Of course, a presumption such as this does not last forever, and although jury members are informed of the presumption of innocence, they also are informed that it can be overturned by proof beyond a reasonable doubt. Presumptions, then, are overturned when they are shown to be contrary to facts.

In summary, the starting points of argument concerned with reality involve facts, truths, and presumptions. These starting points deal with things that are believed to exist in reality. Because starting points dealing with reality enjoy the agreement of the universal audience, they are contrasted with starting points of the preferable, which deal with things as they ought to be.

Starting Points Dealing with the Preferable

In contrast to facts, truths, and presumptions that start with things as they are, a second group of starting points—values, hierarchies, and loci of the preferable—begins with things that are preferable.[60] The statement "Denver is a large city," for example, is classified as a fact in Perelman and Olbrechts-Tyteca's schema. In contrast, the statement that "large cities are undesirable places" is classified as a value judgment, an expressed preference.

Values.   These starting points hold only the adherence of particular audiences. Some values, such as justice or beauty, might seem to be general enough to secure the adherence of the universal audience, but Perelman and Olbrechts-Tyteca claim that values are universal only to the extent that they are not made specific. As soon as the value is applied to a particular case, the adherence of particular audiences is all that reasonably can be expected. They maintain that the claim of values "to universal agreement . . . seems to us to be due solely to their generality. They can be regarded as valid for a universal audience only on condition that their content not be specified; as soon as we try to go into details, we meet only the adherence of particular audiences."[61] Honesty, for example, may be a universal value in general, but most people would not expect someone to tell a thief where the family fortune is hidden.

Perelman and Olbrechts-Tyteca divide values into two types—the abstract and the concrete. Values are abstract when they are not attached to a particular person or institution. Life, liberty, and the pursuit of happiness are examples of abstract values. Values are considered concrete when they are attached to a person, institution, or object. The abstract value of life becomes concrete when it is attached to a particular person, as in the claim, "serial killer Charles Manson has a right to life." Thus, abstract values appear to be universal until attached to a person, institution, or object. Once they become concrete, they lose their universality. Although life, liberty, and the pursuit of happiness seem to be universal values, some persons would balk at a claim that Charles Manson should be liberated from prison so he can pursue happiness.

Individuals who argue for the status quo, according to Perelman and Olbrechts-Tyteca, are more likely to begin their arguments with concrete values because such values are more persuasive when the goal is to preserve institutions rather than to reform them. On the other hand, those who argue for change are more likely to begin their argumentation with abstract values: "Abstract values can readily be used for criticism, because they are no respectors of persons and seem to provide criteria for one wishing to change the established order."[62]

Values are important at some stage of every argument; thus, to some degree, every argument is an argument over values. Even arguments that purport to be over facts—some scientific arguments, for instance—have value implications. Arguments about nuclear power and genetic research are obvious examples. The scientific arguments about both nuclear power and genetic research quickly turn to arguments about the value of human life. Science itself is not value free and, therefore, an argument put forth with science as its basis carries the underlying values of science. Another example is an argument about definition. Definitions are not value free; the definitions chosen for terms carry value implications that are sometimes obvious and other times hidden.

Hierarchies. Values arranged in terms of importance form hierarchies. One reason for ordering values is that the simultaneous pursuit of two values can lead to incompatibilities. Because a fair trial and a free press are absolute values in the United States, an incompatibility of values surfaces when news reports by the press threaten to interfere with the trial of a celebrity. In this situation, one of the values must be compromised for the other. Placing these values in some kind of hierarchy assists in decision making when values clash and allows an arguer to design arguments to persuade an audience.

As in the case of values, hierarchies also can be classified as abstract or concrete. The superiority of humans over animals is a concrete hierarchy because it is related to specific objects. The superiority of the just over the useful is an example of an abstract hierarchy because these values are not applied to particular objects. Value hierarchies help to clarify the interrelationship between abstract and concrete values; an abstract value can be used to establish a hierarchy among concrete values. The abstract value that the individual is more important than society can be used to argue that the U.S. judicial system is preferable to systems that do not offer a presumption of innocence. In this case, the abstract value of individualism is related to judicial institutions in a concrete manner.

Perelman and Olbrechts-Tyteca also classify hierarchies as homogeneous and heterogeneous. A homogeneous hierarchy is one in which values differ only in degree—more of a good thing or less of a bad thing is preferred. According to a homogeneous hierarchy, then, a mild illness is preferred to a severe one. Because the values differ only to the extent that they possess the desired outcome, conflicts involving homogeneous hierarchies are relatively easy to resolve.

A conflict based on a heterogeneous hierarchy is more difficult to resolve because the conflicting values are different in kind. The values of honesty and truth may come into conflict, for example, when a friend wearing an ugly dress asks, "What do you think of my dress?" The answer to this question illustrates a heterogeneous value hierarchy relative to the values of honesty and kindness. Heterogeneous hierarchies involve incompatibilities that force individuals to make choices among them. For instance, although most people value both truth and compassion, these values sometimes come into conflict when medical doctors talk to terminally ill patients and their families.

Loci of the preferable.   Perelman and Olbrechts-Tyteca use *loci of the preferable*, sometimes called *loci communes*, to describe the third starting point of this type of argument. Aristotle uses the term *commonplaces*, and Vico refers to *oratorical themes*[63]; they also are known as *topics* or *topoi*. *Loci communes* are general headings that correspond to the ways in which value hierarchies can be organized. Perelman and Olbrechts-Tyteca point to two types of loci—the general and the special. General loci "are affirmations about what is presumed to be of higher value in any circumstances whatsoever, while special loci concern what is preferable in specific situations."[64] Perelman and Olbrechts-Tyteca consider *loci communes* to be an indispensable stockpile from which arguers can draw when they seek the adherence of an audience.[65]

Perelman and Olbrechts-Tyteca describe six loci of the preferable: quantity, quality, order, existent, essence, and person. If a person's value hierarchies are founded on the locus of quantity, for example, that person probably will argue for the greatest good for the greatest number. On the other hand, a person whose value hierarchies are organized according to the locus of quality probably will argue for something based on its uniqueness or its irreplaceability. Gregg B. Walker and Malcolm O. Sillars use the example of the forestry dispute over the spotted owl in the Pacific Northwest to illustrate this type of argumentation. Environmentalists want the spotted owl to be designated an endangered species, an act the logging industry opposes because it would endanger jobs in the region. The values associated with the spotted owl are "unique and irreplaceable." Therefore, the owl supporters make arguments about "protection, beauty, ecological balance, and the sanctity of each species." The loggers, on the other hand, see protection of a small number of spotted owls as a threat to their livelihood and the economy of the region. As a result, their position is centered in the loci of quantity and order.[66]

Perelman and Olbrechts-Tyteca's system, then, includes starting points of argument that bear on the preferable as well as those that deal with reality. To address any audience properly, an arguer should consider the values, hierarchies, and loci of the preferable that are acceptable to that audience.

Presence

Choice is an important factor in Perelman and Olbrechts-Tyteca's conception of argumentation. Unlike mathematicians or computers involved in analytical reasoning, speakers who engage in argumentation must choose the most promising starting points from among all of the available ones. If they choose starting points that are not particularly salient to the audience, they must begin by securing presence for the selected starting point. The concept of presence, then, is an important element in Perelman and Olbrechts-Tyteca's perspective on rhetoric.[67] When arguers have a variety of elements of argumentation from which to choose, they must select the elements on which to focus attention. To focus attention on something endows it with presence. By skillfully focusing attention on a concept, the arguer can "make present, by verbal magic alone, what is actually absent."[68]

Depending on the situation, certain elements can be perceived as more important or special than other elements. The elements that are present in individuals' minds are the most important, of course, while those that are absent are less important. Presence, then, is "the displaying of certain elements on which the speaker wishes to center attention in order that they may occupy the foreground of the hearer's consciousness."[69] One way to explain the notion of presence is by using the metaphor of figure and ground. A person standing on a mountaintop looking into a valley may see trees, a lake, and a stream, along with other objects. When that person focuses on, for instance, a tree, it becomes the figure, and the rest of the objects become the ground. In this case, the tree has achieved presence in that person's perception.

One role of argumentation is to create presence and thus importance. To illustrate this concept, Perelman and Olbrechts-Tyteca tell a Chinese story in which a "king sees an ox on its way to sacrifice. He is moved to pity for it and orders that a sheep be used in its place. He confesses he did so because he could see the ox, but not the sheep."[70] Other examples of the function of presence can be seen in real objects, such as "Caesar's bloody tunic as brandished by Antony, [or] the children of the victim of the accused."[71] These objects can be presented to an audience to establish presence, and, in these cases, the speaker is acting on the senses of the audience in order to move that audience.

Establishing the presence of that which is absent is a difficult but often important task. Through the use of argumentation, a lawyer can influence a jury to "live" a situation that occurred in the past, a legislator can assist an audience in imagining how much better the world would be if a bill were enacted, and a minister can bring audience members to distant places and times that existed before their birth or will exist after their death. Perelman and Olbrechts-Tyteca warn that the elements of argumentation that are physically present are not always the most persuasive. Often, they claim, the most persuasive ideas, such as freedom or liberty, are abstract and are not represented by physically present objects. In these cases, techniques of presentation designed to create presence can cause those ideas to hold importance for the audience. Perelman and Olbrechts-Tyteca's perspective on rhetoric, then, does not restrict arguers to the use of concrete starting points but allows for the expansion of the variety of appropriate starting points to include those that are intangible and abstract. To use intangible and abstract starting points successfully, an arguer needs to endow them with presence, which involves selecting certain techniques of presentation.

Techniques of Presentation

Certain stylistic ways of arguing can aid the arguer in achieving presence for one or more starting points. Waving the bloody glove found at the scene of the murder of Nicole Brown Simpson in front of the jury, O. J. Simpson's defense attorney Johnnie Cochran repeated the phrase, "If the glove doesn't fit, you must acquit." Although the glove was only one bit of evidence the jury considered in coming to a verdict, Cochran endowed the glove with a presence that gave the jury some of the evidence it needed to return a verdict of not guilty.

Communion is Perelman and Olbrechts-Tyteca's term for establishing commonalities or identifying with the audience. They believe that a speaker who establishes communion is more likely to be persuasive than one who does not. For example, a speaker might establish communion with a group of members of the Veterans of Foreign Wars by referring to personal experiences in World War II. This notion of communion reasserts Perelman and Olbrechts-Tyteca's notion that the starting point of argument is agreement.

Perelman and Olbrechts-Tyteca recognize that the techniques of presentation were developed in traditional rhetoric to the point that their "study came to form the whole material of rhetoric,"[72] but they view them in a substantially different way from how they were viewed in the traditional study of rhetoric. Perelman and Olbrechts-Tyteca do not discuss the stylistic dimensions of the techniques of presentation; instead, they offer an in-depth consideration of how the techniques of presentation assist in the attainment of communion, presence, and adherence.

For Perelman and Olbrechts-Tyteca, the style and form of an argument cannot be separated from its content: "The presentation of data is necessarily connected with problems of language. Choice of terms to express the speaker's thought is rarely without significance in the argumentation."[73] They claim that the argumentative intent of a speaker often is conveyed by the choice of one word over another. For example, when a person is described as "having a tendency to mislead," the meaning communicated is different from when that same person is described as a "liar."[74] In addition to the choice of language as a technique of presentation, Perelman and Olbrechts-Tyteca consider presentation schemes like figures of speech—but always with an eye to how these figures function argumentatively.

For the speaker, argumentation involves the choice of data and techniques of presentation to insure presence and communion. For the listener, it involves choices among various interpretations that might be assigned to the speaker's data. In this respect, argumentation stands in stark contrast to formal logic. In logic, no choice exists because the language of logic is unambiguous; in argumentation, however, many choices exist because human language is symbolic and thus inherently ambiguous. The study of argumentation, then, must take into account the study of human language and matters of interpretation. In Perelman and Olbrechts-Tyteca's words, the "study of argumentation compels us to take into account not only the choice of data but also the way in which they are interpreted, the meaning attributed to them."[75]

The speaker's presentation techniques and the listener's interpretive choices, of course, are related to one another. A speaker's techniques may be aimed at securing a particular interpretation from among several potential interpretations on the part of the listener. The speaker creates presence for a particular interpretation by "setting it in the foreground of consciousness" and pushing "the others into the shadow. The core of many arguments is formed of this play of innumerable interpretations and of the struggle to impose some of them and get rid of others."[76] Argumentation may succeed or fail depending on how successfully the speaker chooses presentation techniques to achieve presence or communion.

Techniques of Argumentation

A substantial portion of Perelman and Olbrechts-Tyteca's perspective on rhetoric is concerned with techniques of argumentation.[77] The two main categories of these techniques are liaison and dissociation. Argumentation in the form of a liaison "allows for the transference to the conclusion of the adherence accorded the premises," while argumentation in the form of dissociation "aims at separating elements which language or a recognized tradition have previously tied together."[78]

Techniques of Liaison

Techniques of liaison are used to establish a bond between an arguer's starting point and thesis. For example, a speaker might begin with the value of life and attempt to create a liaison or bond between life and the act of abortion to convince an audience that abortion is immoral. Perelman and Olbrechts-Tyteca show how liaison can be created by three categories of arguments—the quasi-logical, those based on the structure of reality, and those that establish the structure of reality.

Quasi-logical arguments. Similar to formal logic, much of their persuasive force is achieved because of this similarity.[79] Because people are inclined to accept claims based on logic, this type of argument seems particularly persuasive. A common type of quasi-logical argument is similar in form to the syllogism. Participants in the public debate on abortion frequently use this type of quasi-logical argument when they make statements such as "abortion violates the sanctity of life" or "laws prohibiting abortion violate freedom of choice." In each of these cases, "sanctity of life" or "freedom of choice" is analogous to one term in a syllogism, while "abortion" or "laws prohibiting abortion" is analogous to the other term. In syllogistic form, these arguments might appear as follows:

Major premise: The sanctity of life is an absolute value.
Minor premise: Abortion violates the sanctity of life.
Conclusion: Abortion violates an absolute value.

Major premise: Freedom of choice is an absolute value.
Minor premise: Laws prohibiting abortion violate freedom of choice.
Conclusion: Laws prohibiting abortion violate an absolute value.

Although this kind of argument is similar in form to formal logic, it is different from formal logic in that it is used to gain audience adherence, while formal logic is a mathematical system of demonstration unconcerned with audience adherence.

Another quasi-logical argument is argument from incompatibility. A charge of incompatibility in argumentation is similar to a charge of violating the law of noncontradiction in formal logic. In formal logic, a contradiction consists of two statements that are inconsistent with one another—for example, saying something is simultaneously X and not X or saying that two objects are occupying the same space at the same time. Incompatibility in argumentation occurs when someone is faced with a position that appears to be in conflict with one previously held. A child, for instance, is faced with an incompatibility when told by her mother never to lie and then is told to tell the clerk at the movie that she is 11 years old so she can pay half price. The person who says to another, "How can you be against legal abortion and in favor of capital punishment?" is using an argument of incompatibility. Although incompatibility does not always appear to be a liaison of association, Warnick offers this clarification: "Incompatibility is *associative* because it holds two views as one, and the tension or dissonance that it causes comes from the 'uncomfortable' association."[80]

A major difference between incompatibility and contradiction is that individuals can escape from an incompatibility but cannot break the law of noncontradiction. The child who lies about her age to the movie clerk escapes incompatibility by rationalizing the lie as only a "little white lie"; the anti-abortion advocate can say, "But, you see, I'm only in favor of protecting innocent life." In contrast, X never can be not X, and the law of noncontradiction rightly asserts that two objects cannot occupy the same space at the same time. Olbrechts-Tyteca suggests that incompatibilities function to produce comedy in much the same way as they function in argumentation. In argument, an incompatibility leads to an uncomfortable association; in comedy, it leads to a humorous one. One of her examples involves an incompatibility between a statement and the actual facts to which the statement refers. For example, an explorer asks: "Are there any cannibals in the region?" and hears the reply "No, we ate the last one yesterday."[81] The act of saying "we ate the last one yesterday" is incompatible with denying the presence of cannibals in a way people find humorous.

Perelman and Olbrechts-Tyteca provide other examples of quasi-logical arguments. The ones illustrated here are simply examples of a much larger class of arguments, including argument by ridicule, argument by definition, argument by tautology, argument by reciprocity, argument by transitivity, argument by inclusion of the part within the whole, argument by division of the whole into its parts, argument by comparison, and argument by probability.

Arguments based on the structure of reality.　These arguments make connections between accepted structures of reality and structures that are the conclusions of their arguments. According to Perelman and Olbrechts-Tyteca, associations of sequence and of coexistence are two different ways of structuring reality. The relationships among some elements of reality are based on sequence, such as cause and effect. In these relationships, the phenomena are on the same level and are connected to one another by a sequence in time. Other relationships—such as those between persons and their acts—are based on coexistence. In these kinds of relationships, the phenomena are not on the same level, so time is irrelevant to their connections.

The causal argument is one example of an argument based on a sequential relationship. Causality is argued in a variety of ways, all of which are sequential: by establishing a causal link between two events, by showing that one thing is the cause of another, or by pointing out that something is the effect of a purported cause.[82] These three kinds of causal arguments frequently are used in arguments about human action. In such cases, motive sometimes functions as cause. In attempting to prove someone guilty of murder, for instance, motive frequently is one of the important questions. Asking about someone's motive for committing such an act is like asking what caused him to commit the act. Perelman and Olbrechts-Tyteca claim that one "would not easily admit that someone had acted in a certain way if the accuser did not explain the reasons for the alleged behavior."[83]

The pragmatic argument is a specific example of an argument about causality. Such an argument presumes that the value of an act can be determined by its consequences. To produce a good reason for an action using the pragmatic argument, a speaker argues that the action will lead to good consequences. For example, a speaker might argue that capital punishment is desirable because it is a deterrent to crime. Although the appropriateness of a pragmatic argument rarely is questioned, some believe that the pragmatic consequences of an act are less important than the absolute value associated with the act. Thus, "the pragmatic argument is criticized by those who believe in an absolutist or formalist conception of values and, especially, of morals."[84] Some who take an absolutist position with regard to the moral value of life argue, for example, that capital punishment is immoral regardless of the pragmatic consequences it may have with regard to deterrence.

Other kinds of arguments of sequence involve arguments about ends and means, arguments of waste, and arguments of direction—better known as *slippery slope arguments.* All of these examples are based on structures of reality that are connected to one another by a relationship of sequence. For instance, a slippery slope argument frequently is made against attempts by anti-abortion advocates to ban late-term abortions. According to such an argument, a ban on late-term abortions will be used to justify a ban on middle-term abortions, which ultimately will be used to justify a ban on all abortions. The argument focuses on a sequence of events that its advocates consider ill advised.

A second type of association based on the structure of reality involves relationships of coexistence. Whereas sequential arguments are based on techniques that emphasize the temporal connections between two elements, relationships of coexistence do not depend on time. Relationships of coexistence involve connections among phenomena on different levels, the prototype of which is the relationship between a person and an act. Individuals are more than any single act they commit; for that matter, they are more than the combination of all of their acts. Still, the relationship between person and act assumes that an act is an outward manifestation of the person.[85]

Arguers using an argument based on the relationship between act and person claim that a person can be judged by the quality of the acts she commits. One such argument claims that Adolph Hitler was an evil person because he committed evil deeds. Arguments claiming that people should be judged by the quality of their acts depend on a selection of acts characteristic of the person.[86] To characterize a person as lazy for missing one class during a semester would be an unfair selection of acts, whereas a pattern of skipping class could be a sufficient number of acts to result in a characterization of laziness.

Argument from authority is another example that depends on the relationship between person and act. This argument claims that a proposition should be accepted because it is accepted by important and well-qualified people. For example, someone might argue that capital punishment is a deterrent to murder because George W. Bush says it is. Although frequently dismissed in some theories of argumentation, argument by authority is important to Perelman and Olbrechts-Tyteca and is frequently used as a supplement to other techniques of argument.[87] By itself, however, argument from authority is not sufficient to establish something as true or false.[88]

In their discussion of arguments based on relationships of coexistence, Perelman and Olbrechts-Tyteca also describe relationships between the speaker and the act of speaking, relationships between a person and a group, relationships of act and essence, and relationships between symbols and objects. Arguments of these types are based on the idea that the simultaneous coexistence of two things—for instance, a person and an act—are related to one another in ways that are more than coincidence. For example, the fact that a person belongs to the National Rifle Association may be considered indicative of some of that person's values about private ownership of guns. Perelman and Olbrechts-Tyteca show how techniques of severance and restraint can be used to refute arguments based on the relationship of coexistence. For example, some have argued that former president Bill Clinton was a poor public servant because of his moral transgressions. To refute this argument, which implies a relationship between his public service and his private actions, Clinton used the technique of severance in an attempt to break the relationship between his public duties and his private life.[89]

In summary, arguments based on the structure of reality are of two kinds: arguments based on structures related to one another by sequence and arguments based on structures related to one another by coexistence. Perelman and Olbrechts-Tyteca point to the double-hierarchy argument as one technique that can be applied to both sequence and coexistence. Using an example from Aristotle, Perelman and Olbrechts-Tyteca note: "If *A* be without qualification better than *B*, then also the best of the members of *A* is better than the best of the members of *B*; e.g., if Man is better than horse, the best man is better than the best horse."[90] One hierarchy is used to support another.

Arguments that establish the structure of reality. The third category of arguments rooted in liaison falls into two broad types: (1) argumentation by example, illustration, and model; and (2) argumentation by analogy and metaphor. These two categories differ from one another because the first involves objects or concepts in the same sphere, while the second involves objects in different spheres. A single instance of someone whose profession is professor can be used to support a conclusion about other professors because both the starting point (one professor) and the conclusion (other professors) are in the same sphere. Alternatively, an analogy or a metaphor may compare disparate objects such as a professor and a lion, creating a relationship between objects in different spheres.

Argumentation by example is used in one of two ways—using examples to create a generalization[91] or using one example to reach a conclusion about another example.[92] The first instance presumes the existence of regularities among cases; by presenting several cases, a speaker tries to convince an audience of those regularities. For example, the argument that professors are absent minded can be developed by showing an audience that Professor Martinez constantly loses his keys, Professor Riley constantly misplaces her briefcase, and Professor Hollihan never can find a pen when he needs one. In addition to moving from a particular case to a general statement, argument from example can be used to move from particular cases to other particular cases. For example, a speaker could argue that because capital punishment did not reduce the incidence of murder in Texas, it cannot be expected to do so in Colorado.

Sometimes, an invalidating example can be used to argue against a generalization. Suppose that someone argues through a series of examples that tobacco use leads to health problems. Someone might respond with an invalidating example of a lifelong smoker who outlived several siblings, none of whom used tobacco. Although the invalidating example is useful in preventing unwarranted generalizations, it only weakens the generalization but does not destroy it. The generalization can "always be retained by slightly changing its scope to take into account the newly introduced case."[93] In the example offered here, the generalization can be validated by adding, "all other things being equal, tobacco use is harmful to one's health." The generalization also can be maintained by noting that it is correlative and not universal: "Although everyone who uses tobacco may not be negatively affected, the risks to one's health are increased."

Although argumentation by example is used to establish or refute a generalization, argumentation by illustration simply illuminates that generalization. Argument by example is used when the audience does not agree with the arguer about the generalization. Argument by illustration is used to strengthen a belief in the generalization already held by the audience. Thus, argument by illustration is useful when an arguer needs to add presence to an already accepted generalization. If the audience already accepts the generalization that tobacco is harmful to the health of smokers, the arguer might illustrate that effect with a particularly vivid presentation about a smoker who died a painful death from lung cancer. Perelman explains that the "transition from example to illustration occurs almost imperceptibly in cases in which a rule is justified before being illustrated. The first examples need to be generally accepted, since their role is to give the rule credibility; the others, once the rule is accepted, will in turn be supported by it."[94]

Whereas argument by illustration gives presence to a generalization, argumentation by model is used to convince an audience to imitate the qualities of a particular case. The argument that Professor Davis exhibits the qualities of a superior teacher neither makes a generalization nor establishes that all teachers are excellent. Rather, audience members are provided a model of a teacher they profitably could imitate. Another example of argumentation by model is the ideal of legal precedent: previous court opinions structure future decisions. As several events from the Nixon and Clinton presidencies have demonstrated, argumentation by anti-model also can be used by an arguer who offers them as examples to be avoided rather than imitated.

The second broad category of arguments designed to establish the structure of reality consists of argumentation by analogy and metaphor. An analogy is an argument that can be used to gain adherence about the relationship between two concepts because of its similarity to the relationship that exists in another pair. The most general formulation of the structure of an analogy is *A* is to *B* (the theme) as *C* is to *D* (the *phoros*).[95] The theme and the *phoros* are from different spheres. A football coach might make the analogy that, to win, the players need to behave like animals, focusing on opponents like an animal focuses on its prey before the kill. The structure of this analogy is that winning (*A*) should be to a football player (*B*) what killing (*C*) is to an animal (*D*). Perelman and Olbrechts-Tyteca's view of analogy differs from some other views on analogy in argumentation; theirs is marked by "the fact that the theme and *phoros* must be drawn from different spheres."[96] In argument from analogy, value is transferred from the theme to the *phoros* and vice versa. Some analogies are used to secure audience adherence about the similarities between *phoros* and theme, while others are used to reinforce already existing beliefs.

A metaphor, also important in argumentation, is a condensed analogy in which the theme and *phoros* are fused.[97] In the previous example, the football coach might shout, "All right, animals! Let's go out and kill 'em!" The metaphor is simply a condensation of the analogy. Metaphors sometimes become so commonplace that people forget they are dealing with metaphors. The foot of a mountain and the arm of a chair are both metaphors so commonly used that they tend to be forgotten as metaphorical—they are what Perelman and Olbrechts-Tyteca call *dormant metaphors*.[98] A dormant metaphor sometimes can be more enlightening than an active one because, when forced to add interpretation to the metaphor, individuals reinforce and revitalize its meaning. In the following passage taken from Kant, the dormant metaphor *to shed light on a subject* is awakened: "He [Hume] shed no light on this [metaphysical] kind of knowledge, but he did nonetheless strike a spark from which one might well have got light had the spark fallen on an ignitable wick, whose glow would have been carefully maintained and increased."[99] Metaphor, along with the other examples cited above, illustrates how arguments by association are constructed. Quasi-logical arguments, arguments based on the structure of reality, and arguments that establish the structure of reality are created through liaison.

Techniques of Dissociation

Perelman and Olbrechts-Tyteca also describe arguments established by the process of dissociation, a type of argumentation often ignored in other perspectives on rhetoric. They describe dissociation by differentiating it from the technique of breaking connecting links. When using the technique of breaking connective links, an arguer begins with two concepts and shows how they should remain separate and independent.[100] Perelman and Olbrechts-Tyteca point to John Locke's argument that the government should remain independent from religion to illustrate this technique. Fearful that religion was too involved in government, Locke argued, "Neither the right nor the art of ruling does necessarily carry along with it the certain knowledge of other things, and least of all true religion."[101] Locke's argument is not unlike contemporary arguments advocating the exclusion of prayers from public schools; these arguments by public school officials also attempt to break the link between legitimate educational goals and religious indoctrination. Unlike the breaking of connective links, an argument by dissociation starts with a single concept and splits it into two independent—though related—concepts.

Dissociation often is used to avoid an incompatibility. For example, the belief that to take the life of another human is wrong and the simultaneous belief that abortion is acceptable can create an incompatibility. Argumentation is used to dissociate the concept of life into two concepts: life in general and human life. In such an instance, life in general may be defined to include all organismic growth ranging from an amoeba to plant life to the life of an appendix, while human life is defined as consisting only of those life forms that possess certain qualities of humanity such as free will. With such a dissociation, the incompatibility can be avoided. Abortion can be viewed as destroying life in general (in the same way one destroys life by picking a head of cabbage or removing an appendix from a human) rather than as destroying human life.

Making an argument by dissociation consists of using philosophical pairs, the clearest example of which is the appearance-reality pair. The argument by dissociation divides what Perelman and Olbrechts-Tyteca call *term I* from *term II*. Term I corresponds to appearance (or the lesser of the two concepts), while term II corresponds to reality (or the greater of the two concepts). In the above example, life in general corresponds to term I and is dissociated from human life or term II. Thus, term II is understood only in comparison to term I and aims at "getting rid of the incompatibilities that may appear between different aspects of *term I*."[102] In essence, term II provides a criterion to distinguish the valuable elements of term I from those that are not valuable.[103]

Perelman and Olbrechts-Tyteca show how definitions can be created not just by quasi-logical arguments but by dissociation as well.[104] Some anti-abortion advocates use this technique when they define abortion as the unjustified killing of an innocent human being. They define abortion in this manner to dissociate what they consider to be the unjust act of abortion from the just act of capital punishment. Olbrechts-Tyteca also uses dissociation in her analysis of comedy. Describing the technique she calls *reversal*, Olbrechts-Tyteca explains how comedy can operate by turning a common dissociation on its head. She shows how the comment, "I can't be there in spirit, so I'm coming in person," creates comedy by reversing the value of the real over the possible or contingent.[105]

Olbrechts-Tyteca calls a second dissociative technique *paradox*. Paradox is "made possible by dissociating dissociations so that the apparent and the real become so interchangeable that one cannot be discerned from the other."[106] Thus, reality and appearance become indistinguishable in humorous ways. One of her examples involves a police officer who signals a driver to pull off the road: "Give me your driver's license," he said in a dry tone. When the driver protested "But I did nothing wrong," the policeman answered: "I didn't say you did. But you are driving so carefully that I said to myself that you must not have your driver's license."[107]

The Interaction of Arguments

Perelman and Olbrechts-Tyteca conclude their discussion on rhetoric by addressing the interaction of arguments.[108] They consider topics such as the amplitude or lack of amplitude of arguments and the importance of the order in which arguments are presented. The strength of an overall argumentative strategy is relevant to all of the arguments contained within it. For example, if several distinct arguments independently lead to a particular conclusion, "the value attributed to the conclusion and to each separate argument will be augmented, for the likelihood that several entirely erroneous arguments would reach the same result is very small."[109] For example, opponents of capital punishment make a variety of arguments that independently support their claim that capital punishment should be abolished: capital punishment is not a deterrent to murder, killing a living human being is immoral, and capital punishment is carried out in racist ways. While any one of these arguments alone presents a sufficient case for the abolition of capital punishment, they interact with one another to make the case for abolition even stronger. Amplitude in argumentation can be accomplished by adding new evidence to lines of arguments, increasing the range of kinds of argumentative techniques employed, and adding redundancy.

In many cases, increasing the amplitude of arguments increases their strength; in other cases, the strength of the argument may be affected negatively. For example, in attempting to increase the range of starting points or techniques, arguers may include arguments that are incompatible, although not necessarily inconsistent, with one another. Defense attorneys sometimes use such a strategy when they argue that their client did not commit the murder and, even if she did, she was insane at the time. Such an increase in amplitude can reduce the credibility of the overall argumentative plan: "At first sight, there would seem to be no objection to putting forward a number of different hypotheses to explain an occurrence, even if they are incompatible, for one might imagine that their accumulation would merely make the occurrence seem more convincing." On the other hand, Perelman and Olbrechts-Tyteca continue, "one can often downgrade the opponent by suggesting that the new hypotheses prove that he did not place great confidence in his earlier arguments."[110]

Perelman and Olbrechts-Tyteca also suggest that the order of presentation affects the interaction of arguments. They analyze this topic according to three viewpoints: the argumentative situation itself, the conditioning of the audience, and the way an audience will reflect on the arguments. In terms of the argumentative situation itself, "the premises the audience is progressively led to admit"[111] influence the order of presentation. Thus, the order of presentation largely is determined by the arguer's desire to "bring forward new premises, to confer presence on certain elements, and to extract certain agreements from the interlocutor."[112] A second view of how to order individual arguments involves the conditioning of the audience. Some arguments are included in the introduction to "make the audience well disposed toward the speaker and to secure its goodwill, attention and interest."[113] The arguer then must decide, however, whether to state the thesis at the end of the introduction or to wait for further development. The answer to this question depends, according to Perelman and Olbrechts-Tyteca, on whether the thesis is going to be especially shocking to the audience or whether it contains nothing particularly alarming. In the first instance, the thesis should be delayed, but in the second, it should be presented immediately. A third view for ordering arguments concerns situations when the audience can be expected to reflect consciously on the arguments. In their discussion of order, Perelman and Olbrechts-Tyteca discuss the relative merits of chronological order and natural order.

In summary, Perelman and Olbrechts-Tyteca present a coherent picture of argumentation. An arguer begins by constructing a mental image of an audience and then constructs a thesis for which audience adherence is the goal. The arguer selects starting points related to reality and preference that the arguer believes the audience will accept. Finally, by methods of liaison or dissociation, the arguer connects the starting points to the thesis in an effort to gain the adherence of the audience.

Commentary

Perelman and Olbrechts-Tyteca's work is praised because it helps to justify a rhetorical approach to argumentation—a legitimate counterpart to the logical perspectives on argumentation. David Douglas Dunlap's comment is representative of the praise that rhetoricians have expressed: "The *New Rhetoric* helped to make possible the rebirth of argument as a liberal art. The greatest impact of Perelman's [and Olbrechts-Tyteca's] work to rhetorical theory was the resurrection of reasoning about values from the sepulcher of logical demonstration."[114]

The positive reception Perelman and Olbrechts-Tyteca's work received in the field of rhetoric, however, was not evident in the field of philosophy. According to James Crosswhite, "The reception of Perelman's work by philosophers, especially English-speaking ones, has been a non-reception. . . . Perelman's work is dutifully mentioned in most bibliographies of argumentation and often mentioned in the introduction to books and articles on informal logic or on fallacies. However, it is almost completely ignored in the actual work on argumentation that goes on in these proceedings."[115] According to Crosswhite, many U.S. philosophers interested in argumentation are still working within the traditional framework that Perelman and Olbrechts-Tyteca critiqued. He claims that many of the "features of Perelman's [and Olbrechts-Tyteca's] thought are stumbling-blocks for many philosophers who are engaged in the study of informal argumentation. To accept these ideas may seem tantamount to forsaking philosophy itself. However I believe the opposite is true, that Perelman's thought points the way to a renewal of philosophy."[116]

Dutch scholars Frans H. van Eemeren, Rob Grootendorst, and Tjark Kruiger offer a comprehensive critique of Perelman and Olbrechts-Tyteca's work.[117] They claim that one of the primary difficulties is that the work fails to develop the details of the relationship between the audience and techniques of argumentation and does not address the persuasiveness of argumentative techniques to particular or general audiences.[118] Van Eemeren, Grootendorst, and Kruiger also fault the new rhetoric because the system it uses to categorize argumentation techniques is neither mutually exclusive nor exhaustive.[119] Alone, this is not a particularly serious criticism, but they argue that Perelman and Olbrechts-Tyteca use two different criteria to distinguish among various techniques. For example, form is used to distinguish quasi-logical arguments, while arguments based on the structure of reality and arguments establishing the structure of reality are distinguished by their content. Manfred Kienpointner also finds Perelman and Olbrechts-Tyteca's categories unclear and complains that their argument schemes are not defined with sufficient clarity to allow their use in empirical research. He reconstructs them into formal logic and demonstrates the improvement using argument by division.[120]

Van Eemeren and Grootendorst also argue that Perelman and Olbrechts-Tyteca's schema is unable to account for the important concept of fallacies because of what they regard as the highly relativistic approach in which soundness is "tantamount to effectiveness within the 'target group.'"[121] For this reason, they are not surprised that "no general account or discussion of the fallacies can be found in *The New Rhetoric*, nor, for that matter, in any other publication by Perelman."[122] They argue that the inability to deal with fallacies can be rectified by combining Perelman and Olbrechts-Tyteca's perspective with their own pragma-dialectical approach, in which the "soundness of argumentation is measured against the degree to which it contributes to the resolution of the dispute and against the degree to which it is acceptable to the discussants."[123]

Crosswhite defends Perelman and Olbrechts-Tyteca's system, suggesting that a discussion of fallacies is irrelevant to their project because "the notion of a fallacy suggests a breach of a rule, and the 'techniques' of argumentation offered in *The New Rhetoric* are not rules that can be breached."[124] In a separate essay, Crosswhite argues that although Perelman and Olbrechts-Tyteca's system is silent about the concept of fallacies, it can be used by argumentation theorists to "radically transform the traditional framework for understanding fallacies: a fallacious argument [consistent with the Perelman and Olbrechts-Tyteca's system] is one that seems to persuade a universal audience, but does not. Instead it only persuades a particular audience."[125] Following this analysis, Crosswhite uses the Perelman and Olbrechts-Tyteca system to analyze several common fallacies and then concludes that "Perelman [and Olbrechts-Tyteca] *can* say when argumentation is fallacious *for some audience*. And this is, [they] would claim, the most anyone can do."[126]

Crosswhite also defends Perelman and Olbrechts-Tyteca's argument schema. He writes that van Eemeren and Grootendorst misunderstand "the philosophical motivations and scope of Perelman's [and Olbrechts-Tyteca's] theory, . . . and that the strengths of the pragma-dialectical approach are already incorporated into (and wisely subordinated in) Perelman and Olbrechts-Tyteca's rhetorical theory."[127] Crosswhite claims that "*The New Rhetoric* does not intend to provide the usual sort of theory of argumentation. Its purpose is not to offer mutually exclusive categories of argumentative techniques that can be neatly systematized and applied in a way that emulates modern systems of logic as van Eemeren and Grootendorst seem to believe."[128] Barbara Warnick and Susan L. Kline also come to Perelman and Olbrechts-Tyteca's defense. They conducted an empirical study to see if they reliably could identify arguments based on Perelman and Olbrechts-Tyteca's schema.[129] That they were able to do so with reasonable, although not perfect, consistency supports the validity of Perelman and Olbrechts-Tyteca's categories.

Another important criticism is directed toward Perelman and Olbrechts-Tyteca's conception of the universal audience. Some have found this notion to be so ambiguous that it is almost useless.[130] Johnstone argues that Perelman and Olbrechts-Tyteca's theory would be no worse if the notion of the universal audience (in fact, the entire notion of audience) were ignored completely: "All these ambiguities and perplexities in the concept of the *universal audience* make me wonder whether the concept is after all really necessary to the project that the authors of *The New Rhetoric* have undertaken. What would the book be like without it?"[131] John W. Ray argues that the "universal audience follows in the philosophical tradition of Rousseau's and Diderot's general will and Kant's ethical theory, particularly Kant's emphasis on the categorical imperative. . . . The concept of the universal audience is open to many of the same criticisms leveled against the general will and the categorical imperative."[132] Ray notes that the categorical imperative and the general will are too formal to be useful in providing standards for ethical theory; likewise, the "universal audience is excessively formal and abstract—too formal and abstract to provide a standard for rhetorical theory."[133] Alan Scult notes that Perelman defines the concept of the universal audience differently at different times and that when others attempt to extend that definition, Perelman proceeds "in Zen-master fashion, to let the student know that this or that interpretation is off the mark."[134] Scult attempts to expand the universal audience to the realm of nonphilosophical discourse by suggesting that the universal audience is "made possible by the affirmation by the participants in the discourse of a correlation between the relational quality of the conversational moment and the truth of what is said."[135]

Perelman published an essay in the *Quarterly Journal of Speech* that was designed to respond to some of his critics. In that article, he defends the notion of the universal audience against criticisms such as those by Ray, claiming that his position has been misinterpreted. According to Perelman, the formalist point of view to which he is opposed "was described in *The New Rhetoric* in such a sufficiently convincing manner as to lead certain rhetorical readers to consider it as expressing [his] own ideas." He claims that Ray's criticisms "would certainly be justified if they were not a result of a false interpretation" of *The New Rhetoric*.[136]

Stanley K. Laughlin and Daniel T. Hughes criticize Perelman's distinction between the rational and the reasonable, claiming that Perelman's distinction does not agree with common usage and is not supported in the U.S. judicial system.[137] In addition, William E. Wiethoff examines reviews of Perelman's work from the U.S. and international legal community. He finds mixed reviews of "Perelman's suggested adaptation of rhetoric to law. With varying degrees of accuracy, international scholars have acclaimed Perelman's rationale while questioning the practicability of his suggested method."[138] Wiethoff suggests a potential relationship between Perelman's ideas and those of advocates of critical legal studies: "The ideological gap between Perelman and the advocates of critical legal studies should not be minimized, but each side nonetheless sees a salutary role for rhetorical method in jurisprudence."[139]

Despite these criticisms, the work of Perelman and Olbrechts-Tyteca is particularly useful and influential to scholars interested in rhetorical thought. Walker and Sillars provide an especially readable account of how Perelman and Olbrechts-Tyteca's perspective on rhetoric contributes to an understanding of argumentation and values—"how the arguer develops arguments and the critic of argumentation analyzes argument from this value-centered perspective."[140] Perelman commented on the use of his and Olbrechts-Tyteca's work: "I am happy to state that certain rhetoricians have been able to utilize and extend my works. I think of the texts that I know of Karl A. Wallace, of Louise A. Karon, and of J. Robert Cox, which have certainly enriched the theory of rhetoric. I am convinced that there are works of which I am unaware, but, above all, that there is a great deal more to do in this field."[141]

Bibliography

Works by Chaïm Perelman and Lucie Olbrechts-Tyteca

Book
The New Rhetoric: A Treatise on Argumentation. Trans. John Wilkinson and Purcell Weaver. Notre Dame, IN: University of Notre Dame Press, 1969.

Article
"Act and Person in Argumentation." *Ethics*, 61 (July 1951), 251–69.

Works by Lucie Olbrechts-Tyteca

Book
Le Comique du discours. Brussels, Belg.: Editions de l'Université de Bruxelles, 1974.

Articles
"Recontre Avec la Rhétoric." *Logique et Analyse*, 3 (1960), 49–69.
"Les Couples Philosophiques: Une Nouvelle Approche." *Revue Internationale de Philosophie*, 33 (1979), 81–98.
"Bibliographie de Chaïm Perelman." *Revue Internationale de Philosophie*, 33 (1979), 325–42. (With Evelyne Griffin-Collart.)

Works by Chaïm Perelman

Books
An Historical Introduction to Philosophical Thinking. Trans. Kenneth A. Brown. New York: Random, 1965.

The Idea of Justice and the Problem of Argument. Trans. John Petrie. New York: Humanities, 1963.

Justice. New York: Random, 1967.

Justice, Law, and Argument: Essays on Moral and Legal Reasoning. Trans. John Petrie, Susan Rubin, Graham Bird, Melvin T. Dalgarno, Heather Relihan, and William Kluback. Dordrecht, Neth: D. Reidel, 1980.

The New Rhetoric and the Humanities: Essays on Rhetoric and its Applications. Trans. William Kluback. Ed. Jakko Hintikka, Robert S. Cohen, Donald Davidson, Gabriel Nuchelmans, and Wesley Salmon. Boston: D. Reidel, 1979.

The Realm of Rhetoric. Trans. William Kluback. Notre Dame, IN: University of Notre Dame Press, 1982.

Articles

"Behaviorism's Enlightened Despotism." In *Beyond the Punitive Society.* Ed. Harvey Wheeler. San Francisco: W. H. Freeman, 1973, pp. 13–27.

"The Dialectical Method and the Part Played by the Interlocutor in the Dialogue." *Proceedings of the 30th Indian Philosophical Congress,* 1955, pp. 179–83.

"[Essay] 24." In *Democracy in a World of Tensions.* Proceedings of a UNESCO Symposium. Ed. Richard McKeon and Stein Rokkan. New York: Greenwood, 1951, pp. 295–301.

"The Foundations and Limits of Tolerance." *Pacific Philosophy Forum,* 2 (September 1963), 20–27.

"Fuller's The Morality of Law." *Natural Law Forum,* 10 (1965), 242–45.

"How Do We Apply Reason to Values?" *Journal of Philosophy,* 52 (December 1955), 797–802.

"Interventions." In *Danish Yearbook of Philosophy.* Vol. 7. Ed. Justus Hartnack, Mogens Blegvad, Johs. Witt-Hansen, and Jon Espersen. Copenhagen, Den.: Munksgaard, 1972, pp. 188–90.

"Judicial Reasoning." *Israel Law Review,* 1 (1966), 373–79.

"Justice and Justification." *Natural Law Forum,* 10 (July 1965), 1–20.

"Justice and Reasoning." In *Law, Reason and Justice.* Ed. G. Hughes. New York: New York University Press, 1969, pp. 207–25.

"Justice Re-examined." *Archiv Für Rechts-und Sozailphilosophie,* 66 (1980), 77–84.

"Logic and Rhetoric." In *Modern Logic—A Survey.* Ed. A. Agazzi. Dordrecht, Neth.: D. Reidel, 1980, pp. 457–63.

"Natural Law and Natural Rights." In *Dictionary of the History of Ideas.* Ed. Philip Paul Wiener. New York: Scribner's, 1973, pp. 13–27. (With P. Foriers.)

"A Naturalistic Interpretation of Authority, Ideology and Violence." In *Phenomenology and Natural Existence: Essays in Honor of Marvin Farber.* Ed. Dale Riepe. Albany: State University of New York Press, 1973, pp. 342–51.

"The New Rhetoric." *Philosophy Today,* 1 (1957), 4–10.

"The New Rhetoric." In *The Prospect of Rhetoric.* Ed. Lloyd F. Bitzer and Edwin Black. Englewood Cliffs, NJ: Prentice-Hall, 1971, pp. 115–22.

"The New Rhetoric." In *Pragmatics of Natural Languages.* Ed. Y. Barhillel. Dordrecht, Neth.: D. Reidel, 1971, pp. 145–49.

"The New Rhetoric and the Rhetoricians: Remembrances and Comments." *Quarterly Journal of Speech,* 70 (May 1984), 188–96.

"The New Rhetoric: A Theory of Practical Reasoning." In *The Great Ideas Today.* Ed. Robert M. Hutchins and Mortimer J. Adler. Chicago: Encyclopedia Britannica, 1970, pp. 272–312.

"On Self Evidence in Metaphysics." *International Philosophical Quarterly*, 4 (February 1964), 5–19.

"Philosophical Studies." *Philosophy Today*, 2 (1957), 4–10.

"Philosophy and Rhetoric." In *Advances in Argumentation Theory and Research*. Ed. J. Robert Cox and Charles Arthur Willard. Carbondale: Southern Illinois University Press, pp. 287–97. (With Judy F. Merryman.)

"Philosophy and the Sciences." *Philosophy Today*, 9 (1965), 273–77.

"The Philosophy of Pluralism." *Philosophic Exchange*. Proceedings of the Center for Philosophic Exchange. Brockport: Center for Philosophic Exchange, State University of New York, 1978, pp. 49–56.

"Philosophy, Rhetoric, Commonplaces." *Philosophes critiques d'eux-memes*, 1 (1975), 173–211.

"Polanyi's Interpretation of Scientific Inquiry." In *Intellect and Hope: Essays in the Thought of Michael Polanyi*. Ed. Th. A. Langford and W. M. Poteat. Durham, NC: Duke University Press, 1968, pp. 232–41.

"Pragmatic Arguments." *Philosophy: The Journal of the British Institute of Philosophical Studies*, 34 (1959), 18–27.

"Proof in Philosophy." *Hibbert Journal*, 52 (1954), 354–59.

"The Rational and the Reasonable." *Philosophical Exchange*, 2 (1979), 28–34.

"Remarks on the Papers of Prof. Wild and Dr. Dunham." In *Dialogues on the Philosophy of Marxism*. Ed. J. Somerville and H. L. Parsons. Westport, CT: Greenwood, 1974, pp. 360–64.

"A Reply to Henry W. Johnstone, Jr." *Philosophy and Phenomenological Research*, 16 (December 1955), 245–47.

"Reply to Mr. Zaner." *Philosophy and Rhetoric*, 1 (Summer 1968), 168–76.

"Reply to Stanley Rosen." *Inquiry*, 2 (1959), 85–88.

"Rhetoric." In *Encyclopedia Britannica: XV.* Chicago: Encyclopedia Britannica, 1973, pp. 803–05.

"The Rhetorical Point of View in Ethics: A Program." *Communication*, 6 (1981), 315–20.

"Rhetoric and Philosophy." Trans. Henry W. Johnstone, Jr. *Philosophy and Rhetoric*, 11 (January 1968), 15–24.

"Rhetoric and Politics." *Philosophy and Rhetoric*, 17 (1984), 129–34. (With Winchester James and Molly Black Verene.)

"Self Evidence and Proof." *Philosophy*, 33 (1958), 289–302.

"Some Reflections on Classification." *Philosophy Today*, 9 (1965), 268–72.

"The Theoretical Relations of Thought and Action." *Inquiry*, 1 (1958), 130–36.

"The Use and Abuse of Confused Notions." *ETC.: A Review of General Semantics*, 36 (1979), 313–24.

"Value Judgments, Justifications and Argumentation." Trans. Francis B. Sullivan. *Philosophy Today*, 6 (1962), 45–51.

"What is Legal Logic?" *Israel Law Review*, 3 (1968), 1–6.

"What the Philosopher May Learn from the Study of Law." *Natural Law Forum*, 11 (1966), 1–12.

Endnotes

[1] Barbara Warnick, "Lucie Olbrechts-Tyteca's Contribution to *The New Rhetoric*," in *Listening to Their Voices: The Rhetorical Activities of Historical Women*, ed. Molly Meijer Wertheimer (Columbia: University of South Carolina Press, 1987), p. 69.

[2] Biographical information on Perelman was obtained from the following sources: Carroll Arnold, "Introduction," in Chaïm Perelman, *The Realm of Rhetoric*, trans. William Kluback (Notre Dame, IN: University of Notre Dame Press, 1982); Chaïm Perelman, "The New Rhetoric: A Theory of Practical Reasoning," in *The Great Ideas Today* (Chicago: Encyclopedia Britannica, 1970), p. 272; *Who's Who in World Jewry* (New York: Pittman, 1972), p. 681; Editor's note, "The New Rhetoric and the Rhetoricians: Remembrances and Comments," by Chaïm Perelman, *Quarterly Journal of Speech*, 70 (May 1984), 196; Telephone conversation with Chaïm Perelman's daughter, Noémi Perelman Mattis, May, 1984; and Noémi Perelman Mattis, "Perelman and Olbrechts-Tyteca: A Personal Recollection," unpublished statement read by Ray Dearin at the annual convention of the Speech Communication Association, August 12, 1994.

[3] Perelman, "The New Rhetoric," in *The Great Ideas Today*, p. 273.

[4] Perelman Mattis, "Perelman and Olbrechts-Tyteca."

[5] Perelman Mattis, telephone conversation.

[6] Chaïm Perelman, *The Idea of Justice and the Problem of Argument*, trans. John Petrie (New York: Humanities, 1963), p. 16.

[7] Chaïm Perelman, "The New Rhetoric: A Theory of Practical Reasoning," in *The New Rhetoric and the Humanities: Essays on Rhetoric and Its Applications*, trans. William Kluback, ed. Jakko Hintikka, Robert S. Cohen, Donald Davidson, Gabriel Nuchelmans, and Wesley Salmon (Dordecht, Neth.: D. Reidel, 1979), p. 8.

[8] James Crosswhite, "Is There an Audience for This Argument? Fallacies, Theories, and Relativisms," *Philosophy and Rhetoric*, 28 (1995), 135.

[9] Crosswhite, "Is There an Audience for This Argument?," p. 135.

[10] Crosswhite, "Is There an Audience for This Argument?," p. 137.

[11] Perelman, "The New Rhetoric and the Rhetoricians," pp. 188–89.

[12] Henry W. Johnstone, Jr., "Editor's Introduction," *Argumentation*, 7 (November 1993), 379.

[13] Johnstone, "Editor's Introduction," p. 379.

[14] Michel Meyer, "Foreword: The Modernity of Rhetoric," in *From Metaphysics to Rhetoric*, ed. Michel Meyer (Dordrecht, Neth.: Kluwer, 1989), p. 1.

[15] David A. Frank, "The New Rhetoric, Judaism, and Post-Enlightenment Thought: The Cultural Origins of Perelmanian Philosophy," *Quarterly Journal of Speech*, 83 (August 1997), 313.

[16] Biographic information about Lucie Olbrechts-Tyteca was taken from Noémi Perelman Mattis, "Perelman and Olbrechts-Tyteca"; and Warnick, pp. 69–85. We have been unable to find a photograph of her.

[17] Warnick, p. 71.

[18] Warnick, p. 70.

[19] Perelman Mattis, "Perelman and Olbrechts-Tyteca."

[20] Warnick, p. 83. This point is disputed by Perelman Mattis in "Perelman and Olbrechts-Tyteca." She writes: "Mme. Olbrechts spent all of her time reading away and gathering quotes on file cards. In their joint work the theoretical armature is entirely Perelman's, the examples were mostly Olbrechts's, and they shared the writing. Neither thought of it as an equal collaboration, which is why their names are in reverse alphabetical order and in different type size. Putting her name on *Traité de l'Argumentation* was how Perelman rewarded her for 10 years' unpaid labor." We have chosen to err toward Warnick's interpretation because of Warnick's argument that Olbrechts-Tyteca's single-authored work bears the signs of serious theoretical work that hardly could have been conducted by a person whose only task was to collect examples on cards and help with the writing.

[21] Warnick, p. 71.

[22] Warnick, pp. 70–71.

[23] Warnick, p. 71.

[24] Warnick, p. 71.

[25] Perelman, "The New Rhetoric," in *The Great Ideas Today*, p. 281.

[26] Robert M. Hutchins and Mortimer J. Adler, eds., *The Great Ideas Today: 1970* (Chicago: Encyclopedia Britannica, 1972), p. 272.

27 Perelman, "The New Rhetoric," in *The Great Ideas Today*, pp. 273–77.

28 Chaïm Perelman and Lucie Olbrechts-Tyteca, *The New Rhetoric: A Treatise on Argumentation*, trans. John Wilkinson and Purcell Weaver (Notre Dame, IN: University of Notre Dame Press, 1969), p. 7. Excerpts in this chapter reprinted with permission of the publisher.

29 Aristotle's analysis of epideictic oratory is discussed in Perelman and Olbrechts-Tyteca, pp. 47–51; and Perelman, "The New Rhetoric," in *The Great Ideas Today*, pp. 277–78.

30 Perelman, "The New Rhetoric," in *The Great Ideas Today*, pp. 277–78.

31 Perelman, "The New Rhetoric," in *The Great Ideas Today*, pp. 277–78.

32 Perelman and Olbrechts-Tyteca, p. 4.

33 Perelman, "The Rational and the Reasonable," *Philosophical Exchange*, 2 (1979), 28–34.

34 Perelman, "The Rational and the Reasonable," p. 29.

35 Perelman, "The Rational and the Reasonable," p. 34.

36 Perelman, *The Realm of Rhetoric*, p. 9.

37 References relevant to Perelman's concept of audience include: John W. Ray, "Perelman's Universal Audience," *Quarterly Journal of Speech*, 64 (December 1978), 361–75; Allen Scult, "Perelman's Universal Audience: One Perspective," *Central States Speech Journal*, 27 (Fall 1976), 176–80; John R. Anderson, "The Audience as a Concept in the Philosophic Rhetoric of Perelman, Johnstone, and Natanson," *Southern Speech Communication Journal*, 38 (Fall 1972), 39–50; Perelman and Olbrechts-Tyteca, pp. 11–62; Perelman, *The Realm of Rhetoric*, pp. 9–20; and Perelman, "The New Rhetoric," in *The Great Ideas Today*, pp. 285–86.

38 Perelman, *The Realm of Rhetoric*, p. 10.

39 Perelman and Olbrechts-Tyteca, p. 17.

40 Perelman and Olbrechts-Tyteca, p. 14.

41 Perelman and Olbrechts-Tyteca, p. 15.

42 Perelman and Olbrechts-Tyteca, p. 19.

43 Perelman and Olbrechts-Tyteca, p. 19.

44 Perelman and Olbrechts-Tyteca, p. 21.

45 Perelman, *The Realm of Rhetoric*, p. 14.

46 Perelman and Olbrechts-Tyteca, p. 34.

47 Perelman and Olbrechts-Tyteca, p. 30.

48 Perelman, *The Realm of Rhetoric*, p. 18.

49 Scult, "Perelman's Universal Audience," p. 177.

50 Perelman, "The New Rhetoric," in *The Great Ideas Today*, p. 285.

51 Perelman, *The Realm of Rhetoric*, p. 21.

52 Perelman and Olbrechts-Tyteca, pp. 65–66.

53 Perelman, *The Realm of Rhetoric*, p. 21.

54 The starting points of argumentation are discussed in: Karl R. Wallace, " 'Topoi' and the Problem of Invention," *Quarterly Journal of Speech*, 58 (December 1972), 387–96; Perelman, *The Realm of Rhetoric*, pp. 21–47; Perelman and Olbrechts-Tyteca, pp. 65–114; and Perelman, "The New Rhetoric," in *The Great Ideas Today*, pp. 287–89.

55 Perelman, "The New Rhetoric," in *The Great Ideas Today*, p. 287.

56 Perelman and Olbrechts-Tyteca, p. 67.

57 Perelman and Olbrechts-Tyteca, p. 69.

58 Perelman and Olbrechts-Tyteca, p. 71.

59 Perelman, *The Realm of Rhetoric*, pp. 24–25.

60 Values, hierarchies, and *loci* of the preferable are discussed in Perelman and Olbrechts-Tyteca, pp. 74–99; and Perelman, *The Realm of Rhetoric*, p. 76. For an excellent discussion of Perelman's approach to values, hierarchies, and *loci* of the preferable, see Gregg B. Walker and Malcolm O. Sillars, "Where Is Argument?," in *Perspectives on Argumentation: Essays in Honor of Wayne Brockriede*, ed. Robert Trapp and Janice Schuetz (Prospect Heights, IL: Waveland, 1990), pp. 134–50.

61 Perelman and Olbrechts-Tyteca, p. 76.

62 Perelman and Olbrechts-Tyteca, p. 79.

63 Perelman and Olbrechts-Tyteca, pp. 83–84. For more information about Vico, see the chapter on Ernesto Grassi in this volume.

[64] Perelman, *The Realm of Rhetoric*, pp. 29–30.

[65] Perelman and Olbrechts-Tyteca, p. 85.

[66] Walker and Sillars, "Where Is Argument?," p. 145.

[67] The concept of presence is discussed in Louise A. Karon, "Presence in *The New Rhetoric*," *Philosophy and Rhetoric*, 9 (Spring 1976), 96–111; Perelman and Olbrechts-Tyteca, pp. 115–42; and Perelman, *The Realm of Rhetoric*, pp. 33–40.

[68] Perelman and Olbrechts-Tyteca, p. 117.

[69] Perelman and Olbrechts-Tyteca, p. 142.

[70] Perelman and Olbrechts-Tyteca, p. 116; Perelman, *The Realm of Rhetoric*, p. 34; and Perelman, "The New Rhetoric," in *The Great Ideas Today*, p. 289.

[71] Perelman, *The Realm of Rhetoric*, p. 35.

[72] Perelman and Olbrechts-Tyteca, p. 142.

[73] Perelman and Olbrechts-Tyteca, p. 149.

[74] Perelman and Olbrechts-Tyteca, p. 149.

[75] Perelman and Olbrechts-Tyteca, pp. 120–21.

[76] Perelman and Olbrechts-Tyteca, pp. 121–22.

[77] Perelman and Olbrechts-Tyteca, pp. 187–508.

[78] Perelman, *The Realm of Rhetoric*, p. 49.

[79] For an excellent discussion of quasi-logical argument, see Ray D. Dearin, "Perelman's 'Quasi-Logical Argument': A Critical Elaboration," in *Advances in Argumentation Theory*, ed. J. Robert Cox and Charles Arthur Willard (Carbondale: Southern Illinois Press, 1982), pp. 78–94.

[80] Warnick, p. 74.

[81] Lucie Olbrechts-Tyteca, *Le Comique du discours* (Brussels, Belg.: Editions de l'Université de Bruxelles, 1974), p. 170, quoted in Warnick, p. 74.

[82] Perelman and Olbrechts-Tyteca, p. 263.

[83] Perelman and Olbrechts-Tyteca, p. 264.

[84] Perelman and Olbrechts-Tyteca, p. 269.

[85] Perelman and Olbrechts-Tyteca, p. 293.

[86] Perelman and Olbrechts-Tyteca, p. 299.

[87] Perelman and Olbrechts-Tyteca, p. 307.

[88] Perelman and Olbrechts-Tyteca, p. 306.

[89] The example of Bill Clinton's use of the technique of severance was provided by Kristine Kowalski, an undergraduate student of rhetoric at Willamette University, in her final paper for a seminar about argumentation and values, spring, 2000.

[90] Perelman and Olbrechts-Tyteca, p. 340.

[91] Perelman and Olbrechts-Tyteca, p. 350.

[92] Perelman and Olbrechts-Tyteca, p. 352.

[93] Perelman and Olbrechts-Tyteca, p. 355.

[94] Perelman, *The Realm of Rhetoric*, p. 108.

[95] Perelman and Olbrechts-Tyteca, p. 372.

[96] James S. Measell, "Perelman on Analogy," *Argumentation and Advocacy*, 22 (Fall 1985), 67.

[97] Perelman and Olbrechts-Tyteca, p. 399.

[98] Perelman and Olbrechts-Tyteca, p. 405.

[99] Perelman and Olbrechts-Tyteca, p. 406.

[100] Perelman and Olbrechts-Tyteca, p. 411.

[101] John Locke, quoted in Perelman and Olbrechts-Tyteca, p. 412.

[102] Perelman, *The Realm of Rhetoric*, p. 127.

[103] Perelman and Olbrechts-Tyteca, p. 417.

[104] Perelman and Olbrechts-Tyteca, pp. 444–50.

[105] Olbrechts-Tyteca, *Le Comique du discours*, p. 170, quoted in Warnick, p. 76.

[106] Warnick, p. 76.

[107] Olbrechts-Tyteca, *Le Comique du discours*. p. 170, quoted in Warnick, p. 77.

[108] Perelman and Olbrechts-Tyteca, pp. 460–508.

[109] Perelman and Olbrechts-Tyteca, p. 471.

[110] Perelman and Olbrechts-Tyteca, p. 482.

[111] Perelman and Olbrechts-Tyteca, p. 492.

[112] Perelman and Olbrechts-Tyteca, p. 492.

[113] Perelman and Olbrechts-Tyteca, p. 495.

[114] David Douglas Dunlap, "The Conception of Audience in Perelman and Isocrates: Locating the Ideal in the Real," *Argumentation*, 7 (November 1993), 463.

[115] James Crosswhite, "Being Unreasonable: Perelman and the Problem of Fallacies," *Argumentation*, 7 (November 1993), 385.

[116] Crosswhite, "Being Unreasonable," p. 389.

[117] Frans H. van Eemeren, Rob Grootendorst, and Tjark Kruiger, *Handbook of Argumentation Theory: A Critical Survey of Classical Backgrounds and Modern Studies* (Dordrecht, Neth.: Foris, 1987). See also Frans H. van Eemeren, and Rob Grootendorst, "Perelman and the Fallacies," *Philosophy and Rhetoric*, 28 (1995), 122–33.

[118] van Eemeren, Grootendorst, and Kruiger, p. 254.

[119] van Eemeren, Grootendorst, and Kruiger, pp. 254–55.

[120] Manfred Kienpointner, "The Empirical Relevance of Perelman's New Rhetoric," *Argumentation*, 7 (November 1993), 419–37.

[121] van Eemeren and Grootendorst, p. 121.

[122] van Eemeren and Grootendorst, p. 125.

[123] van Eemeren and Grootendorst, p. 129.

[124] Crosswhite, "Is There an Audience for This Argument?," p. 141.

[125] Crosswhite, "Being Unreasonable," p. 391.

[126] Crosswhite, "Being Unreasonable," p. 401.

[127] Crosswhite, "Is There an Audience for This Argument?," pp. 134–45.

[128] Crosswhite, "Is There an Audience for This Argument?," p. 136.

[129] Barbara Warnick and Susan L. Kline, "*The New Rhetoric's* Argument Schemes: A Rhetorical View of Practical Reasoning," *Argumentation and Advocacy*, 29 (1992), 1–15.

[130] See, for example, Thomas H. Olbricht, rev. of *The Idea of Justice and the Problem of Argument*, by Chaïm Perelman, *Quarterly Journal of Speech*, 50 (October 1964), 323–24.

[131] Henry W. Johnstone, Jr., "The Idea of a Universal Audience," *Validity and Rhetoric in Philosophical Argument: An Outlook in Transition* (University Park, PA: Dialogue Press of Man and World, 1978), p. 105.

[132] Ray, p. 361.

[133] Ray, p. 372.

[134] Alan Scult, "A Note on the Range and Utility of the Universal Audience," *Journal of the American Forensic Association*, 22 (Fall 1985), 83.

[135] Scult, "A Note on the Range and Utility of the Universal Audience," p. 87.

[136] Chaïm Perelman, "The New Rhetoric and the Rhetoricians: Remembrances and Comments," *Quarterly Journal of Speech*, 70 (May 1984), pp. 190–91.

[137] Stanley K. Laughlin and Daniel T. Hughes, "The Rational and the Reasonable: Dialectical or Parallel Systems," in *Practical Reasoning in Human Affairs: Studies in Honor of Chaïm Perelman*, ed. James L. Golden and Joseph L. Pilotta (Dordrecht, Neth.: D. Reidel, 1986), pp. 187–205.

[138] William E. Wiethoff, "Critical Perspectives on Perelman's Philosophy of Legal Argument," *Journal of the American Forensic Association*, 22 (Fall 1985), 95.

[139] Wiethoff, p. 94.

[140] Walker and Sillars, p. 135.

[141] Perelman, "The New Rhetoric and the Rhetoricians," p. 195.

5

STEPHEN TOULMIN

In Stephen Edelson Toulmin's early works, the term *rhetoric* appears rarely; when it does, it is never a central feature of his writing. However, his work has so many implications for the field of rhetoric that many scholars view Toulmin as one of the influential thinkers in the field, and he himself has come to see the importance of rhetoric to philosophy.

Toulmin's recent works have taken a clear rhetorical turn. In *The Abuse of Casuistry: A History of Moral Reasoning* (1988), Toulmin and his colleague Albert R. Jonsen discuss practical argument as a rhetorical rather than a theoretical enterprise.[1] In *Cosmopolis: The Hidden Agenda of Modernity* (1990), Toulmin notes the resurgence of rhetorical studies: "Since the mid-1960s, rhetoric has begun to regain its respectability as a topic of literary and linguistic analysis."[2] The resurgence, he suggests, was due to the fact that a number of "American colleges and universities have departments devoted to 'communication studies,' or 'speech.' These departments are responsible for college debating teams, but their faculty members do serious research on different aspects of oral communication and argumentation."[3] His work *Return to Reason* (2001) shows how the theoretical concepts of rationality and certainty suppressed the rhetorical idea of reasonability.[4]

Stephen Toulmin was born in London, England, on March 25, 1922, to Geoffrey Edelson Toulmin and Doris Holman Toulmin.[5] He received a bachelor of arts degree in mathematics and physics from King's College in 1942. From 1942 to 1945, he was a junior scientific officer for the Ministry of Aircraft Production, where he did technical intelligence work, first at the Malvern Radar Research and Development Station and later at the Supreme Headquarters of the Allied Expeditionary Force in Germany. When World War II ended, he returned to England to earn a master's degree in 1947 and a doctorate in 1948 from Cambridge University, where one of his professors was Ludwig Wittgenstein.

Toulmin's central interest during his graduate education involved the nature of rationality. "From the start," he wrote, "my couriosity drew me toward the subject of 'rationality.' " Wondering if knowledge really were certain and enduring, he asked himself if "intelligent fish learned to do science, . . . must they in the long run end up with the same body of ideas as human beings?"[6] His first major attempt to deal with issues of rationality was his doctoral thesis, "Reason in Ethics," in which he compared and contrasted the ways humans reason about moral and scientific issues.

In 1949, after completing his doctorate, Toulmin was appointed university lecturer in the Department of Philosophy at Oxford University. He published *The Philosophy of Science: An Introduction* in 1953. In 1954, he was appointed to the position of visiting professor in the Department of History and Philosophy of Science at the University of Melbourne in Australia. He returned to England to assume the position of professor and chair of the Department of Philosophy at the University of Leeds from 1955 to 1959.

While at the University of Leeds, Toulmin pursued his belief that traditional logic is incomplete as a tool of rationality and published *The Uses of Argument* in 1958. His primary purpose in writing the book "was to relate traditional philosophical paradoxes to the standing contrast between 'substantive' and 'formal' aspects of reasoning and argument."[7] Because *The Uses of Argument* ran against mainstream thought in analytic philosophy, the book was received poorly in England. Toulmin lamented that Richard

Braithwaite, his graduate advisor at Cambridge, "was deeply pained by the book, and barely spoke to me for twenty years; while one of my colleagues at Leeds, Peter Alexander, described it as 'Toulmin's *anti*-logic book.'" In fact, wrote Toulmin, "a great hush fell upon my colleagues in England. After that, I assumed that the book would (in Hume's words) 'fall stillborn from the press,' so I was a little surprised when it continued to sell in worthwhile numbers: it took me some time to find out why."[8] In fact, he was not to learn the reason until he went to the United States as a visiting professor at New York University, Stanford University, and Columbia University in 1959. At approximately this time, Wayne Brockriede and Douglas Ehninger introduced Toulmin's work to communication scholars in the United States.[9] They interpreted Toulmin's work as useful to scholars of rhetoric and argumentation because it provided "an appropriate structural model by means of which rhetorical arguments may be laid out for analysis and criticism" as well as "a system for classifying artistic proofs which employs arguments as a central and unifying construct."[10]

Since the introduction of Toulmin's work in the United States, rhetoricians have found his ideas about rationality relevant to their thinking about rhetoric. The success of *The Uses of Argument* was due not to professional philosophers but to rhetoricians. In fact, Toulmin learned that people in the United States who had been purchasing his book were the same people who had been keeping the study of practical argumentation and rhetoric alive at the time he was lamenting its death. In his early writings, Toulmin claimed that the study of practical argumentation was dead; he later admitted: "I met people from Departments of Speech and Communication up and down the country, who told me that they used it as a text on rhetoric and argumentation. So, the study of practical reasoning was kept alive after all; but this was done only *outside* the Departments of Philosophy, under the wing of Speech or English, or at Schools of Law."[11]

In 1960, Toulmin returned briefly to London, where he was the director of the Unit for History of Ideas of the Nuffield Foundation. He returned to the United States in 1965 to become a professor of the history of ideas and philosophy at Brandeis University (1965–1969) and later a professor of philosophy at Michigan State University (1969–1972). He then accepted a position as a professor of humanities at the University of California at Santa Cruz (1972–1973), during which time he published *Human Understanding: The Collective Use and Evolution of Concepts*.

In 1973, Toulmin published *Wittgenstein's Vienna* with Alan Janik and joined the faculty at the University of Chicago. From 1975 until 1978, he worked with the National Commission for the Protection of Human Subjects of Biomedical and Behavioral Research established by the United States Congress, collaborating with Jonsen to write *The Abuse of Casuistry: A History of Moral Reasoning*.[12] When he left the University of Chicago, he moved to Northwestern University as the Avalon Foundation Professor of the Humanities (1986–1992). He published *Cosmopolis: The Hidden Agenda of Modernity* in 1990, a work about the modern era in which he proposes a radical revision of ideas about modernity. Toulmin's next position was as the Henry Luce Professor at the Center for Multiethnic and Transnational Studies at the University of Southern California, where he also served as a faculty master with his wife Donna Toulmin in the North Residential College of the university. They lived and ate with students in the dorms "with blaring stereos, errant fire alarms and visitors at odd hours."[13]

In 1998, the National Endowment for the Humanities named Toulmin a Jefferson Lecturer. This appointment, named in honor of Thomas Jefferson, has been described as "the highest honor the federal government bestows for distinguished intellectual achievement in the humanities."[14] Interspersed with his permanent positions, Toulmin has held visiting professorships and lectureships at schools such as Dartmouth College, Southern Methodist University, and Bryn Mawr College. He also has been a Phi Beta Kappa national lecturer, a senior visiting scholar at the Hastings Center, and a Guggenheim Fellow. Published in 2001, _Return to Reason_ carries forward Toulmin's previous arguments about rhetoric, its relations with formal logic, and the ways in which those two ways of analyzing the different forms of argument and/or argumentation can be reconciled. Two chapters on the virtues and defects of disciplines present novel points on the general theme of the book—the need for a philosophical account of reason to strike a proper balance between its rational (calculative) and reasonable (humanistic) aspects.

✳ Theoretical and Practical Argument

The foundation of Toulmin's contribution to rhetoric rests on his classification of two types of arguments. Beginning in *The Uses of Argument*, he distinguishes between what he terms *substantial* and *analytic* arguments; the former are evaluated according to content and the latter according to form. A substantial argument involves an inferential leap from some data or evidence to the conclusion of the argument. In contrast, the conclusion of an analytic argument requires no inferential leap because the conclusion goes no further than the data contained in the argument's premises. Individuals using analytic arguments base their claims on unchanging and universal principles. Those who use substantial arguments, on the other hand, ground their claims in the context of a particular situation rather than in abstract, universal principles.

In their book, Jonsen and Toulmin describe a similar distinction between theoretical and practical arguments: *theoretical* is their term for analytic arguments and *practical* is their term for substantial arguments. The distinction between these two types of arguments lies at the base of "two very different accounts of ethics and morality: one that seeks eternal, invariable principles, the practical implications of which can be free of exception or qualifications, and another that pays closest attention to the specific details of particular moral cases and circumstances."[15] Thus, an analytic argument is based on unchanging, absolute, and invariant principles, while a practical or substantial argument is based on probability and attends to the circumstances of particular cases.

In summary, theoretical and practical arguments represent idealized formal logic and practical, everyday reasoning respectively. Theoretical or analytic argument is consistent with Plato's ideal of formal, deductive logic that leads to absolute truths regardless of context. Practical argument, on the other hand, conforms more closely to the ideas that Aristotle developed in the *Topics* and the *Rhetoric*. Practical argument is judged not by its correspondence to deductive form but by its substance. It deals with matters of probability rather than with universal truths, and it varies according to context.

Part of Toulmin's life work has been developing an account of theoretical and practical argument that emphasizes the poor fit that follows from using theoretical argument in all commonplace situations. These situations range from how individuals consider and decide upon political issues to how they deal with personal moral dilemmas to how scientists describe their concepts. Even though he claims it largely is irrelevant, Toulmin says that theoretical argument has been the dominant mode since the end of the Renaissance. He also claims that too much reliance on theoretical argument has limited the range of methods for appropriate decision making and has created its own sort of tyranny.[16] Toulmin sees his program as an attempt to emancipate people from the domination of theoretical argument.

Domination of Theoretical Argument

If theoretical argument is hegemonic, as Toulmin suggests, it raises the question of why it has been allowed to dominate rationality for so long. Toulmin pursues a historical account of this question in *Cosmopolis: The Hidden Agenda of Modernity* and begins by returning to Aristotle's distinction between theoretical and practical reasoning. Aristotle saw uses for theoretical argument, but he also supported the use of practical argument, particularly in terms of ethics.[17] In fact, prior to 1600, "no one questioned the right of rhetoric to stand alongside logic in the canon of philosophy; nor was rhetoric treated as a second-class—and necessarily inferior field."[18] During the Renaissance, both the theoretical and the practical were regarded as legitimate. According to Toulmin, "theoretical inquiries were balanced against discussions of concrete practical issues, such as the specific conditions on which it is morally acceptable for a sovereign to launch a war, or for a subject to kill a tyrant."[19] These discussions legitimated the place of rhetoric in human affairs during the Renaissance.

Since the end of the Renaissance, most philosophers have been committed to abstract, universal theory to the exclusion of practical issues. A shift occurred "from a style of philosophy that keeps equally in view issues of local, timebound practice, and universal, timeless theory, to one that accepts matters of universal, timeless theory as being entitled to an exclusive place in the agenda of 'philosophy.' "[20] Toulmin's thesis is that the doctrine of absolutism dominated Western civilization throughout the entirety of the modern period (approximately 1650–1950), beginning with the assassination of Henri IV of France in 1610. During his reign, the conflict between the French Catholics and Protestants became intolerable. Because Henri IV wanted to build a kingdom that balanced Catholicism and Protestantism, he "raised toleration to the level of policy, by his Edict of Nantes. This edict called on loyal Catholic subjects to respect the rights of loyal Protestant subjects."[21] Toulmin suggests that "Henri's murder came as the final confirmation of people's worst fears. His disappearance from the scene dashed the last hope of escaping from irresoluble conflicts."[22]

Under Henri's successor Louis XIII and his advisor Cardinal Richelieu, religious "toleration was progressively eroded."[23] Matters then "took a turn for the worse. The toleration for which Montaigne and Henri both worked in different ways no longer had wide appeal: once ideological conflict developed into general war [The Thirty Years' War], the voices of the dogmatists shouted down those of more reasonable people."[24] The Thirty Years' War created so much uncertainty in Europe that an escape was needed. Toulmin noted that "if uncertainty, ambiguity, and the acceptance of pluralism led, in practice, only to an intensification of the religious war, the time had come to discover some *rational method* for demonstrating the essential correctness or incorrectness of philosophical, scientific, or theological doctrines."[25] René Descartes would provide that method.

Descartes's ideas resulted in part from the historical context in which he lived. The Thirty Years' War began when Descartes was in his early twenties and ended only two years before his death. His attempt to avoid relativism and skepticism involved finding a "single certain thing," the *cogito*, that made certainty possible. Toulmin notes that "fifty years later, for a generation whose central experience was the Thirty Years' War, and a social destruction that had apparently become entirely out of hand, the joint appeal of geometric certainty and 'clear and distinct' ideas helped Descartes's program to carry a new conviction."[26]

The position of Descartes affected society's views on everything from the nature of the physical world to the nature of the human being to the role of the nation-state. In terms of the nature of the physical world, "the standard trope was to compare God the Creator to a clock-maker. The phenomena of nature were seen as similar to the movements of the hands of an elaborate clock mechanism, and the unchanging precision with which this operated was evidence of the Creator's omnipotence."[27] In accordance with this mechanistic view of the physical world, humans were viewed mechanistically as well: "If humans must behave in conformity with the natural world, and the natural world is a mechanistic, causally determined system, it follows that humans too are mechanistic, causally determined systems."[28] The absolute certainty that dominated views of the physical world and the human being were transferred to the role of the nation-state. "Historians refer to these claims [of national sovereignty] as a form of 'absolutism.' By this they

A need for certainty

simply mean that each sovereign nation-state was entitled to run its own affairs as it thought best." The individual nation-state "was no longer morally and politically accountable to a larger community beyond its borders."[29] Descartes's position had such influence on intellectual thought in Europe that it lasted well into the twentieth century.

By 1910, the authority of the modern period "was weakening, but its grip outlasted another thirty years of warfare among the nations of Europe, and people were ready to suspend the Quest for Certainty, acknowledge the demolition of modern cosmopolis, and return belatedly to the humane and liberal standpoint of the late Renaissance, only when the Second World War was well behind them."[30] Between the 1920s and the 1970s, Europe and North America were transformed intellectually and culturally by the change from modernity to postmodernity. This transformation was as deep as the transformation that occurred in Europe between the 1590s and the 1640s.

Toulmin draws numerous parallels between the beginning and end of the modern period. Just as the Renaissance was ushered out by the Thirty Years' War, so the modern period ended after another 30 years of warfare in Europe, In fact, changes were conceptualized at the time of World War I but could not be implemented until later. For example, "at the time of the First World War, Norman Angell and Woodrow Wilson dreamed of a new transnational League of Nations; but it was really only after 1945 that the limits to the autonomy of sovereign nation-states were truly acknowledged, and only from the 1960s on that the force of transnational interdependence imposed itself on states."[31] Similarly, just as the assassination of Henri IV ushered in modernity, Toulmin claims that the undoing of modernity "was framed by a new emblematic assassination"[32]—the assassination of John F. Kennedy.

One result of the ideas that dominated the 300 years of the modern period, according to Toulmin, was that philosophy made very little progress, settling on an absolutist, theoretical approach. Rhetoric was banished from much of the intellectual life of modernity. Presently, however, "the formal doctrines that underpinned human thought and practice from 1700 on followed a trajectory with the shape of an omega [Ω]. After 300 years we are back close to our starting point."[33] Science no longer maintains an absolute separation between the observer and observed, independent nation-states are finding the limits of their independence, the certainty of Descartes is being replaced with skepticism, and there is an interest in reviving rhetoric from the rejection of its significance throughout the modern era.

Absolutism is failing.

The Irrelevance of Theoretical Argument

Toulmin's approach to argumentation is rooted in an assumption of the irrelevance of theoretical argument to the assessment of everyday life. The prototypical example of theoretical argument is the syllogism, a method of reasoning that produces absolute knowledge from the combination of two premises. A classic syllogism is the one that combines the major premise *All*

Syllogisms = Absolute certainty

people are mortal with the minor premise *Socrates is a person* to arrive at the conclusion *Socrates is bound to die.* Through a complex analysis of logic, Toulmin shows that what formal logicians call *premises* actually serve different functions and thus cannot be grouped together satisfactorily.[34]

The ideal of formal logic assumes that arguments never vary regardless of their subject matters (Toulmin calls subject matter a *field*). For example, formal logic assumes that the standards for judging an argument in the field of art are the same as those for judging an argument in the field of physics. Formal logic assumes that mathematics (particularly geometry) is the standard by which arguments in all fields can be judged. Arguments constructed according to the standards of mathematics are considered by logicians to be the "first chosen class of arguments" and are displayed "as signs of special merit; other classes of argument, they have felt, are deficient in so far as they fail to display all the characteristic merits of the paradigm class."[35] In other words, formal logicians consider all arguments to be deficient unless they follow the form of deductive logic. But because all fields of human activity are not based on assumptions identical to those of mathematics and geometry, logical arguments are largely irrelevant to the practical world of rationality.

Because they derive from mathematical fields, theoretical arguments are highly impersonal. For example, the person "doing" logic is no more important to formal logic than the person "doing" mathematics is to the formula for determining the circumference of a circle. In contrast, the person engaging in argument is extremely important in rational assessment in the practical world. Rational procedures, according to Toulmin, "do not exist in the air, apart from actual reasoners: they are things which are learned, employed, sometimes modified, on occasion even abandoned, by the people doing the reasoning."[36]

Toulmin claims that theoretical or analytic arguments are not relevant to the world of practical affairs for a variety of reasons. One reason is that practical concerns are rarely—if ever—governed by a single overriding principle. A vast number of the situations individuals face on a day-to-day basis are too complex to yield to a single universal principle. The problems of everyday life are not simple because they vary according to the details of the situation. For example:

> If I go next door and borrow a silver soup tureen, it goes without saying that I am expected to return it as soon as my immediate need for it is over: that is not an issue and gives rise to no problem.
> If, however, it is a pistol that I borrow and if, while it is in my possession, the owner becomes violently enraged and threatens to kill one of his neighbors as soon as he gets back the pistol, I shall find myself in a genuinely problematic situation. I cannot escape from it by lamely invoking the general maxim that borrowed property ought to be returned promptly.[37]

In the first example, the principle requiring return of borrowed goods can be applied without problem. The second situation is more problematic because the principle of requiring the return of borrowed items conflicts with a duty not to harm another person. An analytic argument will not solve this problem because no single, absolute principle exists that does not come into conflict with another equally important principle.

Another reason Toulmin considers formal logic to be largely irrelevant to practical argument is that formal logic assumes concepts do not change with time. For an argument to be considered valid in formal logic, "it must surely be good once and for all."[38] Toulmin believes, however, that most argument fields cannot accommodate timeless claims to knowledge. He phrases this claim as a question to which he provides the answer: "Can one cast into a timeless mathematical mould the relations upon which the soundness and acceptability of our arguments depend, without distorting them beyond recognition? I shall argue that this cannot be done."[39]

Another difficulty with the application of absolutism to practical problems is that answers to many everyday problems are either "probably correct" or "probably incorrect" instead of "absolutely correct" or "absolutely incorrect." Many of the questions that rational procedures are designed to answer cannot be answered with certainty. Did Richard Nixon lie to the American public when he proclaimed, "I am not a crook"? Did George Bush lie to the American public when he said, "Read my lips: No new taxes"? Did Bill Clinton lie when he said, "I did not have sexual relations with that woman—Ms. Lewinsky"? These answers are probably—but not certainly—yes.

As an example of the lack of relevance of theoretical argument to practical problems, Toulmin recalls his service on the National Commission for Protection of Human Subjects of Biomedical and Behavioral Research. The commission, consisting of five members who were scientists and six who were not, was charged with the task of making policies about publicly financed research involving human experimentation. Before the commission began its deliberations, many onlookers believed their discussions would end in deadlock. The commission members, however, came to agreement or very close to agreement on almost all issues. They did so by "taking one difficult class of cases at a time and comparing it in detail with other clearer and easier classes of cases."[40] Serious disagreements occurred only after the commission's members attempted to agree on the underlying principles that justified their conclusions. In other words, "they could agree; they could agree what they were agreeing about; but, apparently, they could not agree why they agreed about it."[41] The failure of their attempt to appeal to principles reflects the difficulty of constructing arguments around single, invariant principles. Although the arguments about certain classes of cases resulted in agreement, their attempts to move to overriding principles "did not add any weight or certitude to the Commissioners' specific ethical findings."[42] The attempt to use absolute principles proved to be irrelevant to the success of the commission.

Theoretical Arguments and the Tyranny of Principles

Argument proceeding from absolute principles is irrelevant to many of the tasks it is designed to accomplish because practical concerns rarely are

Analytic argument is useless in social situations

governed by a single set of principles. Knowledge changes over time, and human affairs are governed more by probabilities than by certainties. In addition to its irrelevance to the success of practical argument, Toulmin believes that appeals to absolute principles can be counterproductive. Reliance on absolute standards of judgment can lead to argumentative deadlocks.

Toulmin uses the abortion issue as an example of a controversy that cannot be resolved by analytic argument. He claims that when people are willing to accept a variety of rights and responsibilities about this issue, they are able to argue temperately and productively. When they proceed in this manner, they balance the issue differently depending on the individual circumstances in which a woman finds herself.[43] When focused on universal laws and absolute principles, however, the abortion debate becomes "less temperate, less discriminating, and above all, less resolvable."[44] Jonsen and Toulmin claim that the activists in the abortion controversy focus their public rhetoric on "*universal* laws and principles, which they could then nail to their respective masts"[45]—a focus that has made the abortion debate unresolvable. In Toulmin's words, "those who have insisted on dealing with the issue at the level of high theory thus guarantee that the only possible outcome is deadlock."[46] Because analytic arguments are used to analyze situations that are properly the domain of substantial arguments, many social debates, such as the abortion controversy, are not resolvable. Jonsen and Toulmin claim that "the zealot's concentration on universal and invariable principles" has created a "practical deadlock" from which there is no escape.[47]

In some cases, the importance of absolute moral standards leads to a tyranny of principles. Toulmin has noticed a "cult of absolute principles" in the argumentative strategies privileged in contemporary society. In this cult of absolutism, one group uses its supposed absolute principle in an attempt to impose these principles tyrannically on all other groups and individuals. Toulmin warns his fellow citizens to "remain on guard against these moral enthusiasts" whom he believes "succeed only in blinding themselves to the equities embodied in real-life situations and problems."[48] A large part of Toulmin's research program is aimed at the emancipation of practical argument from the tyranny of principles.

Toulmin does not conclude that analytic logic needs to be abandoned completely. He simply sees its range of applicability as much narrower than many philosophers have claimed: "This is not to say that the elaborate mathematical systems which constitute 'symbolic logic' must now be thrown away; but only that people with intellectual capital invested in them should retain no illusions about the extent of their relevance to practical arguments."[49] One alternative to theoretical argument is relativism, which, according to Toulmin, has become "extremely popular" in recent decades.[50] Relativism denies the existence of objective standards to evaluate concepts. The only relevant standards are ones shared by groups or communities, and standards vary across these communities. For example, Toulmin explains that, in the field of ethics, relativism involves "the recognition of multiple moral authority, each

claiming its own local validity."[51] The work of R. G. Collingwood is representative of relativistic attempts to deal with the problems of theoretical argument. Collingwood was forced into relativism in his attempt to avoid the
problem of absolute standards. According to Toulmin, the relativistic reaction
of Collingwood "takes good care to avoid the defects of historical irrelevance,
but in doing so . . . it ends in equal difficulties by denying itself any impartial
standpoint for rational judgement."[52]

The choice, then, is seen as limited either to a completely absolutist or a
completely relativistic position—both of which Toulmin views as untenable
and unnecessary. Toulmin believes this choice is based on "the very dilemma
we first set out to escape: the invidious choice between the arbitrariness of
the absolutist and the defeatism of the relativist."[53] Because Toulmin believes that absolutism characterizes mainstream modern thinking, he voices
greater objections to it than he does to relativism. Although he sees absolute
standards of argument as so strict that they are irrelevant to the practice of
rational criticism, he objects to relativistic standards of argument because
they are so imprecise that they constitute no standards at all.

The field of anthropology is one in which practitioners have moved in
the direction of relativism because anthropologists recognize that rational
arguments vary from culture to culture. According to Toulmin, these relativistic standards preclude anthropologists from developing adequate standards of judgment. He uses the example of an anthropologist who comes
across "a tribe with a long tradition of sympathetic magic" that "insists on
using homeopathic medicines in preference to antidotes."[54] The members of
the tribe undoubtedly would be able to give their reasons for this choice. The
question raised by the tribe is whether the anthropologist should consider its
choice of medicine to be rational: "Confronted by this question, anthropologists frequently took the relativist way out: they considered only what was regarded as rational by any particular tribe and avoided the question of
whether that attitude was sound or unsound, well founded or groundless."[55]
Toulmin's concern, then, is that a completely relativist point of view provides
no basis for distinguishing between a good and a poor argument. To avoid
the dilemma of absolutism versus relativism, Toulmin analyzes practical arguments in various disciplines, ranging from the physical sciences to ethics.
Because he believes the very dilemma was created by an identification of rationality with formal logic, he sees the solution in the realm of practical
rather than theoretical argument. In other words, he seeks a middle ground
between the two extremes.

Emancipation of Practical Argument

Between 1950 and 1990, Toulmin authored or coauthored five books
that develop the notion that practical argument can and should be emancipated from the hegemony of theoretical argument.[56] Using a good reasons
approach to ethics, a layout of practical argument, an evolutionary view of

science, a revival of the methods of casuistry, and a view of the humanization of modernity, Toulmin aims to emancipate practical argument—to free argumentation from the extremes of absolutism without falling into the abyss of relativism.

Good Reasons Approach to Ethics

In 1950, Toulmin published his doctoral dissertation under the title *An Examination of the Place of Reason in Ethics*. In this work, he begins his exploration of the emancipation of practical argumentation from theoretical argumentation by focusing on arguments over matters of ethics. He intends to provide an alternative to what he believes are the three most influential approaches to ethics: the objective, subjective, and imperative approaches. The objective approach, most centrally located in the work of George Edward Moore,[57] considers the idea of good or right to be "a property of some kind or other."[58] Toulmin identifies three kinds of properties. Simple properties, such as the colors red or yellow, are "directly perceived by the senses."[59] Complex properties are the kind for which criteria are required that can be "detected by means of a more or less complex routine and the properties can be defined in terms of this routine."[60] For example, the 259 sides of a type of polygon are detected by the routine of counting the sides. A third type of property, scientific qualities, is "detected by means of routines, in the way complex qualities are, but which are not directly perceived—in fact we might say not perceived at all."[61] Accordingly, ethical terms like *goodness* or *right* or *justice* refer to these kinds of properties.

Toulmin argues that values are not directly perceived properties, which is how they are conceptualized in the objective approach. If rightness or goodness could be directly perceived, the extent of disagreement that exists over matters of ethics would not be possible, just as people do not disagree over the fact that the color of a rose is red and a daffodil is yellow. Thus, if the objectivist approach were a sound one, settling a debate about whether capital punishment is good or evil would be just as easy as settling a debate about whether some particular rose is red or white.

The subjective approach, in contrast, is rooted in the belief that in "saying that anything is good or right, we are reporting on the feelings which we (or the members of our social group) have towards it."[62] The evidence produced in favor of the subjective approach is "the variation in ethical judgments and standards, both between individuals within a community and between members of different communities."[63] Toulmin objects to this approach because it cannot provide an "account of what is a good reason for an ethical judgement, or provide any standard for criticising ethical reasoning."[64] If the subjective approach were accepted, no response would be possible when any two people asserted opposite views about a particular value.

A third approach, the imperative approach, "is the doctrine that, in calling anything good or right, we are only evincing (displaying) our feelings towards it."[65] According to this approach, saying something like "X is bad" is the same as saying "do not do X." For example, to say "lying is a bad thing" is the same as commanding someone not to lie. This approach fails because it cannot explain how ethical judgments can be right or wrong, true or false: "there is no disputing about exclamations in the way in which we dispute about questions of fact."[66] Thus, the imperative approach does not allow for argumentation about ethical matters: "When we say that so-and-so is good, or that I ought to do such-and-such, we do so sometimes for good reasons and sometimes for bad ones. The imperative approach does not help us in the slightest to distinguish the one from the other."[67]

As an alternative to these three approaches, Toulmin offers a good reasons approach to ethics. Rather than beginning with questions such as "what is good?" or "what is right?," Toulmin begins with the question, "What kinds of reasons are good reasons in ethics?" He attempts to answer that question based on the function of ethics. Toulmin argues that ethics arise functionally only out of community life. Except for the fact that humans live together in social groups and communities, they would have no reason to think about questions of ethics. In this regard, two types of considerations are relevant to questions of ethics—those about duty and those about a community's moral codes. According to the good reasons approach, one might appeal to duty or to the community's moral code in situations where there is conflict between duties or codes. When a conflict appears, "one has to weigh up, as well as one can, the risks involved in ignoring either, and choose 'the lesser of the two evils.' "[68] In these cases of conflict, the ethics of any action are argued according to its consequences. With his good reasons approach to ethics, Toulmin attempts to steer the middle course between absolutism and relativism.

Layout of Argument

The aspect of Toulmin's theory that is best known is his model of practical argument.[69] This layout of argument was developed from his idea that justification is the primary function of practical argumentation.[70] Practical arguments justify claims rather than infer claims from evidence. Justification is a retrospective activity, while inference is a prospective one. In other words, justification of a claim involves producing reasons for a claim after the fact of mentally arriving at that claim. Inference, on the other hand, refers to the use of reasons to arrive at a claim and is the province of analytic argumentation. Justification involves *testing and sifting ideas critically. It is* concerned with how people share their ideas and thoughts in situations that raise the question of whether those ideas are worth sharing. It is a collective and continuing human transaction."[71] Even in the sciences, where one facet of the scientist's professional work is discovery, Toulmin claims, "the justifying of his discoveries—by the presentation of 'acceptable' supporting arguments—is another, complementary facet of this same work."[72]

The idea that argument involves justification leads Toulmin to discuss the standards by which arguments succeed or fail to justify claims. An argument is sound if it is able to survive the criticism offered by those who participate in the rational enterprises of various fields. In his words, a "sound argument, a well-grounded or firmly-backed claim, is one which will stand up to criticism, one for which a case can be presented coming up to the standard required if it is to deserve a favourable verdict."[73]

Because Toulmin perceives justification to be critical in argument, a prerequisite to comprehending Toulmin's approach to the layout of argument is his consideration of modal terms. Modal terms are terms that frequently occur in arguments, such as *possible, probable, impossible, certainly, presumably, as far as the evidence goes,* and *necessarily.* Toulmin claims that modal terms are characterized by two different aspects—force and criteria. The force of an argument refers to the strength or power of the claim. The claim that a person who jumps from a tall building certainly will hit the ground has a greater degree of force than the claim that a person taking an airline trip from New York to Los Angeles probably will arrive in Los Angeles on time or that a person reading this book possibly will find it interesting. The first claim has a higher degree of probability than the last two claims.

Criteria for an argument refer to the standards used to justify the adequacy of the claim. The standards used to judge the adequacy of a work of abstract art are not the same standards as those used to judge the adequacy of a scientific theory or the wisdom of a president's speech. According to Toulmin, a modal term's force is field invariant, while its criteria are field dependent.[74] Arguments from various fields may carry similar force, but the criteria for assessing them differ.

Toulmin's notion of argument fields[75] helps explain what he means by *field invariant* and *field dependent.* Although other perspectives assume that arguments are the same regardless of the field, Toulmin argues that some elements of argument differ from one field to another. In what ways, for example, is an argument designed to justify the conclusion that Picasso was a great artist similar to an argument designed to justify the claim that liberty is a more important value than life or that Darwin's theory of evolution is a useful explanation for the existence of human life on the planet Earth? In other words, Toulmin is searching for ways to explain how some portions of arguments, as well as the criteria for judging their adequacy, remain the same regardless of field, while other portions of arguments vary from field to field. He believes that "as we move from the lunch counter to the executive conference table, from the science laboratory to the law courts, the 'forum' of discussion changes profoundly."[76] The kinds of arguments that occur in these various forums will be "entirely different in the different situations and so also will be the ways in which possible outcomes of the argument are tested and judged."[77]

Arguments vary from field to field in myriad ways.[78] Some arguments vary according to the degree of formality required in different fields. The degree of formality in an argument between two film critics about the quality of *Erin Brockovich* is much less than that of an argument between defense attorney Johnnie Cochran and prosecuting attorney Marcia Clark about the quality of DNA evidence in the O. J. Simpson case. Arguments also differ according to the degree of precision required in different fields. The amount of precision in an argument about theoretical physics is much greater than that in an argument concerning which applicant for a job is more qualified. Fields of arguments also differ with regard to the modes of resolution that are required. The judicial system of the United States, for example, functions with an adversarial mode of resolution, where one party wins and the other loses. Some forms of negotiation, on the other hand, rely on a compromise or consensus mode of resolution. These are a few of the ways in which practical argument differs from one field to another.

According to Toulmin, one of the ways in which arguments do not vary from field to field is that they all may be analyzed according to his layout of argument.[79] This layout is based on an analog of motion: "an argument is *movement* from accepted *data*, through a *warrant*, to a *claim*."[80] Making an argument is, therefore, analogous to taking a trip, with the traveler trying to get someplace from someplace else.

Toulmin's layout of an argument involves six interrelated components. The first three and most basic elements are claim, grounds, and warrant. The next three components—backing, modal qualifier, and rebuttal—modify the first three. The first component is called a *claim*. The claim is the conclusion of the argument that a person is seeking to justify. It is the answer to the question, "Where are we going?" The claim is the destination of the trip. Toulmin calls the second component of an argument *grounds*—the facts or other information on which the argument is based. Grounds provide the answer to the question, "What do we have to go on?" The grounds constitute the vehicle by which the destination is reached. The third component of an argument is called the *warrant*. This portion of the argument authorizes movement from the grounds to the claim and answers the question, "How do you justify the move from these grounds to that claim? What road do you take to get from this starting point to that destination?"[81] The warrant assesses whether or not the trip from grounds to claim is a legitimate one. These three components are the primary elements of an argument and, in simple arguments, they may be the only components visible.

The three elements of Toulmin's layout can be depicted as follows:

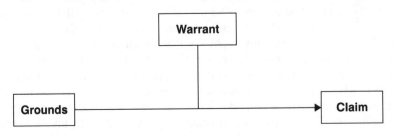

One of the examples Toulmin uses to illustrate his layout concerns a man named Harry and a claim that Harry is a British citizen:[82]

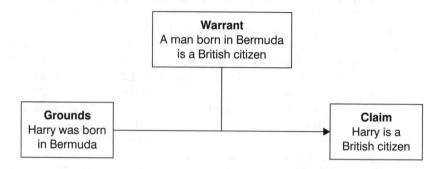

Alone, these three primary elements fail to distinguish analytic from practical arguments. Toulmin's example easily can be transformed into a formal syllogism:

Major premise: A man born in Bermuda is a British citizen.
Minor premise: Harry was born in Bermuda.
Conclusion: Harry is a British citizen.

Three additional elements complete the layout of an argument by showing how practical arguments are contextualized and thus are different from analytic arguments. The first of these is called *backing*. In formal logic, the major premise requires no support because it is seen as a universal principle. In practical argument, sometimes the movement called for in the warrant is not obvious, and backing or additional support for the warrant may be required. While the warrant answers the question, "What road should be taken?," the backing answers the question, "Why is this road a good one?"

Another element in Toulmin's layout of an argument is called a *modal qualifier*. Modal qualifiers indicate the strength of the step taken from data to warrant. Some arguments include qualifiers like *probably* or *certainly*, indicating the strength of the relationship between the data and the warrant. Strength also is indicated when, for example, the weather reporter predicts that the chances of rain are 70%, or a scientist claims results that are significant at the .05 level of confidence. Modal qualifiers answer the question, "How certain are we of arriving at our destination?"

The final element of an argument is called the *rebuttal*, a term that refers to specific circumstances when the warrant does not justify the claim. When using rebuttal, an arguer is presenting claims with a degree of caution. For example, the weather reporter might say that tomorrow will bring rain unless the Pacific front gets stalled over the Rocky Mountains. Using an example from the realm of ethics, a person might argue that suicide is immoral except in cases when a person is in extreme pain and has a disease that has no possible outcome other than a painful and lingering death. The rebuttal answers the question, "Under what circumstances are we unable to take this trip?"

This element emphasizes how practical argument, as opposed to analytic argument, is contextualized—how it is grounded in the specifics of the situation.

The complete diagram of Toulmin's layout of argument is as follows:

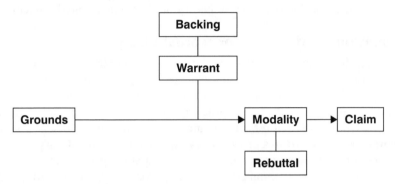

Toulmin's example of Harry, presented earlier, is completed in the following layout:

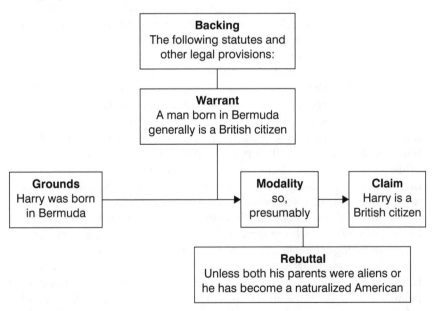

These six elements, considered as parts of an interdependent whole, constitute Toulmin's layout of an argument. Based on legal argument rather than formal logic, Toulmin's layout is modeled on the kind of arguments that typically occur in the courtroom.

When Toulmin first described the layout in *The Uses of Argument*, he did not emphasize and, in fact, did not realize its implications for the field of rhetoric. He did not recognize, for example, that his layout could be adapted to provide a model of how people communicate arguments. Only after he moved to the United States, was introduced to rhetoricians by Brockriede and Ehninger, and had published *Introduction to Reasoning* with Rieke and Janik were the rhetorical implications of his layout of argument stated explicitly.

Evolutionary Model of Conceptual Change

Like his layout of argument, the rhetorical implications of Toulmin's evolutionary model of conceptual change were not readily apparent until scholars began to realize that rhetoric was central to the process of conceptual change. His model of conceptual change provides yet another challenge to the tyranny of theoretical argument. Concepts in all fields, Toulmin claims, are constantly in a process of evolution, and argument is a part of the process of evolutionary change. Prior to discussing his own perspective on conceptual change, Toulmin criticizes the approach of Thomas S. Kuhn, who attempts to account for conceptual change in his seminal work *The Structure of Scientific Revolutions*.[83] Kuhn's thesis is that concepts change when the current scientific paradigm no longer provides useful answers. At such a time, Kuhn claims, a scientific revolution occurs, and new paradigms compete to replace the old. The actors in the competing paradigms are so different that they are unable to communicate clearly with one another.

Toulmin believes that Kuhn's notion of the scientific revolution suffers from the earlier problems of relativism because, in Kuhn's scheme, concepts are not comparable from one paradigm to another. In contrast to Kuhn, Toulmin believes that conceptual change is evolutionary, not revolutionary, and that scientists from competing paradigms are able to—and, in fact, do—argue about the merits of the competing ideas. Toulmin claims that the Copernican Revolution actually took about 150 years to complete "and was argued out every step of the way."[84] The changes in physics and astronomy that resulted were "the outcome of a continuing rational discussion."[85] Once the so-called revolution was complete, the new worldview shared little with the old.

In Toulmin's view, concepts develop according to a pattern of evolution in much the same way that organisms evolve biologically. In fact, he uses Darwin's model of biological evolution to explain conceptual evolution. The development of concepts involves two processes: innovation and selection. Innovative factors account for the appearance of variations in populations of plants and animals as well as for the appearance of variations in scientific theories, while selective factors account for the perpetuation of the healthiest plants and animals and the soundest scientific theories. Innovation occurs when professionals in a particular discipline come to view their concepts in ways that differ from those in which concepts traditionally have been viewed. These innovative concepts then are subjected to a process of debate and inquiry in a forum of competition that involves the process of selection. The ideas that survive the competition are selected as replacements for or revisions of the traditional concepts. As Toulmin explains, "suitable 'forums of competition'" must exist "within which intellectual novelties can survive for long enough to show their merits or defects; but in which they are also criticized and weeded out with enough severity to maintain the coherence of the discipline."[86]

In science, the selection process includes both disciplinary and professional aspects. The disciplinary aspects of a science—the ideas and objects of the science—insure evolution by replacing old theories that no longer offer adequate explanations for the objects of that science. These disciplinary concerns, however, do not comprise all of the factors involved in the evolution of ideas. Professional factors that influence evolution include such things as the political nature of professional organizations, the needs of society for the "products" of the particular science, and the organization and editorship of journals for publishing scholarly work. Toulmin explains that people and organizations "exercise as real a power and influence over the development of science as they do in any other sphere of human life."[87] Thus, an event like the nature of the person elected to office in a professional organization can affect the development of concepts in that scientific discipline.

Toulmin claims that selection processes are rational when "rational enterprises" provide forums of criticism for ideas that are neither absolute nor completely relative. In the court of rationality, clear-headed people with the proper experience assume roles analogous to judges and jurors. He says that from culture to culture, from epoch to epoch, "reasoning may operate according to different methods and principles, so that different milieus represent (so to say) the parallel 'jurisdictions' of rationality. But they do so out of a shared concern with common 'rational enterprises.' "[88]

As concepts change from one period of time to another or from one culture to another, they are either valid or invalid from an absolutist point of view. From a relativistic approach, one concept is neither better nor worse than a competing concept from a different culture or milieu. From Toulmin's perspective, such "evaluations are always a matter of comparison. The operative questions are never of the form, 'Is this concept uniquely "valid" or "invalid"?' . . . Instead, the operative form is 'Given the current repertory of concepts and available variants, would this particular conceptual variant *improve* our explanatory power *more than* its rivals?' "[89]

The fact that Toulmin's approach to argumentation does not distinguish absolutely between the valid and invalid might lead some to the conclusion that he believes that the rational evaluation of ideas is purely subjective and thus not rational at all. Toulmin disputes this view by introducing a concept he calls the *impartial rational standpoint*. The impartial rational standpoint is a significant part of Toulmin's attempt to explain how concept evaluation can be objective without falling prey to the criticisms of absolutism. The impartial rational standpoint is "an 'objective one,' in the sense of being neutral as between the local and temporary views of different historico-cultural milieus; but its conclusions are always subject to reconsideration, and it does not divorce itself from the actual testimony of history and anthropology."[90] It is simultaneously objective and contextual; it is objective in the sense of being neutral and contextual in the sense of considering the relevant facets of history and anthropology. The evolutionary model of argument, then, is Toulmin's attempt to explain how individuals are able to achieve an impartial standpoint of rationality through a process of criticism and evaluation.[91]

Revival of Casuistry

Building on Toulmin's description of an impartial standpoint of rationality as a place between relativism and absolutism in science, Toulmin and his colleague Jonsen describe a similar place for the discussion of ethics in moral controversy. By reviving casuistry, or case ethics, Toulmin believes a path can be found between the extremes of absolutism and relativism in ethical discussions. Casuistry, widely used in the Middle Ages and the Renaissance, fell into disrepute during the modern period but once again is being revived in the postmodern period.[92] In *The Abuse of Casuistry*, Jonsen and Toulmin show how the process of casuistry has been an effective form of practical argumentation: "Human experience long ago developed a reasonable and effective set of practical procedures for resolving the moral problems that arise in particular real-life situations. These procedures came to be known as 'casuistry' and those who employed these procedures were 'casuists.' "[93]

As defined by Jonsen and Toulmin, casuistry is a procedure used to resolve moral problems without resorting to theoretical argument. A theoretical approach to moral problems begins by specifying absolute moral principles and then applying the principle to a specific case. If the sanctity of life is an absolute moral principle and if abortion involves the taking of a life, then abortion is immoral. The approach of casuistry is different, however, and begins with type cases or paradigm cases as objects of reference in moral arguments. These type cases create an initial presumption of moral action for cases that do not contain exceptional circumstances. An individual case then is compared and contrasted with the type case in an attempt to determine whether the specifics of the individual case are comparable to the type case.

Type cases serve as objects of reference. For instance, "willfully using violence against innocent and defenseless human beings, taking unfair advantage of other people's misfortunes, deceiving others by lying to them, damaging the community by your disloyalty, and acting—in general—inconsiderately toward your fellows" were type cases in the classical period of Greece and Rome and are so today. In casuistry, "these type cases are the markers or boundary stones that delimit the territory of 'moral' considerations in practice."[94] Thus, the type case is the starting point for a moral discussion.

In some cases, additional facts surrounding the context may refute the presumption of the rules embedded in the type case. Jonsen and Toulmin discuss three types of problematic situations: a situation in which the type case fits the individual case ambiguously, a situation in which two or more type cases apply to the same individual case in conflicting ways, and a situation in which an individual case is so unprecedented that it defies resolution in terms of existing type cases. In none of these cases is analytic argument helpful because the universal moral principle, like the type case, fits the situation only ambiguously, clashes with another universal moral principle, or does not apply at all to the situation.

The first and second situations that Jonsen and Toulmin discuss can be illustrated by the example of a specific situation occasionally faced by a doctor in a neonatal intensive care unit. Medical science has developed to the point that physicians now have the technical capacity to maintain the breathing of very small, premature infants who, a few years ago, certainly would have died. The doctor is faced with deciding whether Nancy, a very premature infant, should be treated or should be allowed to die without treatment. The procedures the doctor will have to follow may have certain serious side effects; even if Nancy survives, she may live a lifetime of physical pain, or she may be seriously handicapped.

Terminally ill patients who have asked to have their treatments discontinued might be considered a type case relevant to the decision about Nancy. The comparison of this type case to the specific case of Nancy illustrates Jonsen and Toulmin's first example of a problematic moral case because it fits the type case ambiguously. Certainly, the question faced in Nancy's case is similar to the one doctors face in the cases of these terminally ill patients. Should Nancy be treated or should she be allowed to die? Should these terminally ill patients be forced to endure weeks of pain and suffering associated with being tied to mechanical life-support systems or should they be allowed to die?

Because the type case selected to resolve this dispute involves the presumptive rule that a physician should "mercifully refrain" from saving the life of a terminally ill patient who has asked to die, the type case fits Nancy's case ambiguously. The primary difference is that Nancy, unlike terminally ill patients, has no way of telling the doctor whether she would prefer to have her life prolonged or would prefer to be allowed to die. Many other ambiguities exist, such as the fact that, as an infant, Nancy neither can reflect on her physical pain nor anticipate the duration of suffering ahead of her. Terminally ill patients, on the other hand, may be fully cognizant and reflective about their painful physical circumstances.

Nancy's case also can be used to illustrate Jonsen and Toulmin's second example of a problematic moral case in which two different type cases apply to the specific case in conflicting ways. The first type case—the type case just discussed—involves the presumptive rule that a doctor should not take extraordinary measures to save the lives of those patients who choose death over further pain and suffering. The second type case involves a contrary presumptive rule stated in the doctor's oath to "act to preserve life." These two paradigm or type cases apply to Nancy's example in competing ways. The first suggests that the doctor should let Nancy die; the second suggests that the doctor should attempt to save Nancy's life. If Congress were to pass legislation that categorizes withholding care from the newborn as child abuse, the situation would be even more difficult to resolve. Thus, a third consideration—that of the law—would be introduced into Nancy's situation. The dilemma posed when two or more type cases apply to a specific case in conflicting ways is solved not by analytic argument but by personal decision: Which type case best fits the specific situation and under what circumstances should the rules of the type case be set aside?

The third problematic situation involves a moral discussion that is so unprecedented that no paradigm exists to resolve it. Jonsen and Toulmin's example concerns a man who has been married for eight years and has three children. He decides to have hormone therapy and a sex-change operation. This case raises many interesting and unprecedented issues, not the least of which is whether or not this man and his wife still have mutual sexual obligations.

Each of these problematic situations must be resolved by practical argument rather than by analytic argument. In Jonsen and Toulmin's words, "moral experience does not lie in a mastery of general rules and theoretical principles, however sound and well reasoned those principles may appear."[95] Instead of being grounded in rules, moral experience "comes from seeing how the ideas behind those rules work out in the course of people's lives: in particular, seeing more exactly what is involved in insisting on (or waiving) this or that rule in one or another set of circumstances."[96]

A poignant example of the proper place of rules in moral argument was noted by Toulmin as the result of a televised report of some difficulties a young handicapped woman was experiencing with the local Social Security office. Because her Social Security payments were not sufficient to cover her basic expenses, she started a telephone-answering service that she operated from her bedside. When the Social Security office discovered that she was earning income from this service, it lowered her benefits and asked her for repayment of past benefits. In despair, the woman took her own life. The reaction of the television reporter was "there ought to be a *rule* to prevent this kind of thing from happening." For Toulmin, the reporter's reaction reflected an absolutist response to the place of rules in moral deliberation. A more proper reaction—one more consistent with casuistry—would have been that "the local office should be given discretion to waive, or at least bend, the existing rules in hard cases."[97]

Jonsen and Toulmin offer a model of practical argument that explains the procedures of casuistry.[98] This model, similar to the one developed in *The Uses of Argument*, is presented below. It is similar to Toulmin's original layout of argument in many respects, although it has four elements rather than the original six. In this model, grounds apply to the general warrant as well as to the claim, thus eliminating the backing. Modality, or the degree of certainty, has been incorporated into the claim with the phrase *presumably so*.

Practical Reasoning

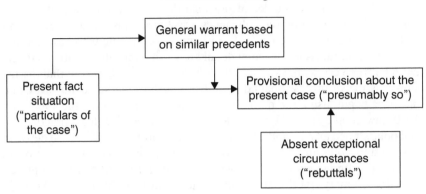

The procedure of casuistry can be illustrated by Jonsen and Toulmin's example, cited earlier, involving whether a person has a moral obligation to return a borrowed pistol to a man who claims that he will shoot his neighbor as soon as he gets the pistol back. The grounds in this case involve data from the context of the particular situation. In this example, the warrant is a general maxim developed from type cases or paradigm cases—that borrowed property ought to be returned. The claim, a provisional conclusion about the present case, is that he ought to return the pistol. But this argument hinges on the rebuttal, where the differences in the specific case and the paradigm case are considered. Thus, the procedures of casuistry involve the interaction of a general warrant developed from a paradigm case, data based on the particulars of the present case, and rebuttals concerning exceptional circumstances that exist in the present case. The conclusion of the argument serves as a guide to future action.[99]

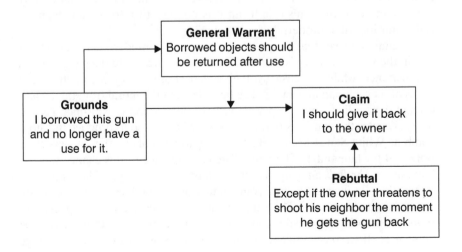

Jonsen and Toulmin claim that, since the 1960s, casuistry has been revived. They provide examples of practical dilemmas where case analysis is used routinely: "Friends and colleagues, psychotherapists and agony columnists, parents and children, priests and ministers: anyone who has occasion to consider moral issues in actual detail knows that morally significant *differences* between cases are as vital as their *likenesses*."[100] They claim that discussion of issues of professional ethics in fields such as medicine, business, and law have begun using the methods of casuistry. In addition, "the 1960s and 1970s saw people enter the moral debates about medicine, legal practice, social policy, nuclear war, and a half a dozen such problems."[101] These debates, Jonsen and Toulmin maintain, always return to the particular situation in which a person faces a moral problem rather than to universal moral principles. In summary, their claim is that "our inquiry confirms what Aristotle taught long ago: that ethical arguments have less in common with formal analytic arguments than they do with topical or rhetorical ones."[102]

Humanizing Modernity

Toulmin not only describes various ways in which society can be emancipated from the tyranny of absolute moral principles but also describes that emancipation in historical terms that he hopes will lead to a humanization of modernity. To succeed in this quest, Toulmin believes that "the hope for certainty and clarity in theory" needs to be balanced "with the impossibility of avoiding uncertainty and ambiguity in practice."[103] This process, already well underway in science and beginning in philosophy, does not involve tossing out all of the progress made during the modern period; rather, it involves reconciling these advances with humanism. As Toulmin states: "We are not compelled to *choose between* sixteenth-century humanism and seventeenth-century exact science: rather, we need to hang on to the positive achievements of them both."[104] The task, therefore, is neither to reject modernity nor to cling to it in its historic form; it is "rather, to reform, and even reclaim, our inherited modernity, by *humanizing* it."[105]

Toulmin believes that the process of humanizing modernity is well underway in the sciences. Today's sciences, Toulmin believes, "are deeply grounded in experience; while, increasingly, their practical use is subject to criticism, in terms of their human impact."[106] The lines dividing the moral from the technical and the applied from the pure have become less and less distinct. As evidence, he cites the concerns of the physicists who worked to produce the atom bomb at White Sands Missile Base in New Mexico about the dangers their work had for humanity: "The immediate consequence of this change was the founding of *The Bulletin of the Atomic Scientists*, which still provides a monthly, transnational nongovernmental commentary on the politics of nuclear weapons and related topics."[107] The humanization of the sciences is, he suggests, responsible for bringing questions about ecology to center stage. If science can be humanized, then so can philosophy. Today, matters of life and death challenge philosophers—specifically, problems of nuclear war, medical technology, and the claims of environment that cannot "be addressed without bringing to the surface questions about the value of human life, and our responsibility for protecting the world of nature, as well as that of 'humanity.' "[108]

Toulmin claims that postmodernity focuses on four elements that were areas of emphasis prior to the seventeenth century's turn from humanism to rationalism. These elements, which largely were considered unimportant during the modern period, are the oral, the particular, the local, and the timely. The oral is the most important of these four elements for the study of rhetoric. Modern philosophers rejected the oral because their scholarly focus was the printed page; they were interested in isolating "literary works, as products, from facts about historical situations and personal lives of their authors, as producers—i.e., to decontextualize the text."[109] In addition, prior to the 1950s, philosophical analysis involved an implicit rejection of the oral for the written because logical propositions—and thus rationality—were analyzed more easily in written form. Since the 1950s, however, Toulmin claims, "questions about oral *utterances* have displaced questions about written *propositions*."[110] The return to the oral is, according to Toulmin, one of the reasons for the resurgence of rhetoric as an academic field since the 1950s.

Accompanying a return to the oral is a return to the particular, the local, and the timely. The return to the particular is signaled by the revival of casuistry. The return to the local has caused a rejection of "Descartes' belief that factual realms of human study like history and ethnography lack intellectual depth, and can teach us nothing of intellectual importance."[111] The return to the timely has meant that, in addition to addressing questions that are timeless, philosophers are concerned with questions of the here and now. In addition, the humanization of modernity brings with it "a renewed acceptance of practice, which requires us to *adapt* action to the special demands of particular occasions."[112]

Toulmin's perspective, then, is that during the modern period, analytic argument replaced practical argument and absolutism replaced relativism. Toulmin argues for an emancipation of practical argument that rejects complete absolutism while avoiding total relativism. Since 1958, he pursued the goal of describing how such an emancipation could be attained. To date, he has argued that good reasons in ethics, practical argument, an evolutionary view of science, the revival of casuistry, and the humanization of modernity demonstrate the possibility of emancipation.[113]

Commentary

Toulmin's works have been the subject of much discussion and critique. Because each of his major ideas for emancipating arguments tends to draw different reactions, this discussion of responses to Toulmin is organized around his works, beginning with his dissertation. Not long after publication of the dissertation under the title of *The Place of Reason in Ethics* in 1950,

Richard Mervyn Hare presented a critique of Toulmin's good reasons approach to ethics.[114] Toulmin claims to be replacing a discussion of moral principles with a discussion of the process of giving good reasons in ethics. Hare believes that Toulmin's argument that reasons are good if they involve "the least conflict of interest attainable under the circumstances"[115] is itself a moral judgment of the kind Toulmin claims not to be making. Kai Nielsen joins Toulmin's side in this debate, claiming that "one need not make any further 'moral decision' to accept Toulmin's criteria for good reasons."[116]

Another critic of Toulmin's good reasons approach to ethics is Patrick McGrath.[117] He argues against what Toulmin claims to be the relationship between ethics and community, objecting to Toulmin's idea that "the scope of one's moral principles is bounded by the limits of one's community." McGrath claims that this idea is clearly incorrect because moral principles should have "equal validity for all. To interpret the principle: 'Promises ought to be kept,' as meaning: 'Promises made to members of one's community ought to be kept,' is obviously absurd."[118] Although controversial, Toulmin's good reasons approach to ethics neither had the influence nor attracted the response that the ideas he developed in *The Uses of Argument* did.

Initially, Toulmin's ideas in *The Uses of Argument*, especially his layout of argument, were not well accepted by philosophers because many of them deal with arguments concerning the nature of formal logic rather than rhetoric or practical logic.[119] J. L. Cowan argues, for example, that formal deductive logic is a useful tool for the criticism of actual discourse, and he denies the distinction Toulmin makes between data and warrants.[120] In general, however, philosophers believe that Toulmin has defined logic too narrowly and that, if defined more broadly, it is more relevant to everyday discourse than Toulmin claims. Albert L. Lewis summarizes this response: "(1) Toulmin erred in his interpretation of traditional logic, (2) his logic was not new since previous logicians had dealt with the problem and, (3) some of the concepts of his new logic were erroneous."[121]

James B. Freeman, in his book *Dialectics and the Macrostructure of Argument*,[122] provides the most comprehensive review of Toulmin's layout of argument. His critique has been called "the most sustained critique of Toulmin's notion of 'warrant' which I know in the literature."[123] Freeman rejects the distinctions Toulmin makes among the concepts of data, warrant, and backing. Still, Freeman accepts the broad outline of Toulmin's idea about practical logic partly because, according to Fisher, Toulmin's work "is the inspiration for Freeman's whole approach."[124]

Despite the negative reading of *The Uses of Argument* by philosophers, the book generally is applauded by teachers of rhetoric. One sign of Toulmin's wide acceptance among rhetoricians in the United States is the number of argumentation textbooks that include the Toulmin layout in part or in whole.[125] Toulmin's layout has gained approval not only for those interested in argumentation and debate but from those who teach communication. For example, James C. McCroskey shows how the Toulmin layout can be used in the basic speech course as an aid to audience analysis and speech organization.[126] Erwin P. Bettinghaus, searching for an adequate model for argumentative speeches, claims that Toulmin's is the "most adequate available model."[127]

Others have used the Toulmin layout of argument as a way to explain the process of persuasion and attitude change. Gary D'Angelo demonstrates that attitude theories, particularly the theory of Carolyn W. Sherif, Muzafer Sherif, and Roger E. Nebergall,[128] can be incorporated within the Toulmin layout of argument to provide a more adequate approach to the study of persuasion.[129] Another attempt to integrate the Toulmin layout of argument into a theory of attitude change can be seen in Gary Cronkhite's paradigm of persuasion.[130] Toulmin's approach also has been shown to be relevant to argumentation in interpersonal communication. For example, Brant R. Burleson extends Toulmin's conception of warrants to show how they are applicable to social reasoning processes evident in argumentation in interpersonal interaction.[131] His model of practical argument from *The Uses of Argument* even has been used to analyze an example of an ethical problem in sports and physical education.[132]

Just as Toulmin has critics among philosophers, he also has them among communication professionals. Jimmie D. Trent, for example, asserts that logic still has some relevance to argument and that Toulmin's ideas should not be allowed to divorce formal logic and practical argument completely.[133] Ray Lynn Anderson and C. David Mortensen, on the other hand, applaud and extend Toulmin's idea that context-invariant forms of logic are not relevant to argument in the "marketplace."[134]

Toulmin's most vocal critic in the field of rhetoric is Charles Arthur Willard, who claims that Toulmin's layout of argument is inadequate for building a descriptive model of argument. Willard claims that the layout contains three sources of distortion: "(1) the process of translation—translating the message into analytic premises; (2) the linguistic bias of argument models; and (3) the model's intrinsic isolation of context—both linguistic and sociopolitical."[135] Willard's claim initiated a debate among Charles W. Kneupper, Burleson, and Willard that extended over a series of convention papers and articles.[136] Willard claims that the study of argument ought to begin with a description of argument as a social phenomenon rather than as a prescription of ways to produce "good arguments." Without denying that prescriptions have their place, he argues that they should flow from carefully constructed descriptions of arguments. He believes that a substantial error in Toulmin's entire project may be that he begins with an attempt to distinguish good reasons from bad ones without first describing the nature of reason giving as a social process.[137]

Although *The Uses of Argument* and *Human Understanding* both make Toulmin's argument about the need to separate logic from rationality, the later work focuses largely on the philosophy of science and, for that reason, draws reactions from philosophers and historians of science. Even his critics speak highly of *Human Understanding*. For instance, R. S. Westfall maintains "historians of science today will recognize the force of Toulmin's argument."[138] He claims that "Toulmin's *Human Understanding* is a work conceived on a heroic scale. It confronts major philosophical questions, and it confronts them in a serious way."[139] Richard J. Blackwell believes that *Human Understanding* represents "a long, and in our opinion overdue and decisive, critique of the identification of rationality with logicality."[140] Still, Blackwell believes Toulmin is unclear about the nature of conceptual selection and variation, with one interpretation placing him "perilously close to the camp of the historical relativists who are sworn enemies" and another interpretation seeing him "captured in the formalist camp, the other group of sworn enemies."[141]

Another of his critics, Struan Jacobs, accepts much about Toulmin's notion of conceptual evolution as presented in *Human Understanding* but rejects his attempt to show specifics about how the process works: "It is easy enough to agree with Toulmin that in scientific *professions* major developments are apt to occur slowly. . . . Yet when we turn to intellectual ideas, there is no attempt by Toulmin to show they are modified by variation and selection, and lead by gradual transitions into new ideals."[142] In particular, some critics question Toulmin's idea of an impartial standpoint of rationality. Burleson, in an article comparing Toulmin's approach to rationality with that of Habermas, finds Toulmin's "impartial standpoint of rationality" unable to accomplish the goal of avoiding the perils of both absolutism and relativism. In Burleson's analysis, Toulmin's system lapses into the relativism it was intended to avoid.[143] Similarly, Jacobs claims that because the concept of impartial rational standpoint is so vague, "Toulmin has failed in his attempt to chart an epistemological middle way between the extremes of cognitive relativism and absolutism."[144]

Jonsen and Toulmin's ideas about casuistry have been the subject of varied responses. Keenan credits Jonsen and Toulmin with "the first methodological study of casuistry."[145] Although Keenan finds casuistry "attractive because of its attention to circumstances and to the uniqueness of the situation,"[146] he is concerned because "why something is right or wrong seems more *displayed* than *explained*. . . . Reasons are lacking."[147] He believes that casuistry as a form of moral reasoning must be able to "determine why certain forms of conduct are correct and others are not" and that "a principle-based ethics could not profitably accommodate the taxonomic method of casuistry."[148]

Another critic of Jonsen and Toulmin's perspective on casuistry, Kevin W. Wildes, believes that the "model of casuistry proposed by Jonsen and Toulmin is ill-suited to secular moral contexts" that exist within a morally pluralistic society that "does not admit a single standard of moral goods and judgment."[149] Wildes claims that Jonsen and Toulmin "assume that there are paradigmatic examples of right and wrong as well as widespread commonalities to be found in the cultural views of right and wrong."[150] In spite of his criticisms, Wildes believes that "a case based reasoning is still possible for clinical ethics" even if its shape is different from "the Catholic casuistry of Jonsen and Toulmin."[151]

James F. Tallmon defends Jonsen and Toulmin's ideas about casuistry in light of the arguments made by Wildes. Tallmon notes that "casuistry is not tied exclusively to Roman Catholic theology [as Wildes asserts]; casuistry also has deep roots in classical thought, roots that Jonsen and Toulmin underscore."[152] Tallmon believes that "the context of Roman Catholic theology can be distinguished from the method of casuistry, permitting that method to be deployed successfully in morally pluralistic contexts."[153] Another of Jonsen and Toulmin's supporters with respect to the issue of casuistry is John D. Arras, who welcomes the development of casuistry in the field of bioethics, claiming that "its account of moral reasoning . . . is far superior, both as a description of how we actually think and as a prescription of how we ought to think, to the tiresome invocation of the applied ethics mantra."[154]

Toulmin's work is important to the study of rhetoric in the last part of the twentieth century. Despite the varied responses to his ideas, they have stimulated a great deal of new work in argumentation, broadening both its concerns and its scope. In Willard's words, Toulmin's work has created "a renegade movement (Informal Logic), a new field (Critical Thinking), and the reinvigoration of an old one (Argumentation)."[155]

Bibliography

Books

The Abuse of Casuistry. Berkeley: University of California Press, 1988. (With Albert R. Jonsen.)

The Architecture of Matter. New York: Harper and Row, 1962. (With June Goodfield.)

Beyond Theory: Changing Organizations Through Participation. Philadelphia, PA: John Benjamins, 1996. (With Bjørn Gustavsen.)

Cosmopolis: The Hidden Agenda of Modernity. New York: Free, 1990.

The Discovery of Time. New York: Harper and Row, 1962. (With June Goodfield.)

An Examination of the Place of Reason in Ethics. Cambridge, UK: Cambridge University Press, 1950.

The Fabric of the Heavens: The Development of Astronomy and Dynamics. New York: Harper and Row, 1961.

Foresight and Understanding: An Enquiry Into the Aims of Science. Bloomington: Indiana University Press, 1961. (With June Goodfield.)

Human Understanding, Volume I: The Collective Use and Evolution of Concepts. Princeton, NJ: Princeton University Press, 1972.

An Introduction to Reasoning. New York: Macmillan, 1979. (With Richard Rieke and Allan Janik.)

Knowing and Acting: An Invitation to Philosophy. New York: Macmillan, 1976.

Metaphysical Beliefs. Ed. Alasdair MacIntyre. New York: Schocken, 1970. (With Ronald W. Hepburn and Alasdair MacIntyre.)

Night Sky at Rhodes. New York: Harcourt, Brace and World, 1964.

Norwood Russel Hanson: What I Do Not Believe and Other Essays. Dordrecht, Neth.: D. Reidel, 1972. (With Harry Wolf.)

The Philosophy of Science: An Introduction. London, UK: Hutchinson University Library, 1953.
Physical Reality: Philosophical Essays on 20th Century Physics. New York: Harper and Row, 1970.
The Return to Cosmology: Postmodern Science and the Theology of Nature. Berkeley: University of California Press, 1982.
Return to Reason. Cambridge, MA: Harvard University Press, 2001.
The Uses of Argument. Cambridge, UK: Cambridge University Press, 1958.
Wittgenstein's Vienna. New York: Simon and Schuster, 1973. (With Allan Janik.)

Articles

"Alan Donagan and Melborne Philosophy."*Ethics,* 104 (October 1993), 143–47.
"Alexandra Trap: 'Thoughts on the Eternal Scientist.' "*Encounter,* 42 (January 1974), 61–72.
"Astrophysics of Berosos the Chaldean."*Isis,* 58 (Spring 1967), 65–76.
"Brain and Language: A Commentary." *Synthese,* 22 (May 1971), 369–95.
"Can Science and Ethics be Connected?"*Hastings Center Report,* 9 (June 1979), 27–34.
"The Case for Cosmic Prudence." *Tennessee Law Review,* 56 (Fall 1988), 29–41.
"Common Law Tradition." *Hastings Center Report,* 11 (August 1981), 12–13.
"The Complexity of Scientific Choice: A Stocktaking." *Minerva,* 3 (Autumn 1964), 343–59.
"The Complexity of Scientific Choice II: Culture, Overheads or Tertiary Industry?" *Minerva,* 4 (Winter 1964), 155–69.
"Concepts and the Explanation of Human Behavior." In*Human Action.* Ed. Theodore Mischel. New York: Academic, 1969, pp. 71–104.
"Concepts of Function and Mechanism in Medicine and Medical Science." In*Evaluation and Explanation in the Biomedical Sciences.* Ed. H. T. Engelhardt, Jr., and S. F. Spiker. Dordrecht, Neth: Foris, 1975, 51–66.
"Concept-Formation in Philosophy and Psychology." In *Dimensions of Mind.* Ed. S. Hook. New York: New York University Press, 1960, pp. 211–25.
"Conceptual Revolutions in Science."*Synthese,* 17 (March 1967), 75–91.
"The Construal of Reality: Criticism in Modern and Post Modern Science."*Critical Inquiry,* 9 (September 1982), 93–111.
"Creativity: Is Science Really a Special Case?" *Comparative Literature Studies,* 17 (June 1980), 190–201.
"Critical Notice of R. Carnap, 'Logical Foundations of Probability.' "*Mind,* 62 (January 1952), 86–99.
"Criticism in the History of Science: Newton on Absolute Space, Time and Motion II." *Philosophical Review,* 68 (April 1959), 203–27.
"Crucial Experiments: Priestley and Lavoisier." *Journal of the History of Ideas,* 18 (April 1957), 205–20.
"Defense of 'Synthetic Necessary Truth.' "*Mind,* 58 (April 1949), 164–77.
"Descartes in His Time." In *Discourse on the Method and Meditations on First Philosophy.* Ed. David Weissman. New Haven: Yale University Press, 1996, pp. 121–46.
"The Language of Morals." *Philosophy: The Journal of the British Institute of Philosophical Studies,* 29 (January 1954), 65–69.
"Ethical Safeguards in Research." *Center Magazine,* 9 (July 1976), 23–26.
"Ethics and Equity: The Tyranny of Principles." *Law Society of Upper Canada Gazette,* 15 (1981), 240–56.

"The Evolutionary Development of Natural Science." *American Scientist*, 55 (December 1967), 456–71.

"Exchange of Letters Between Stephen Toulmin and Ernest Nagel." *Scientific American*, 214 (April 1966), 9–11.

"Exploring the Moderate Consensus." *Hastings Center Report*, 5 (June 1975), 31–35.

"Financing the Universities." *Spectator*, 208 (March 1962), 394.

"From Form to Function: Philosophy and History of Science in the 1950s and Now." *Daedalus*, 106 (Summer 1977), 143–62.

"From Leviathan to Lilliput." In *Celebrating Peace*. Ed. Leroy S. Rouner. Notre Dame, IN: University of Notre Dame Press, 1990, pp. 73–86.

"From Logical Analysis to Conceptual History." In *The Legacy of Logical Positivism*. Ed. Peter Achinstein and Stephen F. Barker. Baltimore, MD: Johns Hopkins University Press, 1969, pp. 25–53.

"From Logical Systems to Conceptual Populations." In *Boston Studies in Philosophy of Science*. Vol. 8. Ed. Robert S. Buck and Roger C. Cohen. Dordrecht, Neth.: D. Reidel, 1971, pp. 552–64.

"Historical Inference in Science: Geology as a Model for Cosmology." *Monist*, 47 (Fall 1962), 142–58.

"How Can We Reconnect Sciences With Ethics?" In *Knowing and Valuing: The Search for Common Roots*. Ed. H. Tristram Engelhardt. Hastings on the Hudson: Hastings Center, 1980, pp. 44–64.

"How Can We Reconnect the Sciences with the Foundations of Ethics?" *Hastings Center Series on Ethics*, 1981, pp. 403–23.

"How Was the Tunnel of Eupalinus Aligned?" *Isis*, 56 (Spring 1965), 46–55. (With June Goodfield.)

"Human Adaptation." In *The Philosophy of Evolution*. Ed. Uffe J. Jensen. New York: St. Martin's, 1981, pp. 176–95.

"In Vitro Fertilization: Answering the Ethical Objections." *Hastings Center Report*, 8 (October 1978), 9–11.

"Inwardness of Mental Life." *Critical Inquiry*, 6 (Autumn 1979), 1–16.

"Koestler's Theodicy: On Sin, Science, and Politics." *Encounter*, 52 (February 1979), 46–57.

"The Language of Morals." *Philosophy*, 29 (1954), 65–69.

"The Layout of Arguments." In *Professing the New Rhetorics: A Sourcebook*. Ed. Theresa Enos and Stuart C. Brown. Englewood Cliffs, NJ: Prentice Hall, 1994, pp. 105–25.

"Logic and the Criticism of Arguments." In *The Rhetoric of Western Thought*. 6th ed. Ed. James L. Golden, Goodwin F. Berquist, and William E. Coleman. Dubuque, IA: Kendall-Hunt, 1997, pp. 221–30.

"Logic and the Theory of Mind." In *Nebraska Symposium of Motivation*. Ed. W. J. Arnold. Lincoln: University of Nebraska Press, 1975, pp. 409–76. (With C. F. Feldman.)

"Ludwig Wittgenstein." *Encounter*, 32 (January 1969), 58–71.

"Ludwig Wittgenstein." *General Semantics Bulletin*, 37 (1970), 19–32.

"Medical Institutions and Their Moral Constraints." In *Integrity in Health Care Institutions*. Ed. Ruth Ellen Bulger and Stanley Joel Reiser. Iowa City: University of Iowa Press, 1990, pp. 21–32.

"The Moral Admissibility or Inadmissibility of Nontherapeutic Fetal Experiments." In *Medical Responsibility: Paternalism, Informed Consent, and Euthanasia*. Ed. Wade L. Robinson. Clifton, NJ: Humana, 1979, pp. 113–39.

"The Moral Psychology of Science." *Hastings Center Series on Ethics*, 1981, pp. 223–42.

"On the Nature of the Physician's Understanding." *Journal of Medical Philosophy*, 1 (March 1976), 32–50.

"Plausibility of Theories." *Journal of Philosophy*, 63 (October 1966), 624–66.

"Pluralism and Responsibility in Post-Modern Science." *Science, Technology, and Human Values*, 10 (Winter 1985), 28–37.

"Principles of Morality." *Philosophy*, 31 (1956), 142–53.

"Problem Statement and Tentative Agenda." In *Argumentation as a Way of Knowing*. Ed. David A. Thomas. Annandale, VA: Speech Communication Association, pp. 1–7. (With Richard Rieke.)

"Qattara: A Primitive Distillation and Extraction Apparatus Still in Use." *Isis*, 55 (September 1964), 339–42.

"Rationality and Reasonableness: From Propositions to Utterances." *Revue Internationale de Philosophie*, 50 (1996), 297–305.

"Reasons and Causes." In *Explanation in the Behavioral Sciences*. Ed. R. E. Borger and F. Cioffi. Cambridge, UK: Cambridge University Press, 1970, pp. 1–41.

"Recovery of Practical Philosophy." *American Scholar*, 57 (Summer 1988), 337–52.

"Rediscovering History." *Encounter*, 36 (January 1971), 53–64.

"Regaining the Ethics of Discretion: The Tyranny of Principles," *Hastings Center Report*, 11 (1981), 31–39.

"Reply." *Synthese*, 23 (March 1972), 487–90.

"Reply, On Prescribing Description." *Synthese*, 18 (October 1968), 462–63.

"Review Essay: A Sociologist Looks at Wittgenstein." *American Journal of Sociology*, 84 (January 1979), 996–99.

"Rules and Their Relevance for Understanding Human Behavior." In *Understanding Other Persons*. Ed. T. Mischel. Totowa, NJ: Littlefield and Rowman, 1974, pp. 25–60.

"Scientific Strategies and Historical Change." In *Philosophical Foundations of Science*. Ed. R. J. Sieger and Robert S. Cohen. Dordrecht, Neth.: D. Reidel, 1974, pp. 401–14.

"Scientist-Overlord." *Spectator*, 209 (July 1962), 104–05.

"Steering a Way Between Constructivism and Innatism." In *Language and Learning: The Debate Between Jean Piaget and Noam Chomsky*. Ed. Massimo Paitelli-Palmarini. Cambridge, MA: Harvard University Press, 1980, pp. 276–78.

"Teleology in Contemporary Science and Philosophy." *Neuve Hefte fur Philosophie*, 20 (1981), 140–52.

"On Teilhard de Chardin." *Commentary*, 39 (March 1965), 50–55.

"Tyranny of Principles." *Hastings Center Report*, 11 (December 1981), 31–39.

"You Norman, Me Saxon (Hamburg, Corsica, Stratford-Upon-Avon and Vermont)." *Encounter*, 51 (September 1978), 89–93.

"You Norman, Me Saxon: Reply." *Encounter*, 53 (August 1979), 80–81.

Endnotes

[1] Albert R. Jonsen and Stephen Toulmin, *The Abuse of Casuistry: A History of Moral Reasoning* (Berkeley: University of California Press, 1988).

[2] Stephen Toulmin, *Cosmopolis: The Hidden Agenda of Modernity* (New York: Free, 1990), p. 187. Excerpts from *Cosmopolis* reprinted with the permission of The Free Press, a Division of of Simon & Schuster, Inc.

3   Toulmin, *Cosmopolis*, p. 187.

4   Stephen Toulmin, *Return to Reason* (Cambridge, MA: Harvard University Press, 2001).

5   Unless otherwise noted, biographic information on Toulmin was obtained from the following sources: Ann Avory, ed., *Contemporary Authors* (Detroit, MI: Gale Research, 1982), p. 533; *Who's Who in America*, vol. 2, 42nd ed. (Chicago: Marquis Who's Who, 1982), p. 3354; and Jacques Cattel Pres, ed., *Directory of American Scholars*, vol. 4, 8th ed. (New York: R. R. Bowker, 1982), p. 541; Stephen Toulmin, "Logic and the Criticism of Arguments," in *The Rhetoric of Western Thought*, 6th ed., by James L. Golden, Goodwin F. Berquist, and William E. Coleman (Dubuque, IA: Kendall-Hunt, 1997), pp. 221–22.

6   Stephen Toulmin, "Logic and the Criticism of Arguments," p. 221.

7   Stephen Toulmin, "Logic and the Criticism of Arguments," pp. 221–22.

8   Toulmin, "Logic and the Criticism of Arguments," p. 225.

9   Wayne Brockriede and Douglas Ehninger, "Toulmin on Argument: An Interpretation and Application," *Quarterly Journal of Speech*, 46 (February 1960), 44–53; and Douglas Ehninger and Wayne Brockriede, *Decision by Debate* (New York: Dodd, Mead, 1963), especially chapter 8.

10 Brockriede and Ehninger, p. 44.

11 Toulmin, "Logic and the Criticism of Arguments," p. 225.

12 Jonsen and Toulmin.

13 Meg Sullivan, "Sharing an Academic Life With Students," *University of Southern California Chronicle*, available at http://www.usc.edu/ext-relations/news_se...2.24.html/Sharing_an_Academic_life_.htm. Accessed November 29, 2000.

14 "Playwright Arthur Miller Named the 2001 NEH Jefferson Lecturer in the Humanities." See http://www.neh.fed.us/news/archive/20010104.html. Accessed April 29, 2000.

15 Jonsen and Toulmin, p. 2.

16 Stephen Toulmin, "Regaining the Ethics of Discretion: The Tyranny of Principles," *Hastings Center Report*, 11 (1981), 31–39.

17 Toulmin, *Cosmopolis*, p. 75–76.

18 Toulmin, *Cosmopolis*, p. 30.

19 Toulmin, *Cosmopolis*, p. 24.

20 Toulmin, *Cosmopolis*, p. 24.

21 Stephen Toulmin, "Descartes in His Time," in *Discourse on the Method and Meditations on First Philosophy*, ed. David Weissman (New Haven, CT: Yale University Press, 1996), p. 124.

22 Toulmin, *Cosmopolis*, p. 48.

23 Toulmin, "Descartes in His Times," p. 127.

24 Toulmin, "Descartes in His Times," p. 143.

25 Toulmin, *Cosmopolis*, p. 55.

26 Toulmin, *Cosmopolis*, p. 62.

27 Toulmin, "Descartes in His Times," p. 133.

28 Toulmin, "Descartes in His Times," p. 135.

29 Stephen Toulmin, "From Leviathan to Lilliput," in *Celebrating Peace*, ed. Leroy S. Rouner (Notre Dame, IN: University of Notre Dame Press, 1990), p. 73.

30 Toulmin, *Cosmopolis*, pp. 160–61.

31 Toulmin, "From Leviathan to Lilliput," p. 81.

32 Toulmin, *Cosmopolis*, p. 161.

33 Toulmin, *Cosmopolis*, p. 167.

34 Stephen Toulmin, *The Uses of Argument* (Cambridge, UK: Cambridge University Press, 1958), pp. 107–22.

35 Toulmin, *The Uses of Argument*, p. 145.

36 Toulmin, *The Uses of Argument*, p. 212.

37 Jonsen and Toulmin, p. 7.

38 Toulmin, *The Uses of Argument*, p. 184.

39 Toulmin, *The Uses of Argument*, p. 182.

40 Toulmin, "Regaining the Ethics of Discretion," pp. 31–39.

41 Toulmin, "Regaining the Ethics of Discretion," p. 32.

42 Toulmin, "Regaining the Ethics of Discretion," p. 32.
43 Toulmin, "Regaining the Ethics of Discretion," p. 32.
44 Toulmin, "Regaining the Ethics of Discretion," p. 32.
45 Jonsen and Toulmin, p. 3.
46 Toulmin, "Regaining the Ethics of Discretion," p. 32.
47 Jonsen and Toulmin, p. 5.
48 Toulmin, "Regaining the Ethics of Discretion," p. 38.
49 Toulmin, *The Uses of Argument*, p. 185.
50 Stephen Toulmin, *Human Understanding, Volume I: The Collective Use and Evolution of Concepts* (Princeton, NJ: Princeton University Press, 1972), p. 66.
51 Toulmin, *Human Understanding*, p. 66.
52 Toulmin, *Human Understanding*, p. 65–66.
53 Toulmin, *Human Understanding*, p. 495.
54 Toulmin, *Human Understanding*, p. 92.
55 Toulmin, *Human Understanding*, p. 92.
56 Stephen Toulmin, *An Examination of the Place of Reason in Ethics* (Cambridge, UK: Cambridge University Press, 1950); Toulmin, *The Uses of Argument*; Toulmin, *Human Understanding*; Jonsen and Toulmin; and Toulmin, *Cosmopolis*. The ideas Toulmin developed in these five books constitute his emancipatory approach to practical argument. To represent his work as authentically as possible, these ideas are presented in the same chronological order in which he developed them.
57 George Edward Moore, *Ethics* (New York: Henry Holt, 1912).
58 Toulmin, *The Place of Reason in Ethics*, p. 5.
59 Toulmin, *The Place of Reason in Ethics*, p. 10.
60 Toulmin, *The Place of Reason in Ethics*, p. 11.
61 Toulmin, *The Place of Reason in Ethics*, p. 11.
62 Toulmin, *The Place of Reason in Ethics*, p. 29.
63 Toulmin, *The Place of Reason in Ethics*, p. 33.
64 Toulmin, *The Place of Reason in Ethics*, p. 29.
65 Toulmin, *The Place of Reason in Ethics*, p. 46.
66 Toulmin, *The Place of Reason in Ethics*, p. 50.
67 Toulmin, *The Place of Reason in Ethics*, p. 60.
68 Toulmin, *The Place of Reason in Ethics*, p. 147.
69 The information for this section is taken from Toulmin, *The Uses of Argument*, chapter 3; and Stephen Toulmin, Richard Rieke, and Alan Janik, *An Introduction to Reasoning* (New York: Macmillan, 1984), chapters 2–7. The information in both sources is similar, although a few terms have been changed. For example, the term *data* in *The Uses of Argument* is *grounds* in *Introduction to Reasoning*. Because *Introduction to Reasoning* is the most recent of Toulmin's writings on the subject, we have used the language of *Introduction to Reasoning* here. This decision was not an easy one because the older source, *The Uses of Argument*, was authored by Toulmin alone, while the more recent source was co-authored with Rieke and Janik. The increased emphasis on communication in *Introduction to Reasoning* is probably more than coincidental.
70 Toulmin, *The Uses of Argument*, p. 6.
71 Toulmin, Rieke, and Janik, p. 10.
72 Toulmin, *Human Understanding*, p. 313.
73 Toulmin, *The Uses of Argument*, p. 8.
74 Toulmin, *The Uses of Argument*, p. 36.
75 Toulmin, *The Uses of Argument*, chapter 1.
76 Toulmin, Rieke, and Janik, p. 8.
77 Toulmin, Rieke, and Janik, p. 8.
78 Toulmin, Rieke, and Janik, chapter 25.
79 Toulmin, *The Uses of Argument*, p. 175.
80 Brockriede and Ehninger, p. 544.

[81] Toulmin, Rieke, and Janik, p. 26.

[82] The content of this and all other examples of the layout of argument are from Toulmin, *The Uses of Argument*, while the form is consistent with Toulmin, Rieke, and Janik.

[83] Thomas S. Kuhn, *The Structure of Scientific Revolutions* (Chicago: University of Chicago Press, 1962); and Thomas S. Kuhn, *The Structure of Scientific Revolutions*, 2nd ed. (Chicago: University of Chicago Press, 1970).

[84] Toulmin, *Human Understanding*, p. 105.

[85] Toulmin, *Human Understanding*, p. 105.

[86] Toulmin, *Human Understanding*, p. 140.

[87] Toulmin, *Human Understanding*, p. 267.

[88] Toulmin, *Human Understanding*, p. 95.

[89] Toulmin, *Human Understanding*, p. 225.

[90] Toulmin, *Human Understanding*, p. 50.

[91] The impartial standpoint of rationality is discussed in Toulmin, *Human Understanding*, pp. 484–85.

[92] The revival of casuistry is discussed in Jonsen and Toulmin, pp. 304–32.

[93] Jonsen and Toulmin, p. 10.

[94] Jonsen and Toulmin, p. 307.

[95] Jonsen and Toulmin, p. 314.

[96] Jonsen and Toulmin, p. 314.

[97] Toulmin, "Regaining the Ethics of Discretion," p. 32.

[98] Jonsen and Toulmin, p. 35.

[99] Jonsen and Toulmin, p. 324.

[100] Jonsen and Toulmin, p. 14.

[101] Jonsen and Toulmin, p. 305.

[102] Jonsen and Toulmin, p. 327.

[103] Toulmin, *Cosmopolis*, p. 175.

[104] Toulmin, *Cosmopolis*, p. 180.

[105] Toulmin, *Cosmopolis*, p. 180.

[106] Toulmin, *Cosmopolis*, p. 181.

[107] Toulmin, *Cosmopolis*, p. 182.

[108] Toulmin, *Cosmopolis*, p. 186.

[109] Toulmin, *Cosmopolis*, p. 187.

[110] Toulmin, *Cosmopolis*, p. 187.

[111] Toulmin, *Cosmopolis*, p. 188.

[112] Toulmin, *Cosmopolis*, p. 192.

[113] Toulmin's latest book, *Return to Reason*, continues the development of his theory of argumentation. Regrettably, this book could not be included in any substantial way in this chapter since *Return to Reason* was published while this chapter was in press.

[114] Richard Mervyn Hare, rev. of *An Examination of the Place of Reason in Ethics*, by Stephen Toulmin, *Philosophical Quarterly*, 1 (1951), 372–75. See also Richard Mervyn Hare, *The Language of Morals* (Oxford, UK: Clarendon, 1952).

[115] Toulmin, *The Place of Reason in Ethics*, p. 224.

[116] Kai Nielsen, "Good Reasons in Ethics: An Examination of the Toulmin-Hare Controversy," *Theoria*, 24 (1958), 28.

[117] Patrick Mcgrath, *The Nature of Moral Judgement: A Study in Contemporary Moral Philosophy* (London, UK: Sheed and Ward, 1967).

[118] McGrath, p. 214.

[119] For a summary of the responses of logicians, see Albert L. Lewis, "Stephen Toulmin: A Reappraisal," *Central States Speech Journal*, 23 (Spring 1972), 48–55.

[120] J. L. Cowan, "The Uses of Argument: An Apology For Logic," *Mind*, 73 (1964), 27–45.

[121] Lewis, p. 50.

[122] James B. Freeman, *Dialectics and the Macrostructure of Argument* (New York: Foris, 1991).

[123] Alec Fisher, rev. of *Dialectics and the Macrostructure of Argument*, by James B. Freeman, *Informal Logic*, 14 (1992), 196.

152   Chapter Five

[124] Fisher, p. 196.

[125] For example, see Ehninger and Brockriede, chapters 8–15; Austin J. Freeley and David L. Steinberg, *Argumentation and Debate: Critical Thinking for Reasoned Decision Making* (Belmont, CA: Wadsworth, 2000); Halbert E. Gulley, *Discussion, Conference and Group Process* (New York: Holt, Rinehart and Winston, 1960), pp. 146–54; Gerald R. Miller and Thomas R. Nilsen, *Perspectives on Argumentation* (Chicago: Scott, Foresman, 1966); Glen E. Mills, *Reason in Controversy: On General Argumentation* (Boston: Allyn and Bacon, 1968), pp. 110–11; John F. Wilson and Carroll C. Arnold, *Public Speaking as a Liberal Art* (Boston: Allyn and Bacon, 1964), pp. 139–42; Russell R. Windes and Arthur Hastings, *Argumentation and Advocacy* (New York: Random, 1965), pp. 157–86; Richard D. Rieke and Malcolm O. Sillars, *Argumentation and the Decision-Making Process* (New York: Longman, 1997); Richard E. Crable, *Argumentation as Communication: Reasoning with Receivers* (Columbus, OH: Merrill, 1976); Karen C. Rybacki and Donald J. Rybacki, *Advocacy and Opposition: An Introduction to Argumentation* (Boston: Allyn and Bacon, 2000).

[126] James C. McCroskey, "Toulmin and the Basic Course," *Speech Teacher*, 14 (March 1965), 91–100.

[127] Erwin P. Bettinghaus, "Structure and Argument," in *Perspectives on Argumentation*, by Gerald R. Miller and Thomas R. Nilsen (Chicago: Scott, Foresman, 1966), pp. 130–55.

[128] Carolyn W. Sherif, Muzafer Sherif, and Roger E. Nebergall, *Attitude and Attitude Change: The Social Judgement-Involvement Approach* (Philadelphia, PA: W. B. Saunders, 1965).

[129] Gary D'Angelo, "A Schema for the Utilization of Attitude Theory within the Toulmin Model of Argument," *Central States Speech Journal*, 22 (Summer 1971), 100–09.

[130] Gary Cronkhite, *Persuasion: Speech and Behavioral Change* (Indianapolis: Bobbs-Merrill, 1969).

[131] Brant R. Burleson, "A Cognitive-Developmental Perspective on Social Reasoning Processes," *Western Journal of Speech Communication*, 45 (Spring 1981), 133–47. See also Marcus L. Ambrester and Glynis Holm Strause, *A Rhetoric of Interpersonal Communication* (Prospect Heights, IL: Waveland, 1984), pp. 310–15.

[132] Earle F. Zeigler, "Applied Ethics in Sport and Physical Education," *Philosophy in Context*, 13 (1983), 52–64.

[133] Jimmie D. Trent, "Toulmin's Model of an Argument: An Examination and Extension," *Quarterly Journal of Speech*, 54 (1968), 252–59.

[134] Ray Lynn Anderson and C. David Mortensen, "Logic and Marketplace Argumentation," *Quarterly Journal of Speech*, 53 (April 1967), 143–50.

[135] Charles Arthur Willard, "On the Utility of Descriptive Diagrams for the Analysis and Criticism of Arguments," *Communication Monographs*, 43 (November 1976), 314.

[136] See, for example, Charles W. Kneupper, "On Argument and Diagrams," *Journal of the American Forensic Association*, 14 (Spring 1978), 181–86; Brant R. Burleson, "On the Analysis and Criticism of Arguments: Some Theoretical and Methodological Considerations," *Journal of the American Forensic Association*, 15 (Winter 1979), 137–47; and Charles Arthur Willard, "The Status of the Non-Discursiveness Thesis," *Journal of the American Forensic Association*, 17 (Spring 1981), 190–214.

[137] Charles Arthur Willard, *Argumentation and the Social Grounds of Knowledge* (Tuscaloosa: University of Alabama Press, 1983), especially chapter 3; and Charles Arthur Willard, *A Theory of Argumentation* (Tuscaloosa: University of Alabama Press, 1989).

[138] R. S. Westfall, "Toulmin and Human Understanding," *Journal of Modern History*, 47 (1975), 69.

[139] Westfall, p. 693.

[140] Richard J. Blackwell, "Toulmin's Model of an Evolutionary Epistemology," *Modern Scholasticism*, 51 (1973), 63.

[141] Blackwell, p. 67.

[142] Struan Jacobs, "Stephen Toulmin's Theory of Conceptual Evolution," in *Issues in Evolutionary Epistemology*, ed. Kai Hahlweg and C. A. Hooker (Albany: State University of New York Press, 1989), p. 521.

[143] Brant R. Burleson, "On the Foundations of Rationality: Toulmin, Habermas, and the *A Priori* of Reason," *Journal of the American Forensic Association*, 16 (Fall 1979), 112–27.

[144] Jacobs, p. 522.

[145] James F. Keenan, "The Casuistry of John Major: Nominalist Professor of Paris (1506–1531)," *Annual of the Society of Christian Ethics*, (1993), p. 205.

[146] Keenan, p. 219.

[147] Keenan, p. 220.

[148] Keenan, p. 220.

[149] Kevin W. Wildes, "The Priesthood of Bioethics and the Return of Casuistry," *Journal of Medicine and Philosophy*, 18 (1993), 34.

[150] Wildes, pp. 34–35.

[151] Wildes, p. 45.

[152] James M. Tallmon, "How Jonsen Really Views Casuistry: A Note on the Abuse of Father Wildes," *Journal of Medicine and Philosophy*, 19 (1994), 103.

[153] Tallmon, p. 103.

[154] John D. Arras, "Getting Down to Cases: The Revival of Casuistry in Bioethics," *Journal of Medicine and Philosophy*, 16 (1991), 47.

[155] Willard, *A Theory of Argument*, p. 14.

6

RICHARD M. WEAVER

Rhetoric has been called the key to Richard Weaver's life work: "The word *rhetoric* was often on his lips. For him it had a rich and vital meaning."[1] He "taught rhetoric, he wrote about rhetoric, and he used rhetoric to present the truths in which he believed."[2] Weaver offers a rhetorical theory that features values, ethics, and culture as core concepts.

Richard Malcolm Weaver, Jr., was born on March 3, 1910, to Richard
Malcolm Weaver and Carolyn Embry Weaver in Asheville, North Carolina,
where his father owned a livery stable and raised thoroughbred horses.
When his father died of a heart attack in 1915, his mother, who was pregnant
with her fourth child, took Richard and his sisters to live with relatives in
Weaverville, North Carolina, a town founded by the family's ancestors. Two
years later, the family moved to Lexington, Kentucky, his mother's home-
town, where she resumed her career as a milliner.

Weaver attended the public schools of Lexington through the eighth
grade and then was sent to Lincoln Memorial Academy in Harrogate, Tennessee, a college preparatory school. He paid for the expenses for his three
years there by working in the school's kitchen. At the age of 17, Weaver returned to Lexington and enrolled in the University of Kentucky, describing
himself at the beginning of his schooling as "gloomy, ardent, stupid."[3] He
was prominent in literary, debate, track, and political circles and was initiated into Phi Beta Kappa in his senior year. After "many wayward choices,"[4]
he emerged from his undergraduate study in 1932 with a bachelor's degree
in English and a minor in philosophy.

Weaver was unemployed during the 1932–1933 school year—the middle
of the Depression—and was "rather bitter"[5] about the experience, which
may have influenced his decision to join the American Socialist Party. He
also was influenced by his professors at the University of Kentucky, most of
whom were social democrats or liberals. "I had no defenses whatever against
their doctrine,"[6] Weaver later explained. Weaver was an active member of
the Socialist Party, serving for a time as secretary of the local chapter. He
discovered, however, that while the "socialist program had a certain intellectual appeal" for him, he "could not like the members of the movement as
persons. They seemed dry, insistent people, of shallow objectives; seeing
them often and sharing a common endeavor, moreover, did nothing to remove the disliking." He performed his duties as secretary "with decreasing
enthusiasm" and began to feel that socialism was not a movement in which
he "could find permanent satisfaction."[7] He quit the party in 1934.

In 1933, Weaver was awarded a scholarship to Vanderbilt University in
Nashville, Tennessee. At that time, Vanderbilt was the chief seat of the
Southern Agrarians, a group of scholars and writers that included John
Crowe Ransom, Robert Penn Warren, Donald Davidson, and Allen Tate.
Their position opposed the doctrines of socialism in almost every way. They
sought to resist the ills of industrialism by a return to the agricultural economy of the Old South and argued against progress, science, and rationalism
as supreme values.[8] Weaver discovered that while he disagreed with the
Agrarians on social and political doctrine, he "liked them all as persons." He
found the "intellectual maturity and personal charm of the Agrarians" unsettling to his allegiance to socialism.[9]

The professor who influenced him most at Vanderbilt was John Crowe
Ransom, who taught literature and psychology, and under whom Weaver

wrote his master's thesis. Ransom "had the gift of dropping living seeds into minds," and Ransom's notion of the "unorthodox defense of orthodoxy"[10] was particularly intriguing to Weaver. He began to understand, after listening to Ransom discuss this idea, that many traditional positions suffered not so much because of inherent defect but because of the inept defense of those positions. Perhaps, he thought, he had been turned away from older, more traditional solutions to problems simply because they had been poorly defended.

Weaver received his master's degree from Vanderbilt University in 1934 and remained as a teaching fellow and doctoral student until 1936, when he left without completing his doctorate to take a position as instructor of English at Alabama Polytechnic Institute (now Auburn University). He then accepted a position as assistant professor at the Agricultural and Mechanical College of Texas in Lubbock in 1937. Weaver dates his "conversion to the poetic and ethical vision of life" from his contact "with its sterile opposite" at Texas A&M: "I encountered a rampant philistinism, abetted by technology, large-scale organization, and a complacent acceptance of success as the goal of life. Moreover, I was here forced to see that the lion of applied science and the lamb of the humanities were not going to lie down together in peace, but that the lion was going to devour the lamb unless there was a very stern keeper of order."[11]

In the fall of 1939, as he was driving across Texas to begin his third year of teaching there, Weaver realized he "did not *have* to go back to this job, which had become distasteful," and that he "did not *have* to go on professing the clichés of liberalism, which were becoming meaningless" to him. At the age of 30, Weaver switched his allegiance from socialism to conservatism, "chucked the uncongenial job,"[12] and enrolled as a teaching assistant in the doctoral program at Louisiana State University. His dissertation was an inquiry into the Southern mind, "The Confederate South, 1865–1910: A Study in the Survival of a Mind and a Culture."

During the 1943–1944 school year, Weaver served as a special instructor at North Carolina State College. In 1944, he joined the faculty at the University of Chicago, beginning as an instructor and working his way up to the rank of professor in 1957. At the University of Chicago, he taught courses in the humanities sequence dealing with history; philosophy; rhetoric; and the criticism of fiction, drama, and poetry. But he gave most of his time to the teaching of lower level, required writing courses such as freshman composition, in which he was dedicated "to helping students increase their skill in using the English language."[13] That he was successful was evidenced in 1949, when he was awarded the Quantrell Prize of $1,000 for best undergraduate teaching at the university. Two of Weaver's works reflect his dedication to the study and teaching of rhetoric and English—*The Ethics of Rhetoric* (1953) and *Composition: A Course in Reading and Writing* (1957).

Weaver's life in Chicago was characterized by order, routine, and simplicity. He lived in an apartment hotel located some distance from campus to give himself the pleasure of the daily walk back and forth. He taught his classes early in the morning, left his office for lunch at the same time every day—eating most of his meals in the university cafeteria—and returned to devote his afternoons to grading papers or taking care of the administrative details of the basic English courses. He then went home to pursue his own scholarly writing. During breaks and summers, which he spent with his mother in the home he had bought for her in Weaverville, he followed a precise schedule as well. His few interests outside of academia were the sport of rifle marksmanship and gardening. The purpose of Weaver's routine was clear to those who knew him: it freed his energies for the reading and writing that mattered to him as a scholar.[14]

Weaver lived a largely reclusive life and never married. He was characterized by privacy and reserve, as described by Eliseo Vivas: "He did not put you off, he did not hold you forcefully at arm's length, as some people do; but somehow you did not breach the reserve that kept his inwardness inviolate and inviolable."[15] But he occasionally gathered with friends and family, especially in North Carolina, as described by his sister Polly: "He enjoyed good food and liked beer. He and my late husband [Kendall Beaton] . . . used to sit up until the early hours talking and drinking beer. They both loved H. L. Menken [*sic*] and I have seen them exchanging Menkian [*sic*] barbs at the foibles of mankind in almost helpless glee. They got into politics and the state of the world, too, and after a number of beers my brother would raise his favorite battle cry: 'keep the barbarians out!' "[16]

Weaver preferred those things that are connected historically to a culture and that embody noble ideals. He did not see all new things and all progress as positive advances. He bought a car with the money won from the Quantrell Prize but gratefully abandoned it to a relative in Weaverville after experiencing difficulty navigating the streets of Chicago; his antimaterialist and antitechnological sentiments undoubtedly contributed to the car's abandonment as well. He traveled by train rather than plane, and he flew only once in his life—from California to Chicago—when he had to meet a schedule. He said he enjoyed the trip and admired the Grand Canyon from the air, but he did not fly again. The train, he felt, had been around for a century and had become part of the landscape and the language, and its continuity was important to him. Similarly, he plowed his land in Weaverville with a horse-drawn plow rather than a tractor. The horse has lived with humans for centuries, and Weaver took such relationships seriously.[17]

Weaver was highly regarded not only as a professor of English and rhetoric but also as a political conservative. Leading conservatives held him in esteem, and Weaver, along with Russell Kirk, Whittaker Chambers, James Burnham, Friedrich A. Hayek, and Ludwig von Mises, often is identified as an intellectual founder of the postwar conservative intellectual movement. The movement contained the libertarian economist, anticommunist, and traditionalist wings, with Weaver associated with the traditionalist philosophy, focused on preserving ancient Western traditions from a valueless material culture. Weaver's politics, then, were primarily cultural; he did not include in his political analyses discussions of issues such as economics or foreign policy.

Instead, he saw the conservative movement as the effort "to conserve the great structural reality which has been given us and which is on the whole beneficent."[18] Recognizing, however, that the conservative cause was "not getting across to the market in sufficient force and volume,"[19] he worked to provide intellectual and political legitimacy for conservatism by providing it with the strongest rhetorical defense possible.[20]

Weaver made numerous speeches defending the conservative cause; served as a trustee of the Intercollegiate Society of Individualists, a conservative youth action group; and helped found the conservative periodicals *National Review* and *Modern Age*. He won a citation from the Freedom Foundation for his pamphlet *Education and the Individual*, and he was honored by the Young Americans for Freedom at Madison Square Garden on March 7, 1962, sharing the stage with former president Herbert Hoover, South Carolina senator Strom Thurmond, and the soon-to-be Republican presidential nominee Barry Goldwater. His books, *Ideas Have Consequences* (1948), an analysis of the fallacies of modern life that launched Weaver's career as a nationally known intellectual conservative, and *Visions of Order* (1964), a description of the modern world that has lost its power to choose between good and evil, were major efforts by Weaver to address the state of the culture and to suggest conservative solutions for its regeneration.

Weaver had just accepted a one-year appointment as a visiting professor at Vanderbilt University when he died of a heart attack on April 3, 1963.[21] In addition to *Visions of Order*, four books by Weaver were published after his death—*Life Without Prejudice and Other Essays* (1965), *A Rhetoric and Handbook* (1967), *The Southern Tradition at Bay* (1968), and *The Southern Essays of Richard M. Weaver* (1987). Weaver's life perhaps best can be summarized as one that focused on the art of rhetoric: "In an age when most lives are divided and compartmentalized, his life had an enviable unity. In an age when words are cheap and the use of words is a skill cheaply held, he believed and taught and demonstrated that rhetoric is the most civilized and civilizing of the arts."[22]

Nature of the Human Being

Weaver's perspective on rhetoric rests on a particular view of the human being. He sees the human as composed of three parts—body, mind, and soul.[23] The body is the physical being that houses the mind and soul during life. It is self-centered and attempts to pull the individual downward toward excessive satisfaction of sensory pleasure. Left unchecked by the other components of the human being, the body is likely to be the cause of unethical behavior.

The second aspect of the human being, the mind, is composed of four faculties or modes of apprehension. The emotional or aesthetic faculty, which is largely contemplative, allows experiences of pleasure, pain, and beauty. The ethical capacity determines what is good and judges between right and wrong, while the religious capacity, which is essentially intuitive, involves a yearning for something infinite and provides individuals with a glimpse of their destiny and ultimate nature. The rational or cognitive capacity provides human beings with knowledge because it allows them to define concepts and order ideas.[24]

The soul or spirit, the third part of the human, is "an integrative power binding the individual into an intellectual, emotional, and spiritual unity which is his highest self."[25] It is composed "of wishes and hopes, of things transfigured, of imaginations and value ascriptions."[26] It is spiritual insight that guides the mind and the body either toward good or evil, depending on whether it has been trained well or ill.

Two additional characteristics complete Weaver's conception of the human being. Human beings are symbol using, which allows them to rise above the sensate level of knowledge to communicate feelings and values and thus to create a culture or civilization. They also are creatures of choice or free agents, and their "dignity arises from" this "power of choice."[27] Yet, for Weaver, freedom does not mean license to do anything desired. Rather, it means freedom to act according to criteria for choice making implicit in the notion of truth held by a culture; freedom is the means to actualize that truth.[28]

Knowledge and Truth

Weaver further divides the rational capacity of the human being into three kinds of knowledge or levels of conscious reflection: ideas, beliefs, and a metaphysical dream. The first level deals with specific ideas about things. These are the thoughts that individuals employ in the activity of daily living or facts about existing physical entities. The measurements of a room or the price of a new computer constitute knowledge at this level. These data direct the "disposition of immediate matters and, so, constitute . . . worldliness."[29] At this level, human beings respond to impinging circumstances in a habitual manner and with little deliberation. For example, the act of turning on a faucet, accomplished by taking physical entities and facts into account, is the result of knowledge at this level. Similarly, the observation that the past winter was not very cold constitutes knowledge at the level of fact.

The second level is that of beliefs, convictions, theories, laws, generalizations, or concepts that order the world of facts. A generalization about average amount of rainfall in an area and the scientific law that water freezes at zero degrees centigrade are examples of this level of knowledge. In the case of the observation about the weather last winter, a theory about that observation might be that global warming is causing higher temperatures during the winter months worldwide. Such theories and beliefs may be inherited from others or may be formulated from personal observations and reflections.

The third level of knowledge is the metaphysical dream, which is "an intuitive feeling about the immanent nature of reality."[30] This is the level of philosophical opinion, statements about the statements on the second level, or ideals. Because it concerns values and ideals, this is the level to which both ideas and beliefs ultimately are referred for verification. The metaphysical dream provides judgmental standards for the evaluation of all other knowledge. A statement about the sacredness of the natural environment and the need to preserve and protect it constitutes knowledge of the third order in the example of winter temperatures and global warming.

With each of the three levels of knowledge, humans impose something on the raw data of the world—they order, shape, and evaluate their experiences of those raw data. The nature of the world in which they live depends on the choices they make in terms of ideas, beliefs, and metaphysical dream. Without such an ordering, reason is impossible, for rational activities begin only after an appropriate perspective is gained that orders and shapes phenomena into a meaningful whole.[31]

Following Plato, Weaver depicts truth as residing in the ideal at the third level of knowledge. Truth is the degree to which things and ideas in the material world conform to their ideals, archetypes, and essences. He contends that "the thing is not true and the act is not just unless these conform to a conceptual ideal."[32] Truth, then, resides at the level of the metaphysical dream, not at the level of individual facts. The enumeration of facts at the first level of knowledge will not lead to truth, for "we do not find the secret of man's life in the study of things."[33]

Facts gain meaning only by reference to a higher conceptual scheme of reality: "Before we can have the idea of relative evaluation at all, we must have a *tertium quid*, a third essence, an ideal ideal, as it were."[34] If the facts used by someone appear to be incorrect, that has no necessary bearing on the truth. Such "wrong" facts simply suggest imperfect skill on the part of the rhetor in finding instances of the truth. In an unpublished essay about Mason Locke Weems, the first biographer of George Washington, Weaver explains the relationship he sees between fact and truth in his discussion of whether or not Weems's biographies are true:

> If they are not true in the sense of fidelity to fact, neither are they false in the sense of presenting a misleading picture. . . . Weems was very shrewd at guessing the integrating principle of man's character; and it is doubtful whether the most plodding scrutiny of the career of Washington, aided by all the apparatus of modern scholarship, has changed the impression of ingrained honesty which Weems sought to convey with his pretty tales and invented speeches.[35]

Weaver suggests that if "a small fact suited not his great fact, he shoved it aside as unfitted for his purpose."[36] The empirical level of facts, then, is interpreted in terms of the ideals of the third level so that a connection always is made between the fact and the ideal.

Nature of Culture

Weaver's notion of the metaphysical dream, or the third level of knowledge at which truth resides, cannot be understood apart from his conception of culture. Culture, for Weaver, does not consist of material goods such as "armrests and soft beds and extravagant bathing facilities," for these "cater to sensation."[37] Factors such as climate, geography, religion, race, liturgy, poetry, and mythology contribute to a culture, but a culture is defined largely by the imagination, the spirit, and inward tendencies: "A culture defines itself by crystallizing around . . . feelings which determine a common attitude toward large phases of experience. . . . They originate in our worldview, in our ultimate vision of what is proper" for humans as higher beings.[38]

At the heart of every culture is a center of authority, which Weaver calls the *tyrannizing image*. This center represents the cultural ideal or vision of perfection for which a society strives: "There is a center which commands all things, and this center is open to imaginative but not logical discovery. It is a focus of value, a law of relationships, an inspiriting vision. By its nature it sets up rankings and orders; to be near it is to be higher; to be far from it in the sense of not feeling its attraction is to be lower."[39] The tyrannizing image may be discerned in part through the uncontested terms of a culture.[40] These are terms that embody beliefs and values that are "fixed by universal enlightened consensus."[41] A term such as *freedom*, for example, was uncontested in America in the nineteenth century and simply was accepted without argument as representing the highest ideals of the culture. In some instances, the tyrannizing image is "a religious ritual; in others a sacred scripture; in others a literature which everyone is expected to know; codes of conduct," but it is always an "inward facing toward some high representation."[42]

The tyrannizing image of a culture contributes to its metaphysical dream because it inserts itself between individuals and their empirical experiences: "a developed culture is a way of looking at the world through an aggregation of symbols, so that empirical facts take on significance."[43] The tyrannizing image exerts subtle, pervasive pressures upon the members of a culture to conform to and to reject that which does not conform to the ideal. Thus, it exerts control over individuals' actions, serving as the "sacred well of the culture from which inspiring waters like magnetic lines of force flow out and hold the various activities in a subservience of acknowledgment."[44]

The tyrannizing image serves another function in a culture. Because it provides a structure for ordering and ranking, it also establishes hierarchy in the culture:

> Civilization is measured by its power to create and enforce distinctions. Consequently there must be some source of discrimination, from which we bring ideas of order to bear on a fortuitous world. Knowledge and virtue constitute this source, and these two things, it must be said to the vexation of the sentimental optimists, are in their nature aristocracies. Participation in them is open to all: this much of the doctrine of equality is sound; but the participation will never occur in equal manner or degree, so that however we allow men to start in the world, we may be sure that as long as standards of quality exist, there will be a sorting out.[45]

Because a tyrannizing image represents an ideal of excellence, it necessarily creates societal distinctions of all kinds according to degree of conformity to that ideal.

Despite the pressure exerted by the cultural ideal, individuals always have freedom of choice in their actions with regard to it. They may uphold the conception of truth of the culture, or they may place their own viewpoints above the expression of the ideal and the welfare of the culture. Proper motivation for action leads people to select the former option and to work to resolve the discrepancy between what is and what should be in the culture. Weaver recognizes, of course, that individuals never can comprehend the cultural ideal perfectly and often will fall short of enacting it. Yet, if the truth in the ideal is recognized and the individuals of a culture work toward its actualization, they will be united in a strong, vigorous culture.

Rhetoric and Dialectic

Language is the process through which the ultimate truth of the metaphysical dream is conveyed to the individuals of a culture. Two means are available for revealing truth through language—dialectic and rhetoric—although they both are imperfect vehicles for the demonstration of truth. For Weaver, dialectic is the means for attaining knowledge of universals and essences at the third level of knowledge; it is "a method of investigation whose object is the establishment of truth about doubtful propositions."[46] It is " 'abstract reasoning' " through such processes as the analysis of fundamental terms, categorization, definition, the drawing out of implications, and the exposure of contradictions.[47]

Weaver's notion of dialectic is limited in its application to dialectical rather than positive terms. Positive terms stand for observable objects capable of physical identification and measurement. They are terms whose referents are things that exist in the world, such as *rock, tree*, and *dog*. Arguments over such terms are not really arguments because the point of dispute can be resolved by accurate observation and reporting.

Dialectical terms, in contrast, are "words for essences and principles, and their meaning is reached not through sensory perception, but through the logical processes of definition, inclusion, exclusion, and implication."[48] *Justice* and *goodness* are examples of dialectical terms. Dialectic, for example, aims to "establish what belongs in the category of the 'just' rather than what belongs in the genus *Canis*";[49] the terms with which it deals concern values. The standard by which to judge competing value positions in dialectic is the ideal or the truth at the third level of knowledge. If the dialectician's "soul has its impulse in the right direction, its definitions will agree with the true nature of intelligible things."[50]

The capacity of dialectic to deal with universals and essences has appeal for Weaver; however, he realizes that limitations to the process exist. One limitation is that dialectic cannot move individuals because it lacks the ability to obtain commitment to a position or action. For instance, the speaker who has arrived at the position, through dialectic, "that 'magnanimity is a virtue' has . . . won our intellectual assent, inasmuch as we see the abstract possibility of this position in the world of discourse. He has not, however, produced in us a resolve to practice magnanimity."[51] As Weaver explains: "In sum, dialectic is epistemological and logical; it is concerned with discriminating into categories and knowing definitions. . . . That would be sufficient if the whole destiny of man were to know. But we are reminded that the end of living is activity and not mere cognition."[52]

A second problem with pure dialectic is that it is not involved with the actual world: "The dialectician knows, but he knows in a vacuum."[53] The dialectician's deliberations occur independently of the facts of a situation and with no necessary reference to reality. In addition, the process occurs apart from the culture in which the dialectician resides. The dialectician does not necessarily share the sentiments of the culture or community. If the dialectician shows no sympathy for or allegiance to the culture's institutions and values, the logic produced breeds distrust in the worth of any of the forms created by the culture because they are judged solely on whether they meet the requirements for logical perfection.

Weaver cites Socrates as an example of a dialectician who worked apart from his culture. Although he was a great dialectician and an ethical teacher, he was charged with and put to death for being a subverter and a corrupter when his dialectic offended the culture. Thus, Weaver asserts, those who believe that dialectic by itself should be practiced "are among the most subversive enemies of society and culture. They are attacking an ultimate source of cohesion in the interest of a doctrine which can issue only in nullity."[54] To "trust all to dialectic is a fast road to social subversion."[55]

Weaver's solution to the subversive nature of extreme dialecticism is rhetoric. He believes that the limitations of dialectic can be overcome and its advantages maintained through the use of rhetoric as a complement to dialectic. Weaver defines rhetoric as "truth plus its artful presentation,"[56] which means that rhetoric takes a "dialectically secured position . . . and shows its relationship to the world of prudential conduct."[57] It instills belief and action and cannot be separated from a concern with values. Weaver explains that "it is the nature of the conscious life . . . to revolve around some concept of value,"[58] which he sees as "the ultimate sanction of rhetoric."[59] The conception of value is derived from the tyrannizing image of the culture, and rhetoric ideally moves individuals in the direction of that image.[60]

Rhetoric is able to move individuals to act because it goes beyond mere scientific demonstration and relates to the world. It is directed to a particular audience in its particular situation. Rhetoric adds a consideration of the character and situation of the audience to the knowledge gained through dialectic: "The honest rhetorician therefore has two things in mind: a vision of how matters should go ideally and ethically and a consideration of the special circumstances of his auditors."[61]

Because rhetoric deals with action in real situations at the same time that it concerns ideals, it "is an essential ingredient of social cohesion";[62] it has an inevitable connection to culture. It functions as a bond for the members of a culture because it emanates from a group's imaginative picture of the world or its tyrannizing image. It conveys the permanent values of the culture and thus serves as a "common denominator of truth" for its members.[63] Rhetoric urges the individuals of a culture to move toward the tyrannizing image by acting in ways that bring them closer to that image. It also enables the members of a culture to talk together because they share basic premises.[64]

Rhetoric is able to serve as a bond for members of a culture because it is a storehouse of universal memory. The uses of words in a culture acquire a significance greater than the meanings individuals have for them and greater than their application to single situations. By embodying the experiences and meanings of the words of all individuals, rhetoric is "suprapersonal, uniting countless minds"[65] in their quest for the attainment of the tyrannizing image.

Although rhetoric should be used to move people toward the ideal, Weaver realizes that it is not always used in this fashion. It also can be neutral—not moving its audience at all—or it can be perverted to the use of base techniques and to serve evil ends. The evil or base speaker conveys attitudes of exploitation, domination, selfishness, superiority, and deception and frequently blocks clear definition and an honest examination of alternatives by discussing only one side of an issue. To lead an audience toward the good, however, requires a noble speaker who exalts the intrinsic worth of the audience and reflects such attitudes as respect, concern, unselfishness, and a desire to help the audience actualize its ideals.[66] Rhetoric, for Weaver, is not a value-free tool. It rests on fundamental assumptions that either do or do not align with the good, the true, and the ideal. Thus, the particular value positions to which rhetors are committed determine whether the rhetoric they employ is good and ethical or evil and base.[67]

Because rhetoric inevitably promotes values by reflecting choices among goods, Weaver sees all rhetoric as sermonic. It always is "a carrier of tendency";[68] it "is never innocent of intention, but always has as its object the exerting of some kind of compulsion."[69] As rhetors, then, "[w]e are all of us preachers in private or public capacities. We have no sooner uttered words than we have given impulse to other people to look at the world, or some small part of it, in our way."[70] If individuals' basic vision of the truth is good, their messages will urge others to virtuous action; if it is evil, they will encourage vice.

Weaver thus asserts that being objective about anything is impossible. A rhetorical or persuasive dimension is present even in a statement that says that a straight line is the shortest distance between two points: "The scientist has some interest in setting forth the formulation of some recurrent feature of the physical world, although his own sense of motive may be lost in a general feeling that science is a good thing because it helps progress along."[71]

Dialectic is abstract reasoning that seeks to establish understanding but does not engage the issues of the actual world. Rhetoric, in contrast, takes a position secured through dialectic and asks individuals to believe and to act on it. To separate the two is dangerous because rhetoric alone does not have knowledge of the truth, and an isolated dialectic does not engage the issues of the empirical world. Weaver explains:

> A failure to appreciate this distinction is responsible for many lame performances in our public controversies. The effects are, in outline, that the dialectician cannot understand why his demonstration does not win converts; and the rhetorician cannot understand why his appeal is rejected as specious. The answer . . . is that the dialectic has not made reference to reality, which men confronted with problems of conduct require; and the rhetorician has not searched the grounds of the position on which he has perhaps spent much eloquence.[72]

A sound rhetoric, then, presupposes dialectic, bringing together understanding and action. Weaver thus affirms an essential connection between dialectic and rhetoric.

Rhetorical Embodiment of Worldview

Weaver's belief that rhetoric expresses the ultimate values and worldview of its users is developed explicitly in his system of sources of arguments, grammatical categories, and ultimate terms.

Sources of Argument

Weaver believes that the type of argument a person habitually uses reveals much about that person and "is a surprisingly effective means of reading the character and intentions of the man behind the argument. . . . Once this truth is appreciated you find that you can judge a man not wholly by the specific thing he asks for but also by the way he asks for it."[73] The type of argument used, in fact, may be a better source of judgment about or "truer index in his beliefs than his explicit profession of principles."[74]

A connection can be made between the source of an argument and the philosophical position of the rhetor because sources of content for rhetoric lie in how individuals interpret and classify their experiences of reality. Sources for arguments are means for interpreting the universe or frames through which the world is viewed, and when speakers use particular arguments, they are asking their listeners not simply to follow a valid reasoning form but to agree with the particular view of reality being presented. Through the use of certain argumentative sources, rhetors say that they believe in and urge acceptance of a particular construction of the universe. They try to persuade the audience to read the world as they do. Weaver also asserts that these sources or types of argument can be ranked or ordered according to their ethical worth. Certain ways of arriving at conclusions and of arguing are better or more noble, in an ethical sense, than others.[75] The most ethical type of argument is that of genus and definition.

Genus and Definition.   One way of thinking about reality or interpreting experience is expressed in the language of philosophy as being, where the world is viewed in terms of things belonging to certain classes and having certain essences. This can be translated into argument by genus or definition. This type of argument relies on the presupposition "that there exist classes which are determinate and therefore predictable."[76] In presenting this type of argument, the rhetor refers the subject of deliberation to its class, and if the audience is sufficiently impressed with the actuality of that class, it grants that whatever is true of the class is true of the subject under consideration.[77] Suppose a robber accosts a woman, threatens her with a gun, and demands her money. Assuming she could get the robber to listen to argument, she might argue by genus or definition that what he is attempting is a crime, which is illegal.[78] Weaver also includes argumentation from example in this category of argument. An example, he suggests, always implies a general class.

Although they function in the same way and reveal similar worldviews, Weaver distinguishes between genus and definition as sources of argument. In argument by genus, a classification already is established and accepted in the minds of audience members. When a minister preaching to a fundamentalist congregation categorizes an action as a sin, for example, the argument is one of genus; the genus of sin is so well established that support for it is unnecessary. Support probably would not be necessary for the definition of crime in the argument to the robber; thus, it also is argument by genus. Argument by definition, in contrast, requires that the classification be established in the course of the argument. The rhetor must define the characteristics of a class and then may use the defined term as a genus. For example, the speaker who wishes to argue that women deserve equal rights with men first would have to establish that all human beings deserve certain rights.[79]

Argument based on definition or genus is the most ethical, according to Weaver, because it involves the interpretation of a subject by defining the fundamental and unchanging properties of its nature or being. It deals with permanent universals and essences: "That which is perfect does not change; that which has to change is less perfect. Therefore, if it is possible to determine unchanging essences or qualities and to speak in terms of these, one is appealing to what is most real in so doing. . . . The realm of essence is the realm above the flux of phenomena, and definitions are of essences and genera."[80] Those who habitually argue from genus are idealists, committed in their personal philosophies to the assumption that things have a nature. Use of this type of argument, according to Weaver, indicates that arguers have used dialectic tempered by rhetoric as a means of analyzing the situation. Thus, they hold knowledge at the level of universals.

Similitude.   A second way of thinking about reality is through relationship: one thing is seen to have a significant resemblance to something else.

This translates into argument by similitude, which involves the interpreta-tion of a subject in terms of similarity and dissimilarity. Here a rhetor draws a conclusion by suggesting that a subject "is like something which we know in fuller detail, or that it is unlike that thing in important respects."[81] This type of argument includes analogy, metaphor, figuration, comparison, and con-trast. Telling the robber that he would dislike his actions if he were the victim of them is argument from similitude. Another example would be arguing that marijuana should be legalized because alcohol is.

Similitude ranks second as an argumentative form in terms of ethics. Al-though rhetors search for the underlying essence or ideal that must be present for the argument to resonate with the audience, they are less confident about the ability to know the truth fully and to produce that essence or ideal for the audience. Because it is based ultimately on essence, however, argument by si-militude still is an ethical argument to use. It simply does not reveal the es-sence at its core as explicitly as does argument by genus or definition.[82]

Cause and Effect.   A third way of thinking about reality is through cause, where something is the known cause of a certain effect. Argument by cause and effect or consequence involves the interpretation of experience in a causal relationship. This type of argument attempts to predict the results of a particular action; the anticipated results then are used to determine whether or not that action should be undertaken. As with arguments from definition, these arguments may involve self-evident and widely accepted causal linkages, or the rhetor may have to establish them. A cause-to-effect argument would be the type used by a politician who argues that war causes inflation. In the case of the robber, the woman could tell him that the act of robbery will result in his having to spend years in prison. Although Weaver recognizes that "we all have to use it because we are historical" people, he sees argument by cause and effect as less ethical than the first two types be-cause it asks the audience to respond to a lower order of reality—"the realm of becoming."[83] This realm, where things are in flux, is a lower state of being than that of essence, the ideal, and the unchanging.[84]

Weaver believes that argument from circumstance is the least ethical type of causal argument that can be used. It reads surrounding circum-stances, accepts them as coercive, and says "Step lively."[85] The key consider-ation in such an argument is not what a thing is but in what directions the forces are piling up. Thus, it is the nearest of all the arguments to pure expe-diency. "I must quit school because I have no money" is argument from cir-cumstance, as is a reply to the robber of "I must surrender all of my money to you because you have a gun, are bigger than I am, and cannot be per-suaded by reason." Present circumstances are the overbearing consideration, and even the bond of cause and effect is not discussed. Weaver asserts this is the least ethical of arguments because it indicates that a subject has been an-alyzed at the level of perception of fact; the rhetor views facts as having philosophical primacy. Use of this type of argument amounts to a surrender of reason, and the arguer expresses an instinctive feeling that, in this situation, reason is powerless.[86]

Authority and Testimony.   Being, relationship, and cause and effect are internal ways of interpreting the world, but a fourth mode of interpretation—authority—is an external one. In this mode, statements made by observers and experts take the place of the direct interpretation of evidence; individuals whom the audience respects vouch for the truth. The force of argument by authority and testimony is not derived from the immediate subject matter of the discourse but from consideration of the competence and integrity of the witness: "If a proposition is backed by some weighty authority, like the Bible, or can be associated with a great name, people may be expected to respond to it in accordance with the veneration they have for these sources."[87] Using an argument from authority, the victim could tell the robber, "The Bible says that stealing is wrong." Arguing that all human beings are created equal because the Declaration of Independence claims they are is another example of such an argument. This type of argument differs from the other three not only in its reliance on external proof but in that it seldom stands alone as the primary source of an extensive argument.

Arguments based on testimony and authority have to be judged in a different way from arguments of definition, similitude, and cause and effect. An argument of this type is as good as the authority on which it is based. Because such testimony often embodies arguments from genus, similitude, and cause and effect, arguments from authority also can be judged by the standards appropriate to such arguments.[88]

Rhetorical-Historical.   Toward the end of his life, Weaver identified another category of argument, the rhetorical-historical argument. This mode of argument exemplifies his view of the essential connection between dialectic and rhetoric and synthesizes the arguments by genus, similitude, and cause and effect. Rhetorical-historical argument is a composite argument that requires a definition of genus or principle and a reference to historical circumstances. Weaver explores this argument in his study of the debate between Robert Hayne, senator from South Carolina, and Daniel Webster, senator from New Hampshire, on the disposition of unsold federal lands in 1830. He cites Hayne's assertion that South Carolina was patriotic to the Union as an example of the rhetorical-historical argument. Hayne first offered a definition of the Union and then turned to the historical record to show South Carolina's loyalty to it. The woman confronted by the robber might use rhetorical-historical argument by pointing out that robbery is legally defined as a crime and that the court's criminal records in the county reveal that numerous individuals like him were convicted and sent to prison for performing actions of the type he is attempting.[89]

In his discussion of rhetoric and dialectic, Weaver advocates that the rhetor hold a vision of the ideal but consider as well the special circumstances of the audience and its particular situation. The rhetorical-historical argument, which involves a synthesis of principle with cause and circumstance and the ideal with the concrete, explicitly points to Weaver's concern both for principle and the circumstances of a particular situation. Thus, it clearly keeps rhetoric and dialectic in their proper relationship as counterparts.

Grammatical Categories

The sources of argument used by a rhetor are not the only indication of philosophical position; grammatical choices also can reveal a rhetor's worldview. Different patterns of expression denote different interests in saying something. Knowledge of the ways in which various grammatical categories function can help a speaker "prevent a loss of force through friction," which "occurs whenever a given unit of the system of grammar is tending to say one thing while the semantic meaning and the general organization are tending to say another."[90] A knowledge of what various grammatical categories suggest in terms of philosophy enables a rhetor to achieve congruence between grammatical form and message content. There "is a kind of use of language which goes against the grain as that grain is constituted by the categories, and there is a kind which facilitates the speaker's projection by going with it. Our task is an exploration of the congruence between well understood rhetorical objectives and the inherent character of major elements in modern English."[91]

Among the grammatical categories that Weaver discusses as indicative of a rhetor's worldview are kinds of sentences. When the mind frames a sentence, it performs intellectual operations of analysis and resynthesis—taking two or more classes and uniting them in some way. The manner in which this unification is accomplished is revealing. A simple sentence, for example, "tends to emphasize the discreteness of phenomena within the structural unity,"[92] for its pattern is that of subject, verb, and object or complement, with no major competing elements. Such a sentence focuses attention on the classes involved, as in "Lillian is a professor" or "The children played." These types of sentences are often the style, Weaver asserts, "of one who sees the world as a conglomerate of things" or "who seeks to present certain things as eminent against a background of matter uniform or flat."[93] Weaver also sees such sentences as indicating an elementary level of perception or an "unclouded perspective."[94]

A complex sentence contains one or more dependent clauses and one independent clause; it is "the branching sentence."[95] In contrast to the simple sentence, it "does not stop with seeing discrete classes as co-existing, but distinguishes them according to rank or value, or places them in an order of cause and effect."[96] The complex sentence, "The students failed the exam because they did not study," for example, goes beyond simple perception. It suggests causal principle and grades elements according to a standard of interest. By the very structure of the sentence, the reader understands which point is primary. Those who use the complex sentence have performed a second act of analysis, in which the objects of perception, after being seen, are ordered.[97]

The compound sentence, which consists of two or more simple sentences joined in some way, may reflect "simple artlessness—the uncritical pouring together of simple sentences." It also may be a " 'mature' sentence when its structure conforms with a settled view of the world."[98] Such a sentence often gives a complete statement by offering two views of a subject—a view with an explanation or a qualifying view that seems to finish off the assertion. A sentence such as "Away is good, but home is best" shows a settled view in which the world is seen as a compensatory system in balance. In such a sentence, an abstract statement often is balanced by a more concrete expression of the same thing—a fact balanced by its causal explanation or a description of one part balanced by a description of a contrasting part. Such sentences convey the completion and symmetry that the world ought to have.[99]

Just as types of sentences selected are revealing of the rhetor, so are the types of words or parts of speech that the rhetor selects. A noun or name word is a word for a material or conceptual substance with a being that is complete rather than in process. Nouns deal with essences, which have a higher degree of being than actions or qualities.[100] Adjectives, in contrast, are words of secondary force and status. They are added to nouns and are attributes conceptually dispensable to the substance to which they are joined. If a thing to be expressed is real, it is expressed through a noun. If it is expressed largely through adjectives, something is defective in its reality because it requires secondary support. For example, the statement "Have some white milk" would make most people curious, and they would suspect "some defect in the original image which is being made up."[101] Of course, in some situations, modifiers do make a useful contribution, but for Weaver, a style that relies heavily on adjectives suggests a lack of confidence about essences and reality on the part of the rhetor.[102]

Verbs, or words that describe actions or states of being, rank with nouns in force. They represent a process or state of becoming whereby things change while still maintaining the essence of their identities. Weaver uses an example of the political state to demonstrate the "paradox of both being and becoming":[93]

> The same process is visible even when we look at the political state. It persists under one name, and it may even affirm in its organic law that it is indestructible. But its old leaders pass on or are removed, and new ones appear. After a twenty-year absence, one would come back and find the leaders looking different in almost any country. But while these individual particles are being shuffled and replaced, "the state" goes on, maintaining some character and identity through all the changes.[104]

A style that uses verbs is a vigorous one because it reflects the rhetor's ability to label the quality of an action while at the same time recognizing the essence of a state of being.[105]

Weaver also examines adverbs, conjunctions, prepositions, and phrases and sees each as serving a rhetor in various ways.[106] A rhetor's use of the various parts of speech and types of sentences allows the creation of rhetoric that functions formally and substantively to create the force desired. At the same time, an audience can use these grammatical categories to assess the worldview of the rhetor.

Ultimate Terms

Yet another way by which rhetors' worldviews can be revealed is through the ultimate terms on which they rely. Ultimate terms are terms to which the highest respect is paid in a culture and to which the populace appears to attribute the greatest sanction. Such terms are rhetorical absolutes in that they generally are uncontested and are widely accepted by members of a culture. Unassailable terms because they represent the ideal or tyrannizing image of a culture, ultimate terms are a primary rhetorical means for motivating individuals to push forward toward that ideal: "We have shown that rhetorical force must be conceived as a power transmitted through the links of a chain that extends upward toward some ultimate source. The higher links of that chain must always be of unique interest to the student of rhetoric, pointing, as they do, to some prime mover of human impulse."[107]

Weaver divides ultimate terms into three major categories: god, devil, and charismatic terms. A god term is a term "about which all other expressions are ranked as subordinate. . . . Its force imparts to the others their lesser degree of force, and fixes the scale by which degrees of comparison are understood."[108] In other words, a god term carries the greatest blessing in a culture and has the capacity to demand sacrifice.

Several terms may compete for the ultimate position if a strong religion is not present in a culture. In the 1950s, when Weaver was writing, *progress* was a god term in American culture. *Fact* also was a god term; "it is a fact" meant it was the kind of knowledge to which all other knowledge must defer. *American* was another god term—one that has maintained its god status. It tends to be identified with that which is destined to be or the goal toward which all creation moves, and a country's civilization often is judged by its resemblance to the American model.[109] *Technology* is currently a god term. Virtually anything gains value by its use of and association with technology.

Devil terms, the counterpart of god terms, are "terms of repulsion" that designate whatever is perceived as the enemy or greatest evil in a culture.[110] In U.S. society, *Communism* is a devil term, as political enemies generally are; *Tory, Nazi,* and *Fascist* all have been devil terms for Americans in the past. *Poverty* and *welfare* also are current devil terms in U.S. culture. These are not ultimate in the way that god terms are, however, because they are the counterfeit of the good and do not represent what is ultimate, unconditional, and true.

Charismatic terms function somewhat differently from god and devil terms. Individuals are able to understand the appeal of god and devil terms through their connection with something they apprehend—something derived from observable aspects of the world. In contrast, charismatic terms seem to operate independently of referential connections. They "have a power which is not derived, but which is in some mysterious way given." Their meaning seems to come from "a popular will that they *shall* mean something. In effect, they are rhetorical by common consent, or by 'charisma.' "[111] As is the case with charismatic leaders, where the populace gives them a power that cannot be explained through their personal attributes alone, the charismatic term is given its load of impulsion without reference and functions by convention. *Freedom* and *democracy* are charismatic terms in U.S. culture. Individuals demand sacrifice in the name of these terms, yet the referents attached to them tend to be obscure and often contradictory. In fact, Weaver says, individuals may resist the attempt to define such terms, perhaps fearing that a term defined explicitly will have its charisma removed.

Just as the ultimate terms used in a culture reveal the ideals held by the members of that culture, the ultimate terms used by a particular rhetor reflect a particular vision of the world. An individual's ultimate terms suggest the degree to which that vision contributes to or detracts from the effort to move the culture closer toward the truth and the perfection embodied in its tyrannizing image. To discover that the god and devil terms of a culture or rhetor are inappropriate, reflecting values out of line with the tyrannizing image, should encourage rhetors to persuade others to see the error, as Weaver himself attempts to do in his critique of culture.

Decline of Rhetoric

Weaver does not write about culture and the role rhetoric plays in it only on a theoretical level. He also applies his ideas to U.S. culture to evaluate and assess it. In this role, he sees himself as "a kind of doctor of culture"— an individual "who may entertain hope of doing something about a culture that is weakening."[112] He explains his concern: "Those who argue that our civilization is advancing are safe as long as they stick to what is above the surface, and they can usually smother you with statistics. But as soon as one peers beneath the surface and looks at what is happening to the only sources of order man has, one sees that those are being seriously weekened [*sic*] if not destroyed, in which case the great superstructure is in danger of collapse."[113] Weaver points to many signs that U.S. culture is degenerating, among them an uncritical homage to the theory of evolution; radical egalitarianism; pragmatism; cultural relativism; materialism; an emphasis on techniques at the expense of goals; idolization of youth; progressive education; disparagement of historical consciousness; the deleterious effects of the mass media; and degenerate literature, music, and art.[114]

For Weaver, one of the most alarming signs of the culture's degeneration is the decline of rhetoric. Weaver sees public rhetoric as reflecting the corrupt and unsound foundations of current thinking. A century ago, rhetoric was regarded as the most important humanistic discipline taught in college. That position of status and value no longer exists: "the wheel of fortune would seem to have turned for rhetoric; what was once at the top is now at the bottom, and because of its low estate, people begin to wonder on what terms it can survive at all."[115]

The decline of rhetoric is evident in who currently is considered qualified to teach it. In the nineteenth century, "to be a professor of rhetoric, one had to be *somebody* . . . a person of gifts and imagination."[116] Now, however, the teaching of rhetoric is left to almost anyone who is willing to teach it: "Beginners, part-time teachers, graduate students . . . and various fringe people, are now the instructional staff of an art which was once supposed to require outstanding gifts and mature experience."[117]

The degeneration of rhetoric further is evidenced in the view that language is relative, "that language, like every other phenomenon, has to be viewed as part of a changing world."[118] Fixed significations for words or an absolutist position from which the application of words can be judged "right" or "wrong," as was the case in earlier times when cultures were more stable, no longer exist. Meanings now depend on the time and place in which the words are used, the perspectives of the users, and estimates as to what the majority of individuals will accept.

Weaver is not arguing that the meanings of words never can change. Change is essential when unsatisfactory terms in a culture are clarified through dialectic. Such changes, however, occur according to two constraints. The first is the convention in effect in the culture. Because individuals are part of a community of language users, a change in language should not be made unless that community endorses it. Words are tied to objects via individuals' minds. Thus, a language—if it is to be shared by individuals—cannot exist unless "a oneness of mind"[119] lies behind it. Language rests on a consensus or common point of view of things and thus serves as a covenant: "It is in the nature of a covenant to be more than a matter of simple convenience, to be departed from for light and transient causes. A covenant . . . binds us at deeper levels and involves some kind of confrontation of reality. When we covenant with one another that a word shall stand for a certain thing, we signify that it is the best available word for that thing in the present state of general understanding."[120]

Weaver provides an example of the notion of a covenant as agreement that a certain symbol shall be attached to a certain object or idea: "It has been agreed that 'sweet' stands for one kind of sensory response and 'sour' for a very different one, and nobody can singly on his own volition switch these two around, anymore than he could tell the clerk in a store that in his lexicon five is more than ten and that therefore he ought to have change for his five dollar bill when he has made a ten dollar purchase."[121] Language cannot be changed by a single individual as a matter of whim but is subject to the convention of the culture concerning language.

A second constraint on changes in language is linked to the ultimate and universal truth embodied in words. From a dialectical perspective, words hold meanings that theoretically are absolutely right. Meanings for words include an awareness of a meaning beyond an everyday, obtuse understanding of a word. This meaning is the one that reflects the high ideals of the culture and that individual members as yet may not understand fully. Thus, words function not as a description of experience at the level of sensation but as a window to glimpse ultimate truth. Individuals cannot change their meanings for words without effecting change at the level of universals and essences. Meanings, Weaver believes, therefore should not change without careful consideration of the consequences.[122]

Finally, the decline of rhetoric is evidenced in the fact that while it once was taught as the art of speaking truthfully, it now has become the art of speaking usefully. According to Weaver, students previously were taught a conception of the true and the ideal through rhetoric. Today, they are taught how to use language to better their position in the world, to get whatever they want, or to prevail with verbal deception. Teachers of rhetoric currently teach sophistry or etiquette rather than the terms that constitute a standard for truth in the culture, and this view is a major enemy of true rhetoric.[123]

In spite of his pessimism about the degeneration of culture, evidenced in part in the decline of rhetoric, Weaver sees hope for the restoration of culture. Such a process would involve the revitalization of memory or the recreation of the value of history as well as a restoration of respect for the right to exist of things not of individuals' own creation, including nature, other people, and the past. Another essential ingredient is a renewed emphasis on the right of private property, which Weaver sees as a relationship or identification between individuals and their substance. Property helps individuals express their being, encourages virtues such as providence in the maintenance of the property, and insures quality in many areas of life as individuals assume responsibility for the products they create and with which their names are connected.[124]

Also essential to the revitalization of culture is the restoration of rhetoric because it is a vehicle of order that enables individuals to understand one another. To restore rhetoric to its proper place in a culture, rhetorical training is needed that features the study of a number of subject areas. Poetry should be studied because great poets are the quickest to apprehend necessary truth. The study of dialectic is important because "it involves the science of naming"[125] or definition. It enables the student to see limitation and contradiction—to learn, in effect, how to think. Foreign languages also should be studied, including Latin and Greek, for their study discourages slovenliness in the use of language: "Focusing upon what a word means and then finding its just equivalent in another language compels one to look and to think before he commits himself to any expression."[126]

Although most teachers of rhetoric probably would agree that the objective of courses in rhetoric is to make students more articulate, Weaver asserts that their duty should not stop there. About what, Weaver asks, do they wish to make students articulate? Those "who instruct in the art of speech are turning loose upon the world a power. Where do we expect the wielders of that power to learn the proper use of it?"[127] Teachers of rhetoric must assume responsibilities they currently do not.

The teacher of rhetoric must be a definer, a namer, and an orderer of the universe of meanings: "The world has to be named for the benefit of each oncoming generation, and who teaches more names than the arbiter of the use of language?"[128] This means that the teacher must discover and show essential values and deal with the subject matter of essences or the structure of reality. If a teacher, for example, assigns an essay or speech on the topic of democracy, that teacher must be able to tell students what the term *democracy* names or means. For Weaver, a teacher of rhetoric is one who names well—someone who gives the proper names for things and reflects the tyrannizing image of the culture. If teachers are going to participate in the redemption of culture, they must "desert certain primrose paths of dalliance and begin the difficult, the dangerous, work of teaching men to speak and to write the truth."[129] Weaver's view of the proper role of the teacher leads him to see the teacher as determining the fate of each student: "I sometimes say to classes: when a teacher walks into a room, part of your fate walks into the room. Because that teacher is going to determine something for you—an attitude, a conviction, or an evaluation. . . . [H]is personality and what he communicates to the class are going to leave their mark or their residue."[130]

Those who oppose Weaver's view of education may argue that the teacher must be very arrogant to know what things really are and to name them. The teacher must transmit respect for the knowledge that has served to construct a providential social order, and this act is an arrogant one, to some degree: "By what act of arrogance do we set ourselves up as teachers? There are two postulates basic to our profession: the first is that one man can know more than another, and the second is that such knowledge can be imparted. Whoever cannot accept both should retire from the profession and renounce the intention of teaching anyone anything."[131] Still others would argue, in opposition to Weaver's position, that teachers should present all sides of a question, giving all possible names previously and currently applied to a thing and allowing students to choose among the names. Weaver's reply is that this position assumes "that there are sources closer to the truth than are the schools and that the schools merely act as their agents. It would be interesting," Weaver muses, "to hear what these sources are."[132]

Weaver's program for teachers of rhetoric, he admits, requires courage. It "is an invitation to lead the dangerous life. Whoso comes to define comes bearing the sword of division."[133] The consequences of these actions, however, are ultimately beneficial: "The teacher will find himself not excluded from the world but related to it in ways that may become trying. But he will regain something that has been lost in the long dilution of education, the standing of one with a mission. He will be able, as he has not been for a long while, to take his pay partly in honor."[134]

Another consequence of such a role for the teacher is that it is incompatible with student-centered education, where everything is adapted to students according to their limitations. In such an approach, no ideals are set by which students are to measure themselves. In contrast, Weaver supports a system in which teachers of rhetoric "will take on an authority which some mistake for arrogance. The student will learn, however, that the world is not wholly contingent, but partly predictable, and that, if he will use his mind rightly, it will not lie to him about the world."[135]

Commentary

Weaver has been described as a "Socialist Party member who became a conservative crusader, a Southern Agrarian who exiled himself to a northern megalopolis, and an academic rhetor who dialectically dissected contemporary culture."[136] This description of Weaver, with its paradoxes, explains why the student of Weaver "appears to be hard put to it to 'classify' Richard Weaver, or to say what he was up to without, pretty soon, sticking his foot in his mouth."[137]

A number of different frameworks have been suggested by which to interpret and understand Weaver's thinking and writing. Many have labeled him a *Platonist*; others have said he only was oriented toward Platonism and held an appreciation for it. Some of his ideas—such as his belief in the reality of transcendentals and the primacy of ideas—clearly are in line with Plato's thinking.[138] Others argue that Weaver's work best is interpreted in a framework of Christian theology. Some interpreters believe that Weaver's thinking reveals a religious foundation and character to his mind, so that while he never explicitly stated he was a Christian, his position is markedly Christian. Another view, exemplified by Robert Hariman, is that Christian language is important in Weaver's work but that his use of that language is doctrinally empty. In other words, he appropriates religious terms to transpose or secularize them to generate rhetorical power.[139] Still others, including Charles Follette, have argued that Weaver's thinking does more than simply appropriate religious terms for his purposes. Follette believes that Weaver takes God seriously and assumes a God-based theological stance that affects his entire perspective on rhetoric.[140]

Christianity and Platonism may not be incompatible as frameworks for interpreting Weaver. The Platonic transcendent ideals on which Weaver focuses may originate, from a Christian perspective, in God. In fact, Weaver aligned himself with both the traditions of Platonism and Christianity in a letter responding to a review of *Ideas Have Consequences* and appeared to see them as quite compatible: "I am quite willing to be identified with the not inconsiderable number of thinkers in the Platonic-Christian tradition who have taken the same stand."[141]

Weaver's capacity to relate his work to a number of conceptual frameworks and to deal with a variety of disciplines has been a point of criticism of his work. He "spent the major part of his working day . . . swimming far from the safe shores of his own competence towards high seas that were beyond his depth," commented Vivas. "A rhetor doing the work of a philosopher, he tackled problems for which he was not equipped."[142] This was evident, his critics have asserted, in that he seemed to be unaware of, to ignore, or to misinterpret relevant material. Richard L. Johannesen, for example, has questioned him for misinterpreting the General Semanticists' position.[143]

Similarly, respondents such as Johannesen, Rennard Strickland, Ralph T. Eubanks, and Russell Kirk have criticized Weaver's use of predominant types of argument to discover a rhetor's philosophical because he seems to ignore the possibility that the form an argument assumes simply may be a rhetorical choice by a rhetor.[144] Other critics have noted that the evidence Weaver uses to support the relationship between form of an argument and worldview is weak. When he attacks science, with its materialistic, mechanistic, and deterministic concepts, Herbert J. Muller points out, he is "seemingly unaware that physicists themselves have scrapped such concepts."[145] Even in his works on rhetoric, he sometimes exhibits a disregard for the rhetorical scholarship of the past, and "the result sometimes is a quite needless tone of ingenuousness." For example, in his essay on the *Phaedrus*, Donald C. Bryant asserts, Weaver discovers "what has long been known, that the *Phaedrus* is a dialogue on rhetoric."[146] Most critics, however, are not willing to dismiss Weaver's entire system of thought because of such problems, for "he nearly always returned from his adventures with something worthwhile to show for them."[147]

Others fault Weaver for the provincialism and ethnocentrism of his thinking—deriving in part from his strong allegiance to his Southern identity. G. Thomas Goodnight, for example, asserts that Weaver's provincialism limits his thinking.[148] "Given any knowledge of the history of civilization," echoes Muller, Weaver's certitudes "look arrogantly provincial."[149] He ignores the great civilizations of the East, and his "universal, eternal truths" are those of Westerners or Southerners. He does not think, as a result of his provincialism, in truly universal terms "of other forms of idealism and other systems of truth" besides his own.[150]

Despite the identification of such problems with Weaver's work, critics recognize his substantial influence on conservatism. He has been called a "powerful intellectual force in the American conservative movement of the post–World War II period,"[151] and his book *Ideas Have Consequences* has been called "the informing principle of the contemporary American conservative movement."[152] Willmoore Kendall suggests that "it and it alone among American Conservative books, is the one that they [conservatives] must place on their shelves beside *The Federalist*, and confer on it, as on *The Federalist*, the political equivalent of biblical status."[153] It will prepare the reader "as no other book, not even *The Federalist* will prepare you, for your future encounters with the protagonists of the Liberal Revolution, above all by teaching you how to drive the debate to a deeper level than that on which our present spokesmen are engaging the Liberals."[154] Weaver, in fact, has been cited as someone who brought conservatives together into a cohesive movement:

That movement had, of course, its roots in the scattered remnants of opposition which remained after Roosevelt's revolution of 1932. But the groups that stood against that tidal wave were diverse, often unidimensional, without cohering principle to hold them together and make a single movement of them. . . .

There did not exist anything in the nature of a broadly principled, coherent conservative movement. In the last fifteen or twenty years such a movement has been welded in thought and action. What is remarkable is the extent to which the attitudes and principles that characterize that movement are prefigured in *Ideas Have Consequences*.[155]

Others have noted that Weaver should be credited for the accuracy of his predictions about the course of Western culture. Joseph Scotchie suggests that Weaver "should be read as one of the great post–World War II prophets of Western decline, especially of an alienated, rootless society."[156] The indicators of the decline of culture to which he pointed have intensified in succeeding decades, evidenced by high divorce rates, the dehumanizing effects of the corporate world and technology, and the destruction of civil communities. What is clear currently is that "the life of discipline and forging, of struggle and error, the grand drama" where the human soul "is at stake is deemed more and more irrelevant."[157]

Weaver's contributions to rhetorical thought are of particular significance. Although he may be criticized for his normative approach, he is considered to have made a solid contribution to re-establishing rhetoric as central among the arts of thought and language. His concepts of god and devil terms, the tyrannizing image, the hierarchy of modes of argument, and the sermonic nature of language continue to be widely used in contemporary rhetorical criticism. His writings on rhetoric were enhanced by his own powerful use of rhetoric. Rhetoric "in Weaver's hands was a gleaming, powerful instrument. He used it on the problems of English scholarship, on language, on politics, and when he was through something new had been established; outlines and interior relationships came into the light."[158]

What characterizes Weaver's thought across all of the spheres in which he worked, however, is the authenticity and consistency of his thought, which came from his coherent and fully examined attitudes. Although his "arguments were not always the best," Vivas explains, "the attitudes from which his rejections and acceptances issued were for the most part unerring. Weaver was authentic in the original sense of the term."[159] Weaver had the courage to stick to his core of values and his own vision, even when they were unpopular: "What he wrote was designed to please no one's fancy but only . . . to make what he thought of as his own modest contribution to the disclosing of a portion of the truth in which a system of values is embedded."[160] He had the talent that would have enabled him "to have had an easy and successful career as a regular professor and a popular writer. . . . He chose the harder path. And he paid the price in slow academic recognition and in the size of the audiences he reached. But in the end he won. He earned promotion in the field, into the leadership of a band of rebels . . . who have been teaching us to value truth and to eschew the lie."[161] Davidson captures this aspect of Weaver's work:

> Weaver's light may at first seem only exploratory and instructive. [The reader] may be tempted to think that it is merely picking out a devious way among heaps of ancient rubbish. But that reader may not realize how deeply his own thought is being engaged—how he is being persuaded to look and look again at what he may have taken for granted or ignored or assumed, in some vain way, that he understood. Presently he is "seeing" (in the sense of understanding or knowing) as never before. He may also feel that he is in the company of a vision that is high and generous and very brave, and that this vision—the vision of Richard Weaver—is making irresistible claims upon his attention, indeed upon his life.[162]

Bibliography

Books

The Ethics of Rhetoric. South Bend, IN: Henry Regnery, 1953.
Ideas Have Consequences. Chicago: University of Chicago Press, 1948.
Life Without Prejudice and Other Essays. Chicago: Henry Regnery, 1965.
Rhetoric and Composition: A Course in Reading and Writing. New York: Holt, Rinehart, and Winston, 1957.
A Rhetoric and Handbook [revision of Rhetoric and Composition]. New York: Holt, Rinehart, and Winston, 1967. (With Richard S. Beal.)
The Southern Tradition at Bay: A History of Postbellum Thought. Ed. George Core and M. E. Bradford. New Rochelle, NY: Arlington, 1968.
Visions of Order: The Cultural Crisis of Our Time. Baton Rouge: Louisiana State University Press, 1964.

Articles and Pamphlets

Academic Freedom: The Principle and the Problems. Philadelphia: Intercollegiate Society of Individualists, 1963.
"Agrarianism in Exile." Sewanee Review, 58 (October/December 1950), 586–606.
"Albert Taylor Bledsoe." Sewanee Review, 52 (January/March 1944), 34–45.
"The American as a Regenerate Being." Ed. George Core and M. E. Bradford. Southern Review, 4 [new series] (July 1968), 633–46.
"Aspects of the Southern Philosophy." Hopkins Review, 5 (Summer 1952), 5–21.
"Contemporary Southern Literature." Texas Quarterly, 2 (Summer 1959), 126–44.
"Humanism in an Age of Science." Ed. Robert Hamlin. Intercollegiate Review, 7 (Fall 1970), 11–18.
"The Humanities in a Century of the Common Man." New Individualist Review, 3 (1964), 17–24.
"Individuality and Modernity." In Essays on Individuality. Ed. Felix Morley. Philadelphia: University of Pennsylvania Press, 1958, pp. 63–81.
"Lee the Philosopher." Georgia Review, 2 (Fall 1948), 297–303.

Letter. *New York Times Book Review*, March 21, 1948, p. 29.
"Looking for an Argument." *College English*, 14 (January 1953), 210–16. (With Manuel Bilsky, McCrea Hazlett, and Robert E. Streeter.)
"Mass Plutocracy." *National Review*, 9 (November 5, 1960), 273–75, 290.
"The Middle of the Road: Where It Leads." *Human Events*, 8 (March 24, 1956), n.pag.
"The Middle Way: A Political Meditation." *National Review*, 3 (January 19, 1957), 63–64.
"The Older Religiousness in the South." *Sewanee Review*, 51 (April/June 1943), 237–49.
"On Setting the Clock Right." *National Review*, 4 (October 12, 1957), 321–23.
"The Pattern of a Life." *Southern Partisan* (Fall 1981), p. 13.
"Realism and the Local Color Interlude." Ed. George Core.*Georgia Review*, 22 (Fall 1968), 300–5.
"The Regime of the South." *National Review*, 6 (March 14, 1959), 587–89.
Relativism and the Crisis of Our Time. Philadelphia: Intercollegiate Society of Individualists, 1961.
"A Responsible Rhetoric." Ed. Thomas D. Clark and Richard L. Johannesen.*Intercollegiate Review*, 12 (Winter 1976-77), 81–87.
The Role of Education in Shaping Our Society. Philadelphia: Intercollegiate Studies Institute, n.d.
"Roots of Liberal Complacency." *National Review*, 3 (June 8, 1957), 541–43.
"Scholars or Gentlemen?" *College English*, 7 (November 1945), 72–77.
"The South and the American Union." In *The Lasting South*. Ed. Louis D. Rubin, Jr. and James Jackson Kilpatrick. Chicago: Henry Regnery, 1957, pp. 46–68.
"The South and the Revolution of Nihilism." *South Atlantic Quarterly*, 43 (April 1944), 194–98.
"Southern Chivalry and Total War." *Sewanee Review*, 53 (April/June 1945), 267–78.
"I. The Southern Tradition." *New Individualist Review*, 3 (1964), 7–17.
"The Tennessee Agrarians." *Shenandoah*, 3 (Summer 1952), 3–10.
"Two Orators." Ed. George Core and M. E. Bradford.*Modern Age*, 14 (Summer/Fall 1970), 226–42.
"Up From Liberalism." *Modern Age*, 3 (Winter 1958–59), 21–32.

Collected Works

Goodnight, Gerald Thomas. "Rhetoric and Culture: A Critical Edition of Richard M. Weaver's Unpublished Works." Diss. University of Kansas 1978.
Language is Sermonic: Richard M. Weaver on the Nature of Rhetoric. Ed. Richard L. Johannesen, Rennard Strickland, and Ralph T. Eubanks. Baton Rouge: Louisiana State University Press, 1970.
The Southern Essays of Richard M. Weaver. Ed. George M. Curtis, III and James J. Thompson, Jr. Indianapolis: Liberty, 1987.

Endnotes

[1] Wilma R. Ebbitt, "Two Tributes to Richard M. Weaver: Richard M. Weaver, Teacher of Rhetoric," *Georgia Review*, 17 (Winter 1963), 417.
[2] Ebbitt, p. 418.
[3] Richard M. Weaver, "Up From Liberalism," *Modern Age*, 3 (Winter 1958–59), 21.

4 Weaver, "Up From Liberalism," p. 22.
5 Fred Douglas Young, *Richard M. Weaver: 1910–1963: A Life of the Mind* (Columbia: University of Missouri Press, 1995), p. 31.
6 Weaver, "Up From Liberalism," p. 22.
7 Weaver, "Up From Liberalism," p. 22.
8 For a description of the philosophy and ideals of the Southern Agrarians, see Richard M. Weaver, "The Tennessee Agrarians," *Shenandoah*, 3 (Summer 1952), 3–10; and M. E. Bradford, "The Agrarianism of Richard Weaver: Beginnings and Completions," *Modern Age*, 14 (Summer/Fall 1970), 249–56.
9 Weaver, "Up From Liberalism," p. 23.
10 Weaver, "Up From Liberalism," p. 23.
11 Weaver, "Up From Liberalism," p. 24.
12 Weaver, "Up From Liberalism," p. 24.
13 Ebbitt, p. 416.
14 Mark Ashin, "Guest Editorial: A Tribute to Richard Weaver," *The Chicago Maroon*, April 5, 1963, p. 3, quoted in Charles Kellogg Follette, "A Weaverian Interpretation of Richard Weaver," diss. University of Illinois 1981, p. 124.
15 Eliseo Vivas, "Introduction to *Life Without Prejudice*," in *Life Without Prejudice and Other Essays*, by Richard Weaver (Chicago: Henry Regnery, 1965), p. ix.
16 Letter from Polly Weaver Beaton to Charles Follette, June 4, 1979, quoted in Follette, p. 132.
17 Eugene Davidson, "Richard Malcom Weaver—Conservative," *Modern Age*, 7 (Summer 1963), 227.
18 Richard M. Weaver, *Life Without Prejudice and Other Essays* (Chicago: Henry Regnery, 1965), p. 159.
19 Richard M. Weaver, "Rhetorical Strategies of the Conservative Cause," speech delivered at the University of Wisconsin, Madison, April 26, 1959, in "Rhetoric and Culture: A Critical Edition of Richard M. Weaver's Unpublished Works," by Gerald Thomas Goodnight, diss. University of Kansas 1978, p. 576.
20 For discussions of the techniques Weaver used to defend conservatism, see: Gerald Thomas Goodnight, "Rhetoric and Culture: A Critical Edition of Richard M. Weaver's Unpublished Works," diss. University of Kansas 1978, pp. 434–37, 460–62, 787–89; Weaver, "Rhetorical Strategies of the Conservative Cause," pp. 574–608; and Follette, pp. 32–34, 407.
21 Additional biographical information on Weaver was obtained from: Follette, pp. 53–55, 65–68, 117, 123, 130–33; Goodnight, pp. 431, 674–75; Ralph T. Eubanks, "Two Tributes to Richard M. Weaver: Richard M. Weaver: In Memoriam," *Georgia Review*, 17 (Winter 1963), 413–15; Russell Kirk, "Richard Weaver, RIP," *National Review*, 14 (April 23, 1963), 308; Henry Regnery, *Memoirs of a Dissident Publisher* (New York: Harcourt Brace Jovanovich, 1979), p. 191; Joseph Scotchie, *Barbarians in the Saddle: An Intellectual Biography of Richard M. Weaver* (New Brunswick, NJ: Transaction, 1997), pp. ix–x, 9–16; and Young.
22 Ebbitt, p. 418.
23 The nature of the human being is discussed in Richard M. Weaver, *Visions of Order: The Cultural Crisis of Our Time* (Baton Rouge: Louisiana State University Press, 1964), pp. 9, 144; and Weaver, *Life Without Prejudice*, pp. 146–47.
24 Weaver, *Visions of Order*, p. 85.
25 Weaver, *Visions of Order*, p. 43.
26 Weaver, *Visions of Order*, p. 9.
27 Weaver, *Visions of Order*, p. 135.
28 Symbol use and choice as features of the human being also are discussed in Richard M. Weaver, "Contemporary Southern Literature," *Texas Quarterly*, 2 (Summer 1959), 143. A summary of these concepts is provided in Follette, pp. 384–98.
29 Richard M. Weaver, *Ideas Have Consequences* (Chicago: University of Chicago Press, 1948), p. 18.
30 Weaver, *Ideas Have Consequences*, p. 18.
31 For additional discussion of the three levels of knowledge, see Richard M. Weaver, *The Ethics of Rhetoric* (South Bend, IN: Regnery/Gateway, 1953), pp. 30–31.

[32] Weaver, *Ideas Have Consequences*, p. 130.

[33] Richard M. Weaver, "Humanism in an Age of Science," ed. Robert Hamlin, *Intercollegiate Review*, 7 (Fall 1970), 17.

[34] Weaver, "Humanism in an Age of Science," p. 17. This view led Weaver to reject empiricism and nominalism. Empiricism is an attitude expressed by two basic doctrines: (1) Words or concepts can be grasped only if connected with actual or possible experiences; and (2) Beliefs depend for their justification ultimately and necessarily on experience—particularly on that of the sense organs. Nominalism denies the existence of universals—words that can be applied to individual things that have something in common. It denies their existence on the ground that the use of a general word such as *humanity* does not imply the existence of a general thing named by it.

[35] Richard M. Weaver, " 'Parson' Weems: A Study in Early American Rhetoric," in Goodnight, p. 295.

[36] Weaver, " 'Parson' Weems," p. 295.

[37] Weaver, *Ideas Have Consequences*, p. 117.

[38] Richard M. Weaver, *The Southern Tradition at Bay: A History of Postbellum Thought*, ed. George Core and M. E. Bradford (New Rochelle, NY: Arlington, 1968), pp. 39–40.

[39] Weaver, *Visions of Order*, p. 12.

[40] Weaver, *The Ethics of Rhetoric*, p. 166.

[41] Weaver, *The Ethics of Rhetoric*, p. 170.

[42] Weaver, *Visions of Order*, p. 11.

[43] Weaver, *Ideas Have Consequences*, p. 19.

[44] Weaver, *Visions of Order*, pp. 11–12.

[45] Weaver, *The Southern Tradition at Bay*, p. 36. The tyrannizing image also is discussed in: Weaver, "Contemporary Southern Literature," p. 133; Weaver, *Ideas Have Consequences*, p. 117; and Weaver, *The Southern Tradition at Bay*, p. 32.

[46] Richard M. Weaver, *Language is Sermonic: Richard M. Weaver on the Nature of Rhetoric*, ed. Richard L. Johannesen, Rennard Strickland, and Ralph T. Eubanks (Baton Rouge: Louisiana State University Press, 1970), p. 71.

[47] Weaver, *Language is Sermonic*, p. 19.

[48] Weaver, *Language is Sermonic*, p. 145.

[49] Weaver, *Language is Sermonic*, p. 72.

[50] Weaver, *Language is Sermonic*, p. 73.

[51] Weaver, *The Ethics of Rhetoric*, p. 28.

[52] Weaver, *Visions of Order*, p. 64.

[53] Weaver, *Visions of Order*, p. 65.

[54] Weaver, *Language is Sermonic*, p. 181.

[55] Weaver, *Language is Sermonic*, p. 164.

[56] Weaver, *The Ethics of Rhetoric*, p. 15.

[57] Weaver, *The Ethics of Rhetoric*, pp. 27–28.

[58] Weaver, *The Ethics of Rhetoric*, p. 213.

[59] Weaver, *Language is Sermonic*, p. 225.

[60] For additional information about Weaver's definition of rhetoric, see Weaver, *The Ethics of Rhetoric*, pp. 25, 27–28, 115.

[61] Weaver, *Language is Sermonic*, p. 211.

[62] Weaver, *Language is Sermonic*, p. 138.

[63] Richard M. Weaver, "The Strategy of Words," speech delivered at the Lake Bluff Woman's Club, Lake Bluff, Illinois, February 13, 1962, in Goodnight, p. 557.

[64] The connection between rhetoric and culture also is discussed in Weaver, *Language is Sermonic*, p. 46; and Weaver, "The Strategy of Words," pp. 556–59. A summary of the connection is provided in Goodnight, pp. 37, 75–92.

[65] Weaver, *Language is Sermonic*, p. 35.

[66] Weaver, *The Ethics of Rhetoric*, pp. 3–26. A summary of the notion of the noble rhetor is provided in Richard L. Johannesen, "Richard M. Weaver on Standards for Ethical Rhetoric," *Central States Speech Journal*, 29 (Summer 1978), 134–35.

[67] For a more comprehensive discussion of Weaver's view of the connection between values and rhetoric, see Follette, pp. 47, 149–206.

[68] Weaver, *Language is Sermonic*, p. 222.

[69] Weaver, *Language is Sermonic*, p. 140.

[70] Weaver, *Language is Sermonic*, p. 224.

[71] Weaver, *Language is Sermonic*, p. 222. The notion that language is sermonic also is discussed in Weaver, *Visions of Order*, p. 69.

[72] Weaver, *The Ethics of Rhetoric*, p. 28. For a summary of examples cited by Weaver of the separation of rhetoric and dialectic in argumentation, see Johannesen, "Richard M. Weaver on Standards for Ethical Rhetoric," pp. 133–34.

[73] Richard M. Weaver, "A Responsible Rhetoric," ed. Thomas D. Clark and Richard L. Johannesen, *Intercollegiate Review*, 12 (Winter 1976–77), 87.

[74] Weaver, *The Ethics of Rhetoric*, p. 58.

[75] Weaver, *Language is Sermonic*, pp. 210–12; and Weaver, *The Ethics of Rhetoric*, pp. 55–57. Although Weaver ranks the sources of argument in these two works, he does not order them in his descriptions elsewhere. See: Weaver, "A Responsible Rhetoric," p. 87; Manuel Bilsky, McCrea Hazlett, Robert E. Streeter, and Richard M. Weaver, "Looking for an Argument," *College English*, 14 (January 1953), 211–14; and Richard M. Weaver and Richard S. Beal, *A Rhetoric and Handbook* (New York: Holt, Rinehart, and Winston, 1967), pp. 136–46.

[76] Weaver, *The Ethics of Rhetoric*, p. 86.

[77] Argument by genus or definition also is discussed in Weaver, *Language is Sermonic*, p. 209; and Bilsky et al., pp. 212–13.

[78] This example is cited by Bilsky et al., pp. 211–12.

[79] The distinction between genus and definition is discussed in Bilsky et al., p. 213; and Weaver, *Language is Sermonic*, pp. 212–13.

[80] Weaver, *Language is Sermonic*, p. 212.

[81] Weaver, *Language is Sermonic*, p. 209.

[82] Argument by similitude also is discussed in Bilsky et al., pp. 212, 214.

[83] Weaver, *Language is Sermonic*, p. 214.

[84] Argument by cause and effect also is discussed in Weaver, *Language is Sermonic*, p. 209; and Bilsky et al., pp. 213–14.

[85] Weaver, *Language is Sermonic*, p. 215.

[86] Weaver discusses argument by circumstance in *Language is Sermonic*, p. 215; and *The Ethics of Rhetoric*, p. 57.

[87] Weaver, *Language is Sermonic*, p. 210.

[88] Argument by authority and testimony also is discussed in Bilsky et al., p. 214.

[89] Richard M. Weaver, "Two Orators," ed. George Core and M. E. Bradford, *Modern Age*, 14 (Summer-Fall 1970), 232, 240. Weaver's connection of genus to history is discussed in Richard L. Johannesen, "Conflicting Philosophies of Rhetoric/Communication: Richard M. Weaver Versus S. I. Hayakawa," *Communication*, 7 (1983), 297.

[90] Weaver, *The Ethics of Rhetoric*, p. 116.

[91] Weaver, *The Ethics of Rhetoric*, p. 117.

[92] Weaver, *The Ethics of Rhetoric*, p. 119.

[93] Weaver, *The Ethics of Rhetoric*, pp. 119–20.

[94] Weaver, *The Ethics of Rhetoric*, p. 120. The simple sentence also is discussed in Weaver, *The Ethics of Rhetoric*, p. 117; and Weaver and Beal, p. 169.

[95] Weaver, *The Ethics of Rhetoric*, p. 124.

[96] Weaver, *The Ethics of Rhetoric*, pp. 120–21.

[97] The complex sentence also is discussed in Weaver, *The Ethics of Rhetoric*, pp. 122–24; and Weaver and Beal, pp. 171–73.

[98] Weaver, *The Ethics of Rhetoric*, p. 124.

[99] Weaver also discusses the compound sentence in *The Ethics of Rhetoric*, pp. 125–27; and Weaver and Beal, pp. 170–71.

[100] See Weaver, *The Ethics of Rhetoric*, pp. 127–28, for Weaver's discussion of nouns.

[101] Weaver, *The Ethics of Rhetoric*, p. 129.

[102] Weaver's discussion of adjectives can be found in *The Ethics of Rhetoric*, pp. 129–33.

[103] Weaver, *Visions of Order*, p. 23.

[104] Weaver, *Visions of Order*, p. 24.

[105] Verbs also are discussed in Weaver, *The Ethics of Rhetoric*, pp. 135–36.

[106] For Weaver's discussion of the other parts of speech, see Weaver, *The Ethics of Rhetoric*, pp. 133–41.

[107] Weaver, *The Ethics of Rhetoric*, p. 211.

[108] Weaver, *The Ethics of Rhetoric*, p. 212.

[109] Weaver provides examples of god terms in *The Ethics of Rhetoric*, pp. 212–22.

[110] Weaver, *The Ethics of Rhetoric*, p. 222.

[111] Weaver, *The Ethics of Rhetoric*, p. 227.

[112] Weaver, *Visions of Order*, p. 7.

[113] Richard M. Weaver, "Making the Most of Two Worlds," commencement address, Gilmour Academy, June 1956, in Goodnight, p. 513.

[114] This summary is provided in Richard L. Johannesen, Rennard Strickland, and Ralph T. Eubanks, "Richard M. Weaver on the Nature of Rhetoric: An Interpretation," in Weaver, *Language is Sermonic*, p. 15. Weaver discusses these ideas in detail in *Visions of Order* and *Ideas Have Consequences*.

[115] Weaver, *Language is Sermonic*, p. 203.

[116] Weaver, *Language is Sermonic*, p. 201.

[117] Weaver, *Language is Sermonic*, pp. 202–03.

[118] Weaver, *Language is Sermonic*, p. 117.

[119] Weaver, "The Strategy of Words," p. 548.

[120] Weaver, *Language is Sermonic*, p. 136.

[121] Weaver, "The Strategy of Words," p. 548.

[122] For Weaver's discussion of the link between language and truth, see *Language is Sermonic*, pp. 123, 136.

[123] Current practices in the teaching of rhetoric are discussed in Weaver, *Language is Sermonic*, pp. 190, 196.

[124] Weaver, *Ideas Have Consequences*, pp. 129–47, 170–87; and Weaver, *Visions of Order*, pp. 40–54.

[125] Weaver, *Language is Sermonic*, p. 54.

[126] Weaver, *Language is Sermonic*, p. 53.

[127] Weaver, *Language is Sermonic*, p. 188.

[128] Weaver, *Language is Sermonic*, pp. 193–94.

[129] Weaver, *Language is Sermonic*, p. 198.

[130] Richard M. Weaver, "The Role of Education in Shaping Our Society," speech delivered at the Metropolitan Area Industrial Conference, Chicago, October 25, 1961, in Goodnight, p. 625.

[131] Weaver, *Language is Sermonic*, p. 194.

[132] Weaver, *Language is Sermonic*, pp. 195–96.

[133] Weaver, *Language is Sermonic*, p. 197.

[134] Weaver, *Language is Sermonic*, p. 197.

[135] Weaver, *Language is Sermonic*, p. 197.

[136] Bruce A. White, "Richard M. Weaver: Dialectic Rhetorician," *Modern Age*, 26 (Summer/Fall 1982), 256.

[137] Willmoore Kendall, "How to Read Richard Weaver: Philosopher of 'We the (Virtuous) People,'" *Intercollegiate Review*, 2 (September 1965), 81.

[138] Among those who classify Weaver as a Platonist or as having an orientation toward Platonic idealism are: James Powell, "The Conservatism of Richard M. Weaver: The Foundations of Weaver's Traditionalism," *New Individualist Review*, 3 (1964), 3; John Bliese, "Richard M. Weaver: Conservative Rhetorician," *Modern Age*, 21 (Fall 1977), 378; John P. East, "Richard M. Weaver: The Conservatism of Affirmation," *Modern Age*, 19 (Fall 1975), 339–42; Robert E. Haskell and Gerard A. Hauser, "Rhetorical Structure: Truth and Method in Weaver's

Epistemology," *Quarterly Journal of Speech*, 64 (October 1978), 236; and Johannesen, "Conflicting Philosophies of Rhetoric/Communication."

[139] Robert Hariman, "Evidence of Things Unseen: Holy Order and the Conservative Mind of Richard Weaver," paper presented at the Speech Communication Association convention, Washington, D.C., November 1983.

[140] Follette, pp. 362–431.

[141] Richard M. Weaver, Letter, *New York Times Book Review*, March 21, 1948, p. 29.

[142] Eliseo Vivas, "The Mind of Richard Weaver," *Modern Age*, 8 (Summer 1964), 309.

[143] Richard L. Johannesen, "Conflicting Philosophies of Rhetoric/Communication," pp. 289–305.

[144] Johannesen, Strickland, and Eubanks, pp. 26–27; and Russell Kirk, "Ethical Labor," rev. of *The Ethics of Rhetoric*, by Richard M. Weaver, *Sewanee Review*, 62 (Summer 1954), 490–91.

[145] Herbert J. Muller, "The Revival of the Absolute," *Antioch Review*, 9 (March 1949), 105.

[146] Donald C. Bryant, rev. of *The Ethics of Rhetoric*, by Richard M. Weaver, *Quarterly Journal of Speech*, 40 (February 1954), 76.

[147] Vivas, "The Mind of Richard Weaver," p. 309.

[148] Goodnight, pp. 780, 784–85.

[149] Muller, p. 103.

[150] Muller, p. 101.

[151] East, p. 338.

[152] Frank S. Meyer, "Richard M. Weaver: An Appreciation," *Modern Age*, 14 (Summer/Fall 1970), 243–44.

[153] Kendall, p. 81.

[154] Kendall, p. 85.

[155] Meyer, p. 243.

[156] Scotchie, p. 139.

[157] Scotchie, p. 139.

[158] Eugene Davidson, p. 228.

[159] Vivas, "The Mind of Richard Weaver," p. 310.

[160] Eugene Davidson, p. 227.

[161] Vivas, "The Mind of Richard Weaver," p. 310.

[162] Donald Davidson, "The Vision of Richard Weaver: A Foreword," in Weaver, *The Southern Tradition at Bay*, p. 13.

7

KENNETH BURKE

"The reason reviewers and editors have had such trouble fastening on Burke's field is that he has no field, unless it be Burkology."[1] This statement by Stanley Edgar Hyman, one of Kenneth Burke's interpreters, captures well the difficulty of characterizing the field to which Burke belongs. In his works, he demonstrates mastery of concepts from the disciplines of philosophy, literature, linguistics, sociology, and economics. As "a specialist in symbol-systems and symbolic action,"[2] Burke focuses on language and its nature, functions, and consequences in his explorations of all of these disciplines. As Burke characterizes himself, "What am I but a word man?"[3]

Kenneth Duva Burke was born on May 5, 1897, to James Leslie Burke and Lillyan May Duva Burke in Pittsburgh, Pennsylvania. He attributed his love of literature to his father who, while working intermittently for Westinghouse in a clerical job, regularly submitted short stories to the *Saturday Evening Post*, although they were never accepted for publication. At Peabody High School in Pittsburgh, Burke was an "unpopular high school intellectual"[4] and member of the literary clique. He spent one summer working in a factory in Pittsburgh and attributed his anti-technological attitude to the experience. It also convinced him that he wanted a different life.

Following graduation from high school in 1916, Burke went to stay with relatives in New Jersey and worked for three months as a bank runner in New York City. He then enrolled at Ohio State University, where he stayed for only one semester. He transferred to Columbia University for a year but was frustrated at having to complete undergraduate courses before he could enroll in the graduate-level courses in which he was interested. Despite hints that he would be asked to join the faculty at Columbia, he dropped out of college a second time: "I didn't want to go into academics, because in those days teachers only taught—I wanted to *write*."[5] As he explained in a letter to his friend Malcolm Cowley: "Suddenly becoming horrified at the realization of what college can do to a man of promise. . . . I don't want to be a virtuoso; I want to be a—a—oh hell, why not? I want to be a—yes—a genius. I want to learn to work, to work like a Sisyphus—that is my only chance. I am afraid, I confess it, but I am going to try hard. This is my final showdown. I am in it for life and death this time. Words, words—mountains of words—If I can do that I am saved."[6]

Burke made a deal with his father: "Let me save you some money. Put me up in the Village [Greenwich Village] with just enough to pull through on, and I'll go on with my studies." His father agreed, and Burke became part of the bohemian subculture of the Village, living in a dingy garret and surviving on oatmeal and milk twice a day. As a member of an informal group of writers that included Malcolm Cowley, Matthew Josephson, Hart Crane, Allen Tate, e. e. cummings, and Edna St. Vincent Millay, Burke settled down to "very serious devotion to study and carousing."[7] The group was dispersed somewhat during World War I, but Burke was not drafted because he failed to pass the Army's medical examination. He spent the war working in a factory, "making gauges to check gauges that were used to regulate the mass production of munitions."[8]

In 1919, Burke married Lillian Batterham. After the arrival of his third daughter, he purchased a dilapidated house on 70 acres of land in Andover, located in the hills of western New Jersey, away from the urban pollution of New York City. By 1928, the Burke family had purchased additional land, dammed a creek to create a lake for swimming, built a tennis court, expanded the house, and built some outbuildings to accommodate guests. Burke always kept the farm rustic, however. He did not install electricity until 1949, and there was no running water until nearly 20 years later. The "agro-bohemian Burkes," as Burke called himself and his family, often invited friends to join them at Andover, sharing with them the bounty of their extensive garden and encouraging spirited conversation.[9] Andover was not a hermitage for Burke, however, and he often commuted to New York City, sometimes maintaining a room there so he could stay in the city during the week, returning to Andover on weekends.

Throughout the 1920s, Burke supported himself and his family with various translating, editing, and writing jobs. In 1921, he was given a steady job as an assistant editor at the literary magazine *The Dial*. There he made himself indispensable in various capacities—proofreading; page design; translations; overseeing the preparation of issues; and contributing book reviews, music criticism, and fiction. During his tenure at *The Dial*, he published his first book, a collection of short fiction called *The White Oxen and Other Stories*, in 1924. He also published numerous essays, poems, and book reviews in various outlets during that time and earned the Dial Award for distinguished services to American letters in 1929.

The Dial ceased publication that year. "I was lost," Burke recalls. "*The Dial* and the whole feeling behind it—that was magic to me, it was my life."[10] Burke went to work for the Laura Spelman Rockefeller Foundation, researching and writing on drug addiction. This prepared him for his later studies of the works of Samuel Taylor Coleridge, in which he analyzed images relating to Coleridge's addiction to opium. Burke also did editorial work for the Bureau of Social Hygiene and was a reviewer and music critic for the *Nation* and the *New Republic*. In 1931, Burke's first book of literary criticism was published. In *Counter-Statement*, he views literature as rhetoric and recommends an attitude of critical openness toward literature, encouraging numerous angles of vision.

In the early 1930s, Burke's personal life was beset by what he called "the trouble." He fell in love with his wife's sister, Elizabeth "Libbie" Batterham. He divorced Lillian to marry Libbie in 1933; two sons were born from this marriage. In 1932, he published a novel, *Towards a Better Life*, a collection of declamations or epistles that the protagonist writes but never sends to his rival for the affections of a woman they both love. The book sometimes is seen as a thinly fictionalized autobiography of Burke's personal and emotional troubles when his first marriage was breaking up and he was arranging his marriage to Libbie, a view Burke confirmed: "I was in bad shape myself, but too pigheaded to see a psychiatrist. I was fictionalizing actual situations, and it scared the life out of me. But I got it all down, and analyzed those situations—and got better."[12] Others suggest that although *Towards a Better Life* may have been a therapeutic exercise for Burke, it was not "drawn directly from his life in any material way" because there are few parallels between the events and characters of the book and Burke's life.[13]

At the time of the Depression, Burke was increasingly attracted to Communism, as were many American writers, although he never became a member of the Communist Party. His writing during the time assumed an ideological cast as he incorporated some of the ideas of cooperation from Communist doctrine. *Permanence and Change*, published in 1935, particularly reflects this ideology as Burke applies his interest in poetry and critical techniques to human relations in general, demonstrating his belief that artists can provide insights into the problems confronting society.

Burke's disillusionment with Communism began with the first Writers' Congress in 1935, a "Communist-sponsored convocation of nearly all the prominent 'committed' literary men in America."[14] Burke presented a paper, "Revolutionary Symbolism in America," in which he argued for the substitution of the term "the people" for "the worker" because it was more "accurately attuned to us," "more of an ideal incentive," and would broaden the appeal of the movement.[15] Some audience members felt that Burke's proposal would transform the revolution into a middle-class movement and weaken its economic thrust, and the reaction to his paper was strong and negative: "But when the time came for criticism—O my god! It was a slaughter! Mike Gold and Joe Freeman—they just tore me apart: 'We have a snob among us'—and so on. And when I was going out of the hall I heard a girl in front of me say: 'And yet he seemed so honest!' "[16] Burke was devastated: "I went home and lay down, but just as I was about to fall asleep, I'd hear 'Burke!'—and I'd awake with a start. Then I'd doze off again, and suddenly again: 'Burke!' My name had become a kind of charge against me—a dirty word."[17] Ironically, Burke discovered the next day that he had been elected a member of the Executive Committee of the newly formed League of American Writers.

Burke read papers at the second and third Writers' Congresses in 1937, but events such as the Stalinist purges, the Moscow trials of 1936-1938, Soviet participation in Nazi Germany's attack on Poland, and the Russian invasion of Finland in 1939 led him to question his commitment to Communism. He subsequently eschewed political affiliation, although he remained anti-Fascist throughout his life and generally adopted an ideology of Agrarian liberalism.

Burke began his teaching career as a lecturer in criticism at the New School of Social Research in New York in 1937. From 1943 to 1961, he held a teaching position at Bennington College in Vermont, interrupted frequently by visiting professor positions at other universities, including the University of Chicago, Harvard University, Northwestern University, and Princeton University. He was granted an honorary doctorate in 1966 from Bennington College.

Writing was Burke's occupation, and his attention was focused on working out the nature and function of language through his writing. In 1937, he published *Attitudes Toward History*, a study of literary attitudes as symbolic action. He distinguishes attitudes of acceptance from attitudes of rejection, with both leading to the development of a comic theory of human relations or an attitude of irony. *The Philosophy of Literary Form*, published in 1941, is a collection of critical essays and reviews written between 1933 and 1940. They are united by a concern with the nature of symbolic action.

In 1945, Burke published the first of what was to be a trilogy of works on motive, using a threefold division of language into grammar, rhetoric, and poetics. *A Grammar of Motives* deals with the intrinsic nature of a work, focusing on dramatism as the key metaphor and the pentad as the method for discovering motivation. The second work, *A Rhetoric of Motives*, published in 1950, deals with strategies of persuasion; Burke suggests that the key term for rhetoric is *identification*. The planned third book of the trilogy, *A Symbolic of Motives*, never was released for publication.[18] Burke's next major work was published in 1961. *The Rhetoric of Religion* explains his shift from poetry to theology as his model for the study of language. *Language as Symbolic Action*, which appeared in 1966, is a collection of works by Burke written from 1950 to 1966. Burke's work as a writer was recognized in 1981 with the National Medal for Literature, an award that honors a living American writer for contributions to American letters.

After Burke's wife's death in 1969, he continued to live on his farm in Andover, surrounded by many children and grandchildren who had vacation homes bordering his farm. One of his grandsons was the singer Harry Chapin, who recorded Burke's song, "One Light in a Dark Valley."[19] Burke died on November 19, 1993. Burke himself provided perhaps the best description of what he was trying "to get cleared up"[20] through his writing. In a poem written in response to Hyman's comment that Burke's field is Burkology, Burke explained: "When I itch/ It's not from fleas,/ But from a bad case/ Of Burke's Disease." He concludes the poem with an announcement of his motive in his work: "What then in sum/ Bedevils me?/ I'm flunking my Required Course/ In Advanced Burkology."[21]

Rhetoric

Burke defines rhetoric as "the use of words by human agents to form attitudes or to induce actions in other human agents."[22] Whatever form rhetoric takes, he sees it as *"rooted in an essential function of language itself... the use of language as a symbolic means of inducing cooperation in beings that by nature respond to symbols."*[23] For Burke, rhetoric is a subset of a larger category, symbolic action, which includes rhetoric, poetics, science, and philosophy. Rhetoric is concerned with persuasion and identification; poetics deals with symbolic action in and of itself; the purview of science is symbolic action in relation to the ends of factual knowledge; and philosophy's concern is with symbolic action in relation to discussions of first principles.[24]

Although Burke's definition of rhetoric, centered in persuasion, appears to be similar to traditional definitions of rhetoric, he introduces other characteristics of rhetoric that expand his definition beyond the traditional one.

With its grounding in the notion of identification, rhetoric makes possible all of human-made order and "designates the very process by which human societies are created, maintained, transformed, destroyed, and recreated."[25]

Identification

Burke's modifications of the definition of rhetoric begin with his concept of identification. Individuals form selves or identities through various properties or substances, which include such things as physical objects, occupations, friends, activities, beliefs, and values. As they ally themselves with various properties or substances, they share substance with whatever or whomever they associate and simultaneously define themselves against or separate themselves from others with whom they choose not to identify. Burke uses the term *consubstantial* to describe this association. As two entities are united in substance through common ideas, attitudes, material possessions, or other properties, they are consubstantial. Men and women, for example, are consubstantial in that they share the substance of humanness. Two artists are consubstantial in that they share an interest in art, artistic talent, and an urge for self-expression through the production of art.[26]

Burke uses the term *identification* synonymously with *consubstantiality*. Shared substance constitutes an identification between an individual and some property or person: "To identify A with B is to make A 'consubstantial' with B."[27] Burke also equates *persuasion* with *consubstantiality* and *identification*, seeing "no chance of our keeping apart the meanings,"[28] for persuasion is the result of identification: "You persuade a man only insofar as you can talk his language by speech, gesture, tonality, order, image, attitude, idea, *identifying* your ways with his."[29] Burke thus expands the notion of rhetoric so that it is a change in attitude or action through identification. In this expansion, Burke does not mean to make *identification* the key term for rhetoric in place of the traditional term *persuasion* but sees the concept of identification as a supplement to the traditional view of rhetoric.[30]

Identification functions in three basic ways. It may be used as a means to an end, as when a candidate for office attempts to win votes by telling an audience of farmers that she was raised on a farm. Similarly, an auto company may attempt to attract buyers for its products through advertisements that depict individuals who share characteristics with the targeted audience for the ad—soccer moms or chic, wealthy sophisticates, for example. In these cases, "insofar as their interests are joined, A is *identified* with B,"[31] and persuasion concerning a desired end occurs.

A second kind of identification features the operation of antithesis and involves the creation of identification among opposing entities on the basis of a common enemy. The United States and Russia, for example, joined forces against Germany in World War II, uniting two ideologically opposed countries on the basis of a shared enemy. Similarly, two faculty members in a university department who are opposed on a number of issues may identify with one another when financial difficulties at the university threaten to eliminate the department. They unite against the common enemy of the possible termination of their department.

A third type of identification—and often the most powerful—"derives from situations in which it goes unnoticed";[32] in this case, identification is used to persuade at an unconscious level. A political party's nominating convention that features many African-American and Hispanic speakers, for example, may create unconscious identification with white voters who do not want to perceive themselves as racist even though their party traditionally has not actively championed civil rights for people of color. In this case, identification subtly and unconsciously is being created between white voters and the party. Although classical definitions of rhetoric, then, focus on "the speaker's explicit designs with regard to the confronting of an audience,"[33] identification includes the possibility of unconscious persuasion, for individuals may not be consciously aware of the identifications they are making.[34]

Identification cannot be understood apart from division, which Burke sometimes calls *alienation* or *dissociation*. Human beings are inevitably isolated and divided from one another as a result of their separate physical bodies. The *"individual centrality of the nervous system"* requires that what "the body eats and drinks becomes its special private property; the body's pleasures and pains are exclusively its own pleasures and pains."[35] Although in the process of identification, "A is 'substantially one' with a person other than himself . . . he remains unique, an individual locus of motives. Thus he is both joined and separate, at once a distinct substance and consubstantial with another."[36]

In division lies a basic motive for rhetoric: people communicate in an attempt to eliminate division. Burke asserts that if individuals were not apart from one another, "there would be no need for the rhetorician to proclaim their unity."[37] Only because of their separation or division do individuals communicate with one another and try to resolve their differences. Paradoxically, then, identification is rooted in division. Rhetoric is an attempt to bridge the conditions of estrangement that are natural and inevitable.[38]

Self as Audience

Persuasion implies an audience. Consistent with traditional views, Burke includes as a condition of rhetoric its "nature as *addressed*."[39] Burke, however, believes that rhetoric also can involve the self as the audience: "A man can be his own audience, insofar as he, even in his secret thoughts, cultivates certain ideas or images for the effect he hopes they may have upon him; he is here what Mead would call 'an "I" addressing its "me" '; and in this respect he is being rhetorical quite as though he were using pleasant imagery to influence an outside audience rather than one within."[40] Burke's notion of the self as an audience for rhetoric means that processes such as socialization are included under the rubric of rhetoric.[41]

Scope of Rhetoric

Rhetoric includes spoken and written discourse, but for Burke it also in-cludes less traditional forms of discourse such as sales promotion, courtship, social etiquette, education, hysteria, witchcraft, and works of art such as lit-erature and painting. Although Burke uses the term *language* in his defini-tion of rhetoric, he sees rhetoric as including nonverbal elements or nonsymbolic conditions that "can themselves be viewed as a kind of symbol-ism having persuasive effects."[42] Although a nonverbal element in itself is not rhetoric, rhetoric is apparent in its meaning. For example, food, "eaten and digested, is not rhetorical," but rhetoric exists "in the *meaning* of food . . . the meaning being persuasive enough for the idea of food to be used, like the ideas of religion, as a rhetorical device."[43] Such "nonverbal conditions or objects can be considered as signs by reason of persuasive in-gredients inherent in the 'meaning' they have for the audience to which they are 'addressed.' "[44] The broad scope Burke sees for rhetoric is summarized in his statement, "Wherever there is persuasion, there is rhetoric. And wher-ever there is 'meaning,' there is 'persuasion.' "[45]

Function of Rhetoric

Rhetoric functions in a number of ways, but one that Burke sees as par-ticularly significant is how it functions to name or define situations for indi-viduals. A speech or a poem, for example, is "a *strategy for encompassing a situation*,"[46] an answer to the question "posed by the situation."[47] Rhetoric sizes up a situation and names its structure and outstanding ingredients. The Constitution of the United States, for example, names a situation concerned with political governance. Calling a person a *friend* or naming the admission standards to a school *rigorous* tells the qualities of the situation that are deemed important by the rhetor.

Rhetoric does not simply provide a name for a situation, however. It also represents a creative strategy for dealing with that situation or for solv-ing the problems inherent in it. Rhetoric offers commands or instructions of some kind, helping individuals maneuver through life and helping them feel more at home in the world. Because rhetoric is a rhetor's solution to per-ceived problems, it constitutes "equipment for living"[48]—a chart, formula, manual, or map that the audience may consult in trying to decide on various courses of action.

Each rhetorical act is not only a strategic answer to a situation but a styl-ized answer to that situation. The rhetor not only names the situation but names it in a particular fashion or style. There "is a difference," Burke ex-plains, "in style or strategy, if one says 'yes' in tonalities that imply 'thank God' or in tonalities that imply 'alas!' "[49] The situation is named with the same response or strategy, but the style is different.[50] Just as the rhetor uses the strategy selected to determine an attitude and the action to take toward it, so the audience is able to use the rhetor's work as stylistic medicine.

A rhetorical work provides assistance to its audience in a number of ways. It may provide a vocabulary of thoughts, actions, emotions, and attitudes for codifying and thus interpreting the situation. It may encourage the acceptance of a situation that cannot be changed, or it may serve as a guide for how to correct a situation. In other instances, it may help rhetors justify their conduct, turning actions that seem to be unethical or absurd into ones considered virtuous or accurate. Rhetoric, then, provides an orientation in some way to a situation and provides assistance in adjusting to it.[51]

Rhetorical Form

Because "form and content cannot be separated"[52] and a rhetor "can't possibly make a statement without its falling into some sort of pattern,"[53] any consideration of the subject or content of rhetoric also must include a consideration of its form. For Burke, how an idea is developed through form is linked inextricably to the effects of rhetoric on an audience. In fact, he sees form as the process of producing such effects.

An effect is produced in an audience, Burke asserts, through the development of an idea in a way that creates and satisfies expectations. Expectation is significant in the process of achieving desired effects because life is structured by expectations: "life itself has form only in so far as you can get a sense of expectancy, and life becomes unreal, and puzzling, and disarrayed when we do not have any way of expecting the next event."[54] In accordance with his emphasis on expectations, Burke defines form as "an arousing and fulfillment of desires"[55] or "the creation of an appetite in the mind of the auditor, and the adequate satisfying of that appetite."[56] "A work has form," he suggests, "in so far as one part of it leads a reader to anticipate another part, to be gratified by the sequence."[57] If, for example, in a novel, an author says something "about a meeting, writes in such a way that we desire to observe that meeting, and then, if he places that meeting before us—that is form."[58]

Identification or persuasion results from an interaction of form and content. Through involvement in its form, a rhetorical work induces tensions or expectations with which the audience identifies. Form "is 'correct,'" in Burke's view, when "it gratifies the needs which it creates."[59] Burke provides an example of the way in which identification or persuasion may result from the form in which a claim or proposition is presented. An audience initially may disagree with a proposition, but it often will yield to the symmetry of the form in which the proposition is being presented, transferring the attitude of assent to the content of the argument:[60]

> "Who controls Berlin, controls Germany; who controls Germany controls Europe; who controls Europe controls the world." As a proposition, it may or may not be true. And even if it is true, unless people are thoroughly imperialistic, they may not want to control the world. But regardless of these doubts about it as a proposition, by the time you arrive at the second of its three stages, you feel how it is destined to

develop—and on the level of purely formal assent you would collaborate
to round out its symmetry by spontaneously willing its completion and
perfection as an utterance. Add, now, the psychosis of nationalism, and
assent on the formal level invites assent to the proposition as doctrine.[61]

Burke sees form as reduced to three primary principles or types: conventional, repetitive, and progressive, with each type relying on the arousal
and fulfillment of expectations managed through different patterns. Conventional form is the expectation of a particular form prior to encountering a
work. It involves the expectations that audiences bring with them to the
form. A sonnet, for example, must follow a certain form, and someone who
reads a sonnet brings to the work the expectation of this form. Similarly, the
audience at an Athenian tragedy expected to see a chorus and attended the
play with this form in mind. Of course, a violation of conventional form
eventually may become "a new convention of its own,"[62] as when the uncon-
ventional editing techniques first used on MTV became the norm in advertising and filmmaking.

A second type of form is repetitive form, "the consistent maintaining of
a principle under new guises. It is restatement of the same thing in different
ways."[63] This type of form involves the ways in which a work embodies a
fixed character or identity and manifests internal consistency. A succession
of images in a poem, each evoking a joyous mood, for example, is repetitive
form. Another example is a town in which numerous elements of the environment—boarded-up buildings, blowing trash, vacant streets, and weeds
growing in the cracks of sidewalks—point to the same conclusion: the town
is not flourishing.

Progressive form involves the use of situations that lead "the audience
to anticipate or desire certain developments."[64] One type of progressive
form is syllogistic progression, "the form of a perfectly conducted argument," advancing step by step.[65] It is called *syllogistic* because it follows the
deductive reasoning pattern of the syllogism, a form of reasoning in which
two statements or premises are made and a logical conclusion is drawn from
them. Upon acquaintance with the premises, the audience is fairly certain
where the work is going to end up: "The arrows of our desires are turned in a
certain direction, and the plot follows the direction of the arrows."[66] In for-
mulaic Hollywood movies, for example, the audience knows from the opening scenes what the ending of the movie will be—that the male hero will win
the affections of the woman and will conquer the villain. Similarly, in a fast-
food restaurant such as McDonald's, the observations the audience makes
upon entering—of plastic surroundings, a limited menu, and low prices—
suggest the conclusion that this is not a place where gourmet dining will take
place. Given the premises it encounters, the audience is likely to draw a particular conclusion.

A second type of progressive form is qualitative progression. This is a
more subtle kind of form than syllogistic progression, for rather than "one
incident in the plot preparing us for some other possible incident of

plot . . . the presence of one quality prepares us for the introduction of another."[67] The tone of scenes or events, rather than the action of the scenes themselves, is involved in this form, so that audience members "are put into a state of mind which another state of mind can appropriately follow."[68] The grotesque seriousness of a murder scene in a play, for example, prepares the audience for the grotesque buffoonery of the scene that follows. Although the action differs, the quality characterizing the scenes is the same.

Another difference between qualitative and syllogistic progressive form is that in qualitative progression, the structure of the form is not anticipated at the outset and is recognized as appropriate only after the work has been experienced. Qualitative progressive form lacks the pronounced anticipatory nature of syllogistic progression, and audiences "are prepared less to demand a certain qualitative progression than to recognize its rightness after the event."[69] In Alfred Hitchcock's film *Vertigo*, for example, the audience is given no clue at the beginning of the film that the woman with whom Scottie Ferguson (the character played by James Stewart) falls in love, Madeleine/ Judy (played by Kim Novak), will be involved in murder and deception and will be killed at the end of the film. After her death, however, the audience realizes how appropriate the ending is. Because of the nature of his character (the internal consistency of repetitive form), Ferguson cannot continue to love someone who is deceptive, but he cannot stop loving her. Her death thus is an appropriate solution to the situation and constitutes a correct end to the film's qualitative progression.

In addition to the three major types of form, Burke discusses minor or incidental forms. Among these are metaphor, paradox, reversal, contraction, expansion, and series. The effect of these kinds of forms partially depends on their function in the work as a whole, and they often serve as parts of the three complex types of form. In some instances, however, these minor forms may appeal and play major roles on their own in the development of tensions and resolution concerning content.

Burke's definition of rhetoric is not unlike traditional definitions of rhetoric that feature persuasion. The uniqueness of his view lies in his equation of identification with persuasion and the expansion of persuasion to include unconscious intent, the self as audience, and nonverbal elements that have meaning for an audience. With the addition of his notion that rhetoric provides equipment for living and generally assumes one of three major forms, the result is a comprehensive examination of rhetoric on which Burke builds an elaborate rhetorical system.

Dramatism

Dramatism is a "philosophy of language"[70] that Burke uses to discover human motivation through the analysis of drama. It is a "technique of analysis of language and thought as basically modes of action rather than as means of conveying information."[71] In a dramatistic perspective, language is seen not just as a means for naming or defining but as a form of action. The key term, then, in Burke's dramatistic approach to the study of motivation is *act*. Dramatism is a study of action as opposed to motion. The major distinction between action and motion lies in the difference between animality—the biological aspect of the human being that corresponds to motion—and symbolicity—the neurological aspect of the human being that corresponds to action.

Animality is that part of the human concerned with bodily processes: "growth, metabolism, digestion, peristaltic 'action,' respiration, functions of the various organs, secretions of the endocrine glands, ways in which elements in the bloodstream reinforce or check one another, and so on."[72] Certain motives arise from the condition of animality—"the desires for food, shelter, mates, rest, and the like, reduced to the most rudimentary forms."[73] Animality "is in the realm of sheer matter, sheer motion";[74] individuals are in motion, rather than acting, at this level. Because motion encompasses the realm of entities that do not respond to words, Burke labels this realm the *nonsymbolic*.

In addition to their biological nature, humans have a neurological aspect, which is the ability of an organism to acquire language. With a symbol system, animality is transcended, and individuals become human, operating in the realm of action, the symbolic, or "symbolic action."[75] Although the "material conditions in which the space program takes place, for instance, are in the realm of motion," the "theorizing, planning, and human coordination involved are in the realm of action" because a symbol system is necessary for these kinds of activities to occur.[76] Just as some human motives are derived from animality, others originate in symbolicity. These motives include the numerous goals toward which individuals strive in areas such as "education, political systems, moral codes, religions, commerce, money, and so on."[77] To be motivated in these areas requires a symbol system that creates the possibility for such desires in the first place.[78]

Three conditions are required for action or symbolicity. Freedom must be involved, for "if an act weren't 'free,' it wouldn't be an 'act.' "[79] Implicit in the idea of action is choice, for if "one cannot make a choice, one is not acting, one is but being moved, like a billiard ball tapped with a cue and behaving mechanically in conformity with the resistances it encounters."[80] Freedom to choose, however, requires adequate knowledge of the act's consequences, so that a person must know the consequences involved in making a particular choice. Human beings never can be completely free because they never know the full consequences of their acts.

A second condition necessary for an act is purpose or will. A person must will a choice. Burke provides an example of the difference between action and motion regarding will, showing how something that begins as motion may be converted to action through the addition of purpose: "If one happened to stumble over an obstruction, that would be not an act, but a mere motion. However, one could convert even this sheer accident into something of an act if, in the course of falling, one suddenly *willed* his fall (as a rebuke, for instance, to the negligence of the person who had left the obstruction in the way)."[81]

A third necessary condition for action is motion. Symbolic action, in other words, ultimately is grounded in the realm of the nonsymbolic. Although motion can exist without action (as when a ball rolls down an incline), action cannot exist without motion. Individuals may use the symbol *bread*, for example, but they "cannot live by the *word* for bread alone"[82]—the word *bread* is grounded in the loaf of bread. Burke elaborates on the importance of the grounding of the symbolic in motion: "Yet, hold! We must never forget that, however social the nature of symbolic action is, the life of the individual as defined by the centrality of his nervous system is grounded empirically in the realm of sheer motion. When his heart stops moving for good, he's through."[83] Although motion is necessary for action, action cannot be reduced to motion. The " 'essence' or 'meaning' of a sentence," for example, "is not reducible to its sheer physical existence as sounds in the air or marks on the page, although material motions of some sort are necessary for the production, transmission, and reception of the sentence."[84]

Once organisms acquire a symbol system, for them to do something purely in the realm of motion without the mediation of symbolicity is virtually impossible. Thoughts and ideas are never free from the language that is used to frame them. Building a house, for example, might be considered motion because it involves the biological need for shelter. To build a house without symbolic conceptions of house entering into that process and turning it into an act, however, is unlikely. Words create orientations or attitudes, shaping individuals' views of reality and thus generating different motives for their actions. If parents define their young child's behavior as *expressive*, for example, they will tend to look upon the child's transgressions as healthy self-disclosure and as signs of the child's intelligence. Consequently, they will put up with the child's interruptions, antics, and screams. If, however, they define the child's behavior as *obnoxious*, those behaviors will be seen as signs of rudeness and lack of respect and the parents will respond differently. The parents' actions toward the child and the child's actions depend on the terminology used to describe that behavior.

Burke suggests that dramatism should be taken literally and not simply as a metaphor. According to Burke, dramatism provides a literal statement about the nature of reality. Burke's term *linguistic realism* summarizes this notion that language is as real as physical objects: "I make a point of insisting that the Dramatistic perspective is *not* a metaphor. For years I myself accepted the Dramatistic perspective as a metaphor, but now I've gone up in my price. I claim that the proposition 'things move, persons act,' is *literal*."[85] He elaborates:

> For instance, a physical scientist's relation to the materials involved in the study of motion differs in quality from his relation to his colleagues. He would never think of "petitioning" the objects of his experiment, or "arguing with them, as he would with persons whom he asks to collaborate with him or to judge the results of his experiment. Implicit in these two relations is the distinction between the sheer motion of things and the actions of persons.

In this sense, man is defined literally as an animal characterized by his special aptitude for "symbolic action," which is itself a literal term. And from there on, drama is employed, not as a metaphor, but as a fixed form that helps us discover what the implications of the terms "act" and "person" *really* are.[86]

Burke's view of dramatism as literal also can be seen in his notion that things are signs of words. The meaning of a word cannot be discovered by looking to reality; instead, language suggests what reality means. Words impose knowledge on human beings and create their reality, and humans often learn words for and thus create realities surrounding objects, places, or situations before they "actually" encounter them, if they ever do. A U.S. citizen who has not traveled outside of the country, for example, develops a version or reality of what Greece is that is as real as the actual country for her. The words connected with Greece literally have created her knowledge. Implicit in Burke's notion of dramatism, then, is the literal function of language to produce reality.[87]

Pentad

Because language use is characterized by freedom and purpose, Burke believes that a rhetor's language can be used to discover motive. Motive is a linguistic product, not some "primal, irreducible datum" hidden within the individual.[88] Motives and language are so closely associated that an analysis of a rhetorical artifact can point to a rhetor's underlying motives. Burke asserts that by inspecting a rhetor's work, "we or he may disclose by objective citation the structure of motivation operating here. There is no need to 'supply' motives. The interrelationships themselves *are* his motives. For they are his *situation*; and *situation* is but another word for *motives*. The motivation out of which he writes is synonymous with the structural way in which he puts events and values together when he writes."[89]

Burke has developed a tool or method of analysis to discover the motivation in symbolic action. The pentad is a critical instrument designed to reduce statements of motives to the most fundamental level, which Burke suggests consists of five terms: *act, agent, agency, scene,* and *purpose*. These five terms are the principles or grammar for the discovery of motive, which is seen as the product of interrelationships or tensions among the terms. Burke explains his rationale for the selection of these five terms: "In a rounded statement about motives, you must have some word that names the *act* (names what took place, in thought or deed), and another that names the *scene* (the background of the act, the situation in which it occurred); also, you must indicate what person or kind of person (*agent*) performed the act, what means or instruments he used (*agency*), and the *purpose*."[90] Burke suggests that the terms be used less as static labels and more as questions that prompt the critic: "At first glance they all might look like quite 'positive' terms—and without thinking explicitly about the problem, I took them to be so. For they are not terms that readily imply logical opposites. But later I came to realize that, though they are not thus 'polar,' neither are they simply 'positive.' They are really *questions*. By *act* was meant: 'What was done?' By *scene*: "In what sort of situation was it done?' And so on. Thus, they are really but a set of *blanks to be filled out*."[91] These elements might be designated in a study of motivation as follows: "The hero (agent) with the help of a friend (co-agent) outwits the villain (counter-agent) by using a file (agency) that enables him to break his bonds (act) in order to escape (purpose) from the room where he has been confined (scene)."[92]

By *act*, Burke means any conscious or purposive action. *Act* prompts the critic to discover what a rhetor did. Thus, "any verb, no matter how specific or how general, that has connotations of consciousness or purpose" constitutes an act. Planting sunflowers, telling a lie, or buying a puppy, for example, are symbolic acts.[93]

Scene asks the critic to name the ground, location, or situation in which the act takes place. Terms for scene include such labels as *5:30 P.M.*, historical epochs such as the *Elizabethan period*, or *Florida in January*. A scenic statement might even be as broad as "in a period following the invention of the atomic bomb but prior to a soft landing of electronic instruments on the surface of the moon."[94] How the scene is designated is important because it indicates the scope or the circumference of the analysis. As Burke explains, "For a man is not only in the situation peculiar to his era or to his particular place in that era (even if we could agree on the traits that characterize his era). He is also in a situation extending through centuries; he is in a 'generically human' situation; and he is in a 'universal' situation."[95] The scene in which the artist is painting, then, could be described as *a studio, New York City, midnight on February 3, the United States, the postmodern era in art,* or *planet Earth*. No particular description of setting is the correct one. Burke simply points out that how scene is labeled affects the scope of the critic's interpretation of motivation.[96]

The term *agent* is the group or individual who performs the act. It includes general or specific words for persons such as *actor, character, hero, villain, mother, doctor*, or *artist*. An agent also may be a collective term such as *nation, race*, or *church*.[97]

Agency is the means used to perform the act or the instruments used to accomplish it. For example, the gardener who is engaged in the act of planting sunflowers seeds might use the agencies of seeds, a trowel, soil, water, and an appropriate season for planting. For the person who tells a lie, the agency might be a false statement. For the individual who purchases a puppy, the agency might be preparations for a puppy, a search for a puppy of a particular kind that includes daily scanning of newspaper classified ads, and the necessary funds.[98]

The *purpose* is the agent's private intention in performing the act. It may be overt, but it is more often covert and unknown to an outside observer. When Dylan Klebold and Eric Harris shot and killed 12 students and a teacher at Columbine High School in Littleton, Colorado, in 1999, their purpose might have been to gain recognition and affirmation in an environment that denigrated and ostracized them.[99] *Purpose* is not synonymous with *motive*. Motive is the much broader, often unconscious reason for the performance of the act. It might be thought of as a "rough, shorthand" description of a situation or the terminology used to interpret a situation.[100] An examination of all five elements of the pentad is needed to discover the motive for a rhetorical act.[101]

In addition to terms for act, scene, agent, agency, and purpose, Burke sometimes includes *attitude* as an element to be considered in the analysis of motivation. Agency denotes the means employed in an act, and attitude designates the manner in which those means are employed: "To build something with a hammer would involve an instrument, or 'agency'; to build with diligence would involve an 'attitude,' a 'how.' "[102] Burke states that "on later occasions I have regretted that I had not turned the pentad into a hexad, with 'attitude' as the sixth term," but he continued to analyze motivation through a pentad, seeing attitude as subsumed under agent: "Where would attitude fall within our pattern? Often it is the *preparation* for an act, which would make it a kind of symbolic act, or incipient act. But in its character as a state of *mind* that may or may not lead to an act, it is quite clearly to be classed under the head of *agent*."[103] In other cases, an attitude may serve as a substitute for an act—as when, for example, "the sympathetic person can let the intent do service for the deed."[104] Simply expressing the "correct" attitude may be enough, and performance of acts of sympathy thus may not be needed.[105]

Burke introduces the term *ratio* to describe the relationships among the elements of the pentad. All of the terms are consubstantial in that they share in the substance of the act. An act inevitably implies, for example, the idea of an agent, and the idea of an agent acting implies the idea of a scene in which the act takes place. Burke formulates 10 ratios that allow for a more detailed examination of the various relationships among the terms: scene-act, scene-agent, scene-agency, scene-purpose, act-purpose, act-agent, act-agency, agent-purpose, agent-agency, and agency-purpose. Reversal of the order of the terms in each pair creates an additional 10 ratios.

Ratios suggest a relationship of propriety, suitability, or requirement among the elements. A scene-act ratio, for example, deals with the kind of act called for by the scene or the modes of response that are required by the situation in which the act occurs. A church scene, for example, determines that only certain acts with certain characteristics will be performed there. Praying, for example, is proper in the scene, while doing cartwheels is not. In a scene of a shipwreck, everyone on the ship responds in some way to the situation, with the scene determining or creating acts in accordance with it. In examining such relationships, the scene is analyzed as "a fit 'container' for the act, expressing in fixed properties the same quality that the action expresses."[106]

The act-agent ratio focuses on a different relationship. It is used to examine how acts can remake individuals in accordance with their nature. The act of betraying a friend, for example, forms the individual to some degree into a traitor. A reversal of the terms to create an agent-act ratio focuses on how a person's character requires the performance of certain acts. A staid professor, for example, is expected to perform acts that exemplify intelligence and seriousness, and this professor would not be likely to perform a comedy routine as part of a local talent night at a bar. Evidence of the act-agent ratio also is seen in how the donning of a clerical garment, a judicial robe, or a police uniform transforms the character of the agent.

According to the relationship of the agency-act ratio, the means selected for carrying out an act confine and restrict it in particular ways. The expression of thoughts in the form of a sonnet, for example, necessarily constrains the act of expression by sculpting it into a particular pattern of rhythm and rhyme. On the other hand, the act-agency ratio suggests that if a particular act is to be accomplished, certain means must be used. An act of forgiveness by one individual toward another requires love and gentleness not hate and violence.[107]

In a pentadic analysis of a rhetorical act, the five elements of the pentad are named and all of the possible ratios explored to discover if one term seems to affect the nature and character of the other terms. The ratios produce a pattern in which one term tends to be the central, controlling, or primary term and defines the other terms in the pentad. In a speech by an anti-abortion advocate on the appropriateness of killing doctors who perform abortions, for example, a rhetor may describe the agent—himself—as a heroic savior, the act as stopping murder, the agency as any means necessary to stop murder, the purpose as saving innocent lives, and the scene as one of desperation in which legal tactics to stop murder have been unsuccessful. Application of the ratios reveals that the dominant term is purpose—to save innocent lives—suggesting that those who are persuaded by his argument accept a definition of the situation as focused on purpose. The motivating force for the rhetor and those who share his definition of the situation is a belief that they are representatives of divine will, doing God's work of honoring human life. The sacredness of this mission sanctifies whatever acts are necessary to fulfill it.

Burke intended the pentad to be used internally—within a rhetorical transaction such as a speech or a poem—so that the pentadic elements are selected from the actual content of the rhetor's discourse. The act is the act discussed by the rhetor, the scene is where the rhetor says the act occurs, and the agent is the person or persons the rhetor sees as engaging in the act. The pentad has been extended, however, to apply as well to the larger context in which the rhetoric studied is seen as the act, with the other elements selected to correspond to it. In this case, a speech is the act, the scene is the place where the speech is delivered, and the agent is the rhetor delivering the speech.[108]

Rooted in a dramatistic perspective, the pentad enables the critic first to name the elements involved in the act and then to investigate the relationships among those elements. As a result, an interpretation of the motivation of the rhetor whose act is the object of study can be formulated. This information can be used to understand the rhetor's particular orientation and the kinds of interpretations she is likely to apply to her current and future actions. It also can be used to discover alternative perspectives for viewing an act. By featuring a different term in the framing of a topic or perspective, the critic can see it from a different viewpoint. The pentad thus can provide a way to detect and correct for bias in an interpretation, serving as the basis for efforts to overcome the limitations of a single critical vocabulary.

Logology

In dramatism, Burke sees drama as representative of symbol use in general. From dramatism, he moves to the analysis of language through logology, seeing theology as representative. *Logology*, a rare word for philology or historical linguistics, is Burke's term for his effort to discover how language works or to discover motivational systems and orientations through the examination of words. It is an approach to the study of symbol systems using a neutralized Christian theology as its model.[109]

Burke studies theological terms not to argue whether or not religious doctrine is true but for the insights that such terms provide into the operation of language. He wants to discover the fundamental truths about the nature and forms of language as a motive, and he seeks the perfect model of the use of words. He chooses theology as this model because he sees it as one field where the resources of language as language have been worked out exhaustively: "religious cosmogonies are designed, in the last analysis, as exceptionally thoroughgoing modes of persuasion. . . . And in order to plead . . . as persuasively as possible, the religious always ground their exhortations (to themselves and others) in statements of the widest and deepest possible scope, concerning the authorship of men's motives."[110] Burke also sees theology as a useful model for the study of language because language creates theology; Burke, then, sees God as a function of language or symbol use. Faith, doctrine, and the notion of an ultimate supernatural being are possible only through language. Theology thus models a basic function of language—the creation of reality through symbol use.[111]

Burke draws six analogies between language and a supernatural being. These analogies reveal principles of language and suggest how such principles underpin ideological and motivational systems, including religion. One such analogy he suggests is that words are to nature as spirit is to matter. Words transcend things as spirit transcends matter; the realm of the symbolic pervades the realm of matter. Another analogy suggests that the relation between the thing and its name is like the relationships among the components of the Trinity. A correspondence or communion exists between the symbolized and the symbol, just as there is between the Father and the Son.

With the development of his notion of logology, Burke has not abandoned dramatism. As William H. Rueckert explains, the "shift from *dramatism* to *logology* is the shift from the smaller category (literature or drama) to the larger category (words) from which the smaller one derives."[112] Logology, then, might be seen as a theory and methodology about words at a higher level of generalization than dramatism. Another difference between dramatism and logology is that dramatism is concerned more with ontology or being, and logology's primary concern is with epistemology or knowledge. Burke sees the nature of the human being in dramatistic terms and answers questions about how reality is known in logological terms: Dramatism "features what we humans *are* (the symbol-using animal). Logology is rooted in the range and quality of *knowledge* that we acquire when our bodies (physiological organisms in the realm of non-symbolic motion) come to profit by their peculiar aptitude for learning the arbitrary, conventional mediums of communication."[113] Burke's notions of the negative, hierarchy, perfection, and the ritual of pollution-purification-redemption are primary concepts developed from his logological perspective.

The Negative

Burke begins his exploration of the negative by examining the world of motion or nature. In this world, he finds, no negatives exist; "everything simply is what it is and as it is."[114] A tree, for example, is a tree; in no way can it be "*not* a tree."[115] The only way something can "not be" something in nature is for it to "be" something else. As Burke explains, "To look for negatives in nature would be as absurd as though you were to go out hunting for the square root of minus-one. The negative is a function peculiar to symbol systems, quite as the square root of minus-one is an implication of a certain mathematical symbol system."[116] The notion of the negative was added to the natural world as a product of language, making it "the ultimate test of symbolicity."[117]

The principle of the negative developed inevitably out of language. When individuals use language, they must recognize that a word for a thing is not that thing: "Quite as the *word* 'tree' is verbal and the *thing* tree is non-verbal, so all words for the non-verbal must, by the very nature of the case, discuss the realm of the non-verbal in terms of *what it is not.*"[118] Language users "must have a *spontaneous feeling* for the negative"—they "must know when something is *not* quite what language, taken literally, states it to be."[119]

Moral action arises as a consequence of the hortatory, judgmental uses of the negative that are possible in language. The negative allows for the establishment of commands or admonitions that govern the actions of individuals—the "thou-shalt-not's" or the "don'ts."[120] The ability to distinguish between right and wrong thus is a consequence of the concept of the negative. Without the negative implicit in language, moral action based on conceptions of right and wrong behavior (such as law, moral and social rules, and rights) would not exist.[121]

Hierarchy

The concept of the negative inherent in language leads to the establishment of hierarchies constructed on the basis of numerous negatives and commandments. Hierarchy also might be called *bureaucracy; the ladder; a sense of order*; or "any kind of graded, value-charged structure in terms of which things, words, people, acts, and ideas are ranked."[122] Hierarchy deals with "the relation of higher to lower, or lower to higher, or before to after, or after to before" and concerns the "arrangement whereby each rank is over-lord to its underlings and underling to its overlords."[123]

Hierarchies may be built around any elements—a division of labor, pos-session of different properties, ages, status positions, stages of learning, or levels of skill, for example. No one hierarchy is inevitable, and hierarchies are constantly crumbling and forming. What is important, Burke empha-sizes, is the inevitability of the hierarchic principle—the human impulse to build society around ambition or hierarchy on the basis of commandments derived from the concept of the negative.

The hierarchic principle motivates individuals to perform a variety of actions. Those on the lowest rungs of a hierarchy fear slipping to even lower rungs, and those at the top fear they will be surpassed. Some seek to attain positions above them on the hierarchy. Others do not actually have to reach higher positions to be satisfied—they may rise vicariously by being used in some way by those in higher positions. A graduate research assistant, for ex-ample, may endure verbal abuse and attack by a professor to assume the professor's status vicariously. Those at or near the top of the hierarchy, on the other hand, are motivated to act by the threat of descending the hierar-chy. For example, in the effort to "keep up with the Joneses," individuals might purchase material goods to avoid falling in the hierarchy that mea-sures success by acquisitions. Individuals also might allow themselves to be used by or grant favors to those below them to reaffirm their own positions, or they might reject those lower on the hierarchy for the same reason.[124]

Perfection

Each member of a hierarchy strives to achieve the perfection repre-sented by the top of the hierarchy. The hierarchy, then, sets in motion a drive for perfection. Burke's notion of perfection is based on Aristotle's concept of entelechy, whereby each being aims at the perfection natural to its kind, and things are seen "according to the perfection (that is, finishedness) of which that kind is capable."[125] Everything, according to Burke, is trying to perfect or complete itself—to bring to completion the kind of thing it is. The seed, for example, " 'implicitly contains' a future conforming to its nature."[126]

The principle of perfection is derived, as is the concept of the negative, from the nature of language. According to Burke, "symbolicity, for all its im-perfection, contains in itself a principle of perfection by which the symbol-using animals are always being driven, or rather, towards which they are al-ways striving, as with a lost man trying to answer a call in a stormy night."[127] This principle of perfection is derived from language in that the "mere de-sire to name something by its 'proper' name, or to speak a language in its dis-tinctive ways is intrinsically 'perfectionist.' "[128] Because language is part of the essence of humans, this perfectionist quality of language also becomes an essential part of humans because they have a tendency to make them-selves over "in the image of" the "distinctive trait, language."[129] As they de-sire to use language correctly, they strive toward perfection in all of their symbolic action—driving toward unattainable ideals and given to excess in their attempts to attain those ideals.[130]

The principle of perfection operates regardless of the ends that individu-als conceive as ultimate, and these ends may be positive or negative, beneficial or destructive. A man may strive to be the perfect criminal, the perfect villain, or the perfect fool, just as he may seek to become the perfect teacher or the perfect husband. Humans attempt to live out the implications of their selected terms, whatever they are. As Burke explains, "Let a man have a gun; and if he shoots it, not because it gives him a sense of power, or because it might pre-pare him to defend himself, or because it has secret analogies with sexual prowess, etc., but simply because *there is a certain range of things that can be done with guns qua guns*—there you have 'perfection' as a motive."[131] Burke recognizes the potentially dark side of perfection, leading, as it can, to events like the Holocaust from the creation of the "perfect" enemy and the destruc-tion that technology allows to be accomplished easily and efficiently. He seeks to undermine the appeal of perfectionism through the adoption of many termi-nologies or terministic screens, played off one another. As Timothy W. Crusius explains: "If language has us rather than we it, yet we can at least choose a dia-logue of vocabularies that should prevent bondage to only one."[132]

Individuals at all ranks share in the principle of hierarchy, accepting the upward and downward movement regardless of the positions they hold on the hierarchy. While the culminating or top stage of the hierarchy best rep-resents the ideal of the hierarchy, each stage of the hierarchy is "infused with the spirit of the Ultimate Stage."[133] Burke explains how this feature of the hierarchy unifies participants: "For if any point, or 'moment,' in a hierarchic series can be said to represent, in its limited way, the principle of 'perfection' of the ultimate design, then each tiny act shares in the absolute meaning of the total act."[134]

The universe thus is filled with entities in various stages of progress to-ward perfection or completion on numerous hierarchies. Whether in phys-ics, Christianity, poetry, seeking revenge, swimming, or growing vegetables, human beings drive uncontrollably and irreversibly toward the end of what-ever line they are on. As they attempt to perfect whatever they do, nothing is free of this entelechial motive. Human beings are always "rotten with perfec-tion"[135] or corrupted by a drive toward perfection.

Mystery

Hierarchy, while unifying its members through the perfection embodied in its ideal, also is characterized by division. As an ordering of classes, hierar-chy results inevitably in estrangement and divisiveness. The differences among members of a hierarchy arise not only from the separateness of their physical bodies but also from their different modes of living.[136] Three concepts used by Burke help explain the existence of such differences among beings and create mystery—occupational psychosis, the terministic screen, and trained incapacity.

Occupational psychosis, a term Burke borrows from John Dewey, is a pronounced character of mind relating to one's occupation or "a certain way of thinking" that accompanies "a certain way of living."[137] Occupational psychosis reinforces particular life patterns: "To equip themselves for their kinds of work, people develop emphases, discriminations, attitudes, etc. Special preferences, dislikes, fears, hopes, apprehensions, idealizations are brought to the fore."[138] By *occupation*, Burke is not limiting his meaning to a trade or career; he means anything with which individuals are occupied. An occupation, for example, might be to have a hunchback, to be religious, to be divorced, or to have rescued a little girl from drowning.[139]

The development of a particular perspective on life results in a framework for seeing, a terministic screen. The terms or vocabularies individuals use as a result of their occupations constitute a kind of screen that directs attention to particular aspects of reality rather than others. Each way of earning a living develops its own distinctive terminology. A person trained in medicine, for example, sees life from a medical point of view or through a terministic screen of medicine, directing the attention in particular ways and producing particular kinds and qualities of observations.[140]

The result of occupational psychosis and its accompanying terministic screen is trained incapacity, the condition in which "one's very abilities can function as blindnesses."[141] As individuals adopt measures in keeping with their past training, the very soundness of that training may lead them to misjudge situations and to adopt the wrong measures for the achievement of their goals—making their training an incapacity. A person trained to work in the competitive business world of the United States, for example, may be unable to cooperate with other businesspersons because of that training, even when cooperative action alone will prevent the failure of a business.[142]

Given different occupations, terministic screens, and the consequent trained incapacity, some differences among members of a hierarchy are likely to be significant—as with a king and a peasant, an accountant and a musician, or a Sunday painter and a renowned professional artist. In other cases, the differences among beings are imaginary. In both cases, members lack knowledge about other beings and see different modes of living by others as implying different modes of thinking. The result of these differences is the unknown, the unexplained, the secret—or what Burke calls *mystery*.[143]

Mystery performs two important functions in a hierarchical system. One is that it encourages the maintenance and preservation of the hierarchy because it encourages obedience:

> For, once a believer is brought to accept mysteries, he will be better minded
> to take orders without question from those persons whom he considers
> authoritative. In brief, mysteries are a good grounding for obedience, inso-

far as the acceptance of a mystery involves a person in the abnegation of his own personal judgment. . . . So, if a man, in accepting a "mystery," accepts someone else's judgment in place of his own, by that same token he becomes subject willingly. That is, subjection is implicit in his act of belief![144]

A second function of mystery is that it enables the members of the hierarchy to identify and to communicate with one another. Mystery allows for the transcendence of differences among members—whether real or imagined—by hiding some of the differences that do exist and allowing beliefs to be held about substances they share. Fans of a rock star, for example, generally have little in common with their idol in terms of lifestyle, values, wealth, or prestige—the musician is substantially higher on a number of hierarchies than they are. But to the degree that mystery cloaks their differences, the fans are able to identify with her and be persuaded by her—whether by adopting her style of dress, learning the words to her songs, attending her concerts, buying the products she advertises, or taking music lessons in preparation for a similar career. Burke summarizes this function of mystery: "Rhetorically considered, Mystery is a major resource of persuasion. Endow a person, an institution, a thing with the glow or resonance of the Mystical, and you have set up a motivational appeal to which people spontaneously ('instinctively,' 'intuitively') respond. In this respect, an ounce of 'Mystery' is worth a ton of 'argument.' Indeed, where Mystery is, we can be assured that the arguments will profusely follow."[145]

For Burke, the concept of the negative, derived from language, is crucial for understanding the communication process. It leads to the establishment of hierarchies in which human beings strive to perfect themselves according to the ideal at the top. Although divided in numerous ways, members of a hierarchy are able to identify with and communicate with one another through the mystery that hides their differences.

Pollution-Purification-Redemption

The negative and its related terms of hierarchy, perfection, and mystery are the foundation for the rhetoric of rebirth, by which individuals deal with the consequences of these linguistic processes to effect redemption, rebirth, or a new identity. The rhetoric of rebirth involves movement through three steps—pollution, purification, and redemption. Pollution is the initial state of guilt, an unclean condition of sins and burdens; purification is the step of cleansing or catharsis, where the guilt is sloughed off; and redemption is the stage of cleanliness in which a new state—whether physical, spiritual, or psychological—is achieved.

Two consequences of the hierarchy are obedience and communication, but there is another consequence as well—guilt or pollution. *Guilt* is Burke's term for the secular equivalent of original sin, an offense that cannot be avoided or a condition in which all people share. It "is intrinsic to the social order as such; and in this sense it is 'inherited' by all mankind, being 'prior' to any individual lapse into 'actual sin.' "[146] Other words for guilt might be *anxiety, social tension, unresolved tension*, or *embarrassment*.[147]

Guilt arises inevitably and in principle from the nature of hierarchy because it is rooted in language. Through the negative, various kinds of hierarchic orders are created, all of them containing hundreds of admonitions and commandments. No person is capable of obeying all of them, and in some way, everyone fails or disobeys: "Once you have a laddered society, then, no matter what you are, no matter where you are, you are unsettled. If you are of low status, there is the 'accusation' that you are not higher. If you are at the top, there is your false relation to those at the bottom. You have a basic, unresolved tension."[148] This failure or disobedience causes guilt, or what Burke sometimes calls the "hierarchal psychosis."[149] Any kind of order automatically creates transgressors who experience guilt, a phenomenon summarized by Burke in one of his poems: "Order leads to Guilt/ (for who can keep commandments!)."[150] Stated succinctly, "Those 'Up' are guilty of not being 'Down,' those 'Down' are certainly guilty of not being 'Up.' "[151]

In connection with his discussion of pollution, Burke introduces the notion of the fecal motive. The purgation of pollution "readily includes connotations of physical excretion"[152] because just as "only by excretion can the body remain *healthy*,"[153] the individual can remain psychologically or spiritually healthy only by getting rid of the guilt or pollution of some aspect of the self. Burke sees a fecal motive in the redemptive process, driving the rhetor to purge from the self the negatively charged persons, places, things, and ideas.[154] The fecal motive is indicated in rhetoric, Burke believes, in images of the Demonic Trinity, the "three principles of the erotic, urinary, and excremental."[155] Images in rhetoric that indicate the presence of the fecal motive include the fecal, sexual, and urinal orifices of the body; their products; anything resembling them in size, shape, or color; and the acts themselves. A character who wears a brown suit might suggest feces, for example, while rain might suggest urination. Puns also might reveal such images; for instance, the word *urn* might suggest urine. Such images, Burke asserts, are symbolic of the desire of an individual to be rid of some guilt and attain redemption.

Burke sees the Demonic Trinity as representing the desire for purgation of pollution because he believes "that *all* bodily processes must have their effect upon human imagery."[156] Natural objects or events are "treated as replicas of corresponding mental states."[157] Sexual and bodily functions are thoroughly infused with negatives, commandments, and taboos that do not allow them to be discussed, so they are discussed in rhetoric in disguise. In movement toward change or redemption of any kind, body imagery is likely to surface, enabling individuals both to purge their guilt and to discuss the unspeakable.[158]

Guilt is a permanent part of the human condition in that it is intrinsic in the negative and the hierarchy produced by language. Some methods of catharsis, purgation, purification, or cleansing are needed to rid individuals of this guilt so that they can achieve redemption. Just as a language system creates guilt, it is the means through which that guilt is purged.[159]

Two primary means for relieving guilt using symbolic action are available—victimage and mortification. Victimage is the process by which guilt is transferred to a vessel or vessels outside of the rhetor. It is the principle of scapegoating, where a victim is selected to be the representative of unwanted evils and is loaded with the guilt of the victimizer. A transfer is made from the polluted, contaminated person to some other person, place, or thing so that others are made to suffer for the sins of the rhetor. The greater the internal inadequacies, the more evils a rhetor is likely to "load upon the back of 'the enemy.' "[160] In the transfer from the self to something else in victimage, the victim may be killed (actually or symbolically), driven away, mocked, or defiled. Hitler's killing of the Jews as scapegoats for the German people exemplifies victimage.

Paradoxically, the scapegoat "combines in one figure contrary principles of identification and alienation."[161] An original state of merger or consubstantiality characterizes victimage in that scapegoats must share some elements with the victimizers. The scapegoat first is included in the group, then assumes the group's sins, and finally is expelled. Division operates, then, "in that the elements shared in common are being ritualistically alienated,"[162] driving the two apart by their differences.

Those who are purified in the process of victimage by defining themselves in opposition to the scapegoat achieve union or identification. If the victimizers can agree on nothing else, they "can unite on the basis of a foe shared by all."[163] Is "it not a terrifying fact," Burke asks, "that you can never get people together except when they have a goat in common? That's the terrifying thing that I begin to see as the damnation of the human race. That's how they have to operate; they get congregation by segregation."[164]

In contrast to victimage, where guilt is transferred to someone or something else, mortification is the process by which individuals make themselves suffer for their guilt or sins. Mortification is self-inflicted punishment, self-sacrifice, or self-imposed denials and restrictions designed to slay characteristics, impulses, or aspects of the self. For example, a person may feel guilt or pollution arising from a low place on a hierarchy of knowledge or prestige. She denies herself free time and pursuit of pleasurable activities to attend classes, write papers, and study for examinations to achieve a college degree and the redemption that comes with a higher place on the hierarchical ladder. Similarly, a person who is dieting denies the body food in an act of mortification to be rid of the pollution of fat and to gain a new identity as a thin person.[165]

The third stage of the rebirth process is redemption, a temporary rest or stasis that represents symbolic rebirth. At this stage, a change has taken place within the rhetor because the self has been purified and redeemed. Redemption may be found in a change of identity, a new perspective, or a feeling "of *moving forward*, towards a *goal*"[166] or a better life in general. The rebirth process is a never-ending one. Once rebirth is achieved, the cycle begins anew as the rhetor experiences pollution yet again either on the same hierarchy or on others. Thus, the process of pollution-purification-redemption is the drama of the self in quest, the human effort to discover and maintain identities so that they can move toward the perfection they seek. It is a life-long process of growth and change.[167]

Definition of the Human Being

Burke's definition of the human being summarizes the major concepts of his theory of rhetoric. The concepts involved in his notions of rhetoric, dramatism, and logology are combined in his definition of the human being:

BEING BODIES THAT LEARN LANGUAGE
THEREBY BECOMING WORDLINGS
HUMANS ARE THE
SYMBOL-MAKING, SYMBOL-USING, SYMBOL-MISUSING ANIMAL
INVENTOR OF THE NEGATIVE
SEPARATED FROM OUR NATURAL CONDITION
BY INSTRUMENTS OF OUR OWN MAKING
GOADED BY THE SPIRIT OF HIERARCHY
ACQUIRING FOREKNOWLEDGE OF DEATH
AND ROTTEN WITH PERFECTION[168]

The concept of the symbol-using animal references Burke's notion that the possession of a symbol system separates human beings from animals and allows them to develop a neurological as well as a biological nature. A symbol system places human beings in the realm of action, where they may engage in symbolic action either wisely or foolishly. Language greatly increases the opportunities humans have for mischief, making possible not only "new divisions, new enemies, and new hatreds" but modern technologies that "enable us to enact our darkest fantasies with unprecedented power."[169]

The human being as inventor of the negative is a crucial concept for Burke. The principle of the negative is inherent in a symbol system, and the conception that something can be not something else is possible only through language. The negative does not exist in nature, where things simply are.

Burke's definition of the human being also includes the notion that humans are separated or alienated from their natural condition by instruments of their own making. By *nature*, Burke means the world of biology, sense perception, and motion. With the tool of language, humans transcend that state of nature and never again can be in a purely natural condition. Once language is developed, it "is ever present,"[170] and individuals "must perceive nature through the fog of symbol-ridden social structures."[171] Reality is constructed through symbols and is not encountered directly:

> But can we bring ourselves to realize just what that formula implies, just how overwhelmingly much of what we mean by "reality" has been built up for us through nothing but our symbol systems? Take away our books, and what little do we know about history, biography, even something so "down to earth" as the relative position of seas and continents? What is

our "reality" for today . . . but all this clutter of symbols about the past combined with whatever things we know mainly through maps, magazines, newspapers, and the like about the present?[172]

By *instruments*, Burke means language and all of the tools that have been invented with language. These tools are not simply devices for performing physical or mechanical work but include all inventions, social structures, systems of governance, and symbolic conceptualizations such as rights, obligations, powers, authorities, awards, technology, and services. In other words, instruments are all those things that humans are able to create because they are symbol users: "Remember always that no modern instrument could have been invented, or could be produced, without the use of a vast linguistic complexity."[173] Burke recognizes that "all animals use tools in the primary sense. But only humans are tool-using in the secondary sense (as when external agencies are used to produce other external agencies)."[174] Only humans use tools to make tools or use symbols about symbols; only humans can remove themselves many times over from their starting point and are able to be "critics-who-write-critiques-of-critical-criticism."[175]

Burke's definition identifies, in addition to language, an element that separates humans from animals: a foreknowledge of death. This foreknowledge of death and the very conception of death are possible only through the acquisition of language. In its biological state—the state of motion—death is a particular biochemical condition, but as a conception of language, death is an idea capable of symbolizing the ultimate negative and serving as a motive for action.

Finally, Burke's definition includes motivation by the spirit of perfection that infuses hierarchy. Human beings desire completion. They continually drive toward the perfection embodied in the god terms at the top of the hierarchy, striving to make their lives perfect. Such efforts, however, cause them to experience guilt and to carry to resolution even those terminologies detrimental to their well-being.[176] Human beings thus are "rotten with perfection."[177]

Commentary

Attempting to summarize the responses to Burke's works and to assess his contribution to rhetoric leads inevitably to paradox and antithesis. A number of critics praise Burke for a particular quality, but an equal number criticize his work for precisely that quality. Rueckert has characterized the two opposing camps as apologists who suffer, "in varying degrees of intensity, from Burke-sickness, a disease which produces hysterical enthusiasm and loss of perspective," and adversaries who "suffer from Burke-nausea, a state which produces hysterical anger and a corresponding loss of perspective."[178] Harry Slochower suggests that the clash of the opposing sides produces consubstantiality in their shared loss of perspective. He explains that Burke strives toward "unification, a unification to be won *through* diversification."[179]

The substance of Burke's work has been praised in terms such as "penetrating" and "rewarding,"[180] "bold, original, energetic, fecund,"[181] "extraordinarily rich and suggestive,"[182] and as representative of "agility of mind,"[183] "intellectual virtuosity,"[184] and a "systematic intellect."[185] "There is no question that Burke is one of the major critical minds of the twentieth century," asserts Rueckert.[186] Others agree, as Alfred Kazin does in his assertion that Burke "is an original. One can't really compare him with other people."[187]

Some critics hold exactly the opposite opinion concerning the quality of Burke's work. Philosophers, in particular, tend not to see much merit in his work. Among the charges raised is that his work appears incapable of "system-building, which at length it craves."[188] Burke's work also has been described as a "vast rambling edifice of quasi-sociological and quasi-psychoanalytical speculation" that rests "on nothing more solid than a set of unexamined and uncriticized metaphysical assumptions."[189] It is seen as "inconclusive,"[190] characterized by "theoretical limitations" that "prevent him from turning up the deeper ground of the fallacies he means to destroy."[191]

The breadth of topics with which Burke deals also is the subject of both negative and positive comment. His work is seen by some as characterized by "a dizzying array of subject matters—among them anthropology, linguistics, religion, oratory, fiction, history, economics, philosophy, and politics."[192] As Eugene Goodheart suggests, "Nothing human is alien to Kenneth Burke. He is the least confined of modern critics."[193] Hyman asserts that, as a result of this breadth, his work "has had the compensatory virtue of endless fertility, suggestiveness, an inexhaustible throwing off of sparks."[194] It also frees his work, argues Bernard I. Duffey, "from the constraints of aesthetics, ontology, or mere semantics which have provided uneasy bounds for the views of other critics."[195]

Burke's breadth, however, is cause for complaint by critics such as Donald A. Stauffer, who asserts that his work "is too eclectic. How long can we read with both attention and pleasure when, opening at random, we come on a single page that refers to, or quotes, Horace Gregory, Wallace Stevens, 'another writer,' Descartes, 'the idealist scientist Shelley,' Leibnitz, an editor, Pascal, and Rabelais? Ambition here surpasses discrimination."[196] Much of the material Burke discusses, Louis Wirth says, "may be regarded as extraneous material from poetry, philosophy, and politics."[197] Recognition of the fact that Burke largely is self-taught and has acquired his breadth through his own study leads critics such as Arthur E. DuBois to suggest that Burke's motive for including so many topics in his work is simply an eagerness to display his learning: "And then Kenneth Burke is doubtless a little over-proud or ostentatious of his self-made learning."[198]

Not only the content of Burke's thought but his style of writing has been criticized, described variously as "too technical and abstract,"[199] "difficult and often confusing,"[200] "turbid,"[201] and "not 'inviting'. . . . The argument often omits the intermediate steps which are expected to be made by the reader himself."[202] "The greatest difficulty that confronts the reader of Burke," Sidney Hook asserts, "is finding out what he means,"[203] a remark echoed in the charge that Burke does not write English.[204] These negative reactions are summarized by Austin Warren, who explains that understanding the point of Burke's writing is difficult: "To discern its drift is another matter; and one has long to wait before the smoke sufficiently clears to let one discover who has won and why."[205]

Two sources of difficulty with Burke's style are mentioned most often. The unusual and specialized terminology Burke employs creates much of his distinctive style. As Marie Hochmuth Nichols explains, "In part the difficulty arises from the numerous vocabularies he employs. His words in isolation are usually simple enough, but he often uses them in new contexts."[206] Goodheart agrees: "If Burke is the adversary of all forms of reduction and de-mystification, he nevertheless proves himself to be an obsessive translator of forms of thought into his own privileged dramatistic vocabulary."[207] Another characteristic of Burke's style is that his discussion of central issues often is drowned out amid discussions and references that appear irrelevant to the main line of thought. The result, Stauffer suggests, is "a style where exceptions, illustrations, by-plays, new ideas, and sudden speculations burgeon from the main stem of the thought."[208] As George Knox explains, Burke seems to have an "overweening sense of responsibility to shovel around a growing heap of apparently uncorrelated documentation."[209]

Yet, some critics argue that Burke "has said something worth saying and said it well."[210] Although some describe his style in positive terms such as "incisive eloquence,"[211] critics more commonly recognize his style as difficult but justify it. Nichols attributes some of the difficulty of comprehension to "the compactness of his writing, the uniqueness of his organizational patterns, the penetration of his thought, and the breadth of his endeavor."[212] Such an undertaking as Burke's, other critics suggest, requires the kind of style Burke employs. Schneider asserts that his "style is seen to be, by the steady and serene progress of its arguments, remarkably suited to its purpose."[213] Barbara A. Biesecker explains, "the series of decisive engagements we call Burke's thought may not be best understood by assuming that a logic of progression obtains between them. For in presuming progression one becomes obliged, wittingly or not, to discount or sublate the false starts, delays, fissures, and detours that, I want to argue, open up for Burke and for us quite unanticipated theoretical and critical possibilities."[214]

All of Burke's critics agree that active participation and the commitment of the reader are required in reading the work of Burke: He "has never dissolved it into pap for the multitude or codified it into tablets for quick absorption by graduate students. He has never made it with a book club."[215] Thus, only the determined push on: "Let anyone avoid it who is not endowed with some philosophic, linguistic, and esthetic training coupled with some power of taut attentiveness";[216] his writing requires that the reader be someone "with a strenuous brain who wishes to go pioneering."[217] If the reader is willing to engage in the adventure, however, the results are "rewarding,"[218] "exhilarating,"[219] and "extraordinarily enriching."[220] James M. Cox suggests that the role required of the reader of Burke's works prompts learning: "I have never felt that I understood him, and I have always found him sufficiently difficult to read, yet I do not hesitate to say that *somehow* I learned more from Burke than from any other critic or teacher."[221] Similarly, Denis Donoghue explains that he regularly reads Burke when he feels "especially inert and stupid; he gets me going."[222] In short, as Benjamin De Mott explains, Burke's work "is generous to its reader: it tells him he has an active mind, is agile and quick, relishes complication, is scornful of emotional posturing and human enough to enjoy being silly now and then."[223]

Burke's contributions to rhetoric are less in dispute than the utility of his style. Trevor Melia argues that he is "probably the most significant contributor to rhetorical theory since Cicero."[224] Similarly, Hugh Dalziel Duncan asserts, "As matters now stand, it is unwise to talk about communication without some understanding of Burke."[225] Four primary contributions Burke makes to rhetorical theory seem to justify such praise. One is his affirmation of the importance of rhetoric and its study in human life. He sees rhetoric as at the very center of life or the ground that underlies all human activity. Rhetoric is not something apart from life or one component of life; it is life. To understand the operation and nature of rhetoric, for Burke, is to understand a great many other things about human beings.

A second contribution Burke makes to rhetorical theory is in the system he creates for explaining rhetoric. Although many earlier rhetoricians attempted but largely failed to build an entire system, theory, or philosophy to explain how rhetoric operates, Burke has come very close to creating one. His work represents near completion of a coherent, thoroughly developed system explaining the operation of rhetoric in human life. As Goodheart suggests, he "is a critic with systematic ambitions"[226] who attempts a "systematic understanding of the workings of language."[227] His system allows for the discovery of the way the mind works and why. He incorporates into his perspective on rhetoric assumptions about the nature of the human being, the human's relation to rhetoric, the nature of rhetoric, and the part rhetoric plays in the motivations of human beings. Burke's work is marked not only by an effort to systematize but by "the need to resist the stultifying consequences of such an effort."[228] Burke makes clear, as Goodheart explains, "that he wants to unsettle things, not tidy them into a neat system. He is concerned with 'how an "orientation" (or general view of reality) takes form. How such a system of interpretation, by its very scope and thoroughness, interferes with its own revision. Why terms like "escape," "scapegoat mechanism," "pleasure principle," and "rationalization" should be used skeptically and grudgingly.' No interpretation is secure: 'We may also interpret our interpretations.' "[229]

Perhaps more than any other contemporary scholar of rhetoric, Burke's works also have contributed to the practice of rhetorical criticism. His concepts have suggested numerous methods to be used in the analysis of rhetoric. The pentad, strategies of redemption, types of form, and identification, for example, all have been used extensively by rhetorical critics in their studies of specific rhetorical acts. Yet, as Burke explicitly suggests and as he demonstrates in his own criticism, the methods arising from his notions should not and do not limit the critic to the units of analysis suggested by these notions alone. They are to be used as guides for the critic to encourage an exploration of various perspectives and interpretations.[230] His methods, more than many others, allow for expansion and freedom rather than reduction and confinement.

Students of rhetoric do not read Burke as often as they once did. As Donoghue suggests: "It is my sad impression that Kenneth Burke has few readers. My students don't read him with much enthusiasm and are dismayed to hear from me that they have to read a lot of him."[231] Nevertheless, his work is seen as relevant to and anticipating numerous trends in current rhetorical scholarship. Goodheart suggests that the "advent of poststructuralism, in particular deconstruction, has revived interest in Burke's logology. Burke anticipates the emphasis in deconstruction on logocentrism, but he proceeds with a wholly different intention. Whereas Burke attempts to show the ways in which language unfolds motives and constitutes structures, deconstruction tries to undo structures and expose the illusoriness of motives (origins)."[232] Burke also anticipates the criticism of all forms of cultural expression that is now standard practice in rhetorical criticism, enabling critics to consider "aesthetic value in popular forms of cultural life."[233]

Other critics suggest that Burke prefigures current explorations of identity in rhetorical and cultural studies. Ann Branaman suggests that Burke explores "the question of if and how identity might serve as an instrument of social critique."[234] "Burke contributes a conception of identity which is both sociologically grounded and critical," she explains. "Rather than ignoring the socially imposed constraints upon the use of identity as a critical instrument, Burke explains how patterns of identification can be critical and transformative rather than merely reproductive despite the fact that experience is always already socially patterned."[235] Biesecker, in a similar vein, suggests that Burke contributes to a theory of social change within a postmodern context, in which "the demise of foundations, not the least of which was the sovereign rational subject of Enlightenment philosophy that served as a point of departure for a whole host of theories of emancipation, seems to have left us without any conceptual foothold whatsoever from which to begin."[236] By "insisting on the constitutive role of rhetoric in the formation of individual and collective subjects," Biesecker claims, "Burke's work productively supplements contemporary understandings of the relations of structure and subject." He thus provides "an alternative theorization of the relations of structure and subject that, in taking rhetoric seriously into account, can admit the role of human agency in the making and unmaking of social structures and history without resurrecting the sovereign subject of Enlightenment philosophy."[237]

The contradictions and paradoxes seem to dissolve when Burke's work is viewed from the perspective that its primary concern is with rhetoric. That his work may lack formal philosophical grounding is less important given his goal of explaining the nature and function of rhetoric, which deals not with formal logic but with the reasoning of humans in their daily lives. His breadth is seen not so much as irrelevant excursion as it is a recognition that the scope of rhetoric is broad, encompassing all of the topics with which he deals. Burke's style, too, seems less formidable when it is viewed as a rhetorical strategy designed to invite the reader to active participation with him in the exploration of the complexities of rhetoric. R. P. Blackmur captures the appropriateness of the rhetorical perspective by which to judge Burke's work when he points out that although some "may object to being called rhetoricians . . . Kenneth Burke must have found it his first cradle-word, and I think he would rather be called Rhetor, as honorific and as description, than anything else."[238]

Bibliography

Books

Attitudes Toward History. New York: New Republic, 1937.
Book of Moments: Poems 1915–1954. Los Altos, CA: Hermes, 1955.
Collected Poems: 1915–1967. Berkeley: University of California Press, 1968.
The Complete White Oxen: Collected Short Fiction of Kenneth Burke. Berkeley: University of California Press, 1968.
Counter-Statement. New York: Harcourt, Brace, 1931.
Dramatism and Development. Barre, MA: Clark University Press, 1972.
A Grammar of Motives. New York: Prentice-Hall, 1945.
Language as Symbolic Action: Essays on Life, Literature, and Method. Berkeley: University of California Press, 1966.
Permanence and Change: An Anatomy of Purpose. New York: New Republic, 1935.
The Philosophy of Literary Form: Studies in Symbolic Action. Baton Rouge: Louisiana State University Press, 1941.
A Rhetoric of Motives. New York: Prentice-Hall, 1950.
The Rhetoric of Religion: Studies in Logology. Boston: Beacon, 1961.
Towards a Better Life: Being a Series of Epistles, or Declamations. New York: Harcourt, Brace, 1932.
The White Oxen and Other Stories. New York: Albert and Charles Boni, 1924.

Articles

" 'Act' as Many-in-One." *Location*, 11 (Summer 1964), 94–98.
"Addendum on Bateson." In *Rigor and Imagination: Essays from the Legacy of Gregory Bateson*. Ed. C. Wilder-Mott and John H. Weaklund. New York: Praeger, 1981, pp. 341–46.
"The Allies of Humanism Abroad." In *The Critique of Humanism: A Symposium*. Ed. C. Hartley Grattan. New York: Brewer and Warren, 1930, pp. 169–92.
"Americanism: Patriotism in General, Americanism in Particular, Interspersed with Pauses." *Direction*, 4 (February 1941), 2–3.
"André Gide, Bookman." *Freeman*, 5 (April 26, 1922), 155–57.
"Approaches to Remy de Gourmont." *Dial*, 70 (February 1921), 125–38.
"An *Arion* Questionnaire: 'The Classics and the Man of Letters.'" *Arion*, 3 (Winter 1964), 23–26.

"The Armour of Jules Laforge." *Contact*, 3 [new series] (1920–23), 9–10.
"Art—and the First Rough Draft of Living." *Modern Age*, 8 (Spring 1964), 155–65.
"The Art of Carl Sprinchorn." *Arts*, 2 (December 1921), 158–59.
"As I Was Saying." *Michigan Quarterly Review*, 11 (Winter 1972), 9–27.
"As One Thing Leads to Another." *Recherches anglaises et américaines*, 12 (1979), 13–17.
"Bankers Arise." *Americana, Satire and Humor*, May 1933, p. 4.
"The Brain Beautiful." *Bennington College Bulletin*, 29 (November 1960), 4–7.
"Catharsis—Second View." *Centennial Review*, 5 (Spring 1961), 107–32.
"Character of Our Culture." *Southern Review*, 6 (Spring 1941), 675–94.
"Chicago and Our National Gesture." *Bookman*, 57 (July 1923), 497–501.
"Colloquy: I. The Party Line." *Quarterly Journal of Speech*, 62 (February 1976), 62–68.
"A Comment on 'It Takes Capital to Defeat Dracula.' " *College English*, 49 (February 1987), 221–22.
"Comments." *Western Speech*, 32 (Summer 1968), 176–83.
"Comments on Eighteen Poems by Howard Nemerov." *Sewanee Review*, 60 (January/March 1952), 117–31.
"Communication and the Human Condition." *Communication*, 1 (1974), 135–52.
"Communications." Letter. *Hopkins Review*, 4 (Winter 1951), 77–79.
"Communications." Letter. *Kenyon Review*, 11 (1949), 310–11.
"Communications to P/T." *Pre/Text*, 8 (Spring/Summer 1987), 156.
"Correspondence." Letter. *Sewanee Review*, 73 (January/March 1965), 173–75.
"Correspondence: Munsoniana." *New Republic*, 69 (November 25, 1931), 46.
"The Correspondence of Flaubert." *Dial*, 72 (February 1922), 147–55.
"Counterblasts on 'Counter-Statement.' " *New Republic*, 69 (December 9, 1931), 101.
"Dada, Dead or Alive." *Aesthete 1925*, 1 (February 1925), 23–26.
"Dancing with Tears in My Eyes." *Critical Inquiry*, 1 (September 1974), 23–31.
"De Beginnibus." *Bennington College Bulletin*, 31 (November 1962), 4–10.
"Doing and Saying: Thoughts on Myth, Cult, and Archetypes." *Salmagundi*, 15 (Winter 1971), 100–19.
"Dramatic Form—And: Tracking Down Implications." *Tulane Drama Review*, 10 (Summer 1966), 54–63.
"Dramatism." In *International Encyclopedia of the Social Sciences*. Ed. David L. Sills. Vol. 7. New York: Macmillan/Free, 1968, pp. 445–52. Rpt. with additional discussion by Burke in *Communication: Concepts and Perspectives*. Ed. Lee Thayer. Washington, DC: Spartan, 1967, pp. 327–60.
"Dramatism and Logology." *Communication Quarterly*, 33 (Spring 1985), 89–93.
"Dramatism and Logology." *Times Literary Supplement*, 4193 (August 12, 1983), 859.
"Dramatism as Ontology or Epistemology: A Symposium." *Communication Quarterly*, 33 (Winter 1985), 17–33. (With Bernard L. Brock, Parke G. Burgess, and Herbert W. Simons.)
"A 'Dramatistic' View of 'Imitation.' " *Accent*, 12 (Autumn 1952), 229–41.
"A Dramatistic View of the Origins of Language: Part One." *Quarterly Journal of Speech*, 38 (October 1952), 251–64.
"A Dramatistic View of the Origins of Language: Part Two." *Quarterly Journal of Speech*, 38 (December 1952), 446–60.
"A Dramatistic View of the Origins of Language: Part III." *Quarterly Journal of Speech*, 39 (February 1953), 79–92.
"An Ecological Proposal." *New Republic*, 161 (December 13, 1969), 30–31.

"Embargo." *Direction*, 2 (November 1939), 2.

" 'Ethan Brand': A Preparatory Investigation."*Hopkins Review*, 5 (Winter 1952), 45–65.

"An Exchange on Machiavelli." *New York Review of Books*, 18 (April 6, 1972), 35–36.

"An Eye-Poem for the Ear: (With Prose Introduction, Glosses, and After-Words)." In *Directions in Literary Criticism: Contemporary Approaches to Literature.* Ed. Stanley Weintraub and Philip Young. University Park: Pennsylvania State University Press, 1973, pp. 228–51.

"The Five Master Terms: Their Place in a 'Dramatistic' Grammar of Motives."*View*, 2 (June 1943), 50–52. Enlarged version in *Twentieth Century English*. Ed. William S. Knickerbocker. New York: Philosophical Library, 1946, pp. 272–88.

"For Whom Do You Write?" *New Quarterly*, 1 (Summer 1934), 8.

"Freedom and Authority in the Realm of the Poetic Imagination." In*Freedom and Authority in Our Time: Twelfth Symposium of the Conference on Science, Philosophy and Religion.* Ed. Lyman Bryson, Louis Finkelstein, R. M. MacIver, and Richard McKeon. New York: Harper, 1953, pp. 365–75.

"A Further View: II." Letter. *Four Quarters* [LaSalle College, Philadelphia], 5 (January 1956), 17.

"Government in the Making."*Direction*, 5 (December 1942), 3–4.

"Human Nature and the Bomb." *University of Chicago Round Table*, 622 (February 19, 1950), 1–11. (With Harrison S. Brown, Herbert Blumer, Helen V. McLean, and William F. Ogburn.)

"Ideology and Myth."*Accent*, 7 (Summer 1947), 195–205.

"The Imagery of Killing." *Hudson Review*, 1 (1948), 151–67.

"In Haste." *Pre/Text*, 6 (Fall/Winter 1985), 329–77.

"In New Jersey, My Adopted, and I Hope Adoptive, State."*New Jersey Monthly*, November 1981, pp. 67–68, 98.

"The Institutions of Art in America."*Arts in Society*, 2 (Fall/Winter 1962), 52–60.

"The Interactive Bind." In *Rigor and Imagination: Essays from the Legacy of Gregory Bateson.* Ed. C. Wilder-Mott and John H. Weaklund. New York: Praeger, 1981, pp. 331–40.

"Intuitive or Scientific?" *Nation*, 146 (January 29, 1938), 139–40.

"Kenneth Burke and Malcolm Cowley: A Conversation." *Pre/Text*, 6 (Fall/Winter 1985), 181–200. (With Malcolm Cowley.)

"Kinds of Criticism." *Poetry*, 68 (August 1946), 272–82.

"Kinds of Sensibility." In *Paul Rosenfeld: Voyager in the Arts.* Ed. Jerome Mellquist and Lucie Wiese. New York: Creative Age, 1948, pp. 100–05.

"*King Lear*: Its Form and Psychosis." *Shenandoah*, 21 (Autumn 1969), 3–18.

"The Language of Poetry, 'Dramatistically' Considered, Part I." *Chicago Review*, 8 (Fall 1954), 88–102.

"The Language of Poetry, 'Dramatistically' Considered, Part II." *Chicago Review*, 9 (Spring 1955), 40–72.

"Last Words on the Ephebe." *Literary Review [New York Evening Post]*, 2 (August 26, 1922), 897–98.

"Letter from a Gentile." *Dialectical Anthropology*, 8 (October 1983), 161–71.

"A Letter from Andover." *Kenneth Burke Society Newsletter*, 2 (July 1986), 3–5.

"Linguistic Approach to Problems of Education." In*Modern Philosophies and Education: The Fifty-Fourth Yearbook of the National Society for the Study of Education.* Ed. Nelson B. Henry. Part I. Chicago: University of Chicago Press, 1955, pp. 259–303.

"Literary Criticism: The Minds Behind the Written Word." *Times Literary Supplement*, September 17, 1954, pp. viii, x.

"The Meaning of C. K. Ogden." *New Republic*, 78 (May 1934), 328–31.

"Methodological Repression and/or Strategies of Containment." *Critical Inquiry*, 5 (Winter 1978), 401–16.

"Motion, Action, Words." *Teachers College Record*, 62 (December 1960), 244–49.

"My Approach to Communism." *New Masses*, 10 (March 20, 1934), 16, 18–20.

"Mysticism as a Solution to the Poet's Dilemma: Addendum." In *Spiritual Problems in Contemporary Literature: A Series of Addresses and Discussions*. Ed. Stanley Romaine Hopper. New York: Harper, 1952, pp. 108–15.

"Negro's Pattern of Life." *Saturday Review of Literature*, 10 (July 29, 1933), 13–14.

"(Nonsymbolic) Motion/(Symbolic) Action." *Critical Inquiry*, 4 (Summer 1978), 809–38.

"Notes on the Lit'ry Life: (Its Quirks and Solemnities)." In *Proceedings of the American Academy of Arts and Letters and the National Institute of Arts and Letters*. Second Series, No. 2. New York: American Academy of Arts and Letters, 1952, pp. 39–50.

"Notes on Walter Pater." *1924*, 2 (1924), 53–58.

"NRT Non-Resident Term." *Bennington College Bulletin*, 28 (November 1959), 16–17.

"On Catharsis, or Resolution." *Kenyon Review*, 21 (Summer 1959), 337–75.

"On 'Creativity'—A Partial Retraction." In *Introspection: The Artist Looks at Himself*. Ed. Donald E. Hayden. University of Tulsa Monograph Series, No. 12. Tulsa, OK: University of Tulsa, 1971, pp. 63–81.

"On Form." *Hudson Review*, 17 (Spring 1964), 103–09.

"On Literary Form." In *The New Criticism and After*. Ed. Thomas Daniel Young. Charlottesville: University Press of Virginia, 1976, pp. 80–90.

"On Motivation in Yeats." *Southern Review*, 7 (1941–42), 547–61.

"On Stress, Its Seeking." *Bennington Review*, 1 (Summer 1967), 32–49.

"On the First Three Chapters of Genesis." *Daedalus*, 87 (Summer 1958), 37–64.

"Order, Action, and Victimage." In *The Concept of Order*. Ed. Paul G. Kuntz. Seattle: University of Washington Press, 1968, pp. 167–90.

"Panel Discussion." In *What is a Poet? Essays from The Eleventh Alabama Symposium on English and American Literature*. Ed. Hank Lazer. Tuscaloosa: University of Alabama Press, 1987, pp. 185–225. (With Gerald Stern, Charles Bernstein, Denise Levertov, David Ignatow, Marjorie Perloff, Helen Vendler, Charles Altieri, Louis Simpson, Hank Lazer, and Gregory Jay.)

"A Philosophy of Drama." *University of Chicago Magazine*, September 1961, pp. 7–8, 20.

"A Plea to Join the Fray and Make It Worth Our While." *Kenneth Burke Society Newsletter*, 11 (October 1984), 1.

"The Poetic Motive." *Hudson Review*, 11 (Spring 1958), 54–63.

"Poetics and Communication." In *Perspectives in Education, Religion and the Arts*. Ed. Howard E. Kiefer and Milton K. Munitz. Albany: State University of New York Press, 1970, pp. 401–18.

"Poetry and Communication." In *Contemporary Philosophical Thought: Vol. 3: Perspectives in Education, Religion, and the Arts*. Ed. Howard E. Kiefer and Milton K. Munitz. Albany: State University of New York Press, 1970, pp. 401–18.

"Poetry as Symbolic Action." In *What is a Poet? Essays from The Eleventh Alabama Symposium on English and American Literature*. Ed. Hank Lazer. Tuscaloosa: University of Alabama Press, 1987, pp. 157–73.

"Policy Made Personal: Whitman's Verse and Prose-Salient Traits." In *Leaves of Grass One Hundred Years After*. Ed. Milton Hindus. Stanford, CA: Stanford University Press, 1955, pp. 74–108.

"The Position of the Progressive: II. Boring from Within." *New Republic*, 65 (February 4, 1931), 326–29.

"Post Poesque Derivation of a Terministic Cluster." *Critical Inquiry*, 4 (Winter 1977), 215–20.

"Postscript." In *Criticism and Social Change*. By Frank Lentricchia. Chicago: University of Chicago Press, 1985, pp. 165–66. (Essay appears in paperback edition only.)

"Progress: Promise and Problems." *Nation*, 184 (April 1957), 322–24.

"A (Psychological) Fable, with a (Logological) Moral." *American Imago*, 35 (Spring/Summer 1978), 203–07.

"Questions and Answers About the Pentad." *College Composition and Communication*, 29 (December 1978), 330–35.

"Questions for Critics." *Direction*, 2 (May/June 1939), 12–13.

"The Reader Critic." Letter. *Little Review*, 9 (Winter 1922), 45.

"Reading While You Run: An Exercise in Translation from English into English." *New Republic*, 93 (November 17, 1937), 36–37.

"Realisms, Occidental Style." In *Asian and Western Writers in Dialogue: New Cultural Identities*. Ed. Guy Amirthanayagam. London, UK: Macmillan, 1982, pp. 26–47.

"Recipe for Prosperity: 'Borrow. Buy. Waste. Want.'" *Nation*, 183 (September 8, 1956), 191–93.

"Redefinitions." *New Republic*, 67 (July 29, 1931), 286–88.

"Redefinitions: II." *New Republic*, 68 (August 26, 1931), 46–47.

"Redefinitions: III." *New Republic*, 68 (September 2, 1931), 74–75.

"Reflections on the Fate of the Union: Kennedy and After." *New York Review of Books*, 1 (December 26, 1963), 10–11.

"The Relation Between Literature and Science." In *The Writer in a Changing World*. Ed. Henry Hart. New York: Equinox Cooperative, 1937, pp. 158–71.

"Responsibilities of National Greatness." *Nation*, 205 (July 17, 1967), 46–50.

"Revolutionary Symbolism in America." In *American Writers' Congress*. Ed. Henry Hart. New York: International, 1935, pp. 87–94.

"The Rhetorical Situation." In *Communication: Ethical and Moral Issues*. Ed. Lee Thayer. New York: Gordon and Breach Science, 1973, pp. 263–75.

"Rhetoric—Old and New." *Journal of General Education*, 5 (April 1951), 202–09.

"Rhetoric, Poetics, and Philosophy." In *Rhetoric, Philosophy, and Literature: An Exploration*. Ed. Don M. Burks. West Lafayette, IN: Purdue University Press, 1978, pp. 15–33.

"The Seven Offices." *Diogenes*, 21 (Spring 1958), 68–84.

"The Study of Symbolic Action." *Chimera*, 1 (Spring 1942), 7–16.

"Surrealism." In *New Directions in Prose and Poetry*. Ed. James Laughlin. Norfolk, CT: New Directions, 1940, pp. 563–79.

"Symbol and Association." *Hudson Review*, 9 (1956), 212–25.

"Symbolic War." *Southern Review*, 2 (1936–37), 134–47.

"Symbolism as a Realistic Mode: 'De-Psychologizing' Logologized." *Psychocultural Review* (Winter 1979), pp. 25–37.

"The Tactics of Motivation." *Chimera*, 1 (Spring 1943), 21–53.

"The Tactics of Motivation." *Chimera*, 2 (Summer 1943), 37–53.

"Thanatopsis for Critics: A Brief Thesaurus of Deaths and Dyings." *Essays in Criticism*, 2 (October 1952), 369–75.

"Theology and Logology." *Kenyon Review*, 1 [new series] (Winter 1979), 151–85.

"A Theory of Terminology." In *Interpretation: The Poetry of Meaning*. Ed. Stanley Romaine Hopper and David L. Miller. New York: Harcourt, Brace and World, 1967, pp. 83–102.

"Thoughts on the Poet's Corner." In *Poetry Therapy: The Use of Poetry in the Treatment of Emotional Disorders*. Ed. Jack J. Leedy. Philadelphia: J. B. Lippincott, 1969, pp. 104–10.

"The Threat of the Trivial." *Nation*, 182 (April 21, 1956), 333.

"Three Definitions." *Kenyon Review*, 13 (Spring 1951), 173–92.

"Three Frenchmen's Churches." *New Republic*, 63 (1930), 10–14.

"Toward a New Romanticism: Proportion is Better than Efficiency." *Films in Review*, 1 (December 1950), 25–27.

"Towards a Post-Kantian Verbal Music." *Kenyon Review*, 20 (Autumn 1958), 529–46.

"Towards a Total Conformity: A Metaphysical Fantasy." *Literary Review*, 2 (1957–58), 203–07.

"Towards Hellhaven: Three Stages of a Vision." *Sewanee Review*, 79 (Winter 1971), 11–25.

"Towards Looking Back." *Journal of General Education*, 28 (Fall 1976), 167–89.

"The Unburned Bridges of Poetics, or, How Keep Poetry Pure?" *Centennial Review*, 8 (Fall 1964), 391–97.

"Variations on 'Providence.'" *Notre Dame English Journal*, 13 (Summer 1981), 155–83.

"Vegetal Radicalism of Theodore Roethke." *Sewanee Review*, 58 (Winter 1950), 68–108.

"War and Cultural Life." *American Journal of Sociology*, 48 (1942–43), 404–10.

"Waste—The Future of Prosperity." *New Republic*, 63 (July 1930), 228–31.

"What is Americanism? Symposium on Marxism and the American Tradition." *Partisan Review and Anvil*, 3 (April 1936), 9–11.

"What's Good About a Bad First Job." *Mademoiselle*, 53 (June 1961), 70–72, 111.

"What to Do till the Doctor Comes: Thoughts on Conscription." *Direction*, 3 (November 1940), 7, 24.

"When 'Now' Became 'Then.'" *Direction*, 5 (February/March 1942), 5.

"Where Are We Now?" *Direction*, 4 (December 1941), 3–5.

"Why Satire, with a Plan for Writing One." *Michigan Quarterly Review*, 13 (Fall 1974), 307–37.

"William Carlos Williams: A Critical Appreciation." In *William Carlos Williams*. Ed. Charles Angoff. Cranbury, NJ: Associated University Presses, 1974, pp. 15–19.

"William Carlos Williams, The Methods of." *Dial*, 82 (February 1927), 94–98.

"Words Anent Logology." In *Perspectives in Literary Criticism*. Ed. Joseph Strelka. University Park: Pennsylvania State University Press, 1968, pp. 72–82.

"The Writers' Congress." *Nation*, 140 (May 15, 1935), 571.

"Your Letters." Letter. *Direction*, 3 (November 1940), 21.

Collected Works

On Symbols and Society. Ed. Joseph R. Gusfield. Chicago: University of Chicago Press, 1989.

Perspectives by Incongruity. Ed. Stanley Edgar Hyman and Barbara Karmiller. Bloomington: Indiana University Press, 1964.

The Selected Correspondence of Kenneth Burke and Malcolm Cowley 1915–1981. Ed. Paul Jay. New York: Viking, 1988.

Terms for Order. Ed. Stanley Edgar Hyman and Barbara Karmiller. Bloomington: Indiana University Press, 1964.

Poetry and Fiction

"Adam's Song, and Mine." *Others*, 2 (March 1916), 184.
"Adam's Song, and Mine" [not identical to above]. *Sansculotte* [Ohio State University, Columbus, OH], 1 (April 1917), 10.
"Anthology." *Little Review* (Spring/Summer 1926), p. 33.
"Bathos, Youth, and the Antithetical 'Rather.'" *Sansculotte* [Ohio State University, Columbus, OH], 1 (February 1917), 7.
"Belated Entrance." *Recherches anglaises et américaines*, 12 (1979), 9.
"But for These Lucky Accidents." *Communication*, 1 (1974), 196.
"Case History." *Nation*, 183 (July 7, 1956), 21.
"A Count-In." *Poetry*, 113 (October 1968), 29–30.
"A Critical Load, Beyond That Door; or, Before the Ultimate Confrontation; or, When Thinking of Deconstructionist Structuralists; or, A Hermeneutic Fantasy." *Critical Inquiry*, 5 (Autumn 1978), 199–200.
"Eye-Crossing—From Brooklyn to Manhattan." *Nation*, 208 (June 2, 1969), 700–04.
"Her Will." *New Republic*, 161 (July 5, 1969), 28.
"Hokku." *Sansculotte* [Ohio State University, Columbus, OH], 1 (January 1917), 4.
"Hymn of Hope." *Slate*, 1 (April 1917), 80.
"Idylls." *Smart Set*, 57 (November 1918), 34.
"In the Margin." *New Republic*, 101 (December 20, 1939), 257.
"Invocation for a Convocation." *Kenyon Review*, I [new series] (Winter 1979), 3–4.
"Invocations." *Sansculotte* [Ohio State University, Columbus, OH], 1 (January 1917), 11.
"A Juxtaposition." *Poetry*, 113 (October 1968), 31.
"La Baudelairienne." *Sansculotte* [Ohio State University, Columbus, OH], 1 (January 1917), 9.
"Modernism So Far is but Peanuts." *New Republic*, 161 (November 8, 1969), 30.
"Nocturne." *Sansculotte* [Ohio State University, Columbus, OH], 1 (April 1917), 9.
"The Oftener Trinity." *Sansculotte* [Ohio State University, Columbus, OH], 1 (February 1917), 7.
"Order, Action, and Victimage." In *The Concept of Order*. Ed. Paul G. Kuntz. Seattle: University of Washington Press, 1968, pp. 167–90.
"Out of Backwards Sidewise Towards Fromwards (An Attitudinizing Winter-Solstitially)." *Kenyon Review*, 2 [new series] (Summer 1980), 92–93.
"Parabolic Tale, with Invocation." *Sansculotte* [Ohio State University, Columbus, OH], 1 (January 1917), 8.
"Poem." In *The Legacy of Kenneth Burke*. Ed. Herbert W. Simons and Trevor Melia. Madison: University of Wisconsin Press, 1989, p. 263.
"Poetry and Communication." In *Contemporary Philosophical Thought: Vol. 3: Perspectives in Education, Religion, and the Arts*. Ed. Howard E. Kiefer and Milton K. Munitz. Albany: State University of New York Press, 1970, pp. 401–18.
"Post-Roethkean Translations." *Hopkins Review*, 6 (Winter 1953), 6–7.
"Revolt." *Sansculotte* [Ohio State University, Columbus, OH], 1 (January 1917), [3].
"Spring Song." *Slate*, 1 (January 1917), 11.
"Two Poems of Abandonment." *New Republic* (May 30, 1970), p. 27.
"Two Portraits." *S₄N*, 4 (December 1922), n.pag.

Interviews

Aaron, Daniel, moderator. "Thirty Years Later: Memories of the First American Writers' Congress." *American Scholar*, 35 (Summer 1966), 495–516. (Conversation among Kenneth Burke, Malcolm Cowley, Granville Hicks, and William Phillips.)

"Counter-Gridlock: An Interview with Kenneth Burke."*All Area*, 2 (1983), 4–32.

Haydn, Hiram, moderator. "American Scholar Forum: The New Criticism."*American Scholar*, 20 (Winter 1950–51), 86–104. (Conversation among William Barrett, Kenneth Burke, Malcolm Cowley, Robert Gorham, and Allen Tate.)

Hook, Sidney. "Kenneth Burke and Sidney Hook: An Exchange: Is Mr. Burke Serious?" *Partisan Review*, 4 (January 1938), 44–47.

Kostelanetz, Richard. "Richard Kostelanetz Interviews Kenneth Burke." Ed. J. Clarke Rountree, III.*Iowa Review*, 17 (Fall 1987), 1–14.

Woodcock, John. "An Interview with Kenneth Burke."*Sewanee Review*, 85 (October/ December 1977), 704–18.

Endnotes

[1] Stanley Edgar Hyman, *The Armed Vision: A Study in the Methods of Modern Literary Criticism* (New York: Vintage, 1955), p. 359.

[2] William H. Rueckert, *Kenneth Burke and the Drama of Human Relations*, 2nd ed. (Berkeley: University of California Press, 1982), p. 227.

[3] Matthew Josephson, *Life Among the Surrealists: A Memoir* (New York: Holt, Rinehart and Winston, 1962), p. 35.

[4] Austin Warren, "Kenneth Burke: His Mind and Art," *Sewanee Review*, 41 (1933), 227.

[5] Ben Yagoda, "Kenneth Burke: The Greatest Literary Critic Since Coleridge?," *Horizon*, 23 (June 1980), 67.

[6] Kenneth Burke and Malcolm Cowley, *The Selected Correspondence of Kenneth Burke and Malcolm Cowley 1915–1981*, ed. Paul Jay (New York: Viking, 1988), p. 56.

[7] Quoted in Warren, "Kenneth Burke," p. 228.

[8] John Woodcock, "An Interview with Kenneth Burke," *Sewanee Review*, 85 (October/December 1977), 706.

[9] Jack Selzer, *Kenneth Burke in Greenwich Village: Conversing with the Moderns: 1915–1931* (Madison: University of Wisconsin Press, 1996), p. 59.

[10] Kenneth Burke, quoted in Yagoda, p. 68.

[11] Burke, quoted in Yagoda, p. 67.

[12] Burke, quoted in Selzer, p. 167.

[13] Selzer, p. 168.

[14] Yagoda, p. 68.

[15] Daniel Aaron, moderator, Conversation among Kenneth Burke, Malcolm Cowley, Granville Hicks, and William Phillips, "Thirty Years Later: Memories of the First American Writers' Congress," *American Scholar*, 35 (Summer 1966), 507.

[16] Woodcock, p. 708.

[17] Burke, quoted in Yagoda, p. 68.

[18] For a description of what purportedly is contained in *A Symbolic of Motives*, see Rueckert, *Kenneth Burke*, pp. 230–35, 288–92.

[19] Biographical information on Burke was obtained from the following sources: Woodcock, pp. 704–18; Warren, "Kenneth Burke," pp. 225–36; Yagoda, pp. 66–69; Carlin Romano, "A Critic Who Has His Critics—Pro and Con," *Philadelphia Inquirer*, March 6, 1984, sec. D, p. 1; "Critic, Poet Kenneth Burke, 84 Will Receive Literature Medal," *Denver Post*, April 20, 1981, p. 32; Armin Paul Frank, *Kenneth Burke* (New York: Twayne, 1969), pp. 19–27; Aaron, p. 507;

Robert L. Heath, *Realism and Relativism: A Perspective on Kenneth Burke* (Macon, GA: Mercer University Press, 1986); Burke and Cowley, p. 56; Grant Webster, *The Republic of Letters: A History of Postwar American Literary Opinion* (Baltimore: Johns Hopkins University Press, 1979); Richard Kostelanetz, "Richard Kostelanetz Interviews Kenneth Burke," ed. J. Clarke Rountree, III, *Iowa Review*, 17 (Fall 1987), 1–23; and Selzer.

20 Romano, sec. D, p. 6.

21 Kenneth Burke, "Know Thyself," in Kenneth Burke, *Collected Poems: 1915–1967* (Berkeley: University of California Press, 1968), p. 208.

22 Kenneth Burke, *A Rhetoric of Motives* (Berkeley: University of California Press, 1969), p. 41.

23 Burke, *A Rhetoric of Motives*, p. 43.

24 Victor J. Vitanza, "A Mal-Lingering Thought (Tragic—Comedic) About KB's Visit," *Pre/Text*, 6 (Fall/Winter 1985), 163–64.

25 Timothy W. Crusius, *Kenneth Burke and the Conversation after Philosophy* (Carbondale: Southern Illinois University Press, 1999), p. 121.

26 Substance is discussed in Burke, *A Rhetoric of Motives*, pp. 20, 24, 64; and Kenneth Burke, *A Grammar of Motives* (Berkeley: University of California Press, 1969), pp. 21–23, 57.

27 Burke, *A Rhetoric of Motives*, p. 21.

28 Burke, *A Rhetoric of Motives*, p. 46.

29 Burke, *A Rhetoric of Motives*, p. 55.

30 Identification also is discussed in Burke, *A Rhetoric of Motives*, pp. xiv, 24, 46; and Kenneth Burke, *Language as Symbolic Action: Essays on Life, Literature, and Method* (Berkeley: University of California Press, 1966), p. 301.

31 Burke, *A Rhetoric of Motives*, p. 20.

32 Kenneth Burke, *Dramatism and Development* (Barre, MA: Clark University Press, 1972), p. 28.

33 Burke, *Language as Symbolic Action*, p. 301.

34 Unconscious persuasion also is discussed in Kenneth Burke, "Rhetoric—Old and New," *Journal of General Education*, 5 (April 1951), 203.

35 Burke, *A Rhetoric of Motives*, p. 130.

36 Burke, *A Rhetoric of Motives*, p. 21.

37 Burke, *A Rhetoric of Motives*, p. 22.

38 For additional discussions of division, see Burke, *A Rhetoric of Motives*, pp. 150, 211, 326; and Kenneth Burke, *The Philosophy of Literary Form: Studies in Symbolic Action* (Berkeley: University of California Press, 1973), p. 306.

39 Burke, *A Rhetoric of Motives*, p. 38.

40 Burke, *A Rhetoric of Motives*, p. 38.

41 Burke also discusses the self as audience in Burke, *A Rhetoric of Motives*, pp. 44, 46.

42 Burke, *A Rhetoric of Motives*, p. 161.

43 Burke, *A Rhetoric of Motives*, p. 173.

44 Burke, *A Rhetoric of Motives*, p. 161.

45 Burke, *A Rhetoric of Motives*, p. 172. Nonverbal rhetoric also is discussed in Burke, *A Rhetoric of Motives*, p. 186; and Burke, *Language as Symbolic Action*, p. 301.

46 Burke, *The Philosophy of Literary Form*, p. 109.

47 Burke, *The Philosophy of Literary Form*, p. 1.

48 Burke, *The Philosophy of Literary Form*, pp. 293–304.

49 Burke, *The Philosophy of Literary Form*, p. 1.

50 Style also is discussed in Burke, *The Philosophy of Literary Form*, pp. 126–30, 309–10; and Kenneth Burke, *Permanence and Change: An Anatomy of Purpose* (Indianapolis: Bobbs-Merrill, 1965), pp. 50–58.

51 Burke discusses the ways in which rhetoric functions to provide assistance in orientation and adjustment in Kenneth Burke, *Counter-Statement* (Berkeley: University of California Press, 1968), pp. 154–56; and Burke, *The Philosophy of Literary Form*, pp. 64, 294, 298–99.

52 Burke, *Language as Symbolic Action*, p. 487.

53 Burke, *A Rhetoric of Motives*, p. 65.

54 Kenneth Burke, "A Philosophy of Drama," *University of Chicago Magazine*, September, 1961, p. 7.

55 Burke, *Counter-Statement*, p. 124.
56 Burke, *Counter-Statement*, p. 31.
57 Burke, *Counter-Statement*, p. 124.
58 Burke, *Counter-Statement*, p. 31.
59 Burke, *Counter-Statement*, p. 138.
60 Types of form also are discussed in: Burke, *Counter-Statement*, pp. 124–29; Burke, *Language as Symbolic Action*, p. 486; Burke, *Dramatism and Development*, p. 16; and Kenneth Burke, "Dramatic Form—And: Tracking Down Implications," *Tulane Drama Review*, 10 (Summer 1966), 54.
61 Burke, *A Rhetoric of Motives*, pp. 58–59.
62 Burke, "A Philosophy of Drama," p. 7.
63 Burke, *Counter-Statement*, p. 125.
64 Burke, "Dramatic Form—And," p. 54.
65 Burke, *Counter-Statement*, p. 124.
66 Burke, *Counter-Statement*, p. 124.
67 Burke, *Counter-Statement*, pp. 124–25.
68 Burke, *Counter-Statement*, p. 125.
69 Burke, *Counter-Statement*, p. 125.
70 Kenneth Burke, "Dramatism," in *International Encyclopedia of the Social Sciences*, vol. 7, ed. David L. Sills (New York: Macmillan/Free, 1968), p. 446.
71 Burke, *Language as Symbolic Action*, p. 54.
72 Burke, *Language as Symbolic Action*, p. 67.
73 Burke, *Language as Symbolic Action*, p. 28.
74 Kenneth Burke, *The Rhetoric of Religion: Studies in Logology* (Boston: Beacon, 1961), p. 16.
75 Burke, *Language as Symbolic Action*, p. 482.
76 Woodcock, p. 709.
77 Burke, *Language as Symbolic Action*, p. 28.
78 The distinction between action and motion also is discussed in: Burke, "Dramatism," in *International Encyclopedia*, p. 445; Burke, *Language as Symbolic Action*, pp. 53, 63; and Burke, *The Rhetoric of Religion*, p. 274.
79 Burke, *The Rhetoric of Religion*, p. 281.
80 Burke, *The Rhetoric of Religion*, p. 188.
81 Burke, *A Grammar of Motives*, p. 14.
82 Burke, *The Philosophy of Literary Form*, p. xvi.
83 Kenneth Burke, "Rhetoric, Poetics, and Philosophy," in *Rhetoric, Philosophy, and Literature: An Exploration*, ed. Don M. Burks (West Lafayette, IN: Purdue University Press, 1978), p. 31.
84 Burke, "Dramatism," in *International Encyclopedia*, p. 447.
85 Kenneth Burke, "Dramatism," in *Communication: Concepts and Perspectives*, ed. Lee Thayer (Washington, DC: Spartan, 1967), p. 331.
86 Burke, "Dramatism," in *Communication*, p. 337.
87 For a discussion of dramatism as literal, see: Burke, "Rhetoric, Poetics, and Philosophy," pp. 16, 25, 27–30; Burke, "Dramatism," in *International Encyclopedia*, p. 448; Burke, *A Rhetoric of Motives*, p. 283; Heath, pp. 2, 121, 145, 156, 166, 167; Bernard L. Brock, Kenneth Burke, Parke G. Burgess, and Herbert W. Simons, "Dramatism as Ontology or Epistemology: A Symposium," *Communication Quarterly*, 33 (Winter 1985), 17–33; and Walter R. Fisher and Wayne Brockriede, "Kenneth Burke's Realism," *Central States Speech Journal*, 35 (Spring 1984), 35–42.
88 Crusius, *Kenneth Burke*, p. 70.
89 Burke, *The Philosophy of Literary Form*, p. 20. For more on Burke's notion of motives, see Burke, *Permanence and Change*, pp. 23–36; and Gerard A. Hauser, *Introduction to Rhetorical Theory* (New York: Harper and Row, 1986), pp. 131–37.
90 Burke, *A Grammar of Motives*, p. xv.
91 Burke, *The Rhetoric of Religion*, p. 26.
92 Burke, *A Grammar of Motives*, p. xx.
93 Burke discusses act in Burke, *A Grammar of Motives*, pp. 14, 227–74.

[94] Burke, *Language as Symbolic Action*, p. 360.

[95] Burke, *A Grammar of Motives*, p. 84.

[96] Scene also is discussed in Burke, *A Grammar of Motives*, pp. xvi, 12, 77, 85, 90. For a discussion of circumference in connection with scene, see C. Ronald Kimberling, *Kenneth Burke's Dramatism and Popular Arts* (Bowling Green, OH: Bowling Green State University Popular Press, 1982), pp. 17–18.

[97] For a discussion of agent, see Burke, *A Grammar of Motives*, pp. 20, 171–226.

[98] Agency is discussed in Burke, *A Grammar of Motives*, pp. 275–320.

[99] Burke discusses purpose in Burke, *A Grammar of Motives*, pp. 275–320.

[100] Burke, *Permanence and Change*, p. 30.

[101] Burke discusses motive in Burke, *Philosophy of Literary Form*, pp. 18, 90; and Burke, *Permanence and Change*, pp. 29–36.

[102] Burke, *A Grammar of Motives*, p. 443.

[103] Burke, *A Grammar of Motives*, p. 20.

[104] Burke, *A Grammar of Motives*, p. 476.

[105] Attitude also is discussed in Burke, *A Grammar of Motives*, pp. 236, 242; and Burke, *Dramatism and Development*, p. 23.

[106] Burke, *A Grammar of Motives*, p. 3.

[107] For discussions of Burke's concept of ratio, see: Burke, *Dramatism and Development*, p. 22; Burke, *A Grammar of Motives*, pp. xix, 3, 15, 18–19, 53; and Vito Signorile, "Ratios and Causes: The Pentad as an Etiological Scheme in Sociological Explanation," in *The Legacy of Kenneth Burke*, ed. Herbert W. Simons and Trevor Melia (Madison: University of Wisconsin Press, 1989), pp. 81–82.

[108] The pentad also is discussed in: Burke, *A Grammar of Motives*, p. xvi; Kenneth Burke, "The Tactics of Motivation," *Chimera*, 1 (Spring 1943), 42; Charles Conrad, "Phases, Pentads, and Dramatistic Critical Process," *Central States Speech Journal*, 35 (Summer 1984), 94–104; Timothy W. Crusius, "A Case for Kenneth Burke's Dialectic and Rhetoric," *Philosophy and Rhetoric*, 19 (1986), 23-37; Joseph R. Gusfield, "The Bridge Over Separated Lands: Kenneth Burke's Significance for the Study of Social Action," in *The Legacy of Kenneth Burke*, ed. Herbert W. Simons and Trevor Melia (Madison: University of Wisconsin Press, 1989), pp. 28–54; and Heath, pp. 184–93.

[109] A summary of the concept of logology can be found in: Rueckert, *Kenneth Burke*, pp. 236, 242; Frank, p. 141; Fisher and Brockriede, pp. 36–37; Heath, pp. 117–20; David Cratis Williams, "Under the Sign of (An)nihilation: Burke in the Age of Nuclear Destruction and Critical Deconstruction," in *The Legacy of Kenneth Burke*, ed. Herbert W. Simons and Trevor Melia (Madison: University of Wisconsin Press, 1989), p. 212; and Kenneth Burke, "Dramatism and Logology," *Communication Quarterly*, 33 (Spring 1985), 91.

[110] Burke, *The Rhetoric of Religion*, p. v.

[111] Theology as a model for symbol use also is discussed in: Burke, *The Rhetoric of Religion*, pp. 33–34; Kenneth Burke, "Words Anent Logology," in *Perspectives in Literary Criticism*, ed. Joseph Strelka (University Park: Pennsylvania State University Press, 1968), 72–82; Frank, p. 142; and Rueckert, *Kenneth Burke*, p. 241.

[112] Rueckert, *Kenneth Burke*, p. 236.

[113] Burke, "Dramatism and Logology," pp. 89–90.

[114] Burke, *Language as Symbolic Action*, p. 9.

[115] Burke, *The Rhetoric of Religion*, p. 283.

[116] Burke, *Language as Symbolic Action*, p. 9.

[117] Burke, *The Rhetoric of Religion*, p. 21.

[118] Burke, *The Rhetoric of Religion*, p. 18.

[119] Burke, *Language as Symbolic Action*, p. 461. Burke also discusses the negative in: Burke, *The Rhetoric of Religion*, pp. 18–22; Burke, *Language as Symbolic Action*, pp. 419–20, 457, 472; and Burke, *A Grammar of Motives*, pp. 295–97. A summary of the concept of the negative can be found in Heath, pp. 98–102.

[120] Burke, *Language as Symbolic* Action, p. 13.

[121] Moral action based on the negative also is discussed in Burke, *The Rhetoric of Religion*, pp. 187, 278, 290–91; and Burke, *Language as Symbolic Action*, pp. 10–13, 421–22.

[122] Rueckert, *Kenneth Burke*, p. 131.

[123] Burke, *A Rhetoric of Motives*, p. 138.

[124] Discussions of hierarchy can be found in: Burke, *A Rhetoric of Motives*, p. 118, 138–41, 265; Burke, *Language as Symbolic Action*, pp. 15–16, 89; and Rueckert, *Kenneth Burke*, pp. 131, 144.

[125] Burke, *A Rhetoric of Motives*, p. 14.

[126] Burke, *The Rhetoric of Religion*, p. 246.

[127] Burke, *The Rhetoric of Religion*, p. 296.

[128] Burke, *Language as Symbolic Action*, p. 16.

[129] Burke, *Permanence and Change*, p. 184.

[130] Perfection as derived from language is discussed in: Burke, *Language as Symbolic Action*, pp. 16–17; Burke, *The Rhetoric of Religion*, p. 296; Burke, *Permanence and Change*, pp. 184–85; Burke, "Rhetoric, Poetics, and Philosophy," p. 25; and Rueckert, *Kenneth Burke*, p. 135.

[131] Kenneth Burke, "Freedom and Authority in the Realm of the Poetic Imagination," in *Freedom and Authority in Our Time: Twelfth Symposium of the Conference on Science, Philosophy and Religion*, ed. Lyman Bryson, Louis Finkelstein, R. M. MacIver, and Richard McKeon (New York: Harper, 1953), p. 367. For additional information about perfection, see Burke, *A Rhetoric of Motives*, p. 14; and Burke, *The Rhetoric of Religion*, pp. 246–47, 297–304.

[132] Crusius, *Kenneth Burke*, pp. 171–72.

[133] Burke, *A Rhetoric of Motives*, p. 118.

[134] Burke, *A Rhetoric of Motives*, p. 195.

[135] Kenneth Burke, "Poem," in *The Legacy of Kenneth Burke*, ed. Herbert W. Simons and Trevor Melia (Madison: University of Wisconsin Press, 1989), p. 263.

[136] For a discussion of the notion of division, see: Burke, *A Rhetoric of Motives*, pp. 139, 147, 211; Burke, *Language as Symbolic Action*, p. 15; and Burke, *The Rhetoric of Religion*, p. 308.

[137] Burke, *Permanence and Change*, p. 240.

[138] Burke, *Permanence and Change*, p. 40.

[139] Burke, *Permanence and Change*, p. 237. Occupational psychosis also is discussed in Burke, *Permanence and Change*, pp. 41–44; and Burke, *The Philosophy of Literary Form*, p. 315.

[140] Burke's discussions of the terministic screen can be found in Burke, *Language as Symbolic Action*, pp. 44–52; and Burke, *Permanence and Change*, p. 240.

[141] Burke, *Permanence and Change*, p. 7.

[142] Burke also discusses trained incapacity in Burke, *Permanence and Change*, pp. 8–11.

[143] Mystery is discussed in: Burke, *A Rhetoric of Motives*, pp. 122, 174; Burke, *The Rhetoric of Religion*, pp. 308–09; and Kenneth Burke, "Mysticism as a Solution to the Poet's Dilemma: II: Appendix," in *Spiritual Problems in Contemporary Literature*, ed. Stanley Romaine Hopper (New York: Harper, 1952), p. 105.

[144] Burke, *The Rhetoric of Religion*, p. 307. Burke also discusses mystery as a source of obedience and cohesion in *A Rhetoric of Motives*, p. 174; and *The Rhetoric of Religion*, p. 309.

[145] Burke, "Mysticism as a Solution," p. 105. Burke also discusses mystery as a source of persuasion in Burke, *A Rhetoric of Motives*, pp. 276, 278.

[146] Burke, *Language as Symbolic Action*, p. 144.

[147] Guilt also is discussed in: Burke, *The Rhetoric of Religion*, pp. 4–5; Burke, *A Rhetoric of Motives*, p. 148; Burke, *Language as Symbolic Action*, pp. 81, 94; and Burke, *Permanence and Change*, p. 283.

[148] Hiram Haydn, moderator, Conversation among William Barrett, Kenneth Burke, Malcolm Cowley, Robert Gorham Davis, and Allen Tate, "American Scholar Forum: The New Criticism," *American Scholar*, 20 (Winter 1950–51), 95.

[149] Burke, *Permanence and Change*, p. 279.

[150] Burke, *The Rhetoric of Religion*, p. 4.

[151] Burke, *Language as Symbolic Action*, p. 15. Burke also discusses the connection between guilt and hierarchy in: Burke, *Dramatism and Development*, p. 44; Burke, *The Rhetoric of Religion*, pp. 222, 294; and Burke, *Language as Symbolic Action*, p. 15.

[152] Burke, *Language as Symbolic Action*, p. 308.

[153] Burke, *Language as Symbolic Action*, p. 341.

[154] A summary of the fecal motive is provided in Rueckert, *Kenneth Burke*, p. 104.

[155] Burke, *A Grammar of Motives*, p. 302.

[156] Burke, *Language as Symbolic Action*, p. 345.

[157] Burke, *The Philosophy of Literary Form*, p. 36.

[158] For additional discussion of the Demonic Trinity, see: Burke, *Language as Symbolic Action*, pp. 340, 477; Burke, *The Philosophy of Literary Form*, p. 36; and Burke, *A Rhetoric of Motives*, p. 256. A summary of the concept is provided in Rueckert, *Kenneth Burke*, pp. 102, 149, 223.

[159] Language as a means of purgation is discussed in Burke, *The Rhetoric of Religion*, p. 231; and Kenneth Burke, *Terms for Order*, ed. Stanley Edgar Hyman and Barbara Karmiller (Bloomington: Indiana University Press, 1964), p. 166.

[160] Burke, *The Philosophy of Literary Form*, p. 203. Burke also discusses victimage in Burke, *Language as Symbolic Action*, pp. 435, 478; and Burke, *The Philosophy of Literary Form*, pp. 39–40. A summary of the concept is provided in Rueckert, *Kenneth Burke*, p. 151.

[161] Burke, *A Rhetoric of Motives*, p. 140.

[162] Burke, *A Grammar of Motives*, p. 406.

[163] Burke, *The Philosophy of Literary Form*, p. 193.

[164] Aaron, p. 499. Identification and alienation in victimage also are discussed in Burke, *A Rhetoric of Motives*, pp. 141, 265–66.

[165] Burke discusses mortification in Burke, *The Rhetoric of Religion*, pp. 190, 206.

[166] Burke, *The Philosophy of Literary Form*, p. 203.

[167] Redemption also is discussed in Burke, *Permanence and Change*, p. 78. A summary of the concept is provided in Rueckert, *Kenneth Burke*, pp. 45, 48, 150.

[168] Burke, "Poem," p. 263. Reprinted by permission of The University of Wisconsin Press.

[169] C. Allen Carter, *Kenneth Burke and the Scapegoat Process* (Norman: University of Oklahoma Press, 1996), pp. 24–25.

[170] Burke, *Language as Symbolic Action*, p. 456.

[171] Burke, *Language as Symbolic Action*, p. 378.

[172] Burke, *Language as Symbolic Action*, p. 5.

[173] Burke, *A Grammar of Motives*, p. 319.

[174] Burke, *A Rhetoric of Motives*, p. 288.

[175] Kenneth Burke, "Creation Myth," in Kenneth Burke, *Collected Poems: 1915–1967* (Berkeley: University of California Press, 1968), p. 5. Instruments or tools also are discussed in Burke, *The Rhetoric of Religion*, pp. 276, 288.

[176] Burke also discusses the motivation of perfection in Burke, *A Rhetoric of Motives*, pp. 187, 299–301, 333.

[177] Burke, *Language as Symbolic Action*, p. 18.

[178] Rueckert, *Kenneth Burke*, pp. 4–5.

[179] Harry Slochower, "Kenneth Burke's Philosophy of Symbolic Action," in *Critical Responses to Kenneth Burke: 1924–1966*, ed. William H. Rueckert (Minneapolis: University of Minnesota Press, 1969), p. 135. Although most of the essays in this book are reprinted from other sources, they are cited from Rueckert's book for the convenience of the reader.

[180] Charles Morris, "The Strategy of Kenneth Burke," in *Critical Responses to Kenneth Burke: 1924–1966*, ed. William H. Rueckert (Minneapolis: University of Minnesota Press, 1969), p. 163.

[181] Donald A. Stauffer, "Salvation through Semantics," in *Critical Responses to Kenneth Burke: 1924–1966*, ed. William H. Rueckert (Minneapolis: University of Minnesota Press, 1969), p. 187.

[182] Abraham Kaplan, "A Review of 'A Grammar of Motives,'" in *Critical Responses to Kenneth Burke: 1924–1966*, ed. William H. Rueckert (Minneapolis: University of Minnesota Press, 1969), p. 170.

[183] Arthur E. DuBois, "Accepting and Rejecting Kenneth Burke," in *Critical Responses to Kenneth Burke: 1924–1966*, ed. William H. Rueckert (Minneapolis: University of Minnesota Press, 1969), p. 83.

[184] Joseph Frank, "Symbols and Civilization," in *Critical Responses to Kenneth Burke: 1924–1966*, ed. William H. Rueckert (Minneapolis: University of Minnesota Press, 1969), p. 403.

[185] Kermit Lansner, "Burke, Burke, the Lurk," in *Critical Responses to Kenneth Burke: 1924–1966*, ed. William H. Rueckert (Minneapolis: University of Minnesota Press, 1969), p. 261.

[186] William H. Rueckert, quoted in Romano, sec. D, p. 6.

[187] Alfred Kazin, quoted in Romano, sec. D, p. 6.

[188] Austin Warren, "The Sceptic's Progress," in *Critical Responses to Kenneth Burke: 1924–1966*, ed. William H. Rueckert (Minneapolis: University of Minnesota Press, 1969), p. 53.

[189] Max Black, "A Review of 'A Grammar of Motives,'" in *Critical Responses to Kenneth Burke: 1924– 1966*, ed. William H. Rueckert (Minneapolis: University of Minnesota Press, 1969), pp. 168–69.

[190] Morris, p. 163.

[191] Harold Rosenberg, "A Review of 'Counter-Statement,'" in *Critical Responses to Kenneth Burke: 1924–1966*, ed. William H. Rueckert (Minneapolis: University of Minnesota Press, 1969), p. 29.

[192] Herbert W. Simons, "Introduction: Kenneth Burke and the Rhetoric of the Human Sciences," in *The Legacy of Kenneth Burke*, ed. Herbert W. Simons and Trevor Melia (Madison: University of Wisconsin Press, 1989), p. 4.

[193] Eugene Goodheart, "Burke Revisited," *Sewanee Review*, 102 (July/September 1994), 424.

[194] Hyman, p. 384.

[195] Bernard I. Duffy, "Reality as Language: Kenneth Burke's Theory of Poetry," in *Critical Responses to Kenneth Burke: 1924–1966*, ed. William H. Rueckert (Minneapolis: University of Minnesota Press, 1969), p. 229.

[196] Stauffer, p. 184.

[197] Louis Wirth, "A Review of 'Permanence and Change,'" in *Critical Responses to Kenneth Burke: 1924–1966*, ed. William H. Rueckert (Minneapolis: University of Minnesota Press, 1969), p. 102.

[198] DuBois, p. 82.

[199] Charles I. Glicksberg, "Kenneth Burke: The Critic's Critic," in *Critical Responses to Kenneth Burke: 1924–1966*, ed. William H. Rueckert (Minneapolis: University of Minnesota Press, 1969), p. 79.

[200] Marie Hochmuth Nichols, "Kenneth Burke and the 'New Rhetoric,'" in *Critical Responses to Kenneth Burke: 1924–1966*, ed. William H. Rueckert (Minneapolis: University of Minnesota Press, 1969), p. 283.

[201] Black, p. 168.

[202] Slochower, p. 131.

[203] Sidney Hook, "The Technique of Mystification," in *Critical Responses to Kenneth Burke: 1924– 1966*, ed. William H. Rueckert (Minneapolis: University of Minnesota Press, 1969), p. 89.

[204] John Simon, quoted in Romano, sec. D, p. 6.

[205] Warren, "The Sceptic's Progress," p. 52.

[206] Nichols, p. 283.

[207] Goodheart, p. 435.

[208] Stauffer, pp. 183–84.

[209] George Knox, "Postscript: Bureaucratization of the Imaginative," in *Critical Responses to Kenneth Burke: 1924–1966*, ed. William H. Rueckert (Minneapolis: University of Minnesota Press, 1969), p. 318.

[210] Wirth, p. 102.

[211] Margaret Schlauch, "A Review of 'Attitudes Toward History,'" in *Critical Responses to Kenneth Burke: 1924–1966*, ed. William H. Rueckert (Minneapolis: University of Minnesota Press, 1969), p. 106.

[212] Nichols, p. 283.

[213] Isidor Schneider, "A New View of Rhetoric," in *Critical Responses to Kenneth Burke: 1924– 1966*, ed. William H. Rueckert (Minneapolis: University of Minnesota Press, 1969), p. 26.

[214] Barbara A. Biesecker, *Addressing Postmodernity: Kenneth Burke, Rhetoric, and a Theory of Social Change* (Tuscaloosa: University of Alabama Press, 1997), p. 16.

[215] Robert M. Adams, Foreword, in *Critical Responses to Kenneth Burke: 1924–1966*, ed. William H. Rueckert (Minneapolis: University of Minnesota Press, 1969), [p. xvi].

[216] Stauffer, pp. 185–86.

[217] Stauffer, p. 185.

[218] Morris, p. 163.

[219] Warren, p. 52.

[220] Slochower, p. 131.

[221] James M. Cox, "Remembering Kenneth Burke," *Sewanee Review*, 102 (July/September 1994), 443.

[222] Denis Donoghue, "K.B.—In Memory," *Sewanee Review*, 102 (July/September 1994), 444.

[223] Benjamin De Mott, "The Little Red Discount House," in *Critical Responses to Kenneth Burke: 1924–1966*, ed. William H. Rueckert (Minneapolis: University of Minnesota Press, 1969), p. 361.

[224] Trevor Melia, quoted in Romano, sec. D, p. 6.

[225] Hugh Dalziel Duncan, "A Review of 'A Rhetoric of Motives,' " in *Critical Responses to Kenneth Burke: 1924–1966*, ed. William H. Rueckert (Minneapolis: University of Minnesota Press, 1969), p. 259.

[226] Goodheart, p. 426.

[227] Goodheart, p. 431.

[228] Goodheart, p. 426.

[229] Goodheart, p. 427.

[230] Burke encourages critical pluralism in Burke, *The Philosophy of Literary Form*, p. 21; and Burke, *A Rhetoric of Motives*, p. 265.

[231] Donoghue, p. 445.

[232] Goodheart, p. 433.

[233] Goodheart, p. 426.

[234] Ann Branaman, "Reconsidering Kenneth Burke: His Contributions to the Identity Controversy," *Sociological Quarterly*, 35 (August 1994), 444.

[235] Branaman, p. 445.

[236] Biesecker, p. 2.

[237] Biesecker, p. 9.

[238] R. P. Blackmur, "The Lion and the Honeycomb," in *Critical Responses to Kenneth Burke: 1924–1966*, ed. William H. Rueckert (Minneapolis: University of Minnesota Press, 1969), p. 245.

8

JÜRGEN HABERMAS

That degree of legal equality should be achieved which will allow at the same time the greatest possible measure of individualism, and this means space for individuals to shape their own lives. . . . Freedom, even personal freedom, freedom of choice in the last instance, can only be thought in internal connection with a network of interpersonal relationships, and this means in the context of the communicative structures of a community, which ensures that the freedom of some is not achieved at the cost of the freedom of others. Interestingly, abstract right is not sufficient for this purpose. One must make the effort to analyse the conditions of collective freedom . . . . The individual cannot be free unless all are free, and all cannot be free unless all are free in community.[1]

With this statement, Jürgen Habermas describes what he hopes will be the practical outcome of his efforts over several decades to construct a theory of communication that explains both the evolution of society and of the individual within it. His project is a quest for a society in which participants collaboratively constitute and competently manage a public sphere of communication by means of unconstrained discourse. He locates human competency and societal evolution in language and develops a theory of communicative action that revitalizes the concepts of freedom, autonomy, and justice from the period of the Enlightenment of the eighteenth century.

Jürgen Habermas is the son of Ernst Habermas and Greta Kottgen Habermas.[2] He was born in Dusseldorf, Germany, on June 18, 1929, but grew up in Gümmersbach, where his father was head of the Bureau of Industry and Trade, and his grandfather was a minister and head of the local seminary. He was four years old when the Nazis seized power in Germany, and as a young man, he joined the Hitler Youth, although he describes his family as neither pro-Nazi nor pro-opposition. Habermas believes this neutral stance was fairly typical of the times, calling it a "bourgeois adaptation to a political situation with which one did not fully identify, but which one didn't seriously criticize either."[3] Habermas was 15 years old at the end of the war, an impressionable age in terms of the development of his political views: "At that point the rhythm of my personal development intersected with the great historical events of the time. . . . The radio was reporting the Nuremberg trials, movie theatres were showing the first documentary films, the concentration camp films."[4] The result was a shattering of cultural complacency about the true nature of the political situation and the Nazi regime: "we saw that we had been living in a politically criminal system."[5] For Habermas, this awareness was the beginning of a lifelong interest in politics.

Habermas graduated from high school in 1949 and attended the universities of Gottingen, Zurich, and Bonn, where he studied philosophy, history, psychology, German literature, and economics. He received his doctorate from the University of Bonn in 1954, writing a dissertation on Friedrich Schelling's philosophy of history. He married Ute Wesselhöft in 1955, and they have three children.

Describing himself as "fed up with intellectual work generally, and philosophy particularly," Habermas spent two years as a free-lance journalist after the completion of his doctorate. During this time, he developed an interest in the "sociology of labour and industrial relations,"[6] which led a friend to introduce him to Theodor Adorno, director of the Institute for Social Research in Frankfurt. As a result, Habermas was offered the position of assistant to Adorno at the *Frankfurt School*, as it is often called,[7] a position he accepted not only because he did not have "a permanent job at the time"[8] but because of the "combination of Frankfurt and sociology." He describes his time at the institute from 1955 to 1959 as one of learning "sociology on the job."[9]

The purpose of the institute is the assessment of institutions and interests in order to provide a critical understanding of the structure and contradictions of society. The contradictions of a society constitute its ideologies—

systems of irrational or distorted beliefs that maintain their legitimacy despite the fact that they cannot be validated if subjected to rational discourse.[10] In general, critical theory is designed to move society in the direction of emancipation from unnecessary domination through the use of reason. Although the earlier generation of critical theorists based its theories of emancipation on Marxist theories of production and the alienation from the production process under capitalism,[11] the current group, of which Habermas is considered the leading spokesperson, devotes more attention to communication, dialogue, and discourse.[12]

In 1961, Habermas began teaching at the University of Heidelberg. In 1962, he published *Strukturwandel der Öffentlichkeit* (*The Structural Transformation of the Public Sphere: An Inquiry into a Category of Bourgeois Society*), in which he describes the conditions for rational argumentation in the public sphere, followed in 1963 by *Theorie und Praxis* (*Theory and Practice*), in which he first presents his distinction between social and political interests.

Habermas became a professor of philosophy and sociology at the University of Frankfurt in 1964, where he was considered one of the intellectual mentors of the *Socialistische Deutsche Studentenbund*, the German equivalent of the Students for a Democratic Society in the United States. In this role, he served as a spokesperson for efforts to radicalize society from within the ranks of the students, arguing that "the only comprehensive conceptions for universities in a democratically constituted industrial society have been worked out by students."[13] The publication of *Protestbewegung und Hochschulreform* (*Toward a Rational Society: Student Protest, Science and Politics*) in 1968 proved a turning point in Habermas's relationship with the student movement, however. Habermas criticized the movement for its disintegration into *actionism*, a term he used to mean a compulsive and unthinking response to all conflict situations. "The new tactics," he suggested, have the advantage of obtaining rapid publicity. But they also bear "the danger of diversion, either into the privatization of an easily consolable hippie subculture or into the fruitless violent acts of the actionists."[14] The students, in turn, criticized Habermas's preference for theory over actual struggle. His *Erkenntnis und Interesse* (*Knowledge and Human Interests*), also published in 1968, was used as evidence of Habermas's retreat into the theoretical realm and represents his first systematic effort to delimit a comprehensive social theory.

Despite his dispute with the students, Habermas still sees the student protest movement as having had significant effects because it "brought about a certain rupture in the normative area, in attitudes, in the cultural value system."[15] He suggests that any effort to transform society will take time:

> We must start from the fact that social systems as complex as highly developed capitalist societies would founder in chaos under any attempt to transform their fundamental structures overnight. . . . I can only imagine a revolution as a long-term process which makes possible: (a) an experimental transformation, guided at every step by its successes and

failures, of central decision-making structures; (b) simultaneously, if not indeed as an actual premise of this change, an "acclimitization" to new democratic forms of life, through a gradual enlargement of democratic, participatory and discursive action.[16]

Habermas now sees social movements as conflicts arising not out of the realm of material production but from efforts to protect identities and lifestyles. [17] According to Habermas, these movements "put forth no revolutionary goals nor advance any totalistic claims. Instead, they tend to advocate structural reforms which would create, protect, or expand space for a plurality of life forms, all the while acknowledging the need for, and allowing for the continuing functioning of, the economic and administrative systems." [18] In spite of the "self-limiting radicalism" of these movements, Habermas sees them as desirable because they encourage an ongoing process of collective discussion within society. [19]

In part because of the conflict with students, Habermas left the University of Frankfurt in 1971 and joined the Max Planck Institute for Research into the Life Conditions of the Scientific-Technical World in Starnberg, West Germany. He assumed the directorship of the institute, serving in that position until 1983, when he returned to Frankfurt and joined the faculty of the Philosophy Department at the Johann Wolfgang Goethe University. [20] He now is retired from that university.

Interspersed throughout Habermas's career have been several visiting professorships to universities in the United States. In 1967, Habermas was the Theodor Heuss professor at the New School for Social Research in New York, a position followed by his appointment as the Christian Gauss Lecturer at Princeton University in 1971. One year later, Habermas served as a research fellow at the Center for the Humanities at Wesleyan University in Middletown, Connecticut; in 1974, he moved to the Department of Sociology at the University of California, Santa Barbara, as a visiting professor. In 1976, he held a joint visiting professorship in sociology at the University of Pennsylvania in Philadelphia and at Haverford College in Haverford, Pennsylvania. In 1980, he served as a visiting professor in both sociology and philosophy at the University of California at Berkeley. In his retirement, Habermas annually serves as a visiting faculty member in the Department of Philosophy at Northwestern University in Evanston, Illinois.

Habermas has received several distinguished awards throughout his career, including the Hegel Prize from the city of Stuttgart, the Sigmund Freud Prize of the Darmstadt Academy for Language and Poetry, the Theodor Adorno Prize from the city of Frankfurt, the Scholl Prize from the city of Munich, and the Wilhelm Leuschner Medal from the state of Hesse. He was awarded an honorary doctorate of law from the New School for Social Research in 1980.

Habermas continues his interdisciplinary theorizing, writing, and political engagement, drawing on whatever ideas from a school or an individual he finds valuable to "open up subjects from the inside out." [21] In this process, his philosophical commitments are many, and he treats Karl Marx, Max Weber,

Wilhelm Dilthey, George Lukács, Sigmund Freud, George Herbert Mead, and Talcott Parsons, among others, as dialogue partners, making use of those parts of their theories that contribute to his own: "Even when I quote a good deal and take over other terminologies I am clearly aware that my use of them often has little to do with the authors' original meaning. . . . I take over other theories. Why not? One should accept others according to their strengths and then see how one can go from there." [22] Habermas also is concerned about the impact of his theorizing on his readers. For him, theoretical matters "are not simply arguments which are absorbed by the scholarly process and then survive or dissolve within it. On the contrary, as published and spoken words, they have an effect on readers and listeners at the moment of their reception which the author cannot revoke or withdraw as if he or she were dealing with logical propositions." [23]

Habermas's evolving approach to and use of Marxism illustrates his eclectic approach to scholarship. Although Marxism was central to the Frankfurt school at the time Habermas studied there, he initially did not use the label of *Marxist* to describe himself. Adorno recalls that Habermas even avoided saying Marx's name; instead, he would ask, "Have a look at this withering away of the state stuff." [24] Ultimately, however, Habermas realized that he had incorporated many aspects of Marxism into his own philosophical approach and that the label fit: "I was taken aback when my friend [Karl-Otto] Apel publicly called me a Neo-Marxist for the first time. Then I thought it over and decided he was right." [25] Habermas offers what he calls a "reconstruction" of Marxism, by which he means "taking a theory apart and putting it back together in a new form in order to attain more fully the goal it has set for itself." [26] Thus, while the core ideas of Marxism appear less frequently in Habermas's later writing, [27] Marxism remains one of Habermas's philosophical commitments and provides a foundation for his own distinctive approach to communication: "Marxism gave me the impetus and the analytical means to investigate how the relationship of democracy and capitalism developed." [28]

Habermas continues to publish prolifically, and his writing can be grouped loosely into four categories. Certain works concern his interest in reason and its validity as a linguistic concept. Books in this category include *Legitimationsprobleme im Spätkapitalismus* [*Legitimation Crisis*] (1973), *Der philosophische Diskurs der Moderne: Zwlf Vorlesungen* [*The Philosophical Discourse of Modernity: Twelve Lectures*] (1985), and *Nachmetaphhsisches Denken: Philosophische Aufsätze* [*Postmetaphysical Thinking: Philosophical Essays*] (1988). Habermas also has many works that describe the particulars of his theory of communication, most notably his two-volume set on communicative action, *Theorie des kommunikativen Handelns: Handlungsrationalität und gesellschaftliche Rationalisierung* (*The Theory of Communicative Action: Reason and the Rationalization of Society*) and *Theorie des kommunikativen Handelns: Zur Kritik der funktionalistischen Vernunft* (*The Theory of Communicative Action: Lifeworld and System: A Critique of Functionalist Reason*), published in 1981 and 1982 respectively.

A third body of works concerns political philosophy and Habermas's interest in German and European politics. Some books in this category include *Die Normalität einer Berliner Republik* [*A Berlin Republic: Writings on Germany*] (1995); *Die Einbeziehung des anderen: Studien zur politischen Theorie* [*The Inclusion of the Other: Studies in Political Theory*] (1996); and *The New Conservatism: Cultural Criticism and the Historians' Debate* (1997), composed of essays and interviews previously published in German that demonstrate Habermas's role as a "passionate commentator" on a wide range of contemporary political themes.[29] German historical revisionism and German reunification, the legacy of Marxist socialism, contemporary social movements, and the nature of world politics after the fall of the Soviet Union and the German Federal Republic are some of the subjects Habermas continues to engage in the political arena.[30] A fourth group of writings reflects Habermas's particular interest in the law as an arena parallel to politics, in which collaborative decision making or "deliberative democracy" occurs.[31] These notions are developed most fully in *Faktizität und Geltung* (*Between Facts and Norms*), published in 1992.

Habermas has been engaged in a systematic and sustained effort to illustrate how a theory of communication is fundamental to and pervades every level of society. The development of Habermas's perspective was evident as early as 1965 in his inaugural lecture at the University of Frankfurt, in which he asserted the fundamental importance of language: "What raises us out of nature is the only thing whose nature we can know: *language*."[32] Habermas's theory of communication begins with the notion of reason in the Enlightenment and proceeds to the level of discourse—of managing situations when rationality fails. His ideas build on one another in the following progression: (1) reason and the public sphere; (2) the nature of human knowledge; (3) lifeworld and system; (4) universal pragmatics; (5) validity claims; and (6) the idea of discourse. At each level, Habermas is interested in the capacity for and manifestations of rationality as they contribute to an emancipated society.

Reason and the Public Sphere

Habermas seeks to complete the project of modernity, which he sees as unfinished since the time of the Enlightenment in the eighteenth century.[33] Habermas finds in the Enlightenment the origins of an approach he believes can correct the present imbalances of society. The Enlightenment, generally characterized by the growth of the idea of reason, a questioning of authority and traditional values, and the rise of empirical science, is especially important for Habermas because it gave birth to a particular conception of reason in the public sphere that Habermas retrieves for his own theory of communication.

The public sphere during the Enlightenment was comprised of private individuals who created a public sphere when they joined in debate about issues bearing on the state. For Habermas, what is distinctive about the conception of the public sphere in the Enlightenment is that the private realm was considered to be the primary and formative sphere. This view differs from the Greek notion of the public sphere of the *polis*, which was considered to be the important place of self-expression and freedom. For the Greeks, the private sphere was unimportant, a conception directly counter to the private sphere of the Enlightenment.[34] Habermas locates the starting point for the emergence of the Enlightenment's version of the public sphere in the private clubs, coffeehouses, salons, learned societies, and publishing houses that arose in opposition to the absolute powers of the state. He dates the origins of this new conception of the public sphere specifically from a revolution in England in 1649 in which the office of the king was declared burdensome and dangerous to the public interest of the people.[35] The recognition of the existence of a sphere distinct both from the private life of the family and from the political authority of the state is crucial to Habermas's notion of the public sphere: "By 'the public sphere' we mean first of all a realm of our social life in which something approaching public opinion can be formed. Access is guaranteed to all citizens. A portion of the public sphere comes into being in every conversation in which private individuals assemble to form a public body."[36]

In addition to a sense of the public as a sovereign body of citizens entitled to access to and deliberation in the public arena, Habermas's conception of the public sphere also contains the notion of publicity. The German word for *public sphere—Öffentlichkeit*—carries connotations of both the public and of publicity. Thus, the term brings together two of the most fundamental political concepts from the Enlightenment—the public as a sovereign body of citizens and the concept of publicity in the sense of openness and access. A third element also was contained in the Enlightenment conception of the public sphere—the idea of individuals as bearers of basic rights given by virtue of their humanity. Such rights do not need to be justified on grounds other than that,[37] and the French revolution was considered "the historical event that for the first time conferred existence and validity on abstract right."[38] For Habermas, then, the citizen is guaranteed the right of access to discussion in the public sphere by virtue of the abstract right of humanness.

During the Enlightenment, the press provided access and openness to the exchange of ideas. Access and openness are critical to Habermas's conception of the public sphere: "Citizens behave as a public body when they confer in an unrestricted fashion—that is with the guarantee of freedom of assembly and association and the freedom to express and publish their opinions—about matters of general interest. . . . Today, newspapers and magazines, radio and television are the media of the public sphere."[39] Thus, Habermas envisions the public sphere as a "sovereign, reasonable public, nourished by the critical reporting of the press and engaged in the mutually enlightening clash of arguments."[40]

With the advent of advanced capitalism, the idealized public sphere Habermas locates in the Enlightenment ceased to exist. As private interests began to take over the political domain, the public sphere no longer existed as a place and space for rational discussion and consensus because all members of society no longer could participate equally in it. Those whose private interests were connected directly with political aims sought to influence how those aims fared in the public sphere, rather than allowing for open discussion about them. In the process, the public sphere lost its ability to monitor the power of the state through the medium of public discussion.[41] Instead, it simply became "an area where competition exists between different interest groups, and publicity is used to gain approval and prestige."[42] These tendencies continue to characterize the public sphere, and even the press is now subject to the influence of private interests because of its dependence on advertising dollars. In addition to providing information for and facilitating public debate, the press also needs to produce audiences for advertisers—a goal that is directly counter to the goal of a free and unrestricted discussion in the public sphere. These conflicting goals are typical, according to Habermas, of the imbalance of interests in the public sphere. He articulates a threefold schema for human knowledge, each dimension of which is necessary for an effective functioning of the public sphere.

Human Knowledge

Habermas suggests that three interests or orientations govern all human activity or constitute the human species and also define the public sphere—work, interaction, and power.[43] Habermas describes these interests as "social media" because they mediate between the natural and human and the private and public realms. Each of these interests stems from basic needs inherent in the human condition: humans work or deal with the physical environment, interact with other humans in social groups, and encounter power relations as a function of these social groups. Habermas views these three orientations as quasi-transcendental. With the term *transcendental*, he suggests that the orientations represent *a priori* and universal conditions underlying human experience: "to the extent that we discover the same implicit conceptual structure in any coherent experience whatsoever, we may call this basic conceptual system of possible experience *transcendental*." The prefix *quasi* suggests that these interests are not completely above any consideration of material existence because they are grounded in fundamental and irreducible necessities of the human condition.[44]

Work, the first domain of human concern, is the basic means by which humans provide for the material aspects of existence by manipulating various aspects of their environment and bringing it under their control. Habermas labels the strategy inherent to the domain of work the *technical interest*. When systematized as a mode of cognition, it culminates in the empirical/analytic sciences. These sciences are simply the logical outgrowth of humans' fundamental interest in controlling various features of their world to provide for the basics of existence. The particular type of rationality associated with the technical interest is means/ends thinking or what Habermas calls *instrumental rationality*.

A second domain in which humans operate is the social realm. Fundamentally, humans are social creatures, and they must learn to live and function in groups to survive. Language and other symbolic forms of communication are the means by which humans create and sustain social groups. Thus, interaction through symbols to achieve mutual understanding is a second domain basic to human life. Habermas calls this realm of social interaction the *practical interest*. It governs the exchange of messages, the internalization of norms, and the institutionalization of social roles that accompany the formation of human societies. The basic form of rationality operating in this realm is that of practical reasoning or reasoning by which humans create shared meanings useful to the conduct of everyday life. It, too, has a systematized counterpart at the cognitive level. When raised to a formal mode of knowing, practical reasoning is realized in the historical/hermeneutic sciences—those that deal with the interpretation of meaning.

The third aspect of life with which all humans must deal is domination or power. Because humans live in social groups, the organization of groups necessarily creates hierarchies and thus differential power arrangements. Although power or domination is just as unavoidable as work and interaction, all humans have a natural or fundamental interest in freeing themselves from unnecessary forms of power and control that manifest as distorted communication or ideologies. Becoming conscious of these ideologies is the first step toward liberation from them and toward greater freedom and autonomy. The desire for greater freedom is what Habermas calls the *emancipatory interest*. Like the other two interests, this one represents a fundamental way of knowing the world, and a particular mode of rationality—critical reasoning or self-reflection—is associated with it. Only through the ability to self-reflect can humans become conscious of the limitations, constraints, and distortions of knowledge. The emancipatory interest takes the form of the critical sciences or critical theory as a mode of cognition.

The following chart summarizes Habermas's conceptualization of the three domains and their various extensions:

Domain	Interest	Form of Rationality	Mode of Cognition
work	technical	instrumental	empirical/analytic sciences
interaction	practical	practical reasoning	historical/hermeneutic sciences
power	emancipatory	self-reflection	critical theory

Habermas sees parallels between Freudian psychoanalysis as a method for treating individual problems and the process of emancipation via critical theory he envisions for society as a whole. At the level of the individual, systematically distorted communication is manifest in neuroses, a process that has parallels at the societal level in terms of ideologies. Just as psychoanalysis is useful when an individual's "texts" are distorted by repressions, so the distorted "texts" or ideologies of society can benefit from the application and reflexivity of critical thought. What Freud provided in terms of the analysis of the individual, then, Habermas wants to provide to society. At both the individual and cultural levels, systematically distorted or deviant communication must be uncovered, penetrated, and reconstructed rationally. [45]

By means of his schema of interests, Habermas suggests that any one-dimensional approach for understanding the world is incomplete. The technical, practical, and emancipatory interests are interconnected and interdependent. For every system of communicative interaction in the practical realm, for example, corresponding systems exist in the technical and emancipatory realms that are affected by the decisions made in the practical arena. Furthermore, no domain of humanity is value free—not even science, despite its goal of objectivity. Each dimension has an agenda that often competes with the others to affect decision making in the public sphere. Habermas acknowledges the "fragmentary and provisional" character of this schema, [46] but for him, it continues to make the point of the "interrelationship" among interacting systems and the fact that each subsystem "is part of the surrounding social systems, which in turn are the result of the sociocultural evolution of the human race." [47]

Habermas ultimately collapses the three kinds of interests into two in part to deal with the overly simplistic divisions they suggest. He now refers to *communicative action* and *strategic action*, each of which is capable of encompassing different interest positions as well as different forms of understanding. Communicative action is consent oriented, relying on consensus to achieve understanding, [48] while strategic action is individualistic and success oriented. Communicative action refers to situations in which "participants are not primarily oriented to their own individual successes; they pursue their individual goals under the condition that they can harmonize their plans of action on the basis of common situation definitions." [49] Strategic action, on the other hand, is primarily instrumental in nature, directed at successfully influencing others to attain a personal end or goal. Habermas folds his third emancipatory interest into the others in that individuals in each form of action have the capacity to communicate self-reflectively, and power itself is embedded in the process of coordinating action through speech. [50]

Lifeworld and System

Habermas's insistence that all forms of knowledge are interrelated and take the form of either communicative action or strategic action leads to his distinction between lifeworld and system. By *lifeworld*, Habermas means the taken-for-granted universe of daily social activity—"the immediate milieu of the individual social actor." [51] The lifeworld consists of the general storehouse of knowledge, traditions, and customs—"cognitive interpretations, moral expectations, expressions, and valuations" [52]—that unconsciously are passed from one generation to the next as well as intuitive know-how and acquired individual competencies. "We can think of the lifeworld as represented by a culturally transmitted and linguistically organized stock of interpretive patterns,"[53] asserts Habermas, who sees the lifeworld as the background consensus of everyday life in that it consists of those aspects agreed upon by a culture that generally go unquestioned.

The lifeworld is the domain of social life—the life of the public sphere—and actions in this sphere are governed by consensus that emerges from the interpretive patterns of the lifeworld: "it is from these [patterns] that contexts for processes of reaching understanding get shaped, processes in which those involved use tried and true situation definitions or negotiate new ones." [54] The lifeworld is a "resource" upon which participants draw for background information or implicit knowledge, but it also is open for discussion; "it is a *topic* about which communicative actors seek to reach agreement." [55] In other words, members of a society make interpretations about the various aspects of the lifeworld by relying on the store of knowledge the lifeworld contains. As participants in the lifeworld, "we cannot divorce ourselves from its influences altogether, but must draw upon it as a resource for our examination. The lifeworld not only constrains our thoughts and actions. It also enables them." [56]

In addition to the lifeworld, societies also consist of a system dimension, the domain dealing with the structural and material features of the world. Habermas describes the components of the system realm as "norm-free" because they are not directly tied to social interaction and cooperation for their functioning. The system domain plays a strong regulative function nonetheless, though it usually is "not even perceived within the horizon of everyday practice."[57] The stock market is one example of a system mechanism that plays a stabilizing function in capitalist societies, according to Habermas. [58] Two other system dimensions that Habermas discusses are money and power.[59] He sees these two elements as especially important because they function as "steering media" with the capacity to exert control over both the system and the lifeworld. "Steering media such as money and power . . . exert generalized strategic influence on the decisions of other participants while bypassing processes of consensus formation in language," explains Habermas. "Because they not only simplify communication in language but *replace it with a symbolic generalization of negative and positive sanctions*, the lifeworld context in which processes of reaching understanding always remain embedded gets *devalued*: the lifeworld is no longer necessary for coordinating actions." [60]

According to Habermas, social pathologies or ideologies arise when attempts to "meet the requirements of system maintenance spill over into domains of the lifeworld."[61] Habermas refers to the influence of system on lifeworld as a process of "colonization,"[62] in which the system side comes to dominate the lifeworld. The process of colonization means that "the lifeworld, which is at first coextensive with a scarcely differentiated social system, gets cut down more and more to one subsystem among others. In the process, system mechanisms get further and further detached from the social structures through which social integration takes place." [63] Such colonization necessarily produces distortions that make free and open decision making increasingly difficult because, once colonization occurs, the goal of understanding is confounded by the instrumental goal of making money and/or achieving power and status. Colonization also means that there is less need to achieve consensus through communication because disputes can be resolved and decisions made by recourse to formal regulations, laws, and established structures of power. Mutual understanding is less likely, and the possibility of personal autonomy declines as the separation from structures of decision making and regulation increases. [64]

The ongoing debate about abortion in the United States provides an example of how lifeworld and system impinge on and affect one another. Lifeworld influences are critical to the abortion debate in that each concerned party brings beliefs about religion, individual autonomy, rights to privacy, morality, and health—all dimensions of the lifeworld—to discussions about abortion. Technological systems also play a role that, paradoxically, is helpful to both sides. Recent developments in medical technology mean that the life of a premature infant can be saved earlier and earlier in the pregnancy, thus raising issues of viability important to pro-life advocates. On the other hand, developments in abortion technology make abortions safer later in a pregnancy, a fact that benefits pro-choice arguments. [65] The resulting technocratization of the debate shows the dominance of system over lifeworld and means that abortion as a right—constitutional or personal—is in fact subordinated to the technical abilities of medical experts.

The prevalence of single-interest groups in society, such as a pro-life or pro-choice organization or Earth First!, illustrates a further effect of the colonization of the lifeworld by system dimensions. Many such groups, believing in the absolute rightness of their positions, use the tools of the system to seal off their particular lifeworlds. Refusing to engage in public debate and largely intolerant of other lifeworlds, they "leave no space for reflection on their relationship to other worldviews with which they share the same universe of discourse."[66] The lack of reasonable disagreement inhibits the full functioning of the legitimate democratic state. The acquisition of advertising and influence through money—another of the system's components—compounds the colonization of the lifeworld even further, obscuring lifeworld claims in deference to the monetary interests of the system.

The notions of lifeworld and system bring together the foundations of Habermas's theory of human society. In the lifeworld, interaction occurs primarily by means of communicative action and depends on consensual decision making in the public sphere for its realization. System coordination, on the other hand, operates in ways that largely bypass the actions of individual agents. Over time, the system has become increasingly "uncoupled" from the lifeworld,[67] meaning that it is increasingly independent and more powerful because it depends less and less on the symbolic processes of the lifeworld. Habermas's critique of the imbalance between lifeworld and system lays the groundwork for the linguistic dimensions of his theory of communicative action.

Universal Pragmatics

Because the knowledge of the lifeworld is contained in language and language is the primary medium of human interaction, Habermas locates a rationality that can rejuvenate the lifeworld in language itself. Habermas turns for this purpose to universal pragmatics, or the study of the general or universal aspects of language use, including an understanding of "the generative nature of rules themselves . . . and the mastery of these rules" that result in "the formation of a competent subject."[68] Habermas's search to discover the conditions for communicative rationality in language use led him to the most elementary unit of communication—the speech act.

Speech-act theory is part of the "ordinary language" approach of Ludwig Wittgenstein, J. L. Austin, and J. R. Searle. These speech-act philosophers believe that the way language is used in interaction is a more important source of meaning than its logical structure or the way words stand for the things they represent. They develop the notion of a speech act, by which they mean that with every utterance, an intentional act is being performed—whether promising, asking, demanding, or simply stating. Usually, a sentence is a speech act, but a word or phrase can be a speech act if it includes intention and follows the rules required of that particular interaction. A word such as "please" is a speech act, as is the sentence "It is five o'clock." In each case, however, the exact meaning of the speech act cannot be determined until the context and intention involved are known.

A speech act also accomplishes an act or does something beyond the utterance itself: "In uttering a promise, an assertion, or a warning, . . . I execute an action—I try to *make* a promise, to *put forward* an assertion, to *issue* a warning—I do things by saying something."[69] A speech act always has two dimensions: propositional content, or the basic factual sense or meaning; and illocutionary force, which gives the speech act its performative dimension. Habermas turns to Austin's approach to speech acts as his point of departure for the analysis of the double structure of speech. Austin refers to the propositional content of an utterance—its meaning—as *locution* and to the speaker's intention as *illocution*. Habermas criticizes Austin for claiming that locutionary and illocutionary meanings are actually different kinds of speech acts. According to Habermas, all speech acts contain two dimensions or levels—propositional content and illocutionary force. Habermas's intent is to analyze this twofold nature of speech acts: "I consider the task of universal pragmatics to be the rational reconstruction of the double structure of speech."[70]

Habermas is concerned with three major types of speech acts: constatives, regulatives, and avowals. Constatives are speech acts that serve primarily to assert a truth claim. "The grass is green," "The meeting is adjourned," and "The 2000 U.S. presidential election was contested" are examples of constatives[71]—statements with which the speaker asserts or claims a certain truth. The speaker, in other words, tells the other how things are, and the listener agrees, at least temporarily, to accept the validity of the asserted truth claim. When this kind of speech act is used, the focus for the speaker is the objective world of facts or states of affairs, the speaker's intention is to be believed, and the external world of objective facts is the focus of discussion between discourse participants.

Regulatives are a second kind of speech act. They govern or regulate in some way the relationship between speaker and hearer in regard to norms—what should or should not be done. Commands, prohibitions, promises, and requests are examples of this type of speech act. The principal validity claim asserted in such acts is to the rightness or appropriateness of a given statement according to shared norms between speaker and listener. Someone who commands another to do something, for instance, must be perceived to have the right to command before that command will be obeyed. This kind of speech act, then, explains and demonstrates the nature of the interpersonal relationship that exists between speaker and listener in terms of the behavioral norms that govern their social world.

Avowals or expressives refer to speech acts that correspond to the function of expression—to the disclosure of feelings, wishes, intentions, and the like. In these speech acts, speakers make a claim of truthfulness about their internal, subjective world. Habermas distinguishes between the "truth" of the constative speech act and the "truthfulness" of avowals by suggesting that truthfulness concerns individual reactions to a situation: Am I being deceived? Will my hopes be realized?[72]

For Habermas, the ability to use speech acts signals communicative competence, which he distinguishes from linguistic competence. Linguistic competence is mastery of the linguistic rules necessary to construct sentences, whereas communicative competence refers to the capacity to employ sentences in utterances.[73] Habermas believes that natural speakers of a language are communicatively competent—they can use sentences in speech acts to communicate their intentions—as part of an "intuitive rule consciousness."[74] That there is a universal capacity to use speech acts appropriately comprises what Habermas calls "*the conditions for a happy employment of sentences in utterances.*"[75]

Validity Claims

Habermas connects speech acts to rationality by showing how each type of speech act stresses a different validity claim. For Habermas, validity is a rational notion that suggests that a speech act is grounded in a particular reality domain and creates a particular relationship to the other participant(s) in the interaction. Habermas posits that these validity claims are recognized by all participants as obligations to fulfill when speaking. When someone performs a speech act, all parties involved accept and operate under certain validity claims.

Validity claims correspond to the three types of speech acts that Habermas describes. Constative speech acts focus on the condition of truth—they contain the offer to refer to actual experiences to determine the certainty of a statement. If someone says, "the grass is green," and someone else doubts the truth of this assertion, the two parties theoretically could go over to the window and look at the color of the grass outside. This type of speech act occurs whenever someone asks for an explanation or clarification of content, as in, "What do you mean by that?" or "How did you arrive at that?" Regulative speech acts are concerned primarily with the appropriateness of the norms operating in a particular context—the socially accepted rules in operation that are binding on all participants. For example, a police officer may have the right to shackle a prisoner, but a prisoner cannot make such a demand of a police officer. If a prisoner says to an officer, "Hold out your hands," the act would be judged invalid according to the norms that are operating in the situation. Finally, avowals raise the validity claim of truthfulness, or the obligation to show that the stated intention behind behavior is the actual motive in operation. The statement "you've hurt my feelings" is an example of an avowal. If intentions are judged to be sincere, the validity claim of truthfulness has been fulfilled successfully. The following chart summarizes the types of speech acts, the corresponding themes, and the validity claims involved:

Type of Speech Act	Focus	Validity Claim
constatives	external, objective world	truth
regulatives	social world	rightness or appropriateness
avowals	speaker's internal world	truthfulness or sincerity

In presupposing the possibility of consensual action in the process of using speech acts, Habermas suggests that every individual, in a situation in which serious argumentation occurs, is anticipating what he calls the "ideal speech situation."[76] This means that all speakers implicitly agree that all participants will have an equal opportunity to employ speech acts, to interact in ways that are free from internal and external constraints, and to seek mutual consensus. Habermas sees this situation as ideal because it is characterized by "(a) a lack of domination, hierarchy, internal neurosis, and external oppression; (b) equality of all participants as asserters and criticizers of truth claims; and (c) the absence of all power except the power of argument itself."[77] The ideal speech situation exists, in other words, when symmetry is evident in terms of access and ability to use the three kinds of speech acts competently.

Equal access to and the ability to use speech acts comprise what Habermas calls the "general symmetry requirement," which consists of three principles. First, no constraints must exist in terms of discussion—all those involved in the speaking situation must have the same opportunity to speak. This is the principle of unrestrained discussion, linked to the capacity to use constatives. A second principle is unimpaired self-representation or the right to use regulative speech acts. For Habermas, this principle suggests that all participants in a speech situation have an equal opportunity to gain individual recognition by expressing their attitudes, feelings, intentions, and motives. A final condition that must be met in an ideal speech situation is that of a full complement of norms and expectations or the use of avowals. This condition requires that all participants have the right to give commands to others—that there are no one-sided obligations—and are required to justify their discourse and actions in terms of mutually recognized norms and rules of interaction. The symmetry among the three dimensions of the ideal speech situation represents a linguistic conceptualization of the ideas of truth, freedom, and justice, respectively.

Habermas's ideal speech situation should not be taken as anything but an ideal.[78] He acknowledges that discourse rarely achieves this level of purity; in fact, he acknowledges that few, if any conversations, meet the criteria of the ideal speech situation. But Habermas does not intend for the ideal speech situation to be realized in a concrete or utopian sense.[79] Its value lies in its function as an assumption that is made whenever individuals enter into a conversation, thus supplying communication with a rational foundation. When all participants in an interaction operate as if "free to speak their minds" and to "listen to reason" without fear of constraints, the possibility for a rationally motivated consensus exists. Such consensus is based not on the arbitrary norms of one interest group or another but on norms inherent in language itself:

> The *design* of an ideal speech situation is necessarily implied in the structure of potential speech, since all speech, even of intentional deception, is oriented towards the idea of truth. . . . Insofar as we master the means for the construction of an ideal speech situation, we can conceive the ideas of truth, freedom, and justice, which interpret each other—although of course only as ideas. On the strength of communicative competence alone, however, . . . we are quite unable to realize the ideal speech situation; we can only anticipate it.[80]

The ideal speech situation is both necessary and unrealized.[81] Because communication would be unnecessary in an ideal speech situation, it functions to regulate the interaction and facilitate the equal access of all participants.[82] At the same time, the possibility of actually achieving such symmetry and equality in all conversational encounters is unrealistic. What is important is that the ideal speech situation sets up the possibility of rationality because it depends on consensus based on the recognition of validity claims that are negotiated and agreed upon by the speakers and hearers themselves.[83] Habermas is able to claim that the "good and true life"—a life of truth, freedom, and justice—is anticipated in every successful act of speech.[84] Thus, he is also able to argue that "the ideal political situation is one in which citizens control their own destiny by taking an active part in the decisions that concern them,"[85] a process that begins with the competent use of language.

Level of Discourse

Habermas does not simply describe the ideal speech situation. He also is interested in what occurs when consensus is not reached through the various speech acts—when the assumptions behind speech acts are called into question and decision making fails. When consensus fails, participants move to another level of interaction—the level of discourse. In discourse, the validity claims that are implicit in communicative action become the explicit topics of discussion: "Discourses are performances, in which we seek to show the grounds for cognitive utterances."[86] In discourse, "we exchange not information, but rather arguments that serve to establish (or reject) problematic validity claims."[87]

Discourse, then, is a mode of communication in which nothing is taken for granted. The participants suspend the usual assumptions about communication and move to the level of argumentation to examine and either accept or reject the problematic claim. Habermas relies heavily on Stephen Toulmin's work to explain how the interactants at this level subject themselves to the force of the better argument. The participants advance conclusions, data, warrants, and backing for warrants in an attempt to make a case for their points of view. "The participants of a discourse," Habermas explains, "no longer seek to exchange information or to convey experiences, but rather to proffer arguments for the justification of problematicised validity claims."[88] Both parties deal with the assumptions behind their validity claims.

The move to discourse involves only two of the three kinds of speech acts and their validity claims: constatives and their truth claims and regulatives and their appropriateness claims. Avowals are not involved at the level of discourse because they cannot be resolved through further discussion. Rather, they depend on the speaker demonstrating, by her future actions, that she means what she says, is reliable, and can be trusted to do what she said she would do. In contrast, when someone questions constatives or regulatives, resolution can be obtained through further discussion.

Habermas calls discourse that deals with the validity claim of truth raised in disagreements over constatives *theoretic discourse*. If, for instance, a speaker asserts that the government has the right to put Timothy McVeigh to death for bombing the Alfred P. Murrah Federal Building in Oklahoma City and another disagrees, both must be willing to suspend judgment and to operate instead as if the statement is a hypothesis that may or may not be valid. Both parties, then, set out to marshal evidence for their respective positions, bringing in different motives and perspectives for establishing the validity of the given proposition as a truth.

When the claim of appropriateness underlying regulative speech acts is under scrutiny, discourse again is operating. Certain norms that guide actions are brought up as grounds for the discussion in what Habermas calls *practical discourse*. In the case of capital punishment, for example, one speaker might argue that killing someone who killed another is appropriately just, while another who is a Christian might insist that such retribution is inappropriate according to the teachings of Jesus. To resolve this debate, participants must deal with the frameworks or grounds from which arguments about the appropriateness and rightness of capital punishment have been formulated.

A level of communication exists beyond practical discourse that Habermas calls *meta-theoretical discourse*. At this level, arguers question the basic conceptual framework underlying their differences or, in Toulmin's terms, the field in which arguments are grounded. The strength of an argument ultimately depends on the system or context in which data and warrants are selected. Paradigm shifts in science are examples of the questioning and overturning of the basic framework of arguments, as when scientists moved from believing the world was flat to believing it to be round. To return to an earlier example, rather than simply marshaling evidence for the assertion that the government does or does not have the right to put someone to death, the participants would look at the sources of their respective assertions—the contexts in which the statements were made—to assess the validity of each.

A final level of discourse—*meta-ethical discourse*—exists in which the structure of knowledge itself is examined and critiqued. This discourse turns on issues of how to conceptualize knowledge, the criteria used to determine what counts as knowledge, and the role of knowledge in everyday life. [89] Whether personal experience counts as knowledge within the social sciences is an issue that might be raised at the meta-ethical level.

The following chart shows the various levels of communication and the corresponding validity claims:

Level of Communication	Validity Claim
theoretic discourse	truth questioned
practical discourse	rightness and appropriateness questioned
meta-theoretical discourse	conceptual field questioned
meta-ethical discourse	knowledge itself questioned

Habermas takes his theory of communication and discourse to yet another level in his book *Between Facts and Norms*. In it, he maintains that the claims of rationality he believes can be discovered in ordinary language—speech acts—also can be found in the field of law in democracies because the law embodies, in a formalized fashion, the consent of the people. The law, however, is a double-edged sword that involves a tension between facts and norms or facticity and validity. Facticity consists of the legal facts of the law that exist as sanctions to limit and manage competing interests in a complex society. Validity refers to the general norms of a society—what is valued, accepted, and upheld by a particular society. [90] In traditional societies, facts and norms were fused by sacred texts and codes, but because of the complexity, pluralism, and disenchantment that characterize modern life, facts and norms exist as separate entities.

The tension between the certainty of law (its facts) and rightness (its validity) is parallel to the distinction Habermas makes between truth and appropriateness claims. The law deals with what is true according to an agreed-upon standard, but it also deals with appropriateness and rightness just as regulatives do. He further suggests that this is also the persistent tension between system and lifeworld. The law embodies the system side of the equation, where money and power reign, while the validity or rightness of the law deals with social norms and expectations.[91] In essence, do people obey the law because of the threat of sanction backed by the state or because they see the law as reasonable and legitimate? Because of the way the law contains elements of both system and lifeworld, Habermas argues that the law should be viewed as a steering mechanism between the two.[92] In this capacity, the law embodies but also is able to resolve some of the tensions between facts and norms, just as moving to the level of discourse in everyday conversations allows participants to resolve tensions between claims and the validity of those claims.[93]

For Habermas, then, communicative action is the ultimate model for and the basis of human action. He makes the process of reaching an understanding fundamental to interpersonal interactions and consensual decision making in the public sphere and grounds it in a rationality inherent to language itself. This rationality is precisely what gives everyday communication its power because it "makes possible a kind of understanding that is based on claims to validity and thus furnishes the only real alternative to exerting influence on one another in more or less coercive ways."[94] Furthermore, he finds in that same model the grounds for democracy because a competent use of speech acts means that speakers are functioning democratically, giving everyone unrestricted access to decision making in the public sphere.

Commentary

Because of his prodigious output and sustained interest in issues over a lengthy period of time, Habermas's ideas have stimulated interest from scholars across fields of inquiry. William Connolly describes the impact and new vantage points offered because of Habermas's work: "The exchange typically begins with specialists . . . complaining about certain misunderstandings on the part of Habermas and ends by many of those ranged on each side viewing their own enterprise in a more refined way."[95]

A project as far reaching and comprehensive as that offered by Habermas necessarily generates considerable criticism as well as praise. By taking on the task of explaining how a communicative rationality undergirds human interaction that ultimately can lead to the emancipation of society as a whole, Habermas does not always provide the degree of detail to satisfy his readers. At the same time, Habermas reminds his readers that his thought is always in the process of development: "That so many competent and distinguished colleagues have dealt so seriously with publications which, as I know only too well, are at best stimulating but by no means present finished thoughts is a source of both embarrassment and pleasure." Habermas acknowledges the "objections to themes and assumptions" that he himself regards "as being in need of clarification."[96] Hanns Hohmann suggests that such calls for clarification essentially assume two forms. Those who disagree with Habermas "find too much content in his paradigm, while those who are supportive may want to ask for more."[97]

Many critics fault Habermas's tendency toward utopianism, which downplays the particulars of political life in favor of abstract and generalized notions of rationality and emancipation. For example, they criticize Habermas for his notion of the ideal speech situation—the foundation of his notion of rationality. The very idea of the ideal is problematic for many scholars because it suggests a perfection not possible in language. In addition, it can lead to the construal of "ordinary communicative practices" as " 'distorted' or 'corrupt' " discourse by comparison.[98]

Other critics suggest that Habermas's notion of an emancipated society also is suspect because of his inability to describe what such a society looks like. Dick Howard is among those who call for greater specificity on this issue: "My point is not that a theory must at every moment tell us what to do. But theory ought *at least* to be able to discuss more than the merry-go-round of continued enlightenment."[99] Similarly, Martin Jay argues that Habermas needs to discuss what else is needed, in addition to a communicative concept of rational action, to realize the good life in which autonomy, understanding, and cooperation can flourish. As Jay explains: "Not only is modernity an uncompleted project, so, too, is Habermas's enormously ambitious attempt to salvage its still emancipatory potential."[100]

In failing to address the nature of emancipation, Habermas also neglects to take into account what happens when the rational decision-making processes he puts in place for an emancipated society fail. Habermas ignores interactions that progress through his levels of discourse but do not end in consensus and resolution. Thomas McCarthy suggests that those "disagreements in *value* commitments and judgments" stemming from "social, cultural, and ideological differences"[101] are especially difficult to manage regardless of the decision-making processes in place. Issues of power are dismissed in Habermas's schema, and yet power differentials may be the dominant factor operating in such situations.

Critics point out that socially and economically disadvantaged individuals may not find Habermas's process accessible. Habermas's privileging of communicative action, in fact, doubly disempowers individuals for whom discussion is not always the preferred mode of managing differences in human interaction. In relegating strategic action to a level below communicative action, Habermas ignores a realm, according to Darryl Gunson and Chik Collins, in which the disempowered often find voice—through legal proceedings, for example.[102] Other strategic possibilities, such as demonstrations and protest, also can be effective in such situations, but Habermas does not address such means as legitimate possibilities for the consensus-driven society he describes. Critics such as Gunson and Collins argue that Habermas needs to recognize the possibility that not only is strategic action a positive option for facilitating the rational society to which he aspires but it also may be the only viable option for certain groups in society. McCarthy summarizes: "Habermas will have to reconsider whether there might not be reasonable, nonviolent alternatives to discursive agreement, hermeneutic consensus, and negotiated compromises other than majority rule and similar mechanisms."[103]

Habermas's apparent unwillingness to consider specifically the case of groups disenfranchised by his rational model carries over to his discussion of the public sphere. Just as his model seems to suggest a universality designed to apply across conditions, so his notion of the public sphere seems unidimensional. In spite of his recognition of the lifeworld as a resource for discussions in the public sphere, Habermas does not adequately address the public sphere as comprised of multiple audiences, some with greater rights of access than others to the role of discourse participant.

Feminist scholars in particular have faulted Habermas for implicitly suggesting that the competent communicator of the ideal speech situation is actually the masculine citizen of liberal political philosophy.[104] Cindy L. Griffin, for example, argues that "the public sphere has been viewed as a particular place to which one goes to engage in debate," but in fact, it is an ideology that manages access to this realm. Individuals need to "enter the market place, take a position at the podium, or enter an arena of objective deliberation in order to arrive at the place of the public sphere." Women and other disempowered groups, however, have "attempted to find this place and enter it for centuries without much measurable success."[105]

Another difficulty with his masculine construction of the inhabitant of the public sphere is that Habermas seems to see the family and the state-regulated official economy on opposite sides of the system/lifeworld line.[106] Feminists suggest that this dichotomy ignores the similarities between the patriarchal, nuclear family and the state and thus perpetuates the lack of access for women in the public sphere: "We require, rather, a framework sensitive to the similarities between them, one which puts them on the same side of the line as institutions which albeit in different ways, enforce women's subordination, since both family and official economy appropriate our labor, shortcircuit our participation in the interpretation of our needs and shield normatively-secured need interpretations from political contestation."[107]

Habermas also is criticized for privileging serious, straightforward, unambiguous language as the only discourse worthy of a democratic culture. John Peters calls him "frankly hostile"[108] to those aspects of language such as humor, irony, and metaphor "that have the capability of sensitizing us to the oppressiveness of whatever categorical distinctions are dominating our thought and social interaction in any given historical period."[109] He is, in other words, "indifferent to the splendour or music of words, to the mind-shaping powers of rhetoric." Hohmann agrees, suggesting that Habermas uses the term *rhetoric* in the "tradition of hostility to the term understood as empty talk or ideologically distorted communication."[110] Lenore Langsdorf makes the same claim, faulting him for his neglect of imagistic dimensions of communication such as "tactile-kinesthetic (nonverbal) and pictorial or im-agistic (unworded) communicative interaction."[111] The singular emphasis on cognitive qualities, then, suggests to many readers of Habermas a limited conception of the human being. Habermas's failure to "attend to rhetorical practice" not only means that Habermas neglects a tradition that has consid-erable bearing on his work but suggests an ignorance of "personal and affec-tive factors that in rhetorical theory appear as inextricably linked with appeals to reason that lead to true conviction."[112] For Habermas, plain speech is the center of democratic life, and communication is "a resolutely sober affair."[113] That rhetoric, narrative, or other alternatives[114] are not even considered for their role in human civic life makes for a lopsided theory.

Another major difficulty with Habermas's writings concerns not con-tent but style. Despite finding Habermas's ideas thought provoking and praiseworthy, his reviewers inevitably comment on the density of his writ-ing. Jonathan Rieder's response is typical: "Wading through prose demands heroic stamina for even the most zealous Frankfurt School devotee."[115] David Held and Lawrence Simon are even more specific in their criticism: Habermas's writing is "often opaque and dense, the language turgid, the ambiguities frequent, the programmatics seemingly endless."[116] Peter Wilby is equally direct in voicing this complaint: "His writing is about as accessible to the average man (even the average honours graduate) as an engineering textbook in Swahili."[117] Hohmann suggests another negative outcome of Habermas's writing style than inaccessibility: it negates the positive empha-sis on rationality that Habermas himself privileges in his theory. Hohmann describes Habermas's style as "dried-up and bleached-out . . . rationalistic academic discourse that is purged of explicit personal and affective ele-ments and thus of any recognizable human context." Hohmann believes that such a style inhibits rather than promotes rationality because it sets up barriers to understanding.[118]

Despite the criticisms, there is no doubt that Habermas has made im-portant contributions to rhetorical theory. That he has written for so long and so extensively means that he has produced a set of concepts about ra-tionality, emancipation, and the communication process that stimulate on-going discussion and debate: "All will find an ordered set of concepts and ar-guments with which to fathom our own social nature and its possibilities. We may not accept what we read, but who dares ask a single scholar to offer more?"[119] His location of rationality in a universal feature of language—the speech act—and his suggestion that democracy can stem from such a basic interaction seem highly idealistic. At the same time, these proposals serve as a reminder that the very language used has a major impact on the kinds of worlds and interactions that are possible. His theory also encourages a search for liberation not just in external schemata but in language itself, which is available to each individual. Whether Habermas's approach will emancipate society remains to be seen, but to contemplate the possibilities he suggests is intriguing. Such reflection and consideration match Habermas's own intentions with his work—not to resolve every possible objection to his theory but to concentrate on helping individuals and societies move toward increasing emancipation: "So much fog lies around today everywhere. I am not giving up the hope that this fog can be lifted. It would be nice if I could do my part to help."[120]

Bibliography

Books

A Berlin Republic: Writings on Germany. Trans. Steven Rendall. Lincoln: University of Nebraska Press, 1997.

Between Facts and Norms. Trans. William Rehg. Cambridge, MA: MIT Press, 1996.

Communication and the Evolution of Society. Trans. Thomas McCarthy. Boston: Beacon, 1979.

The Inclusion of the Other: Studies in Political Theory. Ed. Ciaran Cronin and Pablo De Greiff. Cambridge, MA: MIT Press, 1998.

Justification and Application: Remarks on Discourse Ethics. Trans. Ciaran Cronin. Cambridge, MA: MIT Press, 1993.

Knowledge and Human Interests. Trans. Jeremy J. Shapiro. Boston: Beacon, 1971.

Legitimation Crisis. Trans. Thomas McCarthy. Boston: Beacon, 1975.

Moral Consciousness and Communicative Action. Trans. Christian Lenhardt and Shierry Weber Nicholsen. Cambridge, MA: MIT Press, 1990.

The New Conservatism: Cultural Criticism and the Historians' Debate. Ed. and trans. Shierry Weber Nicholsen. Cambridge, MA: MIT Press, 1989.

Observations on the Spiritual Situation of the Age: Contemporary German Perspectives. Trans. Andrew Buchwalter. Cambridge, MA: MIT Press, 1984.

On the Logic of the Social Sciences. Trans. Shierry Weber Nicholsen and Jerry A. Stark. Cambridge, MA: MIT Press, 1988.

The Philosophical Discourse of Modernity: Twelve Lectures. Trans. Frederick Lawrence. Cambridge, MA: MIT Press, 1987.

Philosophical-Political Profiles: Studies in Contemporary German Social Theory. Trans. Frederick G. Lawrence. Cambridge, MA: MIT Press, 1983.

Postmetaphysical Thinking: Philosophical Essays. Trans. William Mark Hohengarten. Cambridge, MA: MIT Press, 1992.

The Structural Transformation of the Public Sphere: An Inquiry into a Category of Bourgeois Society. Trans. Thomas Burger with the assistance of Fredrick Lawrence. Cambridge, MA: MIT Press, 1991.

Theory and Practice. Trans. John Viertel. Boston: Beacon, 1973.

The Theory of Communicative Action, Volume 1: Reason and the Rationalization of Society. Trans. Thomas McCarthy. Boston: Beacon, 1984.

The Theory of Communicative Action, Volume 2: Lifeworld and System: A Critique of Functionalist Reason. Trans. Thomas McCarthy. Boston: Beacon, 1987.
Toward a Rational Society: Student Protest, Science, and Politics. Trans. Jeremy J. Shapiro. Boston: Beacon, 1970.

Articles

"The Analytical Theory of Science and Dialectics: A Postscript to the Controversy Between Popper and Adorno." In *The Positivist Dispute in German Sociology.* Trans. Glyn Adey and David Frisby. Ed. Theodor W. Adorno, Hans Albert, Ralf Dahrendorf, Jürgen Habermas, Harald Pilot, and Karl R. Popper. New York: Harper and Row, 1976, pp. 131–62.
"Aspects of the Rationality of Action." In *Rationality To-Day.* Ed. Theodore F. Geraets. Ottawa, Can.: University of Ottawa Press, 1979, pp. 185–212.
"Citizenship and National Identity: Some Reflections on the Future of Europe." *Praxis International,* 12 (April 1992), 1–19.
"Comments on John Searle: 'Meaning, Communication, and Representation.'" In *John Searle and His Critics.* Ed. Ernest Lepore and Robert Van Gulick. Cambridge, MA: Blackwell, 1991, pp. 17–30.
"Communicative Freedom and Negative Theology." Trans. Martin J. Matuštík and Patricia J. Huntington. In *Kierkegaard in Post/Modernity.* Ed. Martin J. Matuštík and Merold Westphal. Bloomington: Indiana University Press, 1995, pp. 182–98.
"Concerning the Public Use of History." Trans. Jeremy Leaman. *New German Critique,* 44 (1988), 40–50.
"Consciousness-Raising or Redemptive Criticism: The Contemporaneity of Walter Benjamin." Trans. Philip Brewster and Carl Howard Buchner. *New German Critique,* 17 (1979), 30–59.
"Coping with Contingencies—The Return of Historicism." In *Debating the State of Philosophy: Habermas, Rorty, and Kolakowski.* Ed. Józef Niżnik and John T. Sanders. Westport, CT: Praeger, 1996.
"Discussion on Value-Freedom and Objectivity." In *Max Weber and Sociology Today.* Ed. Otto Stammer. Trans. Kathleen Morris. New York: Harper and Row, 1971, pp. 59–66.
"Emancipatory Knowledge." In *Social Theory: The Multicultural and Classic Readings.* Ed. Charles Lemert. 2nd ed. Boulder, CO: Westview, 1999, pp. 380–81.
"The Entry into Postmodernity: Nietzsche as a Turning Point." In *Postmodernism: A Reader.* Ed. Thomas Docherty. New York: Columbia University Press, 1993, pp. 51–61.
"The Entwinement of Myth and Enlightenment: Re-Reading *Dialectic of Enlightenment.*" Trans. Thomas Y. Levin. *New German Critique,* 26 (1982), 13–30.
"Ernst Bloch—A Marxist Romantic." *Salmagundi,* 10–11 (Fall 1969/Winter 1970), 311–25.
"The Frankfurt School in New York." In *Foundations of the Frankfurt School of Social Research.* Ed. Judith Marcus and Zoltan Tar. New Brunswick, NJ: Transaction, 1984, pp. 55–65.
"The French Oath to Postmodernity: Bataille between Eroticism and General Economics." Trans. Frederick Lawrence. *New German Critique,* 33 (Fall 1984), 79–102.
"Further Reflections on the Public Sphere." Trans. Thomas Burger. In *Habermas and the Public Sphere.* Ed. Craig Calhoun. Cambridge, MA: MIT Press, 1992, 421–61.

"The Genealogical Writing of History: On Some Aporias in Foucault's Theory of Power. Trans. Gregory Ostrander. *Canadian Journal of Social and Political Theory*, 10 (1986), 1–9.

"Georg Simmel on Philosophy and Culture: Postscript to a Collection of Essays." Trans. Mathieu Deflem. *Critical Inquiry*, 22 (Spring 1996), 403–14.

"Habermas: Questions and Counter-Questions." *Praxis International*, 4 (October 1984), 229–49.

"Hannah Arendt's Communications Concept of Power." *Social Research*, 44 (Spring 1977), 3–24.

"Historical Consciousness and Post-Traditional Identity: Remarks on the Federal Republic's Orientation to the West." *Acta Sociologica*, 31 (1988), 3–13.

"History and Evolution." *Telos*, 39 (Spring 1979), 5–44.

"How is Legitimacy Possible on the Basis of Legality?" In *The Tanner Lectures on Human Values*. Vol. 8. Ed. Sterling M. McMurrin. Salt Lake City: University of Utah Press, 1988, pp. 219–79.

"Human Rights and Popular Sovereignty: The Liberal and Republican Version." *Ratio Juris*, 7 (March 1994), 1–13.

"The Idea of the University—Learning Processes." Trans. John R. Blazek. *New German Critique*, 41 (1987), 3–22.

"The Inimitable *Zeitschrift Fur Sozialforschung*: How Horkheimer Took Advantage of a Historically Oppressive Hour." Trans. David J. Parent. *Telos*, 45 (Fall 1980), 114–21.

"Intermediate Reflections: Social Action, Purposive Activity, and Communication." In *Professing the New Rhetorics: A Sourcebook*. Ed. Theresa Enos and Stuart C. Brown. Engelwood Cliffs, NJ: Prentice Hall/Blair, 1994, pp. 204–20.

"Interpretive Social Science vs. Hermeneuticism." In *Social Science as Moral Inquiry*. Ed. Norma Haan, Robert N. Bellah, Paul Rabinow, and William M. Sullivan. New York: Columbia University Press, 1983.

"An Intersubjective Concept of Individuality." *Journal of Chinese Philosophy*, 18 (June 1991), 133–41.

"Justice and Solidarity: On the Discussion Concerning 'Stage 6.'" *Philosophical Forum*, 21 (Fall/Winter 1989–90), 32–52.

"A Kind of Settlement of Damages (Apologetic Tendencies)." Trans. Jeremy Leaman. *New German Critique*, 44 (1988), 25–39.

"Letter to the Editor of the *Franfurter Allgemeine Zeitung*, August 11, 1986." In *Forever in the Shadow of Hitler?: Original Documents of the* Historikerstreit, *the Controversy Concerning the Singularity of the Holocaust*. Trans. James Knowlton and Truett Cates. Atlantic Highlands, NJ: Humanities, 1993, pp. 58–60.

"Martin Heidegger on the Publication of Lectures from the Year 1935." *Graduate Faculty Philosophy Journal*, 6 (Fall 1977), 155–80.

"Modern and Postmodern Architecture." In *Critical Theory and Public Life*. Ed. John Forester. Cambridge, MA: MIT Press, 1985, pp. 317–29.

"Modernity—An Incomplete Project." Trans. Seyla Benhabib. In *The Anti-Aesthetic: Essays on Postmodern Culture*. Ed. Hal Foster. Port Townsend, WA: Bay, 1983, pp. 3–15. (This essay originally was delivered as a lecture in September, 1980, when Habermas was awarded the Theodor W. Adorno prize by the city of Frankfurt. It was published under the title, "Modernity Versus Postmodernity" in *New German Critique*, 22 (Winter 1981), 3–14. It has been reprinted often under both titles.)

"Modernity: An Unfinished Project." In *Habermas and the Unfinished Project of Modernity: Critical Essays on* The Philosophical Discourse of Modernity. Ed.

Maurizio Passerin d'Entrèves and Seyla Benhabib. Cambridge, MA: MIT Press, 1997, pp. 38–55.

"Moral Development and Ego Identity." *Telos*, 24 (Summer 1975), 41–55.

"Morality and Ethical Life: Does Hegel's Critique of Kant Apply to Discourse Ethics?" Trans. Christian Lenhardt and Shierry Weber Nicholsen. In *Kant and Political Philosophy: The Contemporary Legacy*. Ed. Ronald Beiner and William James Booth. New Haven, CT: Yale University Press, 1993, pp. 320–36.

"Neoconservative Culture Criticism in the United States and West Germany: An Intellectual Movement in Two Political Cultures." *Telos*, 56 (Summer 1983), 75–89.

"The New Obscurity: The Crisis of the Welfare State and the Exhaustion of Utopian Energies." Trans. Phillip Jacobs. *Philosophy and Social Criticism*, 11 (1986), 1–18.

"New Social Movements." *Telos*, 49 (Fall 1981), 33–37.

"Notes and Commentary: On the German-Jewish Heritage." *Telos*, 44 (Summer 1980), 127–31.

"Note, February 23, 1987." In *Forever in the Shadow of Hitler?: Original Documents of the Historikerstreit, the Controversy Concerning the Singularity of the Holocaust.* Trans. James Knowlton and Truett Cates. Atlantic Highlands, NJ: Humanities, 1993, pp. 260–62.

"On Hermeneutics' Claim to Universality." In *The Hermeneutics Reader: Texts of the German Tradition from the Enlightenment to the Present.* Ed. Kurt Mueller-Vollmer. New York: Continuum, 1985, pp. 294–319.

"On Social Identity." *Telos*, 19 (Spring 1974), 91–103.

"On Systematically Distorted Communication." *Inquiry*, 13 (Autumn 1970), 205–19.

"On the Internal Relation between the Rule of Law and Democracy." *European Journal of Philosophy*, 3 (1995), 12–20.

"On the Public Use of History: The Official Self-Understanding of the Federal Republic Is Breaking Up." In *Forever in the Shadow of Hitler?: Original Documents of the Historikerstreit, the Controversy Concerning the Singularity of the Holocaust.* Trans. James Knowlton and Truett Cates. Atlantic Highlands, NJ: Humanities, 1993.

"A Philosophico-Political Profile." *New Left Review*, 151 (May/June 1985), 75–105.

"Philosophy as Stand-In and Interpreter." In *After Philosophy: End or Transformation?* Cambridge, MA: MIT Press, 1987, pp. 296–315.

"Paradigms of Law." *Cardozo Law Review*, 17 (March 1996), 771–84.

"The Place of Philosophy in Marxism." *Insurgent Sociologist*, 5 (1975), 41–48.

"A Positivistically Bisected Rationalism." In *The Positivist Dispute in German Sociology.* Trans. Glyn Adey and David Frisby. Ed. Theodor W. Adorno, Hans Albert, Ralf Dahrendorf, Jürgen Habermas, Harald Pilot, and Karl R. Popper. New York: Harper and Row, 1976, pp. 198–225.

"A Postscript to *Knowledge and Human Interests.*" *Philosophy of the Social Sciences*, 3 (June 1973), 157–89.

"Psychic Thermidor and the Rebirth of Rebellious Subjectivity." *Praxis International*, 1 (April 1981), 79–86.

"The Public Sphere: An Encyclopedia Article (1964)." Trans. Sara Lennox and Frank Lennox. *New German Critique*, 3 (Fall 1974), 49–55.

"Questions and Counterquestions." Trans. James Bohman. In *Habermas and Modernity.* Ed. Richard J. Bernstein. Cambridge, MA: MIT Press, 1985, pp. 192–216.

"Rationalism Divided in Two: A Reply to Albert." Trans. Glyn Adey and David Frisby. In *Positivism and Sociology.* Ed. Anthony Giddens. London, UK: Heinemann, 1974, pp. 195–223.

"Remarks on the Development of Horkheimer's Work." In *On Max Horkheimer: New Perspectives*. Ed. Seyla Benhabib, Wolfgang Bonß, and John McCole. Cambridge, MA: MIT Press, 1993, pp. 49–66.

"A Reply to my Critics." Trans. Thomas McCarthy. In *Habermas: Critical Debates*. Ed. John B. Thompson and David Held. Cambridge, MA: MIT Press, 1982, pp. 219–83.

"A Reply to Müller and Neusüss." *Telos*, 25 (Fall 1975), 91–98.

"Reply to Skjei." *Inquiry*, 28 (March 1985), 105–13.

"Response to the Commentary of Bernstein and Dove." In *Hegel's Social and Political Thought: The Philosophy of Objective Spirit*. Ed. Donald Phillip Verene. Atlantic Highlands, NJ: Humanities, 1980, pp. 247–50.

"A Review of Gadamer's *Truth and Method*." In *Understanding and Social Inquiry*. Ed. Fred R. Dallmayr and Thomas A. McCarthy. Notre Dame, IN: University of Notre Dame Press, 1977, pp. 335–63.

"Right and Violence—A German Trauma." Trans. Martha Calhoun. *Cultural Critique*, 1 (Fall 1985), 125–39.

"Social Analysis and Communicative Competence." In *Social Theory: The Multicultural and Classic Readings*. Ed. Charles Lemert. 2nd ed. Boulder, CO: Westview, 1999.

"Some Conditions for Revolutionizing Late Capitalist Societies [1968]." *Canadian Journal of Political and Social Theory*, 7 (Winter/Spring 1983), 32–42.

"Some Distinctions in Universal Pragmatics: A Working Paper." *Theory and Society*, 3 (Summer 1976), 155–67.

"A Speculative Materialist." *Telos*, 33 (Fall 1977), 138–41.

"Struggles for Recognition in Constitutional States." *European Journal of Philosophy*, 1 (1993), 128–55.

"Summation and Response." Trans. Martha Matesich. *Continuum*, 8 (1970), 123–33.

"Talcott Parsons: Problems of Theory Construction." *Sociological Inquiry*, 51 (1981), 173–96.

"The Tasks of a Critical Theory of Society." Trans. Thomas McCarthy. In *Critical Theory and Society: A Reader*. Ed. Stephen Eric Bronner and Douglas MacKay Kellner. New York: Routledge, 1989, pp. 292–312.

"A Test for Popular Justice: The Accusations Against the Intellectuals." *New German Critique*, 12 (1977), 11–13.

"Three Normative Models of Democracy." *Constellations*, 1 (April 1994), 1–10.

"Toward a Reconstruction of Historical Materialism." *Theory and Society*, 2 (Fall 1975), 287–300.

"Towards a Communication-Concept of Rational Collective Will-Formation. A Thought-Experiment." *Ratio Juris*, 2 (July 1989), 144–54.

"Towards a Theory of Communicative Competence." In *Recent Sociology 2*. Ed. Hans Peter Dreitzel. London, UK: Collier-Macmillan, 1970, pp. 114–48.

"Transcendence from Within, Transcendence in this World." In *Habermas, Modernity, and Public Theology*. Ed. Don S. Browning and Francis Schüssler Fiorenza. New York: Crossroad, 1992, pp. 226–50.

"What Does a Crisis Mean Today? Legitimation Problems in Late Capitalism." *Social Research*, 40 (Winter 1973), 643–67.

"What Does Socialism Mean Today? The Rectifying Revolution and the Need for New Thinking on the Left." Trans. Ben Morgan. *New Left Review*, 183 (1990), 3–21.

"Why More Philosophy?" *Social Research*, 38 (Winter 1971), 633–54.

"Work and *Weltanschauung*: The Heidegger Controversy from a German Perspective." In *Heidegger: A Critical Reader*. Ed. Hubert Dreyfus and Harrison Hall. Cambridge, MA: Basil Blackwell, 1992.

"Yet Again: German Identity—A Unified Nation of Angry DM-Burghers?" In *When the Wall Came Down: Reactions to German Unification*. Ed. Harold James and Marla Stone. New York: Routledge, Chapman and Hall, 1992, pp. 86–102.

Collected Works

Cook, Maeve, ed. *On the Pragmatics of Communication: Jürgen Habermas*. Cambridge, MA: MIT Press, 1998.

Seidman, Steven, ed. *Jürgen Habermas on Society and Politics: A Reader*. Boston: Beacon, 1989.

Interviews and Conversations

Bolaffi, Angelo. "Notes and Commentary: An Interview with Juergen Habermas." *Telos*, 39 (Spring 1979), 163–72.

Calhoun, Craig, Leah Florence, and Rekha Mirchandani, eds. "Concluding Remarks." Conversation among Jürgen Habermas, Nancy Fraser, Stephen Leonard, Michael Warner, Lloyd Kramer, Gerald Postema, and Goram Kindem. In *Habermas and the Public Sphere*. Ed. Craig Calhoun. Cambridge, MA: MIT Press, 1992, pp. 462–79.

Carleheden, Mikael, and René Gabriëls. "An Interview with Jürgen Habermas." *Theory, Culture and Society*, 13 (1996), 1–17.

Dews, Peter, ed. *Autonomy and Solidarity: Interviews*. London, UK: Verso, 1986.

Erd, Rainer. "Twenty Years Later: 1968 and the West German Republic." Interview with Jürgen Habermas. *Dissent*, 36 (April 1989), 250–56.

Frankel, Boris. "Habermas Talking: An Interview." *Theory and Society*, 1 (1974), 37–58.

Haller, Michael. *The Past as Future: Jürgen Habermas*. Trans. and ed. Max Pensky. Lincoln: University of Nebraska Press, 1994.

"Herbert Marcuse, Jürgen Habermas and Friends: A Discussion on Democracy and Critical Theory." *New Political Science*, 1 (1979), 19–29.

Honneth, Axel, Eberhard Knödler-Bunte, and Arno Widmann. "The Dialectics of Rationalization: An Interview with Jürgen Habermas." *Telos*, 49 (Fall 1981), 5–31.

Horster, Detlev, and Willem van Reijen. "Interview with Jürgen Habermas: Starnberg, March, 23, 1979." Trans. Ron Smith. *New German Critique*, 18 (Fall 1979), 29–43.

Krzemiński, Adam. " 'More Humility, Fewer Illusions'—A Talk between Adam Michnik and Jürgen Habermas." *New York Review of Books*, 41 (March 24, 1994), 24–29.

Nielsen, Torben Hviid. "Jürgen Habermas: Morality, Society and Ethics." *Acta Sociologica*, 2 (1990), 93–114.

"Theory and Politics: A Discussion with Herbert Marcuse, Juergen Habermas, Heinz Lubasz and Telman Spengler." *Telos*, 38 (Winter 1978-79), 124–53.

"There Are Alternatives." Interview with Jürgen Habermas. *New Left Review*, 231 (September/October 1998), 3–12.

Wolin, Richard. "Jürgen Habermas on the Legacy of Jean-Paul Sartre." Trans. Richard Wolin. *Political Theory*, 20 (August 1992), 496–501.

Endnotes

1 Peter Dews, ed., *Autonomy and Solidarity: Interviews* (London, UK: Verso, 1986), p. 147.

2 Biographical information on Habermas was obtained from the following sources: Detlev Horster and Will van Reijen, "Interview with Jürgen Habermas: Starnberg, March 23, 1979," trans. Ron Smith, *New German Critique*, 18 (Fall 1979), 30; Dews; *1983–84 International Who's Who*, 47th ed. (London, UK: Europa, 1983), p. 532; Axel Honneth, Eberhard Knödler-Bunte, and Arno Widmann, "The Dialectics of Rationalization: An Interview with Jürgen Habermas," *Telos*, 49 (Fall 1981), 5; Martin Jay, *Marxism and Totality: The Adventures of a Concept from Lukács to Habermas* (Berkeley: University of California Press, 1984), pp. 464–68; personal resume obtained from Habermas; and Thomas McCarthy, e-mail to Karen A. Foss, February 9, 2001.

3 Dews, p. 73.

4 Dews, p. 73.

5 Dews, p. 74.

6 Dews, p. 191.

7 The Institute was founded in 1923 by Felix Weil in Frankfurt and thus the origin of the name *Frankfurt School*. In 1933, with the rise of Nazism, its members were forced to flee Germany and emigrated briefly to Geneva, Switzerland, before moving to New York City in 1935. The institute existed under the protective wing of Columbia University until it was reestablished in Frankfurt in 1953.

8 Dews, p. 191.

9 Dews, p. 192.

10 David Held, *Introduction to Critical Theory: Horkheimer to Habermas* (Berkeley: University of California Press, 1980), pp. 65–67.

11 Held, p. 41.

12 David Gross, "On Critical Theory," *Humanities in Society*, 4 (Winter 1981), 92.

13 Jürgen Habermas, *Toward a Rational Society: Student Protest, Science, and Politics*, trans. Jeremy J. Shapiro (Boston: Beacon, 1970), p. 17.

14 Habermas, *Toward a Rational Society*, p. 26.

15 Horster and van Reijen, p. 35.

16 Dews, p. 68.

17 Joan Alway, *Critical Theory and Political Possibilities: Conceptions of Emancipatory Politics in the Works of Horkheimer, Adorno, Marcuse, and Habermas* (Westport, CT: Greenwood, 1995), p. 121.

18 Alway, p. 122.

19 Jean Cohen, quoted in Alway, p. 122.

20 Dews, biographical preface.

21 Peter Wilby, "Habermas and the Language of the Modern State," *New Society*, 47 (March 22, 1979), 667.

22 Honneth, Knödler-Bunte, and Widmann, pp. 7, 30.

23 Jürgen Habermas, "A Test for Popular Justice: The Accusations Against the Intellectuals," *New German Critique*, 12 (1977), 12.

24 Wilby, p. 668.

25 Horster and van Reijen, p. 33.

26 Jürgen Habermas, *Communication and the Evolution of Society*, trans. Thomas McCarthy (Boston: Beacon, 1979), p. 95. For a discussion of where Habermas and Marx disagree, see John P. Scott, "Critical Social Theory: An Introduction and Critique," *British Journal of Sociology*, 29 (March 1978), 7; and William M. Sullivan, "Two Options in Modern Social Theory: Habermas and Whitehead," *International Philosophical Quarterly*, 15 (March 1975), 88.

27 The limited references to Marx and Marxist ideas as Habermas's work has progressed led Wilby to question the appropriateness of calling Habermas a Marxist. Wilby suggests that in terms of Habermas's work, Marx is "only a distant echo, like the Book of Genesis in the writings of radical theologians" (p. 667).

28 Detlef Horster, *Habermas: An Introduction*, trans. Heidi Thompson (Philadelphia, PA: Penn-bridge, 1992), p. 84.

29 Richard Wolin, "Introduction," in *The New Conservatism: Cultural Criticism and the Historians' Debate*, by Jürgen Habermas, trans. and ed. Shierry Weber Nicholsen (Cambridge, MA: MIT Press, 1997), p. vii.

30 Thomas B. Farrell, "Comic History Meets Tragic Memory: Burke and Habermas on the Drama of Human Relations," in *Kenneth Burke and Contemporary European Thought: Rhetoric in Transition*, ed. Bernard L. Brock (Tuscaloosa: University of Alabama Press, 1995), pp. 37–38.

31 William Rehg, "Translator's Introduction," in *Between Facts and Norms: Contributions to a Discourse Theory of Law and Democracy*, by Jürgen Habermas, trans. William Rehg (Cambridge, MA: MIT Press, 1996), p. ix.

32 Jürgen Habermas, *Knowledge and Human Interests*, trans. Jeremy J. Shapiro (Boston: Beacon, 1971), p. 314. Habermas's inaugural lecture is published as the appendix to this work.

33 Jürgen Habermas, "Modernity: An Unfinished Product," in *Habermas and the Unfinished Project of Modernity: Critical Essays on* The Philosophical Discourse of Modernity, ed. Maurizio Passerin d'Entrèves and Seyla Benhabib (Cambridge, MA: MIT Press, 1997), pp. 38–55.

34 Craig Calhoun, "Introduction: Habermas and the Public Sphere," in *Habermas and the Public Sphere*, ed. Craig Calhoun (Cambridge, MA: MIT Press, 1992), pp. 6–7.

35 Margaret C. Jacob, "The Mental Landscape of the Public Sphere: A European Perspective," *Eighteenth-Century Studies*, 28 (Fall 1994), 96.

36 Jürgen Habermas, "The Public Sphere: An Encyclopedia Article," trans. Sara Lennox and Frank Lennox, in *Critical Theory and Society: A Reader*, ed. Stephen Eric Bronner and Douglas MacKay Kellner (New York: Routledge, 1989), p. 136.

37 Dick Howard, "Law and Political Culture," *Cardozo Law Review*, 17 (March 1996), 1402.

38 Habermas, *Theory and Practice*, trans. John Viertel (Boston: Beacon, 1973), p. 122.

39 Habermas, "The Public Sphere," p. 136.

40 John Durham Peters, "Distrust of Representation: Habermas on the Public Sphere," *Media, Culture and Society*, 15 (October 1993), 544.

41 Horster, p. 6.

42 Horster, p. 6.

43 Jürgen Habermas, *Theory and Practice*, pp. 7–40; and A. Brand, "Interests and the Growth of Knowledge—A Comparison of Weber, Popper and Habermas," *Netherlands' Journal of Sociology*, 13 (July 1977), 11.

44 Habermas, *Communication and the Evolution of Society*, p. 21. For a discussion of the difficulties with Habermas's use of the term *quasi-transcendentals*, see Brand, pp. 11–12.

45 Donald McIntosh, "Habermas on Freud," *Social Research*, 44 (Autumn 1977), 562–65.

46 Habermas, *Theory and Practice*, p. 14.

47 Habermas, *Theory and Practice*, p. 14.

48 The German word Habermas uses here is *Verstandigung*, which refers both to linguistic understanding and to the process of reaching agreement, thus extending across a spectrum of meaning from comprehension to consensus. Maeve Cook, *Language and Reason: A Study of Habermas's Pragmatics* (Cambridge, MA: MIT Press, 1994), p. 9.

49 Habermas, *The Theory of Communicative Action, Volume 1: Reason and the Rationalization of Society*, trans. Thomas McCarthy (Boston: Beacon, 1984), p. 286.

50 Stephen K. White, *The Recent Work of Jürgen Habermas* (New York: Cambridge University Press, 1988), p. 45.

51 John Lechte, *Fifty Key Contemporary Thinkers: From Structuralism to Postmodernity* (New York: Routledge, 1994), p. 186.

52 Habermas, *The Theory of Communicative Action, Volume 2: Lifeworld and System: A Critique of Functionalist Reason*, trans. Thomas McCarthy (Boston: Beacon, 1987), p. 327.

53 Habermas, *The Theory of Communicative Action, Volume 2*, p. 124.

54 Habermas, *The Theory of Communicative Action, Volume 2*, p. 125.

55 Kenneth Baynes, *The Normative Grounds of Social Criticism: Kant, Rawls, and Habermas* (Albany: State University of New York Press, 1992), p. 82.

56 Kit-Man Li, *Western Civilization and its Problems* (Aldershot, UK: Ashgate, 1999), p. 173.

57 Habermas, *The Theory of Communicative Action, Volume 2*, p. 150.

58 Habermas, *The Theory of Communicative Action, Volume 2,* p. 150.
59 See Klaus Hartmann, "Human Agency Between Lifeworld and System: Latest Version of Critical Theory," *Journal of the British Society for Phenomenology,* 16 (May 1985), 151.
60 Habermas, *The Theory of Communicative Action, Volume 2,* p. 281.
61 Baynes, *The Normative Grounds of Social Criticism,* p. 174.
62 Habermas, *The Theory of Communicative Action, Volume 2,* pp. 293, 522.
63 Habermas, *The Theory of Communicative Action, Volume 2,* p. 154.
64 Habermas, *The Theory of Communicative Action, Volume 2,* pp. 311, 317.
65 Mathieu Deflem, "The Boundaries of Abortion Law: Systems Theory from Parsons to Luhmann and Habermas," *Social Forces,* 16 (1998), 801.
66 Thomas McCarthy, "Legitimacy and Diversity: Dialectical Reflections on Analytical Distinctions," *Cardozo Law Review,* 17 (March 1996), 1115.
67 Habermas, *The Theory of Communicative Action, Volume 2,* p. 154.
68 Habermas, *Knowledge and Human Interests,* p. 377.
69 Habermas, *Communication and the Evolution of Society,* p. 34.
70 Habermas, *Communication and the Evolution of Society,* p. 44.
71 Habermas, *Communication and the Evolution of Society,* p. 52.
72 Habermas, *Communication and the Evolution of Society,* p. 59.
73 Habermas, *Communication and the Evolution of Society,* p. 26.
74 Habermas, *Communication and the Evolution of Society,* p. 26.
75 Habermas, *Communication and the Evolution of Society,* p. 26.
76 Dews, p. 163.
77 Raymond A. Belliotti, "Radical Politics and Nonfoundational Morality," *International Philosophical Quarterly,* 24 (March 1989), 40.
78 Horster and Van Reijen, p. 97.
79 Dews, p. 163.
80 Jürgen Habermas, "Towards a Theory of Communicative Competence," *Inquiry,* 13 (Winter 1970), 372.
81 Michael K. Power, "Habermas and the Counterfactual Imagination," *Cardozo Law Review,* 17 (March 1996), 1012.
82 Power, p. 1018.
83 Habermas, *The Theory of Communicative Action, Volume 1,* p. 100.
84 Habermas, *Knowledge and Human Interests,* p. 317.
85 Patricia Roberts, "Habermas' Varieties of Communicative Action: Controversy Without Combat," *Journal of Advanced Composition,* 11 (Fall 1991), 412.
86 Habermas, *Theory and Practice,* p. 18. Habermas uses the term *discourse* in a very specialized way, in contrast to most scholars in rhetoric. Generally, the term is used to refer to verbal or written expression.
87 Habermas, quoted in Horster, p. 31.
88 John B. Thompson, *Critical Hermeneutics: A Study in the Thought of Paul Ricoeur and Jürgen Habermas* (Cambridge, NY: Cambridge University Press, 1981), p. 87.
89 Thomas A. McCarthy, *The Critical Theory of Jürgen Habermas* (Cambridge, MA: MIT Press, 1978), p. 305.
90 Power, 1008; John L. Brooke, "Reason and Passion in the Public Sphere: Habermas and the Cultural Historians," *Journal of Interdisciplinary History,* 29 (Summer 1998), 58.
91 Robert Alexy, "Jürgen Habermas's Theory of Legal Discourse," *Cardozo Law Review,* 17 (March 1996), 1027.
92 Howard, "Law and Political Culture," p. 1405.
93 David Abraham, "Persistent Facts and Compelling Norms: Liberal Capitalism, Democratic Socialism, and the Law," *Law and Society Review,* 28 (1994), 943.
94 Jürgen Habermas, *Moral Consciousness and Communicative Action,* trans. Christian Lenhardt and Shierry Weber Nicholsen (Cambridge, MA: MIT Press, 1990), p. 19.
95 William E. Connolly, rev. of *The Critical Theory of Jürgen Habermas,* by Thomas McCarthy, *History and Theory: Studies in the Philosophy of History,* 18 (1979), 398.

[96] John B. Thompson and David Held, *Habermas: Critical Debates* (Cambridge, MA: MIT Press, 1982), pp. 219–20.

[97] Hanns Hohmann, "Rhetoric in the Public Sphere and the Discourse of Law and Democracy," *Quarterly Journal of Speech*, 84 (August 1998), 362.

[98] Farrell, p. 51.

[99] Dick Howard, "A Politics in Search of the Political," *Theory and Society*, 1 (Fall 1974), 300.

[100] Martin Jay, "Habermas and Modernism," *Praxis International*, 4 (April 1984), 12.

[101] McCarthy, "Legitimacy and Diversity," p. 1088.

[102] Darryl Gunson and Chik Collins, "From the 'I' to the 'We': Discourse Ethics, Identity and the Pragmatics of Partnership in the West of Scotland," *Communication Theory*, 7 (November 1997), 298.

[103] McCarthy, "Legitimacy and Diversity," p. 1123.

[104] Pauline Johnson, *Feminism as Radical Humanism* (Boulder, CO: Westview, 1994), p. 105.

[105] Cindy L. Griffin, "The Essentialist Roots of the Public Sphere: A Feminist Critique," *Western Journal of Communication*, 60 (Winter 1996), 32–33.

[106] Johnson, p. 102.

[107] Nancy Fraser, "What's Critical About Critical Theory? The Case of Habermas and Gender," *New German Critique*, 35 (Spring/Summer 1985), 130. Another feminist critique is offered by Isaac D. Balbus, "Habermas and Feminism: (Male) Communication and the Evolution of (Patriarchal) Society," *New Political Science*, 13 (Winter 1984), 27–47.

[108] Peters, p. 562.

[109] White, p. 31.

[110] Hohmann, p. 363.

[111] Lenore Langsdorf, "Refusing Individuality: How Human Beings Are Made into Subjects," *Communication Theory*, 7 (November 1997), 328.

[112] Hohmann, p. 366.

[113] Peters, p. 563.

[114] Peters suggests that this is not surprising, given the Nazi aestheticization of politics; nonetheless, it does ignore the entire realm of traditional rhetoric (p. 656).

[115] Jonathan Rieder, "Review Symposium," *Contemporary Sociology*, 6 (1977), 416.

[116] David Held and Lawrence Simon, "Toward Understanding Habermas," *New German Critique*, 7 (Winter 1976), 136.

[117] Wilby, p. 669.

[118] Hohmann, p. 366.

[119] Michael Pusey, *Jürgen Habermas* (New York: Tavistock, 1987), p. 122.

[120] Honneth, Knödler-Bunte, and Widmann, p. 31.

9

BELL HOOKS

"Passionately concerned with education for critical consciousness, I continually search for ways to think, teach, and write that excite and liberate the mind . . . to live and act in a way that challenges systems of domination."[1] This statement summarizes the commitment of Gloria Jean Watkins, who writes under the name of *bell hooks*[2], to theorizing and creating symbols that resist and transform structures of domination. Situated at the intersection of rhetorical theory and cultural studies, hooks studies the symbolic practices

65

that constitute cultural life. She approaches rhetoric from the perspective of how race, class, and gender inform both the production and the reception of rhetorical/cultural products. Her particular interest is in how such products reinforce domination and, at the same time, can provide productive spaces for its resistance.

Born on September 25, 1952, in Hopkinsville, Kentucky, hooks was one of seven children born to Veodis Watkins, a custodian employed by the U.S. Postal Service, and Rosa Bell Watkins, a homemaker. Hooks's childhood was characterized by an appreciation for various forms of music and art, but her particular interest was poetry. She memorized poems for special events at her church and school; when storms caused power outages, her family would light candles and stage impromptu talent shows, at which hooks would recite the poetry of William Wordsworth, Langston Hughes, Elizabeth Barrett Browning, and Gwendolyn Brooks.[3] For hooks, memorizing poetry "was pure enchantment, for we learned by listening and reciting that words put together just so, said just so, could have the same impact on our psyches as song, could lift and exalt our spirits, enabling us to feel tremendous joy, or carrying us down into that most immediate and violent sense of loss and grief."[4]

Gender was a significant issue in hooks's family life. She grew up with five sisters and one brother and saw her brother given greater rights and privileges than the girls in the family. She learned, along with her sisters, to cater to him. She also learned about the domination and control that accompany gender relations in contemporary culture: "Our daily life was full of patriarchal drama—the use of coercion, violent punishment, verbal harassment."[5] The pattern was evident in her family's daily communication, which she described as living in two social spaces.

> One was a world without the father, when he would go to work, and that world was full of speech. . . . We could express ourselves loudly, passionately, outrageously. The other world was a male-dominated social space where sound and silence were dictated by his presence. . . . We would turn our volumes down, lower our voices; we would, if need be, remain silent. In this same childhood world we witnessed women—our grandmothers, mothers, aunts—speak with force and power in sex-segregated spaces, then retreat into a realm of silence in the presence of men.[6]

Male domination was manifest in hooks's family in even more brutal ways. She remembers her father yelling and screaming, pushing and hitting her mother. One night, he threatened to kill her mother and threw her out of the house. Hooks witnessed her mother—a person she knew as strong, as someone who could get things done, "a woman of ways and means, a woman of action"—sitting paralyzed, waiting for the next blow.[7] Hooks could not "bear the silent agreement that the man is right, that he has done what men are able to do."[8] Her sense that inequity in her household was gender based led her, at the age of 16, to announce to her mother, "I will never marry. I will never be any man's prisoner."[9] Her parents' marriage made marriage "seem like a trap, a door closing in a room without air."[10]

Talking back, or "speaking as an equal to an authority figure . . . having an opinion" became a characteristic way in which hooks responded to such inequities. She felt that "black women spoke in a language so rich, so poetic, that it felt . . . like being shut off from life, smothered to death if one were not allowed to participate."[11] She "could not stop the words, making thought, writing speech."[12] She explains: "To make my voice, I had to speak, to hear myself talk—and talk I did—darting in and out of grown folks' conversations and dialogues, answering questions that were not directed at me, endlessly asking questions, making speeches."[13]

Because she was not silent as children (especially girls) were supposed to be, hooks constantly was punished for her verbosity. She was punished so often, in fact, that she began to feel persecuted. When she learned the word *scapegoat*, she felt it accurately described her role in her family.[14] Persecuted, ridiculed, and punished, she "did not feel truly connected to these strange people, to these familial folks who could not only fail to grasp [her] worldview but who just simply did not want to hear it."[15] Childhood was an experience of estrangement spent dreaming of the moment when she would find her way home: "In my imagination, home was a place of radical openness, of recognition and reconciliation, where one could create freely."[16]

The punishment and persecution hooks experienced as a child pushed her in the direction of critical analytical thought. As hooks explains, "Psychologically wounded and at times physically hurt, the primary force which kept me going, which lifted my spirits was critical engagement with ideas."[17] She found the life of the mind a sanctuary where she "could experience a sense of agency and thereby construct" her own identity.[18] She kept a daily diary or journal while growing up and found that it was a space of critical reflection for her—a place where she struggled to understand herself and the world around her, "that crazy world of family and community, that painful world. I could say there what was hurting me, how I felt about things, what I hoped for. I could be angry there with no threat of punishment. I could 'talk back.' Nothing had to be concealed. I could hold on to myself there."[19] This lived recognition of how critical thought can be used in the service of survival led hooks to value intellectual work "not because it brought status or recognition but because it offered resources to enhance survival and . . . pleasure in living."[20]

One childhood experience in particular gave hooks the courage to take risks—"to assert transgressive critical thoughts that may or may not be popular without debilitating fear."[21] Her grandmother's death in the family's home was very peaceful. This experience liberated hooks and changed her relation to living because it banished any fear of dying. Whenever she was punished for speaking, she was able to hold to her principles by reminding herself that death was not to be feared: "It was an inner secret that enabled me to bear pain and suffering yet hold on to the conviction that I could rebel and resist whenever necessary."[22]

Following graduation from high school, hooks earned a B.A. in English at Stanford University, completing her degree in 1973. Her years at Stanford were difficult ones, and her desire to do intellectual work was not affirmed by her experiences there. She encountered racism, sexism, and classism and continually wondered why she was working to be an academic when she "did not see people in that environment who were opposing domination."[23] Despite hooks's ambivalence about the academy, she went on to graduate school, earning an M.A. degree in English from the University of Wisconsin in 1976 and a Ph.D. in English from the University of California at Santa Cruz in 1983, writing a dissertation on Toni Morrison's fiction. She continued to find life in the academy difficult: "During my graduate years I heard myself speaking often in the voice of resistance."[24] She was told that she did not have the demeanor of a graduate student, but she refused to accept and assume the prescribed subordinate role because the exploitation of graduate school evoked "images of a lifetime spent tolerating abuse."[25]

Following the completion of her doctorate, hooks embarked on a teaching career, serving as an instructor at the University of Southern California, the University of California at Riverside, the University of California at Santa Cruz, Occidental College, and San Francisco State University between 1976 and 1984. She accepted a joint position as an assistant professor in the African-American Studies and English Departments at Yale University in 1985, and she moved to Oberlin College in Ohio as an associate professor of American literature and women's studies in 1988. In 1994, she accepted the position of distinguished professor of English at City College of the City University of New York.

Hooks continues to be disappointed that academia is not a place where the kind of intellectual work she values can take place. She entered academia "assuming it would be a place where a life of the mind would be affirmed"[26] and because she felt "moved, pushed, even, in the direction of intellectual work by forces stronger than that of individual will."[27] Instead of being a place of open-mindedness and critical thinking, however, she found that academia serves "basically a conservatizing function."[28] She also experiences it as a place where the connection between theory and practice is not respected and where the most important work—the work of liberation—is not valued: "To this day, I feel as imprisoned in the academic world as I felt in the world of my growing up."[29] Hooks elaborates: "People have this fantasy (as I did when I was young) of colleges being liberatory institutions, when in fact they're so much like every other institution in our culture in terms of *repression* and *containment*."[30] To be able to function in the academy, hooks "continued to pursue writing as a primary vocation and teaching as a job."[31] She now has left academia to focus on her writing.[32]

Hooks's commitment to intellectual work is demonstrated in her prodigious output. Her first literary efforts were plays and poetry; *And There We Wept*, a chapbook of poems published in 1978, was her first book. Several nonfiction books followed that deal with the relationship between feminism and black women. *Ain't I a Woman: Black Women and Feminism* was written when hooks was 19 years old and an undergraduate at Stanford University,[33] although she was not able to get the book published until 1981. It is "an examination of the impact of sexism on the black woman during slavery, the devaluation of black womanhood, black male sexism, racism within the recent feminist movement, and the black woman's involvement with feminism."[34] In hooks's next book, *Feminist Theory: From Margin to Center* (1984), she proposes new directions for feminist theory from the perspective of black women. In *Talking Back: Thinking Feminist, Thinking Black* (1989), hooks continues to develop feminist theory from this perspective, providing an analysis of issues such as pedagogy, violence, militarism, and homophobia.

Hooks not only theorizes about feminist theory and its intersection with race, but she applies her theoretical perspective to cultural texts in a series of books. *Yearning: Race, Gender, and Cultural Politics* (1990) is an analysis of contemporary culture that focuses attention on phenomena such as Malcolm X, advertising, films such as Spike Lee's *Do the Right Thing*, and the anthropology of Zora Neale Hurston. *Black Looks: Race and Representation* (1992) looks at the depiction of African Americans in film, television, advertisements, and literature; it deals with the persistent hold of racism on the American imagination. In *Outlaw Culture: Resisting Representations* (1994), hooks continues to engage in cultural criticism as a means for "educating for critical consciousness in liberatory ways."[35] In *Art on My Mind: Visual Politics* (1995), hooks imagines new ways to think and write about visual art as a contribution to the process of cultural transformation. Hooks's *Reel to Real: Race, Sex, and Class at the Movies* (1996), is based on the premise that movies change things; she analyzes films such as *Pulp Fiction* and *Waiting to Exhale* from feminist and black perspectives.

Hooks also has written books designed to intervene in specific cultural practices of oppression. *Sisters of the Yam: Black Women and Self-Recovery* (1993) is a self-help book that combines individual efforts at self-actualization with the larger world of collective struggle. In *Teaching to Transgress: Education as the Practice of Freedom* (1994), hooks turns her attention to teaching and constructs a theory of education as the practice of freedom. *Killing Rage: Ending Racism* (1995) is hooks's effort to intervene in practices of racism through an examination of the experiences of domination of all Americans. She provides a similar interrogation of class in *Where We Stand: Class Matters* (2000). *All About Love: New Visions* (2000) offers a rethinking of love and the role it can play in resisting structures of domination. Hooks's exploration of love continues in *Salvation: Black People and Love* (2001), in which she provides a historical review of the transformative power of love in the lives of African Americans.

Four of hooks's books are grounded in her own experiences and serve as potential guides for others in efforts to disrupt oppression. *Breaking Bread: Insurgent Black Intellectual Life* (1991), written with Cornel West, is a personal account about how hooks and West have chosen to lead their lives. *A Woman's Mourning Song* (1993) consists of an essay and a collection of poems in which hooks reveals how death serves as a guide for her in the liberation of the spirit. An autobiography of critical moments in hooks's girlhood, *Bone Black: Memories of Girlhood* (1996) describes the lessons she learned about gender roles, domination, and education while growing up. In *Wounds of Passion: A Writing Life* (1997), hooks documents the context that prepared her to become a writer, linking childhood obsessions with writing to efforts to establish a writing voice in the early years of young adulthood. In *Remembered Rapture: The Writer at Work* (1999), hooks continues her exploration of the writing process, engaging issues of voice, the sacredness of words, and the functions of writing for the writer.

Hooks's use of the name of *bell hooks* when she writes constitutes a conscious political decision. *Bell Hooks* was the name of her great grandmother on her mother's side, a "sharp-tongued woman, a woman who spoke her mind, a woman who was not afraid to talk back."[36] Hooks sees the self that is Gloria Watkins as contemplative and nonpublic; publishing under a different name allows her to claim an identity that affirms her right to speech. She also sees a pseudonym as a reminder that her ideas can change: "Another aspect of this exercise was that the pen name was to serve as a constant reminder to me that I was not my ideas, that they did not represent the voice of a fixed identity."[37] Equally important, the name is a way for hooks to claim a "legacy of defiance, of will, of courage," affirming a link to bold female ancestors who were daring in their speech.[38] The lowercase spelling of the name is a stylistic practice to communicate that the substance of hooks's books is what is important, not who is writing them.

Ideology of Domination

The starting point for hooks's rhetorical theory is substantially different from the starting points for traditional rhetorical theories. The purpose hooks envisions for rhetoric is to facilitate the eradication of the ideology of domination that pervades Western culture. This ideology features a "belief in a notion of superior and inferior, and its concomitant ideology—that the superior should rule over the inferior."[39] This ideology is so pervasive, according to hooks, that "most citizens of the United States believe in their heart of hearts that it is natural for a group or an individual to dominate over others."[40] Western culture is marked by oppression, exploitation, and the devaluation of "reciprocity, community, and mutuality."[41] Acceptance of the naturalness of domination is manifest in the various crises that currently plague the planet: "systematic dehumanization, worldwide famine, ecological devastation, industrial contamination, and the possibility of nuclear destruction."[42]

Hooks calls the current system that promotes domination and subjugation *white supremacist capitalist patriarchy*, a label that suggests interlocking structures of sexism, racism, class elitism, capitalism, and heterosexism. These systems all share the ideological ground of "a belief in domination, and a belief in notions of superior and inferior."[43] In these systems, values are assigned to differences and are ranked hierarchically, fostering hatred, vicious competition, alienation from others, elitism based on position in the hierarchy, and individualism rather than cooperation.

Although hooks sees racism, sexism, classism, capitalism, and heterosexism as grounded in the same ideology of domination, she suggests that sexism and the "struggle to end patriarchal domination should be of primary importance to women and men globally."[44] Sexist oppression "is the practice of domination most people experience, whether their role be that of discriminator or discriminated against, exploiter or exploited."[45] Sexism is also the practice of domination most people are socialized to accept before they ever experience other forms of oppression because "most people witness and/or experience the practice of sexist domination in family settings." Usually, individuals experience and learn to accept domination within the family, whether the experience is one of domination of parent over child or man over woman. In contrast, individuals tend to witness and experience racism and classism as they "encounter the larger society, the world outside the home."[46] Hooks cites her own experience to support her perspective: "Growing up in a black, working-class, father-dominated household, I experienced coercive adult male authority as more immediately threatening, as more likely to cause immediate pain than racist oppression or class exploitation."[47]

Because the various forms of oppression are interrelated and share the same foundation, hooks asserts that any efforts made to free oppressed people must be on behalf of all who are oppressed and not just a particular group: "One would like to think that the more aware you become of one form of institutionalized domination and oppression, the easier it would be for you to see connections. But what we see instead is the capacity of humans to deny the connection of all these."[48] She calls for the oppressed to work together: "It is our collective responsibility as people of color and as white people . . . to help one another. . . . If I commit myself politically to black liberation struggle, to the struggle to end white supremacy, I am not making a commitment to working only for and with black people; I must engage in struggle with all willing comrades to strengthen our awareness and our resistance."[49]

Just as all individuals bear responsibility for working to end all kinds of domination, the "system of white-supremacist capitalist patriarchy is not maintained solely by white folks. It is also maintained by all the rest of us who internalize and enforce the values of this regime"[50] and who "act unconsciously, in complicity with a culture of domination."[51] Because all people within a culture of domination are socialized to embody its values and attitudes, all individuals are agents of domination, helping to perpetuate and maintain its systems. The oppressed are "participants in daily rituals of power where we, in strict sado-masochistic fashion, find pleasure in ways of being and thinking, ways of looking at the world that reinforce and maintain our positions as the dominated."[52] She gives as examples of internalized racism the contempt and low expectations that some black professors have for black students,[53] the preference for light skin on the part of many black people,[54] and the feeling of many successful black people who work in white settings that they are special and different from other blacks.[55] Such practices reinforce practices of domination because they "keep in place racial hierarchies that put white folks on top."[56]

Hooks envisions a culture of love as a replacement for the ideology of domination. By *love*, hooks does not mean a sentimental longing for another person or the domination and possessiveness that often are linked to love. Rather, love is a politicized force that enables movement against dehumanization. It is "the idea of being able to let fear go so you can move towards another person who's not like you."[57] Hooks explains that fear "is the primary force upholding structures of domination. It promotes the desire for separation, the desire not to be known. When we are taught that safety lies always with sameness, then difference, of any kind, will appear as a threat. When we choose to love we choose to move against fear—against alienation and separation. The choice to love is a choice to connect—to find ourselves in the other."[58] Hooks sees love and domination as mutually exclusive: "There can be no love when there is domination."[59] Awakening to love occurs "only as we let go of our obsession with power and domination."[60]

Love, in hooks's view, involves particular kinds of rhetorical practices. Primary is mutual recognition, the "subject-to-subject encounter, as opposed to subject-to-object."[61] In this mutual give and take, individuals "learn to understand, appreciate, and value" the worlds and perspectives of others.[62] Love also involves the ingredients of "care, affection, recognition, respect, commitment, and trust, as well as honest and open communication."[63] She acknowledges how uncommon her perspective is: "This vision of relationships where everyone's needs are respected, where everyone has rights, where no one need fear subordination or abuse, runs counter to everything patriarchy upholds about the structure of relationships."[64] Hooks summarizes: "Commitment to a love ethic transforms our lives by offering us a different set of values to live by."[65]

Marginality as a Site of Resistance

Hooks offers a standpoint for the rhetor and the rhetorical theorist that differs from traditional rhetorical theories in that it explicitly takes into account race, gender, and class. Her theory points to how the standpoint of the rhetorical theorist and rhetor informs the kinds of knowledge generated about rhetoric and the types of rhetoric that are produced. Hooks attends to features of identity that inform rhetoric and privileges those whose identities situate them in the margins of contemporary culture.

Marginality, for hooks, is a "site of radical possibility, a space of resistance . . . a central location for the production of a counter-hegemonic discourse."[66] It offers great potential because individuals located in the margins look "both from the outside in and from the inside out."[67] Their vantage point or structural position provides a bifurcated or double vision of both their own knowledge and the knowledge of the dominant culture. This is a particularly significant standpoint for hooks because it provides an oppositional worldview—"a mode of seeing unknown to most . . . oppressors."[68] For hooks, then, marginality is not a standpoint "one wishes to lose—to give up or surrender as part of moving into the center—but rather . . . a site one stays in, clings to even, because it nourishes one's capacity to resist. It offers to one the possibility of radical perspective from which to see and create, to imagine alternatives, new worlds."[69]

Marginalized rhetors and, in particular, black women, are at the center of hooks's theory.[70] The fact that she features black women is not designed to exclude others but to issue an invitation to "listen to the voice of a black woman speaking [as] subject and not as underprivileged other."[71] Black women have an unusual vantage point. Not only are they "collectively at the bottom of the occupational ladder," but their "overall social status is lower than that of any other group. Occupying such a position," she notes, "we bear the brunt of sexist, racist, and classist oppression. At the same time, we are the group that has not been socialized to assume the role of exploiter/oppressor in that we are allowed no institutionalized 'other' that we can exploit or oppress."[72]

Black women's perspectives also are unique in that their identity has been socialized out of existence, more so than any other group in the United States. Hooks explains: "We are rarely recognized as a group separate and distinct from black men, or as a present part of the larger group 'women' in this culture."[73] She asserts: "When black people are talked about, sexism militates against the acknowledgement of the interests of black women; when women are talked about racism militates against a recognition of black female interests. When black people are talked about the focus tends to be on black *men*; and when women are talked about the focus tends to be on *white* women."[74]

The insights that marginalized rhetors contribute to rhetorical theory derive not from any essential traits or characteristics but from experience. In "certain circumstances, experience affords us a privileged critical location from which to speak."[75] Rhetors with particular identities make use of "a passion of experience"[76] that "cannot be acquired through books or even distanced observation and study of a particular reality."[77] Direct experience is critical to understanding in that it sometimes can be "the most relevant way to apprehend reality."[78] As hooks explains, "imagine we are baking bread that needs flour. And we have all the other ingredients but no flour. Suddenly, the flour becomes most important even though it alone will not do."[79] This is a way to think about the role of experience in the development and use of rhetorical theory.

Acknowledging the perspectives from which rhetoric is produced is one important ingredient in rhetorical theory, but hooks believes that the theories developed need not be confined to particular identities. She encourages rhetors and rhetoricians "to engage multiple locations, to address diverse standpoints, to allow us to gather knowledge fully and inclusively."[80] Hooks summarizes this notion: "My experience as a southern working-class black female from a religious family has shaped the way I see the world. Yet the specificity of that experience does not keep me from addressing universal concerns."[81]

Feminism

Two starting points ground hooks's rhetorical theory—the ideology of domination that she seeks to transform and a designated standpoint of marginality. Both of these starting points derive from hooks's commitment to feminism. Hooks's definition of feminism, however, differs from the popular definition of the term. *Feminism* often is used in the United States as synonymous with *women's liberation*, suggesting "movement that aims to make women the social equals of men."[82] This definition of feminism raises a number of questions for hooks: "Since men are not equals in white supremacist, capitalist, patriarchal class structure, which men do women want to be equal to? Do women share a common vision of what equality means?"[83]

Hooks suggests, then, a broad definition of the term *feminism*. She explains that "to be 'feminist' in any authentic sense of the term is to want for all people, female and male, liberation from sexist role patterns, domination, and oppression."[84] It is "a struggle to eradicate the ideology of domination that permeates Western culture on various levels"[85] and constitutes movement that challenges "an entire structure of domination of which patriarchy is one part."[86] Feminism thus directs attention to the interrelatedness of sex, race, and class oppression.[87] Feminism constitutes a basis for collective struggle among and on behalf of all oppressed people because it "challenges each of us to alter our person, our personal engagement (either as victims or perpetrators or both) in a system of domination."[88] For hooks, feminist movement functions as a constructive, proactive force. It seeks to transform relationships and the larger culture "so that the alienation, competition, and dehumanization that characterize human interaction can be replaced with feelings of intimacy, mutuality, and camaraderie."[89]

Feminism has not achieved its transformative potential, according to hooks, because it has been a reformist, conservative movement, "mainly concerned with gaining equal access to domains of white male privilege."[90] The reforms many feminists have sought have been designed "to improve the social status of women within the existing social structure."[91] This kind of feminism "offers women not liberation but the right to act as surrogate men. . . . The women's movement . . . gives women of all races, who desire to assume the imperialist, sexist, racist positions of destruction men hold . . . a platform that allows them to act as if the attainment of their personal aspirations and their lust for power is for the common good of all women."[92] Feminism, then, must be a radical and revolutionary movement and not a reform movement. It must be committed to forming an oppositional worldview" and to establishing a new social order. The site for the creation of the new order is culture: "Our emphasis must be on cultural transformation: destroying dualism, eradicating systems of domination. Our struggle will be gradual and protracted."[93]

Hooks is optimistic that feminism can be expanded. She acknowledges that most people currently do not hold the positive view of feminism that she does. When she talks with people about feminist theory, "up close and personal—they willingly listen, although when our conversations end, they are quick to tell me I am different, not like the 'real' feminists who hate men, who are angry. I assure them I am as . . . real and as radical a feminist as one can be, and if they dare to come closer to feminism they will see it is not how they have imagined it."[94] Hooks summarizes her optimism about feminist rhetoric to challenge the ideology of domination: "Feminist politics aims to end domination to free us to be who we are. . . . Feminism is for everybody."[95]

Decolonization through Rhetoric

Designed to address the ideology of domination and to be used by rhetors on the margins, the rhetorical options hooks recommends involve the basic process of decolonization. These rhetorical options develop the critical consciousness necessary to challenge and transform the ideology of domination. Colonization is the conquering of the minds and habits of oppressed people so that they internalize and accept inferiority as an inherent trait. Decolonization, in contrast, is the "breaking with the ways our reality is defined and shaped by the dominant culture and asserting our understanding of that reality, of our own experience."[96] The process of decolonization is a "disruption of the colonized/colonizer mind-set,"[97] a letting go of white supremacist capitalist patriarchal assumptions and values that enables rhetors to look at themselves and the world around them critically and analytically. It involves the creation of strategies, visionary models, and imaginative maps that "enable colonized folks to decolonize their minds and actions, thereby promoting the insurrection of subjugated knowledge."[98]

Hooks proposes two primary ways in which marginalized rhetors can use rhetoric to challenge and transform the ideology of domination—critique and invention. Critique is the development of an oppositional perspective that moves against and beyond boundaries. Opposition in the form of critique, however, is insufficient to accomplish decolonization: "In that vacant space after one has resisted there is still the necessity to become—to make oneself anew."[99] This requires the invention of alternative habits—of presenting possibilities for a transformed future.

Critique

Critique contests dominant forms and structures. Critical thinking, "the primary element allowing the possibility of change,"[100] is at the core of critique. It is rhetoric that transgresses "discursive frontiers" to encourage an examination of "ideas in their vital bearing on a wider political culture."[101] Particularly powerful, according to hooks, is critique that focuses on issues of representation in various forms of mass media. Hooks asks that rhetors and rhetorical theorists actively enter the terrain of popular culture because the "politics of domination inform the way the vast majority of images we consume are constructed and marketed."[102] She sees representation as "a crucial location of struggle for any exploited and oppressed people asserting subjectivity and decolonization of the mind."[103]

For hooks, television and film are central texts for an analysis of representation because they, more than any other media, determine how oppressed people are seen and how other groups respond to them. These texts are primary tools used to socialize oppressed people. Through these media, the thoughts and values of the ideology of domination are "projected into our living rooms, into the most intimate spaces of our lives." With the television on, whites "are always with us, their voices, values, and beliefs echoing in our brains. It is this constant presence of the colonizing mindset passively consumed that undermines our capacity to resist."[104]

Hooks explains that colonization through the media is a phenomenon that developed largely with the advent of integration in the United States. Colonization was easier to resist during the period when blacks and whites were segregated: "Significantly, during the worst periods of racial apartheid in the United States, black people were more acutely aware of the need to vigilantly resist internalizing white supremacist thought." In the segregated world, decolonized black people recognized that the expectations of subordination that white people held for them were unjust and "that if we all conformed to them we would be both accepting and perpetuating the notion that it was our destiny to be second-class citizens."[105] She cites as an example many black families' approach to television during the period of segregation:

> Ironically, at that time everyone viewed the lack of black representation in mass media as a mark of racial injustice and white supremacist domination, but in retrospect our self-esteem as black people was stronger then than it is now because we were not constantly bombarded by dehumanizing images of ourselves. When we watched shows like *Tarzan* or *Amos 'n' Andy* that we enjoyed, we were ever aware that the images of blackness we saw on these programs were created by folks who, as Mama would say, "did not like us." Consequently, these images had to be viewed with a critical eye.[106]

At the end of the 1960s, however, "many black people felt they could sit back, relax, and exercise their full rights as citizens of this free nation."[107] Television became a vehicle for propaganda, featuring black programs and characters that reinforced a white supremacist aesthetic.[108]

The kind of critique hooks envisions in the practice of cultural criticism goes beyond "the question of positive or negative representation" or whether the oppressed are portrayed in the media through good or bad images.[109] Hooks acknowledges that she often interacts with "audiences that are enraged by rigorous critique that does not simply celebrate any work done by a black artist or cultural worker."[110] Her notion of critique, however, "intervenes in the kind of essentialist thinking that would have us assume anything done in the name of blackness is righteous and should be celebrated."[111] Simply because a text was created by a black person, for example, does not mean "the representations will automatically have integrity beyond anything a white person can produce."[112] Such texts are "not intrinsically counter-hegemonic."[113] Similarly, the mere visibility of an oppressed group in a cultural product or text does not represent an oppositional life: "Since individuals committed to advancing patriarchy are producing most of the images we see, they have an investment in providing us with representations that reflect their values and the social institutions they wish to uphold."[114] Cultural criticism of media texts, then, requires the development of a critical gaze, moving beyond passive consumption to "be fiercely confronting, challenging, interrogating."[115]

Hooks acknowledges that many marginalized people resist the process of critique she advocates. They may do so because thinking critically about a cultural product threatens the pleasure of consuming a work; other people may not want to work mentally in the way that critique requires. Hooks names another reason for such resistance: "Critical practices in everyday black life are most often deconstructive; they aim to unpack, take apart, dismember. In personal conversation, they are usually used to unmask and expose, often with the intent to belittle, berate, ridicule, or rebuke. Whether one is talking about signifying, 'reading,' or just plain 'dissin' and 'dogging out,' these deconstructive practices are often seen as threatening, as in 'I been played,' or 'she put me on the front street.'" Hostility to critique may arise because "the traditional black modes of practicing the art of critique . . . make it appear solely a negative act."[116]

Hooks responds to the reluctance to engage in critique by asserting that the "function of the critic, to see things that other folks don't and to call them out . . . will be resented if we do not have [in marginalized communities] an appreciation for the sharing of critical insight."[117] We "are not just inspired by affirming, celebratory feedback," hooks continues. "We are also inspired by that vital engagement with our work that is critical, that dares to lovingly unmask, expose, challenge. Such engagement is a gesture of respect; it indicates that the work has been taken seriously. Useful critical commentary offers insights that both reveal aspects of a work—how it is what it is, what it does or does not do—as well as suggest new directions, new possibilities."[118]

The critique hooks encourages involves not only an interrogation of cultural products such as television and film but of the thoughts and actions of individuals. She encourages individuals, in interaction with others, to engage in critique in the form of examination, reflection, exploration of beliefs, and the development of new understandings. Dialogue with others in this way provides "concrete counter-examples" that "disrupt the seemingly fixed (yet often unstated) assumptions" that individuals hold.[119] It also allows rhetors to test their emerging beliefs and theories on others: "In hearing responses, we come to understand whether our words act to resist, to transform, to move."[120]

If dialogue is to prompt individuals to question their own beliefs and to think more critically, it must be characterized by constructive interrogation without censorship. Often, oppressed people who are engaged in critique through dialogue attempt to censor dissenting voices or criticism because they believe such dissent "will play into the hands of dominating forces and undermine support for progressive causes."[121] Others avoid dissent or criticism because they believe it constitutes betrayal of their colleagues in struggle. Hooks believes, however, that criticism of the ideas of others and a willingness to accept criticism of one's own ideas are essential because any "movement grows and matures only to the degree that it passionately welcomes and encourages, in theory and practice, diversity of opinion, new ideas, critical exchange, and dissent."[122] Repression and censorship of ideas simply reinscribe hierarchy and elitism by privileging some voices over others, and they silence just as much as the structures of domination do: "We remember the pain of silence and work to sustain our power to speak—freely, openly, provocatively."[123]

Critique through dialogue must occur not only with colleagues and comrades in the effort to disrupt domination but also with "those who exploit, oppress, and dominate."[124] Engaging in critique with those in privileged positions opens up spaces for greater understanding of the structures of domination and how they function. Such dialogue also has a function for people of privilege in that it allows them to examine their own participation in various forms of oppression. Another advantage hooks sees to critique in this situation is that it is a way for oppressed people to show those who oppress what they can do to help. Often, when people in positions of privilege ask what they can do to resist oppression, the oppressed respond that they "are not willing to teach them." For the oppressed to demand "that those who benefit materially by exercising white supremacist power, either actively or passively, willingly give up that privilege in response . . . and then to refuse to show the way," hooks responds, "is to undermine our own cause."[125]

Hooks's admonition that the oppressed must engage in the process of critique in dialogue with their oppressors does not mean that people of privilege have no responsibility for examining their own beliefs or actions or for doing their own work of changing consciousness. People of privilege should not "give up their *power of knowing*" in such dialogues and ask the oppressed to do the work for them.[126] The willingness to change on the part of the privileged should be reinforced by the oppressed, who can "show the way by [their] actions, by the information [they] share."[127]

Invention

Decolonization means more than simply engaging in the critical interrogation of oppression. It also requires an envisioning and development of "new habits of being, different ways to live in the world."[128] Hooks encourages marginalized rhetors and theorists to create different kinds of texts and different ways of being. In this rhetorical option, hooks explicates and recommends the production or invention of nondominating cultural forms.

The primary means of creating nondominating alternatives is enactment. Rhetors who choose the option of enactment act in nonexploitative, nonoppressive ways of being in their own lives. Enactment is the lived practice of interaction in a nondominating context so that one's life is a living example of one's politics. Hooks explains that critique "counts for very little when critics speak about ending domination, eradicating racism, sexism (which includes the structure of heterosexism), class elitism in our work without changing individual habits of being, without allowing those ideas to work in our lives and on our souls in a manner that transforms."[129] To arrive at a more humane world, hooks asks that rhetors "be willing to courageously surrender participation" in coercive hierarchical domination.[130] According to hooks, lived practices should reject the culture of domination in some way or another every moment of the day.

Hooks suggests that interactions with family members provide an important arena for enactment. She cites as an example her interaction with one of her sisters:

> One day I was talking to my sister who had been having some difficulties in her life and I said: "I think you should get your Ph.D. and you should do this and that . . ." Then she said: "wait a minute, look how you are talking to me!" I then realized that I was trying to impose my values and my agendas on her in a way that was very aggressive. . . . I feel that I have to constantly work against taking in the values of domination and hierarchy, because they are there in every part of our mind.[131]

Parent-child interactions offer another opportunity to enact nondominating ways of living: "When my siblings and I were children," hooks explains, "we vowed that we would not yell at our kids or say mean things the way Mama and Daddy did." During a visit, hooks was shocked when she heard her sister speaking harshly to her children: "It was so much like our childhood, only there was one difference, her children used the same 'nasty' tone of voice when speaking to each other." Hooks and her sister did role playing with the children to see how the talk "could be done differently. . . . At first the kids made fun of . . . her stories about 'noise pollution' and how the way we talk to one another can hurt our hearts and ears, but we could all see and feel the difference."[132]

Enactment of nondomination means that individuals, particularly those from oppressed groups, "practice speaking in a loving and caring manner."[133] Replacing uncivil, exploitive rhetoric with a gentle, compassionate voice "makes it evident to all observers of our social reality" that everyone deserves "care, respect, and ongoing affirmation."[134]

Because many of hooks's efforts to transform the system of domination are directed at representations of oppressed groups, particularly in the media, the creation of new forms that challenge domination also involves the invention of new images. The process concerns "transforming the image, creating alternatives, asking ourselves questions about what types of images subvert. . . . Making a space for the transgressive image, the outlaw rebel vision, is essential to any effort to create a context for transformation."[135] Hooks provides an example of the need for new images: "It's disturbing to me that practically every black woman I know, from every social class, from all walks of life, can talk about the stereotypes of black womanhood. But when I ask these same women to name what types of images they'd like to see, they can't answer that question. That's scary."[136] Rhetors and rhetorical theorists "have to be about the business of inventing all manner of images and representations that show us the way we want to be and are."[137] We "need some wholesale re-envisioning that's outside the realm of the merely reactionary!"[138] If "one could make a people lose touch with their capacity to create, lose sight of their will and their power to make art," hooks suggests, "then the work of subjugation, of colonization, is complete."[139]

Hooks particularly sees aesthetic images as crucial in the effort to develop new representations of oppressed groups. She acknowledges that art does not have a significant place in the lives of many blacks and other oppressed people and that many of them simply do not think about art. She also recognizes that in the cultural marketplace, art usually mirrors "institutionalized systems of domination."[140] "Rather than surrendering our passion for the beautiful," hooks suggests, "we need to envision ways those passions can be fulfilled that do not reinforce the structures of domination we seek to change."[141] Art that is created and engaged outside of formal, institutional structures of domination—art created and enjoyed by the oppressed in their places of work and everyday life—can function "as a force that promotes the development of critical consciousness and resistance movement."[142] Art occupies a radical place in the freedom struggle precisely because it provides a means for imagining new possibilities.

For hooks, the walls of photographs in black homes are an example of art as oppositional. She explains that most Southern blacks grew up in a context where snapshots and photographs taken by professional photographers were hung in their homes: "Significantly, displaying those images in everyday life was as central as taking them. The walls of images . . . were sites of resistance. They constituted private, black-owned and -operated gallery space where images could be displayed to friends and strangers."[143] These images were oppositional because they disproved the representations of blacks created by whites by announcing blacks' visual complexity: "We saw ourselves represented not as caricatures, but in diversities of body, being, and expression."[144] Using these images, black people were able "to construct radical identities, images of ourselves that transcend the limits of the colonizing eye."[145]

The use of an accessible writing style is another way in which a nondominating worldview can be enacted. Translating ideas into forms understandable to audiences that vary in age, sex, ethnicity, and degree of literacy is a critical form of enactment for hooks. If those who develop theory are sincere in reaching as many people as possible, "they must either write in a more accessible manner or write in the manner of their choice and see to it that the piece is made available to others using a style that can be easily understood."[146] A lack of accessibility "diminishes our work's power to make meaningful interventions in theory and practice."[147] An accessible style of writing is important not only because it allows useful ideas to be disseminated but also because it embodies an equality that challenges hierarchy and structures of domination. Work that is difficult to comprehend and linguistically convoluted reinscribes the politics of domination and perpetuates elitism, for "it is indeed the purpose of such theory to divide, separate, exclude, keep at a distance."[148]

In all of her works, hooks writes "with the intent to share ideas in a way that makes them accessible to the widest possible audience."[149] She made a conscious decision not to use footnotes in her first nonfiction book, *Ain't I a Woman*, because she believes that footnotes set class boundaries for readers, determining who a book is for: "I went into various communities and asked non-academic Black people if they read books with footnotes. The majority responded by saying that when they open a book with footnotes they immediately think that book isn't for them, that the book is for an academic person."[150]

Another way in which hooks enacts her commitment to accessibility as a means to transform the ideology of domination is through the use of confession. Confession is the telling of one's personal experience, speaking the truth of one's life, or giving testimony. In confession, rhetors name and give voice to their experiences and "to personal sorrow and anguish, rage, bitterness, and even deep hatred."[151] It involves telling "the past as we have learned it mouth-to-mouth, telling the present as we see, know, and feel it in our hearts and with our words."[152] Hooks uses confessional anecdotes as a strategy to engage diverse readers: "If people felt that your academic language was unfamiliar to them, or even your style of being, they wouldn't listen. That's when I began to think not only about the power of storytelling but about the power of personal testimony. I found that if people could identify with you through the act of personal testimony or confession in some way, they were more open to grappling with different jargon, different paradigms."[153]

Confession has the potential to intervene in structures of domination, however, only if it is connected to a larger political framework that situates the shared experiences in a context of structures of domination and how they function. The self-awareness that results from the confession, hooks asserts, must be linked to "knowledge of how we must act politically to change and transform the world."[154] Without this crucial step of relating one's experience to a critical framework or using one's experience strategically, the confession is simply a narcissistic act that turns the voices and beings of rhetors into a commodity—a spectacle. Without the connection to the political, the self "stays in place, the starting point from which one need never move."[155]

"Private life as exhibitionism and performance," hooks admonishes, "is not the same thing as a politicized strategic use of private information that seeks to subvert the politics of domination."[156]

Hooks also suggests that education can be a site for the enactment of alternatives to domination. Formal education at all levels has the potential to be a place where individuals can unlearn the ideology of domination and where critical thinking in the service of decolonization can occur. In an educational setting, people can be inspired "to have conversion experiences away from their allegiances to the oppressive norms."[157] But this can occur only when pedagogical practices do "not reinforce structures of domination: imperialism, racism, sexism, and class exploitation."[158] She observes that many professors progressive in their politics resolutely refuse to change their pedagogical practice and thus "perpetuate those very hierarchies and biases they are critiquing."[159]

The rhetorical option of revolutionary pedagogy requires that teachers relinquish "traditional ways of teaching that reinforce domination."[160] Such revolutionary practices might include teachers' encouragement of students to influence the agendas of their classrooms, interacting with students according to their individual needs, positioning themselves as learners along with their students, and electing not to assume a stance of omniscience. This kind of pedagogy means that everyone's voice is heard in the classroom and that teachers genuinely value everyone's presence. The potential of education to serve as a site at which the ideology of domination can be disrupted, then, is realized only if education is practiced in nondominating ways.

Hooks is confident about the effectiveness of critique and invention as means to facilitate decolonization and thus to disrupt the ideology of domination: "The programs for change sketched here are the ones that those of us who have come from the bottom, who have decolonized our minds . . . have used. We know they work. They changed our lives so that we can live fully and well."[161]

Commentary

Hooks's works are widely applauded for their "endless struggle toward an ever evolving discourse of liberation."[162] Her primary contribution to rhetorical theory is her linkage of rhetoric "with transformative struggles in society, working against the structures of domination."[163] She conceptualizes and creates rhetoric that analyzes and combats oppression, especially as it relates to the triangle of race, class, and gender. She explicates the role rhetoric plays in the perpetuation of the ideology of domination and how it typically embodies "hierarchial thinking, privileging, and power relations."[164] In doing so, she encourages students and theorists of rhetoric to examine and explore the relationship among "cultural products, cultural critique, and mechanisms which perpetuate oppression."[165] The purpose of hooks's rhetorical theory—to facilitate the eradication of the ideology of domination and to transform it into a culture characterized by equality, mutuality, and respect—contrasts dramatically with the traditional goal for rhetors. Traditionally, rhetors engage in rhetoric in an effort to have their own perspectives prevail and to accomplish their own goals, often at the expense of those of others.

Hooks's ideas transform and reconceptualize basic rhetorical concepts and processes, including the notion of hierarchy. Many basic rhetorical constructs are built on an assumption of hierarchy as both natural and desirable. Rhetoric is used, for example, to ascertain which positions on issues are superior to others, and it is used to assert superiority by level of rhetorical skill or degree of *ethos* or credibility. In some theories of rhetoric, hierarchy is seen as the motivating principle, inducing guilt when advancement to higher positions on various hierarchies does not occur. Hooks, however, seeks to eliminate the hierarchic principle from rhetoric. She asserts that although this principle appears natural, it is not. It can be replaced with an alternative, equally viable ideology of reciprocity, community, and mutuality. A rhetoric built on these values is significantly different in nature and function from a rhetoric rooted in hierarchy.

Hooks's requirement that rhetoric contribute to the disruption of practices of domination has another outcome as well. Her rhetorical theory challenges her audiences to reflect on their daily choices, "as opposed to perpetuating ideologies unconsciously by choices that fail to interrogate debilitating myths and dominations."[166] As Cornel West suggests, her writings "touch our lives. It is difficult to read a bell hooks essay or text without enacting some form of self-examination or self-inventory."[167] One reason hooks's ideas encourage self-inventory is because of her equal treatment of all individuals as rhetors with agency: "No matter whether you are female or male, a person of color or not, rich or poor, hooks finds a way for you to see your contributions to the problems as well as to the solutions. Since everyone is treated equally, I think you are willing to acknowledge your role and consider some of her thoughts on potential changes."[168] The result tends to be an assumption of responsibility: "When I read hooks, the experience is re-affirming at times, extremely disquieting and uncomfortable at others; ultimately however, her books always leave me with a sense of responsibility to at least consider ideas that may push my comfort zones around the way I perceive the world and my place in it."[169]

A second major contribution to rhetorical theory by hooks is her "intentional use of positionality."[170] Although all rhetorical theories are informed by the perspectives of the theorists who created them, hooks develops her rhetorical theory from the "specific rhetorical situations of marginalized people."[171] She avoids creating a theory that is unique to or relevant only to one group of rhetors, however, by enlarging the conception of standpoint beyond essentialist notions of identity. Her identification of her standpoint as a black woman makes visible the largely hidden and normalized standpoints from which most rhetorical theories have been created.

The marginalized rhetors on whom hooks focuses are not accorded *ethos* from a traditional perspective, but hooks sees them as possessing a transformed *ethos*. Their *ethos* is not determined by the degree to which they exhibit intelligence, moral character, and good will (the traditional qualities associated with *ethos*) but by the insights derived from their personal experiences, the dual vision of someone who occupies marginalized status. They are not underprivileged or disqualified as rhetors but, instead, are able to imagine alternatives and to create nondominating relations most easily. They thus are at the forefront in terms of their capacity to create change.

A third contribution hooks makes to rhetorical theory is the rhetorical option of enactment. This option allows rhetors to disrupt domination at a very personal level simply by acting and engaging in rhetoric that is nondominating, nonexploitative, and nonoppressive. Enactment involves making one's life a living example of one's commitment to reciprocity and equality. It is directed not at other rhetors explicitly—although others may observe the rhetor's behavior and choose to engage in it—but primarily at rhetors' own thoughts and actions as they try to live in ways that reflect their commitment to an ideology of equality and respect.

Many critics applaud hooks's efforts to challenge oppression and domination, but the manner in which she presents her ideas generates controversy. Her confrontational style, for example, is noted by critics such as Namulundah Florence, who suggests that "hooks typically adopts a blunt and confrontational, rather than conventional, diplomatic, or 'politically correct,' approach."[172] Kathleen O'Grady explains hooks's stylistic tone in this way: "hooks may be best known for cutting through the crap—be it academic etiquette or high theory jargon—and for her straight forward prose-style that can sum up in a sentence or two what most of us require a life-time to articulate."[173] Some critics suggest that hooks's confrontational style and the "violence of her criticisms" may "alienate the very people she purports to speak for and wishes to attract, people who belong to the social, racial, and economic groups she sharply critiques."[174] At the same time, others acknowledge that her confrontational style "is probably the most effective way to draw attention to the urgency of issues most would rather ignore or gloss over. [H]ooks' candid writing approach communicates the significance and urgency of the issues—racism, sexism, and classism—to marginalized groups."[175]

Another response to the form in which hooks's ideas are presented is frustration with the lack of theoretical connections among ideas and chapters in her books. As Anna Marie Smith suggests, "She does not construct an overall theoretical argument that would link the essays together."[176] Similarly, Haven B. White notes that the essays or chapters in her books are "drawn together in a frankly idiosyncratic fashion. . . . Rather than presenting each thesis with supporting evidence in a linear or 'straightforward' fashion, she frequently jumps from point to point and interest to interest"[177] so that the "path of connection initially seems opaque."[178] Hooks's disorienting style of presentation and organization sometimes is seen as a strength in that it challenges "linear argumentation. She utilizes a postmodern organizational style in making a postmodern cultural critique."[179] White suggests that the "active reading of a cultural product" that is required of hooks's readers "is exactly the kind of cultural training for which hooks is advocating. Rather than spoonfeeding the reader each step along the way to her thesis, . . . hooks leaps from place to place giving momentary views of the terrain she is covering and leaving the reader to view the whole and to connect with her conclusions."[180]

Hooks's later books in the self-help genre, such as *Sisters of the Yam, All About Love,* and *Salvation,* have come under particular scrutiny. O'Grady describes hooks's work in this area as "an eclectic assemblage of new age truisms on the joy of true communion with an other that we all yearn toward but rarely achieve." She continues: "I wish I could say that I found these meditations to be original or even well-written, but they only periodically rise above mediocre platitudes and often fall into an uncritical assumption of New Testament theology ('God is love'). Missing . . . is the voice of the critic that hooks does so very well. Love has made her soft, I suppose, and while these warm-fuzzies are occasionally touching, they lack the intellectual vigor with which hooks is usually associated."[181] Michele Wallace sees hooks as offering in these books "a series of potentially contradictory solutions to what ails us"[182] and describes her ideas as "self-indulgent and undigested drivel that careens madly from outrageous self-pity, poetic and elliptical, to playful exhibitionism, to dogmatic righteous sermonizing."[183]

Keith Byerman suggests that another difficulty with hooks's self-help writing is the "uneasy fit" between the principles of the self-recovery movement and the "historical, economical, and social experiences of black women." He notes: "Self-recovery as a discursive practice assumes a middle-class audience of individuals operating in a competitive, stressful world with few communal resources."[184] Consequently, he asks: "How are black women, the poorest, most denigrated, most abused members of the society, to find the personal and economic resources to even begin to do the kinds of things hooks recommends?"[185]

Another aspect of hooks's style that has drawn comment from critics is her process of drawing on her personal experiences "to shape and explain her theoretical conclusions."[186] Florence describes this characteristic as the ability to avoid "the dichotomy between the 'objective' and 'subjective'" to "highlight the link between the personal and the political."[187] The point is "not to psychologize" her personal life but "to recognize the social location of personal experience."[188] Others are less charitable in their reading of hooks's use of personal experiences; Wallace, for example, describes the practice as epitomizing "the cult of victimization."[189] Smith suggests that hooks "dwells on personal information that in no way advances her argument. . . . While it is true that the personal is political, this does not mean that the totality of the personal is relevant."[190] Others suggest that the experiences hooks recounts of marginality lack authenticity, noting that her "status as distinguished university professor drawing a significant enough salary does raise the issue of her authority on matters of marginality, and her self-proclaimed status of spokesperson for the marginalized."[191]

Many of the stylistic characteristics of hooks's works to which critics respond in various ways are deliberate choices hooks makes in an effort to reach an audience outside of academia. Many commend her for the fact that "she has sought an audience outside the academy and has conceived of her academic role broadly. She has not been confined by narrow disciplinary boundaries that not only limit audience but limit the voice that academics can have in public matters."[192] Although some view her discourse as "highfalutin babble about the movie [she] just saw or the rhyme [she] just heard on the radio,"[193] she "makes use of different literary styles, including (academic) prose, poetry and essays"[194] in ways that most scholars do not. She also frequently engages in a popular form of cultural criticism, film criticism, to disseminate her ideas. Her relation of her ideas to "lived reality"[195] and her accessible writing and speaking style further create appeal of her work for diverse audiences. Hooks's efforts to engage a larger audience have earned her the label of one of the foremost black intellectuals in America today.

Hooks's transformations of rhetorical theory revise and extend traditional constructs and offer new ones to help create a more humane world. She requires of rhetors and rhetorical theorists nothing less than transformation of the cultural values of oppression and domination, an undertaking that is difficult because of their intensity and pervasiveness. Hooks asks individuals to believe, however, that people can change because "what we can't imagine, can't come to be."[196] She asks those who are discouraged to notice the individual incidents of people changing daily and to "bear witness to the reality that our many cultures can be remade, that this nation can be transformed, that we can resist . . . and in the act of resistance recover ourselves and be renewed."[197]

Bibliography

Books

Ain't I a Woman: Black Women and Feminism. Boston: South End, 1981.
All About Love: New Visions. New York: William Morrow, 2000.
And There We Wept. Los Angeles: Golemics, 1978.
Art on My Mind: Visual Politics. New York: New, 1995.
Black Looks: Race and Representation. Boston: South End, 1992.
Bone Black: Memories of Girlhood. New York: Henry Holt, 1996.
Breaking Bread: Insurgent Black Intellectual Life. Boston: South End, 1991. (With Cornel West.)
Feminism is for Everybody: Passionate Politics. Cambridge, MA: South End, 2000.
Feminist Theory: From Margin to Center. Boston: South End, 1984.
Happy to be Nappy. New York: Hyperion, 1999. (With Chris Raschka.)
Killing Rage: Ending Racism. New York: Henry Holt, 1995.

Outlaw Culture: Resisting Representations. New York: Routledge, 1994.
Reel to Real: Race, Sex, and Class at the Movies. New York: Routledge, 1996.
Remembered Rapture: The Writer at Work. New York: Henry Holt, 1999.
Salvation: Black People and Love. New York: William Morrow-HarperCollins, 2001.
Sisters of the Yam: Black Women and Self-Recovery. Boston: South End, 1993.
Talking Back: Thinking Feminist, Thinking Black. Boston: South End, 1989.
Teaching to Transgress: Education as the Practice of Freedom. New York: Routledge, 1994.
Where We Stand: Class Matters. New York: Routledge, 2000.
A Woman's Mourning Song. New York: Harlem River, 1993.
Wounds of Passion: A Writing Life. New York: Henry Holt, 1997.
Yearning: Race, Gender, and Cultural Politics. Boston: South End, 1990.

Articles

"Aesthetic Intervention." In *Emma Amos: Changing the Subject: Paintings and Prints, 1992–1994.* By Emma Amos. New York: Art in General, 1994, pp. 5–12. Rpt. as "Aesthetic Interventions." In *Art on My Mind: Visual Politics.* By bell hooks. New York: New, 1995, pp. 163–70.

"An Aesthetic of Blackness: Strange and Oppositional." In *Women, Creativity, and the Arts: Critical and Autobiographical Perspectives.* Ed. Diane Apostolos-Cappadona and Lucinda Ebersole. New York: Continuum, 1995, pp. 75–86. Rpt. from *Yearning: Race, Gender, and Cultural Politics.* By bell hooks. Boston: South End, 1990, pp. 103–13.

"Altars of Sacrifice: Re-membering Basquiat." *Art in America,* 81 (1993), 68–75, 117. Rpt. in *Outlaw Culture: Resisting Representations.* By bell hooks. New York: Routledge, 1994, pp. 25–37; and in *Art on My Mind: Visual Politics.* By bell hooks. New York: New, 1995, pp. 35–48.

"All Quiet on the Feminist Front." *Artforum,* 35 (December 1996), 39.

"Appearance Obsession: Is the Price Too High?" *Essence,* 26 (August 1995), 69, 70, 112.

"Arguing with the Homeboys." *Village Voice,* 36 (September 17, 1991), 42–43.

"Beauty Laid Bare: Aesthetics in the Ordinary." In *To be Real.* Ed. Rebecca Walker. New York: Anchor, 1995, pp. 157–65.

"Bell Hooks." In *Booknotes: America's Finest Authors on Reading, Writing, and the Power of Ideas.* Ed. Brian Lamb. New York: Times-Random, 1997, pp. 62–65.

"Bell Hooks Speaking about Paulo Freire—the Man, His Work." In *Paulo Freire: A Critical Encounter.* Ed. Peter McLaren and Peter Leonard. New York: Routledge, 1993, pp. 146–54. Rpt. in *Teaching to Transgress: Education as the Practice of Freedom.* By bell hooks. New York: Routledge, 1994, pp. 45–58.

"Between Us: Traces of Love—Dickinson, Horn, Hooks." In *Earths Grow Thick.* Columbus: Wexner Center for the Arts, Ohio State University, 1996, pp. 57–63.

"Black (and White) Snapshots." *Ms.,* 5 (September/October 1994), 82–87.

"Black Students Who Reject Feminism." *Chronicle of Higher Education,* 40 (July 13, 1994), A44.

"Black Is a Woman's Color." In *Bearing Witness.* Ed. Henry Louis Gates, Jr. New York: Pantheon, 1991, pp. 338–48.

"Black Woman Artist Becoming." In *Life Notes: Personal Writings by Contemporary Black Women.* Ed. Patricia Bell-Scott. New York: W. W. Norton, 1994, pp. 181–89.

"Black Women: Constructing the Revolutionary Subject." In*An American Half-Century: Postwar Culture and Politics in the USA*. Ed. Michael Klein. Boulder, CO: Pluto, 1994, pp. 172–91.

"Black Women: Shaping Feminist Theory." In*Words of Fire: An Anthology of African-American Feminist Thought*. Ed. Beverly Guy-Sheftall. New York: New, 1995, pp. 270–82.

"Black Women Writing: Creating More Space."*Sage*, 2 (1985), 44–46. Rpt. in *Talking Back: Thinking Feminist, Thinking Black*. By bell hooks. Boston: South End, 1989, pp. 142–47.

"Breaking Bread: A Dialogue among Communities in Search of Common Ground." In *The New American Crisis: Radical Analyses of the Problems Facing America Today*. Ed. Greg Ruggiero and Stuart Sahulka. New York: New, 1995, pp. 224–38. (With Cornel West.)

"Breaking the Silence between Mothers and Daughters."*Sage*, 1 (1984), 28–29.

"Carrie Mae Weems: Diasporic Landscapes of Longing." In*Inside the Visible: An Elliptical Traverse of 20th Century Art: In, of and from the Feminine*. Ed. M. Catherine de Zegher. Cambridge, MA: MIT Press, 1996, pp. 173–78. Rpt. in*Art on My Mind: Visual Politics*. By bell hooks. New York: New, 1995, pp. 65–73.

"Challenging Men." *Sparerib*, 217 (1990), 12–15.

"Challenging Patriarchy Means Challenging Men to Change."*Z Magazine*, 4 (1991), 33–36.

"Choosing the Margin as a Space of Radical Openness." In*Women, Knowledge, and Reality: Explorations in Feminist Philosophy*, 2nd ed. Ed. Ann Garry and Marilyn Pearsall. New York: Routledge, 1996, pp. 48–55. Rpt. from*Yearning: Race, Gender and Cultural Politics*. By bell hooks. Boston: South End, 1990, pp. 145–53.

"Consumed by Images: Bell Hooks on Spike Lee's*Malcolm X*." *Artforum*, 31 (February 1993), 5–6.

"Critical Reflections."*Artforum*, 33 (1994), 64–65, 100.

"Critical Reflections: Adrienne Kennedy, the Writer, the Work." In *Intersecting Boundaries: The Theatre of Adrienne Kennedy*. Ed. Paul K. Bryant-Jackson and Lois More Overbeck. Minneapolis: University of Minnesota Press, 1992, pp. 179–85.

"Culture to Culture: Ethnography and Cultural Studies as Critical Intervention." In *Rhetoric: Concepts, Definitions, Boundaries*. Ed. William A. Covino and David A. Jolliffe. Boston: Allyn and Bacon, 1995, pp. 328–35.

"Dialectically Down with the Critical Program." In*Black Popular Culture*. Ed. Gina Dent. New York: New, pp. 48–55.

"Dialogue Between Bell Hooks and Julie Dash: April 26, 1992." In*Daughters of the Dust: The Making of an African American Woman's Film*. By Julie Dash. New York: New, 1992, pp. 27–67. (With Julie Dash.)

"Dissident Heat: Fire with Fire." In *"Bad Girls" "Good Girls": Women, Sex, and Power in the Nineties*. Ed. Nan Bauer Maglin and Donna Perry. New Brunswick, NJ: Rutgers University Press, 1996, pp. 57–64. Rpt. from*Outlaw Culture: Resisting Representations*. By bell hooks. New York: Routledge, 1994, pp. 91–100.

"Doing It for Daddy." In *Constructing Masculinity*. Ed. Maurice Berger, Brian Wallis, and Simon Watson. New York: Routledge, 1995, pp. 98–106. Rpt. as "Doing It for Daddy: Black Masculinity in the Mainstream." In*Reel to Real: Race, Sex, and Class at the Movies*. By bell hooks. New York: Routledge, 1996, pp. 83–90.

"Do We Need Kwanzaa?"*Essence*, 28 (December 1997), 68–70.

"Dreams Conquest." *Sight and Sound*, 5 (April 1995), 22–23.
"Eating the Other: Desire and Resistance from *Black Looks: Race and Representation*." In *Forbidden Passages: Writings Banned in Canada*. Ed. Pat Califia and Janine Fuller. San Francisco: Cleis, 1995, pp. 130–47. Rpt. from *Black Looks: Race and Representation*. By bell hooks. Boston: South End, 1992, pp. 21–39; and rpt. in *Eating Culture*. Ed. Ron Scapp and Rian Seitz. New York: State University of New York Press, 1998, pp. 181–200.
"Ending Female Sexual Oppression." In *Women's Studies: Essential Readings*. Ed. Stevi Jackson, Karen Atkinson, Deirdre Beddoe, Teri Brewer, Sue Faulkner, Anthea Hucklesby, Rose Pearson, Helen Power, Jane Prince, Michele Ryan, and Pauline Young. Washington Square: New York University Press, 1993, pp. 245. Rpt. (shortened version) from *Feminist Theory: From Margin to Center*. By bell hooks. Boston: South End, 1984, pp. 147–56.
"Eros, Eroticism and the Pedagogical Process." *Cultural Studies*, 7 (1993), 58–63. Rpt. in *Teaching to Transgress: Education as the Practice of Freedom*. By bell hooks. New York: Routledge, 1994, pp. 191–99.
"Erotic Healing." *Essence*, 24 (July 1993), 60–62, 104–106.
"Expertease: Bell Hooks on Cultural Interrogations." *Artforum*, 27 (1989), 18–20.
"Feminism and Black Women's Studies." *Sage*, 6 (1989), 54–56.
"Feminism and Militarism: A Comment." *Women's Studies Quarterly*, 23 (Fall/Winter 1995), 58–64. Rpt. from *Talking Back: Thinking Feminist, Thinking Black*. By bell hooks. Boston: South End, 1989, pp. 92–97.
"Feminism and Racism: The Struggle Continues." *Z Magazine*, 3 (1990), 41–43.
"Feminism: A Transformational Politic." In *I Am Because We Are: Readings in Black Philosophy*. Ed. Fred Lee Hord (Mzee Lasana Okpara) and Jonathan Scott Lee. Amherst: University of Massachusetts Press, 1995, pp. 329–37. Rpt. from *Talking Back: Thinking Feminist, Thinking Black*. By bell hooks. Boston: South End, 1989, pp. 19–27.
"Feminism: Crying for Our Souls." In *Feminist Foremothers in Women's Studies, Psychology, and Mental Health*. Ed. Phyllis Chesler, Esther D. Rothblum, and Ellen Cole. New York: Haworth, 1995, pp. 265–71.
"Feminism Inside: Toward a Black Body Politic." In *Black Male: Representations of Masculinity in Contemporary American Art*. Ed. Thelma Golden. New York: Whitney Museum of American Art, 1994, pp. 127–40.
"Feminism—It's a Black Thang!" *Essence*, 23 (July 1992), 124.
"From Scepticism to Feminism." *Women's Review of Books*, 7 (1990), 29.
"Future Feminist Movements." *Off Our Backs*, 20 (1990), 9.
"Girls Together: Sustained Sisterhood." In *Sister to Sister: Women Write about the Unbreakable Bond*. Ed. Patricia Foster. New York: Anchor-Doubleday, 1995, pp. 161–69.
"The Hill-Thomas Hearing." *Artforum*, 31 (1992), 13–14.
"How Souls Unfold." *Utne Reader*, 66 (November/December 1994), 143.
"The Imaginary Domain: A Discussion Between Drucilla Cornell and Bell Hooks." *Women's Rights Law Reporter*, 19 (Spring 1998), 261–65.
"In Our Glory: Photography and Black Life." In *Picturing Us: African American Identity in Photography*. Ed. Deborah Willis. New York: New, 1994, pp. 42–53. Rpt. in *Art on My Mind: Visual Politics*. By bell hooks. New York: New, 1995, pp. 54–64.
"In Praise of Student/Teacher Romances." *Utne Reader*, 68 (March/April 1995), 37–38.

"Insurgent Black Intellectual Life: Bell Hooks and Cornel West Break Bread." *Off Our Backs*, 23 (1993), 1–3. (With Cornel West.)

"An Intimate Conversation." *Shambhala Sun*, 4 (1995), 60–67, 72. (With John Barlow.)

"Joining the Dialogue." In *Beyond Political Correctness: Toward the Inclusive University*. Ed. Stephen Richer and Lorna Weir. Buffalo, NY: University of Toronto Press, 1995, pp. 251–52.

"Keeping a Legacy of Shared Struggle." In *Blacks and Jews: Alliances and Arguments*. Ed. Paul Berman. New York: Delacorte, 1994, pp. 229–38. Rpt. in *Killing Rage: Ending Racism*. By bell hooks. New York: Henry Holt, 1995, pp. 204–14.

"Keeping Close to Home: Class and Education." In *Working-Class Women in the Academy: Laborers in the Knowledge Factory*. Ed. Michelle M. Tokarczyk and Elizabeth A. Fay. Amherst: University of Massachusetts Press, 1993, pp. 99–111. Rpt. from *Talking Back: Thinking Feminist, Thinking Black*. By bell hooks. Boston: South End, 1989, pp. 73–83.

"Learning in the Shadow of Race and Class." *Chronicle of Higher Education*, 47 (November 17, 2000), B14–16.

"Let Freedom Ring." In *Why L.A. Happened: Implications of the '92 Los Angeles Rebellion*. Ed. Haki R. Madhubuti. Chicago: Third World, 1993, pp. 241–46.

"Let's Get Real about Feminism: The Backlash, the Myths, the Movement." *Ms.*, 4 (September 1993), 34–43. (With Urvashi Vaid, Naomi Wolf, and Gloria Steinem.)

"Lorna Simpson: *Waterbearer*." *Artforum*, 32 (1993), 136–37. Rpt. (expanded version) as "Facing Difference: The Black Female Body." In *Art on My Mind: Visual Politics*. By bell hooks. New York: New, 1995, pp. 94–100.

"Loving into Life and Death." *The Other Side*, 36 (March 2000), 43. Rpt. (shortened version) from *All About Love: New Visions*. By bell hooks. New York: William Morrow, 2000, pp. 189–205.

"The Magic of Our Moment." *The Other Side* (May/June 1994), pp. 8–11, 30.

"Male Heroes and Female Sex Objects: Sexism in Spike Lee's *Malcolm X*." *Cineaste*, 19 (March 1993), 13–15.

"Marginality as Site of Resistance." In *Out There: Marginalization and Contemporary Cultures*. Ed. Russell Ferguson, Martha Gever, Trinh T. Minh-ha, and Cornel West. Cambridge, MA: MIT Press, 1990, pp. 341–43.

"Men in Feminist Struggle: The Necessary Movement." In *Women Respond to the Men's Movement: A Feminist Collection*. Ed. Kay Leigh Hagan. San Francisco: HarperCollins, 1992, pp. 111–17.

"Micheaux: Celebrating Blackness." *Black American Literature Forum*, 25 (1991), 351–60. Rpt. as "Micheaux's Films: Celebrating Blackness." In *Black Looks: Race and Representation*. By bell hooks. Boston: South End, 1992, pp. 133–43.

"The Oppositional Gaze: Black Female Spectators." In *Black American Cinema*. Ed. Manthia Diawara. New York: Routledge, 1993, pp. 288–302. Rpt. from *Black Looks: Race and Representation*. By bell hooks. Boston: South End, 1992, pp. 115–31; rpt. in *Movies and Mass Culture*. Ed. John Belton. New Brunswick, NJ: Rutgers University Press, 1996, pp. 247–64; and rpt. in *Reel to Real: Race, Sex, and Class at the Movies*. By bell hooks. New York: Routledge, 1996, pp. 197–213.

"Out of the Academy and Into the Streets." *Ms.*, 3 (July 1992), 80–82.

"Performance Practice as a Site of Opposition." In *The Politics of Black Performance*. Ed. Catherine Ugwu. Seattle, WA: Bay, 1995, pp. 210–21.

"Plantation Mistress or Soul Sister?" In *Signs of Life in the U.S.A.: Readings on Popular Culture for Writers*. Ed. Sonia Maasik and Jack Solomon. 2nd ed. Boston: Bedford, 1997, pp. 223–30.

"Point of View: Black Students Who Reject Feminism." *Chronicle of Higher Education*, 13 (July 1994), A44.

"Postmodern Blackness." In *A Postmodern Reader*. Ed. Joseph Natoli and Linda Hutcheon. Albany: State University of New York Press, 1993, pp. 510–18. Rpt. from *Yearning: Race, Gender, and Cultural Politics*. By bell hooks. Boston: South End, 1990, pp. 23–31; rpt. in *Colonial Discourse and Post-Colonial Theory: A Reader*. Ed. Patrick Williams and Laura Chrisman. New York: Columbia University Press, 1994, pp. 421–27; and rpt. in *The Truth about the Truth: De-Confusing and Re-Constructing the Postmodern World*. Ed. Walter Truett Anderson. New York: Jeremy P. Tarcher-Putnam, 1995, pp. 117–24.

"Power to the Pussy: We Don't Wannabe Dicks in Drag." In *Madonnarama: Essays on Sex and Popular Culture*. Ed. Lisa Frank and Paul Smith. San Francisco: Cleis, 1993, pp. 65–80. Rpt. in *Outlaw Culture: Resisting Representations*. By bell hooks. New York: Routledge, 1994, pp. 9–23.

"Pulp the Hype: On the QT: Cool Tool." *Artforum*, 33 (1995), 63. Rpt. (expanded version) as "Cool Cynicism: *Pulp Fiction*." In *Reel to Real: Race, Sex, and Class at the Movies*. By bell hooks. New York: Routledge, 1996, pp. 47–51.

" 'Raisin' in a New Light." *Christianity and Crisis*, 49 (February 6, 1989), 21–23.

"Reading and Resistance: *The Color Purple*." In *Alice Walker: Critical Perspectives Past and Present*. Ed. Henry Louis Gates, Jr. and K. A. Appiah. New York: Amistad, 1993, pp. 284–95.

"Reflections of a 'Good' Daughter." In *Double Stitch: Black Women Write about Mothers and Daughters*. Ed. Patricia Bell-Scott, Beverly Guy-Sheftall, Jacqueline Jones Royster, Janet Sims-Wood, Miriam DeCosta-Willis, and Lucie Fultz. Boston: Beacon, 1991, pp. 149–51.

"Reflections on Homophobia and Black Communities." *Outlook*, 1 (Summer 1988), 22–25.

"Representing Whiteness in the Black Imagination." In *Cultural Studies*. Ed. Lawrence Grossberg, Cary Nelson, and Paula A. Treichler. New York: Routledge, 1992, pp. 338–46. Rpt. as "Representations of Whiteness in the Black Imagination." In *Killing Rage: Ending Racism*. By bell hooks. New York: Henry Holt, 1995, pp. 31–50.

"A Revolution of Values: The Promise of Multi-Cultural Change." *Journal of the Midwest Modern Language Association*, 26 (Spring 1993), 4–11.

"Roundtable Discussion: Christian Ethics and Theology in Womanist Perspective: Bell Hooks." *Journal of Feminist Studies in Religion*, 5 (1989), 102–04.

"Secret Pleasures: An Excerpt from the Memoir *Bone Black*." In *The Bluelight Corner: Black Women Writing on Passion, Sex, and Romantic Love*. Ed. Rosemarie Robotham. New York: Three Rivers-Crown, 1999, pp. 46–55.

"Seduced by Violence No More." In *Transforming a Rape Culture*. Ed. Emilie Buchwald, Pamela R. Fletcher, and Martha Roth. Minneapolis, MN: Milkweed, 1993, pp. 353–56. Rpt. in *Outlaw Culture: Resisting Representations*. By bell hooks. New York: Routledge, 1994, pp. 109–13; and rpt. in *Debating Sexual Correctness: Pornography, Sexual Harassment, Date Rape, and the Politics of Sexual Equality*. Ed. Adele M. Stan. New York: Delta, 1995, pp. 231–35.

"Seductive Sexualities: Representing Blackness in Poetry and on Screen." In *American Feminist Thought at Century's End: A Reader*. Ed. Linda S. Kauffman. Cambridge,

MA: Blackwell, 1993, pp. 65–72. Rpt. from *Yearning: Race, Gender and Cultural Politics*. By bell hooks. Boston: South End, 1990, pp. 193–201.

"Selling Hot Pussy: Representations of Black Female Sexuality in the Cultural Marketplace." In *The Politics of Women's Bodies: Sexuality, Appearance, and Behavior*. Ed. Rose Weitz. New York: Oxford University Press, 1998, pp. 112–22. Rpt. from *Black Looks: Race and Representation*. By bell hooks. Boston: South End, 1992, pp. 61–77.

"Simple Living: An Antidote to Hedonistic Materialism." In *Black Genius: African American Solutions to African American Problems*. Ed. Walter Mosley, Manthia Diawara, Clyde Taylor, and Regina Austin. New York: W. W. Norton, 1999, pp. 125–44.

"Sisterhood: Political Solidarity between Women." *Feminism and Community*. Ed. Penny A. Weiss and Marilyn Friedman. Philadelphia, PA: Temple University Press, 1995, pp. 293–315. Rpt. from *Feminist Theory: From Margin to Center*. By bell hooks. Boston: South End, 1984, pp. 43–65.

"Speech: A Love Rap." *Essence*, 24 (November 1993), 81–82, 155, 156, 160.

"Subversive Desire." *Ms.*, 9 (April/May 1999), 58–59.

"Sorrowful Black Death Is Not a Hot Ticket." *Sight and Sound*, 4 (August 1994), 10–14.

"Standing at the Crossroads: A Conversation between Diamanda Galas and bell hooks." *Village Voice*, September 20, 1994, pp. 15–18. (With Diamanda Galas.)

"Straightening Our Hair." In *Identities: Readings from Contemporary Culture*. Ed. Ann Raimes. Boston: Houghton Mifflin, 1995, pp. 79–88.

"Subversive Beauty: New Modes of Contestation." In *Felix Gonzalez-Torres*. Ed. Russell Ferguson. Los Angeles: Museum of Contemporary Art, 1994, pp. 45–49. Rpt. in *Art on My Mind: Visual Politics*. By bell hooks. New York: New, 1995, pp. 49–53.

"Talking Back." *Discourse*, 8 (1986–87), 123–28. Rpt. in *Talking Back: Thinking Feminist, Thinking Black*. By bell hooks. Boston: South End, 1989, pp. 5–9; rpt. in *Making Face, Making Soul/Haciendo Caras: Creative and Critical Perspectives by Feminists of Color*. Ed. Gloria Anzaldúa. San Francisco: Aunt Lute, 1990, pp. 207–11; and rpt. in *Out There: Marginalization and Contemporary Cultures*. Ed. Russell Ferguson, Martha Gever, Trinh T. Minh-ha, and Cornel West. Cambridge, MA: MIT Press, 1990, pp. 337–40.

"Talk Now, Pay Later." *Sight and Sound*, 8 (June 1996), 18–22

"Theory as Liberatory Practice." *Yale Journal of Law and Feminism*, 4 (1991), 1–12. Rpt. (shortened version) as "Out of the Academy and into the Streets." In *Getting There: The Movement toward Gender Equality*. Ed. Diana Wells. New York: Carroll and Graf-Richard Gallen, 1994, pp. 191–97; and rpt. in *Teaching to Transgress: Education as the Practice of Freedom*. By bell hooks. New York: Routledge, 1994, pp. 59–75.

" 'This Is the Oppressor's Language/Yet I Need It to Talk to You': Language, a Place of Struggle." In *Between Languages and Cultures: Translation and Cross-Cultural Texts*. Ed. Anuradha Dingwaney and Carol Maier. Pittsburgh, PA: University of Pittsburgh Press, 1995, pp. 295–301. Rpt. as "Language: Teaching New Worlds/ New Words." In *Teaching to Transgress: Education as the Practice of Freedom*. By bell hooks. New York: Routledge, 1994, pp. 167–75.

"Tongues of Fire." *Utne Reader*, 63 (May/June 1994), 136–37. Rpt. (shortened version) from *Sisters of the Yam: Black Women and Self-Recovery*. By bell hooks. Boston: South End, 1993, pp. 31–40.

"Touching the Earth." *Orion*, 15 (Autumn 1996), 21–22.

"Transformative Pedagogy and Multiculturalism." In *Freedom's Plow: Teaching in the Multicultural Classroom*. Ed. Theresa Perry and James W. Fraser. New York: Routledge, 1993, pp. 91–97.

"The Universal Resonance of Soul." In *Sacred Encounters: East and West*. By Marcia Lippman. New York: Edition Stemmle, 2000, p. 5.

"Violence in Intimate Relationships." In *Family Matters: Readings on Family Lives and the Law*. Ed. Martha Minow. New York: New, 1993, pp. 200–05. Rpt. from *Talking Back: Thinking Feminist, Thinking Black*. By bell hooks. Boston: South End, 1989, pp. 84–91.

"Virtuous Reality." *Spin*, 11 (November 1995), 86, 140. (With Jaron Lanier.)

"Waking Up to Racism." *Tricycle: The Buddhist Review*, 4 (1994), 42–45.

"White Light." *Sight and Sound*, 6 (May 1996), 10–12.

"The Wisdom of Hopelessness: My Conversation with Pema Chödörn." *Utne Reader*, 81 (May/June 1997), 61–62.

"Wounds of Passion." *Ms.*, 8 (March/April 1998), 56–60.

"Writing from the Darkness." *Tri-Quarterly*, 75 (1989), 71–77. Rpt. in *Essays by Contemporary American Women*. Ed. Wendy Martin. Boston: Beacon, 1996, pp. 152–59.

"Writing the Subject: Reading *The Color Purple*." In *Reading Black, Reading Feminist: A Critical Anthology*. Ed. Henry Louis Gates, Jr. New York: Meridian-Penguin, 1990, pp. 454–70.

Interviews

bell hooks and Tanya McKinnon. "Sisterhood: Beyond Public and Private." *Signs*, 21 (Summer 1996), 814–29.

"Bell Hooks: Critical Consciousness for Political Resistance." In *Talking About a Revolution*. Ed. South End Press Collective. Cambridge, MA: South End, 1998, pp. 39–52.

Carroll, Rebecca. "Bell Hooks Unplugged." *Elle*, December 1994, pp. 78, 80, 81.

Chua, Lawrence. Interview with bell hooks. In *Speak Fiction and Poetry!: The Best of BOMB Magazine's Interviews with Writers*. Ed. Betsy Sussler, Suzan Sherman, and Ronalde Shavers. New York: G + B Arts International, 1998, pp. 108–19.

Cooper, Desiree. "Bourgeois Feminism: Bell Hooks on Why We Aren't All Sisters under the Skin." *Columbus Guardian* [OH], September 8, 1994, p. 15.

Gilroy, Paul. "A Dialogue with Bell Hooks." In *Small Acts: Thoughts on the Politics of Black Cultures*. Ed. Paul Gilroy. New York: Serpent's Tail, 1993, pp. 208–36.

Jones, Lisa. "Sister Knowledge." *Essence*, May 1995, pp. 187, 188, 190, 256, 258.

Juno, Andrea, and V. Vale. "Bell Hooks." *Angry Women*, 13 (1991), 78–97.

Lutz, Helma. "Feminist Theory in Practice: An Interview with Bell Hooks: Encounter with an Impressive Female Academic Fighter against Multiple Forms of Oppression." *Women's Studies International Forum*, 16 (1993), 419–25.

Olson, Gary A. "Bell Hooks and the Politics of Literacy: A Conversation." *Journal of Advanced Composition*, 14 (1994), 1–19. Rpt. in *Philosophy, Rhetoric, Literary Criticism: (Inter)views*. Ed. Gary A. Olson, Carbondale: Southern Illinois University Press, 1994, 81–111; and rpt. (expanded version) in Olson, Gary A., and Elizabeth Hirsh. "Feminist *Praxis* and the Politics of Literacy: A Conversation with Bell Hooks." *Women Writing Culture*. Ed. Gary A. Olson and Elizabeth Hirsh. Albany: State University of New York Press, 1995, pp. 105–37.

Risher, Dee Dee. "Love in the Midst of Babylon." *The Other Side*, 36 (September/ October 2000), 21–24.

Sischy, Ingrid. "Bell Hooks." *Interview*, 25 (1995), 122–27.
Trend, David. "Representation and Resistance: An Interview with Bell Hooks." *Socialist Review*, 24 (1994), 115–28. Rpt. as "Representation and Democracy: An Interview." In *Radical Democracy: Identity, Citizenship, and the State*. Ed. David Trend. New York: Routledge, 1996, pp. 229–36.

Videotapes

Bell Hooks: Cultural Criticism and Transformation. Northampton, MA: Media Education Foundation, 1997.

Endnotes

[1] bell hooks, *Outlaw Culture: Resisting Representations* (New York: Routledge, 1994), pp. 2–3.
[2] Hooks does not capitalize the initial letters of her name. We have capitalized the initial letters of her name only in situations in which any word not usually capitalized would be capitalized—at the start of a sentence, for example.
[3] "Hooks, Bell." *Current Biography Yearbook*, ed. Judith Graham (New York: H. W. Wilson, 1995), p. 253; and bell hooks and Cornel West, *Breaking Bread: Insurgent Black Intellectual Life* (Boston: South End, 1991), p. 67.
[4] bell hooks, *Talking Back: Thinking Feminist, Thinking Black* (Boston: South End, 1989), p. 10.
[5] bell hooks, *Teaching to Transgress: Education as the Practice of Freedom* (New York: Routledge, 1994), p. 119.
[6] hooks, *Talking Back*, p. 128.
[7] bell hooks, "Black is a Woman's Color," in *Bearing Witness*, ed. Henry Louis Gates, Jr. (New York: Pantheon, 1991), p. 345.
[8] hooks, "Black is a Woman's Color," p. 347.
[9] bell hooks, "Challenging Men," *Sparerib*, 217 (1990), 13.
[10] bell hooks, *Bone Black: Memories of Girlhood* (New York: Henry Holt, 1996), p. 98.
[11] hooks, *Talking Back*, p. 5.
[12] hooks, *Talking Back*, p. 7.
[13] hooks, *Talking Back*, pp. 5–6.
[14] hooks, "Black is a Woman's Color," p. 342.
[15] hooks, *Teaching to Transgress*, p. 60.
[16] hooks, *Outlaw Culture*, pp. 9–10.
[17] hooks and West, p. 66.
[18] hooks and West, p. 149.
[19] bell hooks, *Remembered Rapture: The Writer at Work* (New York: Henry Holt, 1999), p. 5.
[20] hooks and West, pp. 149–50.
[21] bell hooks, *A Woman's Mourning Song* (New York: Harlem River, 1993), p. 8.
[22] hooks, *A Woman's Mourning Song*, p. 5.
[23] hooks, *Talking Back*, p. 100.
[24] bell hooks, "Marginality as Site of Resistance," in *Out There: Marginalization and Contemporary Cultures*, ed. Russell Ferguson, Martha Gever, Trinh T. Minh-ha, and Cornel West (Cambridge, MA: MIT Press, 1990), p. 342.
[25] hooks, *Talking Back*, p. 59.
[26] hooks, *Killing Rage: Ending Racism* (New York: Henry Holt, 1995), p. 228.
[27] hooks and West, p. 148.
[28] Ingrid Sischy, "Bell Hooks," *Interview*, 25 (1995), 126.
[29] bell hooks, "Power to the Pussy: We Don't Wannabe Dicks in Drag," in *Madonnarama: Essays on Sex and Popular Culture*, ed. Lisa Frank and Paul Smith (San Francisco: Cleis, 1993), p. 66.
[30] hooks, *Outlaw Culture*, p. 232.

[31] hooks, *Remembered Rapture*, p. 139.
[32] hooks, *Where We Stand: Class Matters* (New York: Routledge, 2000), p. 48.
[33] bell hooks, "Feminism and Black Women's Studies," *Sage*, 6 (1989), p. 54.
[34] bell hooks, *Ain't I a Woman: Black Women and Feminism* (Boston: South End, 1981), p. 13.
[35] hooks, *Outlaw Culture*, p. 6.
[36] hooks, *Talking Back*, p. 9.
[37] hooks, *Remembered Rapture*, p. 114.
[38] hooks, *Talking Back*, p. 9.
[39] hooks, *Talking Back*, p. 19.
[40] hooks, *Outlaw Culture*, p. 200.
[41] hooks, *Outlaw Culture*, p. 202.
[42] hooks, *Talking Back*, p. 19.
[43] hooks, *Talking Back*, p. 175.
[44] hooks, *Talking Back*, p. 21.
[45] bell hooks, *Feminist Theory: From Margin to Center* (Boston: South End, 1984), p. 35.
[46] hooks, *Feminist Theory*, p. 36.
[47] Helma Lutz, "Feminist Theory in Practice: An Interview with Bell Hooks: Encounter with an Impressive Female Academic Fighter Against Multiple Forms of Oppression," *Women's Studies International Forum*, 16 (1993), 422.
[48] Lutz, p. 425.
[49] hooks, *Killing Rage*, p. 194.
[50] bell hooks, *Art on My Mind: Visual Politics* (New York: New, 1995), p. xii.
[51] hooks, *Teaching to Transgress*, p. 173.
[52] bell hooks, *Yearning: Race, Gender, and Cultural Politics* (Boston: South End, 1990), p. 155.
[53] bell hooks, "Keeping Close to Home: Class and Education," in *Working-Class Women in the Academy: Laborers in the Knowledge Factory*, ed. Michelle M. Tokarczyk and Elizabeth A. Fay (Amherst: University of Massachusetts Press, 1993), p. 108.
[54] bell hooks, *Salvation: Black People and Love* (New York: William Morrow-HarperCollins, 2001), p. 59.
[55] hooks, *Salvation*, pp. 72–73.
[56] hooks, *Salvation*, p. 73.
[57] John Perry Barlow and bell hooks, "An Intimate Conversation," *Shambhala Sun*, 4 (1995), 63.
[58] bell hooks, *All About Love: New Visions* (New York: William Morrow, 2000), p. 93.
[59] bell hooks, *Feminism is for Everybody: Passionate Politics* (Cambridge, MA: South End, 2000), p. 103.
[60] hooks, *All About Love*, p. 87.
[61] hooks, *Outlaw Culture*, p. 241.
[62] hooks, *Outlaw Culture*, p. 54.
[63] hooks, *All About Love*, p. 5.
[64] hooks, *Feminism is for Everybody*, p. 103.
[65] hooks, *All About Love*, p. 88.
[66] hooks, *Yearning*, p. 149.
[67] hooks, *Feminist Theory*, preface.
[68] hooks, *Feminist Theory*, preface.
[69] hooks, *Yearning*, pp. 149–50.
[70] hooks, *Feminist Theory*, p. 15.
[71] hooks, *Talking Back*, p. 16.
[72] hooks, *Feminist Theory*, p. 14.
[73] hooks, *Ain't I a Woman*, p. 7.
[74] hooks, *Ain't I a Woman*, p. 7.
[75] hooks, *Yearning*, p. 29.
[76] hooks, *Teaching to Transgress*, p. 91.
[77] hooks, *Teaching to Transgress*, p. 90.
[78] hooks, *Art on My Mind*, p. 12.

[79] hooks, *Teaching to Transgress*, pp. 91–92.

[80] hooks, *Teaching to Transgress*, p. 91.

[81] hooks, *Remembered Rapture*, p. 57. Hooks's focus on marginality is consistent with feminist standpoint theory, first formally articulated by Nancy C. M. Hartsock in 1983. The foundational tenet of feminist standpoint theory is that the position of women is structurally different from that of men and provides women with a particular standpoint from which to theorize. Black feminist theorists challenged feminist standpoint theory, suggesting that it did not acknowledge differences among women, and shifted the focus of feminist standpoint theory to theorizing *standpoints* rather than a feminist standpoint. See, for example, Nancy C. M. Hartsock, "The Feminist Standpoint: Developing the Ground for a Specifically Feminist Historical Materialism," in *Discovering Reality: Feminist Perspectives on Epistemology, Metaphysics, Methodology, and Philosophy of Science*, ed. Sandra Harding and Merrill B. Hintikka (Boston: D. Reidel, 1983), pp. 283–310; D. Lynn O'Brien Hallstein, "Where Standpoint Stands Now: An Introduction and Commentary," *Women's Studies in Communication*, 23 (Winter 2000), 1–15; and Katherine Welton, "Nancy Hartsock's Standpoint Theory: From Content to 'Concrete Multiplicity,'" in *Politics and Feminist Standpoint Theories*, ed. Sally J. Kenney and Helen Kinsella (New York: Haworth, 1997), pp. 7–24.

[82] hooks, *Feminist Theory*, pp. 17–18.

[83] hooks, *Feminist Theory*, p. 18.

[84] hooks, *Ain't I a Woman*, p. 195.

[85] hooks, *Feminist Theory*, p. 24.

[86] hooks, *Talking Back*, p. 25.

[87] hooks, *Feminist Theory*, p. 31.

[88] hooks, *Talking Back*, p. 22.

[89] hooks, *Feminist Theory*, p. 34.

[90] hooks, *Killing Rage*, p. 99.

[91] hooks, *Feminist Theory*, p. 158.

[92] hooks, *Ain't I a Woman*, p. 192.

[93] hooks, *Feminist Theory*, p. 163.

[94] hooks, *Feminism is for Everybody*, p. viii.

[95] hooks, *Feminism is for Everybody*, p. 118.

[96] bell hooks, *Sisters of the Yam: Black Women and Self-Recovery* (Boston: South End, 1993), pp. 1–2.

[97] hooks, *Outlaw Culture*, p. 5.

[98] hooks, *Yearning*, p. 8.

[99] hooks, *Yearning*, p. 15.

[100] hooks, *Teaching to Transgress*, p. 202.

[101] hooks and West, p. 152.

[102] bell hooks, *Black Looks: Race and Representation* (Boston: South End, 1992), p. 5.

[103] hooks, *Art on My Mind*, p. 3.

[104] hooks, *Killing Rage*, p. 110.

[105] hooks, *Salvation*, p. 74.

[106] hooks, *Salvation*, p. 76.

[107] hooks, *Salvation*, p. 76.

[108] hooks, *Salvation*, pp. 76–77.

[109] hooks, *Yearning*, p. 7.

[110] bell hooks, "Dialectically Down with the Critical Program," in *Black Popular Culture*, ed. Gina Dent (New York: New, 1998), pp. 51–52.

[111] hooks, "Dialectically Down with the Critical Program," p. 54.

[112] Lisa Jones, "Rebel without a Pause," *Village Voice*, 37 (October 13, 1992), literary supplement, 10.

[113] hooks, *Yearning*, p. 184.

[114] hooks, *All About Love*, p. 97.

[115] hooks, *Outlaw Culture*, p. 156.

[116] hooks, "Dialectically Down with the Critical Program," pp. 52–53.

[117] hooks, "Dialectically Down with the Critical Program," p. 53.

[118] hooks, "Dialectically Down with the Critical Program," pp. 54–55.

[119] hooks, *Teaching to Transgress*, p. 130.

[120] hooks, *Talking Back*, p. 16.

[121] hooks, *Outlaw Culture*, p. 66.

[122] hooks, *Outlaw Culture*, p. 66.

[123] hooks, *Outlaw Culture*, p. 72.

[124] hooks, *Talking Back*, p. 129.

[125] hooks, *Killing Rage*, p. 193.

[126] hooks, *Outlaw Culture*, p. 219.

[127] hooks, *Killing Rage*, p. 194.

[128] hooks, *Yearning*, p. 218.

[129] hooks, *Remembered Rapture,* p. 42.

[130] hooks, *Outlaw Culture*, p. 6.

[131] Lutz, p. 420.

[132] hooks, *Sisters of the Yam*, pp. 38–39.

[133] hooks, *Sisters of the Yam*, p. 40.

[134] hooks, *Sisters of the Yam*, p. 40.

[135] hooks, *Black Looks*, p. 4.

[136] Jones, p. 10.

[137] hooks, *Sisters of the Yam*, p. 83.

[138] hooks, *Outlaw Culture*, p. 237.

[139] hooks, *Art on My Mind*, p. xv.

[140] hooks, *Art on My Mind*, p. 138.

[141] bell hooks, "Beauty Laid Bare: Aesthetics in the Ordinary," in *To be Real*, ed. Rebecca Walker (New York: Anchor, 1995), pp. 163–64.

[142] hooks, *Yearning*, p. 111.

[143] bell hooks, "Black (and White) Snapshots," *Ms.*, 5 (September/October 1994), 85.

[144] hooks, "Black (and White) Snapshots," p. 86.

[145] hooks, "Black (and White) Snapshots," p. 87.

[146] hooks, *Feminist Theory*, p. 111.

[147] bell hooks, "Critical Reflections," *Artforum*, 33 (1994), 100.

[148] hooks, *Teaching to Transgress*, p. 65.

[149] hooks, "Critical Reflections," p. 65.

[150] hooks and West, p. 72.

[151] hooks, *Talking Back*, p. 129.

[152] hooks, *Talking Back*, p. 3.

[153] bell hooks, "Bell Hooks in Conversation with Deborah Gray White, Charlotte Bunch, and Harriet Davidson," in *Talking Leadership: Conversations with Powerful Women*, ed. Mary S. Hartman (New Brunswick, NJ: Rutgers University Press, 1999), pp. 113–14.

[154] hooks, *Talking Back*, p. 111.

[155] hooks, *Talking Back*. p. 106.

[156] bell hooks and Tanya McKinnon, "Sisterhood: Beyond Public and Private," *Signs*, 21 (Summer 1996), 823.

[157] David Trend, "Representation and Resistance: An Interview with Bell Hooks," *Socialist Review*, 24 (1994), 126.

[158] hooks, *Talking Back,* p.101

[159] hooks, *Teaching to Transgress*, pp. 140–41.

[160] hooks, *Talking Back*, p. 52.

[161] hooks, *Killing Rage*, p. 262.

[162] Pepi Leistyna, "Editors' Reviews," *Harvard Educational Review*, 65 (Summer 1995), 323.

[163] Haven B. White, "Postmodern Communities: The *Yearning* of Bell Hooks, a Review Essay," *International Journal of Group Tensions*, 24 (1994), 443.

[164] Joyce Irene Middleton, "Bell Hooks on Literacy and Teaching: A Response," *Journal of Advanced Composition*, 14 (Fall 1994), 560.

[165] White, p. 435.

[166] Namulundah Florence, *Bell Hooks' Engaged Pedagogy: A Transgressive Education for Critical Consciousness* (Westport, CT: Bergin and Garvey, 1998), xxiii–xxiv.

[167] Cornel West, "Introduction to Bell Hooks," in *Breaking Bread: Insurgent Black Intellectual Life*, by bell hooks and Cornel West (Boston: South End, 1991), p. 62.

[168] Rev. of *Killing Rage* and *Teaching to Transgress*, pp. 317–18.

[169] Rev. of *Killing Rage: Ending Racism* and *Teaching to Transgress: Education as the Practice of Freedom*, by bell hooks, *Journal of Leisure Research*, 28 (1996), 316.

[170] White, p. 435.

[171] Middleton, p. 565.

[172] Florence, p. xxii.

[173] Kathleen O'Grady, rev. of *All About Love: New Visions*, by bell hooks, *WE International*, 48/49 (Summer/Fall 2000), 42.

[174] Florence, p. xxii.

[175] Florence, pp. xxii–xxiii.

[176] Anna Marie Smith, rev. of *Outlaw Culture: Resisting Representations*, by bell hooks, *Ethnic and Racial Studies*, 19 (1996), 937.

[177] White, p. 443.

[178] White, p. 441.

[179] White, p. 443.

[180] White, pp. 441–42.

[181] O'Grady, p. 42.

[182] Michele Wallace, "For Whom the Bell Tolls: Why America Can't Deal with Black Feminist Intellectuals," *Village Voice*, 40 (November 7, 1995), 19.

[183] Wallace, p. 22.

[184] Keith Byerman, "Hip-Hop Spirituality: African-American Cultural Criticism," *College Literature*, 22 (June 1995), 139.

[185] Byerman, p. 140.

[186] White, p. 437.

[187] Florence, p. xxiii.

[188] Joan M. Martin, "The Notion of Difference for Emerging Womanist Ethics: The Writings of Audre Lorde and Bell Hooks," *Journal of Feminist Studies in Religion*, 9 (Fall 1993), 42.

[189] Wallace, p. 23.

[190] Smith, p. 937.

[191] Florence, p. 69.

[192] Tom Fox, "Literacy and Activism: A Response to Bell Hooks," *Journal of Advanced Composition*, 14 (Fall 1994), 564.

[193] Adolph Reed, "What Are the Drums Saying, Booker?: The Current Crisis of the Black Intellectual," *Village Voice*, 40 (April 11, 1995), 35.

[194] Grünell and Saharson, p. 204.

[195] Middleton, p. 560.

[196] hooks, *Talking Back*, p. 176.

[197] hooks, *Killing Rage*, p. 7.

10

JEAN BAUDRILLARD

"I've always had a prejudice against the very word 'communication.' It's always seemed to me to be precisely something like an exchange, a dialogue, a system . . . of contacts, and all the linguistic and metalinguistic functions therein implied. If that is communication, I don't want to know about it." Jean Baudrillard objects to the term *communication* because he does not believe it covers the "really interesting relations between people." He equates communication with information, which only "brings about a relationship between things already in existence."[1] As a process, it is "a little too functional, a little too functionalist, as if the only true purpose of things" is persuasion.[2] Baudrillard prefers the term *symbolic exchange* and finds forms of interaction such as "challenge, seduction, or play" more interesting because they bring "more intense things into being."[3]

Although Baudrillard dislikes the current connotations of the word *communication*, the centrality of the notions of sign and symbolic exchange in his work places him squarely in the field of rhetoric. Baudrillard is interested in "characterizing the structure of communication in a world dominated by the media,"[4] a focus that has earned him the title of the "French McLuhan."[5] Like Marshall McLuhan, Baudrillard starts with the notion that the medium is the message: the media do not communicate an already existing ideology as much as they establish the ideology itself. For Baudrillard, the root of that ideology is a system of signs that is removed from reality by the nature and pervasiveness of mass media and technology. The result is a consumer society in which objects dominate and control humans rather than the reverse.

Baudrillard was born in Rheims, France, in 1929. His parents were civil servants, and his grandparents were peasants. He was the first in his family to earn a university degree, majoring in languages, philosophy, and sociology: "I was the first member of the tribe, so to speak, to do some studying. . . . I was not brought up in an intellectual milieu. . . . It was not a cultural environment." His choice of an intellectual life caused a "rupture" with his parents that Baudrillard recognized as not just one of profession but of entire worldview.[6] With characteristic irony, he recalls: "My grandfather stopped working when he died: a peasant. My father stopped well before his time: civil servant. . . . I never started work, having very soon acquired a marginal, sabbatical situation: university teacher."[7]

Baudrillard began his career by teaching German at the secondary school level. During this time, he wrote book reviews of German and Italian works for *Les temps modernes*, a journal published by Jean-Paul Sartre, and translated into French the works of Friedrich Engels, Peter Weiss, and Bertolt Brecht.[8] Baudrillard returned to school to pursue a graduate degree in sociology at the University of Paris at Nanterre. In his thesis, completed in 1966, Baudrillard focuses on the object, consumerism, and the mediated social order—themes that are ongoing throughout his writing. Baudrillard claims, however, that he did not consciously choose this direction for his life's work: "Nothing begins as a project. It was never a decision or a choice between this and that. . . . It was all a metamorphosis of one into the other. . . . But, fundamentally, I have had the same idea from the beginning. We all have just one idea all our life."[9]

Upon completion of his thesis, Baudrillard assumed the position of assistant lecturer of sociology at the University of Paris at Nanterre, where he remained for his academic career. He completed his doctorate at the Sorbonne; his dissertation became the book *L'autre par lui-même*, although the English title under which it was issued is *The Ecstasy of Communication*. Baudrillard rose to the rank of junior lecturer in the early 1970s but never attained the rank of professor, noting that "as far as the normal stages of a career are concerned, I've always missed them, including the fact that I was never a professor. I say this without any recrimination, because that is how I wanted it. It was a little game of mine to say that I wanted a degree of freedom."[10] Baudrillard served as a visiting professor at universities in San Diego and Los Angeles in 1975 but declined offers of permanent positions in the United States: "It was too much responsibility and I wanted, in a sense, to remain irresponsible."[11] Baudrillard retired from his teaching post in 1987 to what he describes as a permanent "sabbatical."[12] He alternates between a home in the Languedoc region of France and an apartment in Paris.

Baudrillard's career is positioned within the discipline of sociology, and he still considers himself to be a sociologist in the general sense of the term: "Sociology was born with modernity, with the investigation of modernity. Yes, I would be a sociologist in this sense."[13] He also recognizes the limits of the discipline, however. The central focus of his book *In the Shadow of the Silent Majorities* is a critique of sociology. For Baudrillard, sociology "has always had the virtue of being a way of reading things. But it became a kind of stereotype, an analysis for which you have to produce facts. Then, what's the use of producing facts? . . . This sort of conformity to facts, this compliance with truth is clearly never going to contest anything because all it does is constantly verify itself."[14] Despite his association with sociology, Baudrillard does not want to be confined to any traditional disciplinary perspective:

> My particular critical impulse comes from a radical temperament which has more in common with poetry than philosophy. . . . I don't criticize, I'm throwing things up at the same time that I'm greedily devouring them. There does not seem to be much here for the critical subject, does there? Dynamic integration? That's scarcely me! A return to philosophy, and the search for a new conceptual platform . . . ? That doesn't interest me either. Nor can I envisage any kind of compromise position. The only game that amuses me is that of following some new situation to its very limits![15]

Charles Levin, one of Baudrillard's interpreters, summarizes Baudrillard's academic stance by suggesting that he stays "an idiosyncratic course through the world of academic thought."[16]

Just as Baudrillard defies categorization in terms of discipline, so his work raises questions about his positioning within larger intellectual traditions. One such debate involves the question of whether Baudrillard is a postmodernist. To many, Baudrillard is the postmodernist *par excellence*— the "high priest" of postmodernism.[17] In many of his writings, Baudrillard examines themes associated with postmodernism, such as fragmentation, irony, a rejection of grand narratives, and a celebration of multiplicity. Yet, he himself has not embraced the *postmodern* label, largely because it is a word without meaning for him: "It's an expression, a word which people use but which explains nothing. It's not even a concept. It's nothing at all. . . . It's because there is nothing really to express this that an empty term has been chosen to designate what is really empty."[18] He elaborates, suggesting that if postmodernism exists, it must be the characteristic of a universe where there are no more definitions possible. . . . They have been deconstructed, destroyed. In reality there is no more reference to forms. It has all been done. The extreme limit of these possibilities has been reached. It has destroyed itself. It has deconstructed its entire universe. So, all that are left are pieces. All that remains to be done is to play with the pieces. Playing with the pieces—that is postmodern.[19]

Neither does Baudrillard's work fit clearly within the modernist agenda because of its privileging of rationality as the legitimate means of attaining a fixed and objective truth that can lead to progress for humankind. Baudrillard sees himself as associated with modernity to the extent that it is a starting point; he examines and analyzes "this modernity in order to move beyond it."[20] He describes his approach as tracing the "dispersal" of modernist projects throughout the contemporary era of simulation, consumerism, and technology, but he is reluctant to confine himself to either the modernist or postmodernist labels.

Baudrillard's eclecticism also is evident in the other projects and activities in which he has been involved. Political interests and activities characterized Baudrillard's early academic career when he opposed French and U.S. intervention into the Algerian and Vietnamese Wars—a position that aligned him with the French Left.[21] One of the outgrowths of this political involvement was Baudrillard's association, from 1967 into the 1970s, with the journal *Utopie*. He also was a founder and member of the editorial board of *Traverses*, a radical aesthetics journal established in 1975 and housed in the Centre Georges Pompidou in Paris.[22] As a political activist, Baudrillard was inspired by a group of radical writers and artists called the *Situationiste Internationale*, "a neo-Surrealist anti-organization"[23] that became prominent during the revolt in France in May and June of 1968, when 10 million people went on strike, demanding the overthrow of all bourgeois regimes.[24] The Situationists came to prominence in 1967 when they published an attack on the commodification of culture in a treatise called "La société du spectacle"[25] and used art ads to encourage spontaneous action to "cast off the enforced passivity of consumer society."[26] Baudrillard has maintained remnants of the Situationists' approach to life as spectacle throughout his work, claiming he always has been "a Situationist"[27] in his instinctive approach to the political analysis of culture: "the revolution would be a festival or nothing" because a spectacle is a *"social relationship among people, mediated by images."*[28]

Although the notion of the spectacle remains a thread in Baudrillard's work, he has become disillusioned with the political scene and the ability of intellectuals to create social change: "There doesn't seem to be any social movement of the kind we had in the sixties and seventies, which also had theoretical inspiration. . . . It wasn't necessarily a conscious class or mass ideological practice. But movement there was. I think intellectuals felt this energy, and felt it without being affiliated to any group, or being involved in personal terms. . . . All this slowly came to an end during the seventies. This energy used itself up."[29] Baudrillard sees the intellectual life as much more individualistic at present: "Intellectuals are now biding their time because there is no more real dialogue, nor any real discussion. Each person is doing his or her own thing, attached to his or her research or to a group."[30] Baudrillard's present "political strategy, if it fairly may be called that, is to remain equidistant . . . from all parties, to align himself with nothing that exists officially in the present."[31]

Baudrillard's interests and expertise also include design. He became involved with the Centre d'Etudes des Communications de Masse at the Ecole Pratique des Hautes Etudes in Paris, where he lectured on social problems of design and concepts of the environment. His experience with design also resulted in his serving on the jury of the *Compasso d'oro* design prize in Milan and attending the 1970 World Design Congress in Aspen, Colorado.[32]

Cultural criticism is another of Baudrillard's passions, which he pursues through travel, photography, and performance. His travels have taken him around the world, where his "hunting grounds" are the everyday landscapes and places of a country: "Where the others spend their time in libraries, I spend mine in the deserts and on the roads. Where they draw their material from the history of ideas, I draw mine from what is happening now, from the life of the streets, the beauty of nature."[33] His book *America* is a series of ruminations generated as he traveled around the United States, a country that holds a particular fascination for Baudrillard:

> For me there is no truth of America. I ask of the Americans only that they be Americans. I do not ask them to be intelligent, sensible, original. I ask them only to populate a space incommensurate with my own, to be for me the highest astral point, the finest orbital space. . . . I want to excentre myself, to become eccentric, but I want to do so in a place that is the centre of the world. And in this sense, the latest fast-food outlet, the most banal suburb, the blandest of giant American cars or the most insignificant cartoon-strip majorette is more at the centre of the world than any of the cultural manifestations of old Europe. This is the only country which gives you the opportunity to be so brutally naive: things, faces, skies, and deserts are expected to be simply what they are. This is the land of the "just as it is."[34]

Baudrillard has supplemented his knowledge of places with photography, an interest that developed in the 1980s when he was given a camera on one of his trips to Japan: "Before that I was rather indifferent towards photography." He claims it is both "diversion or hobby" and "something serious, in the sense that it offered an alternative to writing."[35] He describes it as "something very intense. It's the form of the object, the form of the appearance of the object, more so than in the cinema. . . . I like photography as something completely empty, 'irreal', as something that preserves the idea of a silent apparition."[36]

Baudrillard's involvement in photography led to an invitation to write an essay to accompany Sophie Calle's book of narratives and photographs called *Suite vénitienne*. Calle followed strangers and photographed them for "the pleasure of following them, not because they particularly interested me. I photographed them without their knowledge, took note of their movements, then finally lost sight of them and forgot them."[37] For Baudrillard, what Calle was able to achieve is an understanding of the contemporary functioning of responsibility: "In comparison with our ideas of liberation, of individual autonomy, which exhaust themselves running after their own shadow . . . , how much more subtle, more amazing, more discreet and arrogant all at once is the idea . . . that someone else looks after your life."[38]

Baudrillard's appearance at a new-age festival called "Chance: Three Days in the Desert," which took place at a casino near Las Vegas in 1997, brings together the many elements that comprise Baudrillard's approach to cultural analysis and criticism. Described as a synthesis of "a rave and summit meeting between artists and philosophers, chaosophists and croupiers, mathematicians and musicians,"[39] Baudrillard discussed his work over the sound of slot machines. A commentator offered this description of Baudrillard at the event: "with his 'diminutive height, wine-and-cheese paunch, nose and self-rolled cigarettes,' 'is there anyone more French than this man?' "[40] Baudrillard returned later in the evening to recite "Motel Suicide," one of his poems, wearing a gold lamé suit and backed by a rock band.

Just as his performances bring together the disparate components of Baudrillard's worldview, so does his writing, which has spanned more than three decades. His writing projects have been remarkably consistent in their analysis of the nature of contemporary society. His works can be grouped into four periods, each of which emphasizes different aspects of his overall project. The first period includes works published between 1966 and 1973 and is the period in which Baudrillard's work is most closely aligned with traditional sociology. In this period, he makes use of Marx's ideas to suggest parallels between Marx's theory of production and his own emergent theory of consumption.

The first work in this period is *The System of Objects*, Baudrillard's thesis, in which he introduces the notion that consumption has become the basis of the social order: the contemporary "subject faces a world of objects which attract, fascinate, and sometimes control his or her perception, thought and behavior."[41] Baudrillard followed the publication of his thesis with *La société de consommation* (The Consumer Society) in 1970, in which he argues that individuals interact with objects not only in terms of their use value or function but as a way of communicating with others. For Baudrillard, "consumer objects are like hysterical symptoms; they are best understood not as a response to a specific need or problem but as a network of floating signifiers that are inexhaustible in their ability to incite desire."[42]

Baudrillard's next two books begin to explore the limits of Marxist ideas of production. *Pour une critique de l'économie politique du signe* (*For a Critique of the Political Economy of the Sign*), published in 1972, is a collection of articles written during the early 1970s in which he describes the collapse of the parallel systems of production and consumption into a single system of signs.

This was followed in 1973 by *Le mirror de la production* (*The Mirror of Production*), the final work of this period, in which Baudrillard is more explicit in attacking the limits of Marxism and its emphasis on production. Baudrillard suggests that Marxism is incapable of describing life before and after the era of production because it does not deal with the symbolic realm: "Failing to conceive of a mode of social wealth other than that founded on labor and production, Marxism no longer furnishes in the long run a real alternative to capitalism."[43] Baudrillard suggests that Marx does not offer a radical critique of capitalism but rather mirrors it, unconsciously providing "its highest form of justification or ideology."[44]

Baudrillard's next collection of writings extends from 1976 through 1983. These works comprise Baudrillard's break with the empirical, academic, and sociological emphases of his earlier writings. Whereas previously he critiqued the traditional components of his training—Marxism as well as psychoanalysis and semiotics—in this second period, he translates his critique into practice, developing and applying his own theories about signs and symbols and the systems of which they are a part. The first book in this period, *L'Echange symbolique et la mort* (*Symbolic Exchange and Death*), focuses directly on his concepts of simulation and symbolic exchange. He surveys how symbolic exchange functions across a number of fields and presents his model of orders of simulation. This book has been called his *magnum opus*, "the definitive formulation and summing up of his ideas to this point";[45] some see it as his last truly theoretical work.[46]

Baudrillard's next two books are short treatises called *L'Effet Beaubourg* (1977) and *A l'ombre des majorités silencieuses* (*In the Shadow of the Silent Majorities*), published in 1978. Both continue his interest in symbolically examining elements of contemporary society. In the former, he critiques the Centre Pompidou in Paris, which to him signifies contemporary culture with its profusion of mixed messages. Not interested in the political implications of the building, he concentrates on its design, finding in the "tangled lattice of the exposed superstructure" images of an "absorptive cybernetic network" that competes with its public function as a "cultural 'attraction' for the 'people.' "[47] *In the Shadow of the Silent Majorities* is a critique of the social concept of "the people" or "the masses" upon which all sociology depends and suggests they do not actually exist. Rather, the masses are fictions produced by polls, surveys, and statistics. Because they are not real and thus cannot be understood or represented by political scientists, sociologists, and the like, the sociology constructed on the basis of this fiction does not exist, either.[48]

Oublier Foucault (*Forget Foucault*) also falls within Baudrillard's second scholarly period. In this book, published in 1977, he attacks Michel Foucault "for giving misplaced concreteness to the concepts of power and repression." In their place, Baudrillard proposes notions such as mobility, irony, and skepticism that foreshadow his fatal strategies. Baudrillard followed *Forget Foucault* in 1979 with *De la séduction* (*Seduction*), in which he presents the principle of seduction as a form of symbolic exchange. He attacks theories such as Marxism, psychoanalysis, and structuralism that privilege hidden structures of rationality and favors instead theories or models such as seduction that play "with the *strategy of appearances*."[49]

In Baudrillard's *Simulacres et simulation* (*Simulations*), published in 1982, he elaborates on the notion of simulation. In particular, he extends his theory of commodity culture, describing a "world constructed out of models or simulacra" that have no referent "in any 'reality' except their own."[50] Baudrillard continues to refine his notions about the end of the representational era and the dominance of simulation in *Les strategies fatales* (*Fatal Strategies*), published in 1983. He suggests that consumers now are subject to the prey of objects and need to rethink the social world from the object's point of view: "let's believe for a single instant the hypothesis that there is a fatal and enigmatic bias in the order of things."[51]

A third period of writing coincides with Baudrillard's 1987 retirement from his teaching position at Nanterre, a period characterized by experimentation with various genres and forms. Works of this stage include the travelogue *America* (1986); the journals *Cool Memories I* and *II* and *Fragments: Cool Memories III*, published in 1987, 1990, and 1996, respectively; a loose survey of his own work, *The Ecstasy of Communication* (1987); and a series of newspaper articles that became a book in 1991, *La guerre du golfe n'a pas eu lieu* (*The Gulf War Did Not Take Place*). Both *America* and *Cool Memories* are whimsical journals of Baudrillard's travels in America, with both the content and form exhibiting the characteristics of "cruising" as a pointless, aimless, and trivial activity.[52] In *Ecstasy*, Baudrillard describes how the pervasiveness of the mass media creates the explicit, the hyperreal, and the obscene, while in *The Gulf War Did Not Take Place*, he suggests not that nothing happened in the Gulf but that what happened was not a war but a deterrence to war. Baudrillard argues that there was no war because there were no warriors, no enemy, and rarely direct conflict—it was a "virtual war of information, electronics, and images."[53]

In Baudrillard's fourth period, which overlaps somewhat with the previous one, he returns to more conventionally structured books. Published in 1990, *La transparence du mal: Essai sur les phenomene extremes* (*The Transparency of Evil: Essays on Extreme Phenomena*) begins with his essay, "After the Orgy," in which he describes how the "orgy of the real, the rational" leads to the pursuit of "every avenue in the production and effective overproduction of objects, signs, messages, ideologies and satisfactions."[54] He describes some of the forms this excess assumes in essays on cancer, AIDS, and terrorism. In the 1992 book, *L'illusion de la fin* (*The Illusion of the End*), he further elaborates on the implications for a culture that has accelerated to excess. *Le Crime Parfait* (*The Perfect Crime*), published in 1994, offers Baudrillard's speculations about how human efforts to uncover reality constitute efforts to avoid confronting the truly random and illusory nature of the world.

Baudrillard sees as a common theme in his work the counter-game, or the effort to provoke new ways of thinking about contemporary culture. For him, this game "destroys things just as they are being constructed. It is not a question of a deliberate, 'subversive' will to deconstruct, but an attempt to identify the curvature of things, the mode in which things try to disappear."[55] He sees his approach as one of attempting "to slim things down, get rid of things, reduce stocks. To escape fullness," he explains, "you have to create voids between spaces so that there can be collisions and short circuits."[56]

Evolution of Simulation

At the root of Baudrillard's notion of simulation is the sign, and he sees all aspects of social life as comprising a system of signs: "The sign is the epicentre. . . . I always tried to analyse it in its actual setting. This is very difficult, of course, because . . . the sign is without doubt a very fragile fact, and it is very hard to force its logic into a hyperlogic without losing the sign itself along the way."[57] Baudrillard's work emphasizes the ways in which signs are not only symbolic expressions in and of themselves—symbols that stand for something else—but also parts of larger systems that have meaning at the societal level. In other words, symbols become "*tools* to facilitate social processes."[58] A sign, then, does not simply stand for its referent—some direct object in reality—but it becomes part of other systems of signs, each of which is further removed from reality. Signs become vehicles not only for the objects to which they refer but for other symbol systems and forms of social interaction. Rhetorically, then, signs and symbols have lost direct reference to reality, creating a world that has no objective referent.

Baudrillard's work focuses on the increasing abstractness of signs from the original contexts that provided the initial meanings for signs. Signs, by their definition, are necessarily abstract because they already are one level removed from the object or concept for which they stand. But contemporary technology has made the distance between sign and referent even greater. The telegraph provides one example. Before the telegraph, there was a "fixed identity between transportation and transmission." Transmission and transportation were the same process because only tangible objects could be transmitted from place to place—most likely through the railroad. The possibility of the instant relay of information in Morse code via telegraph separated transmission from transportation, making transmission faster than and disconnected from the pace of travel.[59]

Simulation derives from the increasing separation of signs from the objects they represent—from the increasing disconnect between the material world and the universes of meaning that are taken for reality. Simulation is a substitution of "signs of the real for the real itself."[60] It is the "sequencing of things as though they had a meaning, when they are governed only by artificial *montage* and non-meaning."[61] Simulation creates a space where literally nothing is real. Baudrillard distinguishes simulation from dissimulation: "To dissimulate is to feign not to have what one has. To simulate is to feign to have what one hasn't. One implies a presence, the other an absence."[62]

Someone who feigns an illness simply can go to bed and pretend to be ill. The person who simulates an illness, however, produces some of the symptoms, raising the question of whether she actually is ill or not. If a symptom can be produced, is the disease real or not? Feigning, or dissimulation, in other words, "leaves the reality principle intact," while "simulation threatens the difference between 'true' and 'false', between 'real' and 'imaginary.' "[63] This characteristic of simulation—the inability to distinguish the real from the fake—is Baudrillard's focus in terms of contemporary society: no longer can the real be distinguished from the simulation of the real because of how the media and technology function.

Baudrillard suggests that there have been four stages in the evolution of simulation—symbolic order, counterfeits, production, and simulation—progressing from the real itself through three levels of simulation. At times, Baudrillard discusses these stages as chronological ones, equated with actual historical periods. At others, he implies that these are stages that coexist to suggest the different ways signs function in relation to reality. What is important is not so much Baudrillard's exact intentions with this typology of signs and meanings but the sense of evolution offered about the emergence and dominance of simulation. With this typology, Baudrillard foreshadows the connections he develops among signs, production, commodification, and the media.

Symbolic Order

The first stage in the evolution of simulation, which Baudrillard calls *symbolic order*, is a pre-simulation stage. In this stage, signs are absolutely clear, referential, stable, and reflect basic reality. Historically, Baudrillard associates this stage with feudal society, an era characterized by actions dependent on rank, duty, and obligation. In such a society, there is little or no room for interpretation of signs. All agree on what something means and are clear about its relation to reality. The sign and the real are equivalent, and each sign carries with it "a reciprocal obligation between castes, clans or persons, so signs are not arbitrary."[64] There is no question, for instance, about what loyalty means and how to behave in the presence of a lord. Any infraction, such as acting above one's station, quickly is agreed upon by all as a wrongful use of signs and is punished immediately.[65] Just as there are no excesses in terms of signs and their meanings, so there is no excess in any aspect of society. In terms of production—a notion that will become critical in the later stages of simulation—only the excesses of production are exchanged in a true needs-based economy. In all aspects, signs are correlated directly to reality, and there are few excesses either in terms of products or symbols.

Counterfeits

The counterfeits stage is the stage at which the first level of simulation occurs. Historically, it extends from the Renaissance of the fifteenth century to the Industrial Revolution of the eighteenth century and signals the advent of the *"arbitrary* sign."[66] Baudrillard calls this period the era of *counterfeits*[67] because signs in this stage are produced "signifieds" without a direct relationship between signs and reality. Instead of "linking two persons in an unbreakable reciprocity, the signifier starts referring back to the disenchanted universe of the signified, common denominator of the real world toward which no one has any obligation." Thus, the signs in this era are only counterfeit—they mimic or copy the symbolic obligations of feudal societies and move from reflecting a basic reality to copying it, masking it, or perverting it: "It is with the Renaissance, then, that the forgery is born along with the natural, ranging from the deceptive finery on people's backs to the prosthetic fork" or fake limb.[68] Because the signs are false, however, a difference always can be detected between semblance and reality.

The counterfeits era is the beginning of a new bourgeois society, characterized by "emancipated signs" in which all classes are able to participate.[69] Signs are non-discriminatory, universally available, and produced according to demand, and Baudrillard cites status, wealth, and prestige as examples of meanings produced or constructed as part of the growth of the new bourgeois society that are available for exchange. Although these signs, as Baudrillard explains, would "dearly love to rediscover an *obligation* in its reference to the real," such obligatory relationships no longer hold.[70] In other words, there never again can be the clear relationship between sign and referent or symbol and reality.

Baudrillard uses the figure of the automaton to capture the nature of signs in this era. The root word *automat* means self-acting or self-regulating, and, for Baudrillard, it is a figure that appears to imitate the actions of humans. Everyone knows, however, that the automaton—whether puppet or machine—is only an imitation of the real human being. In the era of counterfeits, signs are recognized as mimicking reality, but there still is a connection between the two spheres.

Production

Baudrillard's third era is the reign of production, an era in which the technical principle has the upper hand. This is the era of the Industrial Revolution and is the period that best reflects Marx's theories of production and labor. In this phase, production overtakes the symbol and governs the appearance and replication of signs. Baudrillard uses the figure of the robot to clarify this shift in how signs function. What is important about the robot is precisely that it produces or works. In contrast to the earlier period of the counterfeits, where the automaton was the analogue of the human being, the robot is the functioning metaphor here because a robot can be more efficient and capable than the human itself. With the robot, there is no "semblance or dissemblance"—no comparison with reality—because the robot can assume full human functioning.[71] In fact, a whole series of robots—

identical machines—can be created to duplicate human activity and movement exactly. The capacity to duplicate human functioning is crucial, according to Baudrillard, because it means that signs and the ability to control the code have overtaken production itself, and the relationship between production and signs is reversed. In other words, the equivalent of the human being can be duplicated repeatedly, creating an entire level of signs that no longer refers to but surpasses the human.

Simulation

Baudrillard's fourth stage in his typology of signs is simulation. He has chosen the word *simulation* for this level—even though it is also the label he selects for his entire chronology—because it represents the epitome and domination of the process of simulation as it is realized in contemporary society. Whereas the automaton was primary in the counterfeits era and the robot is the metaphor for the production stage, the clone is the figure Baudrillard chooses to suggest the basic principles underlying this final era of simulation.[72] The clone is the representative figure because it does not represent the human but, in fact, creates it by using the model of the human contained in DNA. Just as DNA contains the smallest indivisible elements that comprise the human code and are necessary to create the human, so the bits of information in the digitized code now dominate every area of society. Everything is inscribed, decoded, and produced from discrete units stored digitally in memory banks and command modules. That any given thing can be reproduced through technology by reference to its model or code means it can be reproduced an indefinite number of times, thus giving the model itself prominence over reality.

Simulation actually takes over the original object because of its capacity to reproduce that object.[73] At this point, the system begins to reverse itself, with effects preceding causes. In this case, the model generates the real rather than the reverse. The cycle set up by the constant reproduction according to the code results in the perpetual recreation of the same models and generalization from those models rather than from the real.[74] The model substitutes signs of the real for the real itself: "Never again will the real have to be produced."[75]

The dominance of digitality in the era of simulation has implications for all aspects of communication. The focus of interaction no longer lies with human languages, characterized by complex syntactic structures and possibilities. Interaction now depends on a binary system of stimulus/response, which is the format available in a system in which there is "minimal separation" between two terms or bits of information.[76] Following the model or code produces exactly what is expected, as happens with a stimulus/response format of any kind. Tests are the epitome of this kind of simulation, according to Baudrillard, because the question induces the answer, which is *"design-ated"* in advance. The test "triggers response mechanisms in accordance with stereotypes or analytic models," and the test taker responds appropriately.[77]

When there is virtually no gap between two bits of information in the stimulus/response cycle, the message becomes shorter. The smaller the gap between question and answer, the more the process of signification is reduced to the capacity to produce reactions to a predetermined range of appropriate stimuli. This miniscule management of bits of information dominates reality itself, creating a drastic shift in how signs function in relation to the real. The sign is totally "liberated" from reference to reality. It has its own pure simulacrum because it has the capacity to produce it.

The four stages of signs represent a shift from signs correlated to reality in Baudrillard's first stage, symbolic order, to signs that point to something in the counterfeits era to signs that point to nothing in the present order of simulation. A simple example of how humans change skin color demonstrates the evolution of these layers of simulacra from reality to pure simulation. In pre-simulation societies, skin color simply was; there was no attempt to change it. If it happened to change naturally because of exposure to the sun, that was simply an expectation about reality. There was a direct correspondence between reality and the skin-color changes that occurred. In the next era, the counterfeits, tanning is a process to be deliberately achieved and is one layer removed from that available by means of natural sun exposure. In the third level of production, sun lamps and chemicals produce the effect that the sun once did, but there no longer is any real or direct connection between the sun and the tan that is achieved. The last level of simulation is realized when humans "intervene at the genetic level to get that bronzed look!"—when there is no longer any need of the sun or artificial means for achieving a tan.[78] Michael Jackson may be the closest example currently available to the possibilities of this fourth stage of simulation, according to Baudrillard: "Michael Jackson had his face redone, his hair straightened, his skin lightened. In short, he constructed himself in minute detail. This made him as innocent and pure [as a] child, the artificial androgyne. . . . He/she is a prosthesis-child, an embryo of all the dreamed up forms of mutation which would deliver us from race and sex."[79]

For Baudrillard, the implications of these levels of simulation extend far beyond suntans. He offers as one example the decision of the Filipino government in 1971 to return the remaining Tasaday people—members of an undisturbed stone-age culture that recently had been discovered—"to their primitive state, out of reach of colonists, tourists and ethnologists." In fact, however, the anthropologists were not actually returning the Tasaday to their pure state but rather to one of simulation. The Tasaday stand for Indians in an undiscovered state before their discovery by anthropologists but never truly can return to that state after their exposure to the outside world: "The Indian thereby driven back into the ghetto, into the glass coffin of virgin forest, becomes the simulation model for all conceivable Indians *before ethnology*."[80] The Tasaday in their intact, undisturbed state represent the first of Baudrillard's stages. When discovered by scientists and taken to stand for a pristine and undisturbed state, they represent the second stage. The third stage is the one in which they are returned to the forest to stand not for themselves but for an invented state of virginality. Finally, at the fourth level, the Indians literally or metaphorically are museumized or frozen in time in an environment outside of their own. Although this did not happen with the Tasaday, it did with another Indian—Ishi—the last remaining member of the Yahi tribe, who spent the last five years of his life living at the anthropology museum of the University of California.[81]

Disneyland offers another example of a contemporary application of Baudrillard's layers of simulation. Designed as a constructed fantasy—an imaginary world one level removed from reality with its worlds of pirates, the frontier, and fantasyland—Disneyland suggests the counterfeits, the first order of simulation. On a second level, however, Disneyland "is meant to be an infantile world, in order to make us believe that the adults are elsewhere, in the 'real' world, and to conceal the fact that real childishness is every-where, particularly amongst those adults who go there to act the child in or-der to foster illusions as to their real childishness."[82] The reconstruction of Disneyland Paris in France suggests the final stage of simulacra; the real thing can be reproduced anywhere at anytime.[83]

In every case—whether a suntan, the extinction of an Indian tribe, or Disneyland—the layers of signs in play conceal that reality does not exist. There is nothing but a "network of endless, unreal circulation" that has nothing to do with reality.[84] Baudrillard summarizes the notion that the evo-lution of signs has removed the human from direct contact with reality: "We have already seen signs of the first order, complex signs and rich in illusion, change, with the machines, into crude signs, dull, industrial, repetitive, echo-less, operational and efficacious. What a mutation, even more radical still, with signals of the code, illegible, with no gloss possible, buried like pro-grammatic matrices light-years away in the depths of the 'biological' body— black boxes where all the commandments, all the answers ferment!"[85]

For the human experience and lifeworld, the consequences of simula-tion are enormous. The "natural" or "real" previously could be discovered in what was clearly artificial and counterfeit, but today there is only the "bril-liant ambiance of the simulacra."[86] Everything is artificial—a simulation— far removed from reality. The mass media have considerable bearing on the development and maintenance of this process of simulation and its effects on human society.

The Mass Media

The proliferation and dominance of the media radically transform society and the possibilities for human interaction within it, according to Baudrillard. Like McLuhan, Baudrillard accepts the basic notion that the medium is the message. The real effect of railways is not the particular journey that is made possible but the vision of the world that results. Similarly, just as the format of the book produces a particular kind of culture, so do media of any kind: "in the long run *it is not the ideas which are carried in books which are important in themselves but the discipline they impose.*[87] Baudrillard offers other examples of this phenomenon from contemporary technology: "Television already shapes the angle, the depth and the context which the body uses to select and absorb visual information. Radio produces a similar effect upon the human ear. Computer technology presents simulations of movement which the body already uses to interpret density and mobility." "We believe that we bend the world to our will by means of technology," notes Baudrillard. "In fact it is the world that imposes its will upon us with the aid of technology, and the surprise occasioned by this turning of the tables is considerable."[88]

A basic function of the media is the creation of representations or simulations—reproduced versions of reality. Unlike print or face-to-face interactions, the new media employ the montage principle of film to create a unique reality dominated by simulations or representations that give the appearance of reality. Reality is now "fashioned and ratified" through representational modes of information[89] as the mass media crowd out the world to the extent that we relate to them as the immediate context of reality. For Baudrillard, the "lives of the stars seen on the screen or the 'normal' family selling bread or frozen foods in the TV ads seem real; the lives of viewers seem pale shadows by comparison."[90]

Another feature of contemporary media is that they deal with information rather than with communication. Information is simply a system of emission and reception, while communication, as Baudrillard conceptualizes it, involves a symbolic exchange. Baudrillard distinguishes between communication and information by elaborating on the notion of digitality involved in his orders of simulation. Information consists of encoded digitality that continually "circulates, moves around, makes its circuits"—always favoring circulation over transcendence or discovery.[91] Information depends on an instant replication of an event and its immediate transcription without delay: an "immediate totting up, itemizing and sorting of all these exchanges, precisely as occurs with writing on word-processors."[92] There is no genuine exchange possible with the media; there is no response and thus no responsibility.[93] Baudrillard sees this kind of information as obscene because everything "is given and returned without delay, without that suspense, minute as it may be, which constitutes the temporal rhythm of exchange."[94]

For genuine symbolic exchange or communication to occur, there must be reciprocal space for the interaction and the possibility of shared pleasure in the exchange. Time and rhythm are critical in symbolic exchange, and these are missing in information with its instantaneous interchange of knowledge: "It is, precisely, time which separates the two symbolic moments and holds their resolution in abeyance." Baudrillard suggests that the giving and receiving of gifts exemplify communication in contrast to information. Gift-giving functions according to ritual with agreed-upon norms and expectations that have implications not only for the way the gift is given, received, and reciprocated but for the human relationship involved. Following the

giving of a gift, there must be a time lag between the act and the reciproca-
tion on the part of the recipient of the gift: The rule is "that what is given
should never be returned immediately. It has to be returned, but never right
away. That is a serious, mortal insult. There must never be immediate interaction."[95] Baudrillard also contrasts the exchange of gifts with what occurs
when one person has the power to give "and to whom no return can be
made." That individual has a social monopoly that upsets the reciprocal nature of gift giving, and "the social process is out of balance."[96]

Communication—symbolic exchange represented for Baudrillard by the
gift-giving ritual—has become largely irrelevant precisely because it cannot
compete with the speed of presentation of information. For today's culture,
communication "is too slow; it is an effect of slowness; it proceeds through
contact and speech" and cannot keep up with a culture in which everything
"must occur instantaneously."[97] Furthermore, no response can be made to
mediated communication: "speech occurs in such a way that there is no possibility of a return."[98]

What is significant to Baudrillard about the two systems—the information that characterizes the media and the communication that carries values
of human symbolic exchange—is that they cannot interact with one another:
"there is no relationship between a system of meaning and a system of simulation."[99] The system of meaning, or communication, actually refers to something, while the system of information never does. What Baudrillard mourns
in the shift from communication to information is the loss of denotation or of
a designated referent that comprises reality. The concept of meaning, which
depends on stable boundaries and fixed structures to achieve a shared consensus, no longer is possible. There is "no way 'back' to the real"—no way to
have a stable correspondence between a thing and what it means.[100]

The lack of interaction between the spheres of information and communication, however, does not mean that the mass media have no impact on
reality. Indeed, just the opposite is the case. There never again can be a reality apart from the mass media "because we will never in [the] future be
able to separate reality from its statistical, simulative projection in the media."[101] Thus, there is no way of knowing "if an advertisement or opinion
poll has had a real influence on individual or collective wills, but we will
never know either what would have happened if there had been no opinion
poll or advertisement."[102]

Baudrillard uses the metaphor of the Möbius strip to show how intri-
cately humans are caught up in the information system of the media, even if
direct interaction with the media is not possible. A Möbius strip is a circular,
never-ending band formed by taking one end of a strip and rotating it 180
degrees to connect with its opposite end. A flat surface is constructed that
nonetheless shifts planes as it moves through the strip "with a peculiar conti-
guity of near and far, inside and outside, object and subject within the same
spiral."[103] The relationship between the masses and the media shifts, just as
the surface on a Möbius strip does. On the one hand, individuals are told to

constitute themselves as autonomous subjects, conscious of and responsible for their actions: "to express ourselves at any price, to vote, to produce, to decide, to speak, to participate, to play the game."[104] But equally plausible and sensible is the opposite response—the renunciation of the position of subject and of meaning and the decision not to respond at all. Humans move between these two positions in a never-ending cycle: "the media are the vehicle for the simulation which belongs to the system and for the simulation which destroys the system . . . exactly like a Möbius strip. There is no alternative to this, no logical resolution."[105] An example is the 2000 presidential election in the United States, in which the media prematurely declared Al Gore the winner of Florida's electoral votes. If, from the beginning, the media had declared the state too close to call, the hand counts might have proceeded with less objection. The media simultaneously constructed the conundrum and, with their constant coverage, made resolution of the problem by any logical means virtually impossible.

Although the mass media often are taken to be simply sources of information, their pervasiveness creates changes in the ways in which reality is experienced in that they destabilize "the real and the true."[106] As a result, humans face a kind of uncertainty that has not been present before: "it is a question here of a completely new species of uncertainty, which results not from the *lack* of information but from information itself and even from an *excess* of information. It is information itself which produces uncertainty, and so this uncertainty, unlike the traditional uncertainty which could always be resolved, is irreparable."[107] Subjected to information of all kinds, humans no longer can separate their true desires from those projected on them by the media, and they plunge "into a state of stupor" about their desires, choices, and opinions: "This is the clearest result of the whole media environment, of the information which makes demands on us from all sides."[108]

The Commodity Culture

Baudrillard sees the mass media as creating a commodity culture that increases the separation of individuals from the referents of signs by organizing every possible behavior—tastes, choices, preferences, and needs—as a series of responses to predetermined stimuli. Consequently, individuals no longer can identify their own desires because those desires are almost entirely constructed by the media. There is no longer "the personal transaction of an individual with the view to satisfying a concrete need" but a "response that engages the individual in the collective ritual of consumption."[109]

Baudrillard begins his discussion of consumer culture with an analysis and deconstruction of Marx's thesis of the centrality of production to capitalism. According to Marx, not only are objects produced to be bought and sold, but the producers of these objects—workers or labor—also are commodities on the labor market. The individual human dimension and relationship between consumer and producer are lost as workers are further removed or alienated from the products they produce and from the consumers of those products. Baudrillard believes that a Marxist analysis no longer is relevant in the contemporary mass-mediated climate because "'consumption' has grasped the whole of life."[110] In its place is a new and unprecedented phase of capitalism in which there is no link between consumption and production.

Consumption is *"not* that passive process of absorption and appropriation which is contrasted to the supposedly active mode of production. Rather, consumption now precedes production. Humans used to work "towards something—a car, a refrigerator, a home"—and possessions were rewards. Today, with the ubiquitous availability of credit, objects are consumed before they are earned and anticipate the work they represent.[111] Objects and the satisfaction of needs are the preconditions of consumption, not the end of consumption, and "consumption is *the virtual totality of all objects and messages ready-constituted as a more or less coherent discourse.* If it has any meaning at all, consumption means *an activity* consisting of the systematic manipulation of signs."[112] To consume an object is not so much about consuming that product but about consuming a meaning. The product is sold by grafting onto it meanings with no necessary connection to the product. The basic process of consumption is recognizable in the advertising campaign by Pepsi that featured the slogan, "Drink Pepsi/Get Stuff." The appeal is directed to consumption alone—to acquiring more objects—and the meaning comes from their acquisition. There is no need even to reveal or know what those objects are that will be gotten by buying and drinking Pepsi.

The emphasis on consumption has an impact on the nature of culture in several ways. One consequence is a certain homogenization as individual differences are forfeited in favor of a system that values the consumption of objects over particular objects consumed. What appear to be differences within a culture really are marginal and superficial differences in style and status at best, making the true range of possibilities extremely narrow. Teenagers who insist on wearing Tommy Hilfiger T-shirts rather than ones from Old Navy or who select Nike over another brand of shoes fail to realize that they are, in fact, consuming the same object and, rather than meeting their own needs and desires, they are meeting those of the company, for whom they provide free advertising: "The individual is summoned to choose from a range of objects, and a range of questions, and range of credit companies."[113] The options, however, are highly limited and structured, creating a homogenization of desire. Baudrillard uses the example of the climate-controlled shopping mall that is the same the world over to illustrate the limited options available in commodity culture. Although the mall seems to provide an almost infinite number of choices, it really offers the same set of options. Even the climate, which Baudrillard describes as "'ambiance' in a perpetual Springtime,"[114] is identical worldwide.

A second consequence of the consumer ideology in the age of commodification is the way in which the ideology produces a homogenization of behavior. The consumer who is pressured into trying the latest commodity—

into entering "into the spirit of the latest gadget"[115] in order not to miss out on a recent trend or fashion—may feel personally and uniquely addressed by the advertiser because of the appeals to status and class that are offered. Those who are able to buy a Rolex watch or a Porsche, for instance, feel special and unique. What is distinctive, however, is not the uniqueness of the consumer but that, for the first time in history, these signs are universally recognized and understood because of advertising. Everyone around the world is aware of the same products, even though they may not be capable of purchasing them. Differences previously afforded by nationality, birth, and class are diminished as everyone is socialized to the same code. The images are "self loading, self perpetuating, self referring and they suck everyone into their orbit."[116] On the surface, then, advertising seems to appeal to individual consumers and their personal and status needs, but, in fact, the ideology produces the integration and regulation of the group: "*it already invokes a profound monotony, a uniformula*" among the consuming masses.[117] That consumers are unconscious of the intensity and pervasiveness of this homogeneity makes the hegemony of consumerism even more complete.

The Centrality of the Object

Because objects are critical to the consumption that is fueled by the pervasive nature of the mass media, the object is central to Baudrillard's analysis: "what really appeals to me . . . is to be completely immersed in objects, to have started from objects, from an obsession with them."[118] He is interested in "such questions as how objects are experienced, what needs other than functional ones they answer, what mental structures are interwoven with—and contradict—their functional structures."[119] What is especially significant about objects in contemporary society is that they are abstracted from their social contexts. The object no longer is "an expression emerging from a relationship of symbolic exchange" but is an "interchangeable unit . . . a discrete element in a chain of signification, infinitely transmissible and recombinable."[120]

Baudrillard suggests that objects fulfill two functions—use and possession—both of which demonstrate the chains of signification inherent in objects as signs: "Thus every object has two functions: One of being practical, the other of being possessed."[121] Because there is no longer a natural connection between needs and production, the object is less important for its use value—although this still pertains—than for how it structures humans' experience of the world. Baudrillard chooses the watch as an example that typifies the twofold way in which objects are experienced. On the one hand, the watch functions to provide information "about objective time," but as an object humans can possess, it also becomes an object of consumption. "Not only has knowing the time become a staple diet or reassurance for civilised people," Baudrillard notes, "but also 'having' the time in an object of one's own, having it continually registered before one's eyes."[122]

When humans interact with objects, they inevitably are consuming the two functions of use and possession and, in both cases, believe themselves to be in charge of those objects and the values they embody. In fact, humans are also becoming objectified themselves, subject to the demands of objects on them. They are becoming the "object of the objects," unable to see the hidden structure they are purchasing with the object and to which they are acquiescing.[123] Baudrillard summarizes this objectification process: "We flatter ourselves that we discover the object and conceive it as waiting there meekly to be discovered. But perhaps the cleverer party here is not the one we think. What if it were the object which discovered us in all this? What if it were the object which invented us?" Baudrillard suggests that viruses such as smallpox and AIDS that have plagued the world "discover us at least as much as we discovered them, with all the consequences that follow."[124]

Baudrillard notes with particular fascination the role of kitsch, gizmos, and pets as examples of objects whose use function is purely symbolic—there is no real utility to these objects. Kitsch, which Baudrillard defines as "[k]nickknacks, rustic odds-and-ends, souvenirs, lampshades, and African masks," is perfectly useless,[125] while gizmos, whatsits, or "thingumajigs" are most important for the "vague and limitless functionality"[126] they suggest: "The electrical whatsit that extracts stones from fruit or some new vacuum-cleaner accessory for getting under sideboards are perhaps in the end not especially practical, but they do serve to reinforce the belief that for every need there is a possible mechanical answer, that every practical (and even psychological) problem may be foreseen, forestalled, resolved in advance by means of a technical object that is rational and adapted—perfectly adapted."[127] The functionality and technology that are signified by the gizmo play with the idea of function, but the functionality pales compared to the value of the gadget: "if we can agree that the object of consumption is characterized by a kind of *functional uselessness* (since what is consumed is precisely something other than the 'useful') then *the gadget is indeed the truth of the object in consumer society*. In this sense, *anything can become a gadget*; and everything is one, potentially."[128]

The role played by kitsch and gizmos suggests that signification is moving away from functionality into pure symbolicity. Although objects "do indeed serve specific purposes at times, they are much more commonly good for everything and nothing, and in that case their true utility lies in the very fact that they 'might always come in useful.' "[129] Kitsch and gadgets demonstrate how objects function by parodying functionality because they embody the constant simulation of function with no real practical referent. The true value of kitsch and gadgets is that they show the processes of simulation and acculturation at work, both of which are governing codes of contemporary culture.[130]

The use value of an object does not end with the object itself. What also is purchased along with an object is an entire system of objects that maintains the cycle of consumerism. This ongoing extension of commodification explains why objects are offered in stacks, displays, or collections in stores. When one object is purchased from a stack or collection, what is being bought is an entire network of objects for which the collection stands: It "invokes a psychological chain reaction in the consumer who peruses it, inventories it, and grasps it as a total category." "Washing machine, refrigerator, dishwasher, have different meanings when grouped together than each one has alone," Baudrillard suggests. "The display window, the advertisement, the manufacturer, and the *brand name* here play an essential role in imposing a coherent and collective vision, like an almost inseparable totality."[131] The referential capacity inherent in such a system is exemplified in advertising, which no longer refers to real objects but instead refers "*one sign to another, one object to another, one consumer to another.*"[132] The connections among signs make more likely the purchase of other objects in that system.

Collecting objects also is important beyond its role in a system of display encouraged to promote even more consumption. Collecting—whether antiques, stamps, coins, or miniature cars and whether done formally or informally—involves a process of ranking, sorting, and classifying. The individual assumes a subject position in the process in relation to the object—the one doing the arranging and classifying of the objects. Humans "objectify" these collections of objects, which in turn become ways of reflecting themselves in an idealized way.

Objects fulfill an important function in the reflection process because they accumulate and reflect a particular image back to their owner but never contradict that image. As Baudrillard explains, "objects are the only entities in existence that can genuinely coexist, because the differences between them do not set them against one another, as happens in the case of living beings: instead they all converge submissively upon me and accumulate with the greatest of ease in my consciousness."[133] Even more important for Baudrillard with regard to the object in a collection is that "I can look at it without it looking at me,"[134] making the relationship between human and object the ideal relationship. Thus, the relationship is an unnatural one in which objects function to preserve a static, unchanging image of the human being they surround.

Domestic pets represent the epitome of the objectifying process that is central to possession because, although pets are living beings, they are turned into objects "where subjectivity can be fulfilled in complete tranquility" but with none of the difficulties of other living beings. Their role, according to Baudrillard, is to "exalt rather than limit my person."[135] In this sense, they are like all objects. That they often are neutered makes this objectification even more complete in that they are stripped of their sexuality for the benefit of their human owners. For Baudrillard, objectification is obtained "at the cost of a real or symbolic castration that they can play, at the side of their owners, the role of regulators . . . a role eminently played by all the objects that surround us, for the object is itself the perfect domestic animal."[136]

Whether in terms of utility or possession, what is most important about objects in today's consumer society is that a necessary connection no longer exists between the object and the meanings it has in society. Objects function as signs in a series of increasingly abstract realms and are not simply commodities to be desired, produced, bought, and sold. They also become part of the more abstract discourse of consumption, where they are subject to codes and norms that are increasingly governed by the mass media. That a growing number of the commodities produced are not objects in the tangible sense adds yet another layer of abstraction. Objects such as information "cannot actually be handled." Their purchase and exchange occur only in coded or symbolic form, and their existence is "virtual."[137]

Consumption and the mass media converge in excessive simulation, resulting in an "ascent to extremes" and an "intensifying spiral" at which meanings collapse in on themselves in a process of implosion.[138] Baudrillard describes this implosion as a "contraction," a "fantastic telescoping, a collapsing . . . into one another," an "absorption of meaning."[139] Baudrillard uses the term *ecstasy* to suggest the quality of objects in a system in which the process of excessive consumption that results in implosion is the point. Ecstasy is "the quality of any body that spins until all its sense disappears, until it shines out as a pure and empty form."[140] He also describes the basic state of contemporary culture as *hypertely*, a condition that literally means an extreme degree of excess not based on utility. Baudrillard turns this process into a noun—*hypertelia*—to describe contemporary culture based on the production/consumption process.[141]

The basis of hypertelia is that there is no relation between needs and the purchase of objects to meet those needs. In such a situation, commodification moves in the direction of the superlative toward "the truer than true, the more beautiful than beautiful, the realer than real."[142] In today's world of extremes, meanings do not oppose one another in the dialectic sense—the true and false, the beautiful and ugly—but each meaning is "hyped" or exaggerated into the hyperreal, with each response moving into pure excess. Things are hyperreal, more real than real, and hypertelic, more final than final. There "appears to be no way to turn back to a previous condition of less than *hyper*."[143] This exaggeration or "passion of intensification, of escalation, of mounting power, of ecstasy" means that all objects and systems have absorbed the energy of their opposites, moving toward ever more essential simulations—simulations that contain reality but also embody the ultimate in terms of the fake. Baudrillard describes this process when he asks his readers to "imagine something beautiful that has absorbed all the energy of the ugly: you have fashion. . . . Imagine truth having absorbed all the energy of the false: you have simulation."[144]

Baudrillard sees television as an excellent example of the excesses of contemporary culture, spiraling in on itself until it has lost all meaning and simply radiates as pure and empty form: "Television doesn't even constitute an image. . . . It's a screen and nothing but a screen, and I think that is how we perceive it as without consequence, no emotion, no passion."[145] The screen is the absence of information; it "presents a perpetual void that we are invited to fill."[146] For Baudrillard, the lack of an image on TV stems from television technology itself, which is a series of dots that come together to form what is seen as an image. In fact, there really is no image except that which the human eye creates. According to Baudrillard, nothing on screens—whether television screens or computer screens—"is ever intended to be deciphered in any depth: rather, it is supposed to be explored instantaneously."[147] With television, what is lost is the perspective of the "spectator's distance from the stage—all theatrical conventions are gone."[148] Baudrillard contrasts television with the cinema, which he calls "absolutely irreplaceable" because "that quality of image, of light, that quality of myth, that hasn't gone."[149]

Baudrillard suggests that "the true message delivered by the media of radio and TV, one decoded and 'consumed' at a deep unconscious level, is not the manifest content of sounds and images but a coercive system" divorced from any possibility of reflection and judgment.[150] With sequences of meaning collapsed in the instantaneous nature of the media, the option to step back from the media no longer exists, and the viewer is left only with fascination, a perspective of total immersion and involvement. Where the world used to offer a mirror that could reflect back and allow for contemplation, perspective, and evaluation—transcendence of some kind—television only invites participation: "One is in front of a screen; one is no longer in front of the mirror: it no longer reflects. We are in the screen stage. . . . There's no longer any transcendence in the gaze; there's no longer any transcendence of judgment. There's a kind of participation, coagulation, proliferation of messages and signs etc. And one is no longer in a state to judge, one no longer has the potential to reflect. . . . This is fascination. It is a form of ecstasy."[151]

Baudrillard uses the metaphor of metastasis to describe the notion of hypertelia and how it functions in today's reality of simulation and commodity. The metastasis of cells throughout the body, as with cancer, is an "undisciplined proliferation" not unlike the proliferation of signs in the culture at large. Hyped elements, whether cancer cells or mediated signs, "correspond to the hyperreality" that characterizes the system.[152] At the same time, the trait of excess is revealed in rebellion against that very condition. The body cells essentially are rebelling against "a genetic *decree*, against the commands . . . of DNA. . . . It is as if the species were fed up with its own definition and had plunged headlong into organic delirium."[153] Thus, hyperreality characterizes the system of excess but also contains the possibilities of resistance—features also shared by Baudrillard's rhetorical strategies.

Responses to Hypertelia

Baudrillard's strategies for interacting in contemporary society exhibit the hyperreality of commodity culture, spiraling out ecstatically into pure form. Although they represent the emptiness of commodity culture, they are not purely negative as strategies. In fact, Baudrillard differs from many theorists who simply disparage the impact of technology on culture and stop there. Although he critiques the layers of simulation divorced from reality that rationality and technology have created, he also sees possibilities in hyperreality itself for imaginative, ironic ways of managing hypertelia that signal a return to strategies from a pre-literate era. Baudrillard refers to the strategies used within the rational paradigm as *banal* and the creative possibilities embedded within them as *fatal*. Banal strategies privilege the human as subject, while fatal ones privilege the object.

According to Baudrillard, the dominance of the subject over the object emerged with the invention of rationality, by which the human subject seeks to make sense of the world by ordering, arranging, and dominating. Rationality exists because humans cannot bear the thought that the world is a "radical illusion," so to keep this hypothesis at bay, they "have to realize the world, give it force of reality, make it exist and signify at all costs, take from it its secret, arbitrary, accidental character, rid it of appearances and extract its meaning, divert it from all predestination and restore it to its end and its maximum efficiency, wrest it from its form to deliver it up to its formula."[154] The process of "literally putting the illusion of the world to death" and making sure that "*nothing will be left to chance*"[155] is, in fact, producing a simulation called *reality*. The world constructed through rationality, however, cannot be real because the world, in fact, is not logical and controllable.

Baudrillard suggests that banal strategies are those that function in the world as ordered and constructed by humans. Banal strategies are instrumental approaches grounded in rationality—those strategies that have governed since humans began to see themselves as subjects with the ability to control the world. These strategies "emanate from the subject, and are posed with all the assumptions of the superiority of the subject in its apparent mastery of the world."[156] By means of banal strategies, the world is brought under control through reason, and the "profusion" of signifiers at work in the world is corralled into an "arranged order."[157] For Baudrillard, obedience is at the heart of the banal because obedience signals acquiescence to the rules of logic imposed on a system.

Baudrillard suggests, however, that there is evidence that the world of rationality is losing its grip precisely because of the simulations produced by technology and mass media. "The whole of our history," he asserts, "bears witness to this machinery of reason, which is itself now coming apart. Our culture of meaning is collapsing beneath the excess of meaning, the culture of reality collapsing beneath the excess of reality, the information culture collapsing beneath the excess of information—the sign and reality sharing a single shroud."[158] In particular, the image of an independent subject acting on the world no longer holds when technology acts on humans to the extent that it does in consumer culture. The growing centrality of the object, then, is a primary indicator of a paradigm shift.

Baudrillard offers statistical polling as an example of the ineffectiveness of rational efforts to bring the world under control: "If in fact you consider the inconclusiveness of polls, the uncertainty of their effects, . . . if you consider that they say whatever they want, that everyone already knows it, doesn't believe, does nothing with them (but always demands ever more of them), their capacity of simultaneously validating contradictory tendencies" is what remains in the end. Baudrillard believes that polls are not taken seriously because humans do not truly believe in their ability to control the world: "No one gives up on destiny; this is why no one believes in statistics."[159]

Baudrillard's alternative is not to lament the decline or impossibility of rationality but to consider alternative worlds, and the world he prefers is one of destiny, fate, and chance in which fatal strategies dominate. He prefers this world because it is the way the world really is. Baudrillard suggests that humans approach this world through different lenses from the rational, and humor is of major importance to this task: "There is something like a humorous providence that sees to the derailing of this all too smoothly running machine."[160] He summarizes the perspective embodied in fatal strategies: "But there is perhaps another, more joyous way of seeing things, and of finally substituting for eternally critical theory an ironic theory."[161]

Fatal strategies are those that are and always have been available in the magic of language—nonrational ways of responding that do not privilege the human as in control of the world. These strategies, which include the absurd, the illusory, the secret, and the senseless,[162] are grounded in fate, destiny, or chance—and thus their name. They are more appropriate to a society in which reality is considered to be a series of collisions, juxtapositions, opportunities, and coincidences. In such a world, humans do not assume the position of subject because the world itself and its objects exert control, and "we don't know whether the object or the world isn't just toying with us. Just as, with thought, we don't know if we're thinking the world or if the world is thinking us."[163] The object challenges the subject, constructing a world in which the game—chance or destiny—governs.

Baudrillard prefers the fatal strategies of the nonrational universe over the banal because they provide an alternative perspective to the rational paradigm and suggest other ways than reason to manage and cope with the commodified, technological culture the world has become. He suggests that "we can take the view that there is a double game going on: on the one hand, we play at mastering the world through our technologies . . . but on the other hand we might, without knowing it, be partners in another game"—a game in which humans are not in control.[164] Seeking "to side with the object, to take up the cause of the object,"[165] Baudrillard suggests how different the nonrational or fatal perspective is from the one offered by the rational paradigm: "the only difference between a banal theory and a fatal theory is that in the former the subject always believes itself to be more clever than the object, while in the latter the object is always taken to be more clever, more cynical, more ingenious than the subject, which it awaits at every turn. The metamorphoses, tactics, and strategies of the object exceed the subject's understanding."[166] The fatal strategies that Baudrillard describes manage and resist the world of technical rationality and bring the world of illusion back into play. They provide for what Baudrillard calls the *revenge of the object* or the *revenge of the crystal*. One of Baudrillard's books is titled *The Revenge of the Crystal*, with the word *crystal* representing the object as Baudrillard views it.

A crystal is a hyperreal object in its own right; by definition, it is more transparent and heavier than ordinary glass. It is, in effect, "glassier than glass."[167]

Baudrillard sees parallels between the contemporary world in which fatal strategies have the upper hand and earlier, preliterate societies in which the universe was conceptualized as active, passionate, and magical, to be coped with through ritual and ceremony rather than controlled through rationality. The world, in these earlier societies, was a "cruel theatre of charm and enchantment"[168] in which destiny arrived "without having been produced."[169] Baudrillard anticipates a return to this worldview in the relationship he envisions between banal and fatal strategies in which the banal strategies of reason contain within them fatal possibilities.

Baudrillard suggests that the banal can be read as containing the fatal because of the possibilities of resistance inherent in them. For Baudrillard, the movement from banal to fatal or from obedience to disobedience is a result of the hypertelic excesses that characterize society. As everything spirals into excess, the banal moves into overbanality, and the very excesses involved contain strategies that can resist rationality and privilege the fatal. Baudrillard uses the term *obscenity* to capture these strategies of excess because exaggeration is at the core of the obscene; the shock of obscenity comes because of the exaggeration of the lewd into the grotesque. With the exaggeration of the banal, "all structures are turned inside out and exhibited, all operations rendered visible."[170] The visibility that accompanies excess is precisely what allows banal strategies to move into fatal ones.

Baudrillard offers, among many examples, obesity, terrorism, and hyperconformity to illustrate his point that banal strategies contain the disobedience that can transform them. Obesity, as is true of much of contemporary culture, is about excess. The obese individual exemplifies a system in which there are "no more limits." Obscenity is a process of making the body more than visible, a process in which "unrestrained redundancy prevails." Baudrillard elaborates by making a comparison between obesity and the commodity system. Like the commodity system itself, obese individuals display "something of the system, of its empty inflation"; they are "bloated with information they can never deliver."[171] Just as the obese body does not stop in its pursuit of the ultimate extension, so modernity, "in its frenzy to store and memorize everything, to pass, in the most total uselessness, to the very limits of the inventory of the world and of information," demonstrates the same "monstrous potentiality" that continues without end.[172] Obesity is about absorbing surrounding space and taking in the objects surrounding the body. Obese individuals are "pregnant, symbolically speaking, with all the objects from which they have been unable to separate, or those from which they have not found enough distance to love. They do not separate the body from the non-body."[173]

Contrary to typical stereotypes, however, the obese "have no complexes about how they live, insouciant, as if there was not even an ego ideal left for them. They are not ridiculous and they know it."[174] The body sets its own boundaries of excess and shows "a kind of release" from "all pride of representation."[175] Thus, while the obese demonstrate limitless increase and absorption—characteristics of the current age of excess—at the same time, the obese body offers its own form of truth and resistance to this conceptualization. The obese disobey the expectations about the body and allow it to define who they are. In their excess, the obese reproduce contemporary society but, in that excess, they also disobey it.

Terrorism is another example of a response or resistance to excess that suggests the ways in which the obedience at the core of banality can become disobedience to the entire system. Like obesity, terrorism thrives on excess and lack of meaning. It does not have a productive goal, such as opposing state violence or engaging in acts designed to achieve liberation. Rather, terrorist violence is directed against the excesses that have taken all meaning from society. Terrorism is generated by an absence of events, creating in the void an image that can be captured and broadcast by the media, a point Baudrillard emphasizes by noting that the media often are the first to arrive at terrorist events.[176] Terrorism, like all hijackings and hold-ups, is "inscribed in advance in the decoding and orchestration rituals of the media, anticipated in their mode of presentation and possible consequences." Terrorist acts "function as a set of signs dedicated exclusively to their recurrence as signs, and no longer to their 'real' goal at all."[177] Like obese individuals, terrorist activity is a perfect outcome of a simulation society, but it also offers a kind of resistance to it. Terrorism plays with the media, offering randomness instead of predictability and privileging acts and objects over humans.

Baudrillard also discusses hyperconformity on the part of the masses as an example of the banal and its transformation into the fatal. By hyperconformity, he means the conception of the masses as nonparticipatory and acquiescent. The masses often are conceptualized as "silent majorities," suggesting that they are dominated by the cultural producers who feed them the latest commodities. But a closer look reveals the resistant possibilities of this stance. For the masses, the strategy of hyperconformity often translates into silence or indifference; they deliberately choose not to respond to the pollsters and producers who solicit them. Baudrillard attributes to the masses not alienation but a clear sense of purpose. The masses "know with certainty that they don't need to pass judgment on themselves or on the world, that they don't have to will, know, or desire. The deepest wish is perhaps the wish to hand one's desire over to another."[178]

The masses leave all issues of desire and judgment to the "professionals"—that's what they "are there for." Choice is, after all, an obligation, and the masses are happy to "delegate the faculty of choice to someone else, in a sort of game of irresponsibility, ironic challenge, sovereign lack of will, or secret ruse." They simply decide "to leave it to the advertising or information systems to 'persuade' them, to make a choice for them."[179] Baudrillard summarizes the process by which the hyperconformity of the masses effects a transformation of the banal into the fatal: "All of advertising and information, all of the entire political class are there to tell us what we want, to tell the masses what they want—and we basically assume this massive transfer of responsibility with joy, because it is simply neither obvious, nor of great interest to know, to will, to have faculties, or desires."[180] The masses, then, seduce the advertisers, choosing to play a different game.

Hyperconformity and the abrogation of responsibility that accompanies it are considered appropriate and powerful choices by Baudrillard—much more complex and interesting than their silence appears to be on the surface. Like obesity and terrorism, hyperconformity is consistent with the contemporary consumer culture, which creates the lackluster response in the first place and also contains the roots of its resistance. Although Baudrillard is pessimistic about the layers of simulation and empty symbolicity that constitute contemporary culture, he also recognizes the paradoxical, ironic possibilities that lie just under the surface of this culture.

The specific fatal strategy Baudrillard privileges for responding to the conditions of the current society is the challenge. The challenge contrasts with a rational world in which laws and contracts—concrete evidence of the rational world—prevail. It depends on "an obligation to respond . . . on the basis of its own rhythms; the rule of this exchange is never explicitly formulated or communicated. A law, then, is explicit and controlled; the rule of the challenge is implicit, immanent, immediate and inevitable."[181] Baudrillard suggests that when offered a challenge, individuals generally accept it without much prompting. An element of "madness" or "mystery" distinguishes the challenge from the contractual responses that form the basis of rationality. The challenge sets up the players as partners in a kind of special pact that is outside of formal contracts, structures, or philosophies,[182] creating a kind of exchange that cannot fully be understood, programmed, or coded but that nonetheless is an extremely powerful kind of interaction.

For Baudrillard, seduction is an exemplary type of challenge. Baudrillard's concept of seduction "is highly technical and involves games with signs" and applies to far more contexts than the persuasion of someone to engage in sexual intercourse.[183] Seduction consists of playing with appearances and is a "soft alternative" to traditional efforts to undermine, subvert, or resist. It is a form of exchange that stays on the surface and depends on charms and rituals that lie outside of rationality. Seduction, then, operates in the world of fate and destiny—a world purged of denotation and sense in the way rationality constructs it. Seduction is not, for Baudrillard, "merely an immoral, frivolous, superficial, and superfluous process, limited to the realm of signs and appearances, devoted to pleasure."[184] It is a powerful way of operating in the world.

Seduction challenges the dominant mode of reality by challenging the linearity of that reality. The instrumentality of strategies of reason grounded in cause and effect proceed by steps and stages, but seduction "is an endless refrain. There is no active or passive mode in seduction, no subject or object, no interior or exterior: seduction plays on both sides, and there is no frontier separating them. One cannot seduce others, if one has not oneself been seduced."[185] Seduction also challenges the mode of digitality and circuits of contemporary reality with a circuitry of its own. It is a mode of circulation "that plays by its own rules."[186] This circuitry, then, is not a process of exchange such as that necessary in the current digital world of stimulus and response but a kind of connection through alliance.

Seduction preserves the enigma of the world—its magical, mysterious, inexplicable qualities that are not available with rationality. In the contemporary overabundance and proliferation of signs, in which everything is made visible, seduction preserves the secret: "All other forms, and love in particular, are gossipy and prolix. They say too much, they want to say too much."[187] In a society where everything is said—discovered, uncovered, and revealed—the more subtle spiral of seduction offers an alternative approach that preserves an element of charm and mystery. Seduction is ultimately a defiant strategy—a strategy of resistance—that calls back into play the world before the world of rationality was invented. Seduction violates cause and effect, celebrates appearances and signs, and refuses to reveal everything in a culture that seeks to describe the code behind every interaction. Anytime alliances are relied on to manage a situation or rituals prevail—as in the inauguration of a new president, for example—seduction is at work. Viewers buy into the trappings, the patriotism, and the power with their usual logical perspective in check.

The proliferation of the media and technology has helped create a new consumer culture of simulation that impacts all aspects of society. Baudrillard approaches this culture by playing off the ecstasy of hyperreality and generating from within it fatal strategies that characterize a world governed by chance and destiny. He refers to this world as "an enigma" in which "fatality is at the heart of every strategy. It's what peeks through the heart of more banal strategies."[188] The object and the fatal are privileged, and we "are accomplices in this excess of finality that is there in the object."[189]

Commentary

Baudrillard, one of the "most translated of contemporary French sociologues,"[190] engenders considerable excitement on the part of his followers and critics alike, both because of his ideas and how he chooses to present them. He offers a provocative perspective on new communication forms and media, providing a distinctive theory of symbolic culture as it has developed within the context of an explosion of mediated technology. He frames the emergence of consumption and display since World War II as part of a larger problematic that has changed the nature of human social life significantly.

Baudrillard's willingness to rethink traditional assumptions about society has been an especially important contribution of his body of work. He has not been afraid to challenge thinkers such as Freud, Foucault, or Marx, and the result has been a significant rethinking of taken-for-granted postulates about the nature of contemporary society. He challenges Marxism's emphasis on labor, for example, suggesting that it cannot account adequately for the current commodified society. He also challenges the privileging of rationality that is at the heart of most social theories currently in vogue and refuses to be complacent about the issues that face the highly technological, mass-mediated, consumer culture. As Douglas Kellner, one of his interpreters and critics, notes, Baudrillard writes about "some of the most serious, frightening, and important issues that we are now confronting."[191]

Another hallmark of Baudrillard's work is that it is remarkably consistent over the decades. Although he himself may have been unclear or unaware of the project he was undertaking, "the growing power of the world of objects over the subject" has been Baudrillard's theme from his earliest works.[192] Although he does not always provide the background for an idea that he developed in earlier works, causing confusion for the neophyte reader, he has been engaged in an ongoing contemplation of the subject-object relationship, the nature of the cultural object as it has shifted with the growth of consumption, and the overall evolution of the object against the larger cultural evolution of society.

Baudrillard's focus on the object calls into question the sense of agency that has governed rhetorical theory. Although Baudrillard notes that the subject "has an economy and a history which is quite reassuring," he suggests that it is a concept that has been "overprotected." When called into question, as Baudrillard's focus on the object necessarily does, the subject no longer can manage "a coherent representation of the world."[193] This inability to control the world forces a consideration of objects not simply as part of a static and natural universe but as "constituted by the actions of people operating as historically situated actors and under conditions which they did not choose."[194] The presumed control of the communicator thus is called into question with Baudrillard's description of a universe in which fate and destiny take precedence over rationality. Disillusionment with the rational paradigm is not new, but Baudrillard's approach to it is novel. Rationality is what humans have imposed on the world of fate and illusion to convince themselves that they are in control.

From a rhetorical perspective, Baudrillard provides the opportunity to consider the functions the rational paradigm has served, the way it has dominated communication theory and practice as a mechanism of control, and the possibilities for rethinking traditional arenas of the discipline that have depended on the rational rhetor. The field of persuasion provides an example. How might change be conceptualized if there were no active subject attempting to change others? What groups have been put into the position of objects in a particular time or culture? How can those who have been objectified and commodified be given voice? What if, in the study of social movements, the confluence of factors of coincidence, fate, and destiny were given as much prominence as the actions of movement leaders?

Baudrillard's suggestions for managing the contemporary commodified world of technology also have implications for rhetorical theory. By searching out those features in line with the world of chance—whether the challenge, seduction, hyperreality, or nonresponse—Baudrillard again suggests an exploration of the side of the nonrational. What are the ways in which individuals establish identification that are based not in rational practice but in ritual, ceremony, and obligation? What are the advantages of "playing with appearances" rather than insisting on discovering the logic of all aspects of the world? Baudrillard's work raises useful questions and provocative answers for the rhetorician interested in alternative paradigms to the reason-dominated perspectives of traditional rhetoric.

Despite his thought-provoking ideas, Baudrillard's contributions are mitigated, for some critics, by his lack of systematic analysis of the topics he explores. Paul Foss suggests that his "critical distance has diminished to zero";[195] he is unable or unwilling to deal with contradictory evidence for his claims and sidesteps issues raised by those who attempt more cogent analyses of his ideas. Others suggest that he is given to hyperbole and generalization and fails to define major terms, features that give his work a "totalizing quality."[196] That he criticizes without offering anything affirmative in exchange also is a source of concern for critics. Kellner calls him a "court jester of the society he mocks," suggesting that Baudrillard enjoys "the follies of the consumer and media society of which he is so critical."[197] Foss suggests that when presented with any challenge, Baudrillard simply "becomes 'ecstatic', he takes leave."[198]

The "recklessness"[199] of Baudrillard's approach is seen as undermining his credibility for some scholars at the same time that it is regarded as insightful and interesting by others. Those in the latter group applaud his ability to shock and his unusual writing style as enacting the very conditions about which he writes. His style, in other words, matches his concepts. Bryan Turner sees his work as reflecting "rather than analysing, dissecting and criticizing" the world he is describing and, in so doing, offers a "poetics of the screen image."[200] His writing style flickers like the TV screen, providing the reader with the experience of channel hopping, with its "uncommitted, random overview of a variety of options, to which the viewer/passenger is indifferent."[201]

His inventiveness leads to another benefit of reading Baudrillard, according to Kellner: "It is often simply amusing to read Baudrillard." He can be read "as deadly serious, one can also read him ironically, as a grand joke on social theory and cultural criticism. . . . Baudrillard himself, it seems, wants it both ways and thus opens the way for either a serious or a non-serious reading."[202] As Nicholas Zurbrugg summarizes, Baudrillard perhaps is best approached "in a manner more (or less) Baudrillardian than Baudrillard"—a manner characterized by efforts "to entertain, to interrogate, to adopt, to adapt."[203] Turner suggests that this manner of reading—"sampling the style, tasting the bon mot, admiring the wit, enjoying the topography of his imaginative journey or being dazzled by the outrageous metaphors[204]—can be aesthetically pleasing and satisfying if the relationship between content and form is understood.

what is his functionality?

Baudrillard does not always elaborate on his theories, and he does not offer principles to live by or present panacea by which to manage the challenges of contemporary culture. Anecdotes and maxims sometimes seem to be the only basis for his theorizing.[205] Yet, his unusual style of presentation and the ideas he offers can provide readers with clues as to how they may want to proceed in responding to contemporary mediated consumer culture. He privileges the silent masses, perhaps counting his readers among their membership and wondering what forms their resistance will assume next. Baudrillard uses his own book titles to remind his readers of the choices available to them:

> Keep objects as a system
> Keep production as a mirror
> Keep death as an exchange
> Keep the world as a simulacrum
>
> Keep the evil transparent
> Keep the majorities silent
> Keep your seduction alive
> Keep your memory cool
>
> Keep yourself as an other
> Keep perfection as a crime
> Keep illusion for the end
> Keep on line for the while.[206]

Bibliography

Books

America. Trans. Chris Turner. New York: Verso, 1988.

The Consumer Society: Myths and Structures. Thousand Oaks, CA: Sage, 1998.

Cool Memories. Trans. Chris Turner. New York: Verso, 1990.

Cool Memories II, 1987–1990. Trans. Chris Turner. Durham, NC: Duke University Press, 1996.

The Ecstasy of Communication. Trans. Bernard Schutze and Caroline Schutze. Ed. Sylvère Lotringer. New York: Semiotext(e), 1988.

The Evil Demon of Images. Trans. Paul Patton and Paul Foss. Mari Kuttna Memorial Lecture on Film, 1984. Power Institute of Fine Arts, n.d., pp. 13–31.

Fatal Strategies. Trans. Philip Beitchman and W. G. J. Niesluchowski. Ed. Jim Fleming. London: Pluto, 1999.

For a Critique of the Political Economy of the Sign. Trans. Charles Levin. St. Louis, MO: Telos, 1981.

Forget Foucault. New York: Semiotext(e), 1987.

Fragments: Cool Memories III, 1990–1995. Trans. Emily Agar. New York: Verso, 1997.

The Gulf War Did Not Take Place. Trans. Paul Patton. Bloomington: Indiana University Press, 1995.

The Illusion of the End. Trans. Chris Turner. Cambridge, UK: Polity, 1994.

In the Shadow of the Silent Majorities . . . Or The End of the Social and Other Essays.
Trans. Paul Foss, Paul Patton, and John Johnston. New York: Semiotext(e), 1983.
L'Autre. Trans. Chris Turner. London, UK: Phaidon, 1999. (With Luc Delahaye.)
The Mirror of Production. Trans. Mark Poster. St. Louis, MO: Telos, 1975.
The Perfect Crime. Trans. Chris Turner. New York: Verso, 1996.
Revenge of the Crystal: Selected Writings on the Modern Object and its Destiny, 1968–1983. Trans. and ed. Paul Foss and Julian Pefanis. Concord, MA: Pluto, 1990.
Seduction. Trans. Brian Singer. New York: St. Martin's, 1990.
Simulations. Trans. Paul Foss, Paul Patton, and Philip Beitchman. New York: Semiotext(e), 1983.
Symbolic Exchange and Death. Trans. Iain Hamilton Grant. Thousand Oaks, CA: Sage, 1993.
The System of Objects. Trans. James Benedict. New York: Verso, 1996.
The Transparency of Evil: Essays on Extreme Phenomena. Trans. James Benedict. New York: Verso, 1993.

Articles

"Absolute Merchandise." In *Andy Warhol.* Catalog of an exhibition at Kunstmuseum, Lucerne, Switz., 1995, pp. 18–21.
"The Anorexic Ruins." In *Looking Back on the End of the World.* Trans. David Antal. Ed. Dietmar Kamper and Christoph Wulf. New York: Semiotext(e), 1989, pp. 29–45.
"Art and Value: 'The Contemporary Art Market is Beyond Good and Evil.' "*ArtInternational,* 12 (Autumn 1990), 52–54.
"Desert Forever." Trans. Mark A. Polizzotti. *Semiotext(e),* 13 (1987), 135–37.
"The Ecstasy of Communication." Trans. John Johnston. In *The Anti-Aesthetic: Essays on Postmodern Culture.* Ed. Hal Foster. Port Townsend, WA: Bay, 1983, pp. 126–34.
"Fatality or Reversible Imminence: Beyond the Uncertainty Principle." Trans. Pamela Park. *Social Research,* 49 (Summer 1982), 272–93.
"Hot Painting: The Inevitable Fate of the Image." Trans. Richard Miller. In *Reconstructing Modernism: Art in New York, Paris, and Montreal 1945–1964.* Cambridge, MA: MIT Press, 1990, pp. 17–29.
"Hunting Nazis and Losing Reality." *New Statesman,* 115 (February 19, 1998), 16–17.
"The Implosion of Meaning in the Media and the Implosion of the Social in the Masses." Trans. Mary Lydon. In *The Myths of Information: Technology and Postindustrial Culture.* Ed. Kathleen Woodward. Madison, WI: Coda, 1980, pp. 137–48.
"The Masses: The Implosion of the Social in the Media." Trans. Marie Maclean. Lecture delivered at the University of Melbourne. *New Literary History,* 16 (Spring 1985), 577–89.
"Modernity." *Canadian Journal of Political and Social Theory,* 11 (1987), 63–72.
"Panic Crash!" Trans. Faye Trecartin and Arthur Kroker. In *Panic Encyclopedia: The Definitive Guide to the Postmodern Scene.* New York: St. Martin's, 1989, pp. 64–67.
"Please Follow Me." In *Suite vénitienne.* By Sophie Calle and Jean Baudrillard. Trans. Dany Barash and Danny Hatfield. Seattle, WA: Bay, 1988, pp. 76–87.
"Revolution and the End of Utopia." Trans. Michel Valentin. In *Jean Baudrillard: The Disappearance of Art and Politics.* Ed. William Stearns and William Chaloupka. New York: St. Martin's, 1992, pp. 233–42.

"Simulacra and Simulations: Disneyland." In *Social Theory: The Multicultural and Classic Readings*. Ed. Charles Lemert. 2nd ed. Boulder, CO: Westview, 1999, pp. 481–86.

"Softly, Softly." *New Statesman*, 113 (March 6, 1987), 44.

"The System of Objects." In *Design After Modernism: Beyond the Object*. Ed. John Thackara. New York: Thames and Hudson, pp. 171–82.

"Two Essays." Trans. Arthur B. Evans. *Science-Fiction Studies*, 18 (November 1991), 309–20.

"Transpolitics, Transsexuality, Transaesthetics." In *Jean Baudrillard: The Disappearance of Art and Politics*. Ed. William Stearns and William Chaloupka. New York: St. Martin's, 1992, pp. 9–26.

"The Trompe-l'Oeil." In *Calligram: Essays in New Art History from France*. Ed. Norman Bryson. Cambridge, UK: Cambridge University Press, 1988, pp. 53–62.

"U.S.A. 80's." Trans. Mark A. Polizzotti. *Semiotext(e)*, 13 (1987), 47–50.

"The Virtual Illusion: Or the Automatic Writing of the World." *Theory, Culture & Society*, 12 (November 1995), 97–107.

"When Bataille Attacked the Metaphysical Principle of Economy." Trans. David James Miller. In *Ideology and Power in the Age of Lenin in Ruins*. Ed. Arthur Kroker and Marilouise Kroker. New York: St. Martin's, 1991, pp. 135–38.

"The Xerox Degree of Violence." Trans. Thierry Duval. In *Spectacular Optical*. Catalog of an exhibition at Thread Waxing Space, New York. New York: Passim, 1998, pp, 61–63.

"The Year 2000 Has Already Happened." Trans. Nai-fei Ding and Kuan-Hsing Chen. In *Body Invaders: Panic Sex in America*. Ed. Arthur Kroker and Marilouise Kroker. New York: St. Martin's, 1987, pp. 35–44.

Collected Works

Poster, Mark, ed. *Jean Baudrillard: Selected Writings*. Stanford, CA: Stanford University Press, 1988.

Zurbrugg, Nicholas, ed. *Jean Baudrillard, Art and Artefact*. Thousand Oaks, CA: Sage, 1997.

Interviews

Archard, Pierre. "Politics of Performance: Montand, Coluche = Le Pen?" Interview with Jean Baudrillard. *New Political Science*, 16 (Fall/Winter 1989), 23–28.

Baudrillard, Jean. *Paroxysm: Interviews with Philippe Petit*. Trans. Chris Turner. New York: Verso, 1998.

Boyne, Roy, and Scott Lash. "Symbolic Exchange: Taking Theory Seriously. An Interview with Jean Baudrillard." *Theory, Culture & Society*, 12 (November 1995), 79–95.

Colless, Ted, David Kelly, and Alan Cholodenko. "An Interview with Jean Baudrillard." Trans. Philippe Tanguy. In *The Evil Demon of Images*. By Jean Baudrillard. Sydney, Australia: Power Institute of Fine Arts, n.d., pp. 35–50.

Gane, Mike, ed. *Baudrillard Live: Selected Interviews*. New York: Routledge, 1993.

Gardels, Nathan. "After Utopia: The Primitive Society of the Future." Interview with Jean Baudrillard. *New Perspectives Quarterly*, 6 (Summer 1989), 52–54.

Johnston, John. "Jean Baudrillard." Interview with Jean Baudrillard. Trans. John Johnston. *Art Papers*, 13 (January/February 1989), 4–7.

Lotringer, Sylvère. "Forget Baudrillard: An Interview with Jean Baudrillard." In*Forget Foucault*. By Jean Baudrillard. New York: Semiotext(e), 1987, pp. 65–137.

Moore, Suzanne, and Stephen Johnstone. "Politics of Seduction." Interview with Jean Baudrillard. *Marxism Today*, January 1989, pp. 54–55.

Rötzer, Florian. "Jean Baudrillard." In *Conversations With French Philosophers*. By Florian Rötzer. Trans. Gary E. Aylesworth. Atlantic Highlands, NJ: Humanities, 1995, pp. 17–29.

Shevtsova, Maria. "Intellectuals Commitment and Political Power: An Interview with Jean Baudrillard." *Thesis Eleven*, 10/11 (1984/85), 166–74.

Strand, John. "An Interview with Jean Baudrillard." *ArtInternational*, 12 (Autumn 1990), 55–56.

Zurbrugg, Nicholas. "Fractal Theory: Baudrillard and the Contemporary Arts." Interview with Jean Baudrillard. *Paragraph*, 13 (November 1990), 285–92.

Endnotes

[1] Jean Baudrillard, *Revenge of the Crystal: Selected Writings on the Modern Object and its Destiny, 1968–1983*, trans. and ed. Paul Foss and Julian Pefanis (Concord, MA: Pluto, 1990), p. 24.

[2] Baudrillard, *Revenge of the Crystal*, p. 25.

[3] Baudrillard, *Revenge of the Crystal*, p. 24.

[4] Mark Poster, "Introduction," in *Jean Baudrillard: Selected Writings*, ed. Mark Poster (Stanford, CA: Stanford University Press, 1988), p. 5.

[5] Chris Horrocks and Zoran Jevtic, *Introducing Baudrillard*, ed. Richard Appignanesi (New York: Totem, 1996), p. 121. This does not mean Baudrillard and McLuhan are in total agreement. Baudrillard himself notes that although he and McLuhan both believe that a particular medium communicates via its structure as well as its content, he does not share McLuhan's "technological optimism"—the belief in the ability of technology to move us to the global village, "to the new electronic tribalism—an achieved transparency of information and communication." See Jean Baudrillard, "The Masses: The Implosion of the Social in the Media," in *Jean Baudrillard: Selected Writings*, ed. Mark Poster (Stanford, CA: Stanford University Press, 1988), p. 208.

[6] Mike Gane and Monique Arnaud, "I Don't Belong to the Club, to the Seraglio," interview with Jean Baudrillard, in *Baudrillard Live: Selected Interviews*, ed. Mike Gane (New York: Routledge, 1993), p. 19.

[7] Jean Baudrillard, *Cool Memories II, 1987–1990,* trans. Chris Turner (Durham, NC: Duke University Press, 1996), pp. 6–7.

[8] Gary Genosko, *Baudrillard and Signs: Signification Ablaze* (New York: Routledge, 1994), p. xi.

[9] Rex Butler, "Baudrillard's List," interview with Jean Baudrillard, in *Jean Baudrillard, Art and Artefact*, ed. Nicholas Zurbrugg (Thousand Oaks, CA: Sage, 1997), p. 47.

[10] Gane and Arnaud, p. 19.

[11] Jean Baudrillard, *Paroxysm: Interviews with Philippe Petit*, trans. Chris Turner (New York: Verso, 1998), p. 80.

[12] Jean Baudrillard, *Cool Memories*, trans. Chris Turner (New York: Verso, 1990), pp. 231–32.

[13] Baudrillard, *Revenge of the Crystal*, p. 20.

[14] Baudrillard, *Revenge of the Crystal*, p. 31.

[15] J. Henric and G. Scarpetta, "America as Fiction," interview with Jean Baudrillard, in *Baudrillard Live: Selected Interviews*, ed. Mike Gane (New York: Routledge, 1993), p. 131.

[16] Charles Levin, *Jean Baudrillard: A Study in Cultural Metaphysics* (New York: Prentice Hall, 1996), p. 23.

[17] Gane and Arnaud, p. 21.

[18] Gane and Arnaud, pp. 21–22.

[19] Maria Shevtsova, "Intellectuals Commitment and Political Power," interview with Jean Baudrillard, in *Baudrillard Live: Selected Interviews*, ed. Mike Gane (New York: Routledge, 1993), pp. 94–95.

[20] Baudrillard, *Revenge of the Crystal*, p. 20. For an elaboration of his notion of modernity, see Jean Baudrillard, "Modernity," *Canadian Journal of Political and Social Theory*, 11 (1987), 63–72.

[21] Douglas Kellner, ed., *Baudrillard: A Critical Reader* (Cambridge, MA: Blackwell, 1994), p. 3.

[22] The Centre Pompidou came to be called *The Beaubourg* because it was located on what had been called the *Plateau Beaubourg*; the Centre Pompidou was the subject of Baudrillard's essay, "The Beaubourg Effect" (Levin, p. 65).

[23] Levin, p. 67.

[24] The overriding issue for students and workers alike in this strike was the dominance of consumer society and the meaninglessness of most productive labor—whether in the university setting or the factory. Both groups called for a total reorganization of work relationships, work environments, and the society in which these were situated. Levin, pp. 21, 68.

[25] Levin, p. 67.

[26] Horrocks and Jevtic, p. 11.

[27] Levin, p. 68.

[28] Horrocks and Jevtic, p. 11.

[29] Shevtsova, p. 72.

[30] Shevtsova, p. 73.

[31] Levin, pp. 22–23.

[32] Genosko, p. xiii.

[33] Jean Baudrillard, *America*, trans. Chris Turner (New York: Verso, 1988), p. 63.

[34] Baudrillard, *America*, pp. 27–28.

[35] Nicholas Zurbrugg, "The Ecstasy of Photography," interview with Jean Baudrillard, in *Jean Baudrillard, Art and Artefact*, ed. Nicholas Zurbrugg (Thousand Oaks, CA: Sage, 1997), p. 32.

[36] Gane and Arnaud, p. 23. Although others often make connections between Baudrillard's photographs and the subjects about which he writes, Baudrillard contends that they are entirely separate processes. See Zurbrugg, "The Ecstasy of Photography," p. 32.

[37] Sophie Calle and Jean Baudrillard, *Suite vénitienne*, trans. Dany Barash and Danny Hatfield (Seattle, WA: Bay, 1988), p. 2.

[38] Calle and Baudrillard, p. 82.

[39] Unnamed commentator, quoted in Andrew Hultkrans, "Crap Shoot," *Artforum*, 35 (1997), 21.

[40] Hultkrans, p. 1.

[41] Douglas Kellner, *Jean Baudrillard: From Marxism to Postmodernism and Beyond* (Stanford, CA: Stanford University Press, 1989), p. 8.

[42] Poster, p. 3.

[43] Jean Baudrillard, "The Mirror of Production," in *Jean Baudrillard: Selected Writings*, ed. Mark Poster (Stanford, CA: Stanford University Press, 1988), p. 102.

[44] Poster, p. 4. Baudrillard's critique of Marxism is discussed further in Patrick Murray and Jeanne A. Schuler, "Post-Marxism in a French Context," *History of European Ideas*, 9 (1988), 321–34.

[45] Rex Butler, *Jean Baudrillard: The Defence of the Real* (Thousand Oaks, CA: Sage, 1999), pp. 4–5.

[46] Butler, *Jean Baudrillard*, p. 5.

[47] Levin, p. 66.

[48] Butler, *Jean Baudrillard*, p. 6.

[49] Jean Baudrillard, *Seduction*, trans. Brian Singer (New York: St. Martin's, 1990), p. 8.

[50] Poster, p. 6.

[51] Jean Baudrillard, *Fatal Strategies*, trans. Philip Beitchman and W. G. J. Niesluchowski, ed. Jim Fleming (London, UK: Pluto, 1999), p. 191.

[52] Bryan S. Turner, "Cruising America," in *Forget Baudrillard?*, ed. Chris Rojek and Bryan S. Turner (New York: Routledge, 1993), p. 152.

[53] Horrocks and Jevtic, pp. 118–19.

54 Jean Baudrillard, *The Transparency of Evil: Essays on Extreme Phenomena*, trans. James Benedict (New York: Verso, 1993), p. 3.

55 Patrice Bollon, "Baudrillard's Seductions," interview with Jean Baudrillard, in *Baudrillard Live: Selected Interviews*, ed. Mike Gane (New York: Routledge, 1993), p. 38.

56 Bollon, p. 38.

57 Butler, "Baudrillard's List," p. 44.

58 M. Gottdiener, *Postmodern Semiotics: Material Culture and the Forms of Postmodern Life* (Cambridge, MA: Blackwell, 1995), p. 27.

59 Levin, p. 48.

60 Jean Baudrillard, *Simulations*, trans. Paul Foss, Paul Patton, and Philip Beitchman (New York: Semiotext(e), 1983), p. 4.

61 Jean Baudrillard, *The Illusion of the End*, trans. Chris Turner (Cambridge, UK: Polity, 1994), p. 15.

62 Baudrillard, *Simulations*, p. 5.

63 Baudrillard, *Simulations*, p. 5.

64 Jean Baudrillard, *Symbolic Exchange and Death*, trans. Iain Hamilton Grant (Thousand Oaks, CA: Sage, 1993), p. 50.

65 Horrocks and Jevtic, p. 104.

66 David Ashley, "Habermas and the Completion of 'The Project of Modernity,' " in *Theories of Modernity and Postmodernity*, ed. Brian S. Turner (Newbury Park, CA: Sage, 1990), p. 100.

67 The term *counterfeit* often has negative connotations of a "disquieting foreignness." For Baudrillard, however, it is not a negative term because, with a counterfeit, there is a connection to the real in that the counterfeit is a mirror image of the real. What is more problematic for him are the levels of signs that are detached from the mirror or totally removed from any referent to reality. Baudrillard, *Simulations*, p. 153.

68 Baudrillard, *Symbolic Exchange and Death*, p. 51.

69 Ashley, p. 100.

70 Baudrillard, *Symbolic Exchange and Death*, p. 51.

71 Baudrillard, *Symbolic Exchange and Death*, p. 54.

72 Baudrillard, *Simulations*, pp. 103–05.

73 Butler, *Jean Baudrillard*, p. 25.

74 Baudrillard, *Simulations*, p. 111.

75 Baudrillard, *Simulations*, p. 4.

76 Baudrillard, *Simulations*, p. 145.

77 Baudrillard, *Symbolic Exchange and Death*, pp. 62–63.

78 Horrocks and Jevtic, p. 110.

79 Jean Baudrillard, "Transpolitics, Transsexuality, Transaesthetics," trans. Michel Valentin, in *Jean Baudrillard: The Disappearance of Art and Politics*, ed. William Stearns and William Chaloupka (New York: St. Martin's, 1992), p. 19.

80 Baudrillard, *Simulations*, pp. 13–15.

81 Baudrillard, *Simulations*, p. 15. Ishi walked out of the foothills near Mount Lassen, California, into the town of Oroville in August of 1911; the rest of his tribe had been killed by bounty hunters and vigilantes. The sheriff turned him over to University of California anthropologists Thomas T. Waterman and Alfred L. Kroeber. Ishi chose to remain at the museum as a living interpreter of his culture until he contracted tuberculosis and died on March 25, 1916. In a continuation of the saga that Baudrillard would appreciate, Ishi's brain later was discovered in the Smithsonian, where it had been sent in 1917, following Ishi's autopsy and cremation. Ishi's brain is in the process of repatriation, by which anthropologists return skeletal and cultural remains to Native American groups. In Ishi's case, his brain will be returned to the two surviving Indian tribes most closely related to him and reunited with his cremated body in a traditional burial ceremony. See Bruce Bower, "Ishi's Long Road Home," *Science News Online*, January 8, 2000, www.sciencenewsorg/2000108/bob1.asp. Accessed November, 2000.

82 Baudrillard, *Simulations*, pp. 25–26.

83 Disneyland Paris originally was called *Euro-Disney*. The French were slow to warm up to the concept of Disneyland Paris: "It seems as though no one at Disney had considered whether

or not the French were really interested in American cultural fantasies (fairy-tale castles aren't exactly rare in France, after all). . . . After several mis-starts, Disneyland Paris seems finally to have found a formula that works by focusing more on British, Japanese, and American tourists than on the recalcitrant French. The park contains most of what made the original famous: Main St. U.S.A. at the entrance, and the traditional gateway to Fantasyland, the Sleeping Beauty Castle (called a château here). Rides include: It's a Small World, Pirates of the Caribbean, Indiana Jones, Big Thunder Mountain, and Phantom Manor." See http://msn.expedia.com/wg/europe/france/p13481.asp. Accessed November, 2000.

[84] Baudrillard, *Simulations*, p. 26.

[85] Baudrillard, *Simulations*, p. 104.

[86] Baudrillard, *Simulations*, p. 150.

[87] Mike Gane, *Baudrillard's Bestiary: Baudrillard and Culture* (New York: Routledge, 1991), pp. 49–50.

[88] Baudrillard, *Transparency of Evil*, p. 153.

[89] R. Gibson, "Customs and Excise," in *Seduced and Abandoned: The Baudrillard Scene*, ed. André Frankovits (New York: Semiotext(e), 1984), p. 47.

[90] Chris Rojek, "Baudrillard and Leisure," *Leisure Studies*, 9 (January 1990), 9.

[91] Baudrillard, *The Transparency of Evil*, p. 29.

[92] Jean Baudrillard, "The Masses: The Implosion of the Social in the Media," in *Jean Baudrillard: Selected Writings*, ed. Mark Poster (Stanford, CA: Stanford University Press, 1988), p. 207.

[93] Baudrillard, "The Masses," p. 207.

[94] Jean Baudrillard, *The Perfect Crime*, trans. Chris Turner (New York: Verso, 1996), p. 31.

[95] Baudrillard, *The Perfect Crime*, p. 31.

[96] Mike Gane, *Baudrillard: Critical and Fatal Theory* (New York: Routledge, 1991), p. 82.

[97] Jean Baudrillard, *Fatal Strategies*, p. 8.

[98] Baudrillard, "The Masses," p. 208.

[99] Baudrillard, "The Masses," p. 209.

[100] Meaghan Morris, "Room 101 Or a Few Worst Things in the World," in *Seduced and Abandoned: The Baudrillard Scene,* ed. André Frankovits (New York: Semiotext(e), 1984), p. 101.

[101] Baudrillard, "The Masses," p. 210.

[102] Baudrillard, "The Masses," pp. 209–10.

[103] Baudrillard, *Transparency of Evil*, p. 56.

[104] Baudrillard, "The Masses," pp. 218–19.

[105] Baudrillard, "The Masses," p. 218.

[106] Baudrillard, "The Masses," p. 217.

[107] Baudrillard, "The Masses," p. 210.

[108] Baudrillard, "The Masses," p. 209.

[109] Baudrillard, *Revenge of the Crystal*, p. 69.

[110] Jean Baudrillard, "Consumer Society," in *Jean Baudrillard: Selected Writings*, ed. Mark Poster (Stanford, CA: Stanford University Press, 1988), p. 33.

[111] Levin, p. 197.

[112] Jean Baudrillard, *The System of Objects*, trans. James Benedict (New York: Verso, 1996), pp. 199–200.

[113] Gane, *Baudrillard's Bestiary*, p. 61.

[114] Baudrillard, "Consumer Society," p. 35.

[115] Gane, *Baudrillard's Bestiary*, pp. 58–59.

[116] Rojek, "Baudrillard and Leisure," p. 13.

[117] Jean Baudrillard, "The System of Objects," in *Jean Baudrillard: Selected Writings*, ed. Mark Poster (Stanford, CA: Stanford University Press, 1988), p. 11.

[118] Baudrillard, *Revenge of the Crystal*, p. 18.

[119] Baudrillard, *The System of Objects*, p. 4.

[120] Levin, p. 34.

[121] Baudrillard, *Revenge of the Crystal*, p. 44.

[122] Baudrillard, *Revenge of the Crystal*, p. 50.

[123] Baudrillard, *Fragments: Cool Memories III, 1990–1995*, trans. Emily Agar (New York: Verso, 1997), p. 116.

[124] Baudrillard, *The Perfect Crime*, p. 55.

[125] Baudrillard, *Revenge of the Crystal*, p. 74.

[126] Baudrillard, *The System of Objects*, p. 114.

[127] Baudrillard, *The System of Objects*, p. 116.

[128] Baudrillard, *Revenge of the Crystal*, p. 77.

[129] Baudrillard, *The System of Objects*, p. 118.

[130] Baudrillard, *Revenge of the Crystal*, p. 75.

[131] Baudrillard, "Consumer Society," p. 31.

[132] Baudrillard, *Revenge of the Crystal*, p. 91.

[133] Baudrillard, *The System of Objects*, p. 89.

[134] Baudrillard, *Revenge of the Crystal*, p. 46.

[135] Baudrillard, *The System of Objects*, p. 46.

[136] Baudrillard, *Revenge of the Crystal*, p. 46.

[137] Levin, p. 51.

[138] Baudrillard, "Fatal Strategies," in *Jean Baudrillard: Selected Writings*, ed. Mark Poster (Stanford, CA: Stanford University Press, 1988), p. 194. See also Jean Baudrillard, *In the Shadow of the Silent Majorities . . . Or The End of the Social and Other Essays*, trans. Paul Foss, Paul Patton, and John Johnston (New York: Semiotext(e), 1983), pp. 58–61.

[139] Baudrillard, *Simulations*, p. 57.

[140] Horrocks and Jevtic, p. 148.

[141] Baudrillard, *Fatal Strategies*, p. 13.

[142] Baudrillard, *Fatal Strategies*, p. 9.

[143] Genosko, p. 157.

[144] Baudrillard, "Fatal Strategies," p. 187.

[145] C. Charbonnier, "I Like the Cinema," in *Baudrillard Live: Selected Interviews*, ed. Mike Gane (New York: Routledge, 1993), p. 30. Baudrillard himself did not own a television set until 1980, when he was asked to write an article about simulation and television. Before that time, he notes that "I didn't want the damn thing. I would see it by proxy, at my mother's, or in friends' houses: it wasn't my choice." He admits, however, that "once I had it, I found I liked having it. But I use it in a very random sort of way" (Charbonnier, p. 30).

[146] Baudrillard, *Transparency of Evil*, p. 55.

[147] Baudrillard, *Transparency of Evil*, p. 54.

[148] Baudrillard, *Transparency of Evil*, p. 55.

[149] Charbonnier, p. 31.

[150] Baudrillard, *Revenge of the Crystal*, p. 88.

[151] Gibson, p. 48.

[152] Baudrillard, *Revenge of the Crystal*, p. 169.

[153] Baudrillard, *Revenge of the Crystal*, p. 169.

[154] Baudrillard, *The Perfect Crime*, p. 16.

[155] Baudrillard, *Simulations*, p. 63.

[156] Gane, *Baudrillard*, p. 174.

[157] Baudrillard, *Fatal Strategies*, p. 151.

[158] Baudrillard, *The Perfect Crime*, p. 17.

[159] Baudrillard, *Fatal Strategies*, p. 92.

[160] Baudrillard, *Fatal Strategies*, p. 92.

[161] Baudrillard, *Fatal Strategies*, p. 92.

[162] Morris, p. 104.

[163] Baudrillard, *Paroxysm*, p. 71.

[164] Baudrillard, *Paroxysm*, p. 70.

[165] Baudrillard, *Fatal Strategies*, p. 190.

[166] Baudrillard, "Fatal Strategies," p. 198.

[167] Genosko (p. 149) suggests that Baudrillard may also be playing with crystals in the contemporary sense of "healing crystals." Perhaps Baudrillard is offering an alternative that he believes can be healing for contemporary culture.

[168] Gane, *Baudrillard*, p. 145.

[169] Gane, *Baudrillard*, p. 173.

[170] Baudrillard, *Fatal Strategies*, p. 29.

[171] Baudrillard, *Fatal Strategies*, p. 28.

[172] Baudrillard, *Fatal Strategies*, p. 28.

[173] Baudrillard, *Fatal Strategies*, p. 30.

[174] Baudrillard, *Fatal Strategies*, p. 27.

[175] Baudrillard, *Fatal Strategies*, p. 30.

[176] Baudrillard, *Transparency of Evil*, p. 75.

[177] Baudrillard, *Simulations*, p. 41.

[178] Baudrillard, *Fatal Strategies*, p. 97.

[179] Baudrillard, *Fatal Strategies*, pp. 97–98.

[180] Baudrillard, *Fatal Strategies*, p. 97.

[181] Gane, *Baudrillard*, p. 156.

[182] Baudrillard, *Seduction*, p. 82.

[183] Kellner, *Baudrillard*, p. 14.

[184] Baudrillard, *Seduction*, pp. 83–84.

[185] Baudrillard, *Seduction*, p. 81. Baudrillard contrasts seduction with sexual seduction, which has only a banal conclusion, the accomplishment of desire. See Gane, *Baudrillard*, p. 151.

[186] Baudrillard, *Seduction*, p. 81.

[187] Baudrillard, *Fatal Strategies*, p. 108.

[188] Baudrillard, *Fatal Strategies*, p. 188.

[189] Baudrillard, *Fatal Strategies*, p. 189.

[190] Jacques Delaruelle and John McDonald, "Resistance and Submission," in *Seduced and Abandoned: The Baudrillard Scene*, ed. André Frankovits (New York: Semiotext(e), 1984), p. 24.

[191] Kellner, *Baudrillard*, pp. 17–18.

[192] Kellner, *Baudrillard*, p. 15.

[193] Baudrillard, *Fatal Strategies*, p. 112.

[194] Rojek, "Baudrillard and Leisure," p. 11.

[195] Paul Foss, "Despero Ergo Sum," in *Seduced and Abandoned: The Baudrillard Scene*, ed. André Frankovits (New York: Semiotext(e), 1984), p. 9.

[196] Poster, pp. 5, 7.

[197] Kellner, *Jean Baudrillard*, p. 216.

[198] Foss, p. 15.

[199] Rojek and Turner, "Regret Baudrillard?," p. xi.

[200] Bryan S. Turner, "Cruising America," in *Forget Baudrillard?*, ed. Chris Rojek and Bryan S. Turner (New York: Routledge, 1993), p. 154.

[201] Turner, "Cruising America," p. 153.

[202] Kellner, *Baudrillard*, p. 17.

[203] Nicholas Zurbrugg, "Introduction: 'Just What Is It That Makes Baudrillard's Ideas So Different, So Appealing?,'" in *Jean Baudrillard, Art and Artefact*, ed. Nicholas Zurbrugg (Thousand Oaks, CA: Sage, 1997), p. 5.

[204] Turner, "Cruising America," pp. 155–56.

[205] Richard Vine, "The 'Ecstasy' of Jean Baudrillard," *The New Criterion*, 7 (May 1989), 44.

[206] Baudrillard, *Fragments*, p. 152. Reprinted with permission of Verso.

11

MICHEL FOUCAULT

"I aim at having an experience myself—by passing through a determinate historical content—an experience of what we are today, of what is not only our past but also our present. And I invite others to share the experience. That is, an experience of our modernity that might permit us to emerge from it transformed."[1] These words by Michel Foucault suggest the focus of his work. In whatever subject area he tackles, Foucault's readers have the impression that it is "about them, the world today, or their relations with 'contemporaneity,' in the forms by which the latter is accepted and recognized by everyone. . . . We feel that something contemporary has been brought up for discussion."[2] As "a dealer in instruments, an inventor of recipes, a cartographer,"[3] many of the relations of contemporaneity Foucault explores have a great deal to do with rhetoric.

Foucault was born in Poitier, France, on October 15, 1926, the second of the three children of Paul Foucault, a surgeon, and his wife Anne Malapert Foucault. Following tradition in the Foucault family that an eldest son was named *Paul*, he was named *Paul-Michel* but referred to himself as *Michel*. He was attracted to the scholarly environment at an early age: "We did not know when I was ten or eleven years old, whether we would become German or remain French. We did not know whether we would die or not in the bombing and so on. When I was sixteen or seventeen I knew only one thing: school life was an environment protected from exterior menaces, from politics. And I have always been fascinated by living protected in a scholarly environment, in an intellectual milieu."[4]

Although his father wanted him to study medicine and take over his medical practice, Foucault chose to study philosophy when he enrolled in the École Normale Supérieure (ENS) in Paris, a university designed for the intellectual elite who wished to become teachers. He studied with Jean Hyppolite, Georges Canguilhem, and Georges Dumézil and earned a degree in philosophy in 1948. Foucault completed a degree in psychology in 1949 from the ENS and the diploma course in psychiatry from the Institut de psychologie in Paris in 1952.

Foucault's only participation in an organized political party came in 1950, when he joined the Parti Communiste Français, French Communist Party. His participation was minimal, with his commitment to Marxism largely confined to a general belief that material or economic conditions are a dominant influence on social and political life. Foucault's disillusionment with and eventual departure from the Parti Communiste Français began when he discovered the existence of anti-Semitism in the Soviet Union, which he could not reconcile with his pro-Israeli sentiments. His homosexuality also made him uncomfortable with Communism: "I was never really integrated into the Communist Party because I was homosexual, and it was an institution that reinforced all the values of the most traditional bourgeois life."[5] Foucault never again belonged to an organized political party.

Following the completion of his degrees, Foucault taught psychology for three years at the ENS and the University of Lille, located almost on the Belgian border north of Paris. Like many other professors who did not find towns such as Lille to be as appealing as Paris, Foucault was what the French call a *turbo-prof*, commuting to Lille from Paris, staying in a hotel for two or three nights a week, and fitting all of his teaching into the short periods of time he spent there.

While teaching at the ENS and at Lille, Foucault also conducted research at Sainte-Anne hospital and the Centre National d'Orientation at Fresnes, the prison that houses the penal system's main medical facilities. Foucault published his research on psychiatric practices in mental hospitals in 1954 as *Maladie mentale et personnalité*, a book in which he provides definitions of psychiatric terms and traces the origins of mental illness. In the early 1960s, when the book had gone out of print and a new edition was planned, Foucault changed the title to *Maladie mentale et psychologie* (*Mental Illness and Psychology*) and replaced the second part with new material. Instead of tracing mental illness back to conditions of an individual's development, as he had in the first edition, Foucault understands mental illness in the revised version as a changing, historically conditioned notion. Another reprint of the second edition appeared in 1966, but Foucault would not allow any further editions and attempted unsuccessfully to prevent the publication of the English translation. Foucault removed the book from the lists of "books by the same author" in the front matter of his later books, regarding it as a product of juvenile thinking.

Influenced by his reading of the works of Friedrich Nietzsche, Foucault left France to teach at Uppsala University in Sweden. "Nietzsche was a revelation to me. I felt that there was someone quite different from what I had been taught," explained Foucault. "I read him with a great passion and broke with my life, left my job in the asylum, left France: I had the feeling I had been trapped."[6] During his four years in Sweden, Foucault served as French assistant in the Department of Romance Studies, where he was responsible for teaching courses on French literature, with his nationality his only real qualification for the position. He also was appointed director of the Maison de France, where he was responsible for cultural activities such as organizing play readings and screenings of French films and leading discussions of French poetry. Foucault was disappointed with his experience in Sweden because he found that "a certain kind of freedom" could have "as many restrictive effects as a directly repressive society." Sweden showed him, he said, "what we will be in fifty or a hundred years' time, when we are all rich, happy and aseptisised."[7]

In 1958, Foucault left Uppsala for Warsaw, Poland, where he assumed the position of director of the Centre Français, teaching French language classes and lecturing on French literature. When the French cultural attaché was granted an educational leave, Foucault became his unofficial replacement and then was offered the permanent position. He turned the position down when an affair between Foucault and a man who worked for the police became public, and he was advised by the ambassador to leave Warsaw as soon as possible.

A number of positions were vacant in French cultural institutes in Germany, and Foucault chose to accept an opening in Hamburg. At the Institut Français, he taught French language courses and gave lectures on topics related to French culture. While he was in Germany, Foucault completed the manuscript he had begun in Sweden, *Folie et déraison: Histoire de la folie à l'âge classique* (*Madness and Civilization: A History of Insanity in the Age of Reason*). He submitted it to Georges Canguilhem as his doctoral dissertation in the area of history of science at the Sorbonne in 1960 and defended it in 1961, also the year in which it was published. In the book, Foucault discusses the relationship between the conception of madness and the notion of reason. Once reason was established as supreme in Western culture, he argues, anything that constituted a threat to it was disregarded and excluded from the culture, including the notion of madness.

In 1960, Foucault returned to France to become head of the philosophy department at the University of Clermont-Ferrand, where he taught for six years. Refusing once again to move from Paris, he never lived in Clermont-Ferrand but made the six-hour train journey once a week throughout the academic year. During his tenure at Clermont-Ferrand, Foucault began a close friendship and eventually a nonexclusive sexual relationship with Daniel Defert; they lived together until Foucault's death.

The early 1960s marked the beginning of a productive period of publication for Foucault. He began to contribute reviews and articles to journals, largely on literary topics, and he was in demand as a speaker at conferences and colloquia in France and Western Europe. Just as Foucault had seemed likely to become a psychologist or psychiatrist in the early 1960s, now he seemed likely to become a major literary critic, and the works Foucault wrote during this period give little indication that their author was a professor of psychology and philosophy. Foucault's next book, *Raymond Roussel* (*Death and the Labyrinth: The World of Raymond Roussel*), published in 1963, was his only book devoted to a literary topic. In this book, he examines images, themes, word choice, and order in the works of Roussel, a French writer of the early twentieth century. He did not write other works on literary figures: "I have kept my love of Roussel as something gratuitous and I prefer it that way. . . . I enjoyed doing it, but I am glad I never continued that work. I would have felt, not now, but in those days, that I was betraying Roussel, normalizing him, by treating him as an author like others if after writing about him I had started another study of another writer. Thus he remained unique."[8]

Foucault turned his attention once again to psychology and psychiatry with the publication in 1963 of *Naissance de la clinique* (*The Birth of the Clinic: An Archaeology of Medical Perception*), which focuses on the point in the eighteenth century when medicine based on the classification of diseases gave way to empirical observation that constitutes the medical field today. The birth of the clinic signals a major shift in the understanding of illness and the very concept of disease, and different methods of treatment accompanied this shift, each suggesting entirely different principles of discourse.

Foucault accepted a position in philosophy at the University of Tunis in 1966. He first began to shave his head while in Tunisia, inaugurating a morning ritual that he performed for the rest of his life. He claimed that the practice stopped him from worrying about losing his hair and revealed his true face. Foucault's next major work, *Les mots et les choses* (*The Order of Things: An Archaeology of the Human Sciences*), published in 1966 while he was in Tunisia, immediately became a bestseller, to Foucault's surprise. Foucault's aim in the book is to write a history of order—to discover how a society reflects upon resemblances among things and how differences among things are mastered, organized into networks, and sketched out according to rational frameworks. Foucault identifies three great epochs in European thought; examines the continuities and transformations in the study of living beings, language, and political economy in these epochs; and shows how all three themes are organized according to the same conceptual structure.

Foucault left Tunis in October of 1968 to return to Paris. When the French government dispersed the concentration of the University of Paris in the Latin Quarter and set up a number of autonomous campuses throughout the city, Foucault was offered the position of chair of the philosophy department at the Vincennes Experimental University Centre, where he had the opportunity to create a new department in a new university. An outgrowth of the May 1968 student riots protesting France's system of higher education, the structure of the University of Vincennes responded to many of the students' demands. It was interdisciplinary; introduced novel courses on cinema, semiotics, and psychoanalysis; and was the first French university to open its doors to individuals who had not completed a baccalauréat, thus attracting considerable numbers of wage earners and individuals outside of the normal recruitment pool for students. While at the University of Vincennes, Foucault published *L'archéologie du savoir* (*The Archaeology of Knowledge*), in which he criticizes the traditional method of dealing with history in terms of periods and unifying themes and suggests that it be viewed instead from the perspective of contradictions and discontinuities. In this methodological work, archaeology is not concerned with physical objects but with the process that makes possible objects of discourse such as madness or clinical medicine.

The death of philosopher Jean Hyppolite created a vacancy in the Collège de France; Foucault was elected to fill the chair in 1970. The Collège, the most prestigious institution in France, is unique among French educational institutions. Not part of the university system, it has no student body and awards no degrees. Professors are elected by their future peers, and their appointments are for life. They are required to base their teaching completely on original research, which is presented in the form of 12 two-hour public lectures per year and at related seminars that are open to the public. The Collège was an ideal place for Foucault because he was free from administrative responsibilities and political and bureaucratic interference. Because the Collège's year is short, running from late November to May—and Foucault's lectures often did not actually begin until January—he also was free to travel and to accept visiting professorships elsewhere.

Upon his election to the Collège, Foucault was able to provide his own description for his area of study, and he selected Professor of the History of Systems of Thought. With this title, Foucault suggested that his primary concern was with the location of human beings within systems of thought and practice that become so much a part of them that they no longer experience them as confinements but view them as the very structure of being human. He saw his work as focused on the question: To what extent might it "be possible to think differently, instead of legitimating what is already known?"[9]

Foucault next entered a period where his focus was political activism, in part because his books became part of the cultural infrastructure of those who hoped to create social change. Although *Madness and Civilization*, in particular, had been read primarily as an academic work when it was published in 1961, after 1968, it was read in the context of a social movement of a generalized antirepression. The book's theme of confinement provided the archetype for the confinement of workers in factories, students in universities, and desires in repressive structures. When it was translated into English, it almost immediately became an icon of the counterculture of the late 1960s and early 1970s.

Foucault's personal activism began a few weeks after he delivered his inaugural lecture at the Collège. Hunger strikes began among France's leftist political prisoners, who demanded the special treatment required for political prisoners and initiated a movement of solidarity with all other prisoners. In response, Foucault and others started the Group d'Information sur les Prisons (GIP), designed to help prisoners speak out about prison conditions. The riots that occurred in a number of French prisons in 1972 attested to the GIP's effectiveness, and, at the end of that year, the founders withdrew and handed over the leadership of the struggle to the prisoners themselves. Although the GIP was Foucault's primary political preoccupation, he also was involved in efforts to end the war in Vietnam, oppose racism in France, and improve conditions for immigrants. Foucault's activism between 1971 and 1973 meant he had less time for writing. After *The Archaeology of Knowledge* appeared in 1969, he published no more major works until 1975.

Foucault continued his research activity during his period of activism, however, and it fed both his lectures and his seminars at the Collège. During the 1971–72 academic year, Foucault devoted his course at the Collège to the topic of penal psychiatry. While researching this topic, he discovered the case of Pierre Rivière, a 20-year-old French peasant who was convicted of murdering his mother, sister, and brother in 1836. While awaiting trial, Rivière wrote a 40-page account of his life, and Foucault organized a seminar to study the case. In 1973, with the collaboration of 10 others, he produced *Moi, Pierre Rivière ayant égorgé ma mère, ma soeur et mon frère . . .: Un cas de parricide au XIXe siècle* (*I, Pierre Rivière having slaughtered my mother, my sister and my brother . . . : A Case of Parricide in the 19th Century*), with the title taken from the opening line of Rivière's own narrative. The book consists of essays analyzing the case; contemporary documents, including statements by doctors, newspaper reports of the trial, and transcripts of the legal proceedings; and a transcription of Rivière's account of his actions. The book is intended to show how Rivière's desire, action, and text were made possible by particular discursive practices. In 1975, a film about Rivière was made by René Allio in which Foucault played the role of a judge.

Foucault's continuing study of penal theories and institutions resulted in the publication of *Surveiller et punir: Naissance de la prison* (*Discipline and Punish: The Birth of the Prison*) in 1975. The book charts the emergence of the prison and traces the shift from bodily punishment of criminals to their reform through an investigation of their souls. It also addresses the disciplinary systems that exist beneath the surface of middle-class society and that control individuals' behavior without their knowledge.

In 1975, Foucault traveled for the first time to the United States to assume a visiting professorship in French at the University of California at Berkeley. He returned frequently to the United States, presenting the Tanner Lectures on Human Values at Stanford University in 1979 and returning the following year to give the Howinson Lectures at Berkeley. In October of 1981, he participated in a conference at the University of Southern California, "Knowledge, Power, History: Interdisciplinary Approaches to the Works of Michel Foucault," attracting enormous media attention. In California, Foucault discovered a gay culture that was unknown in France. He enjoyed its sexual openness and began to explore the world of leather and sadomasochism. He also took LSD for the first time. Although he experimented widely, Foucault was not a particularly heavy user of drugs. Drugs afforded an intensity of pleasure which, paradoxically, he sought in disciplined moderation: "Actually, I think I have real difficulty in experiencing pleasure. . . . Because I think that the kind of pleasure I would consider as *the* real pleasure would be so deep, so intense, so overwhelming that I couldn't survive it. I would die. . . . [S]ome drugs are really important for me because they are the mediation to those incredibly intense joys that I am looking for and that I am not able to experience, to afford by myself. . . . A pleasure must be something incredibly intense."[10]

Foucault's homosexuality and his discovery that sexuality has been an issue of power throughout much of history led him to begin a series of books on the history of sexuality. The first volume, *Histoire de la sexualité: La volonté de savoir* (*The History of Sexuality: An Introduction*), was published in 1976. In it, Foucault shows how the history of sexuality, beginning in the seventeenth century, was characterized by a continuous increase in the mechanisms of power. He also charts the shift of the locus of power from the confessional to research laboratories and clinics, showing how the various power mechanisms produced, rather than repressed, discourse on sexuality. Foucault planned the series on sexuality in six volumes, expecting them to appear at the rate of one a year, but none of them appeared on time or in the form announced. In 1984, the second and third volumes were published. Volume 2, *L'usage des plaisirs* (*The Use of Pleasure*), studied problems of sex in classical Greek thought, while volume 3, *Le souci de soi* (*The Care of the Self*), analyzed such problems as they appeared in Greek and Latin texts of the first and second centuries A.D. In the introduction to volume 2, which served as an introduction to his new project, Foucault reconceptualized the aim of his series on sexuality: "instead of studying sexuality at the confines of knowledge (savoir) and power, I tried to investigate at a deeper level how the experience of sexuality as desire had been constituted for the subject himself."[11] The purpose of the series was thus to explore ethics, which he defined as that component of morality that concerns the self's relationship to itself.

The end of 1976 marked the beginning of another period of intense political activism for Foucault. He was involved in demonstrations and campaigns on behalf of dissidents from the Soviet Union and other Eastern-bloc countries. In 1978, he made two visits to Iran and produced reports for the Italian newspaper *Corriere della Sera*. What he saw happening in Iran was "a groundswell, with no vanguard, no party."[12] His belief that he was seeing the emergence of a unified collective will and his underestimation of the power of Ayatollah Khomeini led him to predict mistakenly that there would be no Khomeini party and no Khomeini regime in the future because the Ayatollah was the focal point for more anonymous collective forces. When the prime minister of Poland, Woiciech Jaruzelski, declared a state of war and imposed martial law in December 1981, Foucault protested the action and began a collaboration with the Polish labor union Solidarity.

Foucault's next book was a collaborative effort with historian Arlette Farge that has not been translated into English. In 1982, they published *Le désordre des familles: lettres de cachet des Archives de la Bastille*, a reprinting of police reports or warrants from the archives of the Bastille for the imprisonment without trial of various individuals. The book is divided into two sections, one on marital strife and the other on parent-child relations. The introduction to the section on marital relations is predominantly Farge's work; the piece on relations between parents and children is largely Foucault's.

Foucault returned to Berkeley in April 1983 to lecture on "The Culture of the Self." He discussed the possibility of returning the following autumn to teach a full course, and he also began investigating a long-term arrangement, such as a permanent visiting professorship, that would allow him to return on a regular basis. His enthusiasm about working in the United States and his increasing frustration with his life in France prompted him to talk of resigning his chair at the Collège. These plans ended on June 25, 1984, when Foucault died in Paris of complications resulting from AIDS. Foucault suspected that he might have contracted AIDS, but a positive diagnosis never was made. In 1977, Foucault had told a friend, "When I die, I will leave no manuscripts," and a letter found in his apartment stated these same intentions: "No posthumous publications."[13] His family and friends respected his wishes, and his close friend Hervé Guibert destroyed the preparatory materials and drafts of the final volumes of *The History of Sexuality*—including the fourth volume, which virtually was completed when he died. A great deal of unpublished material by and about Foucault is held in the Bibliothèque du Saulchoir, where it may be consulted but not reproduced.[14]

Foucault's works deal with three primary themes that are relevant to rhetorical theory: knowledge, power, and ethics, developed chronologically through the sequence of his books. These three themes and the method of analysis Foucault proposes and uses for exploring them are the focus of this chapter.

Knowledge

The initial theme Foucault explores in his work is knowledge and the discursive processes that produce it. He describes his interest in this way: "How does it happen that at a given period something could be said and something else has never been said?"[15] He sets out to discover the process by which disciplines such as psychiatry and education create particular knowledge or truths about their subject areas by dictating what can become objects of perception or objects to be known and how new objects are able to enter a domain of knowledge.

Foucault believes that discourse—what others would call *rhetoric*—plays a central role in the creation of knowledge. Everything that can be spoken about in a particular discourse community is knowledge. Foucault's term *discourse* is based on the plural of *statement*. For him, a statement is roughly equivalent to the notion of a speech act and is a set of signs or symbols to which a status of knowledge can be ascribed. It is a type of utterance that, because it follows particular rules or has passed appropriate tests, is understood to be true in a culture. A statement is not the same as a sentence, which is governed by grammatical rules, or a proposition, which is governed by the rules of logic; in contrast, a statement is governed by epistemological rules.[16] "What I call a statement," explains Foucault, "is a set of signs that can be a sentence or a proposition, but envisaged at the level of its existence."[17]

At particular periods in particular discourse communities, Foucault suggests, various domains of knowledge produce various statements that may be related in a single theoretical model. Across domains or disciplines—across widely differing theories, concepts, and objects of study—the "existence of formal relationships, which can indeed be called structures" can be discovered.[18] For example, statements that characterize the domain of medicine, practices of aid to the unemployed, and administrative control over public health may be linked because they obey the same laws or structures. Unknown to themselves, the individuals who participate in these fields employ the same rules to define the objects proper to their own study, to form their concepts, and to build their theories. Foucault's study of the Renaissance in the sixteenth century provides another example of such laws. In this period, knowledge was based on the idea of resemblance or similitude, so that plants resembled stars, the intellect of the human being reflected the wisdom of God, and painting imitated space. Knowledge, then, consisted of the finding of resemblances.[19]

Statements become epistemically significant in their connection to other statements in other domains of knowledge. Foucault first gave the label *episteme* to the relations that link statements in a particular period of time, but with the publication of *The Archaeology of Knowledge*, he replaced the term *episteme* with *discursive formation*, emphasizing the central role of discourse in the process of the creation of knowledge in a community. An episteme or a discursive formation is "the total set of relations that unite, at a given period, the discursive practices that give rise to epistemological figures, sciences, and possibly formalized systems."[20] It is a grouping of statements that suggests a consistent pattern, an order, or a regularity in how those statements function as constituents of a system of knowledge. It is the underground grid or network that allows thought to be organized. As Foucault explains, the discursive formation "is not a formal structure" or "a conceptual coherent architecture; it is not a fundamental philosophical choice; it is rather the existence of rules of formation for all its objects (however scattered they may be), for all its operations (which often can neither be superimposed nor linked together in succession), for all its concepts (which may very well be incompatible), for all its theoretical options (which are often mutually exclusive). There is an individualized discursive formation every time one can define a similar set of rules."[21] A discursive formation, in other words, is a cultural code, characteristic system, structure, network, ground of thought, or style of organization that governs the language, perception, values, and practices of a system, a community, or a historical period.

Foucault postulates a relationship of discontinuity among discursive formations. Only one discursive formation can dominate at any one time because the structure governing the discursive formation is so fundamental that, in the age of one discursive formation, to think by means of another is extremely difficult. The uniqueness of each discursive formation also suggests that no significant relationships exist among different discursive formations. They appear in succession, without any evident rationale or reason, and are neither built on nor created in response to one another. Each discursive formation constitutes a break from the previous discursive formation and thus creates a radically different intellectual framework with which to view the world.[22] Foucault cites as an example a passage from a Chinese encyclopedia

> in which it is written that "animals are divided into: (a) belonging to the Emperor, (b) embalmed, (c) tame, (d) suckling pigs, (e) sirens, (f) fabulous, (g) stray dogs, (h) included in the present classification, (i) frenzied, (j) innumerable, (k) drawn with a very fine camelhair brush, (l)*et cetera*, (m) having just broken the water pitcher, (n) that from a long way off look like flies." In the wonderment of this taxonomy, the thing we apprehend in one great leap, the thing that, by means of the fable, is demonstrated as the exotic charm of another system of thought, is the limitation of our own, the stark impossibility of thinking*that*.[23]

Governing Rules

The nature of a discursive formation can be known through the discovery and articulation of the rules that characterize it. These rules, which are not likely to be conscious and often cannot be articulated without difficulty, determine that one statement rather than another comes to be uttered in a particular discursive formation. They determine the possibilities for the content and form of discourse: "the production of discourse is at once controlled, selected, organised and redistributed according to a certain number of procedures."[24]

Foucault suggests a number of rules that govern the discursive formation. One category of rules controls the fact that something is able to be talked about and governs the appearance of objects of discourse. Rules in this category include, for example, prohibitions against talking about certain things— rules that silence certain dimensions of experience simply by not recognizing them as objects of discourse.[25] In the Victorian Age, for example, children's sexuality simply was not an object of discourse, so children's sexuality was not discussed, and that aspect of children's experience was repressed.

Some rules that govern objects of discourse concern the function of institutional bodies in creating such objects. Particular institutions may be recognized as the ones with the authority to name and thus distinguish one object from another. One such authority was nineteenth-century medicine, which distinguished madness from other concepts and became the major authority that established madness as an object. Educational experts currently recognize and diagnose children with attention deficit disorder, for example, thus making it a condition that can be perceived and about which individuals are able to speak.

A second category of rules concerns not what is talked about but who is allowed to speak and write. Such rules dictate that individuals listen to certain people and reject the discourse of others. The discourse of those who are not heard is considered null "and void, without truth or significance, worthless as evidence, inadmissible in the authentification of acts or contracts." Their words are "neither heard nor remembered."[26] Only those deemed qualified by satisfying certain conditions are heard when they engage in discourse. Among these conditions are legal requirements that give the right to speak in certain ways. Lawyers, for example, must pass the bar examination in order to practice law. Other such rules involve criteria of competence and knowledge. Individuals listen to medical doctors speak about issues involving health because discursive rules attribute competence to them in this area, while the discourse of alternative medicine generally is not heard because its practitioners have not fulfilled the conditions for competence established for speakers of medical discourse.

Another condition imposed on those whose speech is heard is the production of certain kinds of discourse, formulated in certain ways. Those who wish to speak in the academic world, for example, must produce certain types of statements and use certain forms to be allowed to participate in scholarly discourse. An academic paper or article must evidence particular forms of argument and particular kinds of language, put together in complex ways. It also must contain citations to other scholarly articles, and these citations must follow the form of an established style manual such as that published by the Modern Language Association.

Other rules that govern the nature of the speaker define the gestures, behaviors, and circumstances that must accompany speakers as they talk. The wearing of particular clothing and the enactment of behaviors such as genuflection, for example, often must accompany religious discourse if the speaker is to be viewed as legitimate in that role. Judicial discourse also involves rituals that require those participating to engage in certain behaviors. Judges, for example, wear robes in the courtroom and are greeted by the rising of the audience when they enter. To violate such rituals is to be subject to punishment, excommunication, banishment, or some other form of silencing.

Still other conditions imposed on speakers concern the sites from which the discourse must originate. Certain places are seen as appropriate from which to speak, while others are not. For professors, for example, such sites include the university classroom; the field of professional journals, books, and professional conventions; and, if their field of study has application to the business world, the corporate setting. For professors to announce research findings at a press conference rather than in academic journals, for example, generally would not accord them the status necessary to be heard and taken seriously by those who engage in scholarly discourse.

A third category of rules concerns the form that concepts and theories must assume to be accepted as knowledge. Some of these rules govern the arrangement of statements required for a discourse to be seen as knowledge, while others dictate the style and form of that discourse. Still other rules determine which terms are recognized as valid, which are questionable, and which are invalid. They specify the kind of discourse in which the highest truth resides by indicating which statements are true and which are false.[27] Nonlinear perspectives and ways of writing or speaking, for example, generally are not recognized as valid or appropriate, and truth is not seen as residing in such statements.

A particular view of truth accompanies Foucault's concept of the discursive formation governed by rules that prescribe certain objects of discourse, particular types of speakers, and the form that concepts assume. Truth is always dependent on a particular discursive formation. There is no underlying meaning or truth within or imposed on the things of the world. Truth or knowledge about something rests entirely within the relations of statements inside a discursive formation. Foucault, then, approaches truth speaking not from the perspective of formal criteria but as an activity viewed from the content of a discursive formation: "Who is able to tell the truth? About what topics is it important to tell the truth? What are the moral, the ethical, and the spiritual conditions that entitle someone to present himself as a truth-speaker? What are the consequences of telling the truth?"[28] Foucault makes clear that this conception of truth does not mean that the truth of a discursive formation is not real: "I have been seen as saying that madness does not exist, whereas the problem is absolutely the converse: it was a question of knowing how madness, under the various definitions that have been given, was at a particular time integrated into an institutional field that constituted it as a mental illness occupying a specific place alongside other illnesses."[29]

Foucault's notion of the discursive formation and its governing rules led to the popular perception in the 1960s that he was one of the "Structuralist Gang of Four," which also included Jacques Lacan, Roland Barthes, and

Claude Lévi-Strauss. Structuralists attempt to discover the laws according to which the human world in its various manifestations is ordered. Their focus is not on the subjectivity and agency of the human being but on the conditions within which human beings think and act. Foucault often was labeled a *structuralist* because in books, such as *The Order of Things*, he describes the particular configuration of the epistemic field that classifies a variety of different observable entities into a common conceptual space that makes sense and that prevents the conception of other equally possible classifications.[30] Although Foucault acknowledged that a "point of convergence" existed among those to whom the structuralist label was applied—"the calling into question of the theory of the subject"[31]—he vigorously rejected the association and situated his work outside of structuralism: "I think that structuralism is inscribed today within a great transformation of knowledge (*savoir*) in the human sciences, and that this transformation has less to do with the analysis of structures than with a challenge of the anthropological status, the status of the subject, and the privileges of man. And my method is inscribed within the framework of this transformation in the same way that structuralism is—along side of the latter but not in it."[32] "I am absolutely not a structuralist," he asserted. "I have never used any of the concepts which can be considered characteristic of structuralism. I have mentioned the concept of structure several times, but I have never used it."[33]

Power

Foucault turned to the study of power when he came to realize that the treatment of knowledge within discourse cannot be separated from the operation of power. As a result of his study of knowledge as constituted in discourse and characterized by various governing rules, Foucault came to understand that knowledge and power are two sides of the same process. All knowledge is "interested" in that it is engaged in and subject to the exertion of power. Traditionally, the assumption has been that once individuals gain power, they no longer have knowledge: "It has been a tradition for humanism to assume that once someone gains power he ceases to know. Power makes men mad, and those who govern are blind; only those who keep their distance from power, who are in no way implicated in tyranny, shut up in their Cartesian *poêle*, their room, their meditations, only they can discover the truth."[34] This view needs to be abandoned, Foucault asserts, because it "allows us to imagine that knowledge can exist only where the power relations are suspended"—outside the injunctions, demands, and interests of power.[35] Foucault advocates instead a view of power in which "the exercise of power itself creates and causes to emerge new objects of knowledge and accumulates new bodies of information."[36] He explains:

> One can show, for example, that the medicalization of madness, in other words, the organization of medical knowledge around individuals

designated as mad, was connected with a whole series of social and economic processes at a given time, but also with institutions and practices of power. . . . It is also true that mathematics, for example, is linked, albeit in a completely different manner than psychiatry, to power structures, if only in the way it is taught, the way in which consensus among mathematicians is organized, [now it] functions in a closed circuit, has its values, determines what is good (true) or bad (false) in mathematics.[37]

Foucault does not see power and knowledge as identical, however: "I read—and I know it has been attributed to me—the thesis, 'Knowledge is power,' or 'Power is knowledge,' I begin to laugh, since studying their *relation* is precisely my problem. . . . The very fact that I pose the question of their relation proves clearly that I do not *identify* them."[38] The relation Foucault sees between them is one in which power and knowledge imply, implicate, and presuppose one another. There "is no power relation without the correlative constitution of a field of knowledge, nor any knowledge that does not presuppose and constitute at the same time power relations."[39] Power and knowledge relations are superimposed on one another and make one another possible, without either being reducible or subordinate to the other.

Foucault defines power as "a more-or-less organised, hierarchical, coordinated cluster of relations."[40] He sees the term *relations of power* as a more accurate descriptor than *power* for the concept, for it suggests a network of relationships that are systematically interconnected. "Power is relations; power is not a thing,"[41] Foucault explains, and it is exercised from innumerable points and distributed throughout complex social networks. Power is a characteristic of all relationships and, in fact, constitutes those relationships, whether economic, social, professional, or familial: "I mean that in human relationships, whether they involve verbal communication . . . or amorous, institutional or economic relationships, power is always present: I mean a relationship in which one person tries to control the conduct of the other. So I am speaking of relations that exist at different levels, in different forms; these power relations are mobile, they can be modified, they are not fixed once and for all."[42]

The doctor-patient relationship provides an example of Foucault's conception of power as relations. The relationship between these two individuals is defined by a common goal, constituted by a willingness to help on the part of the doctor and a recognition of need for help on the part of the patient. This coming together in a common goal is inseparable from a relation of power that is founded on the presumption that one knows and that the other will take the knower's advice. All individuals exercise power, then, and all are subjected to it: "Power is employed and exercised through a net-like organisation. And not only do individuals circulate between its threads; they are always in the position of simultaneously undergoing and exercising this power."[43]

Foucault's conception of power eschews a number of associations typically linked with power. It requires the abandonment of the legal or judicial view that narrowly defines power as based in the enunciation of the law:

When "one speaks of 'power,' people immediately think of a political structure, a government, a dominant social class, the master and the slave, and so on."[44] In classical judicial theory, power is considered a right, which one is able to possess like a commodity and that can be transferred or alienated through a legal transaction involving a contractual type of exchange. In this conception, "the King remains the central personage,"[45] and even when the legal system no longer relies on control by a monarch, the system is based on challenge to the prerogatives of the sovereign power and the limits of this power: "When it comes to the general organisation of the legal system in the West, it is essentially with the King, his rights, his power and its eventual limitations, that one is dealing."[46] Power in this view is "essentially a right of seizure: of things, time, bodies, and ultimately life itself"[47] as it prohibits, confiscates, or destroys what sovereign judgment pronounces illegitimate.

Foucault clarifies that his conception of power is different: "I am not thinking of this at all when I speak of 'relations of power.' "[48] The notion of power is too limited if it is conceptualized solely in terms of legislation, the constitution or the state, or a concern for rights and justice. We must "break free" of this reduction of power to law, Foucault asserts, "if we wish to analyze power within the concrete and historical framework of its operation."[49] Power is much more complicated, dense, and diffuse than a set of laws or a state apparatus.

Foucault also breaks with a traditional view of power in that he sees power as productive, in contrast to the typical view of power as repressive or prohibitive: "In general terms, I would say that the interdiction, the refusal, the prohibition, far from being essential forms of power, are only its limits: the frustrated or extreme forms of power. The relations of power are, above all, productive."[50] Foucault formulated this conception of power when he began to study prison life and found phenomena that a purely repressive conception of power could not accommodate. He came to believe that repression "is wholly inadequate to the analysis of the mechanisms and effects of power":[51]

> [Repressive power] is poor in resources, sparing of its methods, monotonous in the tactics it utilizes, incapable of invention, and seemingly doomed always to repeat itself. Further, it is a power that only has the force of the negative on its side, a power to say no; in no condition to produce, capable only of posting limits, it is basically anti-energy. This is the paradox of its effectiveness: it is incapable of doing anything, except to render what it dominates incapable of doing anything either, except for what this power allows it to do.[52]

Foucault explains how power operates as a creative force—one that facilitates, produces, and increases qualities and conditions: "If power were never anything but repressive, if it never did anything but to say no, do you really think one would be brought to obey it? What makes power hold good, what makes it accepted, is simply the fact that it doesn't only weigh on us as a force that says no, but that it traverses and produces things, it induces pleasure, forms knowledge, produces discourse."[53] In the prison, for example, power generally produces individuals subjected to habits, rules, order, and authority; delinquency; a high rate of recidivism; and destitution in inmates' families.[54] To Foucault, these are the results of a generative, creative power rather than a repressive, restraining one. Power, then, must be disconnected from the notion of repression: "There are a lot of power-relations which have repression-effects, but there are also a lot of power-relations which have something else entirely as their consequence."[55]

Just as Foucault's conception of power breaks with traditional associations of the term with legal domination and repression, it includes techniques of power not usually associated with the concept. Easily identifiable, spectacular exercises of destructive force such as public executions, the violent suppression of insurrections, and military occupations are replaced in Foucault's view by more subtle types of power imposed in practices of discipline. Foucault sees normalization, the practice of normalizing judgment and the construction of norms, as at the heart of these new practices: "We have entered a type of society where the power of law is not regressing but rather merging into a much more general power: roughly, that of the norm. . . . We are becoming a society which is essentially defined by the norm."[56] He elaborates: "Aren't the powers of normalization, the techniques of normalization, a kind of instrument found just about everywhere today, in the educational institution, the penal institution, in shops, factories and administrations, as a kind of general instrument, generally accepted?"[57]

The impoverishment of human possibilities that constitutes normalization is captured in Foucault's term *bio-power*, by which he means power over life. Normalization "exerts a positive influence on life, that endeavors to administer, optimize, and multiply it, subjecting it to precise controls and comprehensive regulations."[58] The power relations embedded in normalization constitute machinery that defines "how one may have a hold over others' bodies, not only so that they may do what one wishes, but so that they may operate as one wishes, with the techniques, the speed and the efficiency that one determines. Thus discipline produces subjected and practiced bodies, 'docile' bodies."[59] Another way to look at normalization is that it "is the exercise of something that one could call *government* in a very wide sense of the term. One can govern a society, one can govern a group, a community, a family; one can govern a person." Foucault explains that when he says " 'govern someone,' it is simply in the sense that one can determine one's behaviour in terms of a strategy by resorting to a number of tactics. Therefore, if you like, it is *governmentality* in the wide sense of the term, as the group of relations of power and techniques which allow these relations of power to be exercised."[60] The various techniques through which power is enacted in normalization are acceptable only because most of this kind of power is hidden, and individuals usually are unaware of the extent to which this power affects their lives.

Disneyland provides an example of Foucault's notion of normalization as a primary mode of the operation of power. The discursive technologies of

Disneyland are infused with a normative power that comes to control in very subtle ways the behavior of visitors to the amusement park. The breaking up of long lines visually controls the way in which visitors wait in line so that the frustration they normally would experience is dispersed. The constant instructions and lilting, often patriotic music make going along with prescribed activities easy and comfortable. The virtue of cleanliness is created through synthetic materials that suggest easy maintenance (artificial trees do not drop their leaves, for example), the fresh-scrubbed image of the employees, and the litter-free grounds. Individuals usually scorn fakery and imitations of real objects, but at Disneyland, they accept them, relishing copies of furniture, computer-programmed simulations of people, and artificial trees and animals. The rides prevent activity and initiative by visitors, who are offered no choices except trivial ones as they sit passively in containers that transport them in front of and through programmed exhibits. Disneyland, then, is a powerful discursive system that succeeds at making people accept as normal and enjoy experiences they typically would not, at the same time discouraging them from questioning what they typically would. The discursive practices of Disneyland promote wholesome, sterile, and predictable behavior and produce visitors who fill passive, clean, unquestioning roles.[61]

Resistance

Foucault's view of power as omnipresent, dispersed, continuous, and creative raises questions about the nature of resistance and whether reform is possible. Foucault does see resistance as possible: "We are never trapped by power: we can always modify its grip in determinate conditions and according to a precise strategy."[62] He defines resistance as "a centrifugal movement, an inverse energy, a discharge"[63] that "is not anterior to the power which it opposes. It is coextensive with it and absolutely its contemporary."[64] Resistance operates as power does—by being inventive, mobile, and productive. Like power, resistance must "organize, coagulate, and solidify itself. Like power, it would have to come from 'underneath' and distribute itself strategically."[65]

The resistance that coexists with power in Foucault's system is not directed, however, toward the achievement of a particular ideal or utopian society. Every discursive formation is characterized by discourse that both creates and constrains. Thus, to replace one order with another will not bring about greater freedom from discourse. Those who hold a notion of utopia are "blind to the fact that relations of power are not something bad in themselves, from which one must free one's self. I don't believe there can be a society without relations of power, if you understand them as means by which individuals try to conduct, to determine the behavior of others."[66] Furthermore, there is no way of knowing what a "better" discursive formation might be like because each new one produces governing rules for discourse, and there is no particular reason to expect that these will be any better under a new system than the rules that characterize the old one. Foucault opposes the existing order of things, then, but he does not intend to replace what exists. Humans are justified in opposing an order but not in the name of a better order.[67]

Opposition to existing order occurs, according to Foucault, not through the universal intellectual but through the specific intellectual. The universal intellectual is someone who defends natural rights; advocates humanity; and is a bearer of universal moral, theoretical, and political values. In contrast, specific intellectuals are ordinary people who have knowledge of their circumstances and are able to express themselves independently of the universal theorizing intellectual. Because Foucault objects to the idea of a knowledge or a truth outside of networks of power relations, specific intellectuals must work "not in the modality of the 'universal,' the 'exemplary,' the 'just-and-true-for-all,' but within specific sectors, at the precise points where their own conditions of life or work situate them (housing, the hospital, the asylum, the laboratory, the university, family and sexual relations)."[68] The ideals and norms to which specific intellectuals appeal in their work are always internal to the practices they are criticizing. Thus, no transhistorical universals exist in which to ground their critiques, and no theory of global domination guides their revolutionary efforts. Their "progressive politics" recognizes "the historical conditions and the specified rules of a practice."[69] This is the level, then, at which criminals challenge prison conditions; welfare workers and clients seek to change the bureaucracy; consumers organize against corporations; and inmates, attendants, and therapists disrupt the asylum.

The major tool of resistance that Foucault suggests is available to specific intellectuals is critique, which mounts an attack against the existing order of things. Examination of a discursive formation to discover the rules and power relations that undergird it constitutes the act of critique, which problematizes or disrupts commonly held conceptions. Critique "is not a matter of saying that things are not right as they are. It is a matter of pointing out on what kinds of assumptions, what kinds of familiar, unchallenged, unconsidered modes of thought the practices that we accept rest." Criticism is a matter of seeing "that what is accepted as self-evident will no longer be accepted as such."[70] The work of the specific intellectual is "to re-examine evidence and assumptions, to shake up habitual ways of working and thinking, to dissipate conventional familiarities, to re-evaluate rules and institutions."[71] The specific intellectual, then, exercises critical thought through the analysis, description, and criticism of existing power/knowledge relations in specific areas to create an experience of their intolerability, thus opening up a space for change.

Foucault posits a particular role for the specific intellectual who seeks to create change. Engagement in critique does not give specific intellectuals the right to speak for those who have been disqualified from speaking in the discursive formation. Instead, the role of such individuals is to help to create conditions in which the disqualified may express themselves. This can be done by pointing out to the disqualified some places where their particular battles may need to be fought and inviting them to do something about it. "The role of an intellectual is not to tell others what they must do," asserts Foucault. "By what right would he do so? . . . The work of an intellectual is not to mold the political will of others."[72] Foucault envisions his task and that of other specific intellectuals as one of providing tools for others to use in the contexts and struggles in which they find themselves.

Foucault acknowledges that the stance he assigns to the specific intellectual can be criticized because it does not offer specific instructions to the disenfranchised: "On the other hand, it's true that certain people, such as those who work in the institutional setting of the prison . . . are not likely to find advice or instructions in my books that tell them 'what is to be done.' " He explains, however, that his project is to bring them to a place where they " 'no longer know what to do,' so that the acts, gestures, discourses which up until then had seemed to go without saying become problematic, difficult, dangerous."[73] As a result, Foucault believes, those directly involved in the resistance will come to know what to do. If transformation occurs, "it won't be because a plan of reform has found its way into the heads of the social workers; it will be when those who have to do with that . . . reality, all those people, have come into collision with each other and with themselves, run into dead ends, problems and impossibilities, been through conflicts and confrontations; when critique has been played out in the real, not when reformers have realised their ideas."[74] He elaborates:

> But it seems to me that "what is to be done" ought not to be determined from above by reformers, be they prophetic or legislative, but by a long work of comings and goings, of exchanges, reflections, trials, different analyses. If the social workers . . . don't know which way to turn, this just goes to show that they're looking, and hence not anaesthetised or sterilised at all—on the contrary. And it's because of the need not to tie them down or immobilize them that there can be no question for me of trying to tell them "what is to be done." If the questions posed by the social workers . . . are going to assume their full amplitude, the most important thing is not to bury them under the weight of prescriptive, prophetic discourse.[75]

Ethics

Foucault's project began with an examination of the branches of knowledge that constitute human beings as knowable subjects, which he followed with an analysis of the power relations generated by these branches of knowledge. In his last two volumes on sexuality, he adds ethics to his analyses of knowledge and power, excavating the ways in which individuals fashion their subjectivity. What Foucault is calling *ethics* is at odds with the typical definition of the term as an abstract normative code, customary conduct, or duty. For Foucault, the field of ethics concerns who human beings are said to be and the various means through which the notion of being is created.[76] Foucault explains that his interest in this kind of ethics was a part of his earlier projects:

"In actual fact, I have always been interested in this problem, even if I framed it somewhat differently. I have tried to find out how the human subject fits into certain games of truth, whether they were truth games that take the form of a science or refer to a scientific model, or truth games such as those one may encounter in institutions or practices of control."[77]

Foucault's exploration of the self is not a traditional hermeneutics of the self. He does "not plumb the depths of self in order to discover inner truth—an authoritative, authentic experience."[78] Foucault's project takes the form of questioning dominant forms of self-understanding available in the modern West. While his earlier works focus on the anonymous processes through which individuals are constituted by one another, his analyses of the self disclose historical processes or practices that individuals perform on themselves. Foucault's exploration of the technologies of the self begins with the idea that identity is not fixed by nature or rooted in prior knowledge of who the self is. In other words, being the subject of one's own experience is not a given. He then asks how individuals come to be constituted as the subject of their own experience and finds in ethics an area in which he can see the processes by which this happens—the sort of work, attention, knowledge, and techniques that go into self-formation. He sets out to do an analysis of these technologies of the self or the means by which discursive formations incite individuals to use particular means to turn themselves into subjects.

Instead of beginning with *a priori* theories of the subject, Foucault wants to try to show "how the subject constituted itself, in one specific form or another, as a mad or a healthy subject, as a delinquent or non-delinquent subject, through certain practices that were also games of truth, practices of power, etc."[79] Individuals do not have the same relationships to themselves when they constitute themselves as political subjects who vote or when they are seeking to fulfill their desires in a sexual relationship.[80] Because the practices individuals use for such transformation—like those used to create institutions and particular types of roles within them—are patterns in a "culture and which are proposed, suggested and imposed on" the individual by that culture,[81] these practices are not invented by individuals themselves. Ethics is "an activity of disciplined self-knowledge in accordance with certain shared or communal norms,"[82] inherited from historical traditions.

For Foucault, ethics is one part of the study of morals, which consists of three component parts. One element of morals is the moral code, or the rules that determine "which acts are permitted or forbidden and the code which determines the positive or negative value of the different possible behaviors."[83] An example of a moral code is the precept that the individual is not supposed to steal. A second element of morals is the actual activity or behavior in which individuals engage, "the real behavior of people in relation to the moral code (*prescriptions*) which is imposed on them."[84] A third element of Foucault's view of morals is ethics, "the kind of relationship you ought to have with yourself . . . and which determines how the individual is supposed to constitute himself as a moral subject of his own actions."[85]

Foucault divides the realm of ethics itself into four aspects. The first is ethical substance, which is the particular aspect of the self that is seen as the relevant domain for moral conduct. It is the part of the self that is taken into account or subjected to ethics and is the prime material of moral conduct. In various discursive formations, this ethical substance may be feelings, intentions, or desires.

A second component of ethics is mode of subjection, the authority or rationale for moral obligations or "the way in which people are invited or incited to recognize their moral obligations."[86] Mode of subjection is the way in which individuals establish their relation to moral obligations and rules. Moral obligations may be imposed from a wide variety of sources, including divine law, the demands of reason, or convention.

A third aspect of ethics is asceticism or self-discipline, the practical means by which individuals become ethical subjects. Asceticism involves the techniques to be used or the ethical work to be performed to bring the self into compliance with the moral code. It is the "self-forming activity or ethical work that one performs on oneself in order to transform oneself into an ethical subject."[87] Techniques may include a painstaking, detailed checking of progress; confessions; exercises; or deprivations to be endured.

A fourth aspect of ethics is the *telos*, or the image of the right sort of person, life, or soul. *Telos* is the type of being one is attempting to become by means of ethical practices—the state of perfection or completion or the mode of being at which one aims in behaving ethically. Foucault sees this aspect of the ethical system summarized in the question, "Which is the kind of being to which we aspire when we behave in a moral way? For instance, shall we become pure, or immortal, or free, or masters of ourselves, and so on?"[88] In what Foucault calls "the Californian cult of the self," for example, the *telos* is discovery of "one's true self,"[89] which is to be achieved through such modes of subjection as therapy and the reading of self-help books.

The ethical subject, then, is constituted through a focus on a particular aspect of the self as the substance of ethics, the authority for moral obligations, the means by which the self is brought into compliance in the ethical system, and the ideal state toward which the self aims in ethical conduct.[90] Foucault uses the term *game* to describe the relationship he sees between ethics and truth. He explains that game means "a set of rules by which truth is produced. It is not a game in the sense of an amusement; it is a set of procedures that lead to a certain result, which, on the basis of its principles and rules of procedure, may be considered valid or invalid, winning or losing."[91] Care of the self or ethics involves "knowledge of a number of rules of acceptable conduct or of principles that are both truths and prescriptions. To take care of the self is to equip oneself with these truths: this is where ethics is linked to the game of truth."[92]

The practices of sexuality provide a good case study for the exploration of ethics and its link to truth. Foucault believes that throughout the Christian era and perhaps even earlier, individuals have been asked to recognize themselves in relation to sexuality as subjects of pleasure and desire. Various practices related to sexuality such as self-examination, spiritual exercises, avowal, and confession require that individuals apply the game of truth and falsehood to the most private and personal elements of their subjectivity.

Foucault does not explore sexuality or other ethical practices to liberate sexuality. He believes that such a view implies that "there exists a human nature or base that, as a consequence of certain historical, economic and social processes, has been concealed, alienated or imprisoned in and by mechanisms of repression. According to this hypothesis, all that is required is to break these repressive deadlocks and man will be reconciled with himself, rediscover his nature or regain contact with his origin, and reestablish a full and positive relationship with himself."[93] He sees the problem, instead, as one of "defining the practices of freedom by which one could define what is sexual pleasure and erotic, amorous and passionate relationships with others." This act of definition "is much more important than the rather repetitive affirmation that sexuality or desire must be liberated."[94]

Foucault explores transformations in practices of self-formation to reveal their contingency and to free humans for new possibilities of self-understanding, modes of experience, forms of subjectivity, authority, and political identity. His concern is with "the need to escape those prisons of thought and action that shape our politics, our ethics, our relations to ourselves."[95] Thus, the aim of Foucault's self-interrogations is not self-discovery but rather self-refusal—"to become someone else you were not at the beginning."[96]

Analytical Methods

Foucault adopted distinctive terms for his specific methodological approaches to investigating discursive formations and the different emphases he placed on them at the different phases of his career. His early works are called *archaeologies* and focus on knowledge, the subsequent ones are *genealogies* and have as their central theme power, and the volumes on the history of sexuality that focus on ethics Foucault calls *problematizations*. He discovered after each new set of works was written that each new focus was an implicit interest of the earlier focus. Thus, Foucault asserts that the "question of power relations, which characterizes his genealogies, was what his archaeologies were really about and, subsequently, that the issue of truth and subjectivity, the explicit focus of his final works, had been his basic concern all along."[97] As Foucault explains in the introduction to the second volume of *The History of Sexuality*, his previous investigations were the fruit of theoretical shifts that do not exclude one another, and none of the emphases constitutes the complete story.[98]

Archaeology

Foucault initially called his method of investigating epistemes or discursive formations *archaeology*, a term that first appeared in *Madness and Civilization*.

By *archaeology*, Foucault means a "description of the *archive*,"[99] with *archive* defined as "the set of discourses actually pronounced."[100] Archaeology is an analysis of the production of discourse in terms of the conditions of possibility that allow discourse to appear and that govern the system of knowledge and order. It is a way of analyzing systems of thought through a description of what may be spoken of in discourse, which terms are recognized as valid, and what individuals or groups have access to particular kinds of discourse. The aim of archaeology, then, is to enter the interior of discourse to determine the rules that govern it and to describe the various relations among statements in a discursive formation. In short, archaeology is used to discover how, at a given period, something could be said and something else never was said.

Foucault rejects two connotations of *archaeology* that he does not intend to be included in his meaning for the term. One is the notion of "the discovery of a beginning or the bringing to light of the bones of the past."[101] He explains, "Yet I try not to study the beginning in the sense of the first origin, of a foundation starting from which the rest would be possible. I am not searching for the first solemn moment after which all of Western mathematics becomes possible, for example. . . . It's always the relative beginnings that I am searching for, more the institutionalizations or the transformations than the foundings or foundations."[102] He is equally bothered by the connotation of excavations associated with the term: "What I'm looking for are not relations that are secret, hidden, more silent or deeper than the consciousness of men. I try on the contrary to define the relations on the very surface of discourse; I attempt to make visible what is invisible only because it's too much on the surface of things."[103]

Genealogy

In 1972, Foucault introduced the term *genealogy* to describe his method of investigation,[104] adding his new awareness of the importance of power relations to his analyses. Genealogy is the discovery both of the rules that govern discursive practices and of the network of power relations of which these rules are a part. While archaeology involves the identification of the rules of production and transformation for discourse, genealogy's focus is on summarizing "the kinds of power-relations which exist in our society, the ways in which they are related to other systems of relations, and the extent to which power-relations are embedded in our habits, behaviors, institutions, rules, political systems, and the extent to which these relations conform to the goals and values which these institutions, practices and habits take as their justification."[105]

The explicit focus of genealogy is on the imposition of power upon bodies. Foucault's genealogy of the criminal system, for example, centers on the way the "body as the major target of penal repression disappeared"[106] at a certain point in history, only to be subjected to more subtle control by the normalizing techniques of the social sciences in the nineteenth century.

Similarly, the first volume of his genealogy of sexuality reveals "the encroachment of a type of power on bodies and their pleasures" that the Victorian proliferation of "perversions" produced.[107]

Problematization

Foucault characterizes his last works as *problematizations*, a change in terminology that occurred during the eight-year gap between the first and the next two volumes of *The History of Sexuality*. As a result of his work on the last two volumes, he explains that he "now had to undertake a third shift, in order to analyze what is termed 'the subject.' . . . It seemed appropriate to look for the forms and modalities of the relation to self by which the individual constitutes and recognizes himself *qua* subject."[108] He defines problematization as "the ensemble of discursive and nondiscursive practices that makes something enter into the play of the true and the false and constitutes it an object of thought (whether in the form of moral reflection, scientific knowledge, political analysis or the like.)"[109]

Although both archaeological and genealogical dimensions are a part of the experience Foucault analyzes, the distinctive question is the problematizing of activity in the constitution of the moral self. Foucault explains: "If I have studied 'practices' like those of the sequestration of the insane, or clinical medicine, or the organisation of the empirical sciences, or legal punishment, it was in order to study this interplay between a 'code' which rules ways of doing things (how people are to be graded and examined, things and signs classified, individuals trained, etc.) and a production of true discourses which serve to found, justify, and provide reasons and principles for these ways of doing things. To put the matter clearly: my problem is to see how men govern (themselves and others) by the production of truth."[110]

Methodological Tenets

Although Foucault suggests specific concerns for archaeology, genealogy, and problematization, the three complementary modes of analysis share some methodological tenets. These tenets, however, are not ones Foucault advocates for everyone or whose use he tries to limit or control. "Thus I don't construct a general method of definitive value for myself or for others. What I write does not prescribe anything, neither to myself nor to others. At most, its character is instrumental and visionary or dream-like."[111] He emphasizes that his books and their methods are not defined or limited, and he encourages "new, possible, unforeseen uses" for them. "All my books . . . are, if you like, little tool boxes. If people want to open them, use a particular sentence, idea, or analysis like a screwdriver or wrench in order to short-circuit, disqualify or break up the systems of power, including eventually the very ones from which my books have issued . . . well, all the better!"[112]

One methodological tenet that characterizes Foucault's project is the nature of the data he chooses to study. Rather than studying renowned documents such as texts produced by famous philosophers or the documentation surrounding extraordinary events, he studies common, generally unknown documents that typically are considered to be insignificant. The documents he analyzes include records kept by doctors, teachers, and priests; popular prescriptive manuals; grant proposals; and files kept by various bureaucratic agencies. As Foucault explains, he wants to address "a layer of material which had hitherto had no pertinence for history and which had not been recognised as having any moral, aesthetic, political or historical value."[113] Foucault explores these documents to discover what "was done" with, for example, mental patients, criminals, or sick people. He discovers what was done by attending to and analyzing the points "of linkage (*enchaînement*) of what one says and what one does, of the rules one prescribes to oneself and the reason one ascribes, of projects and of evidences."[114] The practices in which Foucault is interested are simultaneously modes of acting and thinking that "establish and apply norms, controls, and exclusions" and "render true/false discourse possible."[115] He studies them to understand "what was constituted as real for those who were attempting to conceptualize and govern it, and of the way in which those same people constituted themselves as subjects capable of knowing, analyzing, and ultimately modifying the real."[116]

As he studies his data, trying to discover common structures in which they are grounded, Foucault seeks to locate events, which he conceptualizes as breaks of self-evidence. An event "is not a decision, a treaty, a reign, or a battle"[117] but "a breach of self-evidence, of those self-evidences on which our knowledges, acquiescences and practices rest."[118] Through the identification of events, Foucault rediscovers "the connections, encounters, supports, blockages, plays of forces, strategies and so on which at a given moment establish what subsequently counts as being self-evident, universal and necessary."[119] He looks for events that show how commonly accepted knowledge is not self-evident—the point, for example, at which "mad people came to be regarded as mentally ill." As he explains, it was not always "self-evident that the only thing to be done with a criminal was to lock him up; it wasn't self-evident that the causes of illness were to be sought through the individual examination of bodies; and so on."[120]

Foucault's analytic method also involves attention to contradictions. Instead of attempting to make disparate views or modes of thought fit into a coherent pattern of discourse, Foucault seeks to discover and investigate such disparities, viewing contradictions as "neither appearances to be overcome, nor secret principles to be uncovered. They are objects to be described for themselves."[121] By determining the extent and form of the gap that separates disparities, Foucault aims to determine if, in fact, they do belong to the same discursive formation. For example, in the eighteenth century, the thesis of the animal nature of fossils was contradicted by the thesis of their mineral nature. The attempt to discover how two statements that now seem contradictory could have been held simultaneously reveals information about the nature of the discursive formation that contained them.

The belief that the analysis of discourse should be a descriptive or transcriptive practice rather than an interpretive one is a foundation for Foucault's method. He does not approach discursive analysis by trying to discover latent and invisible elements or "a hidden element, a secret meaning that lies buried" in manifest discourse.[122] Rather, he hopes to discover the boundaries of acceptability for claims to truth in the discursive formation. Although Foucault recognizes that to avoid interpretation is impossible—in part because of individual perception and the discursive formation in which the observer exists—he seeks to avoid it because crucial content always is lost or suppressed in the process. Interpretation, or what Foucault sometimes calls *commentary*, also is a technique of power in that it selects what is to be suppressed and allows only specially qualified individuals to do the interpreting.[123] Foucault prefers to approach a document or body of discourse in its "raw, neutral state," focusing on what is actually said and done. His aim is simply to give "*a pure description of discursive events*"[124] that allows for the discovery of relationships among statements, the discursive formation in which the events took place, and the kind of conceptual and power changes that accompanied the events.

Another tenet that unites Foucault's archaeologies, genealogies, and problematizations is his rejection of the practice of relating a piece of discourse to its specific author or creator. He is not concerned with the specific person who said or wrote something and does not connect the discourse to the individual who created it. Foucault assumes this position because he views the author as fulfilling a discursive function—playing a role and filling a vacant space that could be filled by many different individuals—with the power of discourse constraining the author's utterances. Foucault quotes Samuel Beckett from *Texts for Nothing* to make his point: "What matter who's speaking, someone said, what matter who's speaking."[125] He seeks to refer "discourse not to the thought, to the mind or to the subject which might have given rise to it, but to the practical field in which it is deployed."[126] He does not move back toward the constitutive subject when seeking an account of an object of knowledge but focuses on the study of the concrete practices by which the subject is constituted in a domain of knowledge. Consequently, in Foucault's writings, no biographical information is presented about the individuals he mentions. What is important for Foucault is the discovery of the role the individual plays and the rules that govern the nature of that role.

Foucault's perspective on the role of individuals in discursive formations is connected to his notion that the human being soon will disappear, by which he means that the current consciousness of the human being soon will disappear. While in the seventeenth and eighteenth centuries the human being was viewed as a function, in the discursive formation of modernity, the human being is regarded as the foundation and origin of knowledge. Foucault sees this epistemological consciousness of the human being as a relatively recent invention within European culture that did not exist in previous epistemes: "Strangely enough, man—the study of whom is supposed by the näive to be the oldest investigation since Socrates—is probably no more than a kind of rift in the order of things."[127] Foucault predicts that this new conception of the human being will change: "It is comforting, however, and a source of profound relief to think that man is only a recent invention, a figure not yet two centuries old, a new wrinkle in our knowledge, and that he will disappear again as soon as that knowledge has discovered a new form."[128] In the discursive formation that he foresees, a sovereign subject who comes from the outside "to animate the inertia of the linguistic codes" and to "constitute the meanings" and then "transcribe them into the discourse" will disappear.[129]

Foucault cites as evidence for the coming disappearance of the modern conception of the human being new trends in the analysis of language that are incompatible with the idea of the human being as a distinct self. These analyses focus not on a theory of the knowing subject but rather on a theory of discursive practices, linguistic structures, and epistemological structures that have no need of the human being as their central presence. In this view, language is seen as a set of formal relationships long antedating individual personal identities. The idea of the human being was built on a system of knowledge that, in itself, has no logical stability and no lasting criteria of truth and validity. As language regains primacy, the human being once again will return to its previous nonexistence as a concept around which to organize knowledge. Foucault asks, "is this not the sign that the whole of this configuration is now about to topple, and that man is in the process of perishing as the being of language continues to shine ever brighter upon our horizon?"[130] Foucault does not find the notion of the disappearance of the human being as the organizing principle of knowledge to be unsettling: "The death of man is nothing to get particularly excited about. It's one of the visible forms of a much more general decease, if you like." It is "the death of the subject, of the Subject in capital letters, of the subject as origin and foundation of Knowledge."[131]

Commentary

Foucault's work has been acclaimed in a number of fields for its originality and insight. It "compels irresistibly [sic]," Vernon Pratt asserts, "illuminating the darkness, not so much a searchlight as a firework display, brilliant, theatrical, bewildering."[132] Meaghan Morris and Paul Patton attribute Foucault's originality to the fact that nothing "less than a new conception of philosophical work is involved."[133] Edward W. Said agrees, calling Foucault's work "a new field of research (or of a new way of conceiving and doing research)."[134]

Although few critics dispute the significance of Foucault's contributions, many complain about his difficult style of writing. Roy McMullen, for example, describes it as "reckless, irritating, and frequently unfathomable";[135] Pratt describes it as "tantalizingly obscure";[136] and Jan Miel views it as "digressive

and repetitive."[137] Hayden White suggests that Foucault's style is characterized by "interminable sentences, parentheses, repetitions, neologisms, paradoxes, oxymorons, alternation of analytical with lyrical passages, and his
combination of scientistic with mythic terminology," which appears "to be
consciously designed to render his discourse impenetrable."[138] White continues, "He cannot *say* anything directly."[139] His terminology, Ronald Hayman
agrees, "presents an undeniable obstacle."[140] The problem, most critics agree,
is that "Foucault uses some deceptively ordinary words . . . in senses that are
highly specialized."[141] Some writers have responded particularly negatively to
the obscure style of Foucault's writing, suggesting that he "is like a magician
forever popping rabbits out of his hat and calling them bluebirds."[142] Still another asks whether understanding his work is "worth the trouble of assimilat-
ing jargon like this."[143]

A number of critics respond to criticisms of Foucault's style of writing by
justifying it in various ways. Eve Tavor Bannet suggests that Foucault's difficult style is a result of his modes of analysis, which "required him to pursue
so many threads at the same time and to encorporate so much specific detail
that the reader is in constant danger of missing the wood for the trees,
branches, twigs and texture of the bark."[144] Foucault tried, she suggests, to
deal with the objections to his style in two ways. He increased his methodological signposting, writing articles and giving interviews to try to clarify his
project and what he meant by particular terms. He also changed his style in
his later works: "The rhetorical and poetical richness of the early books gives
way in the later ones to a much more sparse, straightforward and down-to-
earth style, in which imagery is used much more sparingly for essential ana-
logical purposes."[145]

The evidence that Foucault selects to support the claims he makes is of
concern to other critics. Some have noted that Foucault fails to take into account relevant bits of evidence to support the existence of a particular
episteme or discursive formation—the central importance of Newtonian
physics in the eighteenth century in *The Order of Things*, for example.[146] Others suggest that Foucault ignores evidence that contradicts his thesis—"numerous documents that by sheer number of pages argue vociferously to the
contrary."[147] He has been criticized, for example, for ignoring references to
the conception of the human being in such pre-nineteenth-century writers as
Aristotle, Locke, Pope, Vico, Shakespeare, and Hume when he develops his
thesis that such a conception of the human being did not exist at the time.[148]
R. D. Laing summarizes the complaint, commenting that "Foucault sometimes whirls words into pirouettes which are more to be admired for their
brilliance than trusted for their veracity."[149] Foucault responds to these
charges by noting that he uses "methods that are part of the classic repertory: demonstration, proof by means of historical documentation, quoting
other texts, referral to authoritative comments. . . . From this point of view,
whatever I assert in my writing can be verified or refuted as in any other history book."[150] The end product he sees for his analyses, however, is not the

typical one associated with historical research. Foucault explains that when people say to him that "the things you say are nothing but fictions!," his response is always whoever thinks he is writing anything but fiction?[151]

Another criticism of Foucault's work is that his ideas are inconsistent across his works and that a comparison among his works yields differences in terminology, frameworks, and schema of classification that are conflicting. He devises numerous classification systems for the rules governing discursive formations, for example, with overlaps and discrepancies among them. Mark Poster, however, does not see such variety as a problem and views Foucault's inconsistencies as his refusal "to totalize his position . . . to present a neat and closed theory of history, a formula that would explain the past. . . . The syncopated, uneven character of his books rubs unpleasantly against the sensibilities of those expecting a text that resolves all the main questions."[152]

Other defenders of Foucault's inconsistencies explain them as the result of the very different domains in which he works and the specific demands of those domains. Gary Gutting, for example, argues that specific circumstances occasion the production of Foucault's works: "Each of Foucault's books strikes a specific tone that is muffled and distorted if we insist on harmonizing it with his other books."[153] Gutting suggests that each of Foucault's books has the air of a new beginning; his "theorizing is typically not for its own sake but in response to the demands of a specific historical or critical project."[154] His theories "are temporary scaffoldings, erected for a specific purpose, that Foucault is happy to abandon . . . once he has finished his job."[155]

Foucault himself answers the charge of inconsistency not only by acknowledging but by celebrating the inconsistencies and changes in his thinking: "I'm perfectly aware of having continuously made shifts both in the things that have interested me and in what I have already thought," he explains.[156] "I write precisely because I don't know yet what to think about a subject that attracts my interest. In so doing, the book transforms me, changes what I think."[157] As he reiterates, "Well, do you think I have worked like that all those years to say the same thing and not to be changed?"[158] Foucault summarizes his stance on charges of his inconsistency with this plea: "Do not ask who I am and do not ask me to remain the same: leave it to our bureaucrats and our police to see that our papers are in order."[159]

Divergent responses to Foucault's work do not diminish the many contributions it makes to rhetorical theory. In his early works, he examines the forms of discursive practices that articulated the human sciences, a project in which he explores the relationship between rhetoric and knowledge and thus the notion that rhetoric is epistemic or a way of knowing. A particular discursive formation produces particular kinds of knowledge, just as a particular system of knowledge is inextricably linked to the discourse in which it materializes. Knowledge or truth is created by the rhetorical process and is not possible apart from this process. Foucault's studies of the development of various institutions with their concomitant systems of knowledge provide much historical support for a perspective on rhetoric as epistemic.

Foucault next turned his attention to the notion of power, examining "the manifold relations, the open strategies, and the rational techniques that articulate the exercise of powers."[160] In this effort, he suggests a relationship between rhetoric and power, redefining the notion of power in contemporary society. Power, in his view, is not the explicit domination of one person by another but "the capacity to become or to do certain things . . . exercised by individual or collective human bodies when . . . the actions of one affect the field of possible actions of another."[161]

Foucault's conception of power raises two questions that complicate theorizing about rhetoric in terms of resistance. His focus on the extent to which individuals are subjected to the influences of power raises the question of whether they "are able to operate as agents in the face of disciplinary mechanisms which normalize their behaviour"[162] and alter power relationships. Some critics note that Foucault offers a bleak picture in which the subject always is an effect of power relations and in which there is no possibility of escape from domination of some kind. Nancy Hartsock, for example, asserts that Foucault "fails to provide an epistemology which is usable for the task of revolutionizing, creating and constructing."[163] The issue of the degree of agency Foucault attributes to the individual provides an opportunity for rethinking individuals' capacity to resist power relations and the nature of justification for change in a system, issues that have received little attention in rhetorical theory.

A second contribution Foucault makes to the study of power in the operation of rhetoric concerns the criteria for judgment or norms on which to base critiques of systems in terms of the power relations that characterize them. His "descriptive analyses of power provide us with no criteria for judgement, no basis upon which to condemn some regimes of power as oppressive or to applaud others as involving progress in human freedom,"[164] Patton asserts. Nancy Fraser agrees: "Clearly, what Foucault needs, and needs desperately, are normative criteria for distinguishing acceptable from unacceptable forms of power."[165] Although some critics see Foucault's lack of criteria in this area as an approach that "exposes the limitations of the demand for such criteria,"[166] his work raises the question of how individuals make such judgments and justify them.

In his final works, Foucault saw that his previous emphasis on discursive practices external to individuals needed to be complemented by a consideration of the techniques of the self. He turned to an analysis of ethics and the means by which individuals constitute themselves as subjects, exploring the connection between the self and rhetoric. By defining ethics as the activity of self-constitution, he complicates and broadens the conception of morality and ethics in rhetorical theory. This process of care for the self involves ethical work in that there is "an attempt to transform oneself into a particular type of subject, a process which involved decisions, goals and a certain amount of freedom to choose between different alternatives."[167] Foucault sees his conception of ethics as a useful response to a major problem concerning ethics today: Most "of us no longer believe that ethics is founded in religion, nor do we want a legal system to intervene in our moral, personal, private life. Recent liberation movements suffer from the fact that they cannot find any principle on which to base the elaboration of a new ethics."[168] Foucault offers a rhetorically based means of conceptualizing the self in relation to ethics as a solution to the problem.

Foucault hopes that his work functions to transform those who read it: "An experience is, of course, something one has alone; but it cannot have its full impact unless the individual manages to escape from pure subjectivity in such a way that others can—I won't say re-experience it exactly—but at least cross paths with it or retrace it."[169] His works invite readers to share his experience and thus to experience transformation. The results inevitably challenge the existing order, as Robert J. Ellrich explains, because Foucault "deliberately sets out to do cartwheels on the banquet table, and manages to splash through just about everyone's soup."[170]

Bibliography

Books

The Archaeology of Knowledge and the Discourse on Language. Trans. A. M. Sheridan Smith. New York: Pantheon, 1972.
The Birth of the Clinic: An Archaeology of Medical Perception. Trans. A. M. Sheridan Smith. New York: Pantheon, 1973.
The Care of the Self: The History of Sexuality: Volume 3. Trans. Robert Hurley. New York: Pantheon, 1986.
Death and the Labyrinth: The World of Raymond Roussel. Trans. Charles Ruas. Garden City, NY: Doubleday, 1986.
Discipline and Punish: The Birth of the Prison. Trans. Alan Sheridan. New York: Pantheon, 1978.
Herculine Barbin: Being the Recently Discovered Memoirs of a Nineteenth-Century French Hermaphrodite. Trans. Richard McDougall. New York: Pantheon, 1980. (Collective work edited by Foucault and others.)
The History of Sexuality: Volume I: An Introduction. Trans. Robert Hurley. New York: Pantheon, 1978.
I, Pierre Rivière having slaughtered my mother, my sister and my brother. . .: A Case of Parricide in the 19th Century. Trans. Frank Jellinek. New York: Pantheon, 1975. (Collective work edited by Foucault and others.)
Le désordre des familles: lettres de cachet des Archives de la Bastille. Paris: Gallimard, Julliard, 1982. (Edited with Arlette Farge.)
Madness and Civilization: A History of Insanity in the Age of Reason. Trans. Richard Howard. New York: Pantheon, 1965.
Mental Illness and Psychology. Trans. A. M. Sheridan Smith. New York: Harper and Row, 1976.
The Order of Things: An Archaeology of the Human Sciences. New York: Pantheon, 1970.

This is Not a Pipe. Trans. and ed. James Harkness. Berkeley: University of California Press, 1982.

The Use of Pleasure: The History of Sexuality: Volume 2. Trans. Robert Hurley. New York: Pantheon, 1985.

Articles

"About the Concept of the 'Dangerous Individual' in 19th-Century Legal Psychiatry." Trans. Alain Baudot and Jane Couchman. *International Journal of Law and Psychiatry,* 1 (January 1978), 1–18.

"Afterword: The Subject and Power." Trans. Leslie Sawyer. In *Michel Foucault: Beyond Structuralism and Hermeneutics.* By Hubert L. Dreyfus and Paul Rabinow. Chicago: University of Chicago Press, 1982, pp. 208–26.

"The Catch-all Strategy." Trans. Neil Duxbury. *International Journal of the Sociology of Law,* 16 (May 1988), 139–62.

"Contemporary Music and the Public." *Perspectives of New Music,* 24 (1985), 6–12. (With Pierre Boulez.)

"Dream, Imagination, and Existence: An Introduction to Ludwig Binswanger's 'Dream and Existence.'" Trans. Forrest Williams. *Review of Existential Psychology and Psychiatry,* 19 (1984-85), 29–78.

"An Exchange with Michel Foucault." *New York Review of Books,* 30 (March 31, 1983), 42.

"The Eye of Power." *Semiotext(e),* 3 (1978), 6–19.

"The Flying University." *New York Review of Books,* January 24, 1980, p. 49. (With other members of the International Support Committee for the Freedom of Learning in Poland.)

"Foucault at the Collège de France II: A Course Summary." Trans. James Bernauer. *Philosophy and Social Criticism,* 8 (Fall 1981), 350–59.

"Foucault Responds/2." *Diacritics,* 11 (Winter 1971), 60.

"Georges Canguilhem: Philosopher of Error." Trans. Graham Burchell. *Ideology and Consciousness,* 7 (1980), 51–62.

"Governmentality." Trans. Rosi Braidotti. In *The Foucault Effect: Studies in Governmentality.* Ed. Graham Burchell, Colin Gordon, and Peter Miller. Chicago: University of Chicago Press, 1991, pp. 87–104.

"The Guillotine Lives." Trans. and ed. Paul Auster. *New York Times,* April 8, 1973, sec. 4, p. 15.

"History, Discourse and Discontinuity." Trans. Anthony M. Nazzaro. *Salmagundi,* 20 (Summer/Fall 1972), 225–48.

"History of Systems of Thought, 1979." *Philosophy and Social Criticism,* 8 (1981), 353–59.

"Human Nature: Justice versus Power." In *Reflexive Water: The Basic Concerns of Mankind.* By A. J. Ayer, Arne Naess, Karl Popper, John Eccles, Noam Chomsky, Michel Foucault, Leszek Kolakowski, Henri Lefèbvre, and Fons Elders. London, UK: Souvenir, 1974, pp. 136–97.

"Introduction." In *Fromanger: le desir est partout.* By Gérard Fromanger. Catalog of an exhibition. Paris, Fr.: Galerie Jeanne Bucher, 1975.

"Kant on Enlightenment and Revolution." Trans. Colin Gordon. *Economy and Society,* 15 (February 1986), 88–96.

"Maurice Blanchot: Thought from Outside." In *Foucault/Blanchot.* New York: Zone, 1987, pp. 7–58.

"Monstrosities in Criticism." Trans. Robert J. Matthews.*Diacritics*, 1 (Fall 1971), 57–60.
"My Body, This Paper, This Fire." Trans. Geoff Bennington.*Oxford Literary Review*, 4 (Autumn 1979), 9–28.
"Nietzsche, Freud, Marx." Trans. Jon Anderson and Gary Hentzi. *Critical Texts*, 3 (Winter 1986), 1–5.
"Nineteenth Century Imaginations." Trans. Alex Susteric.*Semiotext(e)*, 4 (1982), 182–90.
"Of Other Spaces." Trans. Jay Miskowiec.*Diacritics*, 16 (Spring 1986), 22–27.
"On the Archaeology of the Sciences." *Theoretical Practice*, 3/4 (Autumn 1971), 108–27.
"On Revolution." *Philosophy and Social Criticism*, 8 (Summer 1981), 5–9.
"Other Spaces: The Principles of Heterotopia."*Lotus International*, 48/49 (1986), 9–17.
"The Political Function of the Intellectual." Trans. Colin Gordon.*Radical Philosophy*, 17 (1977), 12–14.
"The Political Technology of Individuals." In *Technologies of the Self: A Seminar with Michel Foucault*. Ed. Luther H. Martin, Huck Gutman, and Patrick H. Hutton. Amherst: University of Massachusetts Press, 1988, pp. 145–62.
"Politics and the Study of Discourse." Trans. Colin Gordon. In *The Foucault Effect: Studies in Governmentality*. Ed. Graham Burchell, Colin Gordon, and Peter Miller. Chicago: University of Chicago Press, 1991, pp. 53–72.
"The Politics of Crime." Trans. Mollie Horwitz.*Partisan Review*, 43 (1976), 453–59.
"Preface." In *Anti-Oedipus*. By Gilles Deleuze and Felix Guattari. Trans. Robert Hurley, Mark Seem, and Helen R. Lane. New York: Viking, 1977.
"Sexuality and Solitude." *London Review of Books*, 3 (May 21/June 3, 1981), 3, 5–7. (With Richard Sennett.)
"The Simplest of Pleasures." Trans. Mike Riegle and Gilles Barbedette.*Fag Rag*, 29 (n.d.), 3.
"The Subject and Power." *Critical Inquiry*, 8 (Summer 1982), 777–95.
"Technologies of the Self." In *Technologies of the Self: A Seminar with Michel Foucault*. Ed. Luther H. Martin, Huck Gutman, and Patrick H. Hutton. Amherst: University of Massachusetts Press, 1988), pp. 16–49.
"War in the Filigree of Peace: Course Summary." Trans. Ian Mcleod.*Oxford Literary Review*, 4 (1980), 15–19.
"The West and the Truth of Sex." Trans. Lawrence E. Winters.*Sub-Stance*, 20 (1978), 5–8.
"What is an Author?" Trans. James Venit.*Partisan Review*, 42 (1975), 603–14.

Collected Works

Bouchard, Donald F., ed. *Language, Counter-Memory, Practice: Selected Essays and Interviews*. Trans. Donald F. Bouchard and Sherry Simon. Ithaca, NY: Cornell University Press, 1977.
Gordon, Colin, ed. *Power/Knowledge: Selected Interviews and Other Writings 1972–1977*. Trans. Colin Gordon, Leo Marshall, John Mepham, and Kate Soper. New York: Pantheon, 1980.
Kritzman, Lawrence D., ed. *Michel Foucault: Politics, Philosophy, Culture: Interviews and Other Writings: 1977–1984*. Trans. Alan Sheridan and others. New York: Routledge, 1988.
Morris, Meaghan, and Paul Patton, eds.*Michel Foucault: Power, Truth, Strategy*. Sydney, Austral: Feral, 1979.
Rabinow, Paul, ed. *The Foucault Reader*. New York: Pantheon, 1984.

Interviews

Barbedette, Gilles. "A Conversation with Michel Foucault: The Social Triumph of the Sexual Will." Trans. Brendan Lemon. *Christopher Street*, 64 (May 1982), 36–41.

Barbadette [*sic*], Gilles, and André Scala. "Final Interview: Michel Foucault." Trans. Thomas Levin and Isabelle Lorenz. *Raritan Review*, 5 (Summer 1985), 1–13.

Dillon, Millicent. "Conversation with Michel Foucault." *Three Penney Review*, 1 (Winter/Spring 1980), 4–5.

Droit, Roger-Pol. "Michel Foucault, on the Role of Prisons." Trans. Leonard Mayhew. *New York Times*, August 5, 1975, p. 31.

Eribon, Didier. "Is It Really Important to Think? An Interview with Michel Foucault." Trans. Thomas Keenan. *Philosophy and Social Criticism*, 9 (Spring 1982), 30–40.

"Film and Popular Memory: An Interview with Michel Foucault." Trans. Martin Jordin. *Radical Philosophy*, 11 (Summer 1975), 24–29.

Foucault, Michel. *Remarks on Marx: Conversations with Duccio Trombadori*. Trans. R. James Goldstein and James Cascaito. New York: Semiotext(e), 1991.

"Friendship as a Lifestyle: An Interview with Michel Foucault." *Gay Information*, 7 (Spring 1981), 4–6.

Gallagher, Bob, and Alexander Wilson. "Michel Foucault: An Interview: Sex, Power and the Politics of Identity." *The Advocate* [San Mateo, CA], 400 (August 7, 1984), 26–30, 58.

Lévy, Bernard-Henri. "The History of Sexuality: Interview." Trans. Geoff Bennington. *Oxford Literary Review*, 4 (1980), 3–14.

Lévy, Bernard-Henri. "Power and Sex: An Interview with Michel Foucault." Trans. David J. Parent. *Telos*, 32 (Summer 1977), 152–61.

Lotringer, Sylvère, ed. *Foucault Live (Interviews, 1961–1984)*. Trans. Lysa Hochroth and John Johnston. New York: Semiotext(e), 1989.

O'Higgins, James. "Sexual Choice, Sexual Act: An Interview with Michel Foucault." *Salmagundi*, 58–59 (Fall 1982/Winter 1983), 10–24.

"Questions of Method: An Interview with Michel Foucault." In *After Philosophy: End or Transformation?* Ed. Kenneth Baynes, James Bohman, and Thomas McCarthy. Cambridge, MA: MIT Press, 1987, pp. 100–17.

"Questions of Method." Trans. Colin Gordon. In *The Foucault Effect: Studies in Governmentality*. Ed. Graham Burchell, Colin Gordon, and Peter Miller. Chicago: University of Chicago Press, 1991, 73–86.

Rabinow, Paul. "Interview: Michel Foucault: Space, Knowledge, and Power." Trans. Christian Hubert. *Skyline*, March 1982, pp. 16–20.

Riggins, Stephen. "Michel Foucault: An Interview by Stephen Riggins." *Ethos*, 1 (Autumn 1983), 4–9.

Ruas, Charles. "An Interview with Michel Foucault." Postscript to *Death in the Labyrinth: The World of Raymond Roussel*. By Michel Foucault. Trans. Charles Ruas. Garden City, NY: Doubleday, 1986, pp. 169–86.

Simon, John K. "A Conversation with Michel Foucault." *Partisan Review*, 38 (1971), 192–201.

Simon, John K. "Michel Foucault on Attica: An Interview." *Telos*, 19 (Spring 1974), 154–61.

"*Spiegel* Interview with Michel Foucault on 'Paris-Berlin.'" Trans. J. D. Steakley. *New German Critique*, 16 (Winter 1979), 155–56.

Endnotes

1 Michel Foucault, *Remarks on Marx: Conversations with Duccio Trombadori*, trans. R. James Goldstein and James Cascaito (New York: Semiotext(e), 1991), pp. 33–34.

2 Foucault, *Remarks on Marx*, pp. 40–41.

3 Michel Foucault, "Entretien," *Nouvelles littéraires*, March 17, 1975, quoted in Alan Sheridan, *Michel Foucault: The Will to Truth* (New York: Tavistock, 1980), p. 224.

4 Stephen Riggins, "The Minimalist Self," in *Michel Foucault: Politics, Philosophy, Culture: Interviews and Other Writings: 1977–1984*, trans. Alan Sheridan and others, ed. Lawrence D. Kritzman (New York: Routledge, 1988), p. 7.

5 Michel Foucault, quoted in David Macey, *The Lives of Michel Foucault: A Biography* (New York: Pantheon, 1993) p. 40.

6 Rux Martin, "Truth, Power, Self: An Interview with Michel Foucault: October 25, 1982," in *Technologies of the Self: A Seminar with Michel Foucault*, ed. Luther H. Martin, Huck Gutman, and Patrick H. Hutton (Amherst: University of Massachusetts Press, 1988), p. 13.

7 Foucault, quoted in Macey, p. 73.

8 Michel Foucault, *Foucault Live (Interviews, 1961–1984)*, trans. Lysa Hochroth and John Johnston, ed. Sylvère Lotringer (Brooklyn, NY: Semiotext(e), 1989), pp. 405–6.

9 Michel Foucault, *The Use of Pleasure: The History of Sexuality: Volume 2*, trans. Robert Hurley (New York: Pantheon, 1985), p. 9.

10 Riggins, p. 12.

11 Foucault, *Foucault Live*, p. 450.

12 Foucault, quoted in Macey, p. 410.

13 Foucault, quoted in Macey, p. xix.

14 Bibliographic information on Foucault was obtained from the following sources: Sheridan, pp. 4, 8; Otto Friedrich and Sandra Burton, "France's Philosopher of Power," *Time*, November 16, 1981, p. 148; "Philosopher and Author M. Foucault," *Chicago Tribune*, June 26, 1984, sec. 1, p. 12; Riggins; Martin; and Macey.

15 Foucault, *Foucault Live*, p. 66.

16 Michel Foucault, *The Archaeology of Knowledge and the Discourse on Language*, trans. A. M. Sheridan Smith (New York: Pantheon, 1972), p. 86. Other discussions of the statement can be found in: Carole Blair, "The Statement: Foundation of Foucault's Historical Criticism," *Western Journal of Speech Communication*, 51 (Fall 1987), 364–83; Carole Blair and Martha Cooper, "The Humanist Turn in Foucault's Rhetoric of Inquiry," *Quarterly Journal of Speech*, 73 (May 1987), 152–64; and Gilles Deleuze, *Foucault*, trans. and ed. Séan Hand (Minneapolis: University of Minnesota Press, 1988), pp. 2–12.

17 Foucault, *Foucault Live*, p. 63.

18 Foucault, *Foucault Live*, p. 99.

19 Michel Foucault, *The Order of Things: An Archaeology of the Human Sciences* (New York: Random, 1970), pp. 34–36.

20 Foucault, *The Archaeology of Knowledge*, p. 191.

21 Foucault, *Foucault Live*, pp. 34–35.

22 The relationship Foucault sees among epistemes is discussed in David Carroll, "The Subject of Archeology or the Sovereignty of the Episteme," *MLN*, 93 (May 1978), 707, 716; Jan Miel, "Ideas or Epistemes: Hazard Versus Foucault," *Yale French Studies*, 49 (1973), 239; E. M. Henning, "Archaeology, Deconstruction, and Intellectual History," in *Modern European Intellectual History: Reappraisals and New Perspectives*, ed. Dominick LaCapra and Steven L. Kaplan (Ithaca, NY: Cornell University Press, 1982), p. 157; David Carroll, *Paraesthetics: Foucault, Lyotard, Derrida* (New York: Methuen, 1987), pp. 61–62; and Pierre Boncenne, "On Power," in *Michel Foucault: Politics, Philosophy, Culture: Interview and Other Writings: 1977–1984*, trans. Alan Sheridan and others, ed. Lawrence D. Kritzman (New York: Routledge, 1988), pp. 99–100.

23 Foucault, *The Order of Things*, p. xv.

24 Foucault, *The Archaeology of Knowledge*, p. 216.

[25] Rules concerning objects of discourse are discussed in Foucault, *The Archaeology of Knowledge*, pp. 41–44.

[26] Foucault, *The Archaeology of Knowledge*, p. 217. See pp. 224–25 for a discussion of rules concerning who is allowed expression.

[27] Rules concerning the formation of concepts and theories are discussed in: Foucault, *The Archaeology of Knowledge*, pp. 56–57, 68; Michel Foucault, "History, Discourse, and Discontinuity," trans. Anthony M. Nazzarro, *Salmagundi*, 20 (Summer/Fall 1972), 234; and Foucault, "The Discourse on Language," pp. 218–19.

[28] Paul Rabinow, "Modern and Counter-Modern: Ethos and Epoch in Heidegger and Foucault," in *The Cambridge Companion to Foucault*, ed. Gary Gutting (New York: Cambridge University Press, 1994), pp. 204–05.

[29] Foucault, *Foucault Live*, p. 446.

[30] David Paul Funt, "The Structuralist Debate," *Hudson Review*, 22 (Winter 1969–70) 628.

[31] Foucault, *Remarks on Marx*, p. 58.

[32] Foucault, *Foucault Live*, p. 63.

[33] Foucault, *Foucault Live*, p. 99.

[34] Michel Foucault, *Power/Knowledge: Selected Interviews and Other Writings 1927–1977*, trans. Colin Gordon et al., ed. Colin Gordon (New York: Pantheon, 1980), p. 51.

[35] Michel Foucault, *Discipline and Punish: The Birth of the Prison*, trans. Alan Sheridan (New York: Vintage/Random, 1979), p. 27.

[36] The relationship between power and knowledge is discussed in Foucault, *Power/Knowledge*, pp. 51–52.

[37] Foucault, *Foucault Live*, p. 445.

[38] Gerard Raulet, "Critical Theory/Intellectual History," trans. Jeremy Harding, in *Michel Foucault: Politics, Philosophy, Culture: Interviews and Other Writings: 1977–1984*, trans. Alan Sheridan and others, ed. Lawrence D. Kritzman (New York: Routledge, 1988), p. 43.

[39] Foucault, *Discipline and Punish*, p. 27.

[40] Foucault, *Power/Knowledge*, p. 198.

[41] Foucault, *Foucault Live*, p. 410.

[42] Foucault, *Foucault Live*, p. 441.

[43] Foucault, *Power/Knowledge*, p. 98. The omnipresence of power also is discussed in: *Michel Foucault, The History of Sexuality: Volume 1: An Introduction*, trans. Robert Hurley (New York: Vintage, 1980), pp. 93–94; Révoltes Logiques Collective, "Power and Strategies," trans. Paul Patton, in *Michel Foucault: Power, Truth, Strategy*, ed. Meaghan Morris and Paul Patton (Sydney, Austral.: Feral, 1979), p. 55; and Lucette Finas, "Interview with Lucette Finas," trans. Paul Foss and Meaghan Morris, in *Michel Foucault: Power, Truth, Strategy*, ed. Meaghan Morris and Paul Patton (Sydney, Austral.: Feral, 1979), p. 70.

[44] Foucault, *Foucault Live*, p. 441.

[45] Foucault, *Power/Knowledge*, p. 94.

[46] Foucault, *Power/Knowledge*, p. 95.

[47] Foucault, *The History of Sexuality*, p. 136.

[48] Foucault, *Foucault Live*, p. 441.

[49] Foucault, *The History of Sexuality*, p. 90.

[50] Foucault, *Foucault Live*, p. 220.

[51] Foucault, *Power/Knowledge*, p. 92.

[52] Foucault, *The History of Sexuality*, p. 85.

[53] Foucault, *Power/Knowledge*, p. 119.

[54] Foucault, *Discipline and Punish*, pp. 266–68.

[55] Foucault, *Foucault Live*, p. 418.

[56] Foucault, *Foucault Live*, p. 197.

[57] Foucault, *Foucault Live*, pp. 139–40.

[58] Foucault, *The History of Sexuality*, p. 137.

[59] Foucault, *Discipline and Punish*, p. 138.

[60] Foucault, *Foucault Live*, p. 410.

[61] Sonja K. Foss and Ann M. Gill, "Michel Foucault's Theory of Rhetoric as Epistemic," *Western Journal of Speech Communication*, 51 (Fall 1987), 384–401.

[62] Foucault, *Foucault Live*, p. 224.

[63] Foucault, *Power/Knowledge*, p. 138.

[64] Foucault, *Foucault Live*, p. 224.

[65] Foucault, *Foucault Live*, p. 224.

[66] Raúl Fornet-Betancourt, Helmut Becker, and Alfredo Gomez-Müller, "The Ethic of Care for the Self as a Practice of Freedom: An Interview with Michel Foucault on January 20, 1984," trans. J. D. Gauthier, in *The Final Foucault*, ed. James Bernauer and David Rasmussen (Cambridge, MA: MIT Press, 1988), p. 18.

[67] For discussions of Foucault's refusal to envision an ideal society, see: Michael Walzer, "The Politics of Michel Foucault," in *Foucault: A Critical Reader*, ed. David Couzens Hoy (New York: Basil Blackwell, 1986), pp. 51–68; Allan Megill, *Prophets of Extremity: Nietzsche, Heidegger, Foucault, Derrida* (Berkeley: University of California Press, 1985), pp. 195–98; and Nancy Fraser, "Foucault's Body-Language: A Post-Humanist Political Rhetoric?," *Salmagundi*, 61 (Fall 1983), 55–70.

[68] Foucault, *Power/Knowledge*, p. 126.

[69] Foucault, *Foucault Live*, p. 48.

[70] Didier Eribon, "Practicing Criticism," in *Michel Foucault: Politics, Philosophy, Culture: Interviews and Other Writings: 1977–1984*, trans. Alan Sheridan and others, ed. Lawrence D. Kritzman (New York: Routledge, 1988), pp. 154–55. Foucault also discusses the notion of criticism in: Francois Ewald, "The Concern for Truth," in *Michel Foucault: Politics, Philosophy, Culture: 1977–1984*, trans. Alan Sheridan and others, ed. Lawrence D. Kritzman (New York: Routledge, 1988), p. 265; and Martin, p. 10.

[71] Foucault, *Foucault Live*, p. 462.

[72] Foucault, *Foucault Live*, p. 462.

[73] Foucault, *Foucault Live*, p. 284.

[74] Foucault, *Foucault Live*, pp. 284–85.

[75] Foucault, *Foucault Live*, p. 284.

[76] For an excellent summary of Foucault's view of ethics, see John Rajchman, "Ethics After Foucault," *Social Text*, 13/14 (Winter/Spring 1986), 165–83.

[77] Foucault, *Foucault Live*, p. 432.

[78] Jana Sawicki, "Foucault, Feminism and Questions of Identity," in *The Cambridge Companion to Foucault*, ed. Gary Gutting (New York: Cambridge University Press, 1994), p. 287.

[79] Foucault, *Foucault Live*, p. 440.

[80] Foucault, *Foucault Live*, p. 440.

[81] Fornet-Betancourt, Becker, and Gomez-Müller, p. 11.

[82] Christopher Norris, " 'What is Enlightenment?': Kant According to Foucault," in *The Cambridge Companion to Foucault*, ed. Gary Gutting (New York: Cambridge University Press, 1994), p. 161.

[83] Michel Foucault, "On the Genealogy of Ethics: An Overview of Work in Progress," in *The Foucault Reader*, ed. Paul Rabinow (New York: Pantheon, 1984), p. 352.

[84] Foucault, "On the Genealogy of Ethics," p. 352.

[85] Foucault, "On the Genealogy of Ethics," p. 352.

[86] Foucault, "On the Genealogy of Ethics," p. 353.

[87] Arnold I. Davidson, "Ethics as Ascetics: Foucault, the History of Ethics, and Ancient Thought," in *The Cambridge Companion to Foucault*, ed. Gary Gutting (New York: Cambridge University Press, 1994), p. 118.

[88] Foucault, "On the Genealogy of Ethics," p. 355.

[89] Foucault, "On the Genealogy of Ethics," p. 362.

[90] For other discussions of the four aspects of ethics, see: Foucault, *The Use of Pleasure*, pp. 26–28; and Arnold I. Davidson, "Archaeology, Genealogy, Ethics," in *Foucault: A Critical Reader*, ed. David Couzens Hoy (New York: Basil Blackwell, 1986), pp. 228–29.

[91] Foucault, *Foucault Live*, p. 445.

[92] Foucault, *Foucault Live*, pp. 435–36.

[93] Foucault, *Foucault Live*, p. 433.

[94] Foucault, *Foucault Live*, p. 433.

[95] James W. Bernauer and Michael Mahon, "The Ethics of Michel Foucault," in *The Cambridge Companion to Foucault*, ed. Gary Gutting (New York: Cambridge University Press, 1994), p. 152.

[96] Foucault, quoted in Sawicki, p. 288.

[97] Thomas Flynn, "Foucault's Mapping of History," in *The Cambridge Companion to Foucault*, ed. Gary Gutting (New York: Cambridge University Press), p. 28.

[98] Foucault, *The Use of Pleasure*, p. 6.

[99] Foucault, *Foucault Live*, p. 57.

[100] Foucault, *Foucault Live*, p. 57.

[101] Foucault, *Foucault Live*, p. 65.

[102] Foucault, *Foucault Live*, p. 57.

[103] Foucault, *Foucault Live*, pp. 57–58.

[104] *Genealogy* was a term used by Nietzsche, who had a major influence on Foucault's work. Foucault discusses his debt to Nietzsche in *Language, Counter-Memory, Practice: Selected Essays and Interviews*, trans. Donald F. Bouchard and Sherry Simon, ed. Donald F. Bouchard (Ithaca, NY: Cornell University Press, 1977), pp. 139–64. For more on Nietzsche's influence on Foucault, see Megill, "Foucault, Structuralism, and the Ends of History," p. 459; and Sheridan, *Michel Foucault: The Will to Truth*, pp. 114–20.

[105] Foucault, *Foucault Live*, p. 416.

[106] Foucault, *Discipline and Punish*, p. 8.

[107] Foucault, *The History of Sexuality*, p. 48.

[108] Foucault, *The Use of Pleasure*, p. 6.

[109] Foucault, quoted in Flynn, p. 37.

[110] Foucault, *Foucault Live*, p. 280.

[111] Foucault, *Remarks on Marx*, p. 29.

[112] Foucault, *Foucault Live*, p. 149.

[113] Foucault, *Power/Knowledge*, pp. 50–51.

[114] Flynn, p. 30.

[115] Flynn, p. 30.

[116] Maurice Florence [probably a pseudonym for Michel Foucault], "Foucault, Michel, 1926–," in *The Cambridge Companion to Foucault*, ed. Gary Gutting (New York: Cambridge University Press, 1994), p. 318.

[117] Foucault, *Language, Counter-Memory, Practice*, p. 154.

[118] Foucault, *Foucault Live*, p. 277.

[119] Foucault, *Foucault Live*, pp. 277–78.

[120] Foucault, *Foucault Live*, p. 277.

[121] Foucault, *The Archaeology of Knowledge*, p. 151.

[122] Foucault, *The Archaeology of Knowledge*, p. 109.

[123] For a summary of Foucault's position on interpretation, see Carol Blair, rev. of *Michel Foucault: Beyond Structuralism and Hermeneutics*, by Hubert L. Dreyfus and Paul Rabinow, and *Michel Foucault: Social Theory and Transgression*, by Charles C. Lemert and Garth Gillian, *Quarterly Journal of Speech*, 70 (February 1984), 102.

[124] Foucault, *The Archaeology of Knowledge*, p. 27. Description is also discussed in Michel Foucault, *The Birth of the Clinic: An Archaeology of Medical Perception*, trans. A. M. Sheridan Smith (New York: Pantheon, 1973), p. xvii. Foucault discusses his methodological principles in *The Archaeology of Knowledge*, pp. 141–77. For a good summary, see Blair and Cooper, pp. 165–67.

[125] Foucault, quoted in Foucault, *Language, Counter-Memory, Practice*, p. 115.

[126] Foucault, *Foucault Live*, p. 40.

[127] Foucault, *The Order of Things*, p. xxiii.

[128] Foucault, *The Order of Things*, p. xxiii.

[129] Foucault, *Foucault Live*, p. 41.

[130] Evidence for the emergence of a new conception of the human being is discussed in Roy McMullen, "Michel Foucault," *Horizon*, 11 (Autumn 1969), 37; Foucault, *The Order of Things*, p. 386; and Foucault, *Power/Knowledge*, p. 117.

[131] Foucault, *Foucault Live*, p. 67.

[132] Vernon Pratt, "Foucault and the History of Classification Theory," *Studies in History and Philosophy of Science*, 8 (1977), 163.

[133] Meaghan Morris and Paul Patton, "Preface," in *Michel Foucault: Power, Truth, Strategy*, ed. Meaghan Morris and Paul Patton (Sydney, Austral.: Feral, 1979), p. 8.

[134] Edward W. Said, *Beginnings: Intention and Method* (New York: Basic, 1975), p. 291.

[135] McMullen, p. 39.

[136] Pratt, p. 163.

[137] Miel, p. 236.

[138] White, p. 81.

[139] White, p. 92.

[140] Ronald Hayman, "Cartography of Discourse? On Foucault," *Encounter*, 47 (December 1976), 72.

[141] Megill, "Foucault, Structuralism, and the Ends of History," p. 486.

[142] Rev. of *The Archaeology of Knowledge and the Discourse on Language*, *Kirkus Reviews*, 40 (July 15, 1972), 834.

[143] Hayman, p. 74.

[144] Eve Tavor Bannet, *Structuralism and the Logic of Dissent: Barthes, Derrida, Foucault, Lacan* (Urbana: University of Illinois Press, 1989), p. 109.

[145] Bannet, p. 109.

[146] John Mepham, "The Structuralist Sciences and Philosophy," in *Structuralism: An Introduction*, ed. David Robey (Oxford, UK: Clarendon, 1973), p. 106.

[147] Sidonie Clauss, "John Wilkins' Essay Toward a Real Character: Its Place in the Seventeenth-Century Episteme," *Journal of the History of Ideas*, 43 (October/December 1982), 552.

[148] See, for example: McMullen, pp. 38–39; George Huppert, "*Divinatio et Eruditio:* Thoughts on Foucault," *History and Theory*, 13 (1974), 198; David E. Leary, "Essay Review: Michel Foucault, an Historian of the *Sciences Humaines*," *Journal of the History of the Behavioral Sciences*, 12 (July 1976), 291–92.

[149] R. D. Laing, "Sanity and 'Madness': The Invention of Madness," *New Statesman*, 71 (June 16, 1967), 843.

[150] Foucault, *Remarks on Marx*, pp. 32–33.

[151] Foucault, *Remarks on Marx*, p. 33.

[152] Mark Poster, *Foucault, Marxism and History: Mode of Production versus Mode of Information* (Cambridge, UK: Polity, 1984), pp. 146–47.

[153] Gutting, p. 3.

[154] Gary Gutting, "Introduction: Michel Foucault: A User's Manual," in *The Cambridge Companion to Foucault*, ed. Gary Gutting (Cambridge, UK: Cambridge University Press, 1994), p. 16.

[155] Gutting, p. 16.

[156] Foucault, *Remarks on Marx*, pp. 26–27.

[157] Foucault, *Remarks on Marx*, p. 27.

[158] Foucault, "The Minimalist Self," p. 14.

[159] Foucault, *The Archaeology of Knowledge*, p. 17.

[160] Foucault, *The Use of Pleasure*, p. 6.

[161] Paul Patton, "Foucault's Subject of Power," in *The Later Foucault: Politics and Philosophy*, ed. Jeremy Moss (Thousand Oaks, CA: Sage, 1998), p. 67.

[162] Jeremy Moss, "Introduction: The Later Foucault," in *The Later Foucault: Politics and Philosophy*, ed. Jeremy Moss (Thousand Oaks, CA: Sage, 1998), p. 10.

[163] Nancy Hartsock, "Foucault on Power: A Theory for Women?," in *Feminism/Postmodernism*, ed. Linda J. Nicholson (New York: Routledge, 1990), p. 164.

[164] Patton, p. 64.

165 Nancy Fraser, *Unruly Practices: Power, Discourse and Gender in Contemporary Social Theory* (Minneapolis: University of Minnesota Press, 1989), p. 33.

166 Patton, p. 70.

167 Moss, p. 4.

168 Michel Foucault, Paul Rabinow, and Hubert Dreyfus, "On the Genealogy of Ethics: An Overview of Work in Progress," in *The Foucault Reader*, ed. Paul Rabinow (New York: Pantheon, 1984), p. 343.

169 Foucault, *Remarks on Marx*, p. 40.

170 Robert J. Ellrich, rev. of *Language, Counter-Memory, Practice*, by Michel Foucault, *Modern Language Journal*, 62 (April 1978), 206.

INDEX